THE VICTORIA HISTORY OF THE COUNTIES OF ENGLAND

A HISTORY OF OXFORDSHIRE

VOLUME IX

THE VICTORIA HISTORY OF THE COUNTIES OF ENGLAND

EDITED BY R. B. PUGH

THE UNIVERSITY OF LONDON
INSTITUTE OF
HISTORICAL RESEARCH

Oxford University Press, Ely House, 37 Dover Street, London, W.1

GLASGOW NEW YORK TORONTO MELBOURNE WELLINGTON
BOMBAY CALCUTTA MADRAS KARACHI LAHORE DACCA
CAPE TOWN SALISBURY NAIROBI IBADAN ACCRA
KUALA LUMPUR SINGAPORE HONG KONG TOKYO

19 722726 0

PRINTED IN GREAT BRITAIN

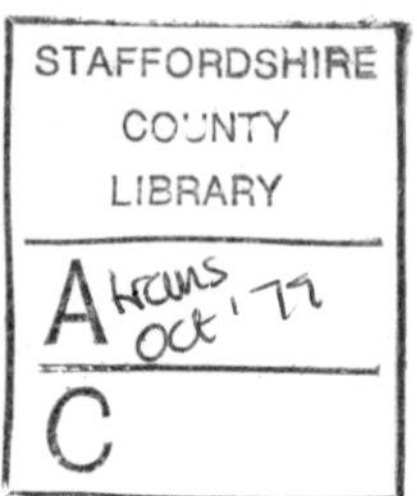

INSCRIBED TO THE

MEMORY OF HER LATE MAJESTY

QUEEN VICTORIA

WHO GRACIOUSLY GAVE THE TITLE TO

AND ACCEPTED THE DEDICATION

OF THIS HISTORY

HORLEY CHURCH: 15th-century 'St. Christopher' fresco

A HISTORY OF THE COUNTY OF OXFORD

EDITED BY MARY D. LOBEL AND ALAN CROSSLEY

VOLUME IX

BLOXHAM HUNDRED

PUBLISHED FOR
THE INSTITUTE OF HISTORICAL RESEARCH
BY THE
OXFORD UNIVERSITY PRESS
1969

Distributed by the Oxford University Press until 1 January 1973
thereafter by Dawsons of Pall Mall

CONTENTS OF VOLUME NINE

LIST OF ILLUSTRATIONS

For permission to reproduce pictures in their possession and for the loan of photographic prints and negatives thanks are due to the Bodleian Library, the National Monuments Record, the Ashmolean Museum, Country Life Ltd., the Oxford Mail & Times Ltd., the Oxfordshire Ironstone Co. Ltd., Miss A. Keyser, and Mr. G. M. Bolton.

LIST OF ILLUSTRATIONS

LIST OF MAPS AND PLANS

The church and house plans were drawn by Laurence Hunt and dated by H. M. Colvin. The church plans were based on surveys by G. Forsyth Lawson and Partners of Banbury. The map of Balscott was drawn by Mary E. Potter, and the other maps by K. J. Wass from drafts by T. G. Hassall. The maps of Bloxham hundred, Adderbury parish, and Bloxham, 1954 are based on the Ordnance Survey with the sanction of the Controller of H. M. Stationery Office, Crown Copyright reserved.

EDITORIAL NOTE

THE preparation of this volume, the eighth in the Oxfordshire set of the *Victoria History* to be published, was initiated at a time when the Oxfordshire Victoria County History Committee, as described in the Editorial Note to the *History of Oxfordshire*, Volume III, was still in being. That Committee was dissolved in 1965 and a new partnership was thereupon concluded between the University of London and the Oxfordshire County Council, similar to those referred to in the Editorial Notes to the *Victoria History of Gloucestershire*, Volume VI, and the *Victoria History of Shropshire*, Volume VIII. The County Council set up an Advisory Sub-Committee charged with local responsibility. Over this committee the late Ivo Murray, 20th Lord Saye and Sele, presided until 1966, when he was succeeded by Mr. C. J. Peers. To the funds provided by the County Council the City of Oxford, the University of Oxford, and several institutions and individuals have added contributions. The University of London here places on record its sincere appreciation of the generous attitude displayed by the Oxfordshire County Council and other contributors.

Mrs. M. D. Lobel continued as local editor after the transfer to the County Council, and Mr. Alan Crossley and Mrs. Mary Jessup continued as her assistants. Mrs. Lobel retired after seventeen years' service at the end of 1965 and took up other work. She was succeeded in 1966 by Mr. Crossley. Mr. T. G. Hassall became Assistant Local Editor in 1966 and on his resignation in 1967 was succeeded by Miss Hilary L. Turner. All of these have in varying degrees played their part in compiling and editing the present volume. The text was originally written under the supervision of Mrs. Lobel, but the revising and final editing of it were carried out by Mr. Crossley and his assistants.

Thanks are gratefully rendered to many institutions and private persons who granted access to documents in their care. Among these special mention must be made of the governing bodies of New College and of Oriel and Trinity Colleges, the Librarian and staff of the Bodleian Library, the incumbents of parishes included in the volume, the Oxfordshire County Archivist and his assistants, the Bishop and the Dean and Chapter of Lincoln, the Archivist of the Lincolnshire Record Office, and the late Ivo Murray, Lord Saye and Sele.

Much valued advice was given by Mr. H. M. Colvin on architecture and by Mr. P. S. Spokes on heraldry and photography. In the gathering of material Mrs. H. M. Colvin, Mrs. Mary Gott, Miss Katherine Price, Mrs. N. E. Selwyn, and Mrs. Frances Walsh performed notable services. All these are likewise sincerely thanked.

LIST OF CLASSES OF DOCUMENTS IN THE PUBLIC RECORD OFFICE

USED IN THIS VOLUME WITH THEIR CLASS NUMBERS

Chancery

	Proceedings
C 1	Early
C 2	Series I
C 3	Series II
C 47	Miscellanea
C 54	Close Rolls
C 60	Fine Rolls
C 66	Patent Rolls
C 78	Decree Rolls
C 93	Proceedings of Commissioners for Charitable Uses, Inquisitions and Decrees
	Inquisitions post mortem
C 132	Series I, Henry III
C 133	Edward I
C 134	Edward II
C 135	Edward III
C 138	Henry V
C 139	Henry VI
C 140	Edward IV
C 141	Richard III
C 142	Series II
C 143	Inquisitions ad quod damnum
C 145	Miscellaneous Inquisitions
C 146	Ancient Deeds, Series C

Court of Common Pleas

	Feet of Fines
C.P. 25 (1)	Series I
C.P. 25 (2)	Series II
C.P. 26	Notes of Fines
C.P. 40	Plea Rolls
C.P. 43	Recovery Rolls

Exchequer, Treasury of the Receipt

E 36	Miscellaneous Books
E 40	Ancient Deeds, Series A

Exchequer, King's Remembrancer

E 134	Depositions taken by Commission
	Inquisitions post mortem
E 149	Series I
E 150	Series II
E 164	Miscellaneous Books, Series I
E 178	Special Commissions of Enquiry
E 210	Ancient Deeds, Series D

Exchequer, Augmentation Office

E 315	Miscellaneous Books
E 317	Parliamentary Surveys
E 326	Ancient Deeds, Series B

Exchequer, Lord Treasurer's Remembrancer's and Pipe Offices

E 368	Memoranda Rolls
E 372	Pipe Rolls

Ministry of Education

Ed. 7	Public Elementary Schools, Preliminary Statements

Home Office

	Various, Census Papers
H.O. 107	Population Returns
H.O. 129	Ecclesiastical Returns

Justices Itinerant, &c.

J.I. 1	Eyre Rolls, Assize Rolls, &c.

Court of King's Bench (Crown Side)

K.B. 26	Curia Regis Rolls
K.B. 27	Coram Rege Rolls
K.B. 28	Crown Rolls

Exchequer, Office of the Auditors of Land Revenue

L.R. 2	Miscellaneous Books

Court of Requests

Req. 2	Proceedings

Special Collections

S.C. 2	Court Rolls
S.C. 5	Hundred Rolls
S.C. 6	Ministers' and Receivers' Accounts
	Rentals and Surveys
S.C. 11	Rolls
S.C. 12	Portfolios

Court of Star Chamber

	Proceedings
Sta. Cha. 2	Henry VIII
Sta. Cha. 4	Mary

State Paper Office

	State Papers Domestic
S.P. 10	Edward VI
S.P. 15	Addenda, Edward VI to James I

Court of Wards and Liveries

Wards 2	Deeds and Evidences

LIST OF PRINCIPAL BODLEIAN LIBRARY MANUSCRIPTS

USED IN THIS VOLUME

MS. Ch. Oxon.	Oxfordshire Charters
MS. dep. deeds	Miscellaneous Oxfordshire deeds from various sources
MS. d.d. Arkell	Deeds collected by Miss Arkell (d. 1953) in the neighbourhood of Banbury
MS. d.d. Dew	Deeds collected by Mr. G. J. Dew
MS. d.d. Ewelme honor	Papers relating to courts leet of the honor, 1712 to 19th century
MS. d.d. Golby	Deeds and papers of the Gardner, Golby, and Wilson families in Adderbury, 1702–1903
MS. d.d. Morrell	Miscellaneous deeds from Messrs. Morrell, Peel, and Gamlen, solicitors, Oxford
MS. d.d. Oxon.	Oxfordshire deeds from various sources
MS. d.d. Par. Adderbury	Churchwardens' accounts, poor law papers, papers of town feoffees, maps and surveys, &c.
MS. d.d. Par. Alkerton	Registers, miscellaneous papers, account book of Alkerton charities
MS. d.d. Par. Bloxham	Deeds of Bloxham town feoffees, 1421–1627
MS. d.d. Risley	Papers of the Barber, Cotton, and Risley families, and miscellaneous papers
MS. Lyell 15	Abingdon Cartulary
MS. North	Papers of the North family from Wroxton Abbey
MS. Oxf. Dioc.	
b 6–18	Parochial returns to bishops' queries, 1793–1824
b 20	Petitions, plans, and correspondence
b 21–23	Oxford diocesan registers, 1737–1868
b 38, 39, 41	Bishops' visitations, 1831, 1834, 1838
b 70	Returns of church, rectory, and school buildings, 1860
b 101	Return of papists, 1767–80
c 16	Banbury Peculiar Acts, 17th century
c 21–31	Attestations and depositions in ecclesiastical courts, 1570–1694
c 49	Episcopal citations, 1688–91
c 66–77	Presentation deeds, 1559–1863
c 85	Registration deeds, 1609–1856
c 93–94	Libels and articles, undated
c 105	Proclamations and draft faculties, *c.* 1670–1740
c 155	Value of livings, 1675–1823
c 206–9	Oxford diocesan ordination papers, 1791–7
c 264	Oxford diocesan register, 1604–23
c 266	Oxford diocesan register, 1699–1736
c 327	Diocese book, 1778–1808
c 332, 341, 344, 350	Bishops' visitations, 1866, 1875, 1878, 1884
c 430	Returns of recusants, 1682–1706
c 433	Return of schools, 1815
c 434–6	Register of faculties, 1737–41
c 441	Return of places of worship, 1810
c 443	Modern papers
c 446	Papers relating to Queen Anne's Bounty
c 448–9	Terriers, early 19th century
c 454–6	Faculty papers, *c.* 1660–1850
c 643–7	Certificates of dissenting meeting houses, 1731–1852
c 649–64	Episcopal correspondence, 1635–1854
c 1692–2086	Oxfordshire parish boxes, 19th–20th centuries
d 14–16	Depositions and attestations in ecclesiastical courts, 1543–93
d 105–6	Oxford diocesan register, 1543–69, 1660–1702
d 178	Bishop Wilberforce's diocese book, 1854–64

d 179, 180	Bishops' visitations, 1857, 1860
d 549	Diocese book, 1807–12
d 555–65	Bishops' visitations, 1759–74
d 566–81	Bishops' visitations, 1802–23
d 702	Notification on non-residence, 1812–13
d 705	Returns of curates' residence and stipends, 1812
d 707	Return of schools, 1808
d 708	Bishop Fell's diocese book, *c.* 1685
e 12	Subscriptions, 1603–24
MS. Oxf. Archd. Oxon.	
b 22–27	Miscellaneous papers about Oxfordshire parishes
b 39	Papers relating to wills, 19th century
b 40–41	Terriers, 17th century
b 53	Transcripts of Hornton parish register
b 60	Transcripts of Horley and Hornton registers
c 2–27	Liber actorum of archdeacon's court, 1566–1761
c 28	Proceedings of Banbury Peculiar Court, 1676–1723
c 30	Penalties, acts of court, *c.* 1566–1777
c 31–33	Allegations, 1645–1791
c 35–44	Archdeacons' articles of enquiry, 1837–68
c 46–115	Churchwardens' presentments, 1730–1844
c 118	Depositions in ecclesiastical courts, 1616–20
c 121	Penalties and excommunications, 1610–20
c 141–2	Terriers
c 155	Horley and Hornton Peculiar Acts, 17th century
c 156	Proceedings of Banbury, Cropredy, and Horley and Hornton Peculiar Courts, 18th century
d 4	Mandates for induction
d 13	Archdeacon's visitation book, 1756–9
MS. Rawl. B 400, b, c, f	Rawlinson's Parochial Collections for Oxfordshire
MS. Top. Eccles. b 14	Collections of sketches of baptismal fonts, *c.* 1832–95
MS. Top. Oxon.	
a 37–39	'Drawings in Oxfordshire': prints and drawings by various hands in the 18th and 19th centuries
a 42	Sketches and water-colours of buildings and places in Oxfordshire, 18th and and 19th centuries
a 48	A guard-book containing mainly drawings of Oxfordshire
a 61	Topographical drawings *c.* 1855 by Joseph Wilkins of Deddington
a 64–69	Drawings by J. C. Buckler and J. Buckler
b 75	Historical notes and papers relating to churches and parishes in Oxfordshire
b 124	Historical notes and extracts relating to Bodicote by C. W. Hurst, 1920–5
b 165	Collections and drawings relating to Oxfordshire, 18th and 19th centuries
b 220	Descriptions and drawings of Oxfordshire churches
c 42–68	Historical collections relating to Oxfordshire by W. H. Turner
c 103–5	Papers about Oxfordshire church restorations, mainly 1860–70
c 165–7	Oxfordshire monumental inscriptions and extracts from parish registers by Col. J. L. Chester, *c.* 1880
c 228	The rental book of the estates of the Draper family, 1693–1747
c 306	Transcript of the churchwardens accounts of Bodicote, 1701–1822 by C. W. Hurst
c 393	Collection of miscellaneous charters
c 449	Collections for Oxfordshire religious houses, including Wroxton, by the Revd. H. E. Salter
d 195–6	Notes on Oxfordshire monumental brasses by Percy Manning
d 351	Enquiry into lands of Oxfordshire recusants, 1700
d 386	Historical notes on the church of Wroxton and chapelry of Balscott by the Revd. R. C. West, 1948
d 460	List of medieval incumbents and patrons from the Lincoln registers and other sources, prepared by the Oxfordshire V.C.H. staff
e 184	Notes and transcripts by Percy Manning
MS. Wills Oxon.	Oxfordshire wills, 16th–19th centuries
MS. Wills Peculiars	Oxfordshire &c. Peculiars, probate records 16th–19th centuries

NOTE ON ABBREVIATIONS

Among the abbreviations and short titles used the following may require elucidation:

Manuscript Sources

Cal. Q. Sess.	Calendar of Quarter Sessions
Ch. Ch. Arch.	Archives of Christ Church, Oxford
Compton Census	William Salt Library, Stafford, MS. 33, 'The census taken in 1676 in the province of Canterbury giving an account of inhabitants, papists and other dissenters in the various dioceses'
Dunkin MS.	Collections of John Dunkin (London Guildhall MSS. temporarily deposited in the Bodleian Library)
Eton Coll. Mun.	Muniments of Eton College, Eton, Bucks.
Gamekprs' deps.	Gamekeepers' deputations
G.D.R.	Gloucester Diocesan Records, in Gloucester City Library, including terriers, tithe awards, and bound volumes of diocesan records.
Hockaday Abs.	The 'Hockaday Abstracts', being abstracts of ecclesiastical records relating to Gloucestershire, compiled by F. S. Hockaday mainly from diocesan records, in Gloucester City Library
Magd. Coll. Arch.	Archives of Magdalen College, Oxford
Methuen Arch.	Archives of the Methuen family, Corsham Court, Wilts.
MS. Oxf. Archd. Oxon.	Bodleian Library, Oxfordshire Archdeaconry Papers
MS. Oxf. Dioc.	Bodleian Library, Oxfordshire Diocesan Papers
MS. Top. Eccles.	Bodleian Library, MS. Top. Eccles.
MS. Top. Oxon.	Bodleian Library, MS. Top. Oxon.
New Coll. Mun.	Muniments of New College, Oxford
N.B.R.	National Monuments (formerly Buildings) Record
Oriel Coll. Mun.	Muniments of Oriel College, Oxford
Oldfield, 'Clerus Oxf. Dioc.'	Bodleian Library, MS. index to clergy by W. J. Oldfield, 'Clerus Diocesis Oxoniensis, 1542–1908'
O.R.O.	Oxfordshire County Record Office, Oxford
Par. Rec.	Parish Records
R.O.	Record Office
Rousham Arch.	Archives belonging to Mr. T. Cottrell-Dormer, Rousham Park
S. & F. colln.	Collection of the records of Messrs. Stockton Sons and Fortescue, in O.R.O.
Trinity Coll. President's Off.	Trinity College, Oxford, President's Office
Trinity Coll. Tower Mun.	Trinity College, Oxford, Tower Muniment Room
Victlrs' recogs.	Victuallers' recognizances

Printed Sources

Adderbury 'Rectoria'	*Adderbury 'Rectoria'. The manor at Adderbury belonging to New College, Oxford: the building of the chancel 1408–1418: account rolls, deeds and court rolls*, ed. T. F. Hobson (O.R.S. viii, 1926)
Archdeacon's Ct.	*The Archdeacon's Court, Liber Actorum 1584*, ed. E. R. Brinkworth
Atkyns, *Glos.*	R. Atkyns, *The Ancient and Present State of Glostershire* (London, 1712)
Baker, *Northants.*	G. Baker, *History and Antiquities of the County of Northampton* (2 vols. London, 1822–41)
Beesley, *Hist. Banbury*	A. Beesley, *The History of Banbury: including copious historical and antiquarian notices of the neighbourhood* (London, 1841)
Besse, *Sufferings*	Joseph Besse, *A Collection of the Sufferings of the People called Quakers, from 1650 to 1689* (2 vols. London, 1753)
Billing, *Dir. Oxon.*	M. Billing, *Directory and Gazetteer of the Counties of Berks. and Oxon.* (Birmingham, 1854)

NOTE ON ABBREVIATIONS

Boarstall Cart.	*The Boarstall Cartulary*, ed. H. E. Salter (O.H.S. lxxviii, 1930)
Brewer, *Oxon.*	J. N. Brewer, *A Topographical and Historical Description of the County of Oxford* (London, 1819)
Bridges, *Northants.*	J. Bridges, *History and Antiquities of Northamptonshire*, ed. Peter Whalley (2 vols. Oxford, 1791)
Calamy Rev.	A. G. Matthews, *Calamy Revised* (Oxford, 1934)
Ch. Bells Oxon.	F. Sharpe, *The Church Bells of Oxfordshire* (O.R.S. xxviii, xxx, xxxii, xxxiv, 1949–53)
Ch. Ch. Arch.	*Cartulary of the Medieval Archives of Christ Church*, ed. N. Denholm-Young (O.H.S. xcii, 1931)
Chant. Cert.	*The Chantry Certificates and the Edwardian Inventories of Church Goods*, ed. Rose Graham (O.R.S. i, 1919)
Char. Don.	*Abstract of the Returns of Charitable Donations made by the Ministers and Churchwardens*, 1786–8, H.C. 511 (1816)
Coll. Top. & Gen.	*Collectanea Topographica et Genealogica* (London, 1834)
Davis, *Oxon. Map*	R. Davis, *Map of the County of Oxford* (1797)
Dom. of Incl.	*The Domesday of Inclosures, 1517–1518*, ed. I. S. Leadam (2 vols. London, 1897)
Dugdale, *Warws.*	Sir William Dugdale, *The Antiquities of Warwickshire* (London, 1656)
Educ. Enq. Abstract	*Education Enquiry Abstract*, H.C. 62 (1835), xlii
Educ. of Poor	*Digest of Returns to the Select Committee on the Education of the Poor*, H.C. 224 (1819), ix (B)
Elem. Educ. Ret.	*Elementary Education Returns*, H.C. 201 (1871), lv
Emden, *O.U. Reg.*	A. B. Emden, *A Biographical Register of the University of Oxford to A.D. 1500* (Oxford, 1957–9)
Evans, *Ch. Plate*	J. T. Evans, *The Church Plate of Oxfordshire* (Oxford, 1928)
Eynsham Cart.	*The Eynsham Cartulary*, ed. H. E. Salter (O.H.S. xlix, li, 1906–8)
Fines Oxon.	*The Feet of Fines for Oxfordshire*, 1195–1291, ed. H. E. Salter (6 vols. London, 1877–80)
Foster, *Alumni*	J. Foster, *Alumni Oxonienses, 1500–1886* (8 vols. Oxford, 1887–92)
Gardner, *Dir. Oxon.*	R. Gardner, *History, Gazetteer and Directory of Oxfordshire* (Peterborough, 1852)
Godstow Eng. Reg.	*The English Register of Godstow Nunnery*, ed. A. Clark (E.E.T.S. orig. ser. 129, 130, 142, 1905–11)
Hasted, *Kent*	E. Hasted, *History and Topographical Survey of Kent* (4 vols. Canterbury, 1778–99)
Hearne, *Remarks*	*Remarks and Collections of Thomas Hearne*, ed. C. E. Doble and others (11 vols. O.H.S. ii &c., 1884–1918)
Hearth Tax Oxon.	*Hearth Tax Returns for Oxfordshire*, 1665, ed. Maureen Weinstock (O.R.S. xxi, 1940)
Kennett, *Par. Antiq.*	White Kennett, *Parochial Antiquities attempted in the history of Ambrosden, Burcester and other adjacent parts in the counties of Oxford and Bucks.* (Oxford, 1695)
L.R.S.	Lincoln Record Society
Lamborn, *Arm. Glass*	E. A. Greening Lamborn, *Armorial Glass of the Oxford Diocese, 1250–1850* (London, 1949)
Land Utilisation Survey	*The Report of the Land Utilisation Survey of Britain*, part 56: *Oxfordshire*, by Mary Marshall (London, 1943)
Lascelles, *Dir. Oxon.*	Lascelles & Co.'s *Directory and Gazetteer of the County of Oxford* (Birmingham, 1853)
Liber Antiq.	*Liber Antiquus de Ordinationibus Vicariarum Tempore Hugonis Wells, Lincolniensis Episcopi, 1209–1235*, ed. A. Gibbons (Lincoln, 1888)
Lipscomb, *Bucks.*	G. Lipscomb, *History and Antiquities of the County of Buckingham* (4 vols. London, 1847)
List of Sch. (1902)	*List of Schools under the Administration of the Board* [Cd. 1277], H.C. (1902), lxxix

NOTE ON ABBREVIATIONS

List of Sch. (1906)	*List of Public Elementary Schools* [Cd. 3182], H.C. (1906), lxxxvi
Luke, *Jnl.*	*Journal of Sir Samuel Luke*, ed. I. G. Philip (O.R.S. xxix, xxxi, xxxiii, 1947–1953)
Lunt, *Val. Norw.*	*The Valuation of Norwich*, ed. W. E. Lunt (Oxford, 1926)
Lyon Turner, *Rec. of Nonconformity*	G. Lyon Turner, *Original Records of Early Nonconformity* (3 vols. London, 1914)
Macnamara, *Danvers Family*	F. N. Macnamara, *Memorials of the Danvers Family* (London, 1895)
Misc. Gen. et Her.	*Miscellanea Genealogica et Heraldica*, ed. J. J. Howard, W. B. Bannerman (London, 1868–1938)
Nichols, *Leics.*	J. Nichols, *History and Antiquities of the County of Leicester* (4 vols. in 8 parts, London, 1795–1811)
O.A.H.S. *Proc.*	*Proceedings* of the Oxford Society for Promoting the Study of Gothic Architecture, 1839–47
O.A.S. *Rep.*, *Trans.*	*Reports* and *Transactions* of the North Oxfordshire Archaeological Society, 1853–86, and of the Oxfordshire Archaeological Society, 1887–1949
O.H.S.	Oxford Historical Society
Ormerod, *Ches.*	G. Ormerod, *The History of the County Palatine and City of Chester* (3 vols. London, 1819)
Orr, *Oxon. Agric.*	J. Orr, *Agriculture in Oxfordshire* (Oxford, 1916)
O.R.S.	Oxfordshire Record Society
Oseney Cart.	*The Cartulary of the Abbey of Oseney*, ed. H. E. Salter (O.H.S. lxxxix–xci, xcvii, xcviii, ci, 1929–36)
Oxf. Jnl.	*Jackson's Oxford Journal*
Oxon. Clockmakers	C. F. C. Beeson, *Clockmaking in Oxfordshire, 1400–1850* (Banbury Historical Society, 1962)
Oxon. Peculiars	*The Churchwardens' Presentments in the Oxfordshire Peculiars of Dorchester, Thame, and Banbury*, ed. S. A. Peyton (O.R.S. x, 1928)
Oxon. Poll, 1754	*Poll of the Freeholders of Oxfordshire taken at Oxford on 17th April, 1754* (Bodl. G.A. Oxon 4° 346)
Oxon. Visit	*The Visitations of the County of Oxfordshire taken in the years 1566, 1574, and 1634*, ed. W. H. Turner (Harl. Soc. v, 1871)
Oxon. Wills	*Some Oxfordshire Wills proved in the Prerogative Court of Canterbury, 1393–1510*, ed. J. R. H. Weaver and Alice Beardwood (O.R.S. xxxix, 1959)
Par. Colln.	*Parochial Collections made by Anthony Wood and Richard Rawlinson*, ed. F. N. Davis (O.R.S. ii, iv, xi, 1920–9)
Parker, *Eccles. Top.*	J. H. Parker, *Ecclesiastical and Architectural Topography of England: Oxfordshire* (Oxford, 1850)
Parker, *Guide*	J. H. Parker, *A Guide to the Architectural Antiquities in the Neighbourhood of Oxford* (Oxford, 1846)
Plot, *Nat.Hist. Oxon.*	R. Plot, *The Natural History of Oxfordshire* (Oxford, 1677)
P.N. Oxon. (E.P.N.S.)	Margaret Gelling, *The Place-Names of Oxfordshire* (English Place-Name Soc. xxiii, 1953–4)
Poor Abstract	*Abstract of the Answers and Returns relative to the Expense and Maintenance of the Poor*, H.C. 175 (1804), i
Poor Law Unions	*Returns relating to Poor Law Unions in England and Wales*, H.C. 81 (1854), lv
Protestation Ret.	*Oxfordshire Protestation Returns 1641–2*, ed. C. S. A. Dobson (O.R.S. xxxvi, 1955)
Pub. Elem. Sch. Ret.	*Return for Each Public Elementary School . . . for the Year ended 1st August, 1893* [C. 7529], H.C. (1894), lxv
Reg. Antiquiss.	*The Registrum Antiquissimum of the Cathedral Church of Lincoln*, ed. C. W. Foster and Kathleen Major (8 vols. L.R.S. 1931–58)
Reg. Sutton	*The Rolls and Register of Bishop Oliver Sutton, 1280–99*, ed. Rosalind M. T. Hill (vols. i–iv, L.R.S. 1948–58)
12th Rep. Com. Char.	*12th Report of the Commissioners for Charities*, H.C. 348 (1825), x

Ret. of Non-Provided Schs.	*Return of Non-Provided Schools*, H.C. 178–xxiv (1906), lxxxviii
Ret. of Sch.	*Return for Public Elementary Schools*, H.C. 403 (1890), lvi
Ross, *Cirencester Cart.*	*The Cartulary of Cirencester Abbey, Gloucestershire*, ed. C. D. Ross (2 vols. London, 1964)
Rot. Graves.	*Rotuli Ricardi Gravesend, 1258–79*, ed. F. N. Davis (Cant. and York Soc. xxxi, 1925, and L.R.S. xx, 1925)
Rot. Grosse.	*Rotuli Roberti Grosseteste, 1235–53*, ed. F. N. Davis (Cant. and York Soc. x, 1913, and L.R.S. xi, 1914)
Rot. Welles	*Rotuli Hugonis de Welles, 1209–35*, ed. W. P. W. Phillimore (Cant. and York Soc. i, ii, iv, 1905–8, and L.R.S. iii, vi, ix, 1912–14)
Rudder, *Glos.*	S. Rudder, *A New History of Gloucestershire* (Cirencester, 1779)
Salter, *Oxford Charters*	*Facsimiles of Early Charters in Oxford Muniment Rooms*, ed. H. E. Salter (Oxford, 1929)
Salter, *Oxon. Recusants*	'Recusants in Oxfordshire, 1602–33', ed. H. E. Salter, O.A.S. *Rep.* 1924
Saxon Oxon.	G. B. Grundy, *Saxon Oxfordshire* (O.R.S. xv, 1933)
Sch. Building Grants	*Statement . . . of Public Elementary Schools which have received Building Grants* [Cd. 1336], H.C. (1902), lxxviii
Schs. Enq.	*Schools Enquiry Commission Reports* 3966–XI, H.C. (1867–8), xxviii (10)
Schs. Ret.	*Return . . . of Number of Children in Inspected Schools in Year ending 31st August, 1867*, H.C. 58 (1867–8), liii
Secker's Visit.	*Articles of Enquiry Addressed to the Clergy of the Diocese of Oxford at the Primary Visitation of Dr. Thomas Secker, 1738*, ed. H. A. Lloyd Jukes (O.R.S. xxxviii, 1957)
Shaw, *Knights of England*	W. A. Shaw, *The Knights of England* (2 vols. London, 1906)
Skelton, *Oxon.*	J. Skelton, *Illustrations of Principal Antiquities of Oxfordshire* (Oxford, 1823)
Stapleton, *Cath. Miss.*	Mrs. Bryan Stapleton, *Oxfordshire Post-Reformation Catholic Missions* (London, 1906)
Subsidy 1526	*A Subsidy Collected in the Diocese of Lincoln in 1526*, ed. H. E. Salter (O.H.S. lxiii, 1905)
Visit. Dioc. Linc. 1517–31	*Visitations of the Religious Houses in the Diocese of Lincoln 1517–31*, ed. A. Hamilton Thompson (L.R.S. xxxiii, xxxv, xxxvii, 1940–7)
Walker Rev.	A. G. Matthews, *Walker Revised* (Oxford, 1948)
Wilb. Visit.	*Bishop Wilberforce's Visitation Returns for the Archdeaconry of Oxford, 1854*, ed. E. P. Baker (O.R.S. xxxv, 1954)
Wood, *Athenae* Wood, *Fasti*	*Athenae Oxonienses, to which are added the Fasti*, ed. P. Bliss (5 vols. London, 1813–20)
Wood, *Life*	*The Life and Times of Anthony Wood, Antiquary of Oxford, 1632–95, described by Himself*, ed. A. Clark (O.H.S. xix, xxi, xxvi, xxx, xl, 1891–1900)
Wood-Jones, *Dom. Archit. Banbury Region*	R. B. Wood-Jones, *Traditional Domestic Architecture of the Banbury Region* (Manchester, 1963)
Woodward's Progress	*The Progress Notes of Warden Woodward Round the Oxfordshire Estates of New College, Oxford, 1659–75*, ed. R. L. Rickard (O.H.S. xxvii, 1945)
Young, *Oxon. Agric.*	A. Young, *General View of the Agriculture of Oxfordshire* (London, 1809 and 1813)

THE HUNDRED OF BLOXHAM

IN 1841, before the addition of Shenington, Bloxham hundred had a population of 9,044 and an area of 27,710 acres.[1] It lies intermingled with Banbury hundred in the valleys between the Cherwell and the Cotswold crest along the modern Warwickshire border, and exhibits the chief characteristics of a wider region centred on Banbury. The Marlstone of the Middle Lias on the higher ground underlies the much-praised corn-producing 'red land',[2] and the clays of the Lower Lias in the valleys of the Cherwell and its tributaries give excellent pasture. The presence of easily worked Marlstone has given the villages striking architectural homogeneity, and the hundred is rich in survivals of vernacular architecture;[3] the 'uncommonly good soil' encouraged a type of mixed farming praised by visitors from Leland onward,[4] and only in three parishes (Adderbury, Broughton, and Drayton) was there extensive early inclosure for specialist farming. Two characteristic features of north Oxfordshire agriculture were a system of convertible husbandry (found at Bloxham from 1552), through leys intermingled with arable strips, and the cultivation of the open field in four quarters. The prosperity derived from agriculture was reflected in three notable houses, Wroxton Abbey, Broughton Castle, and Hanwell Castle, in the rebuilding of local churches in the late 14th century, and particularly in the great medieval churches of Bloxham and Adderbury. The rise of prosperous independent farmers was reflected in their houses, in their opposition to taxes in the early 17th century,[5] in the strength of Puritanism, and the growth of Quakerism in the area. Religious opposition owed much to the leadership of larger landowners, the Copes of Hanwell, the Fienneses of Broughton, and Bray Doyley of Adderbury; the proximity of Banbury was also an important factor. Parliamentary inclosure, beginning in the 1760s, transformed the landscape, and the first influx of 'foreign' building materials came with the completion of the Oxford Canal in 1790. With the growth of Banbury in the 19th century the area ceased to be exclusively agricultural, and in recent years the villages have become 'dormitories' for Banbury and other nearby towns. Since about 1860 large open ironstone workings have become a feature of the landscape.

The hundred is not named in Domesday Book but under the entry for the composite royal manor of Bloxham and Adderbury is the sentence 'the soke of two hundreds belongs to this manor'.[6] There is some evidence of a connexion with a 7th-century Mercian princess, and these two hundreds, like the manor to which they were attached, were probably once royal, as they were again in 1086, though earls Tostig and Edwin had held the manor, apparently in turn, in King Edward's day.[7] Bloxham hundred is first named in 1189–90 in connexion with murder fines.[8] The hundred is not systematically covered in the Hundred Rolls of 1278–9, but the following places are then mentioned as being in the hundred: Bloxham itself, Barford, Wigginton, Wroxton (no doubt including Balscott), Horley and Hornton, Sibford, and Adderbury.[9] Later medieval taxation returns add Alkerton, Bodicote, Broughton and (North) Newington,

[1] *Census*, 1841.

[2] Young, *Oxon. Agric.* 5.

[3] Wood-Jones, *Dom. Archit. Banbury Region*, *passim.*

[4] Leland, *Itin.* ed. Toulmin Smith, ii. 109.

[5] e.g. *Cal. S. P. Dom.* 1636–7, 36, 438.

[6] *V.C.H. Oxon.* i. 400.

[7] See pp. 16, 58–59.

[8] *Pipe R.* 1189 (P.R.S. xxxix), 108.

[9] *Rot. Hund.* (Rec. Com.), ii. 32–33.

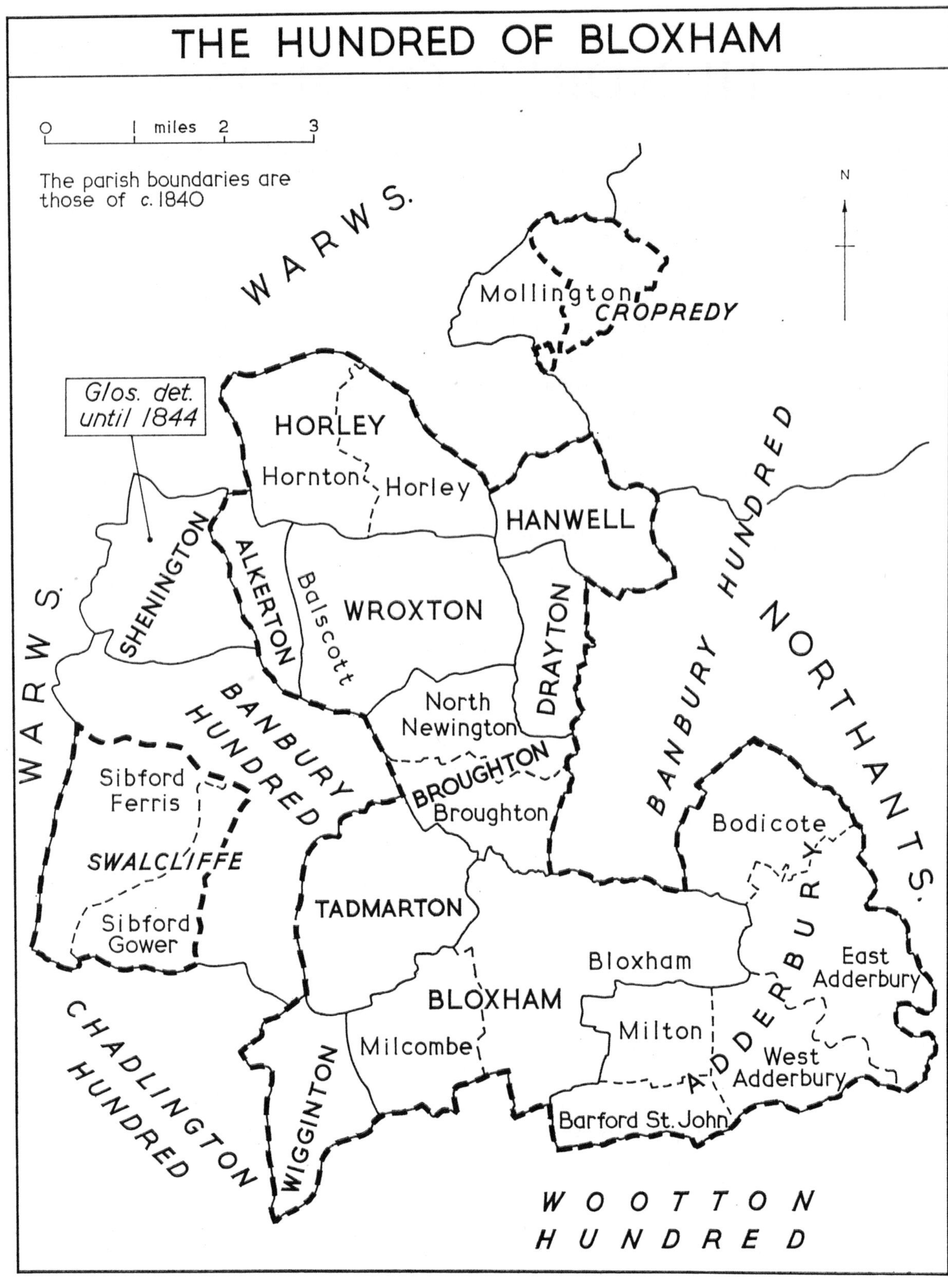
THE HUNDRED OF BLOXHAM
0 1 miles 2 3
The parish boundaries are those of c. 1840
N
WARWS.
Glos. det. until 1844
Mollington
CROPREDY
HORLEY
Hornton
Horley
HANWELL
SHENINGTON
ALKERTON
Balscott
WROXTON
DRAYTON
North Newington
BANBURY HUNDRED
BROUGHTON
Broughton
Sibford Ferris
SWALCLIFFE
Sibford Gower
TADMARTON
Bodicote
ADDERBURY
East Adderbury
West Adderbury
Bloxham
BLOXHAM
Milton
Milcombe
WIGGINTON
Barford St. John
NORTHANTS.
CHADLINGTON HUNDRED
WOOTTON HUNDRED

Drayton, Hanwell, Milcombe, Milton, Tadmarton, the Sibfords (in Swalcliffe), and the Oxfordshire part of Mollington (in Cropredy). The Sibfords and Mollington, however, were omitted in 1306[10] and again in the Protestation Returns of 1642, when they were included in Banbury hundred, to which the rest of Swalcliffe and Cropredy belonged.[11] A list of certainty money of 1651 once again included the Sibfords and Mollington,[12] and the stated composition of the hundred was unchanged in 1841. Shenington (1,628 acres), previously a detached part of Gloucestershire, was added to Bloxham hundred in 1844.[13] The hundred is composed of three separate portions: Epwell, Shutford, and Swalcliffe, none of which is named in Domesday Book, separate the main part of the hundred from the Sibfords and are part of Banbury hundred, although Epwell was part of Dorchester hundred until the 18th century;[14] a projection of Warwickshire separates Mollington from the rest of Bloxham hundred.

It is probable that the two Domesday hundreds dependent on Bloxham and Adderbury already included all the later components of Bloxham hundred. It has been noted that the three entries for Bloxham and Adderbury give a total hidage of 50 for those two places combined;[15] the Domesday hidage of all other later constituents of Bloxham hundred appears to be 162, a total with the 50 for Bloxham and Adderbury of 212. This near approximation to 200 suggests a double hundred of a familiar type. How these two hundreds were made up it is impossible to say, though it may be worth noting that the Sor Brook divides the 162 hides mentioned into two almost equal parts. In any case nothing is heard after 1086 of these twin hundreds; they appear to have coalesced into one, dependent on Bloxham alone.[16]

The region contains a number of Roman sites and ancient trackways and bears many marks of relatively early English settlement. The personal names which lie behind many of the place-names in the hundred are suggestive of early date.[17] Two villages, Adderbury and Tadmarton, are recorded in the 10th century.[18] Moreover, the Domesday assessment proves to be of considerable symmetry. The later hundred contained 5 places assessed in 1086 at 5 hides; these were Balscott, Bodicote (divided into 3 holdings), Drayton, and Hanwell. Wigginton was assessed at 10 hides, and 3 others at about 10 (Alkerton 9½, Barford 10½, Horley and Hornton 11); the total assessment of Mollington (3 holdings) was also 10 hides. Two places (Tadmarton and Broughton) were each assessed at 20 hides, and one (the Sibfords) at 31; the 50 hides of Bloxham and Adderbury have already been mentioned. Only Wroxton, with 17 hides, and Milcombe, with 8, seem to stand outside this pattern. Various permutations of these figures give larger round numbers still. As so much of this kind of calculation is arbitrary it is enough to point out that the 20 hides at Tadmarton with the 31 at Sibford would give a second 50-hide unit in the hundred. The Domesday assessment of Mollington, however, raises a difficult problem: 5 hides are assigned to Warwickshire (Kineton Hundred), 1 to Oxfordshire, and 4 to Northamptonshire, a shire from which Mollington was separated by parts of Cropredy. Part of Mollington is assigned to Northamptonshire on only one other occasion, in 1395,[19] and the Domesday attribution of 4 hides to that county rather than to Oxfordshire may simply be an error; on the other hand it has been thought possible that even this 'extraordinary division' of Mollington between 3 counties may represent 'a complicated piece of administrative geography'.[20] In any case

[10] E 179/161/8, 9, 10.

[11] *Protestation Ret.* 28, 30. The histories of the Sibfords and Mollington are reserved for a forthcoming volume on Banbury hundred.

[12] E 317/Oxon. no. 2.

[13] See p. 139.

[14] *V.C.H. Oxon.* vii. 3.

[15] Ibid. i. 374.

[16] Helen Cam, *Liberties and Communities*, 95, n. 1.

[17] *P.N. Oxon.* (E.P.N.S.), ii. 394, 396, 398, 401, 404, 408, 409.

[18] Ibid. 391, 406.

[19] C 136/85/15.

[20] *V.C.H. Oxon.* i. 392.

it seems that the division of Mollington, which held good for the next 800 years, must have been subsequent to the creation of this particular 10-hide unit.

The hundred has been held by only three families. The king early lost it; in 1283 Amaury de St. Amand alleged that his family had held it since before 1189.[21] In 1235 Annora de Verdun was granted her dower from the revenues of the hundred as she had it in the time of Ralph de St. Amand.[22] The hundred was briefly taken into the sheriff's hands in 1267 *propter defectum ballivorum*.[23] Amaury de St. Amand held the hundred at farm in 1278–9 for 50*s*. yearly; rents of 4*s*. were payable from Barford and from Wigginton, 10*s*. from Wroxton, and 21*s*. 8*d*. from Horley and Hornton.[24] The St. Amand family held the hundred until 1418; John de St. Amand leased the bailiwick before 1333 for a rent of 20 marks.[25] In 1418 Eleanor, relict of Amaury de St. Amand (d. 1402), conveyed the manor and hundred to Thomas Wykeham.[26] From this family they passed by marriage to the Fiennes family, and in 1477 Margaret grand-daughter of Thomas Wykeham and relict of William Fiennes, Lord Saye and Sele (d. 1471), died seised.[27] The Fiennes family of Broughton Castle (Lords Saye and Sele) have held the hundred ever since.

According to the Parliamentary survey of 1651 the issues of the hundred were £5 3*s*., and the whole profits £11 8*s*. yearly.[28] 'Certainty money' was payable in varying amounts from each village at Lady Day; the Hanwell 'certainty money' is mentioned as late as 1904.[29]

The meeting-place of the hundred was probably Bloxham. There is no sign that the hundred was ever sub-divided for the purposes of administration.

[21] *Plac. de Quo Warr.* (Rec. Com.), 667.
[22] *Close R.* 1242–7, 370.
[23] Ibid. 1264–8, 344.
[24] *Rot. Hund.* (Rec. Com.), ii. 32.
[25] *Cal. Pat.* 1330–4, 436.
[26] *Cal. Close*, 1413–19, 508.
[27] *Cal. Inq. p.m.* iv, p. 385.
[28] E 317/Oxon. no. 2.
[29] Bodl. G. A. Oxon. b 91 (2): *Sale cat.*

ADDERBURY

THE ancient parish of Adderbury[1] covered an area of 6,045 a. and included the townships of Adderbury East (2,058 a.), Adderbury West (1,160 a.), Bodicote (1,291 a.), Barford St. John (726 a.), and Milton (810 a.).[2] It was reduced in size in 1855 when Bodicote became a separate ecclesiastical and civil parish, and again in 1932 when Barford St. John was joined with Barford St. Michael to form a new civil parish.[3] The modern civil parish of Adderbury (East and West) with Milton covers 4,028 acres.

The ancient parish was largely bounded by rivers: on the east the Cherwell separated it from Northamptonshire, on the south the River Swere was the dividing line with Deddington parish and Wootton hundred, and on the west the Sor Brook, a tributary of the Cherwell, separated it from Bloxham.[4] The Middle Lias limestone underlies the whole of this area and there is an outcrop of Marlstone over a large part of it.[5] The soil is fertile and its characteristic reddish colour distinguishes the landscape, while the local quarries have provided good building material. There are many disused quarries for both building stone and ironstone.[6] The land lies mostly between the 300 and 400 ft. contours and the landscape is one of undulating hill and river valley. Generations of landowners and tenants have left their mark: it was common practice to stipulate in leases that tenants should plant trees, usually oaks or elms,[7] and well-timbered hedges diversify the natural bareness of the uplands. Resident gentry have created parks and gardens such as those around Adderbury House, and Bodicote and Cotefield Houses; and the needs of fox-hunters have led to the planting of coverts.[8]

Through the centre of the parish runs the main road from the Midlands by Banbury to Oxford (turnpiked in 1755),[9] and the Banbury–Buckingham road branches off it. The course of both these roads was altered by the inclosure award of 1768; their previous course can be seen on Ogilby's map of 1675, where it is noted that there was then 'an indifferent way' from Adderbury to Deddington.[10] Before the award the Buckingham road branched off the Banbury–Oxford road at Weeping Cross east of Bodicote, and ran south-eastwards to Nell Bridge, a line which followed that of the ancient Saltway.[11] After 1768 a minor road, branching off just to the north of Adderbury village, became the main Banbury–Buckingham road. Weeping Cross probably dated from the 15th century; it was repaired and embellished in 1730 and removed in 1803.[12] It might possibly have been a halting place for coffins on their way to the mother church at Adderbury, for Bodicote had no separate burial ground until 1754.[13]

Many of the parish bridges date from the Middle Ages: Aynho or Nell Bridge[14] was kept up by the Bishop of Winchester or his lessees; West Bridge or St. Mary's Bridge (i.e. the bridge over the Sor Brook between the two Adderburys) was the responsibility of New College, Oxford, or its lessees.[15] A bridge called 'Whytesbridge' was built in 1387, and 'Middle Bridge or Grylysbridge' was repaired with stone in the reign of Henry IV.[16] A report on Oxfordshire bridges in 1878 stated that the one wide arch of Adderbury Bridge (i.e. West Bridge) was mainly built of large squared stones dug near Adderbury and was finished with Hornton stone.[17] Ham (or Bloxham) Bridge was rebuilt in 1859 and carries the Milton–Deddington road over the River Swere, here little more than a brook. The repair of this bridge was shared by Adderbury and Deddington. Another bridge across the Swere, carrying the main Adderbury–Deddington road, lies *c.* 1⅓ mile below Ham Bridge.

Communications were greatly improved by the construction of the Banbury–Oxford section of the Coventry–Oxford canal between 1778 and 1790. Tarver's and Nell Bridge Locks, and Twyford, Adderbury, and Nell Bridge Wharfs were built on its course through the parish.[18] In 1887 there followed the construction of the Banbury, Chipping Norton and Cheltenham branch of the G.W.R.[19] It ran through Milton and Adderbury to meet the Oxford and Birmingham line at King's Sutton Junction. There was a halt at Milton and a station at West Adderbury. These were closed to passenger traffic in 1950 and the line was finally closed in 1964.[20]

Apart from the unusually large and scattered parish of Cropredy, Adderbury was the largest parish in north Oxfordshire and was more thickly populated than any other. In 1642 342 of its men took the Protestation Oath compared with 257 in Bloxham parish,[21] and in 1676 871 adults, almost certainly an under-estimate, were recorded in the Compton Census.[22] In the early 19th century

[1] Much of the material for this article was collected by Patricia Hyde.

[2] O.S. *Area Bk.* (1882).

[3] See p. 37; Oxon. Local Govt. Review Order, 1932.

[4] The following maps have been used: O.S. Map 25″ Oxon. V. 16; VI. 9, 13, 14; IX. 4, 8, 11, 12, 15, 16; X. 1, 2, 5, 6, 8–10, 13 (1st edn.); O.S. Map 6″ Oxon. IX, X (1st edn.); O.S. Map 2½″ S.P. 43 (1957).

[5] *V.C.H. Oxon.* i. geol. map.

[6] See p. 29.

[7] e.g. Ct. of John Pope, 20 Nov. 5 & 6 Phil. & Mary: Methuen Archives.

[8] e.g. *Oxf. Jnl.* 7 Apr. 1770: the Duke of Buccleuch's new plantations were damaged.

[9] Act for repairing roads from Banbury to Oxford, 28 Geo. II, c. 46. It was disturnpiked by 1875: 58–59 Vic., c. cxciv.

[10] Ogilby, *Britannia* (1698), plates 12, 82.

[11] Ibid.; P. Overton, *Oxfordshire Actually Surveyed* (1715); Beesley, *Hist. Banbury*, 16.

[12] MS. Top. Oxon. b 124, p. 55: notes by C. W. Hurst. For drawing see Beesley, *Hist. Banbury*, 115, 552 and MS. Top. Oxon. d 282, f. 144.

[13] See p. 37; *P.N. Oxon.* (E.P.N.S.) ii. 196.

[14] New Coll. Mun., Adderbury ct. rolls, 2 Eliz. I, 14 James etc. A family of the name Nel occurs frequently in the records. No evidence has been found for the bridge's reputed connexion with Nell Gwyn.

[15] Eccl. 1/73; *Adderbury 'Rectoria'*, 122.

[16] New Coll. Mun., acct. rolls, *passim*; see also *Woodward's Progress*, 26, 95.

[17] *Oxon. Co. Surveyor's Rep.* (1878), 24–5, 43–4, 85. For drawings see collection in O.R.O.

[18] Coventry to Oxford Canal Act, 9 Geo. III, c. 70; *Oxf. Jnl.* 2 Jan. 1790.

[19] E. T. MacDermot, *Hist. of the G.W.R.*, ii. 365.

[20] Ex inf. British Railways, Western Region.

[21] *Protestation Ret.* 41, 42, 44, 48.

[22] Compton Census. The figure recorded for Bodicote is 109 adults of both sexes of 16 and over, whereas there were at least 91 adult males of 18 and over in 1642.

population increased very rapidly, rising from 1,775 in 1811 to 2,525 in 1841. Thereafter it steadily declined, but changes in the boundary of the ancient parish invalidate any comparison between 20th-century and earlier totals.[23]

Despite the parish's rich soil and plentiful water supply little evidence has been found of pre-historic settlement. There were Romano-British villa sites at Bodicote and near Adderbury West.[24] It is uncertain when the first Anglo-Saxon settlements were made but it is probable that the Upper Cherwell area was overrun in the 6th or early 7th century, possibly by invaders from the east. The double village of Adderbury took its name from an Anglo-Saxon, Eadburga, the earlier form of the place-name being *Eadburgesbyrig*.[25] Since the parish feast used to be on the Saturday before 18 July, the feast day of St. Eadburga of Aylesbury (d. *c.* 650), who may have been the daughter of Penda, King of Mercia,[26] it is likely that the place was named after her.[27] Adderbury's position on the route through Banbury to the Midlands probably encouraged its development. The village was first mentioned in the time of Wynflaed (*c.* 950) and by the 11th century was one of the centres of a large royal estate.[28] In the 13th and 14th centuries Adderbury East and West were the largest settlements in the parish. They lay on opposite slopes of the Sor Brook valley and were together nearly as large and prosperous as the two parts of Bloxham, which were similarly sited on either side of a valley.[29] For the poll tax of 1377 there were 300 contributors.[30] In 1642 114 men from Adderbury East and 61 from Adderbury West took the Protestation Oath compared with 213 at Bloxham.[31] Growth certainly continued in the 18th century, though as incumbents always included Milton in their returns for Adderbury this can only be estimated roughly. In 1768 it was reported that there were 224 families in the three villages and in 1778 300 houses.[32] In 1801 there were 1,144 inhabitants in the two Adderburys, Adderbury East being far the larger; the peak figure was reached in both villages in 1841 when the figures recorded were 1,060 and 442 for Adderbury East and West respectively; in 1961 the figures were 1,312 and 534.[33]

Although the growing population and prosperity of the Adderburys has led to much new building on the outskirts, the villages still retain their regional character. A high proportion of houses and cottages in both date from the prosperous period of the 16th and 17th centuries, and many from the 18th century. Consistent use of local stone and careful restoration and rebuilding in the 19th and 20th centuries in traditional styles of architecture have given the villages a pronounced architectural harmony. Grass verges and low garden walls in front of the cottage rows are a common feature.[34]

The older part of Adderbury East lies partly on the main Oxford–Banbury road, but mainly on both sides of a sinuous branch road which runs westwards down the hill to the Sor Brook. The splendid medieval church, the two manor-houses on either side, the tithe barn, and the Old Vicarage are grouped at the lower end of the village street. It is likely that in the Middle Ages the peasants' houses were mainly around the green at the upper end of the village. The green, notable for its ancient elms and chestnuts, was probably at one time more extensive: in the late 14th century it was prominent enough for the place to be called Adderbury-on-the-Green.[35] The site of the village cross, which once stood there, is known.[36] It was at this end of the village that in the Tudor and Stuart periods the houses of the rising gentry were built — the mansions of the Wilmots, the Cobbs, and perhaps of the Danvers family, and also many farm-houses.

Adderbury East in 1665 had nearly as many taxable inhabitants as the whole of Bloxham or Deddington, a market town, and had a greater number of substantial houses.[37] There were 25 fair-sized dwellings besides the school. Four were assessed on 5 or 6 hearths and the rest on 3 or four.[38] Towards the end of the century Celia Fiennes described Adderbury as a pretty, neat village 'where are two or three good houses; one of Sir Thomas Cobb's and Lady Rochester's looks neat and well with good gardens'.[39] In the 18th century the nearby spa at Astrop (Bucks.),[40] the facilities for hunting, and the proximity of a number of large seats, including Wroxton and Broughton, encouraged aristocratic residents. The Wilmots' house was transformed by stages into the Duke of Buccleuch's palatial mansion and the upper end of the village was greatly altered by the laying out of the duke's grounds and the alteration of the course of the highway at inclosure in 1768. The vicar, writing in 1796, went so far as to say that 90 cottages had gone 'to embellish the environs of the heavy pile'.[41] This destruction followed by rebuilding accounts for the predominantly 18th-century character of the older cottages and houses on the Banbury road and very possibly for the present isolated position of the East End. If the green had once extended further to the east and was taken into the grounds of Adderbury House in 1768, Sydenham Farm, Fleet Farm, and Home Farm, all 17th-century or earlier buildings, would have been cut off from the rest of the village.

The chief 19th- and 20th-century additions to Adderbury East have been the schools, stone-built in the Gothic style in 1831 (the Sunday School), 1854, and 1961;[42] the Wesleyan Chapel (1893);[43] the Institute, given by J. W. Larnach in 1897; and the houses, built both by the R.D.C. and private enterprise, along the main road to Banbury and on Milton road.

[23] *Census*, 1801–1961.
[24] *V.C.H. Oxon.* i. 298, 330.
[25] Ekwall, *Concise Oxf. Dict. of Eng. Place Names*, 2.
[26] MS. Dunkin 438/5, p. 60; Kennett, *Paroch. Antiq.* i. 189–92; *Biog. Dict. of Saints*, ed. F. G. Holweck.
[27] Bicester church was also dedicated to her: *V.C.H. Oxon.* vi. 44.
[28] *Anglo-Saxon Wills*, ed. D. Whitelock, 10; see p. 24.
[29] See p. 66.
[30] E 179/161/44.
[31] *Protestation Ret.* 41, 43.
[32] MS. Oxf. Dioc. d 558, b 37.
[33] *Census*, 1801–1961.
[34] For views see *Country Life*, 7 Jan. 1949, p. 33; N.B.R.
[35] *Cal. Pat.* 1391–6, 382.
[36] O.S. Map 6″ Oxon. X (1881 edn.).
[37] *Hearth Tax Oxon.* 126–27, 131–33, 139–40, 141–42.
[38] Ibid. 139.
[39] *Journeys of Celia Fiennes*, ed. C. Morris, 26.
[40] Baker, *Northants.*, i. 703–4.
[41] New Coll. Mun., Adderbury corresp., vicar's letter to Warden, 27 June 1796.
[42] See p. 42.
[43] See p. 41.

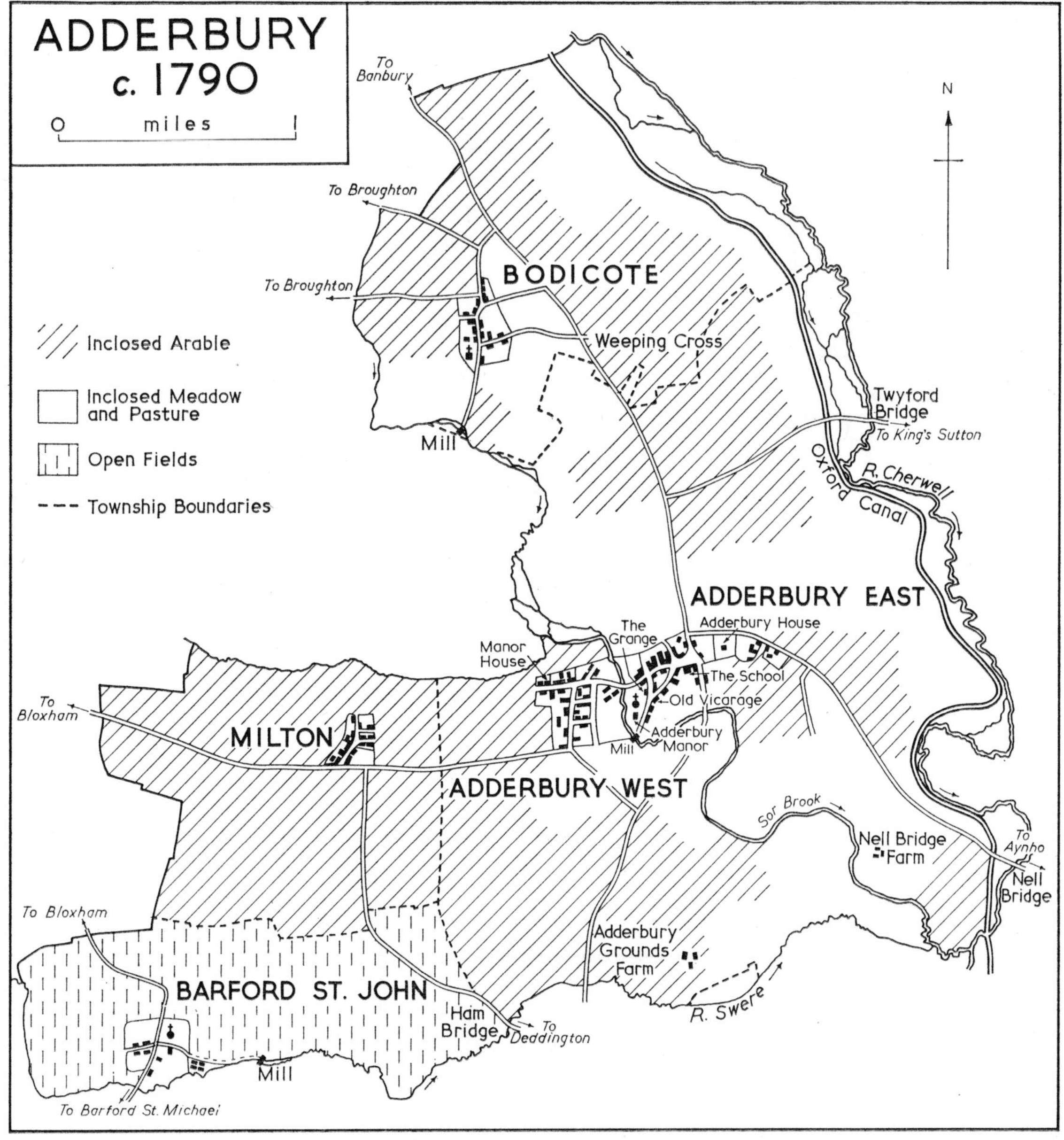

Of the principal houses the 'great house' in the post-medieval period was not one of the medieval manor-houses but Adderbury House. It stands on the east side of the main road to Banbury and is surrounded by extensive, walled grounds. A comparatively small part of the 18th-century house remains and still less ot its 17th-century predecessor. Compared with Wroxton Abbey, Broughton Castle, or even Hanwell Castle, the 17th-century house was small. Its owner, the widowed Ann, Countess of Rochester ,was assessed on 14 hearths for the tax of 1665.[44] After renewing the lease from the Bishop of Winchester in 1661 she is said to have spent £2,000 on building and richly furnishing the house, and on the gardens, so as to make it 'fit for a family who at that time were not possessed of any other save only a house near Scotland Yard'.[45] She evidently did not rebuild entirely, for the additions were described as being 'graft to the old mease'.[46] Dr. Plot, writing in 1676, classed the remodelled house among 'our most stately buildings' and 'among the most eminent in the country',[47] and the Warden of New College reckoned that it had cost £4,000 in all to build.[48] An inventory taken in 1678 mentions the Great and Little Halls, Drawing-Room, Great Room above stairs, Great Square Chamber, Lesser Dining-Parlour, and 11 other rooms, excluding the offices.[49]

Despite Plot's eulogies the house proved to be neither of a scale nor of an architectural design to satisfy John, Duke of Argyll, who obtained the lease in 1717. A constant traveller, seen in most of the courts of Europe, he had 'a head admirably turned to mechanics' and there is reason to suppose that he at once set about making plans for rebuilding. According to Horace Walpole the duke rebuilt the house in several stages.[50] Drawings[51] show that the

[44] *Hearth Tax Oxon.* 139.
[45] C 6/313/46.
[46] Church Com., Add. doc. 155465.
[47] Plot, *Nat. Hist. Oxon.* 266.
[48] Church Com., Add. doc. 155465.
[49] Dalkeith House Charter Room, box xiii. 9.
[50] *Journal of Visits to Country Seats* (Walpole Soc. xvi), 66.
[51] Dalkeith House Charter Room, box xii.

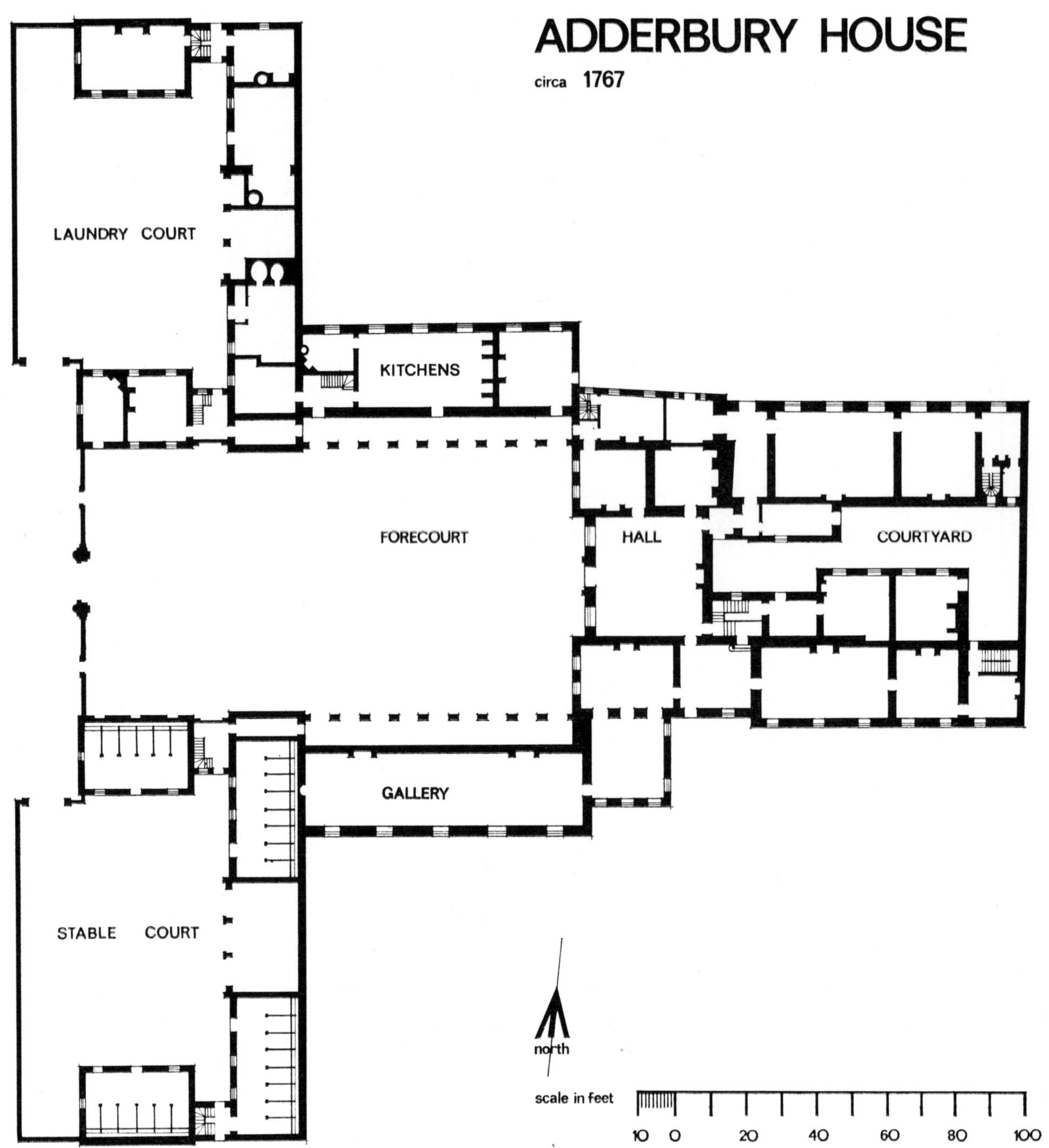

From an architect's survey of *c.* 1767 in the Soane Museum.

existing south front, originally surmounted by 6 Jacobean gables, was remodelled probably in 1722, the date on the rainwater heads. The Georgianization of the north front probably took place at the same period. James Gibbs was subsequently employed to design a new entrance front with a recessed portico, but his plan was not carried out. The arcaded wings were added in or soon after 1731, and were designed by Roger Morris. The southern wing contained a grand gallery nearly 80 ft. long, with a coffered ceiling and other ornamental features. This was in the Palladian style, but the arcades were a Vanbrughian feature which recall Eastbury House, Dorset, then being completed by Morris to Vanbrugh's designs. The stables and other offices were probably added still later.[52] Of this grandiose building only the stable block, the north arcade, and the south front of the main building survive. Before the last alterations in *c.* 1900 the south front had a plain elevation, 3 stories high, with round-headed sash windows.[53] It is evident from the plans that portions of the earlier house were incorporated in the Georgian mansion, and some traces of what may be 17th-century masonry can still be seen on the north side of the existing house.

On the death of John, Duke of Argyll, in 1743 the house was occupied first by his eldest daughter Caroline and then by her son Henry, Duke of Buccleuch.[54] In 1768 the duke was by account 'carrying on great works at Adderbury'.[55] The opportunity, afforded by inclosure that year, to extend the park of Adderbury House may well have been taken, but it also seems likely that there were alterations to the stables, the duke being a well-known rider-to-hounds, and to the interior of the house. The duke's architect was in all probability Sir William Chambers, who was engaged that year on work at the duke's town house in Grosvenor Square.[56] When Adderbury House was sold in 1774 it was said to contain 56 rooms, including a lofty entrance hall, 3 drawing-rooms, a library, and a billiard-room.[57] The whole was later described as a superb mansion worthy of royalty,[58] but Horace Walpole considered it 'large but very inconvenient' and admired the numerous pictures and busts more than the architecture.[59]

The grounds matched the house in magnitude. They covered *c.* 224 a. of flower-gardens and parkland, enclosed with a verge of evergreens and forest trees. There was also a 'fine serpentine stream of water . . . in full view of the house'.[60] The park, like the house, was the work of several owners: it had certainly been enlarged as early as 1734, when land was bought from Sir Edward Cobb, and again by the Rt. Hon. Charles Townshend;[61] later the Duke of Buccleuch employed 'Capability' Brown to make a design for altering the park and gardens.[62]

Early in the 19th century the estate was bought by J. E. Field, who in 1808 decided to pull down most of the building and convert it into 'a handsome dwelling suitable for a family of distinction'.[63] Brewer described the result as a 'happy effort of architectural consistency and adaptation'.[64] An early 19th-century drawing shows that all that remained of the central block was the south front, to which a central doorway and porch were added. Two of the first-floor windows were cut down and provided with iron balconies.[65] The house was bought by W. H. Chamberlin in 1826, but it was not until J. W. Larnach became its owner in 1891 that it was enlarged to its present dimensions.[66] Larnach built additional accommodation to the north of the existing house, and added the pedimented projection in the centre of the south front, together with its Ionic portico. Though corresponding exactly to the style of the 18th-century work, the present east and west elevations are due entirely to Larnach. In 1948 the Oxfordshire County Council acquired the house and grounds for use as an Old People's Home.[67]

The second most important house in Adderbury East was probably the Cobb mansion, of which only the two sets of 17th-century gateposts remain. Drawings exist of the house before its final destruction, and something is known of its history from documents. The 16th-century William Cobb, a freeholder as well as a lessee of New College, may have been the original builder. A stone with the date 1582, which has been inserted in the south side of the eastern gate pier,[68] presumably came from the old house before it was remodelled in the 17th century. William Cobb died in 1598, but his widow Alice lived on there until 1627.[69] Their son William was knighted in 1634 and 7 of his children were baptized in the village church between 1622 and 1637.[70] In 1665 when Sir Thomas Cobb was living at the house it was assessed for the tax on 16 hearths, a higher assessment than that for the Countess of Rochester's house.[71] Warden Woodward of New College, who visited it when on progress in 1668, has left a record of Sir Thomas's hospitality to himself and some of the local gentry. In 1673

[52] An architect's survey was made probably in 1767; one copy is in the Soane Museum (43 v) and is reproduced on p. 8. There was another in the possession of the Duke of Buccleuch, attached to an estate map of 1769: Gepp, *Adderbury*, 62 and corresp. with the duke's Secretary: Bodl. Bradford pps. (uncat.).

[53] See plate facing p. 13.

[54] For the family see *Complete Peerage*, ii, 368–70. Caroline married secondly Charles Townshend, Chancellor of the Exchequer; for a reference to Townshend at Adderbury in 1765 see Hist. MSS. Com. *Buccleuch, I.* 415–16.

[55] *Journals of Lady Mary Coke*, ed. J. A. Home, ii. 28.

[56] Ex inf. Mr. John Harris, who also states that in the Metropolitan Museum of Art, New York, there is a design for a wall mirror attributed to Chambers and inscribed 'for Adderbury'. At Dalkeith House there is an elevation of a proposed new front by Chambers.

[57] *Sale cat.* 1774 (Bodl. uncat.).

[58] Brewer, *Oxon.* 521.

[59] *Journal of Visits to Country Seats* (Walpole Soc. xvi), 66.

[60] *Sale cat.* 1774.

[61] MS. d.d. Risley B I 2/9; New Coll. Mun., drawer 55.

[62] Dorothy Stroud, *Capability Brown*, 213; a plan by Brown is preserved at Dalkeith House.

[63] *Oxf. Jnl.* 25 Jul. 1891.

[64] Brewer, *Oxon.* 522. He notes also (p. 521) that many water spouts attached to the mansion bore the initials and coronet of Wilmot, Earl of Rochester. They are more likely to have been those of the Duke of Buccleuch, of which some remain today.

[65] MS. Top. Oxon. a 37, f. 14.

[66] *Oxf. Jnl.* 25 Jul. 1891; Gepp (*Adderbury*, 63) states that he added one wing.

[67] Ex inf. Clerk to the Oxfordshire County Council.

[68] Ex inf. Mr. P. S. Spokes, who gave a 'squeeze' of this dated stone to the Ashmolean Museum.

[69] For pedigree see *Oxon. Visit.* 320–2.

[70] Par. Rec., register. For a Cobb tomb, once in the chancel of Adderbury Church and now in the Methuen chapel, Corsham church (Wilts.), see Gepp, *Adderbury*, 40–41.

[71] *Hearth Tax Oxon.* 139.

Woodward could not lodge there, as part of the house had been pulled down and had not yet been rebuilt.[72] The remodelled house is depicted in two water-colour copies of an early engraving.[73]

The Cobb family continued to live in this house until the death of Sir George in 1762. His heirs were his two married daughters, one of whom in 1768 leased the house to George Montagu, the bachelor friend of Horace Walpole.[74] Walpole wrote in 1768 that he had heard that Montagu had got 'into an old gallery that has not been glazed since Queen Elizabeth, and under the nose of an infant Duke (of Buccleuch) and Duchess'; he complained that his friend had given himself up 'to port and parsons and would end like a fat farmer, repeating annually the price of oats and discussing stale newspapers'.[75] After one winter in the house Montagu wanted many repairs and alterations, including sash windows 'to let in the sun'.[76] By 1815 it was in ruins; it was partly demolished and the kitchen wing was converted into cottages and a small house.[77]

Close to the Cobb mansion was another of the village's larger houses. Since the 18th century it has been called the 'Rookery'. One side fronts upon the green, the other upon the High Street. It now appears to be a typical 3-gabled Jacobean house, but it is likely that the core of the house is older. Some of the walls in the north-west wing are of a much greater thickness than is usual in this region in 17th-century buildings. The date 1656 on the 2-storied projecting porch with a small powder closet over the entrance is probably the date of a remodelling. Wall-paintings on the upper floors appear to date from the Civil War period. The property was occupied in the 18th century by Samuel Clarson (d. 1802), a descendant of the Clarsons of Horley. On the death of Elizabeth Clarson (d. 1824) the house passed to her cousins, Mary and Elizabeth Wyatt, and finally to the Bradford family, relations by marriage. C. W. Bradford Wyatt, an ornithologist of repute, lived there on the death of his aunt, Elizabeth Bradford Wyatt (d. 1878),[78] and replaced the early-19th-century sash windows by the present stone-mullioned ones.[79] Early in the next century, a large wing containing the present drawing-room and a new stair-case was added. The house is now the home of Godfrey, Lord Elton.

These houses at the upper end of the village have a comparatively short history compared with that of the two manor-houses and the Old Vicarage at the lower end. Adderbury Manor is on the site of the manor-house of the Bishops of Winchester, who acquired their Adderbury estate in 1014 or 1015. The existing house, though much altered in later periods, probably dates in the main from the 16th century, but incorporates medieval walling. The house was occupied successively in the late Middle Ages by the families of Adderbury, Councer, and Bustard, the lessees of the bishop.[80] Anthony Bustard (d. 1568) was wealthy and may have rebuilt the medieval house sometime after 1534, for the initials A. B. were found on the interior woodwork by the Revd. Dr. T. Woolston, who was living in the house in the late 18th century.[81] The Woolstons kept a boarding-school there; the house had 10 bedrooms besides attics, ground-floor rooms, and an underground cellar.[82] It must have been already considerably restored for it had been described as ruinous in 1712, and in the 19th century (in 1887 in particular) it was again carefully restored and modernized.[83] It still retains its mullioned windows, but the stonework has mostly been renewed; there are traces of the original medieval hall-house in the dining-room and bedroom above,[84] and the large open fire-place with 4-centred arch is late 15th- or early 16th-century. This stonework, however, is reported to have been brought from another house.[85]

The second manor-house in Adderbury East, the Grange, though rebuilt in the 17th century, also incorporates medieval features and has a well-preserved medieval tithe barn. The house is on the site of the early medieval rectory-house, but when New College appropriated the church in 1381[86] this house became a secular manor-house or grange and was leased to tenants. The Warden of New College frequently stayed there, held his courts, and entertained the 'best and most substantial' of the parish. In 1395, for instance, he entertained 16 of them.[87] In the 1320s the rector's house had consisted of a great hall with a chamber, a detached kitchen, and other outhouses, all of which were inclosed by a wall. The main entrance into the inclosure was called the Town Gate. The fact that stone was brought for repairs in 1327–8 from Slaughter (Glos.)[88] suggests that the house was of good quality. Between 1386 and 1388 John Wylot, mason, was employed in building the walls, and stone slates were brought from Charlton; in 1388 there is a reference to the thatching of 4 houses 'lying in the rectory' (i.e. in the courtyard); in 1390 a stone porch was constructed; in 1395 a 'great door' and a new room; in 1443 a new gatehouse was built at a cost of over £13. The accounts also refer to the rectory's garden, malt-house, brew-house, granary, hay grange, pig-house, ox-house, and sheepcote, and to the gutters between the hall and the kitchen. The malt-house and brew-house, as well as the main house itself, were all stone slated.[89]

The medieval building was probably still in existence in 1659 when Warden Woodward described the rectory-house as 'very large, containing much building', but 'impossible to be made convenient and handsome without pulling down'. There were 6 mean rooms above stairs and 4 barns.[90]

[72] *Woodward's Progress*, 26, 27.

[73] For illustrations of the remodelled house see Gepp, *Adderbury*, facing p. 64. The originals are now in possession of Godfrey, Lord Elton.

[74] H. Walpole, *Correspondence with George Montagu*, ed. W. S. Lewis and R. S. Brown, ii. 257 and see ibid. index for other references to this house.

[75] Ibid. 259.

[76] Methuen Archives nos. 5653, 5729, 3662, 3665.

[77] Drawing by J. C. Nattes (1815): MS. Top. Oxon. a 37, f. 15; MS. Oxf. Dioc. c 664, f. 43.

[78] MS. notes abstracted from Bodl. Bradford pps. (uncat.) by M. L. Dix Hamilton.

[79] Gepp, *Adderbury*, 71–72. Gepp records an erroneous tradition that the house had been built for a member of the banking house of Montagu.

[80] See p. 15.

[81] *Gent. Mag.* 1792, lxii (1), 111, 112.

[82] Church Com., Adderbury Bk. 8.

[83] Ibid. Add. Doc. 155465; Gepp, *Adderbury*, 68. For a water-colour of the stair-case in 1888 see MS. Top. Oxon. a 48, f. 76.

[84] *Country Life*, 14 Jan. 1949, p. 86.

[85] Local information.

[86] See p. 30.

[87] *Adderbury 'Rectoria'*, 75.

[88] New Coll. Mun., acct. rolls.

[89] Ibid.; *Adderbury 'Rectoria'*, 4, 8, 19, 22.

[90] *Woodward's Progress*, 18.

As the college still kept its courts at the house and the Warden and his 'rider' stayed there, its condition was a matter of frequent complaint.[91] It was not until 1683, however, that Sir Thomas Cobb, the lessee, finally contracted with John Bloxham of Banbury, 'carpenter and surveyor' to rebuild the house for £130. The existing house is substantially the same as the house that Bloxham rebuilt and completed in 1684.[92] It is of 2 stories, with attics, and a cellar. Originally it had 4 gables, but since a fire *c.* 1884, which destroyed the oldest part, the north kitchen-wing, it has had 3 only. The roof incorporates several re-used medieval timbers, including a moulded roof principal, perhaps an indication of the shortage of wood that afflicted the north and central parts of Oxfordshire after the Civil Wars. A large new kitchen block was built in 1829 and the north wing that was burnt down in the 19th century was rebuilt and is now occupied by the library. The college sold the house in 1875 and it has been modernized by the present owner Mr. P. E. Middleton.

The date of the tithe barn is difficult to determine, but differences in construction indicate that the 2 western bays are either an extension or a reconstruction. The architectural character of the remainder suggests a date early in the 14th century for the construction of the barn, but some work may have been carried out in 1421–3, when a mason was paid over £20 for making 17½ rods of masonry and 7 buttresses for a new building at the rectory.[93] It is possible that the buttresses in question were those of the barn, and that the masonry included the 2 western bays in their present form; it is equally possible, however, that the new building was the rectory house itself. In 1877–8 the barn was converted into a stable by Lord Haldon, who inserted a floor and 2 dormer windows.[94]

The Old Vicarage probably stands on the site of the medieval vicarage-house, which was enlarged in 1397.[95] The main part of the existing house probably dates from the 16th and 17th centuries. Warden Woodward of New College noted in 1663 that the house was 'reasonable well' in repairs, but that the vicar would improve it in time.[96] The main range faces north and is of 2 stories with cellars and attics. A square stair-case projection was added at the rear of the house, probably in the late 17th century, and rises to the attics. The roof is partly hipped and retains most of its original rafters. There are dormer windows in it both back and front. Some stone fire-places seem to be of rather earlier date than the house and may have been re-used. One mullioned window remains in the stair-case projection and another in the cellar. The other early windows have been replaced by sash ones, perhaps in 1768 when the vicar was living in college until his house, which was 'very ruinous' could be put right.[97] Considerable alterations were also made in the time of R. R. Stephens (1858–74), who seems to have been responsible for adding the south-east projecting wing and the bays to the ground floor on the south side.[98] The present vicarage-house is a smaller, equally ancient house that was once probably a farm-house. It is **L**-shaped, has 2 stories, cellars, and gabled attics. It retains many original stone-mullioned windows and open fire-places with 4-centred arches and moulded jambs and spandrels.

Another of the smaller houses in Adderbury East belonged to the Danvers family; it was assessed on 4 hearths in 1665[99] but cannot now be identified. Adderbury East has many other houses, inns, and cottages dating from the 16th, 17th, and 18th centuries that deserve notice. Of particular architectural interest is a single-unit house in the main street, of 2 stories with gabled attic. It is very large for this type of house, measuring 19 × 17½ ft. inside and is distinguished by fine details.[1] The school and schoolmaster's house facing the green is a 16th-century building. In 1589 the vicar left money for a free school and begged the inhabitants to help 'cart the material for it with their carts and carriages'.[2] The original building remains largely intact, including some of the original stone-mullioned windows and parts of the original tie-beams and the horizontal struts of the queen-post roof. In 1659 Warden Woodward mentioned the 'school and kitchen, etc. below, with 6 or 7 rooms above, lower and upper', and commented that they might be made very good.[3] For the hearth tax of 1665 as many as 4 hearths were returned for it.[4] The extension on the south side was built in 1847 in a similar Tudor style. In 1965 the house was for sale as a private dwelling having been considerably altered inside.

Among the farm-houses in Adderbury East are Green Farm, the 'Royal Oak' in the High Street and the 'Bell', both once farm-houses, and the Old Mill House. In East End there are 3 farm-houses dating from the 16th or 17th century which have been little altered. Sydenham Farm and the Home Farm, for example, are **L**-shaped in plan, and of 2 stories with attics, and retain many of their original stone-mullioned windows. The 'Plough' and East House (once The Lawn) are 18th-century additions, the latter being built by the Duke of Buccleuch for his Scottish agent.[5]

Adderbury West straggles up the hill from the Sor Brook to the main Bloxham–Deddington road. Except for the 20th-century bungalows, which lie apart from the old village, and the disused Independent chapel, erected in 1829, it is built almost entirely of the local stone and in the regional style. Here also grass verges, climbing fruit trees on the house walls, small unwalled flower gardens, and a

[91] Ibid. 18, 22, 27.

[92] Bloxham's contract is in Methuen Archives; see *Cake and Cockhorse* (Banbury Hist. Soc.), ii, no. 12 for a transcript of the contract and reproduction of Bloxham's elevation.

[93] *Adderbury 'Rectoria'*, 75–78: other workmen were engaged in building a kiln, a bake-house, a pigsty, and a sheep-pen.

[94] Gepp, *Adderbury*, 58; see plate facing p. 13.

[95] New Coll. Mun., acct. rolls.

[96] *Woodward's Progress*, 21.

[97] MS. Oxf. Dioc. d 558.

[98] MS. Oxf. Archd. Oxon. c 46, f. 56; Gepp, *Adderbury*, 56. There was a drawing of the house as it was before Stephens' alterations at the vicarage in *c.* 1900.

[99] *Hearth Tax Oxon.* 140.

[1] Wood-Jones, *Dom. Archit. Banbury Region*, 175.

[2] New Coll. Mun., Adderbury, will of Christopher Rawlins.

[3] *Woodward's Progress*, 17.

[4] *Hearth Tax Oxon.* 139. For a Buckler drawing of the school in 1824 see plate facing p. 12; J. C. Buckler, *Views of Endowed Grammar Schools from original drawings* (1827).

[5] Gepp, *Adderbury*, 73.

green planted with chestnuts, set off the excellence of the buildings.[6]

The largest and most important of the manor-houses was Le Halle Place. It is substantially a 3-gabled 17th-century house remodelled in the 19th century. It contains some medieval work, probably part of the house granted to Walter atte Halle in 1310.[7] The property descended to the Barber family in the 17th century and the parish registers testify to their residence for most of the period from 1629 to 1854. In 1665 William Barber was assessed for tax on 12 hearths;[8] he was connected with Oxford and London merchants and presumably acquired his wealth in trade.[9] Much of the rebuilding probably dates from his day. In 1716, when Edward Barber leased part of the house, among the rooms mentioned were 'two over the hall, commonly called "hall chamber" '.[10] The Barber family ceased to live there on the death of John Barber, known as Squire Barber, in 1854.[11] The present house has a forecourt with a high screen-wall pierced by three pairs of apparently 17th-century stone gateposts. It is possible, however, that these are not all original as in 1730–1 a gatehouse with loft and chamber over it was mentioned.[12] To the west of the house is a 4-gabled square dovecot of the 17th century. On the north is a range of single-storied stabling with attic dormers. It is built of coursed ironstone rubble and may be rather later in date than the dovecot. The house now consists of a coursed-rubble front or west elevation of 2 stories with 2 projecting wings, between which, at eaves level, are 3 gabled dormers. The east elevation has 2 gables. In 1728 some sash windows were inserted in the principal rooms in the front of the house by Edward Barber.[13] In the late 19th century these were replaced by stone-mullioned and transomed windows.[14] The interior contains much 17th- and 18th-century panelling and a fine oak stair-case with panelled walls of the early 17th century; this, however, may have been brought from elsewhere. Leading to the hall there is a stone doorway with 14th-century ball flower ornament in its moulded arch. To the south is another doorway with a pointed arch, and in the passageway leading to it are medieval vaulting ribs.

Of the other large houses Crosshill, standing in a commanding position on the hill-top, has a 3-storied Georgian facade of ashlar, with 7 sash windows with stone key-stoned architraves, and a central stone doorway. The latter has moulded side pilasters and is surmounted by a broken pediment containing a blank cartouche. In the inside there are mid-18th-century panelling and door frames, but most of the fittings appear to be *c.* 1800, when marble fire-places and steel grates were inserted. The house stands on the foundations of a 16th- or 17th-century building of which the cellars and footings remain on the north side. It was lived in in the later 18th century by Christopher Aplin,[15] who was probably responsible for the remodelling of the house and for the stable range. It is possible that it was this house that Mrs. Holford Cotton took on the death of her husband, the vicar, in 1822. In 1823–4 she paid the architect C. S. Smith and others over £4,000 for additions and repairs to an unnamed house in Adderbury.[16]

The house now known as Little Manor may have belonged to the Doyley family. It is an old house, remodelled in the 18th century. In 1665, when Bray Doyley[17] was lord of Adderbury West, he was assessed on 6 hearths for his house.[18] In 1696 his house consisted of 2 parlours, a hall, rooms over the great and little parlours, 3 chambers, and garrets, kitchen, pantry, brew-house, cheese-chamber, and dairy.[19] This may have been the manor-house of the St. Amands, the medieval lords of Adderbury West.[20]

Among the smaller houses and cottages of architectural interest are the 17th-century South Bank, The Leys, the 'Dog and Partridge', and Callary Cottage. The last is dated 1665, but a medieval window of 2 lights, trefoil-headed with a moulded hood, has been incorporated.

Close to Little Manor lies the Friends' Meeting House, which bears the date 1675 and was built at Bray Doyley's expense.[21] It is a plain one-storied building with a gabled attic dormer and is fitted inside with galleries.[22] It is now (1965) disused.

Bodicote lies in the north of the parish, slightly to the west of the main Oxford–Banbury road. It is 2 miles distant from Banbury, by which it was probably much influenced. Its name probably derived from the Anglo-Saxon personal name Boda.[23] Evidence suggesting that Bodicote was an offshoot from Adderbury is set out below.[24] In the Middle Ages Bodicote was apparently a smaller settlement than either of the two Adderburys.[25] By the 16th century it may have outstripped Adderbury West in population, though not in wealth, and by 1642 as many as 91 took the Protestation Oath.[26] Its growth was connected with the development of the weaving industry at Banbury and other north Oxfordshire villages. In 1759 the curate recorded that there were 84 houses, and in 1768 that there were 80 or 100 families.[27] By 1801 Bodicote with 574 inhabitants was far more populous than Adderbury West. In 1831 numbers reached 779, but declined thereafter during the 19th century. Although Bodicote lost 301 a. to Banbury in 1932, its population had reached 1,056 by 1961.[28]

[6] For views see N.B.R.; *Country Life*, 14 Jan. 1949, p. 88; MS. Top. Oxon. c 502.

[7] See p. 21.

[8] *Hearth Tax Oxon.* 136.

[9] For pedigree and family see *Oxon. Visit.* 266; O.R.O. Misc. Pl 1/1, 2, 3. For the vicar's opinion of Barber see MS Oxf. Dioc. c 454, f. 1.

[10] MS. d.d. Risley H iv 1/1; M.I. in church. John Barber had a small but valuable collection of portraits, including those of Sir Samuel Luke, his wife, and son: *Luke Jnl.* i. frontispiece.

[11] For the Barbers see p. 21; C. F. C. Beeson, 'Halle Place . . .' in *Cake and Cockhorse* (Banbury Hist. Soc.) ii. no. 12.

[12] MS. d.d. Risley A ix 1/2.

[13] Ibid. H iv 1/1.

[14] Gepp, *Adderbury*, 72.

[15] For the date of Aplin's residence see Par. Rec., reg. under the year 1780.

[16] MS. d.d. Risley c 15.

[17] See p. 17.

[18] *Hearth Tax Oxon.* 136.

[19] MS. Wills Oxon. 19/1/4.

[20] The Doyleys succeeded the Danvers family as lords of St. Amand's manor in 1565: see p. 17; there is no evidence, however, that the Danvers family ever resided in Adderbury West. For a lease of the house in 1519 to the Fermors see B. M. Eggerton MS. 1938, f. 85.

[21] See p. 39.

[22] For a view see MS. Top. Oxon. c 512, f. 11.

[23] *P.N. Oxon.* (E.P.N.S.), ii. 396.

[24] See pp. 24–25.

[25] See p. 25.

[26] E 179/161/196; *Protestation Ret.* 44.

[27] MS. Oxf. Dioc. d 555; ibid. d 558.

[28] *Census*, 1801–1961; Oxon. Loc. Govt. Review Order (1932).

The parish church from the south-east *c.* 1830

The grammar school in 1824

ADDERBURY

The green, Adderbury East

Adderbury House, south front

The 14th-century tithe barn

The Friends' meeting-house, interior

ADDERBURY

The village lies mainly on either side of a long street, but several small lanes branching off it suggest that as population increased building sites were let on the closes formerly attached to the High Street houses and ran backwards towards the open fields. The High Street was paved with stone as early as the 17th century.[29] A new drainage system was laid down in 1894 and by 1903 the village was lighted by gas supplied from Banbury.[30] The medieval church, the 'Baker's Arms', and a school built in the Gothic style just before 1852[31] are the chief buildings in Church Street. In High Street, a continuation of Church Street, are the 'Plough', various shops, including the Post Office and the Co-operative stores, and some large 18th- and 19th-century mansions, inclosed by high garden walls. Among the large houses are Bodicote House, an 18th-century house which is mentioned in a deed of 1722 and is now the offices of the Banbury Rural District Council; Bodicote Manor, a Georgian house incorporating an older house, Bodicote Grange (since 1932 in the borough of Banbury), and The Elms. Among the surviving 17th-century houses are Broughton House and Paddock Farm, both modernized in the 18th and 19th centuries, and a house immediately to the north of Paddock Farm which has a date panel inscribed 'T.B. 1687' and retains some of its original wood-mullioned windows. It may have been the home of the wealthy Bradford family that had 3 taxable houses in the hamlet in 1665. Thomas Bradford himself then had a 3-hearth house.[32] The south wing of the Old Barn, built in an **L**-shaped plan in two builds, probably dates from early in the 17th century, but the rest of the house is of a later period. The 2 largest houses in the village in 1665, each assessed on 5 hearths, and inhabited by Alexander Hawtrey and William Knight,[33] have not been identified. There are some 17th-century cottages at Farm Place.

Among the 19th-century additions are the Wesleyan chapel (1845) in East Street, a row of houses in East Street dated 1885, and a parish room and library given in 1893 by J. F. Stankey of Bodicote House.[34] A notable 20th-century addition is the crescent of council houses, with a green in front. Bodicote is fast losing its ancient rural character, and traditional building materials of stone and thatch are being superseded by brick, slate, and concrete. The medieval cross, which stood in the middle of the village near the 'Plough Inn' until at least 1841, has now gone, and so also has the 18th-century workhouse, and the Baptist chapel in Chapel Lane, erected in 1817–18 and demolished *c.* 1906.[35] The 'White Hart', mentioned in 1833, has changed its name to the 'Horse and Jockey'.

The hamlet of Milton lies on the western boundary of the parish, on the north side of the road from Bloxham to Deddington; the old part of the hamlet lies well off this road on a branch lane. The name was originally Middleton[36] and was perhaps so named as it lay between Adderbury and Bloxham. The old part of the hamlet consists of farm-houses and cottages, two of them now used as a Post Office and shop. They are built of the local ironstone and date mainly from the 17th century.

For a brief period in the later 17th century Milton achieved importance as a centre of early nonconformity in north Oxfordshire.[37] The Presbyterian chapel has disappeared, but Samuel Cox's cottage, in whose garden it was built *c.* 1708, still stands on the west side of the hamlet.[38] In 1665 Milton had 7 substantial houses, 1 assessed on 5 hearths, 2 on 4 hearths, and 4 on 3 hearths, and there were 14 other smaller houses.[39] This is the only basis for an estimate of Milton's population until the 19th century. In 1801 the population was 105 and rose to a peak figure of 205 in 1831; though numbers fell to 131 in 1881 they had risen to 203 by 1961.[40]

Today there is a 16th- or 17th-century inn, the 'Black Boy', which retains, like many other houses in the hamlet, some of its original mullioned windows. It has a 17th-century stair-case projection at the back but its front has been remodelled. This inn perhaps did a more than local trade in the 18th century when a bridle path ran from Deddington to Banbury through Milton, and probably attracted travellers away from the toll-road.[41] Glebe Farm, once used as a Sunday school, is in origin a late 17th-century house of merit. It has two date-stones, one placed there by the Turner family in 1694, the other inscribed H.J.G. 1876. McGreal's farm-house is a good example of the early-17th-century regional style, a 2-unit plan combining hall and parlour.[42] Manor Farm is a reconditioned house of about the same date; it has 2 stories and cellars and a thatched tithe barn. A nearby cottage has a 14th-century traceried window, and another single-story cottage has a doorway with a stone frame with a pointed chamfered head and plain jambs. These details may have been re-used after Milton's medieval chapel ceased to be used.[43] Now there is a 19th-century church. In the 20th century a row of cottages has been put up.

Barford St. John, the smallest of the hamlets, lies in the extreme south-west of the parish on either side of the Bloxham–Deddington road. Barford, like Adderbury, grew as two villages, Barford St. Michael and Barford St. John, divided by a river, the Swere. Only Barford St. John, generally known in the Middle Ages as North or Little Barford, lay in Adderbury parish and Bloxham hundred. The name Barford derived from the Old English *bere*, meaning barley, compounded with ford because the river was fordable there.[44] Both Barfords lie at *c.* 350 ft. above the valley floor which is liable to flooding, so much so that the road over the bridge is sometimes impassable for motor traffic.[45] In 1784 *c.*30 families lived in Barford St. John, by 1801 there

[29] MS. Top. Oxon. b 124, f. 58.
[30] *Kelly's Dir. Oxon.* (1903).
[31] *Oxf. Jnl.* 6 Mar. 1852.
[32] *Hearth Tax Oxon.* 142–3.
[33] Ibid. 142.
[34] MS. Top. Oxon. b 124, f. 58.
[35] Ibid.; Par. Rec., map of Bodicote in 1833.
[36] *P.N. Oxon.* (E.P.N.S.), ii. 401.
[37] See p. 39.
[38] For a photo of the cottage see *Trans. Unitarian Hist. Soc.* ii (2), facing p. 10.
[39] *Hearth Tax Oxon.* 138.
[40] *Census,* 1801–1961.
[41] G. Herbert, *Shoemaker's Window* (ed. C. S. Cheney), 70.
[42] For a detailed description with plans see Wood-Jones, *Dom. Archit. Banbury Region,* 93–5.
[43] See p. 36.
[44] *P.N. Oxon.* (E.P.N.S.), ii, 393–4. Barford St. John was called 'Barford Plaice' in the early 13th century after its lords, the de Plescy family. Note that Barford St. Michael was always in Wootton hundred and not in Bloxham hundred as there stated.
[45] Local information.

were 100 inhabitants, and by 1901 only 55. In the 1961 census returns it was included with Barford St. Michael.[46]

The manor-house lies close to the church on rising ground. It was largely rebuilt *c.* 1920 on a long rectangular plan facing west with a wing on the north-east. It is of 2 stories and built of coursed ironstone rubble with stone end copings. The south gable end seems least restored and bears a date panel with 1598, W.M.S. The square stone dove-cot was built *c.* 1713[47] and the barn, 175 ft. long, to the south-east of the house, may date from about the same time. It was presumably this house for which William Gamock was assessed on 8 hearths for the tax of 1665.[48] It is likely that the original manor-house lay south-east of the church and nearer the river. There are traces of the moat and earth banks of an early fortified dwelling.[49] Manor Farm or Moat Farm, perhaps the Belcher's house which was assessed on 4 hearths in 1665,[50] dates from 1606 and bears the initials T. and A.B. on the south gable. It, too, is of 2 stories and is built of local material on an **L**-shaped plan with wings to south and east. Originally it consisted of hall and parlour only, but a newel-stair contained in a gabled stair-tower has been added. A 13th-century stone window of 2 lights has been reset in the ground-floor room in the west face.[51] Among other 17th-century buildings are the Crown Inn, remodelled in modern times, Mead and Street Farms, both in the village, and Barford Mill at the bottom of Coombe Hill. In Church Lane, close to the church, there is a house built on the 2-roomed plan, dating from 1680–90. Its doorway has a richly moulded architrave of stone.[52]

The airfield at Barford opened during the Second World War is now (1965) an Anglo-American radio station.

Among the gentry of Adderbury may be mentioned the Danverses, Doyleys, Penistones and Bustards.[53] The Barbers of Adderbury West were prominent from at least 1634, when Robert Barber made proof of his coat,[54] until the mid-19th century. The Dalby family of Milton and Goodwin family of Bodicote, although neither was armigerous,[55] were well-established and affluent. The aristocratic element at Adderbury East brought the parish into contact with a wider world. One notable visitor in 1739 was Alexander Pope, who stayed with John, Earl of Rochester, at Adderbury House and commemorated the visit in a poem;[56] another was Horace Walpole, who visited his friend Montagu in 1770.[57] In the 19th century the villages continued to attract a large number of resident gentry: in 1854 there were 18 in Adderbury East, 5 in Adderbury West, and 12 in Bodicote.[58]

The parish had a number of distinguished vicars[59] and other individuals of note: William (d. 1349) of Adderbury and John (fl. 1445) of Adderbury became Priors of Wroxton;[60] Richard Andrew, born in Adderbury *c.* 1400, was a distinguished royal clerk and Dean of York (1452–77);[61] John Cole (b. *c.* 1624) made a reputation as a translator from French,[62] and his brother William (d. 1662), educated at the grammar school at Adderbury and later at New College, was considered the most famous herbalist of his time;[63] William Oldys, the son of Adderbury's ill-fated royalist vicar,[64] and a distinguished lawyer and Chancellor of Lincoln, was born and educated at Adderbury;[65] Robert Parsons (1647–1714), chaplain to several members of the Rochester family and at one time the vicar's curate, became Archdeacon of Gloucester and was said to be responsible in 1680 for the profligate Earl of Rochester's death-bed repentance.[66] From Bodicote came Regenbald (fl. 1065), Chancellor to Edward the Confessor;[67] the mathematician and author, John Kersey the elder (1616–*c.* 1677);[68] and Hubert Stogdon (1692–1728), a nonconformist divine.[69]

Joseph Tyrell (d. 1878), the 'Bodicote body-snatcher', brought notoriety to the village. In January 1832 he was imprisoned for stealing a corpse from Broughton churchyard in October of the previous year. Local tradition maintains that Tyrell had been helped by other Bodicote men.[70]

In the 17th century the parish was deeply involved in political strife. As early as 1638 Thomas Bodicote made 'undutiful speeches' and refused to pay ship money.[71] Both political parties were represented in the parish. Of the gentry Wilmot was for the king and it was alleged that it was his influence and threats that prevented Adderbury men from going to the aid of Banbury in July 1642.[72] Cobb and Doyley were for Parliament, and along with Lord Saye and Sele and his son were the only men to be excepted from the general pardon offered by Charles I in 1642 to all in the county who had taken arms against him.[73]

Throughout the summer and winter of 1643 and 1644 Royalist or Parliamentary troops were in and about the villages. In May 1643 the Earl of Northampton's troops were at Bodicote; in June and July 2 troops of the King's horse were reported to be at Adderbury; and in August 3 troops of Prince Charles's regiment were there;[74] at the same time Lord Wilmot also had a strong force in this area to prevent the advance of the Earl of Essex to the relief of Gloucester, but the latter's forces later passed

[46] MS. Oxf. Dioc. b 37, f. 113; *Census*, 1801–1961.
[47] E 134/12 Geo. II/East. no. 12.
[48] *Hearth Tax Oxon.* 137.
[49] *V.C.H. Oxon.* ii. 331 and plan.
[50] *Hearth Tax Oxon.* 138.
[51] For further details and plan see Wood-Jones, *Dom. Archit. Banbury Region*, 145–7; and see plate facing p. 46.
[52] Ibid. This house cannot have been the curate's house as that was 'taken down', *c.* 1792: MS. Oxf. Dioc. c 454, ff. 47, 117.
[53] E 179/161/196.
[54] *Oxon. Visit.* 324, 334.
[55] Ibid. 333.
[56] Brewer, *Oxon.* 522.
[57] H. Walpole, *Correspondence with Geo. Montagu*, ii. 311–12.
[58] Billing, *Dir. Oxon.* (1854).
[59] See pp. 32–33.
[60] *V.C.H. Oxon.* ii. 102.
[61] Emden, *O.U. Reg.*
[62] Wood, *Athenae*, iv. 540.
[63] Ibid. iii. 621.
[64] See p. 32.
[65] *D.N.B.*
[66] Ibid.
[67] Ibid.
[68] Wood, *Athenae*, iii. 424; Bodicote Par. Rec., reg.
[69] *D.N.B.*
[70] MS. Top. Oxon. b 124, f. 33; J. H. Fearon, 'The village of Bodicote', *Cake and Cockhorse* (Banbury Hist. Soc.) iii. no. 7. 138–9.
[71] *Cal. S. P. Dom.* 1637–8, 429, 438; 1640–1, 123.
[72] Beesley, *Hist. Banbury*, 302.
[73] Ibid. 329.
[74] Luke, *Jnl.* ii. 105, 117, 121, 135.

through Adderbury without much opposition.[75] In January 1644 Prince Charles's regiment was again at Adderbury;[76] in March Prince Rupert's regiment, quartered at Adderbury, was said to have been 'ruined' by a Parliamentary assault;[77] in the autumn Adderbury was probably permanently occupied either by Parliamentary troops besieging Banbury, or by royal relief forces. The Earl of Northampton with 800 horse and 500 foot was certainly quartered there in October.[78] It may have been at about this time when the Parliamentary troops were in occupation that the vicar, Oldys, was killed by them. In February 1645 Nell Bridge was being guarded by Dutch troops and *c.* 40 men were at Sir William Cobb's houses where they had made some fortifications.[79] The 'bridge between Aynho and Adderbury', i.e. Nell Bridge, was pulled up later by 50 musketeers lodged at Lord Wilmot's house.[80] In March it was reported that all the Earl of Northampton's regiment was quartered at Bodicote and Adderbury preparatory to marching westwards.[81]

A less tragic effect of the war, though nevertheless a serious and probably common one, is illustrated by the action for debt brought in 1652 by a dependant of Lord Wilmot's. She claimed that the steward, though he lent her £30, would not pay her her annuity of £60 in March 1646, on the ground that if the parliamentary forces then besieging Banbury Castle won they would seize the profits of the manor.[82]

MANORS AND OTHER ESTATES. In 1014 or 1015 Athelstan (d. 1016), son of Ethelred II, granted to the Bishop of Winchester land at Adderbury that he had bought from his father for 200 mancuses of gold and 5 pounds of silver.[83] Between 1038 and 1044 Bishop Aelfwine leased the estate to Osgod for life,[84] but in 1086 it was again in the hands of the Bishop of Winchester; at this time it was reckoned as 14½ hides.[85] *ADDERBURY* was one of the manors confirmed to the See of Winchester in 1284.[86] In 1551 Bishop John Ponet surrendered the lands of his see in exchange for an annuity of £1,333 6*s.* 8*d.*,[87] and in 1552 the Crown granted Adderbury to Sir Andrew Dudley (d. 1559).[88] In 1558 the Crown restored the manor to Bishop John White,[89] whose successors held it until the 19th century.[90]

From 1405 onwards the demesne lands were leased at rents which rose from £15 16*s.* to £23 13*s.* 4*d.* in 1478. Among 15th-century lessees were John Adderbury in 1405, John Mason in 1436, Roger atte Welle in 1442, John and Thomas Chedworth in 1478, and William Councer in 1493.[91] John Bustard, who took a 40-year lease in 1511,[92] was the son of William Bustard of Nether Exe (Devon). He married first Elizabeth Fox of Barford (d. 1517) and secondly Margaret, relict of William Pope.[93] He was succeeded in 1534 by his eldest son Anthony, who in 1536 let his Adderbury farm to a creditor, James Merynge of Adderbury.[94] William Bustard, Anthony's eldest son by Jane Horne of Sarsden, succeeded his father in 1568.[95] In 1601 the customary lands of the manor were leased to Thomas Gardner, Thomas Edolf, and William Walter.[96] In 1629, after the death of William Bustard, all the leases were taken up by Charles Wilmot, Viscount Wilmot of Athlone,[97] who was succeeded, probably in 1643, by his son Henry, Viscount Wilmot of Adderbury and later Earl of Rochester, the prominent Royalist commander. Henry's Adderbury estates were sequestrated by the Parliamentarians in 1645,[98] and were sold to Edward Ash,[99] one of the commissioners of the Committee for Compounding, who in 1649 granted them to Joseph Ash and James Wainwright.[1] Henry died in exile in 1658 and in 1661 his relict Anne bought a new lease for 3 lives from the Bishop of Winchester, who had recovered the manor at the Restoration.[2] Anne survived her son John, Earl of Rochester (d. 1680), and her grandson Charles (d. 1681), and in 1683 granted the lease to trustees to the uses of her will, which made Edward Henry Lee, Earl of Lichfield, her residuary legatee. After Anne's death in 1696 the earl successfully maintained his title to the lease against the sisters of Charles Wilmot.[3] At his death in 1716 the lease reverted to the Bishop of Winchester, who sold it to John Campbell, Duke of Argyll and Greenwich.[4] The Duke's relict Jane succeeded to the lease in 1743 and was followed in 1767 by her daughter Caroline, who in the same year was created Baroness Greenwich in her own right. She had married first Francis, Earl of Dalkeith (d. 1750), and secondly Charles Townshend.[5] In 1770 Caroline's Adderbury estates, with others purchased by Townshend, were settled on Henry, Duke of Buccleuch, her son by her first husband, subject to the payment to Caroline of an annuity of £1,000.[6] The duke continued to lease the Winchester manor until 1801 when the estate was split into a number of lots.[7] Richard Heydon, Richard Bignell, and Fiennes Wykeham, all of Banbury, took a lease of the manor in that year,[8] and were succeeded in 1837 by

[75] Beesley, *Hist. Banbury*, 351, 352.
[76] Luke, *Jnl.* iii. 241.
[77] *Letter Bks. of Sir Samuel Luke, 1644–45*, ed. H. G. Tibbutt, p. 628.
[78] Ibid. p. 673.
[79] *Letter Bks. of Sir Samuel Luke, 1644–45*, ed. H. G. Tibbutt, p. 686.
[80] Ibid.
[81] Ibid. p. 694; cf. p. 693.
[82] C 5/377/18.
[83] *Anglo-Saxon Wills*, ed. D. Whitelock, 56.
[84] *Cod. Dipl.* ed Kemble, iv, p. 76.
[85] *V.C.H. Oxon.* i. 401.
[86] *Winchester Cath. Cart.* ed. A. W. Goodman (1927), no. 451; *Cal. Chart. R.* 1257–1300, 274.
[87] *Reg. of Gardiner and Ponet*, ed. H. Chitty (Cant. & York Soc. xxxvii), p. xix.
[88] *Cal. Pat.* 1550–3, 153. For him see *D.N.B. sub* Edmund Dudley.
[89] *Cal. Pat.* 1557–8, 147.
[90] Gepp, *Adderbury*, 10.
[91] Hants R.O. Eccl. 2/159419, 159435, 159438, 155841, 155848.
[92] Ibid. 155861.
[93] *Oxon. Visit.* 196.
[94] P.C.C. 24 Hogen; E 318/2215; C 1/957/53.
[95] P.C.C. 48 Drury.
[96] Hants R.O. Eccl. 2/155943.
[97] Ibid. 155948.
[98] *Complete Peerage*, xi. 45–49; C 5/377/18; *Cal. Cttee. for Compounding*, ii. 938.
[99] *Cal. Cttee. for Compounding*, iii. 2235; C 54/3391/5.
[1] C.P. 25(2)/474/Mich. 1649.
[2] *Complete Peerage*, xi. 45–47; C 6/313/46.
[3] C 6/313/46.
[4] *Complete Peerage*, i. 206–7.
[5] Ibid. ii. 369–70.
[6] C.P. 25(2)/1399/Hil. 12 Geo. III; doc. (uncat.) in Risley colln. at Durham Univ.
[7] Ch. Com., Adderbury doc.; O.R.O., gamekprs' dep.
[8] These and the following names are from ct. bks. *penes* Lord Elton.

Benjamin William Aplin of Banbury, who purchased the manor from the Bishop of Winchester. Aplin was succeeded by Charles Henry Dairds in 1879 and George Bliss in 1882. Oliver Stockton was lord of the manor in 1920,[9] and Godfrey, Lord Elton, has been so since 1954.

In 1381 William of Wykeham, Bishop of Winchester, gave the rectory of Adderbury to New College, Oxford.[10] Although *RECTORY* manor had its own courts[11] it had little land until 1768 when the college received 456 a. for the rectorial tithes.[12] The first lessee (*ante* 1387) of the college's estate was Walter atte Halle, who was followed by John Berewyk (in 1387), Simon Veysey (1418), William Thomelyn (1428), Robert Chedworth (1432), John Knolles (1448), Alice Knolles, widow (1467), Thomas Lynde (1468), and Thomas Smythe (1472). John Cokkys of Weston, lessee from 1494 to 1500,[13] was probably the wool merchant of that name mentioned in 1507.[14] He was succeeded by Thomas and George Smythe (1504). Thomas Penystone, lessee from 1509 to 1527, claimed to have been unfairly ejected by John London, Warden of New College,[15] who replaced him by his brother Ralph London, lessee from 1527 to 1566. Simon Edolf,[16] who next took up the lease, was succeeded at Adderbury by his son Thomas *c.* 1599. Richard Fiennes (d. 1613) was the lessee in 1610, and he was succeeded by his son William, Lord Saye and Sele.[17] Shakerley Marmion of Adderbury leased the manor from 1616 to 1620 when it was taken by Alice and William (later Sir William) Cobb of London. The manor then remained in the Cobb family for nearly a century and a half. Sir William was succeeded in 1659 by his son Thomas, created a baronet in 1662, who died in 1699. Sir Thomas's eldest son Sir Edward died unmarried in 1744, and the latter's brother and successor Sir George died in 1762, leaving 2 daughters: Anne, who married John Blagrave of Southcot (in Reading), and Christian, who married Paul Methuen of Corsham (Wilts.).[18] In 1791 the latter's children Paul Cobb Methuen and Christian, wife of Frederick, Lord Boston, conveyed their share to Richard Heydon,[19] who, with Richard Bignell and Charles Wyatt,[20] appears to have obtained a lease of the whole manor in 1794. Wyatt alone took a lease in 1818 and he was followed by John Whittlesee (in 1828), Nathaniel Stilgoe (in 1850), and Zachariah Stilgoe (in 1875).

In 1086 the Conqueror held in demesne 34½ hides in Adderbury and Bloxham which had formerly belonged to Earl Edwin of Mercia.[21] By the 13th century the Adderbury part of the estate had been split into 3 manors. One of these, later known as *ST. AMAND'S*, was described in 1285 as ½ fee in Adderbury and Milton and was reckoned as 3 hides.[22] This must have been the ½ fee held in Oxfordshire by Richard d'Oilly in 1186, which later evidence shows to have been in Adderbury.[23] By 1199 Richard had enfeoffed Arnold (or Arnulf) de Mandeville,[24] with the manor.[25] In 1205 Richard obtained the wardship of his grand-daughter and heir, the daughter of Ralph d'Oilly,[26] but he evidently died soon afterwards, for in the same year Arnulf had custody of his lands and the heir,[27] whom he married.[28] Arnulf's English lands were seized and restored at least 3 times between 1204 and 1221,[29] and were finally confiscated as *terra Normannorum* in 1224, when Henry III granted Adderbury to Walter de Verdun,[30] lord of Bloxham.[31]

In 1229 Walter was succeeded at Bloxham by his son Ralph,[32] but Adderbury was granted to his nephew Amaury de St. Amand.[33] On Ralph's death in 1230 Amaury obtained his lands also,[34] and in 1239 Amaury's brother William quitclaimed Bloxham and Adderbury to him.[35] Amaury, steward of the king's household from 1233 to 1240,[36] died in 1241 on Richard of Cornwall's crusade.[37] His son Ralph succeeded to Adderbury,[38] and died in 1254;[39] his grandson Amaury[40] came of age in 1256 and held Adderbury until his death in 1285.[41] Amaury was succeeded in turn by his sons Guy (d. 1287), Amaury (II), who died in 1310, and John. Mary, the relict of Amaury (II), held Adderbury in dower in 1316, but his brother John, who married Margaret, daughter of Hugh Despenser the elder, held it at his death in 1330.[42] John's son Amaury (III) came of age in 1335 and meanwhile Adderbury was in the custody of a king's clerk, John of Leicester.[43] Amaury (III), Justiciar of Ireland (1357–9), in 1346 granted a life-lease of Adderbury to John of Evesham.[44] He was succeeded in 1381 by his son Amaury (IV), who died in 1402,[45] leaving as heirs his grandson Gerard Braybroke, son of his daughter

[9] *Kelly's Dir. Oxon.* (1920).

[10] *Adderbury 'Rectoria'*, 89–90; *Cal. Pat.* 1377–81, 621.

[11] *Adderbury 'Rectoria'*, 114 sqq.

[12] For details of the rectory estate see pp. 30–31.

[13] New Coll. Arch., Adderbury acct. rolls. The following names are from the college's calendar of charters and from Bodl. MS. Chs. Oxon. 1068–1081.

[14] *Cal. Pat.* 1494–1509, 535.

[15] C 1/559/45; *Bucks. Visit.* (Harl. Soc. lviii), 98.

[16] *Kent Visit.* (Harl. Soc. liv), 51; P.C.C. 112 Cobham.

[17] P.C.C. 18 Capell.

[18] Ibid. 119 Anstis; G.E.C. *Baronetage*, iii. 268.

[19] C.P. 25(2)/1390/Trin. 31 Geo. III.

[20] Heydon, Bignell, and Wyatt were lessees of the Winchester manor 1801–37: see above.

[21] *V.C.H. Oxon.* i. 400.

[22] *Feud. Aids.* iv. 159; cf. *Cal. Pat.* 1401–5, 24, where the manor is called a third of Adderbury manor.

[23] *Red Bk. Exch.* (Rolls Ser.), 59.

[24] He held lands in Normandy: ibid. 799, where he is spelt Maulai. See also *Rot. Norm.* (Rec. Com.), 68. He is called *flandrenis* in 1230: *Pat. R.* 1225–32, 407.

[25] *Red Bk. Exch.* (Rolls Ser.), 123; cf. *Rot. Litt. Claus.* (Rec. Com.), i. 482.

[26] *Pipe R.* 1205 (P.R.S. N.S. xix), 151; *Rot. de Ob. et Fin.* (Rec. Com.), 298.

[27] *Rot. Norm.* (Rec. Com.) 142.

[28] *Rot. Litt. Claus.* (Rec. Com.), i. 327.

[29] Ibid. 7, 327, 482; *Rot. Norm.* (Rec. Com.) 142.

[30] *Rot. Litt. Claus.* (Rec. Com.), ii. 6; cf. *Bk. of Fees*, 1396.

[31] See p. 60.

[32] *Ex. e Rot. Fin.* (Rec. Com.), i. 182.

[33] *Close R.* 1227–31, 162. For the St. Amand family see *Complete Peerage*, xi. 295 sqq.

[34] *Close R.* 1227–31, 443.

[35] *Cal. Chart. R.* 1226–57, 247; *Fines Oxon.* 235.

[36] See T. F. Tout, *Chapters in Admin. Hist.* vi. 38.

[37] *Close R.* 1237–42, 331.

[38] *Bk. of Fees*, 823.

[39] *Ex. e Rot. Fin.* (Rec. Com.), i. 440.

[40] During his minority he was in the custody of Paulinus Peyvre: *Cal. Pat.* 1232–47, 476; *Bk. of Fees*, 1396.

[41] *Close R.* 1254–6, 278–9; *Cal. Inq. p.m.* ii, p. 350; *Feud. Aids*, iv. 159.

[42] *Cal. Close*, 1279–88, 462; *Cal. Inq. p.m.* v, p. 148; vii, p. 208; *Feud. Aids*, iv. 166.

[43] *Cal. Close*, 1333–7, 382; *Cal. Fine R.* 1327–37, 198.

[44] *Cal. Pat.* 1345–8, 136; cf. *Feud. Aids*, iv. 179.

[45] C 136/21/10; *Cal. Close*, 1402–5, 2; C 137/40/48.

Eleanor, and Ida, his daughter by his second wife Eleanor. In 1395 Amaury (IV) had granted an annuity of £13 6*s.* 8*d.* from Adderbury and Bloxham to Edmund Danvers,[46] and in 1401 he had settled these manors on his wife, Eleanor.[47] In 1418 Eleanor sold them and other property to Sir Thomas Wykeham and others for an annuity of £66. 13*s.* 4*d.*[48]

Sir Thomas (d. 1441) sold the reversion of the property in 1439 to John Danvers, son of Richard Danvers of Epwell, who bought it for the children of his second wife, Joan Bruley of Waterstock. John died *c.* 1449 and Adderbury passed to Sir Thomas Danvers of Waterstock, his eldest son by Joan.[49] The manor was held of Sir Thomas by Thomas Fyfeld on whose death in 1491 it was called 'Fythfelds'.[50] Sir Thomas was succeeded in 1502 by his brother William (d. 1504).[51] William's son John died in 1509, leaving his relict Margaret a life estate in Adderbury,[52] and his son and heir John died in 1517, leaving his 4 sisters as his heirs.[53] Adderbury, however, passed to the younger John's uncle Thomas, who died childless in 1523. At that time a third of the manor was still held in dower by Anne, relict of William Danvers (d. 1504).[54] Thomas's brother William,[55] of Upton (in Ratley, Warws.), succeeded, and was followed in 1558 by his eldest son George who married Margaret, daughter of Thomas Doyley of Hambleden (Bucks.).[56]

In 1565 George Danvers sold St. Amand's to his brother-in-law Robert Doyley of Merton,[57] who in the same year settled the manor on himself and his second wife Katherine Tregyan, with reversion to their heirs male.[58] Robert died in 1577, and Katherine held the manor until her death in 1585,[59] when it passed to her eldest son Robert. By his first wife, Elizabeth Weston, Robert had two sons, John and Nathaniel, but his second wife, Anne Yates of Witney, whom he married in 1598, attempted unsuccessfully to induce him to settle his Adderbury property on her and her children. In 1600, at her suit, Robert was found to be a lunatic; a subsequent petition did not effectively alter that conclusion and the Court of Wards retained the management of his estates.[60] Robert's eldest son John married Anne Bray of Fifield Merrymouth and succeeded his father in 1640.[61] He supported Parliament in the Civil War and was succeeded in 1656 by his eldest son Bray Doyley, a Quaker,[62] who died in 1696 leaving St. Amand's to his nieces Dorothy and Elizabeth, daughters of his brother Robert. Dorothy had married Thomas Oliffe of Aylesbury and Elizabeth married William Markes of North Crawley (Bucks.).[63] In 1701 Bray's surviving brother Edmund unsuccessfully claimed the manor as his heir male.[64] Dorothy and Elizabeth divided the estate, and in 1722 William Markes's trustees gave part of his share to his youngest son Richard. Under an agreement made in 1729 between Doyley and Richard Markes and Thomas Oliffe, the last received the manor-house. In 1751 Doyley Markes left most of his lands to Richard, who with his brother-in-law Thomas Marshall sold St. Amand's manor to Daniel Zachary of London in 1757.[65] Zachary sold it to Charles Townshend in 1766.[66] In 1770 it presumably passed with Towshend's other lands to the Duke of Buccleuch.

A second part of the former royal demesne, later known as *HAGLEY'S* or *BROWN'S* manor, was held in chief as a knight's fee by Oliver de Linguire in the 12th century.[67] A Roger de Linguire is mentioned in connexion with Oxfordshire in 1182,[68] and in 1192 Robert de Linguire paid relief for the Adderbury fee.[69] Robert was succeeded in 1238 by his son Henry,[70] whose daughter and heir Lucy married Henry Hagley, who inherited the manor in her right in 1259.[71] In 1285, however, a William de Linguire held $\frac{1}{3}$ fee in Adderbury of Henry.[72] Henry's son Edmund succeeded his mother at Adderbury in 1297[73] and his father at Hagley (Worcs.) by 1304. He died *c.* 1322[74] and in 1332 his son Edmund granted Adderbury to his own son Henry and Henry's wife Katherine.[75] In 1365 Henry was succeeded by his nephew Henry (II), son of his sister Isabel, who took the name Hagley.[76] In 1409 Henry (II) settled the manor on himself and his wife Alice for life, with remainder to his brother William and his wife Maud.[77] Alice outlived Henry (II) and William, and was succeeded in 1433 by Maud, by then the wife of Humphrey Hay.[78] In 1435 the reversion of the manor was granted by Alice, Humphrey, and Henry (II)'s heir, Thomas Hagley, to John Matthew and another.[79] Thomas alleged that John Matthew was merely to obtain the manor on his behalf[80] but John evidently succeeded Maud, for it was he who in 1460[81] sold

[46] *Cal. Pat.* 1399–1401, 441; *Cal. Close,* 1399–1402, 301, 563.

[47] *Cal. Pat.* 1401–5, 24.

[48] Ibid. 1416–22, 175; *Cal. Close,* 1413–19, 508, 510–11.

[49] *Cal. Close,* 1429–35, 308; *Cal. Pat.* 1436–41, 347; ibid. 1441–6, 344; C.P. 25(1)/191/28/85. For the Danverses see Macnamara, *Danvers Family, passim.*

[50] *Cal. Inq. p.m. Hen. VII,* i, p. 290.

[51] Macnamara, *Danvers Family,* 165, 175, 177.

[52] Ibid. 185–7; C 142/24/62, 63.

[53] C 142/32/36.

[54] C 142/40/62; Macnamara, *Danvers Family,* 188.

[55] Macnamara, *Danvers Family,* 516.

[56] Ibid. 517; C 142/121/140.

[57] *Cal. Pat.* 1563–6, 271; *V.C.H. Oxon.* v. 223.

[58] W. D. Bayley, *House of D'Oyly* (1845), 57.

[59] Ibid; C 142/214/217; MS. Wills Oxon. 186, f. 273.

[60] Bayley, *House of D'Oyly,* 60–61; Wards 1/9/87; Wards 7/24/171; C 142/259/98.

[61] C 142/594/52.

[62] See p. 39.

[63] Bayley, *House of D'Oyly,* 62, 63; MS. d.d. Risley B II 5/3.

[64] C 28/450/62.

[65] MS. d.d. Risley C 39, C 1–36, C 66–72; cf. MS. Dunkin 438/4, p. 196.

[66] MS. d.d. Risley C 39; B I 3/6.

[67] *Red Bk. Exch.* (Rolls Ser.), 305.

[68] *Pipe R.* 1182 (P.R.S. N.S. xxxi), 127.

[69] Ibid. 1191 & 92 (P.R.S. N.S. ii), 274. For other Linguire families see *V.C.H. Hants* iv. 568; *V.C.H. Bucks.* iii. 329, 462; *Red Bk. Exch.* (Rolls Ser.), 638; L. C. Lloyd, *Anglo-Norman Families* (Harl. Soc. ciii), 54.

[70] *Close R.* 1237–42, 28; *Bk. of Fees,* 102, 448, 823.

[71] *Ex. e Rot. Fin.* (Rec. Com.), ii. 310. For the Hagleys of Hagley (Worcs.) see *V.C.H. Worcs.* iii. 133; T. Nash, *Worcs.* i. 487–9.

[72] *Feud. Aids,* iv. 159.

[73] *Cal. Inq. p.m.* iii, p. 256.

[74] *V.C.H. Worcs.* iii. 133.

[75] *Cal. Pat.* 1330–4, 254; cf. *Feud. Aids,* iv. 179. Parts of the manor were leased in the 1330s: *Cal. Pat.* 1330–4, 81; ibid. 1338–40, 84; C 143/212/14; C 143/239/1.

[76] *Cal. Fine R.* 1356–68, 315. Henry leased part of the manor in 1380: *Cal. Pat.* 1377–81, 553.

[77] *Cal. Pat.* 1408–13, 72.

[78] C 139/58/31; *Cal. Close,* 1429–36, 268.

[79] *Cal. Pat.* 1429–36, 494; *Cal. Close,* 1435–41, 38; C.P. 25(1)/191/27/68.

[80] C 1/71/112: Thomas was imprisoned at John's suit and apparently compelled to sell his rights.

[81] C.P. 25(1)/191/28/62.

the manor to William Brome (or Brown) of Holton.[82]

William died in 1461[83] and his son Robert in 1485.[84] Robert's son Christopher came of age in 1498[85] and died in 1509, when the custody of his son John and of his Adderbury estate was granted to Edward Greville.[86] John held no land in Adderbury at his death in 1536[87] and had probably sold Hagley's to the Danverses, who were said in 1586 to have sold it with St. Amand's to Robert Doyley.[88] It followed the same descent as St. Amand's until the 18th century, when it was probably acquired from the Oliffes and Markeses by Christopher Doyley of Twickenham (Mdx.), great-grandson of Christopher, a younger son of Robert Doyley and Anne Yates.[89] Christopher agreed to sell the manor to the Duke of Buccleuch,[90] but only part of the purchase money had been paid by 1779 when he and the duke conveyed the manor to Christopher's nephew Christopher Aplin.[91] Aplin was lord of the manor until 1792,[92] when it was conveyed to Richard Bignell and Charles Wyatt of Banbury, mortgagees of the duke.[93] Thereafter manorial rights appear to have lapsed.

A third manor formed out of the royal demesne and known by the 14th century as *CIRENCESTER*[94] was held in King John's time as ½ fee by Hasculf des Préaux.[95] He sold it to Thomas le Bret *ante* 1212[96] and Thomas later (*c.* 1217–22) enfeoffed Cirencester Abbey for a yearly rent of £7 10*s.*[97] After Thomas's death[98] the rent was granted in 1225 to his nephew William de Brion,[99] whose right was disputed by Robert le Bret, another nephew, in 1230.[1] Robert won his case but in 1232 granted the rent to William,[2] who, while confirming his uncle's gift to Cirencester, reduced the rent to £7.[3] William was succeeded in 1243[4] by his son Simon, who died in 1247.[5] Simon's daughter Margaret married Ralph de Gorges, on whose death in 1290 the rent passed to Richard de Brion, Rector of West Grimstead (Wilts.), Margaret's uncle.[6] In 1294 Richard sold it for £60 to his kinsman and heir Brian de Turberville and his wife Joan.[7] Brian granted it for life to William of Ludford and John, son of Robert of Ludford, in 1306,[8] and in 1325 granted its reversion to Ingram Berenger[9] of Shipton Bellinger (Hants).[10] In 1329 the manor was seized by the king on the pretence that Cirencester Abbey had acquired it contrary to the Statute of Mortmain: it was restored.[11] The rent was not recorded among Ingram's property at his death in 1336,[12] nor was it claimed by his successors, and by 1402 the abbey was considered to hold the manor in chief.[13] Cirencester Abbey held the manor[14] until its dissolution in 1539.[15]

In 1545 the Crown sold Cirencester manor to John Pope,[16] brother of Sir Thomas, founder of Trinity College, Oxford. Pope sold it in 1560[17] to Robert Standard, who was succeeded by his son Henry and his grandson Thomas (d. 1622).[18] In 1662 Thomas's son Henry sold it to Sir Thomas Cobb,[19] and it descended in the Cobb family[20] until the late 18th century when it appears to have been sold by Paul Methuen and John Blagrave, the husbands of the two Cobb coheirs, daughters of Sir George Cobb, to William Steuart of London.[21] He sold it to William Jorns of Barford, who left it to his brother-in-law Richard Jorns (d. 1824). Richard's son William gave it to his own son Richard William Jorns in 1866, and in 1875 the latter sold it to New College.[22]

In 1086 1 hide in *ADDERBURY* was held of Robert of Stafford by one Robert.[23] The overlordship descended in the Stafford family[24] and in 1237 the estate, together with lands in Duns Tew, was held of the honor of Stafford as 1 fee of Mortain,[25] owing the service of ½ knight.[26] The Robert who was tenant in 1086 was very possibly Robert d'Oilly, for in 1166 Henry d'Oilly was mesne lord of the fee.[27] The d'Oillys, moreover, were chief lords of a knight's fee in Duns Tew which included lands in Swerford and Adderbury.[28] The Tew family were probably under-tenants of the Stafford fee in Adderbury by the reign of Henry I. The first known member of the family is Joibert of Tew who was succeeded by his brother Hugh,[29] probably the

82 For the Bromes see *V.C.H. Oxon.* v. 171.

83 E 152/556.

84 *Cal. Inq. p.m. Hen. VII*, i, p. 32; Hagley's was incorrectly said to be held of the honor of Wallingford.

85 Ibid. ii, p. 62.

86 C 142/24/16; *Cat. Anct. D.* v. A 12855.

87 E 150/806/5.

88 C 142/214/217.

89 See above; Bayley, *House of D'Oyly*, 61, 63–4.

90 P.C.C. 76 Newcastle.

91 MS. d.d. Risley C 15; Bayley, *House of D'Oyly*, 65.

92 O.R.O., gamekprs' dep.

93 MS. d.d. Risley C 1–36, 61–72.

94 e.g. *Feud. Aids*, iv. 159.

95 *Bk. of Fees*, 72, 614. A John des Preaux held ¼ fee in Great Tew in 1236: ibid. 447.

96 *Bk. of Fees*, 103, 614.

97 Ross, *Cirencester Cart.* ii, pp. 539–40.

98 For him see *Rot. Litt. Pat.* (Rec. Com.), 121, 130; *Rot. Litt. Claus.* (Rec. Com.), i. 104; *Rot. de Ob. et Fin.* (Rec. Com.), 25.

99 *Rot. Litt. Claus.* (Rec. Com.), ii. 18.

1 *Close R.* 1227–31, 349, 416; cf. *V.C.H. Berks.* iv. 323; Ross, *Cirencester Cart.* ii, pp. 461–2.

2 *Cal. Chart. R.* 1226–57, 151.

3 Ross, *Cirencester Cart.* ii, pp. 540–1.

4 *Ex. e Rot. Fin.* (Rec. Com.), i. 395.

5 *Cal. Inq. p.m.* i, p. 26.

6 Ibid. ii, p. 462; *Cal. Fine R.* 1272–1307, 283.

7 Cirencester Cart., Reg. B, nos. 47, 844–5. The Revd. Potto Hicks, who has transcribed this register of the cartulary (*penes* Lady Vestey, Stowell Park, Glos.) kindly gave access to the documents relating to Adderbury.

8 *Cal. Pat.* 1301–7, 443; *Abbrev. Rot. Orig.* (Rec. Com.), i. 149; Ross, *Cirencester Cart.* ii, p. 838; C 143/59/24.

9 *Cal. Pat.* 1324–7, 88; Cirencester Cart Reg. B, nos. 55, 848; C 143/172/13.

10 *V.C.H. Hants*, iii. 485; iv. 512.

11 *Cal. Close*, 1327–30, 506; Cirencester Cart., Reg. B, no. 849.

12 *Cal. Inq. p.m.* viii, p. 10; cf. ibid. pp. 312 sqq.

13 *Feud. Aids*, iv. 173.

14 For 13th-cent. leases see Cirencester Cart., Reg. B, nos. 850–1.

15 *Valor Eccl.* (Rec. Com.), ii. 467.

16 *L. & P. Hen. VIII*, xx(2), p. 323.

17 C. P. 25(2)/196/Mich. 2 & 3 Eliz. I

18 C 142/397/77.

19 C.P. 25(2)/707/Trin. 14 Chas. II; Bodl. MS. Ch. Oxon. 3816.

20 See p. 16.

21 Ibid.; O.R.O., gamekprs' dep.

22 New Coll. Arch.

23 *V.C.H. Oxon.* i, 412. This was possibly the estate once granted by Wynflaed to Eadmer: *Anglo-Saxon Wills*, ed. Dorothy Whitelock, 10.

24 *Complete Peerage*, xii(1). 168 sqq.

25 *Bk. of Fees*, 447.

26 *Oseney Cart.* iv. 248.

27 *Red Bk. Exch.* (Rolls Ser.), 265. There is no later mention of a mesne lordship.

28 *Bk. of Fees*, 838.

29 *Cur. Reg. R.* vi. 259.

Hugh of Tew who was pardoned 30*s.* danegeld in Oxfordshire in 1130.[30] Hugh was succeeded by his son Walter,[31] who held one fee of the honor of Stafford under Henry d'Oilly in 1166.[32] Walter was succeeded by his son Hugh, whose relict Iseult had received her dower in Adderbury and Tew by 1204.[33] Hugh's successor Walter was probably his nephew.[34] He paid a fine to Aveline, relict of Osbert Longchamp, in 1208[35] and was still alive in 1218.[36] Walter's successor was his elder son Hugh.[37] In 1248 Hugh was pardoned for the murder of Laurence, Archdeacon of York,[38] and he was still alive in 1253.[39] The last of the family to hold in Adderbury was another Hugh, possibly his son. This Hugh settled his Adderbury estate on the marriage of Maud, one of his three daughters, to Roger de Lyons, but later recovered it in exchange for lands in Swerford.[40] Between 1268 and 1270 Hugh sold it for £150 and an annual rent of 6*d.* to Nicholas of Weston, a merchant,[41] who before his death in 1271 sold it to Oseney Abbey for 225 marks.[42] His relict Emma and his son Adam quitclaimed the property before 1277, and the claims of Richard, son of Roger de Lyons, were defeated in 1288.[43] Edward II confirmed the estate to Oseney in 1320,[44] and the abbey held it until the Dissolution.[45]

In 1542 the manor was granted to Christ Church, Oxford,[46] but it appears to have reverted to the Crown. It changed hands frequently, being sold to Sir Thomas Pope in 1535[47] and to Henry Vavassor and Thomas Ward in 1557.[48] In 1586 it was sold by Henry Edmond to Walter Lloyd,[49] a younger son of George Lloyd of Ampney Crucis (Glos.).[50] Walter's descendant Noah Lloyd granted the manor in 1619 to Alice Cobb,[51] whose son William married Noah's daughter Susan.[52] The manor then descended in the Cobb family, which held the Cirencester manor, and seems to have lost its identity after the 1660s.[53]

Walter Giffard, later Earl of Buckingham, held 1⅞ hide, probably in *BODICOTE*, in 1086.[54] Walter died in 1102 and on the death of his son Walter in 1164 the honor of Giffard escheated to the Crown.[55] In 1190 half the honor was granted to William Marshall, later Earl of Pembroke, husband of Isabel de Clare, who was descended from a sister of the elder Walter Giffard.[56] The overlordship of Bodicote then followed the descent of the Earldom of Pembroke: Walter Marshall was overlord in 1243.[57] After the deaths in 1245 of both Walter and his successor Anselm the overlordship appears to have lapsed, for it was not mentioned in the partition of Marshall inheritance.[58]

In 1086 Bodicote was held of Walter Giffard by Hugh de Bolebec, who took his name from Bolbec (Seine Inf.).[59] He was succeeded by his son Walter and his grandson Hugh, who at his death *c.* 1165 held 10 fees in chief and 20 of the honor of Giffard. Hugh's son Walter was a minor in the custody of his uncle Walter in 1165, and in the custody of Reynold de Courtenay in 1168. Walter was dead by *c.* 1175 when Reynold had the custody of the lands of his daughter Isabel. She herself was the ward of Aubrey de Vere, Earl of Oxford, who in 1190 obtained licence to marry her to his son Aubrey. She died childless *c.* 1207, but before 1211 her husband's younger brother Robert married her aunt and coheir, Isabel de Bolebec.[60] Robert succeeded his brother as earl in 1214, and thereafter the mesne lordship (after 1245 the overlordship) of Bodicote followed the descent of the Earldom of Oxford.[61] Robert, Earl of Oxford (d. 1632), was the last recorded overlord.[62]

In the mid-13th century the tenants of Bodicote were the Holcot family of Holcot (Northants.) and Barcote, in Buckland (Berks.). John of Holcot held Bodicote as one knight's fee in 1242,[63] and a John who was alive between 1260 and 1270 and dead by 1284 was apparently his successor.[64] A third John of Holcot and Barcote died *c.* 1316,[65] and by 1346 Bodicote was held by Fulk of Holcot,[66] either John's son or perhaps his grandson.[67] Fulk was still alive in 1371[68] but had died by 1375,[69] and in 1384 his widow Agnes was holding Bodicote.[70] Fulk's son John died before 1428, when his relict held the manor.[71] He left two sons, John and Richard, and it is uncertain which received Bodicote. Holcot passed to John, and to his son John, who died childless in 1482, while Barcote descended through Richard (d. *c.* 1465) to his son Richard, who eventually inherited Holcot from his cousin John.[72] Richard

30 *Pipe R.* 1130 (H.M.S.O. facsimile), 5.
31 *Oseney Cart.* iv. 334; see *V.C.H. Oxon.* v. 125.
32 *Red Bk. Exch.* (Rolls Ser.), 265.
33 *Cur. Reg. R.* iii. 139, 140, 142, 143; ibid. vi. 259.
34 Ibid. vi. 259; *Oseney Cart.* iv. 339.
35 *Rot. de Ob. et Fin.* (Rec. Com.), 432.
36 *Rot. Litt. Claus.* (Rec. Com.), i. 351.
37 *Bk. of Fees*, 447, 840.
38 *Close R.* 1247–51, 27, 85; *Cal. Pat.* 1247–58, 27.
39 *Cal. Pat.* 1247–58, 247.
40 *Oseney Cart.* iv. 253–4.
41 Ibid. 248.
42 Ibid. 249, 252; ibid. ii. 562–5.
43 Ibid. iv. 251, 252, 253–4; see also *Plac. de Quo Warr.* (Rec. Com.), 665; *Abbrev. Plac.* (Rec. Com.), 268.
44 *Cal. Chart. R.* 1300–26, 422.
45 e.g. *Oseney Cart.* vi. 200, 237.
46 *L. & P. Hen. VIII*, xvii, p. 490; S.C. 6/2931, m. 59.
47 E 318/2215.
48 *Cal. Pat.* 1557–8, 275.
49 C.P. 25(2)/197/Mich. 29 Eliz. I; ibid. Hil. 29 Eliz. I; Methuen Archives, no. 5222.
50 Fosbrooke, *Glos.* i. 335.
51 C.P. 25(2)/340/Trin. 17 Jas. I; Methuen Archives, no. 5224.
52 *Oxon. Visit.* 321.
53 Bodl. MS. Ch. Oxon. 3817; C.P. 25(2)/617/Hil. 1656; ibid. 760/Mich. 15 Chas. II; ibid. 865/Mich. 12 Wm. III.
54 *V.C.H. Oxon.* i. 411
55 *Complete Peerage*, ii. 386–7.
56 Ibid. x. 359.
57 *Bk. of Fees*, 833. For the earldom see *Complete Peerage*, x. 365 sqq.
58 *Cal. Pat.* 1364–7, 263–75.
59 *V.C.H. Oxon.* i. 411; L. C. Lloyd, *Anglo-Norman Families* (Harl. Soc. ciii), 17.
60 *Rot. de Dominabus*, ed. J. H. Round (P.R.S. xxxv), pp. xxxix–xli, xlviii; cf. *V.C.H. Oxon.* vi. 315.
61 *Complete Peerage*, x. 208 sqq.; C.P. 40/187/122.
62 C 142/508/15.
63 *Bk. f Fees*, 833.
64 *V.C.H. Berks.* iv. 457; *Feud. Aids*, iv. 5.
65 *Feud. Aids*, i. 52; iv. 22.
66 Ibid. iv. 179; cf. C.P. 25(1)/190/21/24; *Cal. Inq. p.m.* x, p. 519.
67 See pedigree in Baker, *Northants.* ii. 153. A Sir William of Holcot may have held Barcote between John and Fulk: *V.C.H. Berks.* iv. 457 n.
68 *Cal. Inq. p.m.* xiii, p. 98.
69 *Cal. Inq. Misc.* iii, p. 359; *Abbrev. Rot. Orig.* (Rec. Com.), ii. 335.
70 C.P. 25(1)/191/23/39.
71 *V.C.H. Berks.* iv. 457; *Feud. Aids*, iv. 187.
72 Baker, *Northants.* ii. 152–3; *V.C.H. Berks.* iv. 457; *Genealogist*, N.S. xxiii, 243; ibid. N.S. xxv, 37.

held Bodicote at his death in 1503,[73] but its subsequent descent is doubtful, although Richard's great-grandson William described himself as 'of Bodicote' in his will made in 1573.[74] Part of Bodicote seems to have been joined to the Winchester manor in Adderbury, for the Duke of Argyll was said to be lord of Bodicote manor early in the 18th century,[75] and in 1785 the Duke of Buccleuch was the largest proprietor. The latter's Bodicote estate passed by 1795 to Richard Heydon and Charles Wyatt, and by 1796 to James Gardner, who was succeeded *c.* 1818 by William and James Gardner. Another part of Bodicote was held by the Blagrave and Methuen families at the end of the 18th century, and by 1795 passed from them to Heydon and Wyatt, and by 1829 to John Whittlesee.[76] The manorial rights, however, appear to have followed the same descent in the 19th century as the Winchester manor in Adderbury.[77]

In 1086 Berenger de Todeni held 1½ hide in *BODICOTE* of his father Robert.[78] It is likely that this estate became part of the manor of Broughton, also held by the de Todenis.[79] As late as 1836 the Lords Saye and Sele of Broughton included Bodicote among their lordships.[80]

Robert d'Oilly held 2½ hides in *BARFORD ST. JOHN* in 1086.[81] Part of this estate may have been represented in the 13th century by £10 worth of land in Barford held in 1243[82] by Thomas of Warblington.[83] A manor in Barford worth £20 was seized by Thomas in 1265[84] from the Montfortian John de St. Valery, who was probably the son of Henry de St. Valery of Norton (in Wonston, Hants).[85] John attempted to recover his estate in 1267[86] and was evidently successful. No more is heard of the Warblington estate, but in 1293 John's son Richard granted his manor to Roger Beaufeu.[87] Richard, however, had settled part of the estate on his young son John and John's wife Isabel de Navers; although the couple were divorced while still minors Isabel was awarded her half of these lands by the king's court in 1297.[88]

In 1308 Roger Beaufeu settled the manor on the brothers Roger and Thomas Beaufeu and their heirs.[89] The first Roger, who may have been the royal justice of that name,[90] died soon afterwards, perhaps in 1309, when Roger and Thomas called on Richard de St. Valery to warrant the manor to them.[91] In 1314 Roger's relict Joan was awarded damages for the detention of her dower in Barford.[92] Roger and Thomas, who seem to have been kinsmen of the Beaufeus of Waterperry,[93] were succeeded by a Thomas Beaufeu, who held ¼ fee in Barford in 1346,[94] and by a John Beaufeu who held it in 1428.[95] John's son Richard, living in 1449,[96] married Alice, daughter and coheir of Thomas Swynnerton of Whilton (Northants.).[97] Alice held Barford until her death in 1472,[98] when it passed to her son Humphrey (d. 1485),[99] who married Joan, daughter and coheir of John Hagford of Emscote in Milverton (Warws.). Their son John died in 1516[1] and his son John in 1529.[2] He was succeeded by another John Beaufeu (d. 1583),[3] whose son Thomas mortgaged the manor in 1616,[4] and finally sold it in 1624 to Sir Thomas Chamberlayne of Wickham.[5] At his death in 1625 Sir Thomas Chamberlayne left the manor to his heir Thomas,[6] and it appears to have descended in the Chamberlayne family until 1682 when it passed to Sir Robert Dashwood on his marriage to Penelope, daughter and coheir of Sir Thomas Chamberlayne, Bt.[7]

By 1718[8] Barford had passed from the Dashwoods to Col. Fiennes Twisleton of Broughton, son of Cecily, *de jure* Baroness Saye and Sele.[9] Its descent in the 18th century is unknown, but it apparently passed at some time to Twisleton's kinsmen the Viscounts Saye and Sele, for in 1781 Richard Fiennes, the last viscount, left it to Fiennes Trotman of Shelswell, a great-nephew of Lawrence, Viscount Saye and Sele (d. 1742). Fiennes Trotman died in 1782, and his nephew and successor, also Fiennes Trotman, in 1823.[10] The latter's son Fiennes died in 1835,[11] and in 1848 the manor was sold by his widow to Francis Francillon, who in 1850 sold it to Edward Cobb of Calthorpe.[12] In 1879 Cobb sold it to Sir Henry William Dashwood of Kirtlington, and in 1898 the latter's son Sir George sold it to Magdalen College, Oxford,[13] who held it in 1965.

In 1212 Hugh de Plescy held 7 hides in *BARFORD ST. JOHN*, said to have been given to Richard de Meri at the Conquest and by him in marriage to Engelger de Bohun, who had granted them to Hugh's ancestors.[14] There is no mention of this estate in Domesday Book. In 1243 the estate was counted as ½ fee, part of the 2 fees of Ducklington[15]

[73] *Cal. Inq. p.m. Hen. VII*, ii, pp. 478–9.
[74] P.C.C. 25 Pyckering.
[75] *Par. Colln.* i. 50.
[76] O.R.O., land tax assess.
[77] Gepp, *Adderbury*, 16; *Kelly's Dir. Oxon.* (1864 and later edns.)
[78] *V.C.H. Oxon.* i. 417.
[79] See p. 87.
[80] MS. Rawl. B 400f, f. 59v.; O.R.O., gamekprs' dep.
[81] *V.C.H. Oxon.* i. 406.
[82] *Bk. of Fees*, 832.
[83] Of Warblington and Sherfield (Hants): *Close R.* 1234–7, 131; *V.C.H. Hants* iv. 104.
[84] *Cal. Inq. Misc.* i, p. 261.
[85] *Genealogist*, N.S. xxx, 12–13; *V.C.H. Berks.* iv. 464; *V.C.H. Hants* iii. 457. Henry was younger brother of Thomas de St. Valery: *V.C.H. Oxon.* v. 61.
[86] *Close R.* 1264–8, 295, 317.
[87] C.P. 25(1)/188/12/6; Bodl. MS. Ch. Oxon. d 5/59.
[88] K. B. 27/186, m. 52d.; see also C 47/74/1/1.
[89] C.P. 40/170, m. 56d.; 171, m. 86; 174, m. 13; C.P. 25(1)/189/14/19, 32.
[90] *D.N.B.*
[91] C.P. 40/180, m. 20d.; cf. *Cal. Pat.* 1307–13, 256.
[92] C.P. 40/206, m. 180.
[93] *V.C.H. Oxon.* v. 297.
[94] *Feud. Aids*, iv. 179.
[95] Ibid. 187.
[96] *Cal. Close*, 1447–54, 131.
[97] For pedigree of 15th- and 16th-century Beaufeus see Baker, *Northants.* i. 232.
[98] C 140/40/9.
[99] *Cal. Inq. p.m. Hen. VII*, i, p. 52.
[1] E 150/789/6.
[2] E 150/803/2.
[3] C 142/200/27.
[4] O.R.O., Dashwood deeds, box 5.
[5] Ibid.; cf. C 2/Jas. I/B 40/50.
[6] P.C.C. 20 Skynner.
[7] O.R.O., Dashwood deeds, box 5; J. Townsend, *The Oxfordshire Dashwoods*, 9; G.E.C. *Baronetage*, ii. 206–7.
[8] *Par. Colln.* i. 30.
[9] *Complete Peerage*, xi. 492.
[10] P.C.C. 449 Webster; *Trotman Family*, ed. W. P. W. Phillimore (1892), 66; cf. *V.C.H. Oxon.* vi. 74, 287.
[11] J. C. Blomfield, *History of the Deanery of Bicester*, viii. 24.
[12] O.R.O., Dashwood deeds, box 6.
[13] Magd. Coll. Arch., Adderbury recs.
[14] *Bk. of Fees*, 104; cf. *Herald and Genealogist*, vii. 302, 316.
[15] *Bk. of Fees*, 823.

of the d'Oilly's honor of Hook Norton; in the 14th century it was held to make ¼ fee with lands in Kirtlington[16] which also belonged to Ducklington.[17] It is therefore likely that it had always belonged to the d'Oilly honor. Hugh de Plescy was probably succeeded by John de Plescy, Earl of Warwick, whose son Hugh (d. 1292) obtained the honor, which had descended to his stepmother from the d'Oillys. The overlordship remained in the de Plescy family in the 14th century[18] and presumably passed from them through the Lenveyseys and Chaucers to the dukes of Suffolk in the 15th century.[19]

The Roger who held Ducklington under Robert d'Oilly in 1086 was probably Roger de Chesney, and the 2 fees of Ducklington, including the Barford lands, appear to have passed to his eldest son Hugh (d. between 1163 and 1166) who married Denise of Barford, to their son Ralph by 1166 (d. *ante* 1196), and to Ralph's daughter Lucy. Lucy married Guy de Dive (d. 1218), and their son William[20] was the tenant of the Barford lands in 1243.[21] William died in 1261[22] and his son John was probably killed at the Battle of Evesham in 1265.[23] His lands were forfeited but were recovered by his son Henry in 1273.[24] Henry died in 1277[25] and his son John in 1310.[26] It is likely that by this time the manor was held by under tenants of the Dives, who continued as mesne lords. John Dive's son Henry died in 1327[27] and was succeeded by his son John, who was still alive in 1349.[28] The last of the line, John's son Henry, died without issue in 1362, having previously settled much of his property on Roger Mortimer, Earl of March (d. 1360),[29] and no more is heard of the mesne lordship.

In 1316 the Dives' undertenant of Barford appears to have been a Ralph de Bereford.[30] Later the property was said to have descended to the two daughters of a Reynold de Bereford,[31] one of whom was probably Ela, relict of Roger Wyot, who held it in 1327.[32] Robert le Symple and John Wyot, descendants of the daughters, held the manor in 1346, and by 1428 it had passed to Thomas Snareston and Thomas Benet.[33] The later history of this estate is not known.

In 1310 Henry Marwell, Bishop of Winchester, granted a house and 96 a. in Adderbury to Walter atte Halle, brother of Master Thomas Abberbury, and his son Richard.[34] In 1323 Walter's son John paid a fine for acquiring the land without the king's licence.[35] A Walter atte Hall was mentioned from 1355 to 1373,[36] and either he or a successor of the same name leased the rectorial tithes from New College *ante* 1387.[37] John, son of Walter atte Hall, leased the Winchester demesne between 1405 and 1420.[38] The proportion which John's brother and successor Thomas sold to John Fitzalan in 1446–7 probably included his Adderbury lands, for Fitzalan sold to John Goylyn the elder in 1452–3,[39] and at his death in 1485 John Goylyn the younger held Tisoes Place and Hall Place in Adderbury.[40] His son, another John, was succeeded in 1506–7 by his daughter Margaret, wife of John Docwra, who in 1519 sold the estate to Richard Fermor.[41]

In the 17th century the Barber family acquired Hall Place. Robert Barber of King's Walden (Herts.), who purchased many Oxfordshire estates before his death in 1651, obtained the assignment of a mortgage of the Adderbury estate[42] in 1610. It then came by assignments to Robert's son William (d. 1688), who probably held Adderbury before 1651 and lived there in 1665.[43] His son Robert, Sheriff of Oxfordshire in 1697, added to the estate, and his son Edward, sheriff in 1728, died heavily in debt in 1759. A kinsman John, son of the Revd. John Barber of Buscot (Berks.), succeeded and was prominent in Adderbury parish government in the 1760s. He died in 1773 and his son John in 1818, and his grandson John left his property in 1855 to his niece Susannah, wife of the Revd. W. C. Risley. The Risleys were a prominent family in Adderbury in the 19th century.[44]

In 1086 William, Count of Evreux, held a hide and 2½ yardlands in Bodicote.[45] He endowed his foundation of Noyon Abbey with all his English lands,[46] and his grant was confirmed by his grandson Count Simon between 1140 and 1157.[47] Noyon held land in Bodicote[48] until the dissolution of alien priories in 1414. It was then granted to Sheen Priory (Surr.) which held it until the Dissolution.[49]

Clattercote Priory[50] had lands in Bodicote worth 2*s*. 0½*d*. in 1291.[51] By 1535 they were worth 14*s*.[52] In 1538, after the dissolution of Clattercote, they were granted to Sir William Petre.[53] They were later re-purchased by the Crown and in 1546 were granted to Christ Church, Oxford.[54]

LOCAL GOVERNMENT. In the 13th century, besides ordinary manorial jurisdiction, the Bishop of Winchester had gallows and view of frankpledge in his manor. The lord of the St. Amand's manor

16 *Cal. Inq. p.m.* xi, p. 353; *Cal. Close*, 1364–8, 2–3.
17 *V.C.H. Oxon.* vi. 244.
18 *Cal. Inq. p.m.* ix, p. 183; xi, p. 353.
19 For the Plescys see *Complete Peerage*, x. 545 sqq.; cf. *V.C.H. Oxon.* vi. 73.
20 *Eynsham Cart.* i. 411–13, 420–1, where Barford is erroneously said to be Barford St. Michael.
21 *Bk. of Fees*, 823.
22 *Cal. Inq. p.m.* i, p. 299; *Ex. e Rot. Fin.* (Rec. Com.), ii. 364.
23 *Cal. Inq. Misc.* i, pp. 252, 261.
24 Baker, *Northants.* ii. 254.
25 *Cal. Inq. p.m.* ii, p. 139.
26 Ibid. v, p. 145.
27 Ibid. vii, p. 10.
28 Ibid. ix, p. 183.
29 Baker, *Northants.* ii. 254; *Cal. Inq. p.m.* xiii. p. 162.
30 *Feud. Aids*, iv. 166.
31 Ibid. 179.
32 *Cal. Inq. p.m.* vii, p. 10.
33 *Feud. Aids*, iv. 179, 187.
34 *Reg. Hen. Woodlock*, ed. A. W. Goodman (Cant. & York Soc. xliv), 689–90; cf. *Cal. Pat.* 1321–4, 321. For the Abberburys see *V.C.H. Oxon.* vi. 304.
35 *Cal. Close*, 1323–7, 4.
36 Ibid. 1364–8, 229; 1369–74, 605; *Cal. Pat.* 1354–8, 154.
37 See p. 16.
38 See p. 15.
39 B.M. Egerton MS. 1938, ff. 84–87.
40 *Cal. Inq. p.m. Hen. VII*, i, pp. 20–21.
41 B.M. Egerton MS. 1938, ff. 66, 73v. For the Fermors see *V.C.H. Oxon.* vi. 292.
42 A house and 3 yardlands: MS. d.d. Risley C 1–36, 61–72.
43 Ibid.; *Hearth Tax Oxon.* 136.
44 MS. d.d. Risley C 1–36, 61–72.
45 *V.C.H. Oxon.* i. 410.
46 *V.C.H. Berks.* iii. 292.
47 *Cal. Doc. France*, ed. Round, 220.
48 e.g. *Tax Eccl.* (Rec. Com.), 44.
49 *V.C.H. Surr.* ii. 89–94; *Valor Eccl.* (Rec. Com.), ii. 52; S.C. 6/3464, m. 40.
50 *V.C.H. Oxon.* ii. 105.
51 *Tax Eccl.* (Rec. Com.), 44.
52 *Valor Eccl.* (Rec. Com.), ii. 197.
53 *L. & P. Hen. VIII*, xiii (2), p. 490.
54 Ibid. xxi(2), p. 335.

probably also had these rights over his Adderbury tenants.[55] New College, Oxford, later acquired the right to hold the view in its rectory manor. Regular manorial courts were also held by Cirencester Abbey, by Oseney Abbey, and by the lords of Brown's manor.[56] Courts for the Winchester and New College manors were held until the 19th century. The last court leet was held in 1895 and the last court baron in 1898, apart from a special court baron held in 1909.[57]

The courts concerned themselves with the usual business of admissions and surrenders, the exaction of heriots, and the regulation of the open fields. At the view of frankpledge assaults, including those in which blood was shed, and a variety of misdemeanours were dealt with. In the reigns of Elizabeth I and James I presentments included such offences as keeping open a saw pit on the green, charging excessive toll, using false weights or selling beer in unsealed measures, allowing the kiln-house to be ruinous, having defective butts, pillory, or ducking stool, playing unlawful games, and fishing without licence or using a fishing net for trolling the river. Penalties were imposed on those who neglected to attend the court and in one case a tenant forfeited his tenement for prosecuting the lord's tenants out of the lord's court, that is in the hundred and in the county court. As late as the end of the 17th century the homage was often called upon to carry out administrative duties, such as surveying the manor and defining its boundaries, as well as regulating the actual conduct of open-field farming.[58]

The officers of the courts were the usual ones. On the Winchester manor, for example, there were aletasters, affeerors, constables and haywards.[59] Among the recorded customs which were enforced in this court were the following: a tenant was succeeded by his eldest son or eldest daughter; a widow held her husband's land while sole and chaste; a man who married an heiress paid half the entry fine and had a life tenancy of the land; and heriots were due at death, on exchange, surrender to use, and even for mortgages.[60]

Until 1734, when the overseers' accounts begin, little is known of the government of the parish through the vestry; after that date the evidence relates chiefly to Adderbury East and Barford St. John. It is clear, however, that the medieval tithing divisions formed the basis of local government up to modern times and that each of the 5 townships had its own officers and separate administration.[61] Although Adderbury East and Adderbury West, after a dispute lasting from 1852–4, eventually became united in a single vestry for church administration[62] a similar union did not take place for local government.

Besides the normal parish officers Adderbury had a body of 12 feoffees, which was responsible for the town estate.[63] Unlike the Bloxham feoffees, who virtually ruled the town in the 17th century and later, the Adderbury feoffees contented themselves with administering the charity, and their part in local government lay in the grants of money they gave for the use of the poor. In the 18th century this was given either to the overseers to help them to meet their expenses, or to the feoffee elected for each side of the town, so as to buy cloth to be distributed to the poor; in the 19th century it was used for more varied purposes such as education and the support of a village dispensary.[64]

Normally 2 overseers were appointed yearly for Adderbury East, except for the years 1815–19 when there was only one, and 2 surveyors of the highways. The officers were mostly substantial farmers but on one occasion, from 1768 to 1771, the Duke of Buccleuch was surveyor.[65] The surveyor's accounts were approved yearly by 6 or 8 persons and then by the justices. Expenditure varied greatly according to the work in hand; in 1773, when Nell Bridge was repaired, it was £76, in 1785 only £5, and in 1813, when Twyford Causeway was repaired, £116. Long Wall in East End, New Bridge, and Church Bridge accounted for most of the rest of the expenditure. Part of the town estate ($1\frac{1}{4}$ a.), known as Nell Bridge Acre, was used for repairing Nell Bridge. The surveyors received £2 a year rent from that land after inclosure;[66] the rest of their funds came from the inhabitants as composition money for labour due or from levies.

Most of the constable's expenses in Adderbury East between 1801 and 1835 are attributable to the relief of the travelling poor. During the war years this was given chiefly to sailors and soldiers, their wives and families; the amount of relief decreased

[55] *Plac. de Quo Warr.* (Rec. Com.), 667; *Rot. Hund.* (Rec. Com.), ii. 32.

[56] Bodl. MS. Oseney Ch. 276. There is an Oseney roll of 1376: MS. d.d. Ch. Ch. O.R. 86. For St. Amand's manor there are copies of a few ct. rolls (1563–1678) in B.M. Add. MSS. 59667–71; cf. 17th-cent. rolls in O.R.O., Misc. Beds. I/1, Misc. Bull. II/1. For the New Coll. manor's cts. from the 15th century see *Adderbury 'Rectoria'*, 114–126; New Coll. Mun., d.d. Golby d 1(3) for 1731–1838. There are the following records of the Winchester cts.: Hants R.O. Eccl. 1/73/1–6, 85/1–5, 86/4–8 etc.; New Coll. Mun. 12 Wykeham; ct. bks. 1603–35, 1769–1801, 1826–43, and ct. expenses 1841–5, min. bks. 1798–1909 *penes* Godfrey, Lord Elton, Adderbury.

[57] New Coll. Bursary.

[58] Bk. A (*penes* Ld. Elton, Adderbury): cts. of 31 Eliz. I, 1, 2, 3 Jas.; ct. rolls for the 16th and 17th cents. of Adderbury with Milton manor *penes* Lord Methuen, Corsham Court.

[59] Hants R.O., Winchester ct. rolls, *passim.*

[60] Bk. A (*penes* Lord Elton). These customs are transcribed in Bodl. MS. B. Litt. d 473.

[61] Par. Rec. Barford overseers' accts. 1781–1807, 1807–1822, 1832–6; bk. recording receipts and payments to Banbury Union from 1848–65; Vestry Min. Bk. 1809–31. There are no records for Bodicote, but there is evidence that it had its own overseers and dealt with its own poor law administration: J. Wilson, *The New Poor Law a dead letter in the Banbury Union* (Banbury 1844), *passim.* The evidence for Milton is mainly negative. The village does not figure in any of the civil records of Adderbury, and in 1803 the *Poor Abstract* (pp. 400–01) lists it as a township, which usually means a place having its own constable and overseers. For Adderbury West there is a bundle of papers relating to poor relief 1685–1838 in MS. d.d. Risley A I 1/7.

[62] MS. d.d. Par. Adderbury, Vestry Mins. and chwdns' accts. 1826–95.

[63] Ibid., feoffee's accts. 1703–1817 and down to the 20th cent.; ibid., min. bks. 1602–1799; *12th Rep. Com. Char.* 195–200.

[64] MS. d.d. Par. Adderbury, Adderbury East overseers' accts., feoffees' accts. *passim.*

[65] This account of local government in Adderbury East is based, except where otherwise stated, on the following local records: MS. d.d. Par. Adderbury, Adderbury East surveyors' accts., overseers' accts. 1734–74, 1791–1802, 1803–14, 1814–22 (the last three books have no title page, but the sequence of dates and the names of overseers and families relieved make it evident that they belong to Adderbury East), constables' accts. 1801–35 (there is no clear indication to which of the Adderburys these belong).

[66] *12th Rep. Com. Char.* 195, 196, 199.

after 1815, except for the year 1818–19, when the constable's expenditure trebled owing to the extraordinary number of people whom he had to take to the justices at Oxford and elsewhere. The constable also had to pay over the Marshalsea money at Bloxham, although he did not have to raise it, and had to attend many meetings concerned with the militia. On one occasion he went to Birmingham 'after soldiers', probably substitutes, and to various places for baggage waggons. His accounts were normally approved by the church wardens and overseers, and one or two others; he was allowed a yearly salary, by the jury until 1809 and afterwards by the vestry.

The vestry's chief problem was relief of the poor. Of the householders assessed for hearth tax in 1665 as many as 19 were discharged as poor.[67] The poor also figured prominently in the progress notes of Warden Woodward of New College. It appears that the Cobbs were accustomed to give 2*s.* a week in bread to the poor, besides a dinner, and doles at Christmas, and that the College let a house at the nominal rent of 12*d.* a year to the parish for the use of the poor. It had once been used to stack coal for the parish poor, but was now used to house them. The Warden asked for the removal of the occupants because they left filth about. The Warden's reluctance to allow his tenants to divide their houses also reveals that the influx of poor into the parish had already caused trouble. He feared that the justices or the parishioners might force the college to maintain the poor who had been thus encouraged to come in. On the other hand he realized that the natural increase in population made the division of houses a necessity, for otherwise the parish would be obliged to build houses on the waste.[68]

In the year 1734–5 between 13 and 16 people received monthly payments from the Adderbury East overseers, as well as extra payments which included sums for rent, clothing, medical attention, or burials. Expenses fluctuated between £70 and £110 until 1749, when a workhouse was bought and equipped. Although the initial purchase and equipment of the workhouse in 1749 was expensive, by 1756 expenditure on the poor had been reduced to £60 of which more than £30 was paid by the feoffees. The workhouse apparently closed between 1757 and 1759, when the monthly list of payments started again and for the first time payments were made to men 'on the round'. Costs immediately rose to £102 in 1757–8 and to £95 in the first half of 1758–9; the reopening of the workhouse almost halved this expenditure. The workhouse never provided a permanent solution to the problem of the poor; by 1764 monthly payments and payments to 'roundsmen' had begun again, causing a 25 per cent. rise in costs within 10 years.

Disputes arose in 1760 over the levying of a 4*d.* rate; later the same year 44 people were excused poor rates on their houses and it was agreed that all persons occupying houses under the annual value of 40*s.* would henceforth be exempted. The already heavy burden was increased between 1760 and 1770 by a second smallpox epidemic. There had already been an outbreak in 1750, when one of the victims was Francis, Earl of Dalkeith, and it is probable that the pest house, called Carthagena, was built at that time on land belonging to the town feoffees. Once again the overseers had to arrange for the isolation, medical attention, and burial of the victims. By 1775 Adderbury East was spending £272 on poor relief out of £348 raised. Here a comparison is possible with other parts of the parish: in Adderbury West £146 was spent, at Bodicote £132, at Milton £63, and at Barford St. John only £12. By 1785 expenditure at Adderbury East had fallen to £207 and at Milton to £57, but had increased in the other townships.[69]

Poor law costs rose rapidly in the next two decades. In 1792 the total expenses were up by nearly £100 at Adderbury East, and in 1795 they reached over £525. Expenditure fell in the next year to £378 and stayed about this level until 1800, when 'head money', ranging from 12*s.* to 1*s.* 2*d.*, began to be paid to *c.* 22 men. There is no clear indication what head money was; the workhouse payment had ceased in 1796, so it is unlikely to be a capitation fee for that, particularly as it was possible both to draw head money and go on the 'round'. Expenses rose catastrophically to £1,269 in 1801; flour distributed to the poor accounted for £425, monthly payments were high, there were 16 roundsmen in the winter, and 40 persons receiving head money. Expenditure was reduced to £446 by 1809. During this period payments for clothes and rent went on, a doctor received a regular fee of £20 a year, together with £5 5*s.* in 1809 for 'nockalatin the poor'; many bills were paid for the constable, including one of £137, which was possibly spent on substitutes for the militia.

The problem which faced Adderbury East was not unique. In 1802–3, for example, when Adderbury East spent £541 on relief, Adderbury West, with less than half the population, spent £340.[70] Distress was probably greater there as more of its inhabitants were weavers and labourers and there were fewer wealthy ones to bear the cost of relief. The same number of adults and nearly as many children as in Adderbury East received out-relief, while 19 persons compared with 9 at Adderbury East were occasionally relieved. The relief given in Adderbury West was at a much lower level than in Adderbury East where the rate levied was 4*s.* 11½*d.* in the pound compared with 6*d.*[71] Whereas rents from the feoffees' estates were used for the purchase of cloth and linen for the poor in Adderbury East, the portion allotted to Adderbury and Milton was said not to be so well used.[72]

The most striking rise in expenditure, however, was at Bodicote where in 1802–3 relief cost £384, levied by a 6*s.* rate. At Milton £156 was spent at a rate of 4*s.* 2*d.* Barford St. John, though the same size as Milton, had much less of a problem, since 7 persons only were relieved at a cost of £77 compared with 39 at Milton. In the whole parish £1,498 was spent on relief for a total population of *c.* 1,923.[73]

From 1809 onwards expenses in Adderbury East rose again to £1,058 in 1812–13. The overseers bought 12 houses in 1811, which were let at 19*s.* each a year. The end of the war brought little reduction in expenditure; it fell to £732 in 1816, but rose immediately in the next year to £1,036, with

67 *Hearth Tax Oxon.* 136–8, 140, 143.
68 *Woodward's Progress*, 19, 24.
69 *Poor Abstract*, 398–401.
70 Ibid.
71 Ibid.
72 *12th Rep. Com. Char.* 199.
73 *Poor Abstract*, 398–401; *V.C.H. Oxon.* ii. 217.

40 people on the monthly list, and 25 roundsmen in June, and remained at this level until at least 1820.

In 1835 Adderbury East spent only £470 on relief out of £632 raised, and Adderbury West only £302 out of £401. In Bodicote and Milton, however, there had been no improvement, and at Barford St. John relief actually cost more. In all parts of the parish expenditure fell considerably during the following year. By 1835 the parish had been incorporated in the Banbury Union.[74]

ECONOMIC HISTORY. By the 11th century there were 5 settlements in the parish, each with its own fields, but there was no simple equation of manor and *vill*, for several manors contained land in more than one set of fields. The royal manor was reduced before 1086 by 14½ hides granted to the Bishop of Winchester and 1 hide granted to Robert of Stafford.[75] There were 4 small manors, Robert d'Oilly's 2½ hides in Barford St. John and 3 Bodicote manors which together formed a 5-hide unit.[76]

The royal estate in Adderbury was administered with Bloxham as one manor. The chief item of revenue was the corn rent, worth £28 10*s*. a year; there was also 40*s*. from wool and cheeses, over 24*s*. from pannage, and a due of 40 swine when pannage was charged. These money payments were the commuted food rents of an earlier economy and are characteristic of ancient royal demesne in Oxfordshire at this date.[77] The large demesne farm was worked by 27 serfs with 13 ploughs. There was a considerable amount of meadow land (2 leagues, 5 furls. by 4 furls.), pasture (4 sq. leagues), and woodland, and 6 mills. There were 88 customary tenants, 72 *villani*, and 16 bordars; the number of ploughs held was omitted from the record. It is known, however, that in King Edward's time there was land for 48 ploughs. Since that time the estate had risen in value from £56 to £67. The Adderbury part of it almost certainly lay on the western side of the present parish in Adderbury West adjoining Bloxham. This royal estate was not only a large and rich agricultural unit, but was also of administrative importance, for the soke of two hundreds belonged to it.[78]

The other large Domesday estate, the Bishop of Winchester's, had risen in value from £12 to £20; it had land for 20 ploughs, but there were 23 in use: 4 were worked by 9 serfs on the demesne and 19 by the customary tenants, who included 27 *villani* and 9 bordars. There were 36 a. of meadow and 2 mills. The whole estate was additionally described as 3 leagues and 3 furlongs in length and 1½ league in breadth,[79] which suggests that it was a compact estate taken out of the royal manor. Later evidence confirms this interpretation, for Winchester's lands lay in the fields of Adderbury East, Bodicote, and Milton, and not in Barford or Adderbury West.[80]

The Evreux estate at Bodicote was reckoned as 1 hide and 2½ yardlands; there was land for 1 plough and this was on the demesne worked by 2 serfs and 5 bordars.[81] The other two Bodicote manors were undercultivated: one, reckoned as 2 hides less ½ yardland, had land for 2 ploughs but only one was in use, worked by 2 *villani*, on the demesne;[82] the other, reckoned as 1½ hide, had land for 1½ plough but only one was in use, worked by 3 bordars on the demesne.[83] Both the estates, however, had retained their pre-Conquest values of 40*s*. and 30*s*. respectively.[84] At Barford there was land for 1½ plough but 2 were in use on the demesne, worked by 1 serf, and 2 *villani* and 3 bordars had another ½ plough. The estate had increased in value from 30*s*. to 50*s*.[85] No details are given of Robert of Stafford's hide.

By the late 13th century the Adderbury part of the Domesday royal manor had been split into three, the small Stafford manor had passed to Oseney Abbey and had been augmented by various purchases,[86] and only the large Winchester manor remained intact. The last is by far the best documented, but there are some scattered notices relating to the condition of some of the others in the Middle Ages. In 1296 the demesne farm of Hagley's manor consisted of 80 a. of arable and 4 a. of meadow, and free rents amounted to 18*s*. a year.[87] In 1432–3 this manor was said to contain 200 a. of arable and 12 a. of meadow.[88] The Cirencester manor, which does not appear to have had a demesne farm, was probably larger. The abbot was receiving £3 from assized rents in the reign of Henry III, and in the 16th century customary tenants held 8 yardlands of arable and ½ yardland of meadow.[89] The St. Amand manor was more valuable. In 1294 its free tenants were paying rents worth £4 14*s*. 4*d*. and 1 lb. of pepper, and its customary tenants held 10½ yardlands.[90] Some 35 years later the demesne farm consisted of 34 a. of arable and 2 a. of meadow.[91] Week-work may have been commuted on all the manors by the end of the 13th century; this was certainly so on the Winchester manor, where it was commuted before 1208, and on St. Amand's, where the rent for a yardland was 20*s*. On Hagley's manor the rent was 40*s*. in 1433.[92]

An indication of the flourishing state of the Winchester manor in the early 13th century was the royal grant of 1218 allowing the bishop to hold a weekly market.[93] In 1231 there were 452½ field acres of arable in Adderbury East and West and 57½ of meadow.[94] In the late 13th century the tenants held 4½ hides in Bodicote, 38 yardlands, 9 cotlands, 8 acrelands, and 16 cottages in Adderbury. The differences of organization between Bodicote and Adderbury suggest that Bodicote was a later offshoot from Adderbury, developed by free settlers. There was much free land there;[95] the holdings of the customary tenants were measured in hides

[74] *2nd Rep. Poor Law Com.* 292–3, 294–5. Payments to the Union by Adderbury East began in 1835.
[75] *V.C.H. Oxon.* i. 401, 412.
[76] Ibid 406, 410, 411, 417.
[77] Ibid. 375.
[78] Ibid. 400.
[79] *V.C.H. Oxon.* i. 401.
[80] New Coll. Mun., Adderbury, draft Incl. Bill.
[81] *V.C.H. Oxon.* i. 410.
[82] Ibid. 411.
[83] Ibid. 417.
[84] Ibid. 411, 417.
[85] Ibid. 406.
[86] See pp. 18–19.
[87] *Cal. Inq. p.m.* iii, p. 256.
[88] C 139/58/31.
[89] S.C. 12/portf. 18–22; S.C. 6/240, m. 69d.
[90] C 133/43/5.
[91] C 135/21/24.
[92] C 133/43/5; C 139/58/31.
[93] Beesley, *Hist. Banbury*, 91.
[94] The details in the following paragraphs, except where otherwise stated, are taken from a thesis (Bodl. MS. B. Litt. d 473) by Patricia Hyde, which is largely based on the Pipe Rolls, rentals, ct. rolls, etc. of the Bp. of Winchester.
[95] For a freehold of 7½ yardlands see *Fines Oxon.* 21.

rather than in yardlands; and their burdens were apparently lighter than those of the Adderbury customaries. Boon services on each of the 3 hides of nief land in Bodicote were valued at 7*s.* a year, but in Adderbury the services from each of the yardlands was valued at 9*s.* and from each of the cotlands at 6*s.* 8*d.* The Bodicote tenants were burdened with carrying services and paid more for the present given on the institution of a new bishop, but these duties may have entailed an enhanced status. They were obliged to convey the bishop's rent, at their own cost, to the gate of his castle of Wolvesey at Winchester. If the money were stolen they must restore it, a clause which was doubtless intended to ensure that the bodyguard provided was adequate. Also they were to carry the letters of the lord at their own cost if the journey could be made in two days. It was their duty to rescue, if they could, any man of the bishop taken anywhere in England.[96]

In the 13th and 14th centuries the demesne was managed by a reeve and hired labourers, assisted by *operarii* or tenants who worked all the year in specified jobs and whose rent was therefore acquitted. The rest of the tenants owed labour services only in the autumn. The trading accounts for 1245 show that the demesne farm made a profit of *c.* £35 and just over 100 years later the profit was £55. In the same years the income received from rents was £20 12*s.* 9*d.* and £21 10*s.* 4*d.*, while court dues amounted to £10 6*s.* 6*d.* and £20 9*s.* 9*d.* Entry fines rose to £4 or £5 in the early 14th century compared with £2 in 1252. At these dates demesne farming was of greater financial importance than rents, but scarcity of labour after plagues in the 14th century probably encouraged the bishop to lease the demesne lands. The Winchester manor was probably the last in the parish to be directly exploited. All the other manors had absentee landlords who by the 14th century were granting most of their land for life or for a term of years.

The assessment of the parish for early-14th-century taxes made up a large proportion of the total assessment of the hundred.[97] Adderbury village and, to a lesser extent, the hamlets were notable for the high number of inhabitants assessed at substantial sums between 2*s.* and 5*s.* In 1316 48 of the 74 Adderbury contributors came into this category; 17 were assessed at less than 2*s.*, and a handful at sums up to 10*s.* Eight of the 13 Barford contributors were assessed at sums between 2*s.* and the highest contribution of 4*s.*, and 9 of the 16 Milton contributors at sums between 2*s.* and 3*s.* 6*d.*, while one Milton man was assessed at 5*s.* 6*d.*[98] The details of Bodicote's assessment in 1316 are not known, but in 1327 exactly half of the 22 contributors were assessed at sums between 2*s.* and 5*s.* The 1327 assessment for Adderbury, Barford, and Milton confirms the impression of a group of prosperous communities with Adderbury outstanding.[99]

A high death rate in the plague years is suggested by the 62 entry fines and 84 heriots paid between 1348 and 1350 on the Winchester manor alone. By 1351 29½ yardlands out of a total of 38 had changed hands since 1346 as well as 6 cotlands and 25 cottages; the tenant of Bodicote mill died and a new one was not found until 1353; and it was difficult to get tenants for cotlands and acrelands as late as the 1360s. After 1370 there was an improvement, and Winchester was able to exact an increased rent and a small entry fine from its new tenants in return for the commutation of labour services. The poll-tax returns for Adderbury itself are missing; the 43 adults returned for Barford and the 89 for Bodicote[1] may suggest growing population there, since the discrepancy between the number of inhabitants assessed in 1327 and in 1377 is unusually large. The difficulty of securing tenants, however, persisted into the 15th century when some of the copyhold land had to be let for life only, as no other tenants could be found. Between 1375 and 1405 *c.* 50 a. of demesne had been let in separate lots and in 1405, when all labour services were finally commuted, the whole of the remaining demesne was let on a stock-and-land lease to John Adderbury. In 1420 a group of villagers took up the lease. Such was the prevailing agricultural depression that the rent received from the main demesne farm in 1444 was only £21. In 1478 when there were new lessees the rent was only increased by £2 13*s.* 4*d.*[2]

The decline in Adderbury's prosperity is confirmed by variations in the rent of the rectory manor. The annual rent paid by the bailiff from 1387 was normally £66 13*s.* 4*d.*, but in 1394 this was reduced because of the smallness of the corn crop and in 1395 because of the low price of corn. From 1399 to at least 1414 the rent was £54 13*s.* 4*d.* and though there was a £3 increase in 1420–21 the rent was far below that paid in 1387.[3]

The medieval evidence about crops and rotations is for the most part scanty, but it seems that each of the villages had its own set of 2 fields and that the normal system of open-field farming was followed. The 2-field arrangement continued long after estates in the cornbrash belt of Oxfordshire had taken to 3 fields. At Barford, for instance, in the 14th century a yardland of 19¾ a. and 3 *forere* was divided nearly equally between East and West Fields in 46 parcels.[4] The Bodicote yardland seems to have consisted in 1247 of *c.* 30 a., sometimes held in very small parcels: one ¼ yardland consisted of 2 1-a. strips, 10 ½-a. strips, and 1 ¼-a. strip (*roda*).[5] An acre of meadow seems to have been the normal allotment for a yardland.[6]

The crops grown, at least on the Winchester demesne, were wheat, rye, oats, and spring barley; dredge was treated as a separate crop in the accounts of this estate after 1265; less wheat was grown there in the 14th century than in the 13th, but a small crop of peas was sown on the fallow field. Stock rearing was an important part of the economy: horses, oxen, bulls, cows, sheep, pigs, and hens were normally kept both on the demesne and by the tenants. For a short period, 1327–34, no sheep were kept on the demesne, and the reeve paid for tenants'

[96] This custumal is in Book A of the manorial recs. *penes.* Godfrey, Ld. Elton, Adderbury.

[97] See p. 189.

[98] E 179/161/8.

[99] E 179/161/9.

[1] E 179/161/44.

[2] Hants R.O. Eccl. 2/155841.

[3] *Adderbury 'Rectoria'*, 115. The manor was not large: in 1437 there were 8 customary tenants holding 43 a., the largest holding being 16 a., and 5 free tenants were mentioned in 1539–46.

[4] H. L. Gray, *Eng. Field Systems*, 486. Adderbury East also had its E. and W. fields.

[5] *Fines Oxon.* 147; cf. ibid. 157.

[6] Ibid. 147.

sheep to manure the land. Thereafter, until 1348, an inter-manorial system of sheep-farming was in force. The ewes were mainly kept at Adderbury and the lambs were sent thence to Witney, another of the bishop's manors, while most of the hogs were sent back from Witney to Adderbury. The Black Death put an end to this arrangement and the numbers of sheep kept at Adderbury rose until 1405 when the bishop let out his arable demesne and at the same time abandoned sheep-farming. In 1436 a new stock was bought and an arrangement made with the lessee of the demesne to look after them. Bishop Waynflete ended this system in 1444 and thereafter 300 sheep were included in the lease of the demesne. By 1495 much arable seems to have been converted into pasture, for an allowance of £3 was made in that year to the lessee of the rectory manor because 'several of the lands of the Bishop of Winchester and others lay barren and uncultivated'. It is significant that at the close of the century John Cokkys, lessee of the Winchester manor 1494–1500, was a woolman as well as a farmer, and was so described when he was in trouble in 1507 for selling to foreign merchants 'otherwise than for ready money'.[7]

How wide-spread was the increase in sheep-farming on the Winchester and other manors and to what extent it led to early inclosure is uncertain. In 1517 only 70 a. of recent inclosure in the parish were reported,[8] but when parliamentary inclosure came in 1768 it seems that there were 965 a. of old inclosure in the two Adderburys and Milton and 43 a. in Barford. No more than 100 a. of the Winchester estate were still open-field land.[9] The likelihood of some early inclosure on the Winchester estate is supported by the fact that Anthony Bustard, lessee of the manor 1534–68, kept as many as 1,200 sheep.[10] Whether of medieval or of later date there were certainly many inclosures before the Duke of Argyll took the Winchester lease in 1717, and some were then alleged to have existed in 1647.[11]

The later 16th and early 17th centuries were probably a prosperous period: local men profited from the dissolution of the monasteries, acquired their lands,[12] and benefited from rising prices. Their prosperity is reflected in tax lists,[13] in the amount of new building in the villages, in the confirmation of 1635 of the exemption of Adderbury men as tenants of ancient demesne from toll and other dues throughout the kingdom,[14] in the monuments in the church, and in the inventories attached to local wills.

These inventories reveal not only the increasing comfort in the farm-houses but also a great variety in farming practice. Among the lesser men, with chattels valued at sums ranging from £11 to £60, the lowest in the scale had mainly sheep and very little arable; some wealthier men had only arable and kept horses for ploughing or practised mixed farming.[15] Wheat, barley, oats, peas, and grass were the most common crops, though maslin also occurs.[16] Hemp may have been grown then but no mention of it has been found before 1732.[17] Most farmers, but not all, made cheese and butter for sale. Among the richer yeomen the Maule, Bradford, and Jackman families were prominent. The Bradfords provide an example of the rapid fortunes made in this period; Thomas Bradford, who had a small mixed farm, died in 1624 with chattels worth £44; John Bradford died in 1683 with chattels worth the large sum of £701. John, too, had a mixed farm, his grain and hay about equalling in value his stock of horses (£50) cows (£50), and large flock of sheep (£70).[18] Of the Maules, John (d. 1616) was worth £164 in chattels and had a small mixed farm of which a yardland was leased; another John Maule of Milton (d. 1680) kept 80 sheep and a dozen horses and cows, and his goods were valued at £240.[19] The will of Thomas Maule (d. 1680) is of special interest as it shows that he had been making numerous small purchases of land and cow commons from his neighbours.[20] Of the Jackmans, Thomas (d. 1643) left goods worth £241, a trifle more than those left by Robert Doyley, 'gentleman' (d. 1640). About half the value of Jackman's goods consisted of grain, and a quarter of horses and other beasts, while Doyley's crops were also about twice the value of his beasts; a rather higher proportion of his total wealth was in household furnishings.[21] Other members of the Jackman family appear to have been acting as bankers: one had £110 worth of debts due upon bond and £7 in ready money out of a total valuation of £119; another had £150 in money only.[22]

In the absence of estate maps the arrangement of the fields in this period is not clear. As in other north Oxfordshire parishes, however, the original 2-field arrangement seems to have given way to quarters. This change had taken place by 1628 at the latest in the field of Adderbury East, where each quarter was divided into 9 or 11 furlongs.[23] There was leys land or greensward intermixed with the open-field arable, in addition to the inclosed or common meadow and pasture which lay along the river banks and elsewhere. In a terrier of the rectory estate, made in 1628, there is a reference to 11 one-acre parcels of ley ground and also to common meadow, 'always laid out by lot'.[24]

The same terrier shows the continued existence of many minutely sub-divided arable holdings alongside the consolidated bishop's demesne. The rectory estate in 1628 was made up of 54 separate parcels of land scattered in the quarters of Adderbury East. There were 36 one-acre strips (11 being described as 'whole ridged' acres), 14 half acres, described as 'single lands' or 'lands', 3 headlands, and 1 'fore-

[7] *Cal. Pat.* 1494–1509, 535, 569.
[8] *Dom. of Incl.* i. 333, 336.
[9] Detailed analysis of the incl. award by the late L. G. Wickham Legg: Bodl. Libr. (uncat.).
[10] C 1/957/53.
[11] E 134/1 Geo. II/Hil. no. 1.
[12] See pp. 18–19.
[13] E 179/161/196; E 179/163/198.
[14] Beesley, *Hist. Banbury*, 430, n. 32.
[15] e.g. MS. Wills Oxon. 31/1/18; 15/2/8; 129/2/32.
[16] Ibid. 8/2/10; 132/2/1; 132/4/19; 136/3/34; 156/3/4; 2/2/11; 52/3/14.
[17] MS. d.d. Risley B I 2/17.
[18] MS. Wills Oxon. 5/1/23; 7/3/1.
[19] Ibid. 141/2/2; 43/4/21.
[20] Ibid 141/2/1.
[21] Ibid. 136/4/4; 296/4/86.
[22] Ibid. 61/2/9; 72/4/6.
[23] New Coll. Mun., terrier 1628. The names of the quarters were Twifordfield, Marlfield, Sidenham Field, Fellmead Field. In Adderbury West in John Barber's time the quarters were Clayes, Wing furlong, Old Ditch, and Cattle Pit: MS. d.d. Risley A II 5/22. See also terriers of 1632 and 1659 (New Coll. Mun.); MS. Oxf. Archd. Oxon. c 141, f. 453; MS. d.d. Risley A IV 2/1, 3, for other names of quarters. At Milton 4 quarters and greensward occur in a terrier of *c.* 1700: O.R.O., S. & F. colln. (uncat.).
[24] New Coll. Mun., terrier 1628.

shorter land'.[25] Another terrier of 1663 of a half yardland reveals that it was divided into 37 separate arable parcels of land, to which were attached fractions of 17 plots in Mill Mead, and other places, as well as leys in Brook furlong and on the Downs.[26] At this date the stint allowed was 30 sheep and 3 cows to the yardland.[27] The lord's reservation, in a lease, of the pasture in the Berry and in 2 meads suggests that pasture was highly valued,[28] and so also does the requirement in another lease that £5 extra should be paid for every acre ploughed.[29]

New College's relations with its tenants during this period were not altogether happy. Warden Woodward found them 'clamourous and unruly'. They disputed the payment of fines, 'exceedingly low ones' in the college's view; they demanded a dinner as of right when the courts were held, and also the killing of a bull at Christmas, as a free gift to the poor, along with the dole of 3*d*., bread, and beer to each poor man. Both demands proved to be unjustified as it was established that the dinner and the bull had been given as a courtesy only by the Cobb family, who were the lessees of the college, and by their predecessors.[30] The warden was also worried about immigration into the parish, encouraged by the dividing up of houses.[31]

This movement of population, however, was not all in one direction. Apprenticeship certificates and other records show that Adderbury people were constantly moving out of the village either temporarily or permanently, in order to better themselves.[32] In the late 17th century the eldest son of an Adderbury miller entered the church and another son became a citizen and wine-cooper of London.[33] A Bodicote man, Richard Wise, became a London clock-maker.[34]

Inclosure of the open fields of Adderbury East and West in 1768 was facilitated by extensive purchases, in the years 1717–67, by John, Duke of Argyll, and his son-in-law Charles Townshend, a trustee for the Duke of Buccleuch: they spent at least £12,000, paying sums varying between £2,300 for the St. Amand manor and £30 for the acres of small freeholders. Much of the property was bought on the assignment of mortgages and included at least 16 'lands' in the common fields that were bought to make the park of Adderbury House.[35] These purchases reduced the number of freeholders, which had been particularly high since the Doyley family sold much of their land in Adderbury West in the 17th century.[36]

The movement to inclose was initiated by Charles Townshend and supported by Warden Hayward of New College and Paul Methuen; it was opposed by the vicar and John Barber, the squire of Adderbury West,[37] and others. Townshend, the grandson of 'Turnip Townshend', was a strong believer in the merits of inclosure and Hayward, who had already promoted the inclosure of Shutford, was to acquire a great reputation in his college as an estate manager.[38] He argued that the arable land would not only be improved but would double in value, while the price per acre of meadow and common pasture would be trebled. The land at Bodicote would be even more greatly improved as there was more extensive common pasture. He claimed that some of the most respectable farmers were in favour of inclosure and that the vicar's opposition was based merely on 'general dislike of the practice'.[39] Paul Methuen considered that the breeding of sheep and black cattle would be the 'chief improvement'; it was calculated that there would be a rise in the Methuen receipts from rents of £480 over the existing rental of £672.[40] The vicar got up a petition which he claimed was signed by nearly two-thirds of the principal landholders. There were 29 signatures; except for John Barber's they were mostly those of small property-holders. They claimed that inclosure would tend 'to the ruin and destruction of a populous village'. The cost of ditching and fencing would be one of the chief difficulties, particularly with regard to the glebe. The vicar also feared that the vicarage would lose by the commutation of tithes.[41] Opposition, however, was overcome and the award was made in 1768.

Out of 4,310 a. allotted New College received 544 a.,[42] the vicar received 312 a., and the Duke of Buccleuch, 682 a. for the lands purchased by John, Duke of Argyll, and 100 a. as the lessee of the Bishop of Winchester. Townshend was awarded 340 a. There were 6 allotments of between 200 and 100 a., and 126 smaller allotments, 97 of which were of less than 20 a.[43] The Buccleuch estate, valued at £54,000 in 1774, was divided into a number of medium-sized tenant farms, and when the property was sold in 1801 many of the tenants were able to buy the freehold of their farms.[44] The parish has never since been dominated by one landowner.

After inclosure New College's property consisted of a consolidated holding, still known (1965) as Bodicote Grounds Farm. The fines paid on this estate between 1774 and 1820 throw light on the state of agricultural property in this period of war. The fine rose from £791 in 1774 to £1,327 in 1794 and to over £2,118 in 1810. It apparently remained at the last figure until 1822 when it dropped to £1,694.[45] The Methuens also received higher rents; there was an increase of £15 8*s*. on the freehold land and £227 on the leaseholds.[46] It was reckoned that the lands allotted in exchange for leasehold tithes in Adderbury East, Bodicote, and Cote Field would let for £134 more, and that an increase of £142

[25] Ibid.
[26] MS. d.d. Oxon. C 1/1; cf. MS. d.d. Risley B II 14/1; ibid. A IV 13/2.
[27] In 1698 the stint in Adderbury East was 20 sheep to the yardland: Methuen Archives, no. 5258.
[28] MS. d.d. Oxon. C 1/1: sale by Bray Doyley.
[29] MS. d.d. Risley B I 1/5.
[30] *Woodward's Progress*, 18, 25.
[31] See p. 23.
[32] Par. Rec., apprentice certificates.
[33] MS. d.d. Risley B II 6/8, 20, 21.
[34] Beesley, *Hist. Banbury*, 55.
[35] MS. d.d. Risley, *passim*; Ch. Ch. Arch., Adderbury box 36, A 1–12. As early as 1714 Argyll inclosures valued at £300 were mentioned in a tithe case: E 134/12 Geo. I/East. no. 4.
[36] e.g. MS. d.d. Oxon. C 1/1; *Oxon. Poll, 1754*; O.R.O., land tax assess. 1789 sqq.
[37] New Coll. Mun., Adderbury corresp. and misc. papers.
[38] Ibid.
[39] Ibid. cf. Methuen Archives, no. 5764.
[40] Methuen Archives, nos. 5321, 3654, 5730b.
[41] New Coll. Mun., Adderbury corresp.
[42] See p. 31.
[43] O.R.O., incl. award.
[44] Ch. Com., Adderbury docs., sale of 1801. See also Ch. Ch. Arch., Adderbury box 36, A 12 for John Bellow's purchase.
[45] MS. notes by L. G. Wickham Legg in Bodl. (uncat.).
[46] Methuen Archives, no. 5730.

would be realized from the exchange in Adderbury West and Milton.[47]

Barford St. John was not inclosed until 1794. Of the six proprietors the two largest were Sir Henry Watkin Dashwood who was allotted 287½ a. for his 20½ yardlands, and Michael Corgan who received *c.* 148 a., including 10 a. for tithes.[48]

In the 19th century farming methods were improved. The land was considered especially suitable for the 'turnip and barley system of husbandry' and a variety of new cropping systems was tried throughout the parish. A 5-course system of husbandry was prescribed on the Winchester estate: the course was barley, clover, vetches, and turnips, wheat, and then fallow; a 6-course rotation, followed by a 5-course, was laid down in a Bodicote lease of 1843.[49] The 6-course rotation was summer fallow followed by turnips, barley and clover, clover (12 months), clover (2 years), wheat, barley, beans, and peas or vetches. Small quantities of hops were also grown. This may be compared with the course used a century earlier by Edward Barber (d. 1759): he sowed corn, pulse, oats, and vetches, whereas his father had previously sown wheat, barley, and peas with one quarter of his land fallow each year.[50] Arthur Young comments fairly favourably on the courses used in the early 19th century, though he regretted the failure to grow beans on the rich Adderbury soil: he had praise for one farmer who cultivated spring wheat with success, for another, John Wilson of Bodicote, who drilled peas with a special drill so that the seed was not trampled on, and for this same farmer who got a crop of 6 qr. an acre, whereas the county average was 4 qr. an acre.[51] He commented on the great improvement in production brought about by inclosure; he thought that the red sand was among the finest soils in the country and marvelled at the remarkable ignorance of the commissioners, who had valued the clay of which the parish had some small amount at 12*s.* to 14*s.* an acre higher than the sand, which as everyone now knew was far more valuable and could be let in some parts of the country for as much as £3 an acre.[52] Although good crops were grown, however, the parish remained essentially a stock-raising area throughout the 19th century. In 1809 Arthur Young noted that there was nearly as much grass as arable, and that it was 'under dairies and fatting cows'; that both long- and short-horned cattle were kept, the former being hardier and better for fattening, the latter better for milk.[53] Experiments with sheep breeds had been made: farmers had switched from the 'Warwick breed' to a cross of the New Leicester, which were far more profitable. Breeding flocks were kept and folded, sometimes for as much as 9 months in the year.[54] John Barber (d. 1818) has recorded that he penned his sheep at night all the year round on the pulse stubble.[55] Later in the century the Adderbury flocks of Oxford Down sheep gained a wide reputation,[56] while most farms continued to be noted for their good grazing land and stock.[57]

After *c.* 1777 Bodicote had a special enterprise, the cultivation of rhubarb and other medicinal plants, such as henbane, belladonna, and poppies. The cultivation of rhubarb was first introduced by Dr. William Hayward, an apothecary of Banbury. He died in 1811 and his farm was carried on by the Usher family for many generations.[58] In 1833 two fields in Bodicote were growing rhubarb. The business was greatly improved and enlarged by Richard Usher (d. 1898) and became a company trading as R. Usher & Co. They grew and prepared pharmaceutical extracts, dried herbs, and the like; the firm's activities later declined and it finally closed in 1946.[59]

Although there was much tenant farming in the 19th century the break up of the Buccleuch estate led to a temporary increase in owner-occupiers. In 1786 the duke was paying one third of the land tax of the two Adderburys; there were 45 other landowners in Adderbuy East, of whom 25 were owner-occupiers; at Adderbury West the proportions were 26 and 10, at Milton 19 and 6, at Bodicote 34 and 12, and at Barford there were 5 owners.[60] Soon after inclosure the duke sold his estate, and Paul Methuen and John Blagrave followed suit.[61] It is possible that some of the smaller allottees were squeezed out on account of the expenses of inclosure.[62] By 1831 the number of landowners had been reduced to 82, none of them paying more than *c.* £17 in tax, and owner-occupiers to 35. In Adderbury West at this date all the holdings were freehold, although copyhold still survived in Adderbury East.[63]

Another change was brought about by the completion of the canal in 1790. It enabled farmers to send their corn further afield for sale and so to get a better price. This, however, caused hardship to the poor at the outset.[64] The poor profited on the other hand from being able to get cheap coal from the Wednesbury collieries.[65] The introduction of machinery also caused hardship, and there seems to have been some local discontent. When the Banbury men rioted in 1830 a mob marched to Bodicote and burnt machinery on an estate there. The yeomanry were routed and regular troops from Coventry had to be called in to restore order.[66] The influence of Banbury, however, was generally on the side of improvement. The importance of the agricultural market there had a stimulating effect;[67] so also had the Banbury branch of the National Farmers' Union, which worked hard to raise the common level of farming.[68]

The percentage of arable under wheat decreased between 1909 and 1914, and the amount of per-

[47] Methuen Archives, no. 5730b.
[48] O.R.O., incl. award.
[49] Ch. Com., Adderbury leases.
[50] MS. d.d. Risley A II 3, 5/22.
[51] Young, *Oxon. Agric.* 111, 162, 106, 147–8, 138.
[52] Ibid. 4.
[53] Ibid. 281.
[54] Ibid. 312.
[55] MS. d.d. Risley A II 5/22: Barber's notebook contains much other information on practical farming.
[56] Orr, *Oxon. Agric.* 66.
[57] e.g. Bodicote Grange (270 a.), Little Barford Manor farm (160 a.): Bodl. G. A. Oxon. b 85[a].
[58] Gardner, *Dir. Oxon.* (1852); *Kelly's Dir. Oxon.* (1885, 1939).
[59] *Kelly's Dir. Oxon.* (1903, 1920, 1939); ex inf. Mr. J. H. Fearon, Bodicote.
[60] O.R.O., land tax assess.
[61] MS. notes of L. G. Wickham Legg.
[62] Ibid., comparison made by Wickham Legg between incl. award and land tax assess.
[63] O.R.O., land tax assess.
[64] F. M. Eden, *The State of the Poor*, ii. 591.
[65] *V.C.H. Oxon.* ii. 205–6.
[66] Beesley, *Hist. Banbury*, 79, 128.
[67] Orr, *Oxon. Agric.* 69–70, 72.
[68] Ibid. 75.

manent pasture increased.[69] In 1962 the main crops were wheat, barley, oats, beans, swedes, and potatoes.[70] Poultry production on an intensive scale was a recent development.[71] The size of farms as elsewhere in Oxfordshire had considerably increased.[72]

The proximity of markets at Banbury and Deddington probably encouraged a small trading element in Adderbury even in the Middle Ages. A merchant held a house and land in Adderbury at the end of the 13th century,[73] a wool merchant lived in Adderbury in the late 15th century,[74] and in the 16th century a merchant was buried in the church.[75] The development of Banbury as a centre of the weaving industry and later of Shutford as a centre of the plush industry, together with the construction of the Banbury–Oxford canal encouraged non-agricultural pursuits.[76] In 1841 Bodicote had at least 10 families of plush-weavers, a linen-weaver, a stocking-weaver, a blanket-maker, a machine-maker, and a dyer; at Milton there were 6 plush-weavers; there were 26 weavers in Adderbury East and West.[77] Later in the century the industry declined and many weavers left the district for Coventry.[78]

Both the Adderburys and Bodicote had a great variety of other skilled craftsmen and women, as well as tradesmen and professional men. In 1841 there were 3 coal merchants, whose living depended on the canal, a seedsman, a land agent, a road surveyor, 3 surgeons, and 4 solicitors. Among the craftsmen were several stone-masons, a rope-maker, a brick-maker, a basket-maker, a printer, and a clock-maker.[79] Since the 16th century Adderbury had had some outstanding clock-makers. The craft was closely connected with the Quaker community; Richard Gilkes (1715–87) was the best-known practitioner.[80] Another Richard Gilkes, perhaps his father, had been apprenticed in 1678 to William Hancorne, a member of the Clock-makers' Company of London.[81] Joseph Williams and Richard Tyler practised the craft at the end of the 18th century.[82] Another noted craftsman who came from London to live in Adderbury East and whose work was known far outside was Charles Harris (d. 1851), violin-maker.[83] George Herbert of Banbury had a 'good fiddle' made by him.[84] Herbert has also commemorated another Adderbury craftsman who 'turned' the blocks for the silk hats made by Herbert's father.[85]

The local stone quarries were noted in the 17th century, and also a 'spongy chalk' used at Adderbury and Milton for pointing.[86] Ironstone quarries began to be worked intermittently after 1859 and regularly after the opening of the Banbury and Cheltenham railway in 1887.[87] The workings were in Adderbury East near Sydenham Farm and in Adderbury West on either side of the Banbury–Oxford road. There were brick works near Twyford Bridge *c.* 1880.[88]

In the 20th century other industrial undertakings have been sited on the outskirts of the villages. The largest, Twyford Mill Ltd., seed merchants, took over the war-time buildings of the Northern Aluminium Co. and in 1955 were employing some 2,000 men and girls. Twyford Vale, an offshoot of this company, opened a pre-packaging factory in 1958. A staff of 31 was employed to wash and pack potatoes and vegetables from Twyford Mill's 3,000 a. of local farm land.[89] Another industrial undertaking was Modern Conveyors Ltd.[90]

MILLS. In 1086 2 mills, each worth 30*s.* a year, were attached to the Winchester manor.[91] These were probably in Adderbury East and in Bodicote. By the 13th century their tenants held them by payment of an entry fine and not on an annual lease.[92] The fine for the Adderbury mill between 1305 and 1474 was £6 13*s.* 4*d.* and thereafter £5.[93] In the 16th century this mill was held by Anthony Bustard and then by his son John.[94] Between 1558 and 1579 3 Adderbury men brought an action in Chancery, alleging that Anthony Bowlestred (Bustard?) had purchased land from the Bishop of Winchester and built a mill on it which he called Lord's Mill; he now demanded suit of mill from the Winchester tenants who 'always did maulte at home'.[95]

The Bodicote mill was held at the beginning of the 14th century by Hugh the miller, who was among the highest contributors to the tax of 1327.[96] Bodicote's miller died in the Black Death and was not replaced until 1353.[97] In the 16th century the mill was held for a time by Edward Councer of Bloxham, who owned nearby Grove mill in Bloxham, then by William Dauntesey of London.[98]

The king had 6 water-mills on his estate in Adderbury and Bloxham in 1086; one of these was probably the mill belonging to the St. Amand manor, originally a royal manor, which was worth 13*s.* 4*d.* in 1294 and 30*s.* in 1330 when it was let to John of Leicester.[99] In 1616 Robert Doyley sold 2 water-mills, one from the St. Amand's manor and one from Brown's manor, also originally a royal manor, to William Westley, who sold them in 1629–30.[1]

About 1250 the Abbot of Cirencester granted his share of a mill with the multure of all his tenants in Adderbury and Milton to the brothers John and

[69] Ibid., statistical plates.
[70] Local information.
[71] *Oxf. Mail*, 6 Jan. 1958.
[72] Local information.
[73] Bodl. Oseney Ch. 272, 273–5.
[74] *Cal. Pat.* 1494–1509, 535. Agnes Fuller occurs in a ct. roll of 14 Ed. IV: New Coll. Mun.
[75] See brass in Adderbury church.
[76] See MS. d.d. Risley A IV 7/8 and *passim* for trades.
[77] H.O. 107/875.
[78] *V.C.H. Oxon.* ii. 246.
[79] H.O. 107/875.
[80] *Oxon. Clockmakers.*
[81] Gepp, *Adderbury*, 76.
[82] *Oxon. Clockmakers.* These men were all buried in the graveyard of the Adderbury meeting-house.
[83] Par. Rec., letter from A. F. Hill, 1926; J. M. Flemming, 'Violins and their Value', *Bazaar, Exchange and Mart.*, 4 Jan. 1905, p. 8. See also C. C. Brookes, *Steeple Aston*, 88–89 for Harris's connexion with Steeple Aston.
[84] G. Herbert, *Shoemaker's Window*, ed. C. S. Cheney, 24.
[85] Ibid. 4.
[86] Plot, *Nat. Hist. Oxon.* 66, 78.
[87] *V.C.H. Oxon.* ii. 225, 268.
[88] O.S. Map 25″ Oxon. X. 6 (1st edn.).
[89] *Oxf. Times*, 6 Jan., 24 Mar. 1958.
[90] Ibid.
[91] *V.C.H. Oxon.* i. 401.
[92] Hants R.O. Eccl. 2/159270 sqq.
[93] Ibid. There is a complete list of tenants.
[94] Adderbury recs., Book A (*penes* Godfrey, Lord Elton, Adderbury).
[95] C 3/35/29.
[96] E 179/161/9.
[97] Hants R.O. Eccl. 2/159270 sqq.
[98] Ibid.
[99] *V.C.H. Oxon.* i. 400; C 142/214/217; *Abbrev. Rot. Orig.* (Rec. Com.), ii. 8.
[1] C.P. 25(2)/340/Mich. 14 Jas. I; ibid. 473/Trin. 5 Chas. I.

Simon de Briddesthorne who were to pay 8*s.* rent and each of their heirs 6*s.* 8*d.* relief.[2] This too may once have been one of the king's mills.

In 1675 there were at least 3 mills in Adderbury and one in Bodicote.[3] The Duke of Argyll had the mill in Adderbury East removed to its present position because it interfered with the landscaping of his grounds.[4] By 1920 Adderbury mill had become a steam-mill, and was run by a miller and a baker. It was still in use in 1924, but had ceased to function by 1939.[5] The derelict buildings were still standing in 1963. Bodicote had 2 mills in 1854, one owned by a corn-miller, the other by a miller and maltster.[6] By 1869 only the corn-miller remained, and in 1887 Bodicote mill, as it was called, had become a bakery as well.[7] It had ceased working by 1915.

The mill at Little Barford, or Barford St. John, was first mentioned in 1307, when it was held by Roger Beaufeu.[8] In 1327 the lessee paid the second highest contribution to the tax.[9] The mill followed the descent of the Beaufeu manor and was sold by Sir George Dashwood to Magdalen College, Oxford, in 1898.[10] This mill too had ceased working by 1915.[11]

CHURCHES. The likelihood is that Adderbury church was founded before the Conquest: the village was named after St. Eadburga[12] and in 1270 the Bishop of Winchester claimed that Athelstan had given the church to his see in 1014 or 1015.[13] Moreover, Adderbury in the Middle Ages was the mother church of a wide area, including the chapelries of Milton, Bodicote, and Barford St. John. Milton chapel probably did not survive the Reformation, Bodicote became a separate parish in 1855, and Barford St. John was amalgamated with Barford St. Michael in 1890.[14]

The descent of the advowson is complicated,[15] partly perhaps because of the wealth of the living. The Bishop of Winchester's ancient right was not disputed, but in 1257 the king successfully claimed his right to present during a vacancy in the see.[16] The first papal provision was made in 1297 at the request of the Bishop of Winchester when Adderbury's rector, Edmund of Maidstone, died on a visit to Boniface VIII; the Pope provided Robert of Maidstone.[17] In 1330, on the death of one of the king's presentees,[18] the advowson appears to have reverted to the Pope; Itherius de Concoreto, papal nuncio, seems to have been the next rector and on his resignation or marriage the Bishop of Winchester presented in 1344 his own nephew, Master Thomas de Trillek.[19] This led to a papal protest that the benefice was reserved to the papacy and at the bishop's request the Pope provided Trillek and remitted the fruits received.[20] The king ratified this papal provision in the same year.[21] When Trillek became Bishop elect of Chichester in 1363, the Pope presented John, Cardinal of St. Mark's.[22] Whenever a vacancy occurred in the See of Winchester, however, the king claimed his right:[23] in 1365 he was successful in a suit with the Cardinal of St. Mark's over this but ratified the cardinal's estate in Adderbury in the following year.[24] In 1371 the king again presented and Cardinal John, 'unjustly incumbent' of Adderbury, was summoned to Westminster and so also in 1373 was William of Wykeham, Bishop of Winchester.[25] In 1374 the king made a presentation but revoked it immediately on the grounds that it had been made in the belief that Cardinal John was dead.[26] The cardinal died between 1377 and 1379,[27] when William of Wykeham presented. The king confirmed the presentation in 1380, notwithstanding the judgment whereby Edward III had recovered his right of presentation against the then Bishop of Winchester on the grounds that the temporalities of the see were in his hands.[28] In 1381, when the living again became vacant, the controversy was ended by Bishop Wykeham's grant of the advowson to New College, Oxford.[29]

Papal licence for the appropriation of the church had been obtained in 1379 and royal licence was granted in 1381.[30] Thereafter New College regularly presented to the newly created vicarage Fellows or members of the college.

Valuations of the rectory in 1254, 1291, 1341, and 1535 give the following figures: £41 4*s.*, £46 13*s.* 4*d.*, £48 15*s.* 8d. with portions, and £56 5*s.* 2*d.* Of the last sum £1 5*s.* 2*d.* came from the rent of customary tenants and the rest from tithes.[31] Allowing for several small expenses the net income was £52 18*s.* 5*d.* in 1535.[32] In 1794 the rectory was worth £1,327, by 1810 the net annual value was £10 more, and in 1827 it was valued at £1,250.[33]

In 1381, when the rectory was granted to New College, it consisted of land and tithes.[34] The tithes included most of the great tithes from the Adderburys and Bodicote, and the lesser tithes from the demesne of the Winchester manor and of the New College rectory manor. The great tithes of Barford St. John and Milton were excluded.[35] Various

[2] Cirencester Cart., Reg. B, no. 850.
[3] Ogilby, *Brittania* (1675), 82.
[4] Gepp, *Adderbury*, 63.
[5] *Kelly's Dir. Oxon.* (1903–1939).
[6] Billing, *Dir. Oxon.* (1854).
[7] *Kelly's Dir. Oxon.* (1869).
[8] C.P. 40/107.
[9] E 179/161/9.
[10] See p. 20; ex inf. Magd. Coll. (Oxf.) Bursary.
[11] *Kelly's Dir. Oxon.* (1915).
[12] See p. 6.
[13] *Reg. Pontissara* (Cant. & York Soc. xxx), 609. A royal quitclaim of the advowson was obtained in 1284: ibid. 420.
[14] See below.
[15] For a list of presentations see MS. Top. Oxon. d 460.
[16] K.B. 26/165/30; 169/37; cf. *Cal. Close*, 1259–61, 266, 279.
[17] *Cal. Papal Regs.* i. 570.
[18] *Cal. Close*, 1330–3, 223; Kennett, *Par. Antiq.* ii. 206, quoting Reg. Dalderby; *Cal. Pat.* 1317–21, 421.
[19] *Cal. Papal Pets.* i. 52.
[20] Ibid.
[21] *Cal. Pat.* 1334–8, 88.
[22] *Cal. Papal Pets.* i. 470.
[23] e.g. *Cal. Pat.* 1361–4, 512; ibid. 1370–4, 145, 401.
[24] Ibid. 1364–7, 325.
[25] *Adderbury 'Rectoria'*, 111–112; *Cal. Pat.* 1370–4, 145.
[26] *Cal. Pat.* 1370–4, 401; cf. *Cal. Close*, 1374–77, 28.
[27] *Cal. Pat.* 1377–81, 35.
[28] Ibid. 438.
[29] *Adderbury 'Rectoria'*, 88–89.
[30] Ibid. 84–8, 88–9.
[31] Lunt, *Val. Norw.* 310; *Tax. Eccl.* (Rec. Com.), 31*b*, 215*b*; *Inq. Non.* (Rec. Com.), 139; *Valor Eccl.* (Rec. Com.), ii. 257.
[32] *Valor Eccl.* (Rec. Com.), ii. 257.
[33] New Coll. Mun., Adderbury Misc.
[34] For the descent of the rectory manor see p. 16.
[35] *Adderbury 'Rectoria'*, 99–103. The allotment of tithes to New College is not specifically stated in the ordination of the vicarage, but it can be worked out. In 1685 the rectory had 7 yardlands in Bodicote field: MS. Oxf. Archd. Oxon. c 141, ff. 449–50.

deductions from the tithes had to be made: Oseney Abbey had a claim to tithes worth 13*s.* 4*d.* and the owners of the former Oseney manor were still claiming tithes in 1700.[36] Eynsham Abbey claimed tithes worth 6*s.* in 1291 and 26*s.* 8*d.* in 1535.[37] After the Dissolution the Eynsham tithes were leased for 21 years; but the freehold evidently went to Lord Saye and Sele, who already held land in Bodicote, and later to Robert Barber.[38] Another claimant to the share of the rectory tithes was the Rector of Barford St. Michael. His share was valued at 5*s.* in 1291,[39] but payment later appears to have lapsed. The origin of this charge is not known, but it is possible that certain lands or common rights in the township of Barford St. John once belonged to the founder of the church of Barford St. Michael. As late as the 18th century tenants of certain lands in Barford St. John claimed right of burial in the churchyard of Barford St. Michael without paying special fees and the inhabitants of Barford St. Michael claimed a right of common in the same lands.[40] At inclosure in 1768 New College received 456 a. in lieu of rectory tithes of open-field land, 33 a. for tithes of old inclosures, and 55 a. in lieu of open-field glebe.[41]

Before the ordination of a vicarage in 1381 there had been a temporary vicarage on at least two occasions: in the early 12th century William Giffard, Bishop of Winchester (1107–29), granted a house to Master Geoffrey, the vicar, and in 1262–3 Wybert of Kent, the rector, presented a vicar. The vicarage then consisted of all the altarage, but the rector received the great tithes and tithes of hay.[42] By the ordination of 1381 the vicar was assigned the great tithes of Barford, the small tithes from the whole parish (i.e. 5 tithings), except those from the rectory manor and the tithes of hay from the Winchester manor. The vicarial tithes were augmented in 1397 by the addition of the great tithes of Milton.[43] By the ordination of 1381 the vicar was also allowed all customary offerings and oblations from the chapels of Barford and Bodicote and mortuary dues from all parishioners buried in Adderbury cemetery. He was to have as his vicarage the house with a croft and meadow land which William Giffard, Bishop of Winchester, had once given to Master Geoffrey, at an annual rent of 6*s.* The vicar was also to have 8 a. in the fields of Barford, a house which belonged to Adderbury church, 16 a. in the field of Adderbury West and 18 a., called 'le Chirchelonde', lying in the demesne of the Bishop of Winchester in Adderbury East, meadow in Bodicote called 'Parsonsham', and 2 a. in Barford belonging to the church; also a house and 1 yardland at Bodicote belonging to the church. The vicar was to pay tithes great and small on this Bodicote property but not on his other land. He was to support all the burdens of his office, to pay procurations and synodals, to be responsible for the cure of souls of his parishioners in Adderbury and the dependent chapels, to celebrate mass and other divine offices, and to administer the sacraments in the church and chapels either himself or by chaplains provided by himself; he was also to provide a lamp for the chancel of Adderbury church, bread, wine, and wax for all services, and 2 processional candles and 2 other candles for the high altar. All repairs were his responsibility except those of the chancel and the rectory-houses.[44]

In 1535 the vicarage was worth £21 4*s.* 9*d.* net. The rent of 6*s.* a year for the vicarage was paid to the Bishop of Winchester and was still paid in 1805, and procurations cost 11*s.* 8*d.*[45] The living has never been augmented.[46] With the chapels of Bodicote and Barford St. John its gross value in 1852 was *c.* £750.[47] In 1883, after Bodicote had become a separate parish, Adderbury was worth £522.[48]

The main sources of income were the tithes and glebe. In 1765 these were valued at £263 15*s.* by the vicar, who considered that the improved value of the vicarage after inclosure would be £418.[49] In 1768 the vicar was allotted 43 a. in lieu of open-field glebe and 269 a. for tithes. When Barford was inclosed in 1794 the vicar received 3½ a. for glebe and 78 a. for small tithes.[50] In 1874 the glebe consisted of 130 a. at Adderbury, 206 a. at Milton and Barford, and 60 a. at Bodicote.[51] In 1965 some 56 a. were left.[52]

The payment of tithes after the Reformation became an increasing cause of quarrels, which were undoubtedly encouraged by the nonconformist element in the parish. There was a dispute over tithes with a Barford farmer in 1617–18, and again in 1621 when the rectorial lessee brought a case against a tenant for avoiding payment of tithes on wool. The issue was the length of time sheep brought in from outside could stay in the parish without payment of tithe. Payment was of vital importance to the curate, for the tithes formed the main part of his income.[53] Again in 1661[54] and in Edward Somervill's time (1721–4) there were other lawsuits.[55] Somervill tried to exact tithes in kind from Bodicote and break a *modus*, made by one of his predecessors, which, owing to the rise in prices, had turned out disastrously for the living. A parishioner brought an action for trespass against him and he was obliged to accept 8*s.* a yardland for his hay tithe and was allowed tithe milk for 3 months a year only. Even this unfavourable arrangement was unpopular in the village and the vicar alleged that the men of Bodicote had laid stones in the road to upset his carter's waggon, and had flung dung into the milk and rotten eggs at those who milked the

[36] *Tax. Eccl.* (Rec. Com.) 31*b*; C.P. 25(2)/865/Mich. 12 Wm. III.
[37] *Tax. Eccl.* (Rec. Com.) 31*b*; *Valor Eccl.* (Rec. Com.), ii. 257.
[38] New Coll. Mun., Reg. Evid., deeds 27, 33, 37; MS. d.d. Risley C 3.
[39] *Tax. Eccl.* (Rec. Com.), 31*b*.
[40] E 134/2 Geo. II/East. no. 12.
[41] O.R.O., incl. award.
[42] New Coll. Mun., Reg. Evid. ii. 220; *Rot. Graves*, 217.
[43] *Adderbury 'Rectoria'*, 99–103; MS. Top. Oxon. c 60, f. 1.
[44] *Adderbury 'Rectoria'*, 94–8.
[45] *Valor. Eccl.* (Rec. Com.), ii. 164; MS. Oxf. Dioc. c 448, f. 1.
[46] Bacon, *Liber Regis*, 798.
[47] MS. Oxf. Dioc. c 1693: petition for non-residence by C. Alcock.
[48] *Kelly's Dir. Oxon.* (1883).
[49] New Coll. Mun., Adderbury Misc.: vicar's valuation of 1765 with details of how the total was made up.
[50] O.R.O., Adderbury and Barford incl. awards.
[51] Par. Rec., vicar's MS. note.
[52] Ex inf. the Vicar of Adderbury.
[53] MS. Oxf. Archd. Oxon. c 118, ff. 131, 135, 142v.–146v.; ibid. c 10, ff. 20–23.
[54] E 134/13 Chas. II/Mich. no. 40.
[55] New Coll. Mun., Adderbury corresp. 1723–9; E 134/1 Geo. II/Hil. no. 1.

tithe milk.[56] In 1751 another vicar was at issue with the inhabitants of Adderbury when it was successfully argued that a *modus* had been made in Elizabeth I's reign or earlier.[57] His successor was faced with a different anxiety: 13 Quaker families in Adderbury had been excused Easter offerings and so the Churchmen paid very unwillingly.[58] The damage that might be done to the vicarage by a single easy-going vicar is brought out in the comments of Warden Hayward of New College, who complained that Cox, a man of a 'generous disposition', had greatly underlet his tithes. The Warden was of the opinion that the college must insist on good terms for the vicarage as Cox was so adverse to doing so.[59]

As the living before its appropriation was often in the hands of royal and papal officials the rectors were mostly absentees and the cure was frequently left to ill-paid curates. Among the rectors were the pluralists Peter de Cancellis (fl. 1232),[60] Robert of Maidstone (1297–1319), chaplain to the Bishop of Winchester,[61] and Thomas Trillek (1344–63), later Bishop of Chichester, who was able to spend £200 on the rectory-house.[62] Others such as Wybert of Kent (fl. 1260), a king's clerk,[63] and John, Cardinal of St. Mark's (1363–*c.* 1378),[64] probably used the living only as a source of income. The latter's proctor was engaged in a lawsuit in 1377 over 30 a. in Adderbury which he claimed had been granted to the church long before the Statute of Mortmain.[65]

The appropriation of the living by New College meant that the parish not only acquired a number of resident, educated vicars, but was also in contact with the Fellows. Visits of Fellows are recorded, for example, in 1388, 1390, and 1392; the expenses of one of these and of 'other good parishioners' eating with him are entered in the college accounts, as are the expenses of the Warden's dinner with numerous men of the parish.[66] Not all vicars were resident; soon after the death of the first vicar, who served for 14 years, there was probably a return to non-residence. Master John Monk,[67] instituted in 1395, made an exchange after two years and the next vicar after one year. Then Monk, who had resigned to become a chaplain of Canterbury, was again instituted as vicar and held office until his death in 1414, but it is doubtful whether he resided. Of his successors one resigned in less than a year, and each of the next two after six years. There followed two vicars who each spent 20 years in the parish and a third who was there for nearly thirty. One of these, Martin Joyner (1462–81), refused the wardenship of New College in 1475.[68]

Little direct evidence has been found of the effect on Adderbury of the religious change of the 16th century, but certainly the distinguished John London, Vicar of Adderbury from 1526, was conservative in his views and played an active part in putting down 'heresy' both inside and outside the University. He was Warden of New College, canon of four churches, and a royal commissioner for the dissolution of the monasteries.[69] The parish was well provided with curates at this time: London had two to help him at Adderbury as well as having a curate both at Bodicote and at Barford.[70] In 1540, however, the latter was found to be inadequate.[71] William Binsley (vicar 1551–4), was chancellor to Cardinal Pole and a persecutor of all Protestants,[72] and as late as 1566 the college's influence was against radical changes, for in that year the Warden and many Fellows were accused of being crypto-papists.[73]

The policy of Protector Somerset, however, had inevitably brought about changes. In 1547, for instance, the college contributed to the cost of Bibles for Barford and Bodicote.[74] An effect of the Anglican settlement under Elizabeth I may be seen in the vicar's foundation of a free school,[75] and the growing strength of Puritanism in the neighbourhood may account for the acceptance of the living by John Pryme (1589–96), a noted Puritan preacher at Oxford and the author of several sermons and treatises. At the visitation of 1576, when he was a New College Fellow, he was accused of being 'seditious and factious', probably because of his zealous Puritanism; at Adderbury he was 'much followed for his edifying way of preaching'.[76] The influence of Puritanism is more clearly seen in the later controversy surrounding Francis Wells, Curate of Bodicote,[77] which probably had an impact on the whole parish. Of the Vicar of Adderbury at that time it is known only that he presented the churchwardens for neglecting to provide a decent communion table and for placing the reading desk in an unsuitable position.[78]

The Civil War heightened religious differences. Hostility to the Established Church was violently expressed by a village carpenter who went into the church and tore in pieces both the book of Common Prayer and the Bible.[79] It was probably at this time, too, that much of the coloured glass, in which the medieval church was particularly rich, was destroyed.[80] William Oldys (vicar 1626–45), a Royalist, was killed in Adderbury in 1645 by Parliamentary soldiers who had been informed of his movements by one of his parishioners.[81] His successor William Barker, another Royalist, was sequestered for 'malignancy and other scandals' in 1646,[82] and the Puritan Curate of Bodicote, Francis Wells, was put in as 'minister', only to be removed at the Restoration, after a chancery action. During his ministry at Adderbury it is evident that he steered a middle

[56] E 134/12 Geo. I/East. no. 4.
[57] E 134/24 Geo. II/East. no. 1.
[58] MS. Oxf. Dioc. d 558.
[59] New Coll. Mun., Adderbury corresp.
[60] *Rot. Welles*, ii. 39.
[61] *Cal. Papal Regs.* ii. 3; *Reg. Woodlock* (Cant. & York Soc. xliii, xliv), 55, 687.
[62] *Cal. Papal Pets.* i. 52, 114–15, 180, 251.
[63] *Close R.* 1259–61, 279.
[64] *Cal. Papal Pets.* i. 470; *Cal. Pat.* 1367–70, 17; ibid. 1377–81, 35, 438.
[65] *Cal. Pat.* 1377–81, 35.
[66] New Coll. Mun., account rolls.
[67] Emden, *O. U. Reg.*
[68] MS. Top. Oxon. d 460; Kennett, *Par. Antiq.* i. 190.
[69] *D.N.B.* and H. Rashdall and R. S. Rait, *New Coll. Hist.* 100–110.
[70] *Subsidy 1526*, 269, 271.
[71] See below.
[72] Wood, *Fasti*, i. 102.
[73] H. Rashdall and R. S. Rait, *New Coll. Hist.* 116–133.
[74] New Coll. Mun., account rolls.
[75] See pp. 11, 41.
[76] Wood, *Athenae*, i. 572, 215; H. Rashdall and R. S. Rait, *New Coll. Hist.* 135.
[77] See p. 37.
[78] MS. Oxf. Archd. Oxon. c 12, ff. 278v.–279.
[79] Ibid. f. 363v.
[80] See below.
[81] For Oldys see *Walker Rev.* 323.
[82] Ibid. 295.

course, thus offending both sides in the religious and political controversy. In 1661 he was charged by some of his parishioners with refusing to administer the sacrament, with allowing it to be administered 'in an indecent and irreverent manner' by a 'mere lay parson', and with denying baptism and burial. Consequently, it was alleged, 60 inhabitants went elsewhere to church. This dispute, which arose in part out of the vicar's claim to mortuary and other dues was exacerbated by the political situation. Some accused the vicar of preaching against Charles I and others declared that he had so strongly condemned the king's execution that they were surprised that he had not lost his cure. He was quoted as saying that he had read of kings putting saints to death, but never of saints putting kings to death. He was also said to have described the king's execution as 'a most horrid act', and those responsible as 'bloody minded men'.[83]

The institution of William Beau (1661–1706) meant that the vicarage became once again a stronghold of Royalist opinion. Ejected from New College, he had become a major in Charles I's army and later fought in Poland. When made Bishop of Llandaff in 1679, through the influence of Charles, Earl of Rochester, he was licensed to hold Adderbury *in commendam*.[84] He was careful of his church's temporal interests but less so, it seems, of its spiritual ones. He tried to ensure the proper payment of tithes and brought a suit in 1661 over this matter, but his parishioners countered by accusing him of failing to serve Bodicote adequately.[85] In 1686 the vicar was accused of similar neglect at Barford.[86] The task of the vicars of Adderbury was made more difficult by the strength of nonconformity: the parishioners' tendency to frequent both Church and Presbyterian services led the curate to write in 1682 that they seemed to be 'like the borderers between two kingdoms', uncertain 'what prince they are subject to'.[87] He found at Adderbury not only indifference to religion and worldly-mindedness but also 'a factious, schismatical spirit'.[88]

Difficulties grew during the course of the 18th century. The large parish with its growing population received inadequate attention from its vicars, who found the endowments of the living insufficient to pay for proper clerical assistance. In 1755, however, the position was probably no worse than elsewhere. The archdeacon made a number of orders both for Adderbury and Barford, which suggested that there had been minor but not serious neglect.[89] At this time there were 2 services and a sermon at Adderbury every Sunday, prayers were read twice a week and on Holy days, the sacrament was administered 3 or 4 times a year, and children were catechized only between Easter and Whitsun.[90] A real decline began after 1778: the vicar was non-resident until 1802, and duty was performed by a curate, whose answers to visitation questions were often meagre in the extreme.[91] Many families absented themselves from church, the poor pleading lack of decent dress; and there were also middle-class absentees who had no such excuse.[92] Even with resident vicars the number of communicants continued to drop: there were 40 in 1823 compared with 50 in 1814, despite an increasing population, and the newer nonconformist sects grew in strength.[93] Bodicote also was badly served at this period.[94] The church's ministry reached perhaps its lowest level after 1823 when the incumbent went mad and because of financial difficulties no resident curate was appointed until 1829.[95] In the interval the church was served by the Vicar of Bloxham for a modest charge. When he was unable to continue, the bishop was advised that legally half the gross value of the vicarage could be assigned to curates for Adderbury and the chapelries.[96] A curate was appointed to Adderbury at a stipend of £130 with the use of the vicarage-house; Bodicote had its own curate and neighbouring incumbents did duty at Barford.[97]

Adderbury's new curate was zealous for innovations and suggested to the bishop that instead of preaching a second sermon on Sundays he might revive the ancient custom of catechizing publicly or the custom of expounding considerable portions of the scriptures by means of a popular running commentary.[98] There followed the first major restoration of the church building, and the curate's report of 1831 shows a great revival of church activity: he had a Sunday afternoon congregation of nearly a third of the population and 70–90 communicants; he had a thriving Sunday school and had started a private lending library as well as circulating 180 tracts a week.[99] In 1836 the parish obtained a resident vicar and there is further evidence of renewed vigour in the conduct of the parish. By 1854 the churches of Barford St. John and Bodicote had been restored[1] and in Adderbury itself there were 6 regular weekly services, catechism every Sunday in the boys' and girls' schools alternately, and monthly communions. During Lent and Advent there were services every day. Some lightening of his burden and better provision for the hamlets was long over-due: Bodicote was made into a separate ecclesiastical parish and Milton chapel was built.[2] About this time a reorganization of parochial government was carried out. Hitherto the vicar had appointed the warden for Adderbury East and the parishioners of Adderbury West the other. In 1852 the parishioners of Adderbury East claimed the right to vote with Adderbury West and after much discussion it was proposed to end the old division between the two villages and have one common rate, one vestry, and one warden.[3]

During the incumbency of Henry Gepp (1874–1913) there were daily matins and evensong on Fridays besides a full complement of Sunday services. Bible and communicant classes were held and a parish-room opened in Water Lane in 1890.[4] Gepp took an active part in organizing educational

[83] MS. Oxf. Dioc. e 9, f. 183v.; E 134/13 Chas. II/Mich. no. 40; *Calamy Rev.* 519.
[84] Wood, *Ath.* iv. 889–90.
[85] MS. Top. Oxon. c 56, f. 73 and see p. 37.
[86] See p. 37.
[87] MS. Oxf. Dioc. c 430, f. 1.
[88] E 134/12 Geo. I/East. no. 4.
[89] MS. Oxf. Archd. Oxon. d 13, f. 10.
[90] MS. Oxf. Dioc. d 558.
[91] MS. Oxf. Dioc. b 37; ibid. d 566.
[92] MS. Oxf. Archd. Oxon. b 22, f. 57.
[93] Ibid. d 574; ibid. d 580
[94] See p. 38.
[95] MS. Oxf. Dioc. c 664, ff. 5, 20–21, 23, 27, 31, 34.
[96] Ibid. f. 27.
[97] Ibid. ff. 20, 26.
[98] Ibid. ff. 8–9.
[99] MS. Oxf. Dioc. b 38 and see p. 42
[1] See below.
[2] See below.
[3] Par. Rec., parish mag.
[4] Ibid.

projects in the parish and in many of the social clubs which flourished in the late 19th century.[5] He was responsible for letting out allotments in Barford on his own ground; all tenants were to maintain a character for morality and sobriety, and it was hoped that tenants would attend church at least once a day on Sundays.[6]

from the earlier 13th century when a church with transepts and a nave of 5 bays was apparently built: in the east wall of the north transept are remains of 13th-century lancet windows with wall paintings on the splays and on the north wall there are the remains of an arcade. It is probable that there was once a 5-light lancet window in this wall.

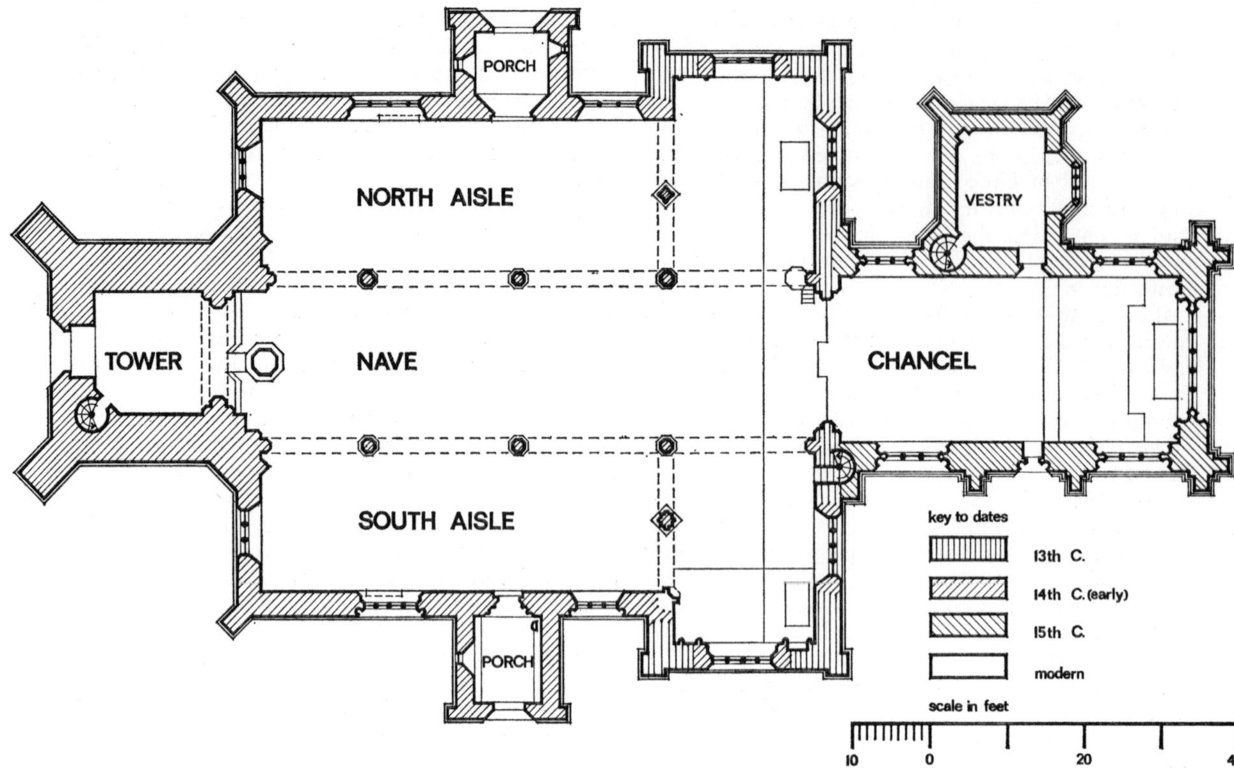

THE CHURCH OF ST. MARY THE VIRGIN, ADDERBURY

Despite his efforts the vicar noted that about half the population, including dissenters, was habitually absent from church. The large number of prescriptive and facultied pews, which left only 136 free sittings, was considered a barrier to church-going among the less privileged.[7] The principle on which pews had once been granted is expressed in a 17th-century vicar's petition to the bishop for an enlarged pew for Mr. Barber, the High Sheriff, stressing 'his public relation besides his private quality and reputation amongst us'.[8] In 1830 the occupiers of 36 houses in the parish were granted exclusive use of certain sittings.[9] In 1885, after a petition by *c.* 150 inhabitants,[10] the plans for restoration included provision for at least 170 free sittings.[11]

The church of *ST. MARY THE VIRGIN* is a large cruciform building with chancel, north and south transepts, nave, north and south aisles with porches, and a western tower with a spire.[12] The spire is celebrated, along with Bloxham and King's Sutton, in a local rhyme.[13] The earliest work dates

Similarly in the south transept there are traces of lancets in the east wall and of arcading on the south wall. Of the original 13th-century nave arcade the capitals alone remain. The piers and arches were reconstructed in the 14th century, only the westernmost bay probably retaining its original proportions.

Extensive alterations were made in the late 13th or early 14th century. The tower and spire were added. The nave arcade was reconstructed: the arches of the eastern bays appear to have been enlarged so that there were 4 arches instead of an original 5 arches.[14] The aisles were so much widened that they are now broader than the nave.

The similarity between the carving of the capitals of the columns that support the 2 arches separating the aisles from the transepts and that executed in other north Oxfordshire churches suggests that the same mason may have been employed. The capitals are carved with the heads and shoulders of women or knights with arms linked.[15] At this period Decorated windows, of which the original tracery

[5] See p. 42.
[6] Par. Rec., allotment agreement of 1883.
[7] MS. Oxf. Dioc. c 341.
[8] Ibid. c 454, f. 1.
[9] Ibid. c 1692.
[10] Ibid.
[11] Ibid.
[12] For earlier accounts of the building see *Trans. Bristol and Glouc. Arch. Soc.* xx. 359–64; ibid. lii. 58–63; Gepp, *Adderbury* (1924), 22–38; *Country Life*. 1949, 30–32, 86–89; *Gent. Mag.* 1834, N.S. i. 161–5.
[13] See p. 76.
[14] Five arches with the span of the existing Early English western arch would just fit the space now occupied by the 4 bays, according to measurements made by J. D. Sedding in 1885: Gepp, *Adderbury*, 22.
[15] cf. Capitals at Bloxham and Hanwell, Hampton Poyle, and Steeple Aston; and see *Antiq. Jnl.* iv(1). 1–3.

has since been destroyed, were inserted in the walls of the transepts in place of the former lancets. North and south porches were added, the north one sheltering a fine doorway with elaborate mouldings and carved decorations. Over the entrance is carved a shield charged with the emblems of the Crucifixion. A notable addition was the continuous frieze round the exterior walls of the aisles: the one on the north side depicts a lively series of musicians and their instruments interspersed with grotesque figures. This kind of work is also found in other north Oxfordshire churches.[16]

Later in the 14th century a clerestory was added to the nave and a new roof was constructed. This roof is remarkable for its original moulded arched braces supporting the tie-beams.[17] At a later date clerestories were added to the transepts and so the easternmost windows of the nave clerestory were turned into interior windows.

The chancel, with a vestry on the north side, is a notable example of Perpendicular architecture. It was built between 1408 and 1419 at the expense of New College, and the building accounts show that the chief mason was Richard Winchcombe, later to be the builder of the Divinity School at Oxford, and that a carpenter named John was responsible for the timber roof.[18] Taynton freestone was employed for the dressed stonework. The total cost to the college was *c.* £400. The wooden chancel screen was also made at this time. It is similar to a screen in Winchester Cathedral and may possibly have been made by Winchester craftsmen.[19] No major alterations were made before the 19th century, but some repairs were done between 1722 and 1727.[20] The stone work of the spire was repointed by White of Witney in 1766, but part of it fell in 1777 and in 1815 John Cheshire of Over Whitacre (Warws.) rebuilt 17 ft. of it.[21] Meanwhile the chancel had fallen into a bad state. In 1770 3 of the chancel windows were taken out and the space walled up; apparently the steward of Sir John Cobb, who, as lesseee of the rectory, was responsible for the upkeep of the chancel, refused to do more after a quarrel with the vicar.[22] Later the tracery was removed from the other 3 chancel windows and between 1787 and 1789 the churchwardens had all the tracery removed from the windows in the body of the church and replaced by plain stone bars.[23] A contemporary wrote that the way in which the church had been treated furnished a 'deplorable instance of the economy which seeks to avoid the expense of repair by the total destruction of its object.'[24] Late-18th-century drawings show the extent of the mutilation: one from the south-east shows a chancel window and all the transept windows in the south and east walls barred, while 2 chancel windows are entirely blocked: one from the north-east shows the north-east window of the chancel blocked and the transept windows without their tracery.[25]

Outraged public opinion probably caused the first major restoration, which was carried out at an unusually early period. Between 1831 and 1834 J. C. Buckler restored the chancel at the expense of New College.[26] The tracery inserted in the 6 windows was modelled on the Early Perpendicular style; the mutilated stone reredos was repaired and the canopied niches filled with figures; the fine workmanship of the sedilia and piscina was restored after the large Cobb monument, which had been placed in front of them, had been removed. At the same time the nave was repaired. It was not, however, until 1866–70 that the body of the church was thoroughly restored by Sir Gilbert Scott. New tracery was designed for the windows of the transepts, based on examples at Bloxham and on a drawing showing the original windows before their destruction. The musicians' gallery was taken down, the tower arch opened, and the south transept restored.[27] In 1886 there were further extensive alterations in accordance with the plans of J. O. Scott. The north and south aisles and the north transept were re-roofed, the old timber being used where possible; the pitch was raised to the original gables which still survived. The north and south porches were restored, the floor was re-laid, a new heating system was installed, and the church was re-seated.[28] The builders were Messrs. Cooper & Co. of Aylesbury.

The tower was restored in 1927; in 1952 the spire, partly rebuilt in 1922, was again repaired by the Souwestone Restoration Co. and in 1956 4 pinnacles were restored and other work was carried out by the same firm. In 1955 a successful experiment in re-roofing the church with aluminium instead of lead was carried out.[29] Electric lighting was installed in 1944 and improved electric light was installed in the choir in 1955.[30]

Various changes were made in the 18th and 19th centuries in the fittings of the church. Growing population in the 18th century and an increasing desire for comfort led to the erection of private galleries. In 1832 John Plowman of Oxford was employed to put up a large west gallery for the musicians,[31] and a smaller one beneath it for the school children.[32] A private gallery in the middle of the church was made for the vicarage but was taken down in 1831.[33] About this time the wooden Communion table of 1634[34] was removed from the east

[16] For drawings made in 1781 see Gough Maps 26, f. 60v.

[17] The roof is illustrated in Bloxham, *Principles of Ecclesiastical Gothic Architecture*, i. 197, and in *Arch. Jnl.* lxxi. fig. 26.

[18] *Adderbury 'Rectoria'*, 7–21. For Winchcombe see J. Harvey, *English Medieval Architects*, 41, 296.

[19] For an account and illustrations of the screen see *Arch. Jnl.* lxvii, 171 and plate facing p. 173.

[20] MS. d.d. Par. Adderbury, chwdns' accts.

[21] Ibid.

[22] *Gent. Mag.* 1800, lxx(1), illustration facing p. 209. See illustration facing p. 12

[23] MS. d.d. Par. Adderbury chwdns' accts.; *Gent. Mag.* 1800, lxx(1), illustration facing p. 209; ibid. 1834, N.S. i(1), 161.

[24] *Gent. Mag.* 1834, N.S. i(1), 161.

[25] For Buckler drawings of 1802 and 1825 see MS. Top. Oxon. a 65, nos. 29, 30. Drawings were also made by W. Woolston of Adderbury in 1797: MS. Top. Oxon. a 37, nos. 10, 11.

[26] MS. Oxf. Archd. Oxon. c 46, f. 124; cf. *Gent. Mag.* 1834, N.S. i(1), 161–5.

[27] MS. d.d. Par. Adderbury chwdns' accts.; MS. Oxf. Archd. Oxon. c 35, f. 29.

[28] Bodl. G. A. Oxon. c 22(3): appeal for funds; MS. Oxf. Dioc. c 1692: faculty; MS. d.d. Par. Adderbury, chwdns' accts.; specifications by J. O. Scott, 1884.

[29] *Oxf. Mail*, 2 Apr. 1956.

[30] For all faculties see MS. Oxf. Dioc. c 1692.

[31] The instruments provided included a bassoon and a hautboy: MS. d.d. Par. Adderbury, chwdns' accts.

[32] Ibid.

[33] Gepp, *Adderbury*, 35.

[34] MS. Oxf. Archd. Oxon. c 12, f. 363. It was later moved to the N. transept.

end of the chancel to the vestry and was replaced by a stone altar; in 1832 the 17th-century box pews were removed and the nave was re-pewed and a new pulpit, reading desk, and clerk's seat were erected.[35] In 1870 New College gave the oak stalls on the south side of the chancel; in 1886 the church was again re-seated with oak benches; in 1905 more choir stalls, designed by J. O. Scott, were installed; and in 1956 oak panelling was erected in the north transept.[36]

At the restoration of 1866 the early-15th-century screen, which had been cut down to the level of the Jacobean pews of the Cobb and Wilmot families, standing on either side of the central aisle, was restored; its original tracery, which had been removed, was replaced. A loft to surmount it was designed by Sir Gilbert Scott and the Cobb pew removed, but the Wilmot pew remained until 1906.[37]

In 1877 a new organ, made by Messrs. Walker & Sons, London, was bought. The case was designed by G. G. Scott, the room over the vestry was used as an organ-chamber, and an archway was made in the chancel wall.[38]

The medieval font was replaced in 1831 by one designed by John Plowman and given by the Revd. W. C. Risley.[39]

There is now no stained glass of earlier date than the 19th century though Rawlinson recorded armorial glass in the south chapel and in a window in the north aisle.[40] Some armorial glass (1834), formerly in the east window and now in one of the south windows, is by Thomas Willement. Two windows (1870 and 1888) in the transepts are by Ward and Hughes, and one (1905) by Clayton and Bell. The west window (1912) is by Messrs. Powell & Sons.[41]

A brass inscription set in the floor near the pulpit commemorates Roger Welles, merchant of Adderbury and 'special benefactor' of the church.[42] There are also two 15th-century brasses to an unidentified knight and lady, and one of 1508 to Jane Smith. There is a memorial to Edmund Birch, *informator publicae scholae de Adderbury* (d. 1620). There were once two fine monuments. One commemorated John Bustard (d. 1534) and his wife Elizabeth (d. 1517) and Jane (d. 1568), wife of Anthony Bustard. An inscription, once part of that monument, is on the south wall of the south transept.[43] The other monument was to Alice (d. 1627), relict of William Cobb. Twelve of her children and the family arms were depicted on it. It was removed from the chancel in 1831 and was later restored at the expense of Lord Methuen, her descendant, and set up in Corsham church (Wilts.).[44] Sir George Cobb, her last lineal descendant, was buried in the chancel in 1762.

The only early silver is a silver-gilt chalice of 1692.[45]

There is a ring of 8 bells of which all but one date originally from 1789. The sanctus bell dates from 1681. The vicar H. J. Gepp, recorded some interesting customs in connexion with bell-ringing.[46]

The churchwardens accounts have many references to the clock, which was ordered in 1684.[47]

Registers are complete from 1598 for baptisms, burials, and marriages.[48]

Milton had a chapel of St. John in the Middle Ages which seems to have been abandoned after the Reformation, the inhabitants thereafter attending Adderbury, but probably keeping their own parish officers.[49] The chapel was described in 1783 as *destructa*.[50] A 13th-century doorway in a cottage opposite to Manor Farm is likely to be a survival from it.

The 19th-century religious revival led in 1851 to plans for a new church at Milton. A former nonconformist meeting-house there was used temporarily for services held by the Curate of Barford.[51] The new church was consecrated in 1857.[52] During Gepp's incumbency the chapelry was well served: there were celebrations monthly of Holy Communion, and matins and evensong were held on alternate Sundays.[53] The Glebe farm-house was restored and a room was reserved in it as a parish-room with a library.[54]

The church of *ST. MARY THE VIRGIN*, Milton, was built in 1856–7 after the design of W. Butterfield. The builders were Franklin & Hopcraft and the site was part of the vicar's glebe.[55] The church comprises a nave, south porch, and chancel. It is in the early Decorated style and has a small central tower with 2 bells. Electric light was installed in 1948 and repairs supervised by J. M. Surman, architect, were carried out in 1953.[56] The church plate and bells are 19th-century. The east window is by F. Preedy of London.

Barford's ancient chapel, valued at £4 6*s.* 8*d.* in 1291,[57] survived the Reformation and continued to be served by the Vicar of Adderbury or his curate until it was annexed to Barford St. Michael in 1890.[58]

The chapel is known to have had its own curate with a stipend of £5 6*s.* 8*d.* in 1526,[59] and to have still had one in the late 16th century and at various dates in the 17th century. In 1540 the curate was charged with not reading the royal injunctions, not making any sermons or processions, and with being unable to administer the sacraments.[60] In 1618 he was engaged in a struggle over the payment of tithes

35 MS. Oxf. Arcd. Oxon. c 664, f. 36.

36 MS. Oxf. Dioc. c 1692.

37 Ibid. For an illustration of the Wilmot pew see A. Fea, *Picturesque Old Houses*, facing p. 142.

38 Par. Rec., corresp. between J. O. Scott and the vicar; report by G. G. Scott.

39 Gardner, *Dir. Oxon.* (1852), 611. For Buckler drawings of the medieval font see MS. Top. Oxon. a 65, no. 31.

40 *Par. Colln.* i. 4.

41 Par. Rec.

42 For other brasses see *Jnl. Oxf. Univ. Brass Rubbing Soc.* i(2), 79–80; Bodl. Wood MS. E 1, f. 222. Welles was a lessee of the rectory.

43 For notes on the Bustard memorials see *Par. Colln.* i. 3; *Gent. Mag.* 1800, lxx(1), 209. For a water-colour of 1801 by J. C. Buckler see MS. Top. Oxon. a 64, no. 1.

44 *Par. Colln.* i. 1–2; Gepp, *Adderbury*, 39; for the blazons of the arms on the monuments see G. A. Oxon. 16° 215, p. 506; ibid. 16° 217, pp. 40–1, 44; ibid. 8° 1270, pp. 31, 44, 45, 94; ibid. 4° 685, pp. 1–4.

45 Evans, *Ch. Plate.*

46 *Ch. Bells Oxon.*; Gepp, *Adderbury*, 39.

47 MS. d.d. Par. Adderbury, chwdns' accts.

48 Par. Rec.

49 See p. 22.

50 Bacon, *Liber Regis*, 800.

51 MS. d.d. Risley, letter of John Barber.

52 MS. Oxf. Dioc. c 748, p. 165.

53 Ibid. c 344.

54 Adderbury Par. Rec., par. mag.

55 Adderbury Par. Rec.; MS. Top. Oxon. c 104, ff. 53–5. There are water-colours of the church *c.* 1880 in Bodl. MS. drawings Gen. c 8, f. 10; Gen. c 9, f. 9.

56 MS. Oxf. Dioc. c 1693: faculties.

57 *Tax. Eccl.* (Rec. Com.), 31*b*.

58 MS. Oxf. Dioc. c 1718.

59 *Subsidy 1526*, 271

60 'A visitation of Oxon. 1540', O.A.S. *Rep.* 1930, 296.

which formed part of his stipend,[61] and is mentioned in the complaints brought by the villagers later in the 17th century. The villagers alleged in 1686 that the chancel had been ruinous for 24 years and that the vicar refused to admit responsibility for its repair or to hold services until forced to do so by legal action; that no service was conducted round Christmas because of the mud and rain; and that burials and marriges were conducted at Adderbury only.[62] In the mid-18th century there was no resident curate but prayers and a sermon were held every Sunday. In 1792 the vicarage-house was said not to have been used as such in the memory of man; it was ruinous and was taken down.[63] By 1805 at the 4 annual celebrations there were only 8 communicants. There was no Sunday school, but children went to the school at Barford St. Michael, just across the river.[64] The restoration of the church in 1849 was a sign of new life, but in the 1850s Bishop Wilberforce evidently feared that the curate, 'cynical and non-resident', was unsuitable.[65]

The chapel of *ST. JOHN*, Barford consists of a nave, chancel, and south porch with an octagonal bell-turret over it. Of the original 12th-century church there remain the south doorway with chevron ornament and possibly the font.[66] The chancel appears to have been rebuilt in the 13th century, the chancel arch and a two-light window in the south wall being of this date. The decorated nave windows and two piscinae were inserted in the 14th century. The church formerly had a tower which stood inside the nave at its south-west corner. Buckler's drawing shows that it was of medieval character, though possibly of post-Reformation date.[67] The date 1622 was carved on the highest stage of the tower.[68]

Repairs to the chancel were ordered in 1684,[69] and these were evidently carried out for in Rawlinson's time there was a tablet bearing the names of the churchwardens and the date 1684.[70] The chancel was again recorded as out of repair in 1752, 1755, and 1844.[71] A restoration of the church was proposed in 1855[72] and carried out in 1864 in accordance with the plans of G. E. Street.[73] The tower was removed and was replaced by a bell-tower standing over the new south porch.

A new oak Communion table was provided in 1861.

There is an armorial tablet to James Belcher (d. 1722).[74]

William Cumming, M.D., gave a silver chalice with paten cover in 1746.[75] The bells are 19th-century.

The churchyard was opened in 1838 on land given by the vicar.[76]

[61] MS. Oxf. Archd. Oxon. c 118, ff. 131, 135, 142v.
[62] Ibid. c 31, 98–98v.; ibid., c 29, ff. 33–4, 152.
[63] MS. Oxf. Dioc. d 558; c 454, f. 47.
[64] Ibid. c 568.
[65] Ibid. d 550.
[66] For drawings see MS. Top. Oxon. a 65, nos. 72, 73.
[67] Ibid. no. 71 (S.E. view).
[68] Adderbury Par. Rec., MS. notes.
[69] MS. Oxf. Archd. Oxon. c 29, f. 53.
[70] *Par. Colln.* i. 31.
[71] MS. Oxf. Archd. Oxon. c 50, f. 131; d 13, f. 10; c 36, f. 84.
[72] Adderbury Par. Rec., note at back of marriage reg.
[73] MS. Top. Oxon. c 103, f. 53. Drawings and notes by J. C. Buckler, made before the restoration of the church, are among the late Miss M. Bradford's papers: Bodl. (uncat.).
[74] For blazon of arms see G. A. Oxon. 16° 217, p. 270*b*.
[75] Evans, *Ch. Plate.*

The registers are complete from 1771 for births, 1784 for marriages, and 1839 for deaths.[77]

Bodicote's ancient chapel continued to be used after the Reformation and became a separate parish church in 1855.[78] The new vicarage was worth £270 net with residence and was in the gift of New College. There were 12 a. of glebe.[79]

In 1526 Bodicote had its own curate at a stipend of £5.[80] After the Reformation the curate at times did duty at Adderbury also.[81] The chapelry had its own wardens and its own registers, but burials took place at Adderbury until the early 18th century; at least between 1754 and 1837 marriages too were celebrated at the mother church. The vicar was not bound to attend burials, but he was often invited to do so when 'notables' were buried and was paid a mortuary fee of 10*s*. Five members of the Wise family, for example, were buried by the vicar between 1725 and 1730.[82] In 1754, after a petition by the vicar and others, Bodicote churchyard was consecrated.[83] Ground adjoining the chapel had long been used but never consecrated. The question arose as early as 1713 when the vicar was willing to have a churchyard at Bodicote if 10*s*. a time was paid for burials and a sermon as well, the poor being exempted from any payment.[84]

In the early 17th century Bodicote had a notable curate, Francis Wells. In 1634 he was charged with preaching against 'the king's Declaration and Book'. He denied this, but said that he had admonished the congregation to beware of the abuses done in church ales and that he thought God would not have his Church upheld and repaired by them.[85] He was also presented for failing to wear a surplice when perambulating the bounds, failing to follow the usual custom of reading a chapter at various stages of the perambulation but substituting instead the singing of psalms by the people, and preaching too often and too long. His Sunday sermons numbered two, each lasting about 1¼ hour. When his churchwarden forbade him to preach on a certain Sunday, saying it was against the canons and against the churchwardens' oath, he took away the pulpit cushion.[86] In the 1660s the Vicar of Adderbury was accused of having neither prayers nor sermon in Bodicote chapel for several Sundays and of having prayers at 'unseasonable and uncertain times'.[87] He admitted that the chancel of the chapel was ruinous.[88]

In the later 18th century the congregation seems to have been somewhat neglected: the curate lived at Adderbury, where he did part duty, and Bodicote had only one Sunday service and sermon; the children were catechized in Lent only and the sacrament was administered no more than 3 times a year.[89]

[76] MS. Oxf. Dioc. c 436, ff. 381–90.
[77] Adderbury Par. Rec.
[78] MS. Oxf. Dioc. c 1738.
[79] Ibid.
[80] *Subsidy 1526*, 271.
[81] One was buried there in 1580: Par. Rec., register; another took the Protestation Oath in 1642: *Prot. Ret.* 45. For curates of Bodicote and Adderbury see Oldfield's 'Clerus Oxf. Dioc.' in Bodl.
[82] Par. Rec., register.
[83] MS. Oxf. Dioc. c 454, ff. 83–5.
[84] New Coll. Mun., Adderbury corresp., letter from Somervill, *c.* 1722.
[85] MS. Oxf. Archd. Oxon. c 12, ff. 278v.–279.
[86] Ibid.
[87] MS. Top. Oxon. c 56, f. 73.
[88] MS. Oxf. Archd. Oxon. c 31, f. 98.
[89] MS. Oxf. Dioc. d 555; ibid. d 558; ibid. d 561.

The visitation returns of 1768 and 1771 suggest that both the vicar and his curate were ignorant of Bodicote affairs.[90]

In the early 19th century, although neglect continued, there seems to have been a revival of interest among the villagers. Much was done to beautify the church and to keep it clean.[91] The curate did not reside, however, as there was no vicarage-house; in 1808 the vicar was himself serving the cure and the number of communicants had fallen from 40 to *c.* 25.[92] The growing population of Bodicote led to requests for more services and for a better paid curate, but financial and other difficulties prevented anything from being done.[93] The curate from 1818, James Nutt, served Barford also but wished to resign his 'arduous duties' there to the Curate of Barford St. Michael without any diminution in his stipend of £70. Nutt stressed the strength of nonconformity in Bodicote where the chapel had 3 Sunday services.[94] By at least 1831 he was resident in the village and conducted two services on Sundays and on Christmas Day and Good Friday, attended by congregations of 200 or 300 out of a possible 600. From *c.* 1820 he had had a well-attended Sunday school.[95] In the 1850s, after the rebuilding of the church, Wilberforce thought that the low church curate was 'pretty good' and his wife 'invaluable'.[96] From the vicar's visitation return of 1866 it appears that Bodicote had benefited from becoming a parish; the vicar was resident and held no other benefice; there were 2 Sunday services, monthly Communion services, and weekly Sunday school. There was an average Sunday congregation of 200 and numbers were increasing; by 1878 it was thought they were over 250. Communion services were then being held twice a month, there was morning prayer every Friday, and 7 voluntary teachers assisted the vicar with the Sunday school.[97]

The church of *ST. JOHN THE BAPTIST*,[98] Bodicote, is a stone building, largely rebuilt in 1843–4. It comprises a chancel, nave of 3 bays, aisles, and a western tower. The earliest surviving feature is the chancel arch, which dates from the early 13th century. The building was much altered at later dates: the chancel was rebuilt in the 14th century and the aisles were also probably added then. Buckler's drawing of 1823 shows that the chancel roof had once been steeply pitched. It was subsequently lowered, but traces of the former level remained on the east face of the tower.[99] An embattled tower was added in the 15th century. It stood on the north side of the nave in the middle of the north aisle.[1] A medieval rood-loft survived until 1843.[2]

In 1766 a west gallery was built for the singers.[3] In 1809 a new roof and in 1812 a clerk's seat and a pulpit were provided.[4] In 1837 the chancel was repaired and tracery which had been taken out of the windows in the 18th century, in order no doubt to economize on repairs, as at Adderbury, was again put in the east window.[5] The rapidly increasing population led to an enlargement in 1843–4. The medieval tower was removed, and a new tower was built at the west end of the nave. The north aisle was rebuilt, and the whole church was much altered and re-seated. The architect was John Plowman and the builder Robert Franklin of Deddington.[6] Further changes followed: in 1866 a north porch was added,[7] and in 1878 the organ was moved from the west end to the chancel, new seats were placed in the chancel, a new pulpit was built, and a new vestry was made at the base of the tower. A new organ was given in 1914.[8]

There is a medieval font and a 17th-century wooden eagle lectern. There were once several inscriptions to two 17th-century families, the Huckles and the Wises;[9] only an inscription to Hawtrey Huckle (d. 1784) remains.[10]

The church plate dates from the 19th century.[11]

There were once 3 bells, but in 1843 5 new bells were cast. The saunce bell was originally cast in 1624.[12]

A piece of charity land attached to Bodicote chapel was exchanged at inclosure in 1768 for 2 a., subsequently let at £7 a year. This land was probably given and used for repairs to the building. In 1907, however, the income was given to the Nurses' Fund.[13]

The registers are complete from 1563 for baptisms and marriages, and from 1567 for deaths.[14]

ROMAN CATHOLICISM. Thomas Moore and Michael Bustard both appeared on a list of recusants remaining at liberty in the county in 1592,[15] and *c.* 1640 another Roman Catholic family was mentioned.[16] The Compton Census of 1675 listed one family in each of the two Adderburys, and throughout the 18th century the vicars recorded one or two papist families.[17] In 1768 they were described as 'of no great note'.[18] There was still one family in 1817 which worshipped at Warkworth (Northants.).[19] In the 20th century there was a considerable Roman Catholic community. Services were held in the 1940s in a room at 'The Court', the house of Lady Bedingfeld, a member of an ancient Roman Catholic family. She left Adderbury *c.* 1955.

The church of *ST. GEORGE* in Adderbury West was built in 1956 and is served from Banbury.

[90] MS. oxf. Dioc. d 558; ibid. d 561.
[91] MS. Top. Oxon. c 306; chwdns' accts.
[92] MS. Oxf. Dioc. d 570.
[93] Adderbury Par. Rec., Bodicote MS.
[94] MS. Oxf. Dioc. c 664, ff. 3–3v.; see p. 40.
[95] Ibid. b 38.
[96] Ibid. d 550.
[97] Ibid. c 332.
[98] In the early 18th century and later the village wake was held on the Sunday following that feast: *Par. Colln.* i. 50.
[99] MS. Top. Oxon. a 65, no. 108.
[1] Ibid. nos. 108, 109 (NE. & SE. views by Buckler).
[2] Parker, *Eccles. Top.*, no. 126.
[3] MS. Top. Oxon. c 306.
[4] Ibid.
[5] Ibid. For a drawing of 1825 showing the window before restoration see MS. Top. Oxon. a 65, no. 108.
[6] MS. Top. Oxon. b 124, ff. 13–15; MS. Oxf. Dioc. c 2166(7).
[7] MS. Oxf. Dioc. c 332.
[8] MS. Top. Oxon. b 124, f. 40.
[9] *Par. Colln.* i. 50.
[10] For all other inscriptions up to 1924 see MS. Top. Oxon. b 124, ff. 17–23.
[11] Evans, *Ch. Plate.*
[12] *Ch. Bells Oxon.*
[13] *12th Rep. Com. Char.* 200; Char. Com., G file corresp. and accts.
[14] Par. Rec., regs.
[15] Stapleton, *Cath. Miss.* 3.
[16] Ibid. 64–65.
[17] Compton Census; MS. Oxf. Dioc. d 561; c 327, ff. 116, 120; b 37, f. 7.
[18] MS. Oxf. Dioc. d 558.
[19] Ibid. d 576.

PROTESTANT NONCONFORMITY. The strength of Puritan feeling in the parish before the Restoration, the institution of an undistinguished vicar in 1661,[20] and the influence of some of the most outstanding ejected ministers of the neighbourhood facilitated the early growth of nonconformity in Adderbury. In 1669 the vicar reported that *c.* 200 of his parishioners, some Quakers, some Presbyterians, and some Anabaptists, attended weekly meetings in the houses of Bray Doyley, William Gardener, and Widow Swift.[21]

Milton became a centre for Presbyterians from a large area. Their early teachers were Christopher Newell, ejected Vicar of Bloxham, Samuel Wells, ejected Vicar of Banbury, and Thomas Whately, formerly Vicar of Sutton-under-Brailes (Warws.) and son of the eminent Puritan Vicar of Banbury.[22] Samuel and Josiah Cox's house in Milton was licensed in 1672[23] and in 1682 the Vicar of Adderbury stated that the Presbyterian 'conventicle' at Milton was 'peopled from all quarters roundabout'; and that Whately and Stedham of Banbury preached there. The social and political importance of this Presbyterian group is made evident by the vicar's comment that the meeting was 'a great exchange for politics' and that 'by reason of our numerous freeholders herabouts the county knights are generally chosen in it'.[24] In the early 18th century the decision to create a permanent chapel was taken and a building of 3 bays was erected on land in Milton belonging to the yeoman farmer, Samuel Cox, the elder. The trustees in 1708 included 4 yeomen, a weaver, and 2 gentlemen of Bloxham.[25] When a permanent chapel was acquired at Bloxham, the Milton and Bloxham chapels shared the same pastor, and Bloxham, being the larger village and having a more influential and richer congregation, seems to have taken the leadership of the movement later in the 18th century.[26] The reports of vicars and curates of Adderbury in the 18th century are brief and ill-informed: in 1768 it was said that there were 11 Presbyterian families of 'no great note', who had a meeting-house at Milton and a teacher, but whether either was licensed was not known;[27] in 1790 there were said to be *c.* 50 Presbyterians, Independents, or Baptists, no regular teacher, but sometimes a tailor, a weaver, or a farmer who officiated;[28] by 1811 the numbers of Presbyterians had been reduced to 2 families of 6 persons,[29] and Milton chapel ceased to be used by the Presbyterians *c.* 1842.[30] By 1851 it had been taken over temporarily by the Church of England for services held by the Curate of Barford.[31]

Presbyterianism also developed in Bodicote, where in 1699 Alice North's house was licensed for worship.[32] In 1759 7 Presbyterian families were said to reside in Bodicote, 'none above the rank of middling farmer'; the same number was reported in 1781 and a 'few' in 1817.[33] This small group was strengthened in 1814 by the arrival of Peter Usher, unordained Presbyterian minister of Banbury from 1796 to 1814, who farmed at Bodicote until 1844.[34] A son, W. R. Usher, who still lived on the family farm, was a leading Presbyterian and a trustee of the Banbury meeting-house in 1863.[35]

The Quaker community at Adderbury, because of its leading member Bray Doyley, lord of Adderbury West, was unusually important in the county as a whole. Doyley's social standing clearly contributed to the comparative leniency with which he was treated by the magistrates. In an attack on Quakerism in 1660 William Fiennes, Viscount Saye and Sele, addressed himself first to Doyley, 'a sober and discreet gentleman and a neighbour of mine', and grieved that he had been 'wrought upon by these seduced and seducing people'.[36] When Doyley refused to pay a fine after his arrest in 1665 at a Banbury meeting the magistrate paid for him and he was released from prison.[37] It was alleged in 1684 that the justices were so favourable that many Quakers came to live in north Oxfordshire to avoid prosecution, although this was clearly an exaggeration.[38] Doyley was first prosecuted for non-payment of tithes in 1661 and he refused to pay them up to his death in 1695.[39] He was three times arrested for attending meetings and on the third occasion it was at North Newington in Lord Saye's own parish and on the orders of Sir Thomas Cobb of Adderbury, 'who had a mind to hasten his preparation for banishment' in accordance with the Act prescribing banishment for the third offence.[40] Sir Thomas Chamberlain, however, sent him to prison for two months only, as if for a second offence, and finally got him released despite the wishes of his fellow magistrates.[41]

Doyley played a prominent part in Quaker affairs both at local and national levels. He organized the counter-attack on Viscount Saye and Sele's pamphlet against the Quakers in 1659.[42] In 1675 he built a meeting-house on his estate at Adderbury West and was so zealous in his support of the movement that the vicar complained in 1682 that he filled any of his vacant houses with Quakers from outside the parish and would have no other tenants.[43] He was frequently appointed to act for the Banbury Division in financial matters, or to attend the

[20] See p. 33.

[21] Lyon Turner, *Recs. of Nonconformity*, iii. 826. Bray Doyley's house was in Adderbury West, William Gardener's probably in Adderbury East and Widow Swift's probably in Milton: *Hearth Tax Oxon.* 136, 138, 139.

[22] Lyon Turner, op. cit. iii. 826; *Calamy Revised.* Whately lived on his own property at Hempton in Deddington parish and in 1690, by then 'aged and infirm' was receiving a regular stipend of £20–£30: Gordon, *Freedom after Ejection*, 85.

[23] Lyon Turner, op. cit. iii. 829, 830. Milton-under-Wychwood is clearly a mistake for Milton in this parish: cf. A. D. Tyssen, 'The Presbyterians of Bloxham and Milton', *Trans. Unitarian Hist. Soc.* ii(2). 10. For the house see p. 13.

[24] MS. Oxf. Dioc. c 430.

[25] *Trans. Unitarian Hist. Soc.* ii(2). 10.

[26] See p. 80.; Dr. Williams's Libr. MS. Evans gives the names of two preachers of Bloxham and Milton in *c.* 1730.

[27] MS. Oxf. Dioc. d 558.

[28] Ibid. b 22, ff. 57–60.

[29] Ibid. d 572.

[30] *Trans. Unitarian Hist. Soc.* ii(2). 25.

[31] MS. d.d. Risley: letter of John Barber.

[32] O.R.O. Cal. Q. Sess. viii. 803. Thomas North of Bodicote was a trustee of Milton chapel in 1708: *Trans. Unitarian Hist. Soc.* ii(2). 10.

[33] MS. Oxf. Dioc. d 555; ibid. c 327, f. 120, d 576.

[34] *Trans. Unitarian Hist. Soc.* ii(2). 29.

[35] Ibid.

[36] Wm. Fiennes, Ld. Saye and Sele, *The Quakers Reply Manifested to be Railing* (Oxf. 1660).

[37] MS. Sufferings.

[38] *Cal. S. P. Dom.* 1683–4, 84.

[39] MS. Sufferings. Doyley usually paid about £20, but in 1664 a fine for attending meetings cost him £40 and 20 cows.

[40] Ibid.

[41] Ibid.

[42] Saye and Sele, *Quakers Reply*.

[43] Oxon. Q. M. Min. Bk. (1671–1746); MS. Oxf. Dioc. c 430.

assizes to look after the presentments and indictments of Friends.[44]

Other Adderbury Quakers were fined and imprisoned for attending meetings either in the village or elsewhere in the county. Thomas Baylis and Christopher Barret were taken at a meeting at Banbury in 1660 and were imprisoned for two months before being released by Sir Anthony Cope.[45] Members of the families of Poultney, Treppas, Aris, and Garner were all fined for being at meetings at Milcombe, Banbury, Adderbury, and Milton between 1660 and 1674.[46] Prosecutions for non-payment of tithes began in 1659 when Timothy Poultney was imprisoned for 15 months.[47] Imprisonment, however, was exceptional after *c.* 1666, but distraint of goods went on until well into the later 18th century.[48] Barret and 5 other Quakers were constant offenders up to the end of the 17th century; from 1692 to 1766 the Maules, father and son, of Milton, paid fines each year, and in 1766 a Maule paid as much as £25. Other recurring 18th-century offenders were from the families of Stow, Gilkes, Halkes, King, Trafford or Turford, Robinson, and Pottinger.[49] It is noticeable from the 'Book of Sufferings' that after the immediate post-Restoration years Adderbury Quakers were more often prosecuted for the non-payment of tithes than urban Banbury. On the other hand, after the disappearance of the Maules of Milton, Adderbury Quakers ceased to bear witness in this way.[50]

The Quaker community in Adderbury in the 17th century included 27 family names. Four of these names (Maule of Milton, Soden, Barrett, and Williams) recur down to the 19th century and 15 other names are continued into the 18th century. For the 18th century the Quaker registers give 50 family names, of which 6 persisted into the 19th century. Most of these Quakers lived in Adderbury itself; only 9 families are known to have lived in Milton, 8 in Bodicote, and there is one reference for Barford.[51]

Adderbury Particular Meeting was one of the most important in Banbury Division, until the 19th century second only to Banbury itself. Monthly divisional meetings were regularly held there and, in the 17th century, occasional Quarterly Meetings. The Monthly Meetings appointed overseers of the poor for the Quakers of Adderbury and the earlier minute books give their names and the names of those who received relief — 3 persons in 1737 and 5 in 1739. The Monthly Meeting also let the grazing of the burial ground and organized the repair of the meeting-house in 1746. In 1770 the Division disowned William Halford, a prominent Quaker in the village, for insolvency caused by 'sloth and want of care';[52] in 1783 another Quaker was disowned for joining the army and 10 years later a man who procured a substitute for the militia was reprimanded.[53]

The general decline in the local Quaker community started in the last quarter of the 18th century. In 1786 proposals were made for the union of several meetings, Adderbury, Shutford, and Bicester among them; in 1790 it was decided that Bicester's few remaining members should be deemed to belong to Adderbury meeting.[54] By 1811 there had been a considerable decline in numbers and in 1851 only 16 persons attended on Census day.[55] At Banbury meeting in 1870 there were 3 regular members and 5 attenders from Adderbury. Tabular statements of Banbury Monthly Meeting for 1905–9 record only 1 member and 4 attenders from Adderbury, which thereafter ceases to be mentioned.[56] It is not known when the Adderbury meeting-house ceased to be used.

Although Anabaptists were recorded at Adderbury in 1669[57] the sect appears to have made little progress until the end of the 18th century. In 1759 and 1781 the vicar reported 2 Anabaptist families, neither above the rank of 'middling farmer', living at Bodicote.[58] In 1793 John Claridge and 2 others applied for a licence for Claridge's house in Bodicote, probably for use by Baptists. A house in Adderbury was probably registered at the same time.[59] Growth in the next few decades was very rapid and should be related to factors such as the increase of population, the spread of radical ideas, the inadequate arrangements made in the 1820s by the vicars of Adderbury for serving the outlying villages, and possibly to the dying-off of the Presbyterians.[60] By 1817 it was reckoned that one third of the village of Bodicote was Baptist.[61] There was a resident minister and a new chapel was being built.[62] The chapel, which stood in Chapel Lane, was later described as a handsome building of three stories with its front built of ashlar from the demolished mansion of the Cobb family at Adderbury, and with a well for baptisms.[63] In 1820 the vicar called the community 'a conventicle of Anabaptists', in 1841 Beesley termed it Strict or Particular Baptist, and the 1851 Census recorded it as Baptist and Independent.[64] The congregation was only 50 in 1851.[65] This was doubtless drawn partly from the surrounding villages, and the vicar's report in 1854 that there were only 4 Baptists in the parish may not have been very inaccurate.[66] In 1866 the Baptist meeting-house was only occasionally opened,[67] and having ceased to be used regularly was sold in 1902 and demolished a few years later. According to the original trust deed,

[44] Oxon. Q. M. Min. Bk. (1671–1746).
[45] MS. Sufferings.
[46] Besse, *Sufferings*, i. 566–576; MS. Sufferings.
[47] Besse, *Sufferings*, i. 566.
[48] MS. Sufferings.
[49] Ibid.
[50] Ibid.
[51] Banbury Quaker reg.
[52] Banbury Prep. M. Min. Bk. 1696–1720 (with accts. from 1661); Banbury M. M. Min. Bk. 1736–78, 1778–93, 1793–1804.
[53] John Busby and William Lamb: Banbury M. M. Min. Bk. 1736–78, 1778–93.
[54] Banbury M. M. Min. Bk. 1778–93.
[55] MS. Oxf. Dioc. d 572; H.O. 129/163.
[56] List and Tabular statements *penes* Secretary of the Society of Friends for N. Oxon.
[57] Lyon Turner, *Recs. of Nonconformity*, iii. 826.
[58] MS. Oxf. Dioc. d 555; b 37 f. 113.
[59] Ibid. c 644, no. 20.
[60] See p. 33; a few certificates were sent in for dissenting meetings whose denomination has not been identified: 1 for Adderbury dated 1813 (MS. Oxf. Dioc. c 644, no. 132) and 2 for Bodicote (MS. Oxf. Dioc. c 645, nos. 75, 143).
[61] MS. Oxf. Dioc. d 576.
[62] *Baptist Mag.* x. 240.
[63] MS. Top. Oxon. b 124, ff. 31, 60; *Baptist Mag.* ix. 279.
[64] MS. Oxf. Dioc. d 578. The visiting preacher also served Barford St. John; Beesley, *Hist. Banbury*, 558; H.O. 129/163.
[65] H.O. 129/163.
[66] *Wilb. Visit.*
[67] MS. Oxf. Archd. Oxon. c 332.

the money should have been divided amongst the subscribers, but as the list was lost it was divided between other Baptist chapels and the Building Fund.[68]

In 1828 the minister of the Independent church at Banbury and George Cakebread, a Particular Baptist of Bloxham, sent in a certificate for a private house in Adderbury West.[69] Two years later a certificate for a newly built meeting-house was signed by the same minister and Jonathan Dury.[70] As George Cakebread had been baptized by the Presbyterian minister Joseph Jevans in 1803 and one of the Dury family had married into the Presbyterian Usher family,[71] it looks as if the Adderbury Independents were closely allied with the declining Presbyterian groups as well as with the Baptists. The deed of 1827 conveying the land for the chapel, burial ground, and manse, states that it was for the use of Paedo-Baptists or allied denominations.[72]

In 1842 the chapel received a small endowment from Thomas Cox: £3 for the minister and £2 for the Sunday school.[73] The average congregation in 1851 was 80–100 and the vicar reported in 1854 that there were at least 60 'Independents'.[74] In 1870 the manse for the minister was pulled down and replaced by a school. The chapel was closed at the end of 1955 and was sold two years later.[75] The minister used to have three services on Sunday and a Sunday school as well as meetings during the week.[76]

Although Methodism was not mentioned in the reports of 18th-century vicars it had probably taken root in the hamlets before the end of the century. In 1851, when the Primitive Methodists at Milton had a congregation of over 60, including 28 Sunday-school children, the steward said that the chapel dated from before 1800, in which case it pre-dated the beginnings of Primitive Methodism.[77] At Bodicote the vicar reported the existence of a lively group of Methodists in 1802: many there were 'tinctured with Methodism'; they had a resident teacher, two occasional visiting teachers, and a meeting-house.[78] This meeting was probably a licensed private house, for a chapel was built in Bodicote in 1845, and in 1851 it was stated that on Census day the evening congregation was 60.[79] Adderbury East had a small chapel from 1810; a licensed preacher with a small congregation was recorded in 1811; and by 1851 there was a congregation of 30–40.[80] As the vicar estimated that there were only 20 Wesleyans in the whole parish in 1854 it may be that both at Bodicote and Adderbury the chapels were attended by people from outside the parish and by churchgoers.[81] The movement, however, was evidently growing, for in 1893 Adderbury chapel was rebuilt to seat 200.[82] The chapels at Adderbury and Bodicote were still in use in 1965. The Methodist community was flourishing, with a membership of 45 at Adderbury and 38 at Bodicote.[83]

SCHOOLS. The first school to be founded in the parish was the free grammar school in Adderbury East, endowed by the will of Christopher Rawlins in 1589. Although the essential function of this school was to teach grammar to boys who had already received some elementary education, the Warden and Fellows of New College, Oxford, who were the trustees of the bequest, decided that if the parishioners would pay for an usher to teach reading, writing and arithmetic, he might lodge in the school house and prepare boys for entry to the master's class. The school continued on these lines for at least two centuries.[84] Three of the 17th-century masters, one of whom is buried in the chancel of the church, were graduates. In 1768 the vicar reported that the school was kept according to the design of the founder.[85] There is, however, no record of Latin or grammar being taught after this date. The master's salary, originally fixed at 20 marks a year, had risen to £20 by 1771 and to £25 with a rent-free house in 1818.[86] The overseers appear to have made payments of 2*s*. 6*d*. to various parishioners to help with school fees at this time.[87] New College continued to pay the salary, but it was complained that the parishioners had no deed of endowment and did not know how large the funds were.[88] By 1833 the master was paid £30 and had 50 boys in the school,[89] by 1860 the salary was £50, and in 1939 the college was still contributing this amount.[90]

There was some hesitation about starting a public elementary school for girls as it was feared that it would ruin the dame schools of which there were 7 in 1831.[91] Some also thought that education of any kind would spoil the girls for domestic service. Their objections were overcome, however, and a girls' school was founded by public subscription in 1832, starting with 76 pupils.[92] Prejudice against the idea of educating working-class girls, however, persisted in the parish for many years, and it may have affected the average attendance at the girls' school, which was sometimes lower than normal. In 1874, a year in which this feeling was commented on as being very strongly held by the upper classes, only 51 out of 82 girls in the school had attended the required 250 times.[93]

In the mid-19th century the reorganizing zeal of the recently appointed resident vicar was turned towards education. By 1854 he claimed to have been much occupied in starting an infant school for 70 children and the supervision of its buildings and

[68] Char. Com., file B 75921; Unrep. vol. chapels, p. 221.
[69] MS. Oxf. Dioc. c 645, nos. 102, 95.
[70] Ibid. no. 153.
[71] *Trans. Unitarian Hist. Soc.* ii(2). 27, 29; see also under Bloxham, p. 80.
[72] Char. Com. E 105, 266; cf. Banbury where the Independents likewise called themselves Paedo-Baptists at this period.
[73] Char. Com. Unrep. vol., p. 184.
[74] H.O. 129/163; *Wilb. Visit.*
[75] Char. Com. G file (corresp.); file E 105, 266.
[76] *Oxf. Mail*, 2 Dec. 1955.
[77] H.O. 129/163. No further mention of this chapel has been found.
[78] MS. Oxf. Dioc. d 568.
[79] H.O. 129/163.
[80] MS. Oxf. Dioc. d 572; H.O. 129/163.
[81] *Wilb. Visit.*
[82] *Kelly's Dir. Oxon.* (1939).
[83] Ex inf. Revd. A. J. Davis, Secretary of the Oxf. and Leic. District Synod.
[84] For a fuller account see *V.C.H. Oxon.* i. 458–9. For the building see p. 11.
[85] See p. 36; MS. Oxf. Dioc. d 558.
[86] *V.C.H. Oxon.* i. 458–9; *Educ. of Poor*, 717.
[87] MS. d.d. Par. Adderbury, overseers' accts. 1814–22.
[88] *Educ. of Poor*, 717.
[89] *Educ. Enq. Abstract*, 738.
[90] *V.C.H. Oxon.* i. 458–9.
[91] MS. Oxf. Dioc. b 38.
[92] Par. Rec., misc. pps.; *Educ. Enq. Abstract*, 738.
[93] Par. Rec., par. mag. 1875; corresp.

this, he observed, on top of his constant care of 1,470 people, left him no time for instituting evening classes as he intended.[94] By 1866 this situation had been remedied and an evening class for men was tolerably well attended. In this year the three separate elementary schools in Adderbury East had a total attendance of 226 children,[95] 90 of whom were at the infant school which was taught by one uncertificated mistress. This school, and the girls' school, were supported by voluntary contributions, the boys' school still by endowment and fees.[96] Fees paid by the parents were raised in 1877 from 1*d*. a week to 2*d*. a week each for two of a farm labourer's family, 3*d*. a week each for three of an artisan's family, 4*d*. for each child of a farmer occupying under 50 a. or of a tradesman, and 6*d*. for each child of a farmer occupying over 50 a.[97] Further funds were provided by a Scheme of 1871, by which a fifth of the revenue of £350 a year from the foeffees' land in Adderbury and Milton was spent on education. The schools were managed by committees which were elected by the subscribers and maintained a high standard. Reading, writing, and arithmetic were taught, as well as grammar, geography, history, needlework, drawing, singing, and drill. The government inspectors commended the work and the schools were exempted from annual examination. The vicar and curate both taught in the day schools as well as holding Sunday schools in which they were assisted by 10 voluntary helpers. They also taught in the adult evening school and gave cottage lectures in Lent. Additional stimulus to education was also given by the opening of a reading library in 1879 and a parochial library the following year.

In 1899 the schools' committees were appealing for further support in order to avoid 'the costly expedient of having a school board', which would not be 'welcomed' in the village.[98] By 1896 evening classes were being supported by a parliamentary grant.[99] In 1939 the boys' school had the status of a non-provided elementary school. In 1962 the Church of England Schools for girls, boys, and infants were all transferred to the new Christopher Rawlins school building. The church found £4,500 towards the cost of £22,000 to secure continuation of 'aided' status. The school was managed by a board of 6, of whom 2 were appointed by New College and 4 by local bodies. There were 146 pupils in 1965.[1]

The earliest recorded Sunday school in Adderbury East was in 1802.[2] In 1833 it was attended by 68 boys and 66 girls, while another Sunday school, started in Adderbury West in 1829, took 25 children.[3] Classes were being held on Sundays in 1854 in both the boys' and the girls' school premises in Adderbury East and were attended by *c*. 30 more children than the 117 usual daily pupils.[4] This state of affairs was officially recognized when, by a Scheme of 1874, the vicar was empowered to use the boys' elementary school as a Sunday school and for other parochial purposes.[5] The girls' and infants' schools in Adderbury East were also still being used for Sunday classes.[6]

Adderbury has also had a number of private schools. The fact that Rawlins's school was originally intended for boys who could already read suggests that there were dame schools in the 17th century providing elementary education. In 1663 it is recorded that an old paralytic man earned his living by teaching children English[7] and there were probably dame schools in the 18th century. In 1808 there were said to be 2 dame schools, and in 1818 6 schools for boys and girls had 142 pupils.[8] A daily school for 30 boys and girls at Adderbury West, who were being educated at their parents' expense, was no doubt also an elementary school.[9]

The superior social character of Adderbury East village encouraged the setting up of private schools for older children. In *c*. 1780 Dr. Woolston, a clergyman, opened a boarding school for boys at the Manor-house, then known as Adderbury House.[10] It was probably this school which was advertised in 1829 as a school where boys were prepared for commercial and professional situations.[11] In 1833 it had 58 pupils;[12] it was closed just before 1851.[13]

In 1808 a boarding school for girls had 17 pupils and was perhaps Miss Weller's school, which moved to Oxford in 1825.[14]

Children from Bodicote had always been eligible for Rawlins's boys' school at Adderbury.[15] Otherwise the only education available there in the early 19th century seems to have been supplied by Sunday schools and dame schools, charging small fees. A Sunday school was mentioned in 1814 and again in 1823, when it was said to be supported by voluntary subscriptions.[16] In 1833 there were 2 Sunday schools, one Church of England with an attendance of 72 children under 16 years of age, the other Wesleyan, with a roll of 40 boys and girls.[17] In 1831 the vicar stated that most children went to dame schools, and in 1833 the existence of 2 daily schools for 50 children was officially reported.[18] There was also a day and boarding school, the Bodicote Classical, Mathematical, and Commercial Academy, possibly the same as the Gentlemen's Boarding and Day School kept at Draycot House by Richard Hartley.[19]

A National school was built in Bodicote in 1852 on land given by the vicar with the consent of New College; in 1857 it was described as a mixed voluntary school and by 1866 was receiving a parliamentary grant and had between 40 and 50 children on the books.[20] It was still partly supported by voluntary subscriptions, partly by school pence,

[94] *Wilb. Visit.*
[95] MS. Oxf. Dioc. c 332.
[96] Ibid. Ed. 7/101/75.
[97] Par. Rec., par. mag.
[98] Ibid.
[99] *Schs. in receipt of Parl. Grants*, [8179], p. 363, H.C. (1896), lxv.
[1] Ex inf. Oxfordshire County Council, Educ. Cttee. and the Revd. J. P. Vyvyan, Vicar of Adderbury.
[2] MS. Oxf. Dioc. d 566.
[3] *Educ. Enq. Abstract*, 738.
[4] *Wilb. Visit.*
[5] *Ret. of Non-Provided Schs.* (1906), 29.
[6] Ed. 7/101/75.
[7] MS. Oxf. Dioc. c 454.
[8] Ibid. d 570; *Educ. of Poor* 1819.
[9] *Educ. Enq. Abstract*, 738.
[10] For Woolston's school see p. 10.
[11] *Oxf. Jnl.* 12 Jan. 1822, 3 Jan. 1829, 10 Jan. 1833.
[12] *Educ. Enq. Abstract*, 738.
[13] The *Census* (1851) notes this closure as a cause for the drop in numbers of children at school.
[14] *Oxf. Jnl.* 20 Dec. 1825.
[15] Foundation deed.
[16] MS. Oxf. Dioc. c 433; ibid. b 7.
[17] *Educ. Enq. Abstract*, 738.
[18] MS. Oxf. Dioc. b 38; *Educ. Enq. Abstract*, 738.
[19] *Oxf. Jnl.* 1832, *passim*; *Rusher's Banbury List* (1831, 1833).
[20] Ed. 7/101/25; MS. Oxf. Dioc. b 70; ibid. c 332.

and partly by the vicar, who met any deficit.[21] Four pupil teachers assisted and evening classes were held.[22] A public elementary school was established by a deed of 1875: it was under Church of England control, the vicar being empowered to use it as a Sunday school.[23] The average attendance at the school was 105 in 1879, and 110 out of 124 children registered as pupils attended regularly in 1890,[24] a particularly high rate. The school was managed by a local committee. School pence were paid by the children, and this, together with subscriptions and a government grant, covered salaries and other expenses.[25] The managers had to make continual efforts to raise money to keep up with the demands of the government inspectors.[26] The school was enlarged in 1892 and again in 1900 to accommodate 180 children.[27] In 1961 it had the status of a controlled school, but numbers had dropped to 76, though by 1965 they were up to 118.[28]

Barford was the worst served village in the parish. In 1815 there were 25 children needing education, but the numbers were too small and the tenant farmers were not well enough off to contribute towards the cost of a school. Some of the children went to a school at Barford St. Michael, which adjoined Barford St. John,[29] but there were complaints in 1818 that the poor had not the means to educate their children.[30] In 1852 a Church of England mixed school was established for the two Barfords at Barford St. Michael and a certificated mistress who had previously taught at Adderbury school was appointed.[31] This school was closed in 1957 and the children were transferred to Deddington primary and secondary schools.[32]

CHARITIES. In 1603 a body of feoffees in Adderbury and Milton held land and money given at various dates from at least 1462 for several town purposes, chiefly payments of fifteenths, repair of the church, and relief of the poor.[33] In 1603 the administration of the feoffees' estate was regularized by the Commissioners for Charitable Uses. It was decreed that income from land called 'Town Hook' in Milton was to be used, as it had been time out of mind, for Milton only, and that the following charities should be used as the donors intended: £4 stock given by Anthony Bustard and Richard Gill in their lifetime (*c.* 1540) for a coal charity, a quarter of maslin yearly given by Anthony Bustard for a bread charity out of his lease of the demesne of Adderbury manor,[34] and a sum of 3*s.* yearly given for a bread charity by Thomas Hall of Bodicote. Hall's charity was still being distributed in 1824, in the form of penny loaves given away by the overseers on Good Friday.[35]

A decree of 1627 regularized the following additional bequests: by will dated 1605 John Sadler gave 40*s.* for a coal charity; in 1617 by their wills Christopher Jakeman gave the feoffees £5 and Thomas Herbert gave £10, the interest to be used for the poor; by will dated 1624 John Adkins gave £10 for the same purpose; William Bustard gave a cottage in Adderbury East for the poor there, though there is no record that it was used exclusively for that hamlet; John Baylis gave £1 by will; and Mary Green gave £20 in her lifetime, the interest to be spent on cloth for 6 poor persons of Adderbury.[36] Only Mary Green's gift was separately mentioned after 1627; after inclosure it formed part of an allotment in Adderbury West let for £2 10*s.* a year. Up to this time, according to existing records, there seems to have been a fairly regular distribution of coats and gowns.[37] The other charities, all of which were supposed to have been laid out in lands, were merged in the town estate which in the 18th century comprised 6 yardlands and some houses, including several alms-houses where lodging was provided free.[38]

The cost of inclosing the town estate in Adderbury West in 1767–8 was met by a loan of £150 from Ann Harrison of Bodicote, which was largely repaid by 1774; the inclosed estate was let for £55.[39] In 1786 the feoffees' income from the whole town estate was £130 and in 1800 £155.[40] In 1811 the feoffees paid £203, of which £164 10*s.* was raised by sale of land, to redeem the land tax on the estate.[41]

In 1823 the amount received from Milton (*c.* £60) was distributed there among 28 families in the form of clothing coupons to be used in local shops. In Adderbury East *c.* £82 out of a total income of *c.* £116 was distributed at the rate of 7*s.* worth of linen to the head of each poor family, and *c.* £21 was given in money to the more careful and sober poor.[42] In Adderbury West from 1804 to 1817 almost the whole income was distributed in linen at Michaelmas and Lady Day. In 1804 linen was given to 78 families. Every poor person in the division received the charity in turn; at times money or additional clothing was given to persons in special need.[43]

In about 1817 a coal fund was established with £45 from the income of the feoffees' estate. Each summer 40 or 50 tons of coal were bought and retailed to the poor in winter at a small profit. The profit was insufficient to maintain the stock, but in 1825 it was found that a Mr. Spencer had made up the deficiency.[44]

By a scheme of 1871 the income from the 11 cottages and 109 a. of the town estate was divided into 5 portions, each of £70, for church repairs, education, provident club, coal and clothing club, and for the benefit of the poor in case of special distress or emigration. To the amount allotted to the provident club was added the 3*s.* rent charge given before 1603 by Thomas Hall of Bodicote for bread.

21 MS. Oxf. Dioc. c 332.
22 Ibid. c 338.
23 *Ret. of Non-Provided Schs.* (1906), 18.
24 Par. Rec., annual rep. (1879); *Ret. of Sch.* (1890), 213.
25 Par. Rec., annual rep. (1879).
26 Par. Rec., par. mag. (1899).
27 *Kelly's Dir. Oxon.* (1820).
28 Ex inf. Oxfordshire County Council, Educ. Cttee.
29 MS. Oxf. Dioc. c 433.
30 *Educ. of Poor*, 717.
31 Ed. 7/101/13.
32 Ex inf. Oxfordshire County Council, Educ. Cttee.
33 *12th Rep. Com. Char.* 195; for charities other than those for the poor see pp. 38, 41.
34 *12th Rep. Com. Char.* 195–6.
35 Ibid. 200.
36 Ibid. 196–7.
37 MS. d.d. Par. Adderbury, feoffees accts.
38 *Char. Don.* 976.
39 MS. d.d. Par. Adderbury, feoffees accts.
40 Ibid.
41 *12th Rep. Com. Char.* 198. Feoffees accts. exist for the years 1703–36, 1767–78, 1804–17. The poor's book (1680–1726) was said to have been retained by a feoffee. The accts. were amalgamated after inclosure.
42 *12th Rep. Com. Char.* 199.
43 MS. d.d. Par. Adderbury, feoffees accts.
44 *12th Rep. Com. Char.* 196 sqq.

The distribution of bread has ceased *c.* 1850. A further Scheme of 1897 increased the portion given to the sick and provident clubs at the expense of the portion given for eleemosynary purposes.[45]

In 1874 and 1890 4 cottages belonging to the town estate in Adderbury East were sold and the money spent on building 3 new ones. In 1920 a farm and 72 a. at Milton and in 1949 the Pest House and a cottage in Adderbury East were sold.[46] Between 1954 and 1960 more land and 7 cottages were sold.[47]

One charity was confined to Bodicote. Alice Pittam, by will dated 1723, left her house and land with a rent charge of 15*s.* a year to be given on Good Friday to landless poor not receiving relief. In 1824 the money was given to 15 poor widows. Between 1923 and 1926 17*s.* 4*d.* a year was spent on coal.[48]

ALKERTON

THIS narrow, spear-shaped parish (2¼ miles long by ¼ to ¾ mile wide) of 742 a. is unusually small and its boundaries have apparently remained unaltered since they were laid out.[1] It lies on the Warwickshire border in the Middle Lias clay belt at a height of between 400 and 500 feet.[2] Until Shenington was incorporated in Oxfordshire in 1845 the Sor Brook marked both Alkerton's western boundary and the Gloucestershire border.[3] The landscape, though still bare in aspect for the most part, was improved in the 18th and 19th centuries by tree planting around the village and on the northern borders, where there were two coverts of *c.* 4 a. each by 1882. Afforestation schemes were also being carried out in the 1960s on the Upton estate at Shenington Hirons and Christmas Gorse.[4] Extensive heath in the north of the parish, where the poor once had the right to cut furze, was brought under cultivation in the 18th century.[5]

Banbury, the nearest market town, lies 5½ miles to the south-east and the main road connecting it with Warwick crosses the northern end of Alkerton parish; the road was turnpiked in 1743–4.[6] The 'White Lion', licensed in 1782,[7] may have been on this road; the 'New Inn' now stands at the point where the road enters Wroxton parish.[8] A secondary road branches off the main one and runs southward towards Shutford and Newington and another connects with Alkerton village and Shenington.

Alkerton was probably always the smallest village in Bloxham hundred;[9] in 1641 it was expressly stated that 29 was the number of all the men (of 18 and over) in the parish, while 69 adults (of 16 and over) were recorded in 1676.[10] The usual growth in population and increase in dwellings took place in the 18th century: incumbents reported that in 1738 there were 6 farm-houses and *c.* 'eight town-houses besides'; in 1759 5 farm-houses and 10 cottages; in 1768 23 houses; and in 1831 38 houses.[11] The population increased from 135 in 1801 to 201 in 1871 and then fell during the agricultural depression to 105 in 1901.[12] By 1951 it had dropped to 88.[13]

In the 17th century there were several gentlemen and substantial farmers living in the village; in the 18th century there was 'no one of note';[14] for most of the 19th century not even the rector resided there and the village consisted of tenant-farmers and labourers.[15] In the 20th century agricultural changes, such as the introduction of machinery and the amalgamation of farms, again entirely altered the character of the village. It attracted a number of professional people, either retired or working outside Alkerton, and its 17th-century farm-houses and cottages have been modernized and restored as private residences. They are strung out along a terraced road, which is cut out of a hill-side of red ironstone, and look across the Sor Brook valley to Shenington on the crown of the opposite slope. The road runs southward from the 12th-century church, 17th-century Rectory, and manor-house (Tanner's Pool), past Alkerton House to Barn House.[16]

There is no trace now of the Town Green, mentioned in the 18th century.[17] The houses and cottages, including the 19th-century school, are all built of local rubble or ironstone ashlar and are mostly thatched or stone-slated in the traditional manner. One cottage of 1½ story, built on a two-unit plan with parlour and kitchen, has an inscription I.E. 1716.[18] Brook Cottage still retains its stone-mullioned windows. Both were probably built for small farmers. The 'poor cottages' commented on in a parliamentary report of 1867, which are likely to have been put up for labourers after inclosure of the open fields in 1777, have been pulled down.[19] Electricity was brought to the village in 1939.[20]

Of the 6 sizeable houses assessed for the hearth tax of 1665 4, including the rectory-house, were owned by the Lydiat family.[21] Christopher Lydiat, a citizen of London, acquired the manor in 1567 and retired there. His son lived at the manor-house after him.[22] Their house was probably the present Tanner's Pool, which was a farm-house in 1852.[23] It seems to have been originally built on an **L**-shaped plan, like so many other houses in the

[45] Par. Rec.; Char. Com., G file corresp., B 26525, B 41784.

[46] For the Pest House see p. 23.

[47] Char. Com., G file corresp.

[48] *12th Rep. Com. Char.* 200; Char. Com., G file corresp. and accts.

[1] O.S. *Area Bk.* 1882; O.S. Map 2½″ S.P. 34 (1959); *Census,* 1951.

[2] *V.C.H. Oxon.* i. map facing p. 1.

[3] O.S. Map 6″ Oxon. V (1st edn.).

[4] Ex inf. the Viscount Bearsted.

[5] See p. 48.

[6] *Act for repairing the road . . . Buckingham . . . to Warmington,* 17 Geo. II, c 43.

[7] O.R.O., victlrs' recogs.

[8] Ibid.; O.S. Map 25″ Oxon. V. 1 (1st edn.).

[9] See p. 189.

[10] *Protestation Ret.* 42; Compton Census.

[11] *Secker's Visit.*; MS. Oxf. Dioc. d 555; ibid. d 558; ibid. b 38.

[12] *Census,* 1801–1901.

[13] *Census,* 1951.

[14] *Secker's Visit.*; MS. Oxf. Dioc. d 555; ibid. d 558; ibid. b 38.

[15] MS. Top. Oxon. c 105, ff. 9, 18.

[16] O.S. Map 25″ Oxon. V. 1 (1st edn.); for photos of Barn House etc. see MS. Top. Oxon., c 483 nos. 4366–67.

[17] O.R.O., incl. award.

[18] For plan (dated 1710 in error) see Wood-Jones, *Dom. Archit. Banbury Region,* 191.

[19] *Agric. Employment Women and Children,* 351.

[20] Localinformation.

[21] *Hearth Tax Oxon.* 146.

[22] Wood, *Athenae,* iii. 185–189.

[23] Gardner, *Dir. Oxon.* (1852); Plot, *Nat. Hist. Oxon.* 222.

neighbourhood, with the entrance on the north, rooms on either side of the hall, and an extension at right-angles on the south side. Later wings have been added on the north and east.[24] There are fishponds nearby.

Another of Christopher Lydiat's sons was the 17th-century mathematician, Thomas Lydiat, who was rector from 1612.[25] He rebuilt the rectory-house in 1625.[26] A contemporary account says that it had three bays with a lean-to of one bay, a largish barn of four bays, and an orchard on either side.[27] The present house is of two stories and is built of iron-stone ashlar with a stone coping. It is entered on the north side by its original moulded doorway with cambered arch and lozenge-shaped stops to the label mould. The two ground-floor rooms (17 ft. square) were once the hall and kitchen. They are separated by a central double fire-place, of which one has the date 1625 in the spandrels. A similar but smaller fire-place, is in the bedchamber above, and this would account for the return of 3 hearths for the tax in 1665.[28] Lydiat's house was repaired in 1692, when the roof was slated, and enlarged in 1748,[29] when a two-storied kitchen wing was added at right-angles. The present Alkerton House may have belonged to the Goodwin family, another of Alkerton's principal families, since it has the letters B.G. 1633 on the end wall.[30] The Goodwins, later found in several north Oxfordshire villages, were settled in Alkerton in the early 16th century. Thomas Goodwin (d. 1531) and his son Richard (d. 1560) were both buried in the churchyard. Thomas was of sufficient standing to leave money to eight churches, of which Alkerton was one, and his grandson, another Thomas (d. 1581), left a legacy to the poor of the village. In the 16th century the Goodwins had two houses in Alkerton and in 1665 were living in one of the two largest houses there.[31] Alkerton House was partly rebuilt at the end of the 18th century when it belonged to John Anderton, in whose family it remained until 1883.[32] It was restored in 1834; the date is carved on the Gothic porch which was added at that date.

Alkerton Heath Farm and Alkerton Grounds Farm were built in the north-east of the parish in the late 18th century after inclosure.

During the Civil War the village was several times raided by Parliamentary troops based on Compton Wyniates.[33]

MANORS. In 1086 Miles Crispin held an estate assessed at 6 hides in Alkerton.[34] From it descended *ALKERTON MANOR* which was reckoned as a ½ fee and was first recorded in the 13th century. The overlordship followed the descent of other of Crispin's lands under Wallingford honor.[35]

In 1086 the mesne tenant was Richard Fitz Reinfrid, Miles Crispin's tenant also at Appleton and Eaton (Berks.), and at Chearsley, Draycott, and Ickford (Bucks.), with which Alkerton continued to be associated as a feudal holding.[36] Fitz Reinfrid died at Alkerton in 1115 or 1116 and his heir was his son Hugh of Appleton and Eaton.[37] In 1166 Alkerton was evidently included in the 2 fees Hugh held under Wallingford honor.[38] He was succeeded by his son Richard of Appleton,[39] and by 1201 by his grandson Thomas of Appleton (d. *ante* 1209).[40] Thomas's heir Geoffrey held the 2 fees in 1211, but he may have forfeited his Alkerton property, as he certainly did Appleton, for his part in the revolt of 1215 against John.[41] He was still alive in 1217, when he had letters of safe conduct to parley with the Earl Marshal, but he had died by 1218.[42] In 1226 his heir was still a minor, but by 1235 he was evidently of age, for a Thomas of Appleton was in possession of the Buckinghamshire property and presumably also of Alkerton.[43] In 1270 Thomas included Alkerton among property which he alienated to Denise de Stokes.[44] In about 1293 Denise and her son Master Robert de Stokes alienated their holdings, which included a carucate in Alkerton, reckoned as ½ fee, to the king, receiving them back as his tenants.[45] Master Robert still held the fees in 1300, [46] but there is no further mention of the family in connexion with Alkerton.

By the mid-13th century the Alkerton ½ fee was held by under-tenants. In 1242 Hugh son of Henry of Abingdon, a member of a family closely connected with Abingdon Abbey, was returned as tenant.[47] In 1247 he sold 1 carucate in Alkerton and 2 yardlands in Balscott to Master Simon of Walton, who already had property in Balscott; Simon and his heirs were to hold it for a ½ fee's service and homage, but Hugh was not to claim relief or custody of the land and heirs.[48] Simon became Bishop of Norwich in 1258 and before his death in 1265 granted Alkerton to his son Sir John Walton.[49] The Walton's main estate was in Walton, a hamlet of Wellesbourn Hastings (Warws.), which was encumbered with debts contracted to the Jews by a previous tenant.[50] In 1271

[24] See architect's plan *penes* Lt.-Col. R. Bartram and for this type of house see Wood-Jones, *Dom. Archit. Banbury Region*, 125 and *passim*.

[25] See p. 50.

[26] MS. d.d. Par. Alkerton d 1.

[27] MS. Top. Oxon. c 60, 24 sqq.

[28] *Hearth Tax Oxon.* 146; for other details see Wood-Jones, op. cit. 152 and index; see illustration facing p. 46.

[29] Par. Rec., reg.

[30] It is possible the 'B.G.' stands for Bret Goodwin, who later became Lord of Epwell manor.

[31] For the Goodwins see Alkerton Par. Rec., reg.; *Misc. Gen. et Her.* 4th ser. ii. 150–152, 190–192; and Wood, *Life*, ii. 106; *Hearth Tax Oxon.* 146.

[32] Deeds of Alkerton House *penes* Mr. D. N. Hoddinott, the owner.

[33] Wood, *Athenae*, iii. 187.

[34] *V.C.H. Oxon.* i. 382, 419. Two hides were in Wroxton: *Chron. Abingdon* (Rolls Ser.), ii. 108–9. Their connexion with the Alkerton manor ceased in the early 12th century: see pp. 177–8.

[35] *V.C.H. Oxon.* viii. 3–4.

[36] *V.C.H. Oxon.* i. 419; *V.C.H. Berks.* i. 355; *V.C.H. Bucks.* i. 261; *Boarstall Cart.* 320, 322.

[37] *Chron. Abingdon* (Rolls Ser.), ii. 108–9; *Oseney Cart.* ii. 404.

[38] *Red Bk. Exch.* (Rolls Ser.), 309. The composition of the 2 fees in 1166 is uncertain. There was probably a rearrangement of holdings later: cf. *Boarstall Cart.* 320–1, 322.

[39] *Oseney Cart.* iv. 404.

[40] *Rot. de Ob. et Fin.* (Rec. Com.), 150; *Pipe R.* 1209 (P.R.S. xxiv), 8.

[41] *Pipe R.* 1211 (P.R.S. N.S. xxviii), 204; *Rot. Litt. Claus.* (Rec. Com.), i. 240.

[42] *Cal. Pat.* 1216–25, 49; *Rot. Litt. Claus.* i. 351; *Bk. of Fees*, 254.

[43] *Boarstall Cart.* 321; *Bk. of Fees*, 555. The Oxfordshire property is listed for the 1220 carucage, but is not in the list of Wallingford honor fees in 1235–6: *Bk. of Fees*, 313, 554–5.

[44] *Fines Oxon.* 244.

[45] *Cal. Inq. Misc.* i, p. 449.

[46] *Cal. Inq. p.m.* iii, p. 481.

[47] *Bk. of Fees*, 823; see also ibid. 845, 953, 1278; *V.C.H. Berks.* iv. 442.

[48] *Fines Oxon.* 141.

[49] *Reg. Godfrey Giffard* (Worcs. Hist. Soc.), 443–4; *Cal. Fine R.* 1272–1307, 89.

[50] *V.C.H. Warws.* v. 195.

Walter Giffard, Archbishop of York, purchased the debts and thus obtained a claim against the Walton's property, including Alkerton. Sir John was obliged to convey Alkerton and other property to Giffard, receiving them back as tenant.[51] After John's death in 1277 his relict Isabel, Henry le Foun, her second husband, and John's heir Maud made similar acknowledgments to the archbishop.[52] On Giffard's death in 1279 his heir was his brother Godfrey Giffard, Bishop of Worcester, who claimed custody of Maud Walton.[53] He granted Alkerton to Walter de Mandeville (d. by 1288) with reversion to himself if Mandeville should die without heirs.[54] There is no later reference to the Giffard or Mandeville interest in Alkerton.

Another claim to the manor, however, was put forward by Thomas, son of Gervase Walton. His relationship to other members of the family is unknown, but he derived what rights he had in Alkerton from Master Simon of Walton; in 1285 he sold them to Sir John of Ladbrooke, a Warwickshire landowner and neighbour of the Waltons.[55] Until his death in *c.* 1310 Sir John of Ladbrooke was recorded as a mesne tenant of the manor and ½ fee,[56] but there is no record of his descendants claiming it.

For the next century or more Alkerton followed the descent of the Walton estate in Walton. Maud Walton married successively,[57] Sir John de Stradling, Sir John Lestrange (d. 1309), who became Lord Strange of Knockin (Salop.) in 1299, and Sir Thomas Hasting of Leamington Hastings (Warws.), recorded as one of the lords of Alkerton in 1316. The last was dead by 1348,[58] and Maud's property reverted to the Lestranges, descendants of her second husband. In 1376 John Lestrange, lord of Walton, apparently a member of a collateral branch of the Lestranges of Knockin, granted his Alkerton estate to a Roger Lestrange and others, perhaps as part of a settlement.[59] No record of Alkerton's descent for the next century and a half has been found, but it probably continued to follow that of Walton.[60] Thomas Lestrange, lord of Walton (d. 1485),[61] left two daughters who must have been heirs to Alkerton also: in 1542 Anne, one of the daughters, and her heirs, and Barbara, daughter of Anne's sister Margaret, with her husband Robert Mordaunt, sold Alkerton manor to Robert Hopper of Henley.[62] Hopper's descendants held the manor for over a century and the following were lords: Robert's son Thomas (d. 1573), his grandson Thomas (d. 1596),[63] and his great-grandson also Thomas (d. 1618), whose brother John sold the manor in 1619 to another member of the family, Timothy Hopper (d. 1628).[64] There were Hoppers in the parish in the 17th and early 18th century[65] and in 1719 Elizabeth Hopper, widow, and John Hopper granted their rights in the manor to George Wheeler and John Barnesley.[66] There is no further record of these manorial rights and it is likely that the manor was merged in the other Alkerton manor.

A second *ALKERTON MANOR* descended from a 3½-hide estate granted after the Conquest to Bishop Odo of Bayeux. In 1086 it was recorded as of his fief, although he himself had been under arrest and his property confiscated since 1082. His tenant was one Ralph.[67] The Conqueror redistributed many of Bishop Odo's fees, and it is reasonable to suppose that this Alkerton manor was granted to Wadard, a tenant of Odo at South Newington, since the two estates of Alkerton and South Newington were held by Wadard's descendants as a knight's fee.[68] Wadard's son was probably Walkelin Wadard, whose heirs were his two daughters Eloise and Denise; in 1168 Walkelin Hareng, the son of Eloise by her first husband, was in possession of the fee.[69] He was dead by 1190 when Ralph Fitz Geoffrey, the husband of Maud de Lucy, niece and coheir of Walkelin Hareng, was holding the fee.[70] Walkelin's other heirs were Miles of Fritwell, the husband of another niece, and William le Brun, who was probably a nephew. In 1200 the three coheirs were summoned to warrant the ¾ fee in Alkerton and ¼ fee in South Newington to the respective tenants.[71] They gave up their rights in the ¾ fee in Alkerton and the tenant William of Alkerton did homage directly to the king.[72]

William's father Walter of Alkerton (d. *c.* 1201) had been tenant of Alkerton since at least 1194, and William himself or a son still held in 1230.[73] In 1233 the land of Thomas, son of Walter of Alkerton was in the king's hands, presumably because of a minority.[74] In 1235 Amaury de St. Amand was returned as lord of one fee.[75] His possession was warranted by David, son of Thomas of Alkerton, who lived in Scotland.[76] The overlordship of Alkerton for the rest of the Middle Ages remained with the St. Amand family and until the 15th century followed the descent of their Adderbury manor.[77] Like Adderbury Alkerton was sold in 1418 by Eleanor, the relict of Amaury (d. 1402),

[51] *Cal. Pat.* 1266–72, 567; *Reg. Giffard*, 445.

[52] *Feet of Fines Warws.* i (Dugdale Soc. xi), pp. 203–4; *Reg. Giffard*, 137.

[53] *Cal. Inq. p.m.* ii, pp. 183–4; *Reg. Giffard*, 137, 472.

[54] *Cal. Inq. p.m.* ii, p. 414: incorrectly indexed as Offerton in Hindlip (Worcs.). In 1281 Bishop Robert Burnel, who was granted the other estates, renounced all claim to Alkerton: *Reg. Giffard*, 137.

[55] *Cat. Anct. D.* iv. A 7592; *V.C.H. Warws.* v. 195–6; vi. 144.

[56] *Cal. Inq. Misc.* i, p. 450.

[57] She is incorrectly identified as Maud Deiville in *Complete Peerage*, xii (1), 352 n.; see *V.C.H. Warws.* v. 195.

[58] *Feet of Fines Warws.* ii (Dugdale Soc. xv), p. 25; *Cal. Inq. Misc.* i, p. 450; *Cal. Inq. p.m.* v, p. 111; *Feud. Aids*, iv. 166; *Complete Peerage*, vi. 341–3.

[59] *Cal. Close*, 1374–7, 455, 461; *V.C.H. Warws.* v. 196.

[60] *V.C.H. Warws.* v. 196; *Cal. Inq. p.m. Hen. VII*, i, p. 370.

[61] *Cal. Inq. p.m. Hen. VII*, i, p. 370.

[62] Ibid.; C.P. 25(2)/52/377/9.

[63] MS. Wills Oxon. 185, f. 47; C 142/168/11; C 142/258/138.

[64] C 142/377/64; C.P. 25(2)/340, Hil. 17 Jas. I; ibid. Mich. 19 Jas. I; ibid. 473/East. 4 Chas. I; MS. Wills Oxon. 297/5/19.

[65] MS. d.d. Par. Alkerton d 1: par. reg.; *Hearth Tax Oxon.* 146; MS. d.d. Ewelme hon. d 1, 3/7/11.

[66] C.P. 25(2)/1050/Trin. 5 Geo. I.

[67] *V.C.H. Oxon.* i. 379, 406.

[68] Ibid. 379; *Eynsham Cart.* iv. 413; *Cur. Reg. R.* i. 258.

[69] *Eynsham Cart.* iv. 94–95, 413; *Pipe R.* 1168 (P.R.S. xii), 207.

[70] *Pipe R.* 1190 (P.R.S. N.S. i), 14; *Eynsham Cart.* i. 95–97.

[71] M. V. Taylor, 'Woodeaton', O.A.S. *Rep.* 1917, 100; *V.C.H. Oxon.* v. 311; *Cur. Reg. R.* i. 216.

[72] *Cur. Reg. R.* i. 258.

[73] *Pipe R.* 1194 (P.R.S. N.S. v), 94; *Chanc. R.* 1196 (P.R.S. N.S. vii), 74, 75; *Pipe R.* 1201 (P.R.S. N.S. xiv), 213; 1211 (P.R.S. N.S. xxviii), 11, 12; 1230 (P.R.S. N.S. iv), 249.

[74] *Cal. Pat.* 1232–47, 16.

[75] *Bk. of Fees*, 448.

[76] *Bracton's Note Bk.* ed. Maitland, iii. 173.

[77] See pp. 16–17.

Alkerton: the rectory-house

Barford St. John: Manor Farm

to Sir Thomas Wykeham, who was returned as lord in 1428;[78] similarly Alkerton passed to John Danvers of Epwell, who was building up a large estate in north Oxfordshire. After his death *c.* 1448 Alkerton's history diverged from that of Adderbury, Alkerton passed to John Danvers's son Sir Robert, Recorder of London, a noted judge, and M.P. for Oxfordshire and London.[79] In 1473 two of Sir Robert's daughters and coheirs quitclaimed their thirds, probably as part of a settlement on another daughter Joan Danvers.[80] Joan had married Sir Henry Frowicke of Gunnersbury (in Ealing, Mdx.) and their daughter Margaret, wife of Sir Michael Fisher (d. 1549) of London and Clifton (Beds.), inherited.[81] The Fisher's son died before them and their grand-daughter Agnes succeeded to their property. She married Oliver St. John of Bletsoe (Beds.).[82] They were in possession of Alkerton in 1556 and 1559, the year Oliver was created Baron St. John of Bletsoe, but by 1567 he had sold Alkerton to Christopher Lydiat.[83] Lydiat died in 1612 or soon after and his son Richard, being imprisoned for debt, mortgaged the manor in 1625 and then sold it in 1630 to Robert Burden of Balscott, yeoman.[84] Robert Burden died aged 81 in 1677.[85] In 1703 William Burden of Braunston (Northants.) mortgaged land in Alkerton and in 1706 Richard Burden, clerk, of Braunston and Francis Burden of Rugby sold Alkerton manor and advowson to Richard Capel of Shenington.[86] Capel (d. *c.* 1712) left his property in trust for his two sisters, and Alkerton eventually became the portion of Susannah, wife of William Townshend of Oxhill (Warws.).[87] Townshend was lord of the manor in 1718, but died before his wife, who was succeeded in 1751 by their son John Capel Townshend.[88] The latter was obliged to mortgage the property, which had been encumbered with various charges, and in 1778 he sold the manor to Robert Child of 'Childs', the banking house, who had an estate in the neighbouring hamlet of Upton in Ratley (Warws.).[89] Robert Child died before 1783 when his widow Sarah was in possession.[90] She married Francis Reynolds-Moreton, Baron Ducie of Tortworth, in 1791, but after her death in 1793 the property eventually came to Robert Child's grand-daughter and heir Sarah Sophia Fane.[91] Sarah Fane, one of the great heiresses of her day, married George Villiers, later Child-Villiers, Earl of Jersey (d. 1859).[92] She retained Alkerton until her death in 1867 and was succeeded by her grandson Victor Child-Villiers, Earl of Jersey (d. 1915).[93] He was lord of the manor in 1891, but had sold it by 1903 to A. R. Motion of Upton (Warws.).[94] On Motion's death in 1934 the Upton estate, which extended into several parishes on the Oxfordshire–Warwickshire border, was sold to Walter Horace Samuel, Viscount Bearsted (d. 1948) and in 1959 was held by his son Marcus Richard Samuel, Viscount Bearsted.[95]

Another Alkerton manor was recorded in the 13th century and followed the descent of the lay manor of Horley and Hornton.[96] It was held in the mid-13th century by Henry Lexington, Bishop of Lincoln (d. 1258), and passed to his nephew William Sutton who held *ALKERTON MANOR* in 1258.[97] There is no further record of the Suttons in Alkerton, but the Horley manor, held by the Grevilles, had appurtenances in Alkerton in 1398, which may represent this holding.[98]

LOCAL GOVERNMENT. In 1775–6 £28 out of £37 10*s.* raised was spent on poor relief; but by 1783–5 the sum had more than doubled. In contrast to the position in neighbouring parishes the amount spent on relief had dropped slightly by the beginning of the 19th century to £38 on out-relief and £14 on removals and law charges. The rate was 2*s.* in the £. In 1802–3 5 adults and 2 children received permanent out-relief, and 2 adults occasional relief, 4 of this total being either over 60 or disabled by illness.[99]

Expenditure had risen sharply by 1834–5, however, and must have been even higher in the intervening years: of £185 raised £106 was spent on relief in that year. The parish became part of the Banbury Union after the 1834 Poor Law Act. In 1835–6 £100 out of £112 was spent on poor relief[1] and £74 in 1851–2.[2]

ECONOMIC HISTORY. It is evident that the expansion of arable cultivation was slow in both the Anglo-Saxon and medieval periods. In 1086 much of Alkerton's soil was uncultivated; although there was land for 11 ploughs, only 6 were recorded, and the fact that the value of Alkerton had remained unchanged since before the Conquest suggests that under-stocking was not a recent development. Of the two estates in the parish in 1086 the larger one of Richard Fitz Reinfrid had 4 out of a possible 6 ploughs working, but a third of his land may have been in Wroxton.[3] The smaller one, later the St. Amand manor, had only 2 out of a possible 5 ploughs. The only other asset mentioned was meadow (10 a.) on Fitz Reinfrid's holding. The recorded population of 4 *villani* and 11 bordars was small and confirms the picture of a comparatively unprosperous village.[4]

There is no record of Alkerton in the hundredal survey and other information about its development in the 12th and 13th centuries is meagre. In 1220

78 *Feud. Aids*, iv. 187.

79 Macnamara, *Danvers Family*, 102–112; *Cal. Close*, 1468–76, 274.

80 C.P. 25(1)/76/650/82, 84; Macnamara, *Danvers Family*, 115–16 and table facing p. 103.

81 *Cal. Inq. p.m. Hen. VII*, iii. pp. 260–1; *Cal. Pat.* 1548–9, 160: *V.C.H. Beds.* ii. 277. Margaret Fisher's will was proved in 1552: P.C.C. Powell 29.

82 *Complete Peerage*, xi. 334.

83 Ibid.; MS. Oxf. Dioc. d 105, pp. 171, 177, 239; Wood, *Athenae*, iii. 185.

84 MS. Oxf. Dioc. c 264, p. 48; C.P. 25(2)/473, Mich./Chas. I; ibid. Hil. 5 Chas. I; *Par. Colln.* i. 5. For Richard Lydiat and his financial difficulties see Foster, *Alumni*; *D.N.B.* under Thomas Lydiat; Bodl. MS. Bodley 313, f. 99; O.R.O., S. & F. colln. (uncat.).

85 *Par. Colln.* iii. 361; *Hearth Tax Oxon.* 147.

86 O.R.O. J.IIIa/104; cf. O.R.O., S. & F. colln. (uncat.).

87 O.R.O. J.III a/6: copy of Richard Capel's will; ibid. a/13, 14.

88 *Par. Colln.* i. 5; O.R.O., J.III a/14, 24, 30.

89 O.R.O. J.III a/32–34.

90 O.R.O. J.III b.

91 *Complete Peerage*, iv. 475; vii. 92; O.R.O., land tax assess. 1785–1805.

92 *Complete Peerage*, vii. 92.

93 Ibid. 92–93; *Kelly's Dir. Oxon.* (1864 and later edns.).

94 *Kelly's Dir. Oxon.* (1903); Burke, *Land. Gent.* (1939).

95 *V.C.H. Warws.* v. 145; *Debrett's Peerage*; *Who's Who* (1959).

96 See p. 126.

97 *Feet of Fines Essex* (Essex Arch. Soc. x), 232–3.

98 C.P. 25(1)/190/24/71.

99 *Poor Abstract*, 398.

1 *2nd. Rep. Poor Law Com.* 29.

2 *Poor Law Unions*, 21.

3 *V.C.H. Oxon.* i. 419; see p. 45 n.

4 *V.C.H. Oxon.* i. 406, 419.

the two estates were assessed on 4½ and 3 ploughlands respectively.[5] When the Walton manor was surveyed in 1279 it was worth £9 2*s*. 9*d*. a year: 60 a. of demesne (£1 10*s*.), assized rent (£7 4*s*. 9*d*.), and works (8*s*.).[6] In 1310 this manor had a manor-house worth 6*s*. 8*d*. and 60 a. still in demesne, but said to be worth only 20*s*. a year or 4*d*. an acre. There were 3 a. of meadow worth 2*s*. an acre, some several pasture, a water-mill worth 13*s*. 4*d*., 3 free tenants paying 7*s*. 3*d*. a year, and 10 customary tenants who paid £5 a year. The total value of the manor was £7 16*s*. 9*d*.[7]

A survey of the other manor was made in 1331, when there was a manor-house worth 12*s*. a year and 1 carucate of land. As the arable (*c*. 91 a.) was only worth 2*d*. an acre when sown, the soil cannot have been very productive. Meadow (4 a.), valued at 1*s*. 8*d*. an acre, was of less than normal value in the neighbourhood. Pasture worth 1*s*. was inclosed from 25 March to 1 August. The manor had 6 free tenants, who together paid 4*s*. 1½*d*. rent a year, 3 customary tenants (*nativi*) and 2 cottars (*cotelli*), whose combined rent came to £1 10*s*. At Christmas the *nativi* paid churchscot and bread to the lord worth 15*s*. a year. Their works were valued at 3*s*. 11½*d*. a year. Any week-work there may have been seems to have been commuted since only harvest and carrying services were enumerated.[8]

In 1316 there were 19 contributors to the sixteenth, two-thirds of whom paid between 2*s*. and 4*s*., while the lord of the Walton manor paid 8*s*.[9] In 1327 there were 20 contributors to the twentieth, most paying between 1*s*. and 2*s*.[10] Alkerton's assessment was fixed at £1 16*s*. 2*d*. in 1334 and was the lowest in the hundred except for Drayton.[11]

The village clearly declined like many other small townships during the 14th century, for in 1428 it was returned as having fewer than 10 households.[12] It is possible that the population had decreased since the poll tax of 1377 when 39 adults were returned.[13] The greatest loss, however, is likely to have resulted from the Black Death, which raged in the north of the county in 1349. As elsewhere there was definite recovery in the 16th and 17th centuries. Population increased but the subsidy lists with their small number of contributors provide evidence for the increasing concentration of wealth in the hands of a few husbandmen. Apart from the tenant of the manor there were 8 names in the assessment of 1523, all assessed on goods, and there were not more than 5 contributors to the later-16th-century taxes.[14] In 1665 only 6 householders were assessed for Hearth Tax: all had fair-sized houses of 3 to 5 hearths, while the cottagers described as labourers in the parish register were evidently not taxed.[15]

A selection of 17th-century inventories gives totals for the value of some of the parishioners' chattels ranging from £11 to over £165 for Timothy Hopper, lord of an Alkerton manor. One of the Lydiat family, whose ancestors had owned much of Alkerton, was worth £73 in goods when he died in 1715.[16]

There is no evidence for early inclosure and Alkerton remained an open-field village until 1777. The yardland seems to have been of normal Oxfordshire size of *c*. 24 field-acres, since in 1331 a carucate consisted of some 91 a., and in 1776 there were said to be 38 yardlands or *c*. 1,000 field-acres.[17]

The medieval field system is not known, but early-17th-century terriers show that the fields were divided into lands, ridges, 'hades' and leys, lying in furlongs and described as being either on the south or north side of the town.[18] One yardland of glebe, for example, was divided in 1647 into 21 pieces lying on the south side and 19 pieces on the north side.[19] By 1725, if not earlier, the furlongs were grouped into four 'quarters'. In Alkerton in 1725 the quarters were North, South, East, and West.[20] In both the 17th and 18th centuries much land in the open fields was in leys, i.e. laid down to pasture. In 1647 3 of the leys of the glebe land had been recently ploughed up, but on the whole leys seem to have been fairly permanent pasture.[21] Eight lands were also in the Water-furrows, which indicated that there were water-meadows in Alkerton.[22] At least some meadow land was lot meadow: in 1619 lot meadows lay north and south of the town, and there was a meadow called 'Three Lots'.[23] There were also lots both of fuel and furze in the heath, which covered at least 90 a. as late as 1774.[24] Crops grown in the parish included wheat, rye, barley, pulse, and oats.[25]

The small number of farmers made it comparatively easy to inclose in 1777. The total allotment was 689 a. of which 32 a. were common or waste. Two acres were awarded for manorial rights to plant and cut timber on the waste land. The rector received some 104 a. as rector, and 99 a. were allotted for his 8-yardland holding; there were five allotments of 40 to 99 a. and nine of 1 to 20 a.[26] The immediate result of inclosure was an increase in production. Davis's map of 1797 shows that even Alkerton heath was used for arable,[27] and in 1809 Arthur Young cited Alkerton as a parish where the wheat yield had increased.[28] The cultivation of turnips, for which the soil was well suited, probably also increased.

A casualty of the re-organization following inclosure may have been the mill. It was transferred by Timothy Hopper, lord of the Walton manor, to Richard Lydiat, lord of the St. Amand manor, in 1624;[29] it was recorded in early-18th-century deeds,[30] but had disappeared by 1778.[31]

Inclosure appears to have had little effect on the pattern of landholding: at the beginning of the 19th

[5] *Bk. of Fees*, 313, 317. [6] C 133/22/9. [7] C 134/16/6.
[8] C 135/21/24. [9] E 179/161/8. [10] E 179/161/9.
[11] See p. 189. [12] *Feud. Aids*, iv. 201. [13] E 179/161/44.
[14] E 179/161/196, 198; ibid. 162/238, 285, 341, 345.
[15] *Hearth Tax Oxon.* 146; MS. d.d. Par. Alkerton d 1.
[16] MS. Wills Oxon. 163/1/8, 61/1/16, 297/5/19, 83/2/34.
[17] C 135/21/24; Alkerton Incl. Act, 16 Geo. III, c 37 (priv. act).
[18] MS. Top. Oxon. c 60, f. 25; terriers 1715, 1720 at Williamscote House; see also A. Ballard, 'Notes on the Open Fields of Oxfordshire', O.A.S. *Rep.* 1908, 24.
[19] MS. Top. Oxon. c 60, f. 25.
[20] O.R.O., S. & F. colln. (uncat.): terrier 1725.
[21] MS. Top. Oxon. c 60, f. 25; O.R.O., S. & F. colln.; terriers 1619, 1628 at Williamscote House.
[22] MS. Top. Oxon. c 60, f. 24.
[23] Terrier 1619 at Williamscote House.
[24] O.R.O., J IV/5: estate map. For an example of lots in the heath in 1725 see ibid., S. & F. colln. (uncat.).
[25] e.g. O.R.O., S. & F. colln. (uncat.): deed 1730; MS. Wills Oxon. 297/5/19.
[26] O.R.O., incl. award. [27] Davis, *Oxon. Map* (1797).
[28] Young, *Oxon. Agric.* 89.
[29] C.P. 25(2)/340/Hil. 21 Jas. I.
[30] e.g. O.R.O., J III/a33; ibid. 60 I/k/kk.
[31] MS. d.d. Par. Alkerton d 1.

century there were usually about 6 chief proprietors, who on the whole let out their land to tenant-farmers.[32] In 1851 there were 5 farmers, 4 with farms of 100 to 150 a. and a fifth with only 16 a.,[33] and until the 1920s the parish continued to be divided into 5 or 6 farms.[34] Labourers' wages averaged 12*s.* to 13*s.* a week; in summer, however, there was free beer, and produce from cottage gardens and allotments supplemented the low wages.[35]

By the end of the 19th century difficult communications added to the difficulties of the farmers. It was stated in an agricultural survey of 1916 that Alkerton was too distant from Banbury and too hilly for large quantities of feeding stuffs and manures to be brought, or for frequent sending away of produce.[36] More recently there have been considerable changes: traditional village craftsmen, such as the cooper, carpenter, basket-maker, and stonemason enumerated in the 19th century,[37] have disappeared, as also has the small farmer. The greater part of the farm land in 1959 was held by two land-owners. Alkerton Heath Farm and Manor Farm were farmed as part of the Upton estate which lay partly outside Oxfordshire. The Oxfordshire Ironstone Company was the other chief proprietor; its land was leased and farmed by Passmore & Nunnelly of Balscott.[38]

CHURCH. There is no documentary evidence for the history of the church until 1233,[39] but there are some features in the church building which point to a 12th-century origin at least. No change in status occurred, apart from the institution of a temporary vicarage in the 13th century,[40] until the living was united to the neighbouring rectory of Shenington in 1900. The new rectory came to be known as Shenington with Alkerton.[41]

From at least the early 13th century the advowson was attached to the St. Amand manor. The first recorded presentation was a royal one in 1233, proabably during the minority of the lord of the manor.[42] After two further presentations by Sir Mathew de Coudray, the guardian of the St. Amand's heir, the advowson descended with the manor until the late 19th century.[43] When the manor passed out of the Earl of Jersey's family the advowson was retained. As Shenington was also in the patronage of the Earl of Jersey the union of the two parishes in 1900 did not affect the patronage.[44] It was transferred to the Diocesan Board of Patronage in 1952.[45]

Although in about 1087 Miles Crispin granted the demesne tithes of his Alkerton manor to Bec Abbey[46] there is no record of the abbey receiving them, possibly because Alkerton church was already in existence and the grant was disputed. The rectory was in fact endowed with all the tithes in the parish and with a small glebe, but because the parish was so small the rectory has always been poor. In 1291 it was valued at £4 6*s.* 8*d.* and in 1535 at £6 3*s.* 8*d.*[47] In 1716 its annual value was £60.[48] At inclosure in 1777 the tithes were commuted for about 92 a., and the yardland of open-field glebe was exchanged for 11 a.[49] This farm, containing some of the best land in the neighbourhood, formed from this time until its sale in 1901 the endowment of the rectory.[50] Its value varied with the price of agricultural land: in 1808 it was rented for over £130, in 1869 a rent of £175 was considered too low by £45, but by 1900 only £104 could be obtained.[51] When in that year the living was annexed to Shenington, the value of the new benefice was more than three times that of Alkerton rectory.[52]

In the 13th century Alkerton had two educated rectors: Master William (1233–43/4), who was surgeon to Henry III and to Bishop Grosseteste,[53] and Master Robert of Clifton (1291–8), an Oxford graduate.[54] On the other hand another rector, Reinotius, presented in 1250–1, was found on examination by Bishop Grosseteste to be poorly educated (*minus literatus*) and barely able to speak English. The bishop insisted that a temporary vicarage be ordained and that a better qualified minister should serve the church. The vicar was to receive all the income from the parish and bear all the expenses, but was to pay 5 marks a year (half at least of his income) to the rector as long as the latter was well behaved in orders, and did not accept another benefice.[55]

As the living was a poor one, it did not attract members of the St. Amand family; only one, John de St. Amand (resigned 1250–1), held it, nor were any university graduates rectors between the end of the 13th century and the late 16th century.[56] Except for the case of Reinotius there is no direct evidence for either pluralism or non-residence during the Middle Ages. Possibly one 15th-century rector, who was a Canon of Wroxton,[57] may have lived at the abbey. Two early-16th-century rectors, on the other hand, were certainly resident. One had his brother and sister-in-law living with him in the rectory house at the time of the bishop's visitation *c.* 1520;[58] the other, Thomas Williams (1537–56), started the parish register,[59] left 12*d.* to every house

[32] O.R.O., land tax assess. 1785–1832.
[33] H.O. 107/1733.
[34] *Kelly's Dir. Oxon.* (1864 and later edns.).
[35] *Agric. Employment of Women and Children*, 581.
[36] Orr, *Oxon. Agric.* 65.
[37] H.O. 107/1733; *Kelly's Dir. Oxon.* (1864 and later edns.). A weaver's wife was buried at Alkerton in 1701: MS. d.d. Par. Alkerton d 1. A family of weavers was recorded in 1751: O.R.O., S. & F. colln. (uncat.).
[38] Local information.
[39] *Cal. Pat.* 1232–47, 16.
[40] See below.
[41] MS. Oxf. Dioc. c 1997, Order in Council; *Crockford* (1957–8).
[42] *Cal. Pat.* 1232–47, 16.
[43] In 1310, the year Amaury (II) de St. Amand died, the patron was Master John de St. Amand: MS. Top. Oxon. d 460 (list of medieval presentations prepared by the Oxon. V.C.H. staff).
[44] MS. Oxf. Dioc. c 1997, Order in Council.
[45] Ex inf. Oxf. Dioc. Registry.
[46] *E.H.R.* xl. 75.
[47] *Tax Eccl.* (Rec. Com.), 32; *Valor Eccl.* (Rec. Com.), ii. 164. It is not clear what is meant by the valuation of 1254 which gives both 3 and 10 marks: Lunt, *Val. Norw.* 309.
[48] MS. Oxf. Dioc. c 155, f. 45.
[49] O.R.O., incl. award. For 17th-cent. terrier of glebe see MS. Top. Oxon. c 60, ff. 24–25.
[50] MS. Oxf. Dioc. c 1695, letter of 16 Apr. 1870; ex inf. Church Commissioners.
[51] For 1808 terrier see MS. Top. Oxon. c 60, f. 26; MS. Oxf. Dioc. c 446, f. 31; ibid. c 1695, letter of 16 Apr. 1870 and 1900.
[52] MS. Oxf. Dioc. c 1695, letter of 1900.
[53] *Cal. Pat.* 1232–47, 16; *Rot. Grosse.* 482.
[54] Emden, *O.U. Reg.*
[55] Lunt, *Val. Norw.* 309; *Rot. Grosse.* 499–500.
[56] For list of rectors see MS. Top. Oxon. d 460.
[57] Linc. Reg. xx, f. 243.
[58] *Visit. Dioc. Linc.* (*1517–31*), i. 126.
[59] This part of the register is a later copy.

in the parish, and was buried in the chancel.[60] He was a witness of the Reformation changes, among them the disappearance of the church light; in 1549 its endowment (4 a. of land worth 6*d.* a year) was sold.[61]

In the 17th and 18th centuries when the patrons often lived in the parish, they frequently presented their connexions to the living. During the 17th century, in particular, this system gave the parish several able rectors and one outstanding one, Thomas Lydiat, commemorated in *The Vanity of Human Wishes*.[62] He was presented to the living in 1612 by his father, Christopher,[63] and spent most of the rest of his life in the village. From the rectory-house, 'my home', he corresponded with his friend Archbishop Usher and there wrote many of his chronological and astronomical works as well as 600 sermons on the harmony of the gospels. Many of these sermons he probably preached in Alkerton church.[64] After rebuilding the rectory-house,[65] he fell into grave financial difficulties and spent from at least 1629 to 1632 in prison for debt, partly at Oxford.[66] Lydiat had friends on both sides in the religious controversies of the 17th century:[67] but during the Civil War he was a royalist and episcopalian. In a petition of 1644 to the governor of Banbury castle, about his house in Banbury, he wrote that he had tried to keep 'true allegiance' to the king and to persuade others to do the same. His house had been four times pillaged by Parliamentary forces and he had been twice imprisoned. He signed himself as the 'old and weak minister' of Alkerton[68] and two years later he died there.[69] He left goods valued at only £169, of which £50 was for books.[70]

Lydiat was followed by several other learned rectors: the first, Richard Burden, had studied seven years at Oxford and come in 1646 to Alkerton with the reputation of being a 'painful and diligent' minister.[71] His successor was Thomas Lydiat's nephew Timothy (d. 1663), a former Fellow of New College, and a 'faithful pastor',[72] and after him came John Pointer (1663–1710), the son of a Puritan preacher of the same name.[73] He repaired the chancel and the rectory-house in 1692 and his neat handwriting in the parish register shows that he was usually resident.[74] His elder son John later acquired a reputation as a learned antiquary[75] and his younger son Malachy succeeded his father as rector (1711–20).[76]

Although residence continued to be the rule in the earlier 18th century there was some falling off in zeal. Francis Townshend (1733–42), a younger son of the squire, usually held two services on Sunday, administered the sacrament three times a year 'according to the custom of the parish', and frequently catechized the children[77] but his successor decreased the number of services to one, since he also served Shutford chapel. He never had more than five or six communicants,[78] he catechized only in Lent, and refused to repair the churchyard wall or the church fabric.[79] The dispute over the repair of the wall was long: in 1752 the churchwardens reported it as constantly out of repair for the last ten years.[80]

By this time there was only one churchwarden, instead of the two wardens of the 16th century,[81] perhaps as a consequence of a declining population. The wardens changed frequently until 1780, when it became customary for the person chosen, usually one of the leading farmers, to serve for many years.[82] In the 19th century, if not before, the warden was chosen by the rector or his curate.[83] One of the warden's responsibilities was the handling of the lands given for the repair of the church.[84] These are mentioned in the early 18th century, when they had been used to lower the rates,[85] and by 1809 they were of sufficient value to make a church rate unnecessary. The churchwardens also managed a small coal fund.[86] The parish clerk had an endowment: before inclosure this had been a cow-common and the right to cut furze on the heath. By the inclosure award he received over 2 a., and this land, which in 1831 was worth about £3 and in 1869 about £10,[87] made him comparatively well paid.

When John Capel Townshend, the lord of the manor, became rector in 1775, there began the long association with Shenington which was to lead to the union of the two parishes. The Jacobean rectory-house at Alkerton was too small for him and he lived 'with every convenience' in his own house at Shenington. As it was in an elevated position overlooking Alkerton he was perhaps correct in saying that 'not a bell can ring or anything happen but I hear it from my own house'.[88] He also stated that he was often in Alkerton two or three times a day, yet he held only one service on Sundays and catechized once a year.[89] Nor did he at once display great energy about the

[60] MS. Wills Oxon. 181, f. 52.

[61] *Chant. Cert.* 35; *Cal. Pat.* 1549–51, 85.

[62] Cf. *Boswell's Life of Johnson*, ed. G. B. Hill, revised L. F. Powell, i. 194 *n.*

[63] MS. Oxf. Dioc. c 264, f. 55v. For Christopher Lydiat see Wood, *Athenae*, iii. 185–9, and *D.N.B.* which states that Thomas Lydiat would not take up the living while his father was alive.

[64] *Ad Henricum Savilum Epistola Astronomica* (1621), 52; Wood, *Athenae*, iii. 186; MS. Rawl. J 4, f.232. Many of his sermons are in MS. Rawl. E 75–6, E 168.

[65] See p. 45.

[66] MS. Bodley 313, ff. 23, 56v., 99.

[67] He dedicated one work to the Puritan, Sir Anthony Cope of Hanwell. *Defensio Tractatus . . . contra J. Scaligeri* . . . (1607). He was also on good terms with John Dod and Robert Cleaver, the Puritan rectors of Hanwell and Drayton; on the other hand he owed his release from prison, in part, to Archbishop Laud: MS. Bodley 313, f. 58; Wood, *Athenae*, iii. 186.

[68] MS. Bodley 313, f. 82.

[69] MS. d.d. Par. Alkerton d 1. For his gravestone in the churchyard, which had gone by 1798, see *Gent. Mag.* 1798, lxviii (2), 1028; A. Wood, *Historia Universitatis Oxoniensis* (1674), ii. 149.

[70] MS. Wills Oxon. 139/2/32.

[71] *L.J.* viii. 293; Hist. MSS. Com. *6th Rep. App.* 115.

[72] M.I. in church; for a letter from him to his uncle see MS. Bodley 313, f. 40, and for his will see MS. Wills Oxon. 41/4/17.

[73] For him see *Calamy Rev.* 397; M.I. in church. For the family see *Genealogist*, N.S. iii. 101–7, 232–40.

[74] MS. d.d. Par. Alkerton d 1.

[75] *D.N.B.*

[76] Foster, *Alumni.*

[77] *Secker's Visit.*

[78] MS. Oxf. Dioc. d 555.

[79] Ibid. c 652, f. 68; MS. Oxf. Archd. Oxon. c 47, ff. 17–19.

[80] MS. Oxf. Archd. Oxon. c 47, f. 16.

[81] *Visit. Dioc. Linc.* (*1517–31*), ii. 42.

[82] MS. Oxf. Archd. Oxon. c 47, *passim.*; O.R.O., land tax assess.

[83] MS. Oxf. Dioc. b 38.

[84] Ibid. d 578.

[85] *Par. Colln.* i. 5; MS. Oxf. Dioc. c 1695, petition.

[86] MS. Oxf. Dioc. d 578.

[87] O.R.O., incl. award; MS. Oxf. Dioc. b 38; c 1695, petition.

[88] MS. Oxf. Dioc. c 656.

[89] Ibid. c 327, pp. 117, 282.

upkeep of the church. There were no Commandments, Lord's Prayer, or 'Belief' painted up in the church in 1755 and the same complaint was made in the next year, when the porch was also out of repair. Later Townshend remedied these things.[90] From 1804 he sometimes had a curate at Alkerton since he spent much time at Wroxton Abbey as domestic chaplain to Lord Guilford.[91] He died in 1821, leaving a somewhat unclerical reputation behind him. It was later said that he used to play whist in Alkerton church porch while waiting for a funeral, and that after afternoon service he always finished the day playing whist with Lord Guilford at Wroxton.[92]

After Townshend's death the church was served by the rectors of Shenington.[93] By 1866 the number of communion services had been increased from four in 1854 to twelve a year, and the church was 'tollerably well filled' although much of the congregation came from Shenington, because most of the religious poor of Alkerton were dissenters.[94] When in 1869 both Alkerton and Shenington livings became vacant, Lord Jersey presented his friend Arthur Blythman to Shenington and proposed to unite the livings.[95] A protest was signed by over 70 people, however, 10 from Shenington and the rest from Alkerton.[96] Their case was that the villages were 'perfectly distinct' and a deep valley lay between them, making the journey from one to the other 'most tedious and difficult', especially for the old and infirm and those from outlying farmhouses. 'Through the forethought of our ancestors' each village had its own church, and the petitioners could see no reason for the union except to increase the value of Shenington rectory, 'already amply sufficient'. They thought Alkerton a suitable living for a clergyman 'of modest means and views'; and that a rector constantly resident among his people would 'confer many benefits', and would be preferable to a curate. Behind the petition was apparently the fear that Alkerton church would eventually be closed and pulled down.

Blythman, supported by the churchwarden of each parish, answered the petition by pointing out that of the signatories one of the leaders was a Roman Catholic, about half were dissenters, and some were non-resident landowners. He promised to appoint a resident curate, and stressed the advantage of a well-paid rector and a curate over two poorly paid rectors.[97] He was defeated, however, when the Bishop of Worcester (in whose diocese Shenington lay)[98] withdrew his support after the petition was sent in, largely, it was thought, because by transferring Shenington to Oxford diocese his officers would lose parochial fees.[99] Alkerton therefore obtained its last resident rector, Benjamin J. Smith (1870–1900), who held the two desired Sunday services. By 1878 the number of communicants had risen to 26, but he was dissatisfied with the small size of his congregations, which he attributed to the strength of dissent and the rise of the Agricultural Union.[1] He laboured unremittingly to get his church building restored, contributed handsomely himself, and collected funds over a period of fourteen years, a difficult task as the parish had no resident gentry.[2]

In 1900, when the living was again vacant, no objection was raised to its union with Shenington, or to the transference of Shenington to Oxford diocese.[3] Blythman, who was still at Shenington, served the two churches until his retirement in 1926 at the age of 85.[4] Although there is only one parochial church council, Shenington and Alkerton technically remain separate ecclesiastical parishes.

The church of *ST. MICHAEL* is built of local iron-stone and consists of a nave with south aisle and porch, a central tower, and a chancel.[5] The chancel is at a considerably higher level than the nave; there are steps between the chancel and the

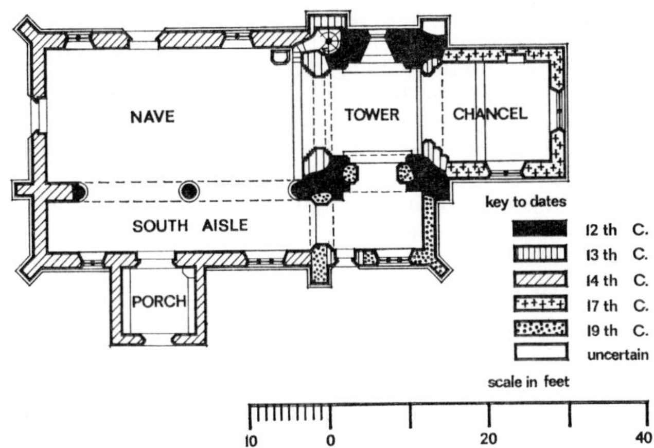

THE CHURCH OF ST. MICHAEL, ALKERTON

[90] MS. Oxf. Archd. Oxon. c 47, ff. 18, 74, 87.
[91] *Complete Peerage*, vi. 216; MS. Oxf. Dioc. c 327, p. 282; d 705, f. 318; d 578; c 429.
[92] MS. Oxf. Dioc. c 1695, letter of 5 Mar. 1869.
[93] MS. Oxf. Dioc. b 38, b 39; *Wilb. Visit.*
[94] *Wilb. Visit.*; MS. Oxf. Dioc. c 332.
[95] MS. Oxf. Dioc. c 1695, letter of 5 Mar. 1869.
[96] Ibid. petition.
[97] Ibid. draft of answer.
[98] It was thought that there had never been a union of parishes in different dioceses: MS. Oxf. Dioc. c 1695, letter of 29 Mar. 1869.
[99] Ibid. letters of 13 Dec. 1869, 2 Feb. 1870.
[1] Ibid. c 344.
[2] MS. Top. Oxon. c 105, ff. 9, 17v., 21.
[3] MS. Oxf. Dioc. c 1997, Order in Council.
[4] Ibid. Consecration pps. 1948–9.
[5] Early accounts of the building in Beesley, *Hist. Banbury*, and the report by Bodley and Garner (*c.* 1878) in MS. Top. Oxon. b 75, ff. 48–49 are misleading.

tower, and between the tower and the nave. The earliest part of the building is the tower, its lower story dating from the 12th century. Its north and south walls stand on plain Romanesque arches. The northern arch is blind, as was the southern until 1889, and there is no evidence that transepts were ever built. Towards the end of the 12th century the nave was enlarged by the addition of the south aisle of two pointed arches, and early in the 13th century the Romanesque arches in the east and west walls of the tower were replaced by Gothic arches. The western of these two arches is elaborately moulded and springs from slender clustered columns of 'Early English' design. The present chancel dates wholly or largely from the 17th century, but probably stands more or less exactly on the foundations of its medieval forerunner.

Early in the 14th century the two upper stories of the tower were added, and later the nave was rebuilt. It is lighted by a clerestory consisting of four windows on the south side and two on the north. It is roofed by a low-pitched timber roof resting on corbels, and decorated externally by a parapet resting on a cornice of Hornton stone sculptured with grotesque figures of men and animals. The cornice resembles those at Adderbury, Hanwell, Bloxham, and elsewhere in north Oxfordshire. Although its iconographical significance is obscure, it is unlikely that, as has sometimes been supposed, any allusion to the life of the Black Prince was intended.[6] The porch appears also to be an addition of the 14th century.

In the early 17th century Thomas Lydiat (rector 1612–47) 'rebuilt'[7] or partially rebuilt the chancel in a Perpendicular style. No further large-scale alterations were executed before the general restoration of 1889, but the following parts of the church underwent minor repairs: the nave roof in 1683;[8] the porch in 1756;[9] the roof in 1813 and 1814;[10] the north wall of the tower in 1833;[11] and the foundations in 1843 when they were underpinned.[12] The lower part of the south wall was also rebuilt, externally only, before 1824 and two windows were blocked up.[13] All the whitewash and plaster was removed from the interior and the windows were repaired in the early 1840s.[14]

The poverty of the parish prevented a general restoration before 1889, although the roof was reported to be decayed both in 1855 and 1868.[15] The architects Bodley and Garner reported in *c.* 1878,[16] and the Diocesan Church Building Society was applied to for a grant in 1889. It was proposed to rebuild the roofs, restore the mullions of the windows and other stonework, underpin the walls and tower, build an organ chamber and a vestry, put in new floors, new sittings in place of the existing high pews, and install heating. The bells were to be rehung, the west gallery, probably an 18th- or early 19th-century addition, removed, and an organ provided.[17] When the diocesan architect reported on the plans he noted that the south porch had fallen away from the aisle wall and that extreme care would be necessary in restoring the tower. The architect employed for the restoration was J. A. Cossins of Cossins and Peacock, Birmingham.[18] All this work appears to have been carried out and the southern tower arch now opens into the vestry and organ chamber: the ancient south doorway of the tower was re-erected in the south wall of the vestry.[19]

In the chancel there is a stone effigy of an unknown knight in armour, dating probably from the early 13th century.

There are memorial inscriptions to the following: John Pointer, rector (d. 1710); Malachy Pointer, rector (d. 1720); Timothy Lydiat, 'faithful pastor' (d. 1662/3); and Hannah, the wife of Richard Burden, pastor (d. 1653/4).[20] Thomas Lydiat was buried in the chancel (1646/7) beside his father and mother. In 1669 the Warden of New College had an inscription put over Lydiat's grave but it has been obliterated.[21]

The silver Elizabethan chalice with paten cover is considered to be the work of a provincial goldsmith whose work is found in many Oxfordshire and Northamptonshire churches.[22]

There is a chime of four bells of which one is a fine medieval bell *c.* 1400 and one is of 1618.[23]

Apart from a small gap in the marriage register for the period 1784–1803, the registers are complete from 1544.[24]

NONCONFORMITY. There were 6 Protestant nonconformists in 1676[25] but the only others recorded in the 17th or 18th centuries were a few Quakers,[26] an Anabaptist gentleman farmer in 1768 (his wife and family went to church), and a dissenter of unknown sect in 1784.[27] In 1802 there was one Presbyterian.[28] Probably Alkerton people were attending the Methodist chapel in Shenington from the time of its foundation in 1819.[29] In 1854 a cottage in Alkerton was being used as 'a meeting-house for Ranters',[30] and by 1866 most of the poor were said to be Primitive Methodists.[31] In 1869 the rector blamed the 'historically Puritanical associations' of the neighbourhood and pointed to the proximity of Shenington Primitive Methodist chapel, built 'as nearly as may be between the two villages'.[32] It is not known what proportion of that chapel's congregation came from Alkerton.

SCHOOLS. In 1811 there was a small subscription school.[33] A Sunday school was established in 1813, supported by voluntary subscriptions; there were 20 girls and 16 boys attending in 1815. It was stated that the teachers were willing to learn and practise

[6] *Antiq. Jnl.* iv (i). 1–3; *Trans. Birmingham Arch. Soc.* xxxix. 63–70.
[7] MS. d.d. Par. Alkerton d 1.
[8] Ibid.
[9] MS. Oxf. Archd. Oxon. c 47, ff. 18, 19.
[10] Ibid. f. 87.
[11] Ibid. f. 118.
[12] Ibid. f. 84.
[13] See Buckler's drawing in MS. Top. Oxon. a 65, no. 37.
[14] MS. Oxf. Archd. Oxon. c 47, f. 118; ibid. c 35, f. 89.
[15] Ibid. c 35, ff. 92, 96.
[16] MS. Top. Oxon. b 75, ff. 48–9.
[17] Ibid. c 105, ff. 9–26.
[18] Ibid.
[19] The architect's plans are in Alkerton church chest.
[20] For M.I.s in the church see *Par. Colln.* i. 6; MS. Top. Oxon. c 165, ff. 207–9.
[21] Wood, *Athenae*, iii. 189.
[22] Evans, *Ch. Plate.*
[23] *Ch. Bells Oxon.*
[24] MS. d.d. Par. Alkerton d 1, reg. (1544–1742), and Par. Rec.
[25] Compton Census.
[26] Banbury Quaker Reg. Two family names occur in the late 17th century.
[27] MS. Oxf. Dioc. d 558; ibid. b 37.
[28] Ibid. d 566.
[29] See p. 149.
[30] *Wilb. Visit.* Nothing further is known of this meeting-house.
[31] MS. Oxf. Dioc. c 332.
[32] Ibid. c 1695.
[33] MS. Oxf. Dioc. d 572.

the National Society's new plan of instruction, but that if more children were collected from neighbouring villages to profit by it, the small chancel of the church, where classes were held, would no longer be adequate as a schoolroom.[34]

The problem was only partially solved in 1818, for although the parish had joined with Shenington in establishing a National school, supported partly by subscription and partly by the parish rates, it was stated that the poor were 'without means of affording their children education'.[35] In 1834 Alkerton children still attended, both daily and on Sundays, the school at Shenington, which was within half a mile of most of their cottages.[36] They paid only fines for non-attendance, which were divided once a year, either among the good ones or those who were most regular.[37] In 1861 Sophia Hughes and Mary Wilson bequeathed £269 and £223 15*s.* 6*d.* respectively to the National school for the poor children of Alkerton and Shenington. In 1905 sufficient stock from Sophia Hughes's bequest was sold to produce £50, which was gradually replaced by the accumulated dividends of the remaining stock.[38]

By 1868 education at Shenington National school was supplemented by a night school held in the winter at Alkerton, but the rector, while admitting the existence of such a school, disclaimed all knowledge of its operation. He thought that it would have been possible to retain many more children in the Sunday school after leaving day school if a larger building had been available.[39] At the age of 9 boys were apt to leave school to work a 12 or 13 hour day in the fields, where, it was said, their health benefited from the excercise. Girls were not employed as agricultural labourers in Alkerton.[40]

In 1871 Alkerton's first mixed elementary school was established in conjunction with the National Society and the Church of England: it had accommodation for 58 children,[41] but was attended by no more than seventeen. The rector gave daily religious instruction and there was a certificated schoolmistress. The school was built by the ratepayers' subscriptions.[42] By 1890 half the financial support was received from a Government grant; rates and subscriptions and the small endowment mentioned above provided the rest. The average attendance had dropped to fourteen.[43] In 1905 the school was closed. The children returned to the school at Shenington, which continues as a mixed elementary school now known as the Shenington with Alkerton school.[44]

CHARITIES. At inclosure in 1777 *c.* 7 a. worth £5 a year was given for fuel for the poor.[45] This was the 'Poor Land', one parcel of which was sold in 1906 for £93 and another in 1945 for £280. In 1963 interest on this invested capital was bringing in £11 which was distributed in coal.[46]

By will proved 1855 Mary Wilson left £50, the interest to be given yearly in bread and money to the aged.[47] By 1963 the distribution of bread had ceased.[48]

BLOXHAM

BLOXHAM parish lies on gently rising ground 3 miles south-west of Banbury.[1] The ancient parish, out of which the parishes of Bloxham (3,142 a.) and Milcombe (1,254 a.) were formed in 1854, covered 4,397 a. and included Milcombe township.[2] Its boundaries partly followed the meandering course of the Sor Brook in the north and east, and of the River Swere in the south. The soil and scenery are varied: the parish is covered for the most part by Middle Lias Marlstone; in the north and south, where the land lies on the 325 ft. contour, there are wide and fertile river valleys; in the centre the land rises gradually to 500 ft. at Hobb Hill, which is capped by Oolite rock, and to 525 ft. at Fern Hill and Rye Hill. Between a feeder of the Sor Brook, which crosses the centre of the parish, and the northern boundary lies a fertile plateau at *c.* 275 ft. There are no woods in this upland parish, but there has been considerable planting of trees in the hedges, probably in the 18th and 19th centuries. There are a number of disused quarries in the parish; the Oolite and Middle Lias rock was used for building stone and the Marlstone for its iron ore.[3]

The principal road in the parish is a route of historic importance for it ran from Banbury to Chipping Norton and the wealthy wool producing area of the Cotswolds. Several roads connect Bloxham with the neighbouring villages of Barford, South Newington, Wigginton, Milton, Adderbury, and Tadmarton, and also with the road from Banbury to Shipston-on-Stour that skirts the western boundary of the parish. The chief bridges, for the upkeep of which money was left from medieval times on,[4] were the Great Bridge (later Old Bridge) on the old High Street, and the Little Bridge to the west of the old High Street; there were also Cumberford Bridge, Wickham Bridge, and Bridle Road Bridge near Grove Mill.[5]

[34] Ibid. c 433.

[35] *Educ. of Poor*, 717. Shenington has been confused with Cherrington (Glos.).

[36] MS. Oxf. Dioc. b 39; *Agric. Employment of Women & Children*, 351.

[37] *Educ. Enq. Abstract*, 738.

[38] Char. Com., Unrep. vol. 34, p. 379; file E 79465; file 84346.

[39] MS. Oxf. Dioc. c 335; Par. Rec.

[40] *Agric. Employment of Women & Children*, 329–30.

[41] *Elem. Educ. Ret.* 326.

[42] MS. Oxf. Dioc. c 344.

[43] *Ret. of Sch.* (1890), 212.

[44] Ex inf. Oxon. Educ. Cttee.

[45] Char. Com., Unrep. vol. 92, p. 178; *Char. Don.* 976. Amounts are given to the nearest £. Deeds referring to this endowment were removed by a churchwarden before 1870: letter from rector, 1895, in Char. Com., file B 65991.

[46] Char. Com., file B 65991: G file accts.

[47] Ibid., Unrep. vol. 34, pp. 378–9.

[48] Ex inf. the local trustee.

[1] Maps used include the following: O.S. Map 25" Oxon. IX. 6–13 (1st edn.); 6" Oxon. IV. (1st edn.); 2½" SP 43 (1957). Much other local information, particularly field work, is contained in an MS. account of some aspects of Bloxham's history by P. J. F. Wade-Martins, Bloxham School.

[2] O.S. *Area Bk.* (1882).

[3] See p. 71.

[4] See p. 64.

[5] O.R.O., Bloxham townsmen's accts., *passim.*

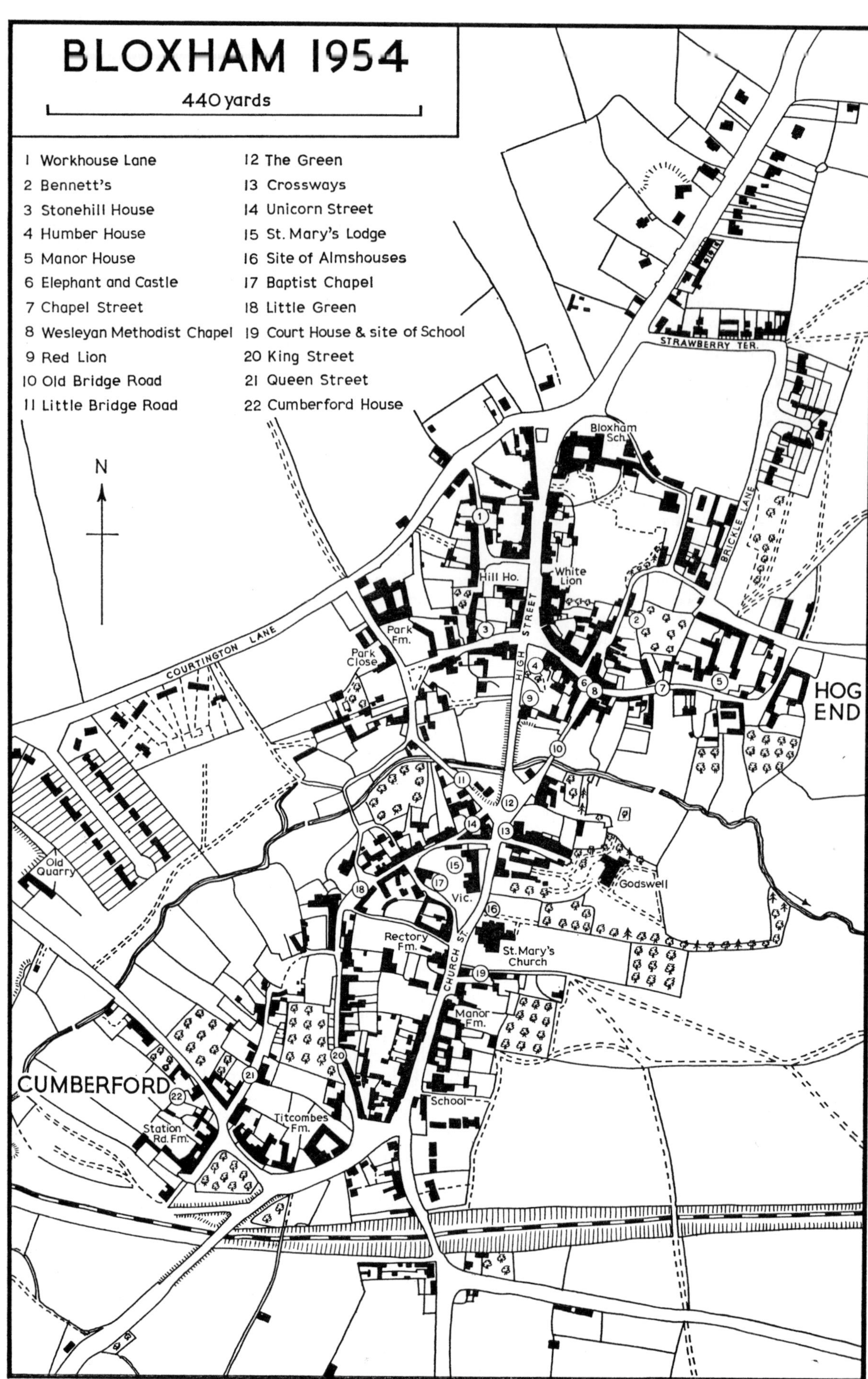

BLOXHAM 1954
440 yards
1 Workhouse Lane
2 Bennett's
3 Stonehill House
4 Humber House
5 Manor House
6 Elephant and Castle
7 Chapel Street
8 Wesleyan Methodist Chapel
9 Red Lion
10 Old Bridge Road
11 Little Bridge Road
12 The Green
13 Crossways
14 Unicorn Street
15 St. Mary's Lodge
16 Site of Almshouses
17 Baptist Chapel
18 Little Green
19 Court House & site of School
20 King Street
21 Queen Street
22 Cumberford House
N
STRAWBERRY TER.
Bloxham Sch.
BRICKLE LANE
White Lion
Hill Ho.
HIGH STREET
Park Fm.
Park Close
COURTINGTON LANE
HOG END
Old Quarry
Godswell
Vic.
Rectory Fm.
CHURCH ST.
St. Mary's Church
Manor Fm.
School
CUMBERFORD
Station Rd. Fm.
Titcombes Fm.

Several inns, built with courtyards and stabling sufficient in size to provide for travellers, lay on the main road as it passed through Bloxham. Five were licensed in 1753, and in 1782 and 1783 there were six.[6] The 'Hawk and Partridge', 'Joiners' Arms', 'Elephant and Castle', and 'Red Lion' were among the six. Three of these still flourished in 1965. The 'Red Lion' seems to have been the leading 18th-century inn and was used by the town feoffees for meetings. A Friendly Society was founded there in 1769.[7] The present 'Red Lion', which is on a site different from that of 1783,[8] was evidently built in the 1830s to serve travellers on the new highway, when the course of the main road through Bloxham was altered. The 'Bull and Butcher', the 'Crown', the 'Hare and Hounds', and the 'Unicorn', all 18th- or early-19th-century inns, have since disappeared. The 'Railway Tavern' in Queen's Street came into being after 1855 when work began on a single-line railway track between Banbury and Cheltenham. The line was completed by 1887 with a station at Bloxham; but it was closed in 1950 for passenger traffic, and finally abandoned in 1964. The station has been demolished.[9]

Although the fertility of the soil and plentiful water supply probably attracted early settlements, little evidence has been found. An earthwork near Upper Grove Mill, marked as a castle on a map of 1882,[10] has not been excavated and its date is not known. Of the 4 Romano-British sites found in the parish the most important was a settlement on the Bloxham–Tadmarton road *c.* ½ mile west of Bloxham village; this was inhabited from the 1st to the 5th century by a poor community engaged in agriculture.[11] The Anglo-Saxon settlers, however, chose the valley slopes both to the north and to the south of a small stream, and an unknown Saxon, named Blocc, gave Bloxham its name.[12] Double settlements of this type are found at Adderbury and the Barfords.[13] In the late Anglo-Saxon period Bloxham was part of a large estate, belonging to the earls of Mercia, stretching from the boundary with Tadmarton and Wigginton in the west to the River Cherwell.[14] As the head of a hundred it had clearly been important at least since the time of Edward the Elder.[15] A 'mural mansion' in Oxford was attached to Bloxham manor.[16]

Bloxham's importance survived the Conquest: in the Middle Ages it was a large parish with 403 contributors to the poll tax of 1377 of whom 78 lived in Milcombe.[17] In 1642 213 names were listed on the Protestation Returns for Bloxham and 44 for Milcombe,[18] and in 1676 the Compton Census gave a total of 880 inhabitants for the whole parish.[19] As in other parishes in this region there seems to have been a steep rise in population in the late 17th century. In 1738 the incumbent estimated that there were 192 families, and in 1805 that there were 230, figures that are unlikely to have been more than guesswork.[20] The population of the parish rose steadily from 1,358 in 1801, of which only 201 lived in Milcombe, to a peak 19th-century figure of 1,759 in 1881.[21] In the 20th century Bloxham has become a dormitory town for Banbury: building development has been extensive, farm-houses have been converted into urban residences, and farmers have moved out of the centre of the town. In 1961 the population of Bloxham was 1,359, a slight reduction of the 1951 figure; Milcombe's population, however, rose from 169 to 415 in the same period.[22]

Modern Bloxham forms a continuous village. In the Middle Ages, however, its north and south sections, separated by the brook, were distinct communities known as 'le Crowehead Ville' and 'le Downe End'.[23] There is no evidence of any correlation between the two villages and the manors of Bloxham Beauchamp and Bloxham Fiennes.[24] By the 17th century the two villages were known as Bloxham North and Bloxham South.[25]

Bloxham retains to a large extent its medieval street plan.[26] This was extemely irregular and consisted of a network of winding streets or alleys lying on either side of the present main street, which runs down the hill from the cross-roads in the north, across the brook, and up the hill to the exceptionally fine church, and to the Manor and Rectory Farms on the crest. This road was straightened before 1815 when the trustees of the Banbury and Chipping Norton turnpike purchased two cottages on the brook in order to alter the tortuous line of the old road.[27] It originally turned left at the church, passed along Unicorn Street, and came out by the Green. It then ran down Old Bridge Street to the Great Bridge and on to the 'Elephant and Castle', where it again turned left to join the present stretch, of the main road in Bloxham North.[28]

The focal point of the northern village seems to have been the cross-roads by the 'Elephant and Castle', though Park Close and Park Farm on the hill-top would have formed another nucleus. In the south the church, the vicarage-house,[29] the alms-houses,[30] the Court House, the St. Amand or Fiennes manor-house, with the Manor and Rectory Farms formed an important group of buildings, but the real heart of the village seems to have been the green and 'little green', into which King Street runs. If Hog End and Cumberford were comparatively late developments, the evidence of surviving houses shows that the outskirts of the Bloxham of today were, by the 16th century, at least partly

6 O.R.O., victlrs' recogs.

7 O.R.O., Bloxham townsmen's accts. *passim*; Cal. Q. Sess. iii. 615.

8 The present 'Red Lion' cannot be on the same site as the 18th-century one as it is on the new road made *c.* 1810.

9 E. T. MacDermot, *Hist. G.W.R.* ii. 365; ex inf. British Railways, Western Region.

10 O.S. Map 25″ Oxon. IX. 4 (1st edn.).

11 O.A.S. *Rep.* (1929), 229–32; W. F. J. Knight, 'A Romano-British Site at Bloxham', *Oxoniensia*, iii. 41–56.

12 *P.N. Oxon.* (E.P.N.S.), ii. 394.

13 See pp. 6, 13.

14 See pp. 58–59.

15 See p. 1.

16 *V.C.H. Oxon.* i. 396.

17 E 179/161/44.

18 *Protestation Ret.* 43–4.

19 Compton Census.

20 *Secker's Visit.*; MS. Oxf. Dioc. d 568.

21 *Census*, 1801–81.

22 Ibid. 1961.

23 Bloxham ct. rolls, 1514, 1544, *penes* Ld. Saye and Sele, Broughton Castle.

24 For the manors see pp. 59–60.

25 e.g. *Hearth Tax Oxon.* 138–9.

26 O.S. Map 25″ Oxon. IX. 7, 8 (1st edn.).

27 The new line of the road is shown in the plan of the new vicarage (1814–15): MS. Oxf. Dioc. b 102, no. 3.

28 See O.R.O., photostat map of 1801: Bloxham feoffees own the original.

29 At one time on the west side of the churchyard: ibid. and see pp. 57, 75.

30 Now destroyed. For site see O.R.O., photostat map of 1801; and see p. 83.

occupied. Until changes made by the R.D.C. most of the village street names dated from about this period or earlier. Tank Lane, now King Street, occurs in 1513 and was so named after the family who had the chief farm there. Humber Lane and the Humber family occur in 1536,[31] and other lanes were likewise called after the families of Doughty, Job, and Budd. These too may have been of medieval origin, but the earliest documentary evidence for them dates from *c.* 1700.[32] Church Lane (now Street), Great Bridge, and Little Bridge Street are medieval names which have survived.[33] Chapel Street takes its name from the Methodist Chapel, but contains many cottages dating from the 16th–17th century and a farm-house of still older date. Similarly Queen (formerly Grub) Street has many dwellings dating from the 17th century and earlier. Until at least 1802 the main streets leading into the village were all gated.[34]

In 1665 29 houses in Bloxham North were assessed for hearth tax and of these, excluding the manor-house, 8 had 3 hearths and 1 had four.[35] In Bloxham South 28 houses were assessed and of these, excluding the manor-house and another largish house with 5 hearths, there were 7 with 4 hearths and 6 with three.[36] The sites of the two manor-houses are uncertain, but it seems probable that the present Park Close is roughly on the site of the Beauchamp manor-house and that Godswell is roughly on the site of the St. Amand house.[37] The medieval house of the Beauchamp manor stood in an extensive inclosure, walled and hedged; in 1314 Queen Margaret, who was then in possession, complained that her close and house had been broken into, the trees felled, and that the intruders had hunted and fished there.[38] When the manor was surveyed in 1592 the site of the manor-house, with gardens, orchard, and park covered 24 a.[39] Between 1601 and 1612 Sir Thomas Garway, a London merchant of the Staple, who was the lessee of the two manors, built himself a new mansion on the premises. It was later inhabited by John Griffith, who by will dated 1632 left 'the chamber wherein I now lye myselfe in my house at Bloxham . . . with the gallerie thereunto adjoining and the outward chamber wherein my men lie'.[40] The house was probably lived in by John (II) Griffith (d. 1662), two of whose children were baptized in the church in 1643 and 1649.[41] In 1665 Mrs. Margaret Griffith, probably his relict, owned the house, which was assessed on 13 hearths and was the only large house in Bloxham.[42] Shortly afterwards it passed to the Cartwrights of Aynho, whose deeds often refer to it as the 'Great House'.[43] In 1667 John Cartwright gave it as a marriage portion to Ursula Cartwright (née Fairfax) on the occasion of her marriage to his son William.[44] In 1714 a 'Madame Balle' and a 'Madame Husney' were living there rent-free.[45] William Cartwright of Aynho still had this house in 1718.[46] It may have been rebuilt about this time, since the present Park Close, formerly Cartwright property and now the house of the headmaster of Bloxham School, has an early-18th-century façade, remodelled in the 19th century.[47] The rear of the house is still in the main an early-17th-century building, and retains its stone-mullioned windows. At the end of the 19th century the house was standing in a small park.[48]

The St. Amand manor-house, which later passed to the Fiennes family, had a prison, either attached to it or within it, which almost certainly served for Bloxham hundred, of which the St. Amands were lords.[49] The ground for connecting Godswell with this manor is that the site of this 19th-century house was once owned by the Councers, who had long farmed the manor-house from the Cartwrights.[50] In the 18th century their house was somewhat to the west of the present Godswell[51] and was presumably the one with 6 hearths on which Jonathan Councer was assessed for hearth tax in 1665.[52] The remains of a dovecote in the grounds of the adjoining Manor Farm reinforces the argument that the manor-house was sited hereabouts.

Pike Hall, which was part of Eton College's rectory estate, stood opposite the south end of the church in 1801. John and William Davis were lessees in 1819 and 1829 respectively.[53]

Although Bloxham contains no outstanding house the village has an exceptional number of good yeoman houses dating from the 16th and 17th centuries. One of the best examples is Seal Cottage (formerly Blue Gates)[54] in King Street, which dates from the mid-16th century; it has been comparatively little altered, apart from the addition in the 18th century of an upper floor, stairs and dormer-windows, and the closing of the street entrance on the west side by the construction of an oven. The original doorway with carved spandrels was then rebuilt in the rear wall. The 'Joiners' Arms' in Old Bridge Street dates from the mid-16th century and resembles Seal Cottage in size, structure, plan, and detail. The 13th-century moulded doorway standing in a wall in its yard formed part of a later cottage, now demolished, in which this feature had been incorporated.[55] Station Road Farm is another 16th-century farm-house with a re-used medieval feature, a 2-light 13th-century window built into the rear wall.

In connexion with the building or rebuilding of houses in the 16th century an Elizabethan lease of some interest has survived.[56] A yardland was granted on condition that the tenant built a house

[31] Bloxham ct. rolls, 1513, 1536, 1532, and *passim*.
[32] The family name Doughty occurs in 1532 (ct. roll, Mar. 25).
[33] Bloxham ct. rolls, *passim*.
[34] Ibid. 1514; O.R.O., Bloxham townsmen's accts.
[35] *Hearth Tax Oxon.* 138–9.
[36] Ibid. 141–2.
[37] See below.
[38] *Cal. Pat.* 1313–17, 137.
[39] MS. Rawl. D 892, f. 169.
[40] P.C.C. 45 Audley.
[41] *Oxon. Visit.* 294; see p. 60.
[42] *Hearth Tax Oxon.* 138.
[43] Northants. R.O., Cartwright Mun.
[44] Ibid., indenture. Portraits of Ursula and William by Lely are in the Soane Drawing Room at Aynho Park.
[45] Northants. R.O., Cartwright Mun., rental 1696 etc.
[46] MS. Rawl. B 400 B, f. 134.
[47] It belonged to the Bartletts for *c.* 100 years: local information.
[48] O.R.O., 1801 map.
[49] *Close R.* 1242–7, 313 and see p. 4.
[50] Northants. R.O., Cartwright Mun.
[51] O.R.O., 1801 map.
[52] *Hearth Tax Oxon.* 141.
[53] O.R.O., 1801 map; Eton Coll. Mun.; cf. also the plan of the vicarage house in MS. Oxf. Dioc. b 102, no. 3.
[54] For a detailed description and photos of this house, and Bennett's, 'Joiners' Arms', Sycamore Terrace etc. see Wood-Jones, *Dom. Archit. Banbury Region*, index.
[55] Wood-Jones, op. cit. 42 and fig. 82.
[56] O.R.O., Bloxham feoffees' recs.

All Saints' Grammar School in 1857

Ancient building adjoining the churchyard, 1823

BLOXHAM

Bloxham parish church from the south-west in 1802

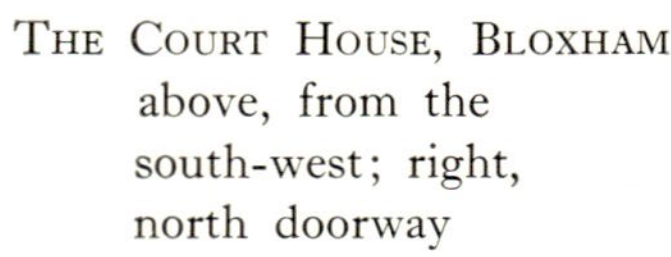

The Court House, Bloxham
above, from the
south-west; right,
north doorway

on it by 1590 'fit for the owner of a yardland to live in'. It was to have 2 bays and so, presumably, was to be built on the 2-unit pattern commonly found in this region.[57] Park Farm, built on a 2-unit plan with the fire-place backing upon the through passage, dates from the early 17th century. Cheese House or Painter's Farm (now called 'Manor House') is a similar house with cellars and attics. Though it was modernized in the 18th century, it retains some of its mullioned windows. Its stables bear William Cartwright's initials 'W. C. Esq. 1759'. The 'Elephant and Castle' was originally of the same date: one stone-mullioned window and a door with a stone label and dripstone of this period remain. The 'Hawk and Partridge' is also a 17th-century house in origin and retains its original rubble walling at the rear. Bennett's can be dated to *c.* 1630–40; it is of the through passage type but with 3 ground-floor rooms instead of the earlier two. All 3 rooms — kitchen, hall, and parlour — have wide fire-places with timber bressumers. The house has a cellar and a cock-loft over the parlour, with a stair-case leading from one to the other. A second stair-case from the first floor leads to two attic chambers over the hall and kitchen. The hall fire-place is placed against the rear wall, thus bringing the hall entrance nearer to the doorway from the village street. This improved plan was to become common in the region in the second half of the century.[58]

The large farm-house immediately south of the church is similar in size but of a slightly advanced type and may have been built *c.* 1640 or later. It had a kitchen, hall, and parlour, but the hall had lost its former significance and was the smallest of the 3 rooms. A newel staircase in a projecting turret leads from the cellar to the attics. The house was modernized in the 18th century and has been completely remodelled internally in the 20th. Titcombe's Farm is another fine house of *c.* 1650 with an arched stone doorway. Like many of Bloxham's farm-houses it lies parallel to the road with an extended wing and farm-yard at the rear of the house. The Court House (or Town House), on the south edge of the churchyard, was probably rebuilt in 1685 and 1689. In the latter years as much as £90 was spent on it.[59] It incorporates an earlier doorway of medieval character. In the 19th century the building housed the parish fire-engine. The schoolhouse which once adjoined it has been demolished except for the south doorway which bears the almost illegible inscription: 'G.C.:T.W.:T.M. Townesmen Anno. 1610'.[60] Until at least the early 19th century an important ancient building of unknown function stood to the east of this school;[61] the stone corbels once supporting the timber studding of its second story survive in the churchyard wall.

Of the cottages the row of 8 under one thatched roof in King Street are among the earliest and least altered. They are 2-storied, built of coursed ironstone rubble, and have a number of original 3-light and 2-light stone-mullioned windows in moulded frames with square moulded labels over them. On no. 3 there is a sculptured stone, found in the flagged floor, and reset in the road elevation. Campbell Cottage and a cottage opposite are also good examples of the period; so also is the end cottage in Sycamore Terrace. This last house and the rest of the terrace were perhaps used as weavers' cottages in the 19th century; in 1956 they were completely modernized. Six 4-story cottages on the north side of Queen Street, which were certainly weavers' cottages, were demolished *c.* 1950.[62]

The growing size of families and increasing standards of comfort and wealth led to the building of a number of 'gentlemen's residences' in the town in the 18th century. Stonehill House, for example, now divided into flats, is an 18th-century enlargement of an earlier building. The Georgian part is a building of 6 bays, faced with ashlar. Adjoining is a 2-storied range with 3-light stone-mullioned windows dating from the 17th century. St. Mary's Lodge, once a girls' boarding school,[63] is a house of 2 builds, partly late-18th-century and partly 19th-century. Crossways is a 2-storied 18th-century house with contemporary sash and casement windows on the ground floor. Hill House has an 18th-century wing added to a 17th-century house and Cumberford House was modernized in 1742. This date and the letters R.P. are cut on a date-stone over the lowest window in the south gable; its stone fire-place dated 1619 was brought from a house in Adderbury. Among the many 18th-century cottages may be mentioned an effective row of 6 to the east of Crossways; they are 2-story buildings of coursed rubble and mostly retain their 18th-century casement windows.

The chief 19th-century building is Bloxham School. The school, originally known as All Saints' School, was founded in 1853 by the Revd. J. W. Hewett as a Church of England boarding school for the sons of 'the professional classes'. It was housed originally in the vicarage-house and from 1854 in a farm-house. In 1857 Hewett went bankrupt, his school came to an end and the derelict building was bought by P. R. Egerton, Curate of Deddington, who re-opened the school in 1860. With the financial help of his wife's family (Gould) and of the Duke of Marlborough he built it up until in 1896 he handed it over to the Society of the Woodard Schools. The original building was extended in 1860–3 at a cost of £28,000. The architect was G. E. Street and he built in the local stone in the Gothic style. The building was enlarged in 1864, 1869, and 1871, when the school chapel was built, and now dominates Bloxham North and the outskirts.[64]

Other 19th-century buildings were the new vicarage-house designed by the vicar George Bell (1811–15),[65] the Baptist chapel (1859), and the Wesleyan chapel,[66] both built of red brick with stone facings, and the infant school at the south end of the village. In the late 19th century residential houses were built along the Banbury road and in Strawberry Terrace to the north of the village. In the 20th

[57] See Wood-Jones, op. cit., *passim.*
[58] Ibid.
[59] O.R.O., townsmen's accts.
[60] Wood-Jones, op. cit. 97, 268–9, 271.
[61] See plate facing p. 56.
[62] Ex inf. C. Butler, Esq.
[63] O.R.O., townsmen's accts. 1758–1869.
[64] For accounts of the school see J. S. W. Gibson, 'All Saints' Grammar School, Bloxham, 1853–7', *Cake & Cockhorse* (Banbury Hist. Soc.), ii. no. 6; *All Saints', Bloxham, Centenary History*. For further details see *The Bloxhamist* (1875–1965).
[65] MS. Oxf. Dioc. b 102, no. 3 has a plan of the house. The new building of 5 rooms was added on to an old house adjoining the old vicarage garden. Ephraim Randle of Bloxham was the builder.
[66] See pp. 81–82.

century there has been housing development both by private enterprise and the R.D.C. The earliest council estate of 12 houses was built in 1919 in Courtington Lane to the north of the village near the Tadmarton road, and was extended in 1936 and 1961 with a further 84 brick houses. Another council estate of 18 stone and roughcast houses was built in Buckle Lane in 1951. A group of 12 well-designed houses on the Barford road were put up in 1924.[67]

The village obtained a recreation ground of *c.* 5 a. given by George Allen in 1910[68] and there are local teams for football, cricket, and athletics. The first village hall was erected by the Co-operative Society in 1899–1900 in Workhouse Lane. The Ex-servicemen's Hall was opened after the First World War, and the Ellen Hinde Memorial Hall, built in the 1930s by the daughter of the founder of All Saints' School, was given to the village *c.* 1946. The last has become a new social centre and is doing something to counteract the pull of Banbury.[69]

Various town properties shown on a map of 1801 have since been demolished. Besides the almshouses on the edge of the churchyard, there were the poor-houses on the green where Unicorn Street once joined Old Bridge Street, the workhouse, whose site is still commemorated by the street name Workhouse Lane, and the pest-house near the railway line beyond the station.[70]

Milcombe village, which lies 1½ mile to the south-west of Bloxham seems always to have been very scattered; it now straggles along the road to Wigginton and on a branch road. The chief buildings in 1882 were the church, the school (1832), the Baptist chapel (built in 1824),[71] and the 'Horse and Groom' on the former road, the manor-house and the smithy on the latter.[72] After 1871, when Milcombe's population reached its 19th-century peak,[73] the agricultural depression caused a decline and in the first decade of the 20th century the village was 'dilapidated' and full of empty houses.[74] During and after the Second World War prosperity returned. By 1964 Milcombe had ceased to be a remote village and had become a dormitory for Banbury industrial and business workers. Council houses, built of honey-coloured brick and of good design, had been built and a new estate of 'continental' houses and bungalows was being rapidly developed off New Road by private enterprise.

The manor-house, Milcombe Hall, was mostly demolished in 1953, and the remnant that still stands was converted in 1964 into a modern dwelling. It is of 2 stories and retains some 2- and 3-light mullioned and transomed windows both at the back and front. A pair of 17th-century gateposts remains. So does the early-18th-century octagonal dovecot.[75] It has an octagonal roof of stone slates with 4 dormers and a small leaded cupola at the summit. The manor-house was lived in by the Dalby family. Between 1564 and 1629 19 of the family were baptized in the church and 14 were buried there between 1563 and 1625. In the early 18th century the Thornycrofts remodelled part of the house. Lady Thornycroft died there in 1704 and Sir John in 1725.[76] Manor Farm has a 19th-century Gothic front of 3 stories, but the back of the house, which was probably once the front, is early-17th-century. The entrance doorway, now blocked, has a square label and the date 1630.

A cottage at Milcombe of late-18th-century date is typical of many single-cell cottage plans in the region; it measures only 12 ft. 6 in. by 10 ft. 6 in. internally.[77] It forms the nucleus of a terrace of cottages each with their fire-place, bread-oven, and winding stair.[78] These were the homes of the landless labourer, a class enlarged by inclosure in 1794 and 1802.

The chief house outside the villages was once Bloxham Grove, a 17th-century house largely rebuilt in the 19th century. It is very possibly on the site of the 'Logge' (Lodge) conveyed in 1528 with the Warren by Edward Fiennes to James Merynge on a repairing lease.[79] It was owned by Sir James Dashwood in 1738. The Revd. George Warriner, a principal landowner, who lived there in the 19th century[80] may have been responsible for planting the avenue of beeches between it and Adderbury. In 1852 it was described as a 'good modern mansion',[81] but in 1964 was in poor condition. Nearby is a small derelict wooden windmill. There are 5 isolated farms but none is older than the inclosure of the common fields in 1794 and 1802.

Bloxham and Milcombe rarely had resident lords of great standing and in the post-medieval period it was the lesser gentry and yeomen farmers who were the leaders of society, except possibly for a short period in the 17th century when the Cartwrights used their 'Great House' at Bloxham for junior members of the family.[82] This dominance of the local farmers may have encouraged the growth of nonconformity, and Bloxham was notable in the 17th century and later for the strength, in particular, of its Presbyterian and Baptist communities; it also accounted for the stout resistance offered on more than one occasion to high-handed actions by men of authority, as both the Fienneses of Broughton and Sir John Thornycroft of Milcombe found to their cost.[83] The local leaders in the 17th century and later were members of the Councer, Dalby, Sabell, Stranke, and Youick families. In the 18th century the Davis family was notable for its progressive farming and for its clerics, including a Vicar of Bloxham.

The impact of the Civil War on Bloxham seems to have been small; in June 1643 the royalists built some small fortifications at Bloxham[84] and in 1647 John Cartwright complained that none of the small rents due to Bloxham parsonage had been paid since 1640.[85]

MANORS AND OTHER ESTATES. Before the Conquest Bloxham and part of Adderbury formed a large estate held by Edwin, Earl of Mercia;[86] before Edwin's time it seems to have belonged to Tostig,

67 Ex inf. Banbury R.D.C.
68 *Kelly's Dir. Oxon.* (1915).
69 Local information.
70 O.R.O., map of 1801.
71 See pp. 82–83.
72 O.S. Map 25″ Oxon. IX. 10 (1st edn.).
73 *Census*, 1801–1901.
74 Orr, *Oxon. Agric.* 74.
75 See plate facing p. 182.
76 M.I. in the church; Par. Rec., reg.
77 Wood-Jones, *Dom. Archit. Banbury Region*, 132, fig. 39.
78 Ibid. 197–8.
79 MS. Rawl. D 82, ff. 294–24v.
80 *Secker's Visit.*; *Kelly's Dir. Oxon.* (1864, 1887).
81 Gardner, *Dir. Oxon.* (1852).
82 See above.
83 See pp. 68, 75.
84 Luke, *Jnl.* ii. 105.
85 Northants. R.O., Cartwright Mun.
86 *V.C.H. Oxon.* i. 400. For him see *D.N.B.* under Morcar.

Earl of Northumbria, who was deposed by his thegns in 1065 and replaced by Edwin's younger brother Morcar. It was from Morcar, presumably, that Edwin obtained the estate.[87] In 1086 Bloxham, with part of Adderbury and a hide and a yardland in Ledwell and Sandford St. Martin, formed a royal manor, which was assessed at 34½ hides, had the soke of two hundreds, and the duty of helping to keep the defences of Oxford in repair.[88] Edwin's estate may have passed to the Crown by 1067; certainly Bloxham church was in the king's hands at that date.[89]

BLOXHAM remained a royal manor until King Stephen granted it to Waleran, Count of Meulan.[90] Waleran was in Oxford in 1140 and his two charters about Bloxham may date from then.[91] In 1141 he made terms with the Empress and after 1142 was never in England again.[92] He clearly lost Bloxham, either then or at the general resumption of Crown lands on the accession of Henry II, for the manor was in the king's hands in 1155–6, except perhaps for 1 knight's fee.[93] Thereafter the manor was divided into two parts.

One part, known later as the manor of *BLOXHAM BEAUCHAMP*, was held from 1156 by the justiciar Richard de Luci until his death in 1179.[94] It was then in the sheriff's hands for a few years.[95] It was then held successively by Walter de L'Espalt (1191–4),[96] William de Ste. Mère Eglise (1196–7),[97] Imbert de Carenci (1197–1202),[98] and Ingram des Preaux (1202–4).[99] Then it was again in the sheriff's hands for several years,[1] except for a period after 1218 when it was granted during pleasure to Walter de Verdun, the holder of the second Bloxham manor.[2]

During the reign of Henry III various ways of managing this manor were adopted. Sometimes it was in the hands of a bailiff, as in 1236 when Walter of Tew was appointed keeper of Bloxham and Woodstock.[3] In 1242 it was held by Engelard de Cygoniac,[4] and in 1251 Bloxham, with several other manors, was farmed to John of Handborough and Peter of Leigh, bailiffs of Woodstock, for 6 years at £98.[5] In 1226 Peter of Leigh was ordered to hand the manor over to Amaury de St. Amand,[6] the holder of the second Bloxham manor, to whom the king had committed it at will.

In 1269 this Bloxham manor was granted to Queen Eleanor, together with other property, in exchange for the honor of Richmond,[7] and for most of the next 50 years it was held by the queens of England. Eleanor held the manor until her death in 1291; it then reverted to the Crown and on Edward I's marriage in 1299 to Margaret, sister of Philip IV of France, was given together with Oxford and Headington as part of the Queen's dowry.[8] After Margaret's death in 1318 Bloxham was again assigned in dower, this time to Edward II's wife Isabel.[9] She held it for a year only for in 1319 it was granted for life and rent-free to John of Weston the younger because he had been maimed in the king's service.[10] In 1338, before John of Weston's death, Edward III granted the reversion of the manor to Roger de Beauchamp, his yeoman, first at the usual rent and afterwards rent-free.[11] Later he was granted it in fee but Beauchamp's heirs were to pay the usual rent.[12] When Roger de Beauchamp obtained possession in 1343, on John of Weston's death,[13] Bloxham's history as a royal demesne manor ended, although the king still expected an income from it.

Roger de Beauchamp, lord of Ditchley (in Spelsbury) and chamberlain of Edward III's household,[14] died in 1380, leaving as heir his grandson Roger, a minor;[15] Roger died in 1406, and his son John in *c.* 1412, leaving a son John, who died young and unmarried,[16] thus bringing the male line of the family to an end. In 1406 Bloxham had been enfeoffed on John de Beauchamp and Margaret, the daughter of John of Holland of Northamptonshire,[17] perhaps a fiancée who died before marriage, since his later wife was Edith Stourton.[18] After John de Beauchamp's death Edith, who later married Sir Robert Shottesbrooke, held Bloxham in dower until her own death in 1442.[19] It was discovered in 1421 that only £20 a year rent had been paid since the time of Edward III whereas in Edward I's reign the rent had risen from £20 to £35. The Shottesbrookes were, however, forgiven any arrears and were allowed to hold the manor for life at the old rent.[20] The Beauchamp property descended on the death of Edith Shottesbrooke to her daughter Margaret Beauchamp. She married first Oliver St. John (d. *c.* 1435), secondly John Beaufort, Duke of Somerset, and finally Leo Welles, Lord Welles, a Lancastrian slain at the Battle of Towton in 1461.[21]

On Margaret's death in 1482[22] Bloxham descended to John de St. John of Bletsoe (Beds.),

[87] *Complete Peerage*, ix. 703–4; *V.C.H. Oxon.* i. 401.
[88] *V.C.H. Oxon.* i. 396, 400.
[89] *Cal. Chart. R.* 1327–41, 332: inspeximus.
[90] For him see *Complete Peerage*, vii. App. I; ibid. xii (2). 829–37; G. H. Whitt, 'Career of Waleran, Count of Meulan', *Trans. R. H. S.* 4th ser. xvii. 19–48.
[91] *Eynsham Cart.* i. 52–53. His initial there is given as E. and G. but clearly Count Waleran is meant.
[92] Whitt, op. cit. 36–37.
[93] C. S. Hoyt, *Royal Demesne 1066–1272*, 95; *Red Bk. Exch.* (Rolls Ser.), 674; and below.
[94] *Pipe R.* (P.R.S.), *passim.* For Richard de Luci see *D.N.B.* During 1157 the manor was held by William de Chesney: *Pipe R.* 1156–8 (Rec. Com.), 82; *Eynsham Cart.* i. 415–18.
[95] e.g. *Pipe R.* 1181 (P.R.S. xxx), 116.
[96] Ibid. 1191 (P.R.S. N.S. ii), 99; Ibid. 1193 (N.S. iii), 121.
[97] Ibid. 1195 (N.S. vi), 142; *Chanc. R.* 1196 (P.R.S. N.S. vii), 70.
[98] *Pipe R.* 1197 (P.R.S. N.S. viii), 33; ibid. 1201 (P.R.S. N.S. xiv), 205–6.
[99] Ibid. 1202 (P.R.S. N.S. xv), 204; ibid. 1203 (P.R.S. N.S. xvi), 187; *Rot. Lib.* (Rec. Com.), 91.
[1] e.g. *Pipe R.* 1206 (P.R.S. N.S. xx), 119; ibid. 1230 (P.R.S. N.S. iv), 245.
[2] *Rot. Litt. Claus.* (Rec. Com.), i. 381*b*.
[3] *Cal. Lib.* 1226–40, 241; *Cal. Pat.* 1232–47, 141.
[4] *Pipe R.* 1242 (ed. H. L. Cannon), 49.
[5] *Close R.* 1253–4, 88; *Cal. Pat.* 1247–58, 87; *Close R.* 1256–9, 358.
[6] *Close R.* 1261–4, 314–15; *Cal. Pat.* 1258–66, 628.
[7] *Cal. Pat.* 1266–72, 311, 433–4; *Close R.* 1268–72, 316.
[8] *Cal. Pat.* 1292–1301, 453; ibid. 1307–13, 217.
[9] Ibid. 1317–21, 115, 131, 201; *Cal. Close*, 1318–23, 57.
[10] *Cal. Pat.* 1317–21, 397, 401. For John of Weston see C. Moore, *Knights of Edw. I*, v. 182–3.
[11] *Cal. Fine R.* 1337–47, 68; *Cal. Pat.* 1338–40, 48.
[12] *Cal. Pat.* 1338–40, 96; ibid. 1377–81, 183.
[13] *Cal. Close.* 1343–6, 189.
[14] *Complete Peerage*, ii. 44–45.
[15] C 136/8/3.
[16] *Complete Peerage*, ii. 45.
[17] *Cal. Pat.* 1405–8, 123.
[18] *Complete Peerage*, ii. 45.
[19] *Cal. Pat.* 1416–22, 369; ibid. 1441–6, 102.
[20] For the rent in the Shottesbrookes time and later see *Cal. Pat.* 1416–22, 369; 1441–6, 102; 1452–61, 466; 1461–7, 150; 1476–85, 4; *Cal. Close*, 1461–8, 340; 1476–85, 46.
[21] *Complete Peerage*, ii. 45; xii(1). 47–48.
[22] C 140/82/7.

her son by her first husband.[23] He, or more probably his son, died in 1525,[24] and his grandson John[25] sold Bloxham in 1545 to Richard, Lord Saye and Sele,[26] who was already owner of the second Bloxham manor.

The second part of Bloxham manor, known later as *BLOXHAM FIENNES*, was held from 1158 to 1174 by Engelard de Bohun,[27] a powerful Norman supporter of Henry II. In 1175 it was given to Ralph, the son of Walter de Verdun,[28] and was subsequently always held by his family. Ralph was succeeded by his son William in 1198 or 1199,[29] and William by his brother Walter in 1203 or 1204.[30] Walter, who was a justiciar, died in 1229 and his son Ralph paid relief as his successor in Bloxham.[31] The next year Ralph died abroad, probably in Poitou, and his property went to his relative Amaury de St. Amand.[32] From this time until the 15th century Bloxham descended with the St. Amand manor of Adderbury.[33] The holding was generally designated as a third of Bloxham: Amaury de St. Amand held a fee in 1242, while the king had 2 fees in demesne, and in 1254 he held a third of the manor 'which had once been in the king's hands'.[34] There are later references to the St. Amand manor as a third of Bloxham, notably in 1285 when the king brought a plea of *quo warranto* against Amaury de St. Amand, demanding why he withheld the hundred and a third of the manor which had once belonged to the king's father.[35] Amaury defended his right and the matter was ordered to be settled by precedent.[36] He seems to have won his case, for the third of the manor continued to descend in the St. Amand family and all connexions with the royal demesne ceased.

In 1418 this Bloxham manor was sold with part of Adderbury to Sir Thomas Wykeham.[37] Sir Thomas sold his Adderbury land in 1439 but kept Bloxham, which passed on his death in 1443 to his son William.[38] William was still alive in 1455 when he made a settlement of the manor,[39] and on his death this Bloxham manor and Broughton were inherited by his daughter Margaret, wife of William Fiennes, Baron Saye and Sele.[40] From this time Bloxham Fiennes descended with Broughton and the barony of Saye and Sele.[41]

On the death of Richard Fiennes, Lord Saye and Sele, in 1501, the manor was held in dower by his relict Elizabeth until her death in 1527.[42] In 1545, when Richard, Lord Saye and Sele, purchased Bloxham Beauchamp, the two manors were united.[43] Bloxham is still (1965) in the family's possession. Lt.-Col. Ivo Murray Twisleton-Wykeham-Fiennes, Lord Saye and Sele, is the present lord.[44]

Much of the manor's land, however, was sold in the 17th century. In 1601 Richard Fiennes (d. 1613) sold the 2 manor-houses of Bloxham Beauchamp and Bloxham Fiennes with 16 yardlands and 2 mills to Sir Thomas Garway, merchant of the Staple. In 1612 this property, together with the new dwelling-house built by Sir Thomas Garway, was sold to John Griffith, a descendant of William Griffith, Chamberlain of North Wales. On John's death in 1632 the property probably passed to his brother Richard (d. 1636) and to Richard's son John (d. 1662).[45] John conveyed the property to Ambrose Thelwell in 1653. The conveyance, however, may have been a mortgage, for Mrs. Margaret Griffith, probably John's relict, was assessed for tax on the new house in 1665. Before 1667, however, the house and various closes passed to John Cartwright of Aynho, and was absorbed in his other property in the parish.[46]

In 1086 William, Count of Evreux, was holding a *MILCOMBE* manor assessed at 4½ hides. In 1108 he and his wife Helewis granted it with his other English estates to Noyon Priory (Noyon-sur-Andelle).[47] The priory was returned as one of the lords of Milcombe in 1242, and in 1291 held 30*s.* rent there.[48] In 1414, on the dissolution of the alien priories, Noyon's possessions were granted to Sheen Priory (Surr.) and Sheen retained 30*s.* rent in Milcombe until the Dissolution.[49] There is no record of a grant by Henry VIII of this Milcombe estate and it presumably passed to the tenant.[50]

Noyon Priory had been leasing the estate from the 12th century. The earliest recorded tenant was Master Robert de Inglesham (fl. 1168), Archdeacon of Surrey and perhaps also of Berkshire.[51] He was succeeded by John de Inglesham and Roger de la Dune, who quitclaimed their rights to Milcombe and other property in 1208 and restored the charters concerning them to the monks.[52] In 1232 the Prior of Noyon was involved in a lawsuit with Race FitzAlexander of Milcombe over customs due there.[53] It is probable that John of Milcombe, who was returned with the Abbot of Eynsham and Ralph de Bereford as one of the lords of the parish in 1316,

[23] For family see *Complete Peerage*, xi. 334; and J. Brownbill, 'St. John of Bletsoe', *Genealogists' Mag.* v. 355–9. The number of generations is uncertain.
[24] P.C.C. 33 Bodfelde.
[25] For him see *Select Cases in Star Chamber*, ed. Leadam (Selden Soc. xxv), ii. 25–7.
[26] C.P. 25(2)/34/230/25; C.P. 40/1127, m. 169.
[27] *Pipe R.* 1156–8 (Rec. Com.), 142; ibid. 1174 (P.R.S. xxi), 174.
[28] Ibid. 1175 (P.R.S. xxii), 10; Ross, *Cirencester Cart.* ii, p. 650.
[29] *Pipe R.* 1198 (P.R.S. N.S. ix), 182; ibid. 1199 (P.R.S. N.S. x), 219.
[30] Ibid. 1203 (P.R.S. N.S. xvi), 188; ibid. 1204 (P.R.S. N.S. xviii), 106, 111.
[31] *Ex e Rot. Fin.* (Rec. Com.), i. 182. For Walter see *Cal. Pat.* 1216–25, 32; *Rot. Litt. Claus.* (Rec. Com.), i. 147*b*, ii. 6.
[32] *Ex e Rot. Fin.* (Rec. Com.), i. 204.
[33] e.g. *Bk. of Fees*, 824; *Cal. Inq. p.m.* ii, p. 350; *Feud. Aids*, iv. 179; and see pp. 16–17.
[34] *Bk. of Fees*, 824; *Rot. Hund.* (Rec. Com.), ii. 32.
[35] *Feud. Aids*, iv. 159.
[36] *Plac. de Quo Warr.* (Rec. Com.), 667.
[37] *Cal. Pat.* 1416–22, 175.
[38] C 139/113/16. For settlement of 1441 see *Cal. Pat.* 1436–41, 514.
[39] C.P. 25(1)/191/28/45; C.P. 25(1)/191/28/42; C.P. 40/778, m. 71d.
[40] *Complete Peerage*, xi. 482.
[41] e.g. C 140/62/45; and see pp. 88–89.
[42] *Cal. Inq. p.m. Hen. VII*, ii. pp. 272, 401; *Complete Peerage*, xi. 483.
[43] See below.
[44] *Complete Peerage*, xi. 488.
[45] Northants. R.O., Cartwright Mun.; *Oxon. Visit.* 294.
[46] Northants. R.O., Cartwright Mun.; *Hearth Tax Oxon.* 138; see pp. 61–62.
[47] *V.C.H. Oxon.* i. 410; cf. v. 107; *Cal. Doc. France*, ed. Round, 220.
[48] *Bk. of Fees*, 832; *Tax. Eccl.* (Rec. Com.), 44.
[49] Dugdale, *Mon.* vi(1). 29, 31, 33.
[50] cf. *V.C.H. Oxon.* v. 107; and see below.
[51] *Memo. R.* 1208 (Pipe R. Soc. N.S. xxxi), 109; *Pipe R.* 1168 (P.R.S. xii), 201; *Ancient Chart.* (P.R.S. x), 77; *Oxon. Chart.* no. 18.
[52] *Memo. R.* 1208 (Pipe R. Soc. N.S. xxxi), 109.
[53] *Close R.* 1231–4, 140.

was tenant of the priory's land[54] and that it descended with his family until 1370 when John, son of John of Milcombe, sold his lands to Sir Thomas of Broughton, lord of Broughton.[55]

The manor thereafter descended with the Broughton lordship:[56] in 1534, for example, tenements in Milcombe were stated to be held of Broughton manor and their tenants did suit at Broughton,[57] and the lords of Broughton were lords of Milcombe in the 18th century.[58] After 1836, however, there is no record of a connexion between this manor and Broughton, and it may perhaps be identified with the manor which Mrs. Selina Hosford held in 1869,[59] and which Christ Church, Oxford, purchased in 1872 and have since retained.[60]

In 1086 a second *MILCOMBE* manor, assessed at 3½ hides, was held by Alfric, lord also of Ascot (in Great Milton), Chastleton, Rollright, and Stonesfield.[61] Alfric's successors in all five places were the d'Oillys, who held Ascot by 1100 and probably Milcombe as well, since by 1109 Niel d'Oilly, lord of Hook Norton, had granted this Milcombe estate to Eynsham Abbey.[62] It was valued at 40*s.* a year and was clearly intended for the maintenance of a monk whom Niel d'Oilly had nominated.[63] The grant was confirmed by Henry d'Oilly in the last quarter of the 12th century.[64] The property was added to in the course of the Middle Ages;[65] it was valued at £3 10*s.* in 1291 and at £5 6*s.* 8*d.* in 1535.[66] In 1539 the king made a grant of Eynsham's property to Sir George Darcy and a further grant of it in 1543 to Darcy and Sir Edward North, Treasurer of the Court of Augmentations.[67] By 1551, however, John Croker (d. 1569), lord of Hook Norton manor, was in possession.[68] Before 1563 he settled a part of the property on his younger son Gerard;[69] his heir John succeeded to the other part in 1569.[70] In 1584 John Croker the younger conveyed his part of the manor to Thomas Hawten of the Lea, in Swalcliffe,[71] a family that was allied by marriage with the Crokers since Margery Croker, sister of John Croker, had married an Edward Hawten.[72] Thomas Hawten sold his Milcombe estate in 1603 to Edward Hawten and in 1606 Edward sold it to John Bonner of Swerford,[73] who was already in possession of Gerard Croker's share of Milcombe manor. Sir Gerard Croker of Steeple Barton had sold it to John Bonner's father, also John, some time before 1563.[74] The elder John had also acquired more Milcombe land (described as a manor) from John Dormer in 1566.[75] His son John succeeded in 1589 and appears to have run into debt for he sold a part of the estate in 1625 to Roger Snelson, a London dyer, and in 1628 he and his son William sold 'the manor and lordship of Milcombe' to Christopher Allanson of London.[76] Allanson devised this property in 1631 to his brother and to some of the children of his sister Judith, and it was later partitioned between four members of the family. No manorial rights were mentioned. In 1647 Snelson sold his interest to William Bonner of Milcombe and in 1656 William Bonner of Henley-on-Thames sold 'Milcombe manor or lordship' to John Cartwright of Aynho.[77]

A third *MILCOMBE* manor first recorded as such in the early 16th century, evidently descended from the estate of the judge Ralph de Bereford (d. *c.* 1329), who was one of the principal landowners in the hamlet in the early 14th century and was returned as one of the lords of the vill in 1316.[78] His relict Agnes was in possession in 1333 when she was licensed to have an oratory.[79] Ralph had held Milcombe with an estate in Mollington (in Cropredy) which descended to Robert de Bereford (fl. 1327, 1340), and to Edmund Waldyff, who married Robert de Bereford's daughter Margery.[80] Edmund's son Thomas, a minor on his father's death in 1395, was granted livery of his parents' lands in 1404.[81] He can be identified with the Thomas Waldyff recorded in Warwickshire in the late 15th century. His connexion with Milcombe is not noted although he still held Mollington in 1428.[82] The Milcombe estate passed, probably by marriage, to Humphrey Willingham, described in 1464 as of Mollington and Milcombe.[83] Willingham was still alive in 1482 when a commission was issued to arrest him, but by 1506 his estates, described as the manors of Milcombe and Mollington, were held by his daughter and heir Grace and her husband Robert Halse.[84] Halse put the manor in trust for himself and his wife, but after his death Grace and her second husband, William Saunders, were involved in a lawsuit with the heirs of the trustees who maintained that Milcombe had been sold outright to Edmund Hall.[85] Edmund Hall's heirs were his daugher Elizabeth, wife of Laurence Woodhull (Odell) of Mollington,

54 *Feud. Aids*, iv. 166.
55 *Cal. Close*, 1369–74, 194.
56 See pp. 87–89.
57 C 142/56/5.
58 *Par. Colln.* ii. 209; MS. d.d. Oxon. Milcombe 1781; O.R.O., gamekprs' deps.
59 *Kelly's Dir. Oxon.* (1869). One third was conveyed to her husband Dr. J. S. Hosford of Stratford, West Ham, Essex, in 1870: O.R.O., OR. VIII/i.
60 Ch. Ch. Treasury, schedule of title deeds of Chapter estates, pp. 113–19.
61 *V.C.H. Oxon.* i. 412, 424; vii. 126.
62 Ibid. vii. 126; *Eynsham Cart.* i, pp. xxxv–xxxvi, 36; I. J. Sanders, *English Baronies*, under Hook Norton.
63 *Eynsham Cart.* i. 36.
64 Ibid. 78.
65 e.g. ibid. 212.
66 *Tax Eccl.* (Rec. Com.) 44; *Valor Eccl.* (Rec. Com.) ii. 208.
67 *L. & P. Hen. VIII*, xiv(1), p. 417; ibid. xviii(1), pp. 446, 540.
68 *Cal. Pat.* 1550–3, 63; M. Dickins, *Hist. of Hook Norton*, 162–3.
69 C 142/152/118.
70 For the date of Croker's death see P.C.C. 76 Leicester. He appears also to have settled 'a third of Milcombe manor' on Bridget Strange, the only child of John Croker of Barton (Warws.). In 1575 she and her husband were in possession: C 60/391/34.
71 C.P. 25(2)/197/Mich. 26 Eliz. I.
72 *Oxon. Visit.* 138, 185. One return gave her husband as John Hawten, Edward's son: ibid. 137.
73 C 145/512/11; C.P. 25(2)/473/East. 4 Chas. I; Northants. R.O., Cartwright Mun. indentures.
74 In 1563 John Bonner put a Milcombe manor in trust for himself and his wife Margaret: Bodl. MS. Ch. Oxon. 418. For the relationship between the Crokers and Bonners see *Oxon. Visit.* 185.
75 See below.
76 Northants. R. O., Cartwright Mun.
77 Ibid.
78 E 179/161/8, 10; *Feud. Aids*, iv. 166; *D.N.B.*
79 MS. Top. Oxon. c 394, f. 198.
80 E 179/161/9; *Feud. Aids*, iv. 179; C 136/85/15.
81 *Cal. Pat.* 1391–6, 535; 1401–5, 405.
82 *Feud. Aids*, iv. 187. For 15th-century references see *Cal. Pat.* 1452–61, 680, 1461–7, 236, 531.
83 *Cal. Fine R.* 1461–71, 131; *Cal. Pat.* 1461–7, 278, 293.
84 *Cal. Pat.* 1476–85, 320; *Warws. Feet of Fines III* (Dugdale Soc. xviii), pp. 221–2; C 1/358/1.
85 C 1/362/57; C 1/358/1. It was alleged that Anthony Hall of Swerford held the 'evidences' and would not surrender them.

and Alice, wife of Richard Harcourt.[86] The outcome of the lawsuit is not known, but the manor was evidently divided into moieties. One moiety was probably that moiety of a Milcombe manor which Thomas Langrich and his wife Joan sold in 1515 to a Thomas Westall and his heirs for 100 marks, for a John Hall was one of the feoffees.[87] The later descent is not clear, but it may have been that moiety which Roger Becket and Alice his wife, perhaps Edmund Hall's coheir, conveyed in 1532 to Robert Dormer of Wing (Bucks.).[88] In 1566 John Dormer, who may have been a son, granted a Milcombe manor to John Bonner, and thereafter it was merged with Bonner's other Milcombe estate.[89]

Another moiety of a Milcombe manor was granted in 1530 by Edmund Peckham, Treasurer of the Mint, and Ann his wife to William Billing of Deddington.[90] Billing died in 1534 holding tenements in Milcombe, said to be parcel of Milcombe manor and to be held partly of the Prior of Merton (Surr.) and partly of Broughton manor, as well as a mill and tenements described as the rest of Milcombe manor.[91] It is doubtful whether any manorial rights were attached to this land and no such rights were mentioned when the land was sold to George Dalby in 1556.[92]

The rectory estate was granted first to Westminster Abbey in 1067.[93] Nevertheless Henry II granted it *c.* 1180 to Godstow Abbey, and after an appeal to Rome by Westminster Abbey a settlement was made whereby the nuns retained the rectory subject to a payment by them to Westminster of a pension out of the benefice of £3 6*s.* 8*d.*[94] The abbey then held the rectory until its dissolution in 1539,[95] when it was farmed by a tenant, Anthony Bustard, who was still holding it in 1546.[96] In 1547 the estate was granted by the Crown to Eton College, which continued to lease it after the Godstow lease expired and still owned it in 1965.[97]

At first Eton leased the property on 21-year leases and until 1605 entry fines were charged. Rents were paid partly in money and partly in kind and these rents remained virtually unchanged until 1793;[98] a typical lease was that to Sir Anthony Cope of Hanwell in 1605; he paid an entry of £40 and his rents were 14 qr. of wheat, 4 bushels of malt, £16, and 40 fat wethers.[99] Another distinguished family to hold the lease were the Cartwrights of Aynho (Northants.); Richard Cartwright entered into the property in 1624 and his son, John, ten years later.[1] The latter endowed two scholarships at Brasenose College, Oxford, with £10 a year issuing out of Goodwin's farm in this estate.[2] In 1683 William Cartwright's relict, Ursula, was lessee.[3] Thomas Cartwright sold the lease in 1713 to Dr. George Freeman, Rector of Steeple Aston, but Thomas Cabell of Bloxham remained the actual tenant until 1737.[4] By this time the 10-year lease had replaced the former long leases. The Davis family became the chief lessees in the 1770s when John Davis of Bloxham took up the lease; in 1793 it was renewed by his executors, and the rent, raised for the first time since 1602, was set at £16, 2,340 gallons of wheat and malt, and 40 fat wethers. In 1793 the lease was taken up by Harry Davis, and in 1797 by Samuel Davis, the Revd. Henry Davis, John Davis the younger, and others; again the rent was raised since Eton had the redeemed land-tax.[5]

By 1819 the rectory estate had been divided, although both halves were still leased by the Davis family. In 1819 John Davis of Bloxham and Samuel Davis paid a fine of £684 for a 10-year lease of the rectory-house and the Bloxham land for which they were to pay £23 8*s.*, 702 gallons of wheat and malt, and 12 fat wethers or £9 12*s.* a year. This land was leased again to the Davis family in 1822 and in 1826. The Milcombe part of the estate was also leased on 10-year leases, the lessees in 1820 being the Revd. Henry Davis and Samuel Davis. A £456 fine was levied and they paid £7 17*s.*, 468 gallons of wheat and malt, and 8 fat wethers in rent. The lease was renewed in 1822 and in 1826 but in 1829 the two estates were reunited and leased to William Davis, Samuel Davis of Hampshire, and John Davis the younger. The fine for a 10-year lease was then nearly £1,000, and Eton continued to lease the estate to the Davis family until at least 1856, a fine being regularly levied for each renewal.[6]

A small estate in Milcombe belonged to Merton Priory (Surr.). Roger Fitz Ralph (fl. early 12th century), probably the nephew of Niel d'Oilly, granted 2 hides to the priory in free alms;[7] the prior was one of the lords of the fee of d'Oilly in 1242 and held £1 10*s.* 8*d.* rent in Milcombe.[8] In 1538 the priory held 24*s.* assized rent in Milcombe.[9] After the Dissolution the estate was probably held by the former tenants.[10] In 1534 William Billing held tenements in Milcombe partly of Merton Priory and these may well have been among the proprety sold by John Billing to George Dalby in 1556.[11]

The Dalbys, a yeoman family, evidently profited by the break-up of the monastic estates in Bloxham and the 16th-century price revolution. Alice Dalby held a house and yardland under Eynsham Abbey in 1530; a John Dalby was resident in Milcombe in 1536; and in 1556 George Dalby, a yeoman of Milcombe, added to his holding by buying a farm-house, 4 yardlands, and Milcombe mill from John Billing.[12] On his death in 1570 he had a house in

[86] C 1/358/1; C 1/362/57; *Oxon. Visit.* 266.
[87] C.P. 25(2)/34/225/32.
[88] C.P. 25(2)/51/369/13.
[89] C.P. 25(2)/196/Hil. 8 Eliz. I; and above.
[90] C.P. 25(2)/34/227/2; C 136/85/15. For Peckham see *D.N.B.*
[91] C 142/56/5.
[92] C.P. 25(2)/76/651/10; *Oxon. Visit.* 223; and below.
[93] *Cal. Chart. R.* 1327–41, 332: inspeximus. For the make-up of the estate see p. 73.
[94] *Godstow Eng. Reg.* i, pp. 227–9.
[95] *V.C.H. Oxon.* ii. 74; *Valor Eccl.* (Rec. Com.), ii. 193.
[96] *L. & P. Hen. VIII*, xxi(1), p. 783.
[97] Eton Coll. Mun., Bloxham, no. 2. At the end of the 16th century the glebe and tithes were allegedly leased to 7 different persons: C 3/217/37.
[98] Eton Coll. Mun., Bloxham, nos. 4, 35.
[99] Ibid. no. 7.
[1] Ibid. nos. 11–15.
[2] *B.N.C. Monographs* (O.H.S. lii), no. IV, p. 25.
[3] For her see pp. 56, 74.
[4] Eton Coll. Mun., Bloxham, no. 183.
[5] Ibid. nos. 16, 22, 25, 26.
[6] Ibid. nos. 36, 38–40, 42, 44–46, 48, 50–61.
[7] *Recs. of Merton Priory*, ed. A. Heales, 16; *Godstow Eng. Reg.* i, p. 351.
[8] *Bk. of Fees*, 832; *Tax Eccl.* (Rec. Com.), 44.
[9] *Recs. of Merton Priory*, ed. A. Heales, app. clii, p. cxxx.
[10] In the 12th and 13th centuries the tenants were Elias son of William le Haneswell and his son Adam of Milcombe: *Recs. of Merton Priory*, ed. A. Heales, 16, app. lxvi, p. xlv.
[11] C 142/56/5; and see below.
[12] *L. & P. Hen. VIII*, xi, p. 481; Bodl. MS. Ch. Oxon. 3706, 3707.

Milcombe, held of Broughton manor.[13] His son John (d. by 1616) and grandson George Dalby (d. by 1626) succeeded.[14] Some of the Dalby estate, like the mill,[15] was sold in 1651 to John Youick and so came to the Cartwrights. In 1653, however, a John Dalby still held 5 yardlands in Milcombe.[16] A Dalby married George Violet of Sandford,[17] who in 1667 acquired from John Dalby of Sandford a 1,000-year lease of the farm-house where John Dalby of Milcombe had lived, and 14 yardlands in Milcombe.[18] This lease was held under the Cartwrights. In 1673 Joseph Key of London bought the freehold.[19] Josiah Key's daughter and heir Elizabeth married John Thornycroft and so brought the estate to that family.[20] Thornycroft, who was created a baronet in 1701 and became Sheriff of Oxfordshire, lived at Milcombe. He died in 1725 and his son Sir John Thornycroft died in prison in 1743 without heirs.[21] An Edward Thornycroft was still one of the chief landowners in Milcombe in 1793.[22]

Another farm in Milcombe was held by the Goodwins, a wide-spread family of gentry of yeoman origin in north Oxfordshire. In 1653 Richard Goodwin of the Lea in Swalcliffe, who had recently acquired 3 yardlands of the Allanson estate in Milcombe,[23] granted 5 yardlands there to the use of William, his son and heir. In 1656 John Cartwright bought from William Goodwin the freehold of 9 yardlands and a house.[24]

From *c.* 1180 until 1201 or 1202 Osbert of Headington held Crown land in Bloxham worth 32*s.* a year.[25] He was no longer in possession in 1203, and in 1219 Walter de Verdun had the custody of his heirs.[26] In 1230, after the death of John, Osbert of Headington's eldest son, his younger son William, born posthumously, claimed it from his cousin Ralph, son of Osbert's brother Richard, and in 1235 they agreed to divide 6 yardlands and 5*s.* rent in Bloxham and 2 yardlands in Headington.[27] They were no doubt the 6 yardlands held in demesne in 1284–5 by Adam of Headington and Ralph de Flore for $\frac{1}{7}$ fee.[28]

Ralph, son of Richard the Clerk of Milton, granted in free alms to the Hospital of St. John the Baptist in Oxford a house and 70 a. in Bloxham and Milton, with meadow in Bloxham, a grant confirmed by the king in 1240.[29] By 1270 the hospital had added to its land a house and 2 yardlands.[30] This land, like the hospital, went to Magdalen College, Oxford, in the 15th century; it was valued at 36*s.* 8*d.* in 1535.[31]

In the later 12th century Walter de Verdun gave Cirencester Abbey, in free alms, $\frac{1}{2}$ yardland in Bloxham, and his son Ralph added the other half. The yardland was held by Richard de Bereford who was also given to the abbey with his family and his service.[32] Walter later added another $\frac{1}{2}$ yardland, quit of all service except to the king.[33] Amaury de St. Amand confirmed this grant and freed the $\frac{1}{2}$ yardland of royal service.[34] Cirencester Abbey's Bloxham land was probably attached to its Adderbury manor.[35]

LOCAL GOVERNMENT. For most of the Middle Ages there were 4 manorial courts in Bloxham: the holders of the St. Amand (later Fiennes) manor, the royal (later Beauchamp) manor, and the rectory estate had assize of bread and ale and gallows,[36] while Eynsham Abbey held an ordinary manorial court for its Milcombe tenants.[37] These courts dealt with the usual business of manorial courts, for instance tenure, infringements of manorial custom, breaking of the assizes, overcharging, and assaults.[38]

When the Fienneses acquired both the principal manors they continued to hold the manorial courts separately, except on very rare occasions, as in July 1598, when a joint court of Bloxham Fiennes and Bloxham Beauchamp was held. Between 1631 and 1648 the courts leet and baron were held in the Town House before Lord Saye and Sele; when a joint court was held it was usually a court baron. The courts were held until 1925 but their work had long been confined mainly to the admission of tenants.

The main sources for local government in the 17th and 18th centuries are the constables' and overseers' accounts, beginning in 1684 and 1706 respectively, and the extensive records of the feoffees of the town estates.[39] For the purposes of local government Bloxham itself was divided into two distinct districts north and south of the river, and Milcombe formed a separate tithing. Two overseers were annually appointed for Bloxham, one each for the north and south sides of the river.[40] Two constables were similarly appointed to serve for a year, one for each side, and payments for ale to the surveyors of highways suggest that in 1686–7 there may have been 2 surveyors for each side of the river.[41]

[13] C 142/158/38.

[14] C 142/392/97; *Cat. Anct. D.* vi. C 7936; P.C.C. 74 Hele; C 3/400/8.

[15] See p. 72.

[16] Northants. R.O., Cartwright Mun.

[17] *Par. Colln.* ii. 209. For other Milcombe property acquired by Violet see Bodl. MS. Ch. Oxon. 40911.

[18] Northants. R.O., Cartwright Mun. A lease was also made in 1671.

[19] Ibid. For Key see G.E.C. *Baronetage*, iv. 186.

[20] *Par. Colln.* ii. 209.

[21] G.E.C. *Baronetage*, iv. 186.

[22] O.R.O., Milcombe incl. award.

[23] Northants. R.O., Cartwright Mun. and see above.

[24] Northants. R.O., Cartwright Mun.

[25] *Pipe R.* 1182 (P.R.S. xxxi), 123; ibid. 1201 (P.R.S. N.S. xiv), 206.

[26] Ibid. 1202 (P.R.S. N.S. xv), 204; *Bk. of Fees*, 252.

[27] P.R.O., Harrison Extracts, xiii. 231; *Fines Oxon.* 98.

[28] *Feud. Aids*, iv. 159.

[29] *St. John's Hosp. Cart.* (O.H.S. lxix), ii. 393; *Cal. Chart. R.* 1226–57, 254.

[30] *Cal. Chart. R.* 1257–1306, 135; *St. John's Hosp. Cart.* (O.H.S. lxix), ii, 400.

[31] *Valor Eccl.* (Rec. Com.), ii. 275.

[32] Ross, *Cirencester Cart.* ii, pp. 541–2.

[33] Ibid., p. 542.

[34] Ibid., pp. 542–3.

[35] The two were valued together: *Tax Eccl.* (Rec. Com.), 43*b*; *Valor Eccl.* (Rec. Com.), ii. 467.

[36] *Rot. Hund.* (Rec. Com.), ii. 32; *Plac. de Quo Warr.* (Rec. Com.), 663.

[37] *Eynsham Cart.* ii. 149.

[38] There are ct. rolls for Bloxham Beauchamp and Bloxham Fiennes from 1350 *penes* Lord Saye and Sele, Broughton Castle; B.M. Add. MSS. 9283–9289 (for 1658–60); B.M. Harl. MSS. 58, E 9, 11, 12 (extracts, Bloxham Beauchamp, 1479, 1499, 1505); B.M. Harl. Roll A 24 (for 1513); B.M. Harl. Rolls I 18–19 (Eynsham manor).

[39] Par. Rec., overseers' accts. 1706–1722, 1723–52, 1774–1813; constables' accts. 1684–1707, 1708–51; vestry mins. 1852–1942; O.R.O., Bloxham feoffees recs., townsmen's accts. 1674–1934 (8 vols.).

[40] In 1774 and 1801 4 overseers were appointed.

[41] Par. Rec., constables' accts.

Bloxham North and South were united for highway purposes in 1883.[42] Bloxham and Milcombe each had 2 churchwardens. All parish officials, except the tithingmen, were appointed in the Vestry. Office was normally held for one year, but between 1868 and 1880 the same overseers served for 2 or even 3 years. The constables in Bloxham dealt with the payment of muster masters for the militia, land tax, and carriage of the king's goods, and with the care of the vagrant poor. At some periods they also paid the Marshalsea money. Funds were raised by a levy on the yardland. From 1691 the levy was made on 94 yardlands for the north side and 62 for the south side.[43]

A great part in local government was played by the feoffees of the town estate, which had been given and was used for many town purposes as well as for the poor,[44] for example two sums of 3*s.* 4*d.* which Richard Dalby and John Samon each gave before 1602 as a stock for highway repairs. From 1627 the estate's income was divided into thirds, one of which was reserved for payments of fifteenths and other town charges, and part of another third was for the upkeep of the Great and Little bridges.[45]

The present consitution of the feoffees dates from two decrees of 1627 and 1635. Having criticized the old feoffees' administration of the estate the Charity Commissioners in 1627 appointed 16 new feoffees, of whom 3 were to serve annually as 'townsmen' to receive and disburse the profits; one townsman was to be elected by Viscount Saye and Sele and his heirs,[46] and the others by 6 holders of yardlands, the vicar, churchwardens, and overseers. These electors were to approve the accounts before they were inspected by the lord's steward at Broughton, and to appoint new feoffees when the number fell to eight. After 1635, because of the difficulty of finding 6 holders of yardlands willing to elect, all tenants and copyholders of over 20*s.* yearly were to elect 2 townsmen, and the lord's steward the third.[47] One townsman acted for the north side of the town, another for the south, and the third, elected by the steward, seems to have functioned as a watchdog on the other two. The vicar, churchwardens, and overseers continued to approve the accounts. In 1824 it was found that new feoffees were not elected but co-opted.[48]

The feoffees regularly repaired the bridges, and met most, if not all, the cost of rebuilding the Town House in 1689, paid for work on the school-house and pest-house, and built in 1781 new town houses, which were let at low rents to the poor. They paid for and sowed the furze seed on the common, counted the cattle there, and saw that the driftways to and from the common were kept clear. They paid for the scouring of the brooks and streams, particularly the Washbrook, the town ditch and gutters, and for cleaning the streets. In 1750 they completed the purchase of a fire-engine from a London manufacturer, and in 1846 assisted with the purchase of 'two new water carts in case of fire'. Regular payments were made from 1880 to 1929 for the upkeep and repair of the fire engine and town pump, and after that date they gave a yearly donation to the Bloxham Fire Brigade.[49]

The activities of the feoffees up to 1895, when the Local Government Act of 1894 was adopted, were supplemented by those of the vestry. In the 19th century there were constant disputes over the choice of parish officers, and between 1860 and 1873 over re-rating after the adoption of the Tenements Act. In 1863 the vestry sent a petition to Quarter Sessions asking that no steps be taken under the Provisional Order for the better management of highways with reference to Bloxham. In 1866 the parish favoured the continuation of the Turnpike Trust (Banbury, Chipping Norton, and Burford) even though it would cost them £232 yearly to take over their section.

Although threatened with an injunction in 1873 for alleged pollution of drinking water at Adderbury the vestry was unwilling to pay for an adequate drainage scheme, and opposed the view that one was necessary implied in a report of 1874; instead they declared that Broughton was to blame for pollution of the Sor Brook, that Bloxham's privies did not pollute the stream, and that the brook below the sewer was not used because there were springs. The cost of the drainage scheme was considered excessive and the vestry was hardly prepared to pay the £1,800 for which the rate had already been levied. They declared that there was 'no more healthy, cleanly, well cared for village in the whole of the Union than that of Bloxham'.[50]

If this was so, the feoffees are probably to be thanked. During the 19th century they laid down a drainage system of 6 cesspits, emptied by contract labour twice a year. When the Bloxham Gas Company started in 1870, they decided to provide street lighting, with 21 lamps, and until 1937 the village continued to be lit at their expense. They paid half the cost of repairing the Court (formerly Town) House in 1885–6, and £10 for fitting up the library there. After 1888 the Court House was used as a club and reading-room and the feoffees paid for the lighting until 1934 at least. By 1900 most of the streets were paved with York stone, at their expense.[51]

The primary responsibility for poor relief rested until 1834 with the vestry and its officers, the overseers of the poor, but much assistance was also given by the feoffees. The townsmen's records throw light on the treatment of the poor before 1700, when the overseers accounts begin. In 1700 tenants of 6 town houses were let off arrears of rent through their poverty. It was argued that if they had been turned out, the town would probably have found them other houses and paid the rent, and this 'would have been a much greater charge to the town'. Earlier, in 1678, the townsmen bought hemp to set the poor to work. Throughout the period for which there are records the feoffees provided rent free or very cheap housing for some paupers including paying for much repair work; after inclosure, which deprived the poor of their right to gather fuel on the commons and of common grazing rights, land for allotments was

[42] Par. Rec., vestry mins.

[43] Par. Rec., constables' accts. The overseers did not adopt this practice till 1810.

[44] For the history of the estate see pp. 83–84.

[45] *12th Rep. Com. Char.* 203.

[46] Ibid. The town estate was copyhold of the manor of which Viscount Saye and Sele was lord.

[47] Ibid. 203–4.

[48] Ibid. 207.

[49] Ibid. For the townsmen's role in poor relief see below.

[50] Par. Rec., vestry mins.

[51] O.R.O., Bloxham feoffees recs. and ex inf. Mr. C. Butler, Townsman, Bloxham.

provided, a small rent being charged to those who could afford it; money for apprenticeships was given; in 1758 the poor received £83 distributed in summer and winter at the rate of 1*s.* each to *c.* 346 adults who were neither property owners nor tradesmen and 6*d.* each to 416 children; in 1796 the townsmen paid £60 to the bakers to reduce the price of bread and in 1800 they were again forced to do this.[52]

The townsmen also handed over money to the overseers to assist in ordinary poor relief expenditure. These sums were occasionally considerable; in 1724 the overseers got £70, nearly two thirds of their expenditure, but the contribution normally varied between £20 and £40. After 1792, however, there was often no contribution at all, probably because the feoffees were giving more in direct relief. The total expenditure of the overseers in 1706 was £80 and up to 1740 the average annual total was *c.* £110. In the 1740s the sum fell to under £100 but in 1752 it was nearly £132 and it evidently continued to increase as, after a 22-year gap in the accounts, the average spent between 1774 and 1792 was over £400. Thereafter the figure rose steeply from £517 in 1793 to over £1,290 ten years later and the peak came in 1810 when £2,222 was spent. This was very heavy expenditure for a parish which throughout the period had just over 1,000 inhabitants. After the 1834 Act Bloxham became part of the Banbury Union and in 1835 only £1,185 was spent on relief;[53] in 1851–2 the figure had fallen to £496.[54]

The main item of the overseers' expenditure was the workhouse, first mentioned in 1736 when 24 people were living there. It seems to have been farmed out for monthly payments, at first for £7–£9, paid alternately by the overseers of the North and South sides. The reduction in the total spent on relief in the 1740s is reflected in the reduction of the monthly payment to under £5 but in 1774 the master of the workhouse was getting £26 5*s.* a month. In 1782 the workhouse costs were based on actual disbursements but two years later it was farmed out again, though after some discussion the parish reverted to actual bills in 1786, when the master got a salary of ten guineas. In the spring of 1800 the workhouse was costing up to £94 a month and in 1801 £152 but the figure went down to £60 in 1802 and in 1804 the workhouse was again let, at £60 a month.[55] Later an extra allowance was made for the increase in the price of bread. In 1811 a new form of contract was used; the master received 3*s.* 3*d.* a head a week for each of the 21 paupers. Workhouse costs were considerably reduced and the emphasis was probably shifting from in to out relief. Payments to roundsmen first appear in 1776 but they were not a regular feature in the accounts until *c.* 1803 when they were costing £3 5*s.* a month. In that year accounts for the South side were divided under the headings 'Account extraordinary', 'By the list', 'Workhouse Bills', 'Roundsmen and Boys', and 'For Soldiers' Wives'. Money was spent throughout on clothes and rent, on coals and medical care, and on apprenticeship fees, and the accounts also included lump sums for the constables' expenditure and the county rates. A pest-house was mentioned in 1813;[56] it seems to have been started in 1766 and was still in use in 1836.[57]

Milcombe's overseers, like the township's other officers, seem to have been quite independent of Bloxham; their accounts have not survived. In 1776 £49 14*s.* was spent on out-relief from a total of £61 6*s.* 8*d.* raised from rates.[58] There was the usual heavy increase in expenditure at the end of the 18th century; in 1802–3 £249 was spent on out-relief out of a total of £309 raised at a rate of 4*s.* 9¼*d.* At that date 14 adults and 58 children were receiving permanent relief, and 14 adults were occasionally relieved.[59] After 1834 Milcombe formed part of Banbury Union; in 1851–2 £126 was spent on the poor.[60] Milcombe, like Bloxham, had a town estate, administered by 2 elected townsmen and used partly for the poor and partly for the upkeep of public roads and bridges. It seems that the money was rarely used for the poor.[61] In 1825 the income from the estate was *c.* £22, which was applied, after necessary expenditure on repairs, in discharge of the constable's and churchwardens' expenses. In 1855 a third of the income of £33 went to the surveyor of highways and a third to the churchwardens.[62]

In 1602 Milcombe had 3 charities for mending the highways: Richard Dalby bequeathed and John Farthinge and John Stranke gave 6*s.* 8*d.* apiece.[63] No further reference to these sums has been found.

ECONOMIC HISTORY. In 1086 Bloxham formed only a part of a royal estate of 34½ hides, the details of which, as given in Domesday Book, apply to the whole. The food renders once paid to the king had been commuted for a corn rent almost equal in amount to that paid by the royal manor of Benson. The total rent had increased from £56 in 1065 to £67. The demesne was worked by as many as 27 serfs. The tenants included one free man, 72 *villani*, and 16 bordars. The free man, a thegn named Saiet, had served as a free man in the time of Earl Tostig, was later given by Earl Edwin to the Norman Ralph d'Oilly, and was finally returned to the royal demesne.[64]

Milcombe was established as a hamlet by at least 1065 and in 1086 comprised 2 estates, the 4½-hide manor of the Count of Evreux and Alfric's 3½ hides: this clearly represents the division of a single estate, for each held half the mill, half the meadow (30 a. in all), and half the pasture. The arable was divided into 3-plough lands on the Evreux estate and 2 on Alfric's, which was fully cultivated with 1½ plough on the demesne and ½ plough held by tenants. The Evreux estate, however, had only 1 plough and had decreased in value from £2 in 1065 to 30*s.* in 1086,

[52] O.R.O., Bloxham feoffees recs. For assistance given by the townsmen after 1805, when the poor's third was accounted for in a separate account, see p. 84.

[53] Par. Rec., overseers' accts.; *2nd Rep. Poor Law Com.* 290.

[54] *Poor Law Unions*, 21.

[55] Par. Rec., overseers' accts. As the high totals for workhouse at the turn of the century account for the bulk of poor relief expenditure, it is possible that some out-relief as well as in-relief was being farmed out to the master of the workhouse.

[56] Par. Rec., overseers' accts.

[57] O.R.O., Bloxham feoffees recs.

[58] *Poor Abstract*, 398.

[59] Ibid.

[60] *Poor Law Unions*, 21.

[61] For the history of the estate see pp. 84–85.

[62] *12th Rep. Com. Char.* 208; Char. Com., file B 70163.

[63] MS. d.d. Par. Bloxham b 1.

[64] *V.C.H. Oxon.* i. 395, 400–01.

while Alfric's farm retained its value of 30*s*. Three serfs and 4 bordars are recorded on the two estates and in addition 3 *villani* on Alfric's estate.[65]

The demesne farm of the royal manor in 1266 included 14 a. of meadow and 8 a. of pasture.[66] In the late 14th century this manor included a home farm with 200 a. of arable, 12 a. of meadow worth 2*s*. an acre, and 20 a. of separate pasture worth 30*s*. in all.[67] The St. Amand estate in 1285–6 also had a large demesne farm with 200 a. of arable worth 6*d*. an acre, 8 a. of meadow worth 3*s*. an acre, and 4 a. of pasture at 1*s*. 8*d*. an acre, a dovecot, and a water-mill.[68]

A fragmentary description of the royal manor in 1266 mentions sokemen, holding at least 60 yardlands, and cottars. In 1275–6 one free tenant held 9 a. another (the Abbess of Godstow) 100 a., and a third (Elias of Tingewick) 58 a., the mill, and 6 yardlands.[69] The standard holding of the sokemen was one yardland, but their rents and services are not known. There were at least 4 cottars on the royal manor who owed works.[70] On the St. Amand manor in 1285–6 there were 25 virgaters, each paying 4*s*. rent and services worth 2*s*. 8*d*. The services, which could be commuted, included harrowing and sowing for 1 day in Lent, ploughing for 1 day with 1 man, lifting and carting the lord's hay, and harvesting his corn with 1 man for 8 days and carting it for 2 days. The rents and works of cottars were worth 11*s*. 11*d*. and 14*s*. 8*d*.[71] On land held by Amaury de St. Amand in chief of Queen Eleanor were a further 8 tenants holding 1 yardland each in socage, paying 6*s*. rent together with reaping service for 8 days with 1 man, valued at 2*d*. a day.[72]

In both Bloxham and Milcombe were wealthier tenants able to sell and exchange lands freely; their grants are recorded in many Eynsham and Godstow charters.[73] In the tax assessments of the early 14th century large numbers of tenants were assessed at between 6*s*. and 2*s*. In 1316 23 tenants of the St. Amand manor were assessed at this rate, and in 1327 (the only complete tax list) two-thirds of the contributors paid over 2*s*., the highest paying 14*s*. and four others 7*s*. or 8*s*.[74] Milcombe too was a prosperous hamlet: more than half the 29 contributors in 1316 paid between 2*s*. and the highest contribution of 11*s*., whilst the total of £4 12*s*. was more than those of some of the smaller parishes in the hundred.[75]

The return of 1327 suggests that Bloxham town itself was more flourishing than any other rural community in north Oxfordshire. It had 70 contributors compared with Adderbury's 76, while its total assessment was over £2 more. As a parish Adderbury with its 3 hamlets was richer than Bloxham and Milcombe together.[76] This position was reversed, however, after the re-assessment of 1344.[77]

Milcombe had a separate field system, and it is possible that, as later, Bloxham had 2 sets of fields, divided by the brook.[78] A grant *c*. 1210 of 3 a. in the East Field and 3 a. in the West Field[79] suggests a 2-field system which probably still existed in the 14th century when 200 a. were equally divided into fallow and sown land.[80] Milcombe, however, had 3 fields *c*. 1235 when land in the South, West, and North fields was granted.[81] The lack of woodland on the Bloxham highlands was compensated for by the attachment to Bloxham manors of 2 woodland areas in Wychwood forest.[82] The valuation of Bloxham meadowland in 1286 at 3*s*. an acre suggests that it was scarce, whereas pasture may have been plentiful since ½ yardland in Milcombe carried with it 100 sheep commons.[83] In 1180–1 stock purchased for the royal manor included 250 sheep, and in 1194 300 sheep were bought in a half-year.[84] The existence of inclosed pasture on the demesne in the 14th century also suggests that sheep-farming for the wool market was important. Court rolls of the 14th century, however, suggest that on the whole farming practice was conservative. There seems to have been very little consolidation of holdings; one holding of 8 a. was distributed in 6 separate pieces.[85]

There is no clear indication that the population of the parish was reduced by the plague in the 14th century. In 1377 there were as many as 403 contributors to the poll tax.[86] That there had been some decline may perhaps be inferred from the policy of leasing adopted in the early 15th century. In 1431–2 the demesne of Bloxham Beauchamp manor was leased to 4 men for 12 years at £13 6*s*. 8*d*. a year, and in 1435–6 to 4 others for £13 a year. By the terms of the first lease the tenants were to hand back the demesne in the West Field well fallowed and manured; the fallow was to have been ploughed for the third time. By the second lease 20 a. were to be returned well fallowed, 7 a. ploughed for the third time, and 29 a. manured.[87] A close, the rabbit warren, the manorial courts, and feudal dues were excepted from the leases, but all houses on the manor were included and were to be kept in good repair. Roughly the same terms occur in a third lease of 1443–4,[88] but when the manor was leased a century later (1526–7, 1534–5) for 40 years, both warren and courts were also leased.[89]

Leasing was the rule, too, on the property of Eynsham Abbey by the 15th century; in 1438 the abbey received £3 12*s*. from assized rents, 7*s*. 6*d*. from other 'foreign' rents, and £1 10*s*. for customary aid. The total assized rent and aid of £13 13*s*. was the same 30 years later. Profits of court brought in an additional £4 10*s*.[90]

If there was any conversion to sheep-farming it was on a comparatively small scale. No inclosures were reported in 1517 and when the 2 main manors

[65] *V.C.H. Oxon.* i. 410, 424.
[66] C 145/131/3.
[67] C 136/8/3.
[68] C 133/43/5.
[69] C 145/13/13.
[70] Ibid.
[71] C 133/43/5.
[72] Ibid.
[73] e.g. *Eynsham Cart.* i, p. 212; *Godstow Eng. Reg.* i, pp. 352–9.
[74] E 179/161/8, 9, 10.
[75] E 179/161/9.
[76] E 179/161/10.
[77] See p. 189.
[78] See below.
[79] MS. Rawl. D 892, f. 1v. For date see *Rot. de Ob. et Fin.* (Rec. Com.), 461, where witnesses are pledges together in 1208.
[80] C 136/8/3.
[81] *Godstow Eng. Reg.* i, pp. 353–4.
[82] *Eynsham Cart.* i, pp. xiv, 52; ii, p. 93; *Rot. Hund.* (Rec. Com.), ii. 41–42; *Cal. Inq. p.m.* (Rec. Com.), ii, p. 81. Bloxham Wood is now represented by King's Wood and King's Wood farm and is part of Woodstock manor: see *Top. Oxon.* ed. A. W. Blanchett, nos. 5, 10.
[83] C 133/43/5; *Godstow Eng. Reg.* i, p. 357.
[84] *Pipe R.* 1181 (P.R.S. xxx), 110; ibid. 1194 (P.R.S. N.S. v), 88.
[85] B.M. Add. R. 41, 641; cf. *Godstow Eng. Reg.* i, pp. 358–9.
[86] E 179/161/44.
[87] MS. Rawl. D 892, ff. 9v.–11v.
[88] Ibid., f. 17v.
[89] Ibid. ff. 22v.–23, 24–24v., 26v.–27.
[90] B.M. Harl. R. I 17; ibid. G 2.

were surveyed in 1592 the only large demesne inclosure was 211 a. of pasture and meadow called the Grove, attached to the manor of Bloxham Fiennes. The rest of the manor consisted of 1,702 a. of 'fields, meads, and closes', less the area covered by the Fiennes part of Bloxham town. No closes at all were mentioned in the account of the 939 a. of Bloxham Beauchamp, which was described as consisting of fields and meads only, and of part of the town.[91] The date of the inclosure of the Grove is not known but it was presumably after 1421 when pasture at the Grove called 'cotemanlese' was recorded in connexion with a tenant's 12-acre holding.[92]

The date of the re-organization of the field system into 'quarters' is also unknown, but it was probably completed at the latest by 1542 when the term Broughton Quarter first occurs in the court rolls.[93] Whether the medieval fields were ever divided into 4 in accordance with the common practice found both in north Oxfordshire and elsewhere, or whether some more complicated arrangement based on furlongs was adopted at Bloxham is not altogether clear. Bloxham South field certainly seems to have been divided into the conventional 4 quarters. The 17th-century names Milcombe, Milton, Cowhill, and Ovenhill Quarters[94] survived until the inclosure of 1802.[95] Their position can be plotted and they evidently correspond to the 4 principal divisions of the field. In Bloxham North field, however, the arrangement was far more complicated. The names of 9 'quarters', undoubtedly in the North Field, occur in 16th- and 17th-century documents, and 7 of them at least are distinct 'quarters', and not merely alternative names.[96] A terrier of 1663 describing how 2 holdings of $1\frac{1}{2}$ yardland had been 'divided out of three yardlands in open court' throws some light on the problem of this re-organization.[97] The yardlands and $\frac{1}{2}$ yardlands

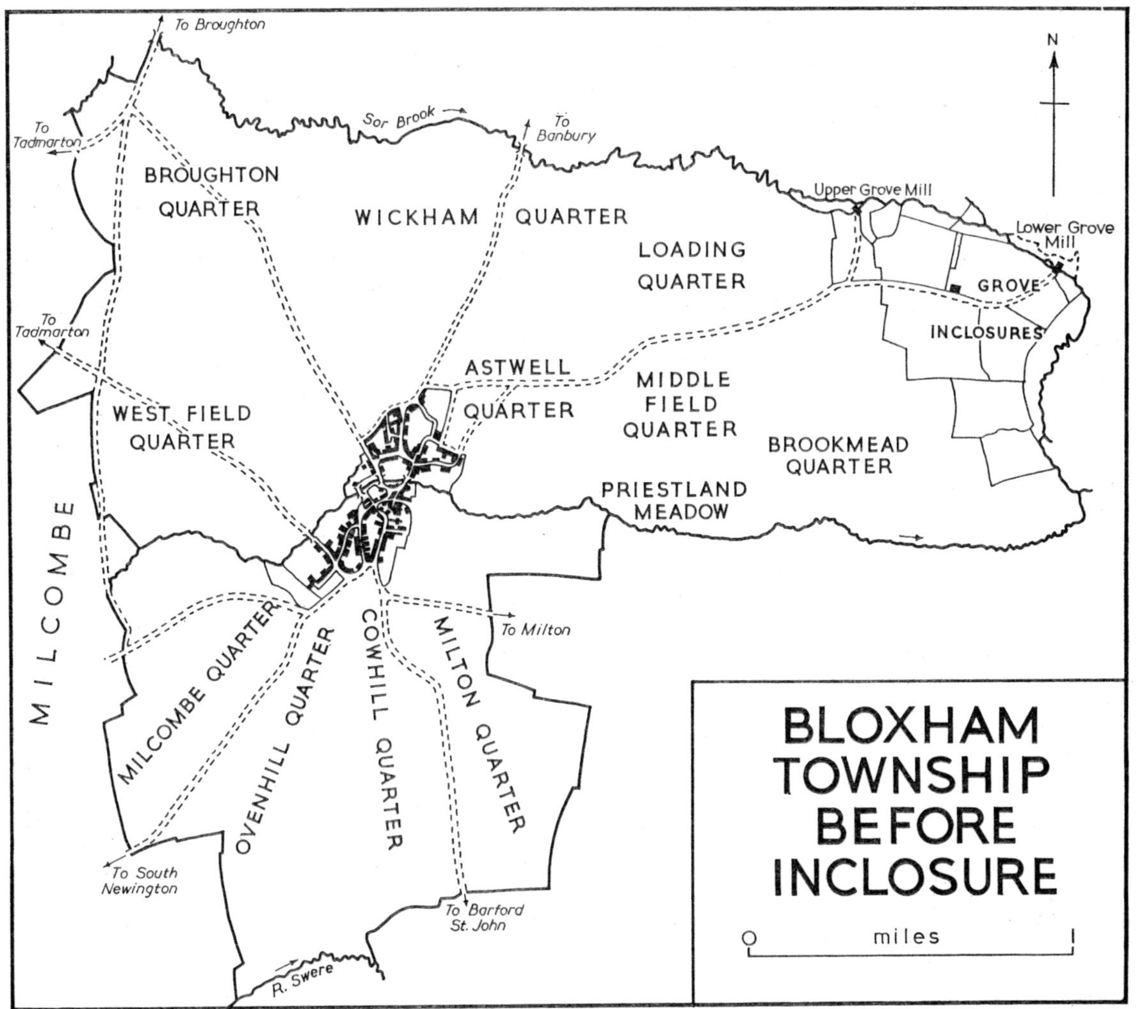

Based on Davis, *Oxon. Map* (1797) and the inclosure award and map (1801).

[91] MS. Rawl. D 892, f. 165v.

[92] Bloxham Beauchamp ct. roll, 1421–2. Rolls for the Beauchamp and Fiennes manors are at Broughton Castle, and are cited as Beauchamp or Fiennes ct. rolls.

[93] Fiennes ct. roll, Apr. 1542.

[94] Beauchamp ct. roll. Oct. 1655.

[95] O.R.O., incl. award and map.

[96] The 7 quarters are as follows: Broughton (Fiennes ct. roll, Apr. 1542), Grt. Lodyn (MS. d.d. Par. Bloxham b 1), Wickham (Fiennes ct. roll, Mar. 1602), Astwell and Brookmead (Beauchamp ct. roll, Oct. 1636), Middle Field and West Field (1663 deed). Grove, Southway, and Middle Path quarters may be alternative names (Beauchamp ct. rolls, Apr. 1618, Oct. 1665).

[97] O.R.O., Bloxham feoffees' recs.

were dealt with separately, but in each case the arable strips were divided into 4 groups. In one terrier these were Middle Field, Broughton and Astwell Quarters, Wickham and Westfield Quarters, and Loading (i.e. Lodyn) and Brookmead Quarters; in another terrier the fourth group was Loading and Westfield Quarter. It is possible, though evidence is lacking, that the quarters in Bloxham North were arranged to provide 2 separate rotation courses, and in such a large and dispersed area this would have been convenient. Peas were grown and there was some leys farming: a number of references to a tenant holding leys occur between 1513 and 1552,[98] while a peas field was mentioned in 1598.[99] Despite re-organization some holdings at least were in 1663 still minutely sub-divided: 1 yardland contained 25 strips and a ½ yardland 30 strips.[1]

At Milcombe the old 3-field organization had given way by the end of the 16th century to a complicated system based on quarters. These seem to have been in 2 sets, one on the north side, the other on the south side. In 1592 3 divisions of the field were specifically called quarters, of which one was the old South Field, presumably much diminished. These divisions all contained furlongs and leys ground, while water furrows were mentioned in one. In a terrier of 1769 6 quarters and South Field were mentioned, all apparently on the south side; in 1752 there were at least 3 quarters on the north side and 4 on the south side. Milcombe Field, as a whole, had an estimated 1,200 a.[2]

A custumal of 1552 for the 2 main Bloxham manors, then both in the hands of the Fiennes family, described the elaborate arrangements for the rights of the lord and tenants to several and common rights. It confirms the existence of leys farming and seems to point to a 2-year rotation, though there is also some evidence of a 4-year cycle. Some tenants, for instance, had common in Priestlands every second year when it lay fallow. Other land in the west part of Bloxham North was described as fallow every other year. On the other hand Chalcott Leys was several to the lord of Broughton 3 years together from Lady Day to Lammas and then common to the tenants of the north side. Various meadows were several for part of the year and common every other year. There is also a reference to the special rights of occupiers of 'ancient cottages' in Bloxham. They had the right to keep a cow on the common and one breeder. All tenants had the right to take the manure of beasts (heardlyme) going into 'Neelands' from Lady Day to St. John the Baptist's day.[3]

Over some of the customs of 1552 there were subsequent disputes. In 1556 Richard Fiennes was sued in Chancery by some of his tenants led by Anthony Councer. They complained about damage done to their corn by rabbits from the warren in the Grove, and about fines of 1*s.* and 2*s.* an acre of arable and meadow, which they claimed was more than the customary rate. Richard Fiennes proved that he had clear right to warren there, that damage by rabbits was less than ever before, and that the fines he charged were long since approved by custom. In 1569 it was agreed that he should henceforth breed rabbits within a limited area, which must be walled round, and that any rabbits found outside this area could lawfully be killed by the inhabitants. Anyone losing land when the Grove was walled was to be compensated with land elsewhere in the manors.[4]

The court rolls throw additional light on the husbandry of this period. Sheep were obviously kept in large numbers, for in 1514 it was ordered that a tenant should have no more than 90 sheep and another 100 commoning in the fields.[5] Each tenant was limited to a stint of 4 cows or 50 sheep to a yardland in 1535, and no 'ancient cottage' was to keep more than 1 cow and 2 pigs.[6] The number of sheep to a yardland was reduced in 1538 to 40, but exceptions were allowed.[7] Even so the increased allowance of 60 sheep to a yardland for the tenants of the north side in 1542 seems to have been a temporary measure; the reductions of stints on Bloxham Beauchamp manor to 20 sheep and 2 beasts in 1552 and 20 sheep and 8 lambs in 1617,[8] and presentations at the end of the 16th century for overloading the commons, keeping sheep on the fallow field, and sheep in the peas field, show that there was a growing pressure on the available commons.[9] Flocks of between 90 and 180 sheep and lambs are recorded in the 17th century and in 1717 John Youick had sheep valued at over £90 and beasts worth £66 6*s.*[10] As for crops, a farmer who died in 1615 was growing 28 a. of peas as well as barley, wheat, and maslin; another (d. 1667) had wheat, barley, peas, beans, oats, and vetches.[11] In 1718 the incumbent described Bloxham as fertile, champion, and having 'more corn than pasture'. In fact the only inclosure, apart from small inclosures in and on the outskirts of the town, was still the inclosure at the Grove. When surveyed in 1609 the Grove covered 206½ a. and included 4 fields and a number of meadow closes along the river banks.[12]

After the Reformation there were no long-standing resident landowners in Bloxham and the yeoman freeholders and copyholders were the dominant element in the community. The position of Bloxham tenants is fully defined in the 1552 custumal. It was there laid down that, since their status was especially privileged because Bloxham claimed to be ancient demesne, tenants could surrender their lands to whom they wished, in fee simple, estate tail, or for a term of life or lives, year or years. The words *ad voluntatem domini* were not to be inserted in the copies made by the lord's steward, as this was 'against the custom and repugnant to their estate'. These words had certainly appeared in the court rolls of 1536 and 1539, and this abuse was now rectified. No tenant could lease his land for more than one year; otherwise a lease was to be void but the land was not to be forfeit, although in 1543 a man who had leased his land for 20 years was declared to have forfeited it. A fixed scale of fines

[98] Beauchamp ct. roll, Oct. 1513; Mar. 1532, Mar. 1534; MS. d.d. Par. Bloxham b 1.
[99] Fiennes ct. roll, Oct. 1598.
[1] O.R.O., Bloxham feoffees recs., terrier 1663.
[2] Eton Coll. Mun., Bloxham, nos. 139, 140, 145, 147.
[3] MS. d.d. Par. Bloxham b 1.
[4] Ibid.; O.R.O., Bloxham feoffees' recs. (uncat.).
[5] Beauchamp ct. roll, May 1514.
[6] Ibid. Apr. 15 35.
[7] Ibid. Apr. 1538; Oct. 1541.
[8] Ibid. Fiennes ct. roll, Apr. 1542; Beauchamp ct. roll Mar. 1552; Fiennes ct. roll, Apr. 1617.
[9] Ibid.; Fiennes ct. roll, Oct. 1598.
[10] MS. Wills Oxon. 85/4/28; 12/3/21; 78/2/4; 132/3/6; 159/5/19.
[11] Ibid. 30/2/24; 78/2/4.
[12] MS. Rawl. B 400b, f. 134. feoffees' recs.

was set down; only one heriot was payable even if many separate tenements were held, and this rule applied whether the tenant had died, or had surrendered his land to another, when heriot was also taken. Where land had been handed over to a group of tenants or to feoffees, no heriot was to be paid until the death of the last tenant or feoffee.

Descent was to the heirs at common law, including daughters, and a married man holding land in the manor could surrender it to his wife for her life, and to her heirs. But no tenant could take a surrender from a woman without the presence of the steward. Elaborate precautions were laid out to ensure that any heir who was sick, imprisoned, or 'letted in the Kinge's warres' could appoint a deputy to enjoy the profits of the land until he was able to come to take his oath of fealty. If he was able to come and did not do so, the lord might seize the land until fealty was taken. All cases relating to land were to be brought to the lord's court, unless a writ of right close had been taken out.[13]

It appears to have been necessary to re-affirm the rights and privileges of the tenants of Bloxham in 1606 when Richard, Lord Saye and Sele, sold some land to a syndicate of Banbury drapers. He covenanted with all his tenants, the feoffees of Bloxham, Adderbury, and Deddington town lands, and 94 others, that in spite of the sale they would still hold their lands by the payment of the ancient and accustomed yearly rents, and all fines and heriots would be extinguished. This extinction of fines had first been applied to the 23 properties of Bloxham town estate in 1602 and was now extended to all tenants. It was still to be lawful for them to surrender land to others, the new owner being admitted without fine or heriot, and heirs to copyholds would be admitted without fines too. Tenants were to be free of reeveship and gathering the lord's rent, and could have a court baron if they wished and if they bore the cost.[14]

Out of 81 contributors to the subsidy of 1523 there was a group of 15 who were assessed at comparatively high rates — 6 at between £20 and £25 and 9 at between £10 and £20. At the other end of the scale were 32 labourers paying the lowest possible rate of 4*d.*[15] Of those assessed William Councer, taxed on £60, was outstanding and his family illustrates the rapid rise of a yeoman family into the ranks of the lesser gentry. William appeared regularly in the court rolls of the 16th century and was already occasionally styled 'gentleman'. He was followed by Anthony and Edward Councer, both of whom played a large part in Bloxham affairs.[16] The family owned two mills and when George Councer died in 1629 his estate was worth £957.[17] Although George Councer was undoubtedly more prosperous than most of his fellow townsmen, there were several yeoman farmers who had by this time acquired considerable wealth. John Lovell (d. 1634), for example, had chattels worth £385; John Stranke of Milcombe (d. 1617) left goods valued at £305, and Clement Stranke (d. 1639) left £205 worth.[18] In the second half of the 17th century the Councer family was still pre-eminent, for Jeremy Councer (d. 1667) left well over £1,000 in chattels, but there was still a flourishing group of yeoman farmers, such as Willam Huckle (d. 1681), whose inventory totalled £280.[19]

In the later 18th century rather more than half the 90 landowners in Bloxham South were tenants and 72 of the total number held only small properties assessed for land tax at under £1. Of the 42 owner-occupiers William Davis and George Councer held the largest estates, paying taxes of over £16 and £14 respectively, while 2 tenant farmers paid £11 2*s.* and £9 17*s.* 8*d.* No others were assessed above £5. In Bloxham North all the large farms were held by tenants: one belonging to George Warriner was rated at £23; another held by Elizabeth Cartwright at over £22. Of the remaining 30 properties assessed at over £1 6 were assessed at between £5 and £15 and 24 between £1 and £5. There were 7 owner-occupiers in this group, of whom 4 were assessed at between £7 and £11.[20]

In Milcombe the chief proprietors were Edward Thornycroft, with land assessed at over £18, and William Cartwright of Aynho and the Revd. Henry Davis with land assessed at £11 and £8 16*s.* respectively. There were 7 farms rated at *c.* £5, and 9 at under £1, most of which were owner-occupied.[21] Inclosure in 1794 made little immediate difference to this pattern in Milcombe. After allotments for tithes and glebe, most of which was leased by the Davis family,[22] the main allotments were to William Cartwright, lord of the manor (255½ a.), and Edward Thornycroft (308 a.). There were 4 of between 122 and 79 a. The remainder were much smaller. John Davis had 22½ a., the feoffees of Bloxham town land 22½ a., the feoffees of Milcombe town land 12½ a., and the poor 16 a. In all 1,135½ a. were inclosed and there were approximately 119 a. of old inclosure.[23]

In Bloxham the pattern of landholding was confirmed by the inclosure of 1802. There were 2,773 a. to be inclosed; old inclosures, including roads and house plots, amounted to only 366 a. After allotments for tithes and glebe,[24] John Preedy and George Warriner received 386 a., George Councer, Robert Potter, Henry Davis, and the Bloxham feoffees received between 118 and 98 a., and 6 others received between 50 and 100 a. Of the allottees 89 had under 50 a., and two-thirds of those had less than 20 a.[25]

Arthur Young visited Bloxham 10 years after inclosure and was particularly impressed by 2 farmers, Warriner and Davis. The latter he described as an excellent practical farmer, who had had a great deal of experience as an inclosure commissioner, 'having been employed upon 26 at the same time'. Davis thought that inclosure had greatly increased arable production and that as much could now be grown on half the number of acres as on the whole before, with turnips and grass taking up the other half. Though much grass-land had been ploughed up, much had been laid down, and he considered the position was practically unchanged. He claimed that although rents had gone up the effect

[13] MS. d.d. Par. Bloxham b 1.
[14] O.R.O., Bloxham.
[15] E 179/161/196, 198.
[16] Bloxham ct. rolls, *passim.*
[17] See p. 72; MS. Wills Oxon. 12/3/21.
[18] MS. Wills Oxon. 139/2/7; 85/4/28; 148/4/1.
[19] Ibid. 75/2/4; 132/3/6.
[20] O.R.O., land tax assess. 1785–1831.
[21] Ibid.
[22] See p. 62.
[23] O.R.O., Milcombe incl. award; Gray, *Engl. Field Systems*, 537.
[24] See pp. 73–74.
[25] O.R.O., Bloxham incl. award; see also Bloxham Incl. Act, 39 & 40 Geo. III, c. 12 (priv. act).

on the poor had been small, since only the inhabitants of 'ancient' cottages had had the right to graze cows on the common; others, however, disagreed with this view.[26] Both farmers experimented with new crops and machinery. Warriner had introduced a threshing-mill, as well as two Rotherham ploughs and a Nottinghamshire ploughman to work them. Davis drilled everything, all white corn, peas and beans, and turnips; drilling was condemned by his neighbours but produced an astonishing wheat crop. Young did not fully approve of the rotation adopted by either. Davis planted first turnips, then barley, followed by 2 lots of seeds, then wheat, and finally two-thirds oats and one-third peas and beans. Warriner grew turnips, followed by clover, then barley or spring wheat, and lastly wheat. He did not grow oats since he did not think that two white crops should immediately succeed one another. Both men experimented with new crops; Warriner had made a great success of spring wheat where his neighbours had failed, and his crop was good and worth more than barley. Over all he took 4 qr. per acre of wheat, compared with the county average of three. He had grown 6 a. of cabbage in 1806 and 5 in 1807, which was unusual in Oxfordshire. He 'ate them off' with sheep, getting better corn crops afterwards. He had also successfully grown carrots to feed his horses and cows, and parsnips with less success. Davis had tried swedes, grew turnips to 'eat off' with sheep, and had successfully reversed the common practice by feeding his clover to animals the first year and mowing it the second. Warriner laid down 2½ a. with meadow fescue in 1806 and from the seed was planting 14 more in 1807, mixed with Dutch clover. He also followed the Bloxham practice of laying 15 to 25 qr. per acre of loamy sand or lime on the red land and found it successful. As for stock Davis was changing to shorthorns since they gave more milk and butter. He had a cross between Leicestershire and Gloucestershire sheep, bought after inclosure; he did not fold them but kept them on large tracts of land in summer and normally got more rams than ewes. Altogether Young gave a picture of 2 able farmers, keeping abreast of the times and willing to experiment, and no doubt exercising considerable influence on Bloxham agriculture.[27]

Twenty years after inclosure Bloxham South remained much the same as before. In 1826 there were 81 proprietors, 42 of them owner-occupiers, of whom 36 had houses or land assessed at less than £1. Most of the land was held by copyhold or 'college hold'. The rents of the various properties were given with this 1826 assessment; there were 5 over £100, of which the highest were the former Councer estate at £250 and another estate at £235. In Bloxham North there were 83 proprietors, 34 of them owner-occupiers, 26 having only a house or a house and a small piece of land. The chief proprietors were George Warriner, occupying his own land at a rent of £458, and Eton College, which leased its property at a rent of £405. There was one other large farm with a rent of £228, 4 with rents between £100 and £200, and 10 with rents between £50 and £100.[28]

In Milcombe the former Cartwright estate was leased at £320 and the Thornycroft estate was leased at £332. There were 3 other farms at rents between £160 and £93 and the rest were below £50. The 1831 assessment shows that most of these properties were freehold.[29]

Although there was some agricultural progress in Bloxham in the early 19th century there was also much distress. There were many unemployed weavers, and large sums were spent on poor relief up to 1835.[30] The townsmen allowed 15 per cent. discount on the rent of some of the town's tenants in 1821, 1823, and 1830.[31] The effects of the introduction of the Speenhamland system and of the inclosures were felt keenly: an unknown author in 1834 addressed the inhabitants of Bloxham on the inadequate supply of allotments, on pauperization, and the ill effects of inclosure.[32] Nevertheless, the feoffees and other responsible officers and inhabitants of Bloxham managed to keep the poor of Bloxham from participating in the disturbances at Banbury in the winter of 1830. The poor were rewarded for their law-abiding behaviour by a distribution of 20 fat sheep and 11 tons of coal which had been paid for by private subscription.[33] The feoffees also acted quickly by making more land available for allotments. This, however, only partly solved the problem, for there were cases of arson and on one occasion the Court House was stormed and a meeting of the feoffees broken up.[34]

Later in the century the agricultural depression brought further economic distress to both farmers and labourers. One of the effects was the growth of larger farms. As early as 1851 this trend was clearly visible:[35] there was one large estate farm of 359 a. at the Grove on which 12 men were employed, 4 farms between 200 and 300 a., and 4 between 100 and 200 a. Most of the small farms were under 40 a. and included one at Milcombe which evidently specialized in medicinal plants. The owner, described as a farmer and druggist, employed 6 men and a boy on a 36 a. farm. In 1867 and 1876 there were 19 farms of under 100 a. The 3 largest farms at Milcombe were owned in 1876 by New College (418 a.), Christ Church (282 a.), and Eton College (173 a.). There were 7 farms at Bloxham of between 120 and 350 a., the largest being that owned and occupied by George Warriner.[36] At Milcombe there were only 5 farmers in 1903,[37] compared with 8 in 1851. The farming was, and remained, mainly mixed. In 1914 44 per cent. of each cultivated acre was arable and of this, 24 per cent. in Bloxham was under wheat, 17 per cent. in Milcombe. Barley was the next most important crop, in Bloxham as important as wheat, in Milcombe more so. Oats, swedes, turnips, mangolds, and potatoes made up the rest. Of the cultivated area in both parishes 56 per cent. was permanent pasture and in both places for every 100 a. cultivated there were 21 head of cattle; there were 7 cows and heifers per 100 a. in Bloxham and 5 in Milcombe. Sheep were much more important, with

[26] See below.

[27] Young, *Oxon. Agric.* 4, 86, 93, 94, 95, 106, 109, 138, 142, 148, 153, 161, 175, 184, 189, 218, 260–1, 263, 280, 312.

[28] O.R.O., land tax assess. 1826–30.

[29] Ibid.

[30] Young, *Oxon. Agric.* 44; and see p. 65.

[31] O.R.O., Bloxham feoffees' recs., townsmen's accts. 1797–1846.

[32] Pamphlet printed by Messrs. Cheney & Sons in 1834.

[33] *The Herald*, 8 Jan. 1831.

[34] O.R.O., Bloxham feoffees' recs.

[35] H.O. 107/1733.

[36] O.R.O., Bloxham feoffees' recs., valuation lists 1867, 1876.

[37] *Kelly's Dir. Oxon.* (1903).

52 and 71 per 100 a. in 1909 and 45 and 54 in 1914. Small numbers of horses and pigs were kept in both areas.[38]

By 1963 there were 15 farms, and a smallholding of 40 a. belonging to the feoffees. Most Bloxham farms were under 150 a., and therefore small, but Bloxham Grove had *c.* 350 a., Ells farm 300 a., and Rectory farm 240 a., while Manor farm at Milcombe had 300 a. The increasing traffic on the main road, which cut off farmers living in Bloxham from their land, combined with the high prices being offered for building sites, was leading many farmers to sell part of their land for housing.[39]

Although Bloxham was predominantly a farming community its size and its proximity to Banbury encouraged other occupations. Medieval evidence is scant: fine stone quarried in Bloxham was used for the seats of the priory church at Bicester in 1296,[40] a fishmonger was living in the town in 1467, and there may have been an early fulling mill in Bloxham.[41] A wool-winder occurs in 1636 and by 1768 at least there was a woollen manufactory employing a number of weavers.[42] A master hemp dresser and weaver, Matthew Jellyman, occurs in 1773.[43] In the early 19th century there were shag-weavers and plush-weavers in the town,[44] and the 1851 census listed 13 weavers, of whom 5 were employed in Edward Gascoigne's plush manufactory; the other 4 plush-weavers, 3 linen-weavers and a ribbon-weaver probably worked for Banbury masters.[45] In 1864 there was a rope and twine maker in Bloxham.[46]

The building trade continued to be important. In 1851 there were 11 stone-masons, 15 slatters, thatchers, carpenters and plasterers, and a brick-maker.[47] One marble-mason, George Cakebread,[48] was outstanding and was responsible for an elaborate classical monument to the Hitchcock family in the churchyard at Deddington; throughout the later 19th century the Adkins family of masons was particularly prominent. In 1851 one master carpenter employed 6 men, and the Butler family of carpenters later introduced a saw-mill and timber-yard which by 1900 employed 40 men.[49]

After the First World War ironstone was exploited. In 1918 the Bloxham and Whiston Iron Co. were in possession of 191 a. of land in Bloxham, in 1919 Lord Saye and Sele leased more land to the Brymbo Steel Co.,[50] and by 1939 the Claycross Coal and Iron Co. was established in Bloxham.[51] Since the Second World War other industries have started. In 1947 I. & C. Steele and Co. Ltd. established a carpet-mill with 3 looms and 6 employees, choosing Bloxham because of its central position and good rail connexions. In 1964 it was specializing in Wilton carpets of high quality, partly hand-made. There were 6 looms and *c.* 30 employees, most of whom lived in the parish.[52] The firm of Tibbett & Co., which manufactured ready-to-build concrete structures, expanded rapidly after it came to Bloxham in the late 1950s and in 1964 there were 30–40 employees.[53]

The growth in trade and industry, and the existence of a boys' public school and girls' private school in Bloxham, led in the 19th century to an increased demand for shops. Already in 1851 there were 4 grocers and 15 tailors, besides several shoemakers and bakers, dress-makers and milliners, a coal dealer, and a watch and clock maker.[54] By 1864 a chemist's shop had opened; later the Banbury Co-operative and the Gas Light and Coke Co. were established. In the 19th century 3 carriers plied daily to and from Banbury[55] and apparently the innkeepers and the maltsters flourished. The use of private cars and the opening of a bus service between Bloxham and Banbury in 1910 gradually increased the dependence of the town on Banbury, but by 1964 the growing residential population had encouraged the opening of new shops. There was still a post office and a Co-operative Stores; there were also 5 general stores, 6 other shops, and 6 public houses.

MILLS. In the late 19th century there were 3 water-mills in the parish: Upper Grove Mill and Lower Grove Mill lay on the Sor Brook in the north and there was a third mill in Milcombe.[56] The 2 Bloxham mills probably descended from 2 of the 6 mills which belonged to the royal estate at Bloxham and Adderbury in 1086.[57] Their descent is confused, however; leasing and sub-leasing was common[58] and it is not clear whether references to Bloxham mills relate only to the 2 Grove mills under various names or to other ephemeral water-mills.

In 1241–2 William de St. Amand was farming one or more Bloxham mills along with other royal mills.[59] In 1273 Elias of Tingewick held 2 Bloxham mills. One had been held of the Crown by William de Mategrey in the time of Henry III, and had been granted to Elias by Queen Eleanor; the other was granted by Elias to Amaury de St. Amand.[60] On Amaury's death in 1285 it was valued at 13*s.* 4*d.*[61] and it descended with the St. Amand manor until it was sold by Eleanor de St. Amand to Thomas Wykeham shortly before 1431–2, the year in which Wykeham granted it to trustees.[62] It was then known as Clare Mill, and is not to be confused with another of Thomas Wykeham's mills, called Wykham Mill, which also lies on the Sor Brook, but just within the parish of Banbury. Clare Mill presumably passed with the manor from the Wykehams to the Fiennes family in *c.* 1455.[63] Deeds of the mill are

[38] Orr, *Oxon. Agric.*, statistical plates.
[39] Local information.
[40] J. C. Blomfield, *Deanery of Bicester*, ii. 139.
[41] MS. Rawl. D 892, f. 11: William Fuller mentioned.
[42] O.R.O., feoffees' recs., indenture; MS. Oxf. Dioc. d 558.
[43] *Oxf. Jnl.* 11 Dec. 1773.
[44] R. P. Beckinsale, 'The Plush Industry of Oxfordshire', *Oxoniensia*, xxviii. 58; Young, *Oxon. Agric.* 44.
[45] H.O. 107/1733.
[46] *Kelly's Dir. Oxon.* (1864).
[47] H.O. 107/1733.
[48] Gunnis, *Dictionary of Sculptors*.
[49] *Kelly's Dir. Oxon.* (1864 and later edns.).
[50] Broughton Castle, Saye and Sele loose deeds.
[51] *Kelly's Dir. Oxon.* (1939).
[52] Ex inf. the Manager.
[53] Ibid.
[54] H.O. 107/1733.
[55] *Kelly's Dir. Oxon.* (1864 and later edns.).
[56] O.S. Map 6″ Oxon. IX (1st edn.).
[57] *V.C.H. Oxon.* i. 400.
[58] Bloxham Beauchamp and Bloxham Fiennes ct. rolls at Broughton Castle.
[59] *Pipe R.* 1242 (ed. H. L. Cannon), 123–4.
[60] *Rot. Hund.* (Rec. Com.), ii. 32; MS. Rawl. D 892, f. 3v.
[61] C 133/43/5.
[62] MS. Rawl. D 892, f. 8v.; Clare Mill is also mentioned in the early 15th century: C 1/17/181.
[63] See p. 60.

mentioned in a Chancery suit of *c.* 1500,[64] but no later reference to the name Clare has been found; it is likely that it was this mill that Richard Fiennes leased for 41 years in 1581–2 to Thomas Blyth, miller of Bodicote, under the name of Bloxham Grove Mill.[65] In 1602–3 Sir Richard Fiennes granted a water-mill, presumably this one, to Thomas Chamberlain[66] and 20 years later Sir Thomas Chamberlain was in possession of 2 Bloxham water-mills, which he leased to 3 tenants.[67] His grandson Sir Thomas held it in 1681.[68] This mill was almost certainly the later Lower Grove Mill for a lease of 'Grove Mill' was made by the Dashwoods to Robert Marriot, who was tenant in 1797.[69] Marriot's mill is marked on Davis's map on the site of the modern Lower Grove Mill.[70]

A Bloxham mill described as Grove Mill belonged to the Beauchamp manor in 1473.[71] By 1513 William Councer was the lessee, and he was still in possession in 1532 with Thomas Perkins and James Merynge,[72] who was leasing the manor by 1534.[73] Councer, however, sublet his share first in 1533 and then again in 1535–6 to Anthony Bustard of Adderbury who took it on an 80-year lease.[74] George Councer was seised of 2 water-mills in 1635 and in 1662 Jeremy Councer surrendered them to Michael Bellow and his heirs.[75] The second water-mill might have been purchased from Sir Thomas Chamberlain, who, as has been said, was holding 2 mills in the 1620s.

The Grove mills were named in the 1851 census and in 1869. By 1887 Upper Grove Mill had passed to the Cherry family who worked it until at least 1939. Bloxham Grove (or Lower Grove) Mill did not operate after 1903.[76]

Richard Madsey, recorded as the holder of a horse-mill in 1513 and of a water-mill in 1516[77] may have been a tenant of one of the Grove mills. There was at least one other water-mill in Bloxham, however: in 1544–5 Roger Carroll obtained a 21-year lease of a mill which had once belonged to Chacombe Priory (Northants.). It was regranted to Richard Pettifer in 1554.[78] Finally frequent references to Windmill Hill occur in court rolls from 1618 and the remains of a windmill are visible on the hill next to Upper Grove Mill.

Milcombe Mill was situated in the extreme south-east corner of the township. In 1086 it was divided between the Count of Evreux and Alfric, each drawing 2*s.* from it yearly.[79] By the 14th century it had passed to Eynsham Abbey, the tenant being Margery, daughter and heir of Robert de Bereford of Milcombe; it remained on her death, by the courtesy of England, to her husband Edmund Waldyff (d. 1394).[80] In the 15th century the mill was in the hands of the Eburton family; in 1547 it was transferred from Alice Eburton of Milcombe, widow, and her son Thomas, to her son Richard Eburton, a London draper,[81] and later descended to Edmund Peckham, a relation by marriage.[82] In 1530 it was sold with half the manor to William Billing.[83] At this time it was held partly of the Prior of Merton and partly of Richard Fiennes.[84] The Billings continued to hold Milcombe Mill until 1556, when John Billing of Deddington granted it to George Dalby of Milcombe.[85] It remained in the Dalby family until 1651, when John Dalby of the Middle Temple sold his estate in Milcombe to John Youick.[86] In 1665 Youick sold the mill to John Cartwright, and in 1667 Cartwright leased this water-mill and a windmill to John Parsons of South Newington.[87] The water-mill was still in operation in 1887, but had closed down by 1903.[88]

CHURCHES. The earliest evidence of the existence of a church at Bloxham is a charter of 1067 by which William I granted it to Westminster Abbey.[89] Since Bloxham was an important royal manor in the late Anglo-Saxon period,[90] however, its church was probably founded before the Conquest. Milcombe was a dependant chapelry of Bloxham until it became a separate parish in 1854. Until at least the 13th century there was a chapel on part of Bloxham manor in Wychwood forest.[91]

About 1180 Henry II granted the church to Godstow Abbey;[92] it was held by the abbess and convent until the Dissolution when it passed first to the Crown and in 1547 to Eton College.[93] In the Middle Ages presentations were normally made by Godstow;[94] in 1312, however, the Pope provided, and in 1349 the king presented while Godstow was vacant.[95] Out of the next 8 presentations at least 5 were made by Godstow. At the end of the 14th century the patronage appears to have been granted to Sir Thomas West, for in 1407 the king presented during the nonage of Sir Thomas's heir.[96] In 1487 the abbess granted the right of presentation to a group of persons.[97] In 1504 the Archdeacon of Lincoln and others presented by reason of a grant made to them by the late Abbess of Godstow, but the patronage was again exercised by the abbey in 1511 and 1519. Before its dissolution the abbey granted the next turn to the Bishop of Lincoln who exercised his right in 1545;[98] in 1547, however, the advowson passed with the rectory to Eton College,[99]

64 C 1/17/181.
65 Broughton Castle, misc. deeds.
66 C.P. 25(2)/198/Mich. 44 Eliz. I.
67 C.P. 25(2)/340/Trin. 19 Jas. I.
68 O.R.O., Dashwood deeds (uncat.).
69 Ibid.; Act for . . . sale of estates of late Sir James Dashwood, 37 Geo. III, c 101 (priv. act).
70 Davis, *Oxon. Map* (1797).
71 Bloxham Beauchamp ct. roll, Oct. 1473.
72 Ibid. Oct. 1513; Mar. 1532.
73 MS. Rawl. D 892, f. 26.
74 Bloxham Beauchamp ct. roll, Mar. 1533; ibid. June 1538.
75 Bloxham Beauchamp ct. roll, Oct. 1635; ibid. Apr. 1663.
76 H.O. 107/1733; *Kelly's Dir. Oxon.* (1869 and later edns.).
77 Bloxham Beauchamp ct. roll, Sept. 1516.
78 *Cal. Pat.* 1553–4, 482.
79 *V.C.H. Oxon.* i. 410, 424.
80 C 136/85/15; *Cal. Inq. p.m.* iii, p. 185. In 1422–3 the rent was 6*s.* 8*d.*; B.M. Harl. R. I. 18.
81 *Cal. Close*, 1454–61, 258.
82 For him see *D.N.B.* and p. 62.
83 C.P. 25(2)/34/227/East. 21 Hen. VIII.
84 C 142/56/5.
85 MS. Ch. Oxon. 3706.
86 MS. Ch. Oxon. 3708.
87 Northants. R.O., Cartwright Mun.
88 Billing, *Dir. Oxon.* (1854); *Kelly's Dir. Oxon.* (1869 and later edns.).
89 *Cal. Chart. R.* 1327–41, 332: inspeximus.
90 See pp. 57–58.
91 See below.
92 *Godstow Eng. Reg.* i, p. 227.
93 *V.C.H. Oxon.* ii. 74; *Cal. Pat.* 1547–8, 9.
94 e.g. *Rot. Grosse.* 443; *Reg. Sutton*, i. 341. For a list of presentations see MS. Top. Oxon. d 460.
95 *Cal. Pat.* 1348–50, 300; *V.C.H. Oxon.* ii. 75.
96 *Cal. Pat.* 1405–8, 384, 457.
97 MS. Top. Oxon. c 394, p. 205.
98 MS. Oxf. Dioc. d 105, p. 13.
99 *Cal. Pat.* 1547–8, 9.

which regularly presented until the union of the benefices of Bloxham and Milcombe in 1921, when the Rector of Wigginton was granted one turn in four.[1]

The rectory was valued in 1254 at £13 13*s.* 4*d.*[2] and in 1291 at £23 6*s.* 8*d.*, after the deduction of a pension of £3 6*s.* 8*d.* paid to Westminster Abbey.[3] In 1535 it was farmed for £21 a year, and there were a few payments from tenants which appear also to belong to the rectory.[4] In 1679 its net value was £200 and in 1769 £406.[5] The rectory comprised tithes and glebe. The tithe customs of the parish were complex and until inclosure in the late 18th century there were disputes from time to time with the Vicar of Bloxham over small tithes, and with the Rector of Wigginton over tithes in Milcombe.[6] Godstow's share of the tithes was increased *c.* 1270 by the grant by Amaury de St. Amand of the great and small tithes of his demesne and tenant land in Bloxham, and a similar grant in 1346 by Sir Roger Beauchamp whose aunt Maud was the abbess.[7] Sir Roger also gave the tithes of his own and his tenants' woodlands and assarts in Queenwood in Wychwood forest.[8] In 1608 the rectorial tithes, by then in the hands of Eton College, included tithe of corn on any land then greensward, inclosed or not, which should be broken up or sown thereafter.[9] In 1793 Eton College was paying the Rector of Wigginton £15 a year, presumably the product of an agreement over Milcombe tithes.[10] At inclosure in 1794 Eton was allotted 114 a. for Milcombe tithes, and in 1802 423 a. for Bloxham tithes, and the long dispute with Wigginton's rector was resolved by the allotment to him of a total of 32½ a. in Milcombe.[11] The rectorial glebe comprised 1½ hide, a meadow, and a house in 1067;[12] in 1285 it was said that at the time of the original grant to Godstow the glebe was 100 a.[13] In 1200 Eynsham Abbey granted to Godstow a house in Milcombe for the use of a chaplain; in 1210 a rent-charge of 2*s.* and before 1235 16 a. of land were given by the family of Alexander of Milcombe.[14] Later Maud, wife of Race Fitz Alexander, gave up her dower, and her son Robert confirmed to the abbey leases made by his mother of 2½ yardlands and pasture for 100 sheep.[15] In 1287 Ralph Ben granted a house and 8½ a. of land in Bloxham in return for a corrody and a pension.[16] There is little evidence for the administration of the Godstow estate, but the control was probably not very great since in 1297 the abbey brought an action against 14 inhabitants of Bloxham to recover possession of a house, 32 a. of arable, and 1 a. of meadow.[17] The abbess suffered from the 'great might' in the county of Sir Thomas Wykeham of Broughton, who apparently claimed overlordship of some of her Bloxham land. In 1535 the Godstow estate comprised 3 yardlands in Bloxham and 2 in Milcombe; the whole was regarded as rectory glebe after the Dissolution.[18] At inclosure Eton College were allotted for glebe 115 a. in Bloxham and 56 a. in Milcombe. Thus after inclosure the rectory estate was over 700 a.[19] In 1965 the estate (832 a.) comprised 5 farms in Bloxham and Milcombe and 16 a. in Milton (in Adderbury).[20]

Apart from the usual burdens of the church expenses and responsibility for the upkeep of the church it seems that the rectors had another: in the 14th century the parishioners claimed that, by custom, since the appropriation of the church, Godstow Abbey was bound to distribute to the poor weekly half a quarter of grain. For lack of written evidence it was decided that Godstow had no such obligation.[21] A later composition must have been made, however, for in the 16th century the abbey was distributing £1 6*s.* 8*d.* a year to the poor, as was Eton College in the early 17th century and in 1824.[22]

About 1176 the Rector of Bloxham established a curacy, supported by altar dues, tithe of flax, and certain other small tithes.[23] About 1180 when the church was granted to Godstow Abbey, however, no curate was mentioned. The life interest of a rector was reserved, he paying to the abbey a pension of 2*s.* a year.[24] After the appropriation of the church by Godstow a chaplain was installed, but before 1221 a vicarage was ordained by Hugh of Welles, Bishop of Lincoln. It was at that time prescribed that, besides the vicar, 2 chaplains were necessary.[25]

In 1254 the vicarage was worth only £2 13*s.* 4*d.* but in 1291 was valued at £6 13*s.* 4*d.*[26] It rose in value during the Middle Ages and in 1535 was worth £17 9*s.* 4*d.*[27] In 1658 the Trustees for the Maintenance of Ministers augmented the living with a grant of £40.[28] This probably did not survive the Restoration and in 1675 the vicarage was worth only £25.[29] In 1721 the living was augmented by a grant of £200 from Queen Anne's bounty which was used to buy a yardland in Barford St. Michael.[30] In 1814 the vicarage was valued at £310 and in 1831 at £262 net from which a curate received £100,[31] so that the vicar was not rich. The loss of the income from Milcombe after 1854 was consequently serious; in 1888 Bloxham's net value of £158 was lower than that of Milcombe.[32] In 1917 the net value was only *c.* £207 and the union of Bloxham and Milcombe benefices a few years later was almost inevitable.[33]

The income of the vicarage came from tithes and glebe. It was endowed at its ordination with a house belonging to the rectory estate, the altarage of Bloxham and Milcombe, except for Bloxham's tithe wool and lambs, and the grain (ground small)

[1] MS. Oxf. Dioc. c 1735 and see below.
[2] Lunt, *Val. Norw.* 309. For the descent of the rectory estate see p. 62.
[3] *Tax Eccl.* (Rec. Com.), 32, 42, 61. For the origin of this pension see p. 62.
[4] *Valor Eccl.* (Rec. Com.), ii. 193.
[5] Eton Coll. Mun., Bloxham, 144, 147.
[6] See below and p. 166.
[7] *Godstow Eng. Reg.* i, pp. 230–2.
[8] *Rot. Welles*, ii. 9.
[9] C 5/15/49.
[10] Milcombe Incl. Act, 33 Geo. III, c 74 (priv. act).
[11] O.R.O., Milcombe and Bloxham incl. awards.
[12] *Cal. Chart. R.* 1327–41, 332.
[13] *Plac. de Quo Warr.* (Rec. Com.), 666.
[14] *Godstow Eng. Reg.* i, pp. 352–3.
[15] Ibid. 357–8.
[16] Ibid. 233.
[17] Ibid. 236–7.
[18] *Valor Eccl.* (Rec. Com.), ii. 193.
[19] O.R.O., Bloxham and Milcombe incl. awards.
[20] Ex inf. the Bursar of Eton College.
[21] *Godstow Eng. Reg.* i, p. 231.
[22] *Valor Eccl.* (Rec. Com.), ii. 193; MS. Top. Oxon. c 50, f. 99; *12th Rep. Com. Char.* 201–2; and see p. 83.
[23] *Godstow Eng. Reg.* i, pp. 226–7.
[24] Ibid. 227.
[25] *Rot. Welles*, i. 179; *Lib. Antiq.* 6.
[26] Lunt, *Val. Norw.* 309; *Tax Eccl.* (Rec. Com.), 32.
[27] *Valor Eccl.* (Rec. Com.), ii. 164.
[28] *Cal. S. P. Dom.* 1658–9, 47.
[29] MS. Oxf. Dioc. c 155, f. 15.
[30] Ibid. c 448, f. 19.
[31] Ibid. c 435, p. 58; *Eccl. Comm.* H.C. 285, p. 25 (1843), xl.
[32] MS. Oxf. Dioc. c 1735, letter of 1888.
[33] Ibid., order in council.

called 'chirchsede' given to the two churches. Godstow Abbey was to pay all church expenses except synodals.[34] In 1601 the endowment of the vicarage consisted of small tithes, apparently of the whole parish, a small meadow close, and church dues; the vicar received 4*d.* for churchings, 6*d.* for a marriage, 2*d.* from every communicant at Easter, 4*d.* for a dove-house, 1*d.* for a garden, and so on.[35] After the Restoration, in common with many Anglican clergy, Bloxham's vicar, Nicholas Page, found difficulty in establishing his right to certain of his proper endowments. In the Exchequer of Pleas he pressed his claim to Bloxham mortuaries (certainly part of the vicarage's endowment in 1601) and to tithes in Milcombe. By 1683 according to his curate's evidence, Page was unable to recover mortuaries from several parishioners, although they had paid them for 10 years past. Ursula Cartwright, lessee of the rectory and arbitrator in the case, decided that mortuaries were not anciently owed to the vicar and that they had been paid to Page only out of fear, 'he being a very passionate man'. Her suggested compromise, whereby the town should pay the vicar £20 of which she would contribute £5 5*s.*, was met by a reminder from Page that she was 7 years in arrears with procurations out of the rectory.[36] The outcome of the dispute is not known. In 1708 37 parishioners declared that Milcombe's tithes (presumably the small tithes in this case) were divided between the Vicar of Bloxham and the Rector of Wigginton, who held services at Milcombe every fourth Sunday.[37] In 1794, when Milcombe was inclosed, the vicar's share of tithes there was commuted for 65 a. in Milcombe Heath and Combe. When Bloxham was inclosed in 1802 the small tithes were commuted for 79 a. in Bloxham North and 7 a. in the Great Leys. At the same time the vicar's glebe was exchanged for 1 a. in the Great Leys.[38] In the early 19th century these 3 pieces of land in Bloxham, Milcombe, and Barford St. Michael, formed the main endowment of the vicarage. In addition the vicar received £20 a year from Eton College and Easter dues amounting to between £3 and £5.[39]

Bloxham's earliest known rector was Seffrid, Archdeacon of Chichester from 1176 to 1178, and Bishop of Chichester from 1180, by which date he had probably resigned the rectory.[40] Although he was clearly non-resident he took pains to establish the curacy mentioned above. The earliest known Vicar of Bloxham was John of Verdun, who held the living by 1221.[41] Another early vicar was referred to in a letter from the Franciscan Adam Marsh to Bishop Grosseteste as a 'pestilent priest'; apparently he had an illegitimate child at Barford St. John and had been ordained not, as he claimed, by the Bishop of Salisbury but in Ireland.[42] In the early 15th century the living was frequently exchanged: 3 vicars were instituted in the years 1406–8, for example, and each one made an exchange.[43] The first known graduate to serve Bloxham died in 1474,[44] and between then and 1546 there were at least 8 vicars of whom 5 were graduates.[45]

The Reformation seems to have encountered some opposition at Bloxham. At the visitation of 1540 it was reported that one man was refusing to attend church and had threatened the vicar with 'words of insult', but this may have been only a personal quarrel.[46] The vicar instituted in 1545 was Lewis Thomas, last abbot of the Cistercian Abbey Cwmhir (Radnor),[47] who may have exerted a conservative influence, since bequests were still made for rood lights, the Jesus altar, the high altar, and for dirges and masses.[48] The vicar's curate, John Wade, was strongly conservative: he took an active part in the opposition to the first prayer book of Edward VI and was condemned to be hanged from the steeple of Bloxham church.[49] The execution does not appear to have taken place for Wade lived to make his will in 1553.[50] No record has survived of the visit of the Chantry Commissioners in 1545, but it seems that, as at Thame,[51] steps were taken to forestall the commissioners: the town lands, given originally for the maintenance of a morrow-mass priest and lights before the altar of St. Peter, were diverted to other uses.[52]

The early bias of Eton College towards Puritanism is shown by its choice of Bloxham incumbents in the later 16th century. Thomas Lovell, for instance, who became vicar in 1578 after being curate, and died at Bloxham after nearly 20 years of office,[53] published a strongly Puritan discussion of dancing and minstrelsy.[54] The book was dedicated to Robert Crawley who was in prison for creating a disturbance about the wearing of surplices in church.[55] Lovell was a strict disciplinarian and an ardent preacher and catechizer. One parishioner was accused in 1584 of being absent from divine service and of failing to receive the Eucharist for 12 months; another made his communion elsewhere because the vicar refused to let him do so at Bloxham unless he could say the catechism without the book, and this he thought he was not bound to do, as he could and did read it.[56] Lovell's successor John Lancaster[57] did not wear a surplice until he was charged with not doing so in 1598, and though he then complied, saying he had 'no scruples on the matter', his orthodoxy remained suspect and 7 years later he was deprived by the Bishop of Oxford.[58] The strength of nonconformity in north Oxfordshire generally, and in particular at Banbury, made this a difficult period for the church. Roger Matthew, who was presented in 1605 and was at Bloxham for 50 years,

[34] *Rot. Welles*, i. 179; *Lib. Antiq.* 6.
[35] MS. Oxf. Archd. Oxon. c 141, f. 461.
[36] E 134/Trin. 35 Chas. II, no. 6; Eton Coll. Mun., Bloxham, nos. 167–82.
[37] MS. Oxf. Dioc. c 454, f. 78. For date see ibid. f. 76.
[38] O.R.O., Bloxham and Milcombe incl. awards.
[39] MS. Oxf. Dioc. c 448, f. 19.
[40] *D.N.B.*
[41] *Rot. Welles*, ii. 9.
[42] *Monumenta Franciscana* (Rolls Ser.), 114, 117.
[43] MS. Top. Oxon. d 460.
[44] Ibid.; Emden, *O.U. Reg.*
[45] MS. Top. Oxon. d 460.
[46] O.A.S. *Rep.* 1930, 395–6.
[47] For him see ibid. 1916, 61.
[48] MS. Top. Oxon. c 47.
[49] *V.C.H. Oxon.* ii. 36.
[50] A. Vere Woodman, 'The Bucks. and Oxon. rising of 1549', *Oxoniensia*, xxii. 83.
[51] *V.C.H. Oxon.* vii. 160.
[52] MS. Rawl. D 892, f. 164 and see p. 83.
[53] O.A.S. *Rep.* 1916, 62, 63.
[54] Anon., *Dialogue between Custom and Veritie* (J. Alde, 1581).
[55] *D.N.B.*
[56] *Archdeacon's Ct.* 159, 241. See also *Acts of P.C.* 1580–81, 208 for a false charge of recusancy.
[57] Sir Wasey Sterry has identified (*Eton Coll. Reg.* 1441–1698, 204) this John Lancaster as the Bishop of Waterford (1607–19) for whose life see *D.N.B.* This, however, seems doubtful; cf. O.A.S. *Rep.* 1916, 63.
[58] MS. Oxf. Dioc. c 264, f. 19v.; MS. Top. Oxon. c 56, f. 21.

was a learned theologian,[59] 'cruelly ejected by the Oliverians'. He too seems to have been disinclined to conform altogether to the Established Church. He was cited in 1633 for reading the prayers in a 'confused and abrupt' manner, not reading them in the correct order, and saying one part of the litany procession one Sunday and another part the next.[60] He kept a register of preachers from 1606 to 1631 and he noted in the parish register in 1638 'the outbreak of the Scotch Puritan rebellion'.[61] He published a treatise on the reciprocal duties of clergy and laity as well as a sermon preached at Bloxham. At and before his death in 1657 he left bequests for the poor and to the parish for church uses.[62] Two years later the Puritan Christopher Newell, member of a prominent south Oxfordshire family, was instituted, but was replaced in 1663 by Nicholas Page, who was vicar for 34 years.[63] Although Page's career was stormy, this may have been only because of the complex tithe customs and not because of his theological views.[64] After Page's death in 1696 Mordecai Pointer, a 'puritanical popular preacher', canvassed the town to petition the college to present him to the living. 'His principles and these unworthy practices' led some of those present at Page's funeral to recommend to Eton Thomas Fletcher, 'a very sensible and civil man', and he was accepted.[65]

In 1708 there was a dispute between Sir John Thornycroft and a group of parishioners over Sir John's burial vault and over his proposal to block one of the windows in an oratory in the church with a monument to Lady Thornycroft. Apparently he had dug up the ancient burial place of the Dalbys without authority, and had cast out the bones 'in an indecent manner'; it was thought, moreover, that others with more property in the parish had better right to the aisle. As for the monument the parishioners asserted that the vicar had no right to decide such matters without the consent of the churchwardens and 'some other of the most substantial inhabitants concerned'. They also begged the bishop to prevent the mutilation of one of the finest churches in England.[66]

The poverty of the living and meanness of the vicarage house before its enlargement in the early 19th century[67] probably accounts for the fact that before the 19th century only one Etonian, Robert Pargiter (1724–41), was vicar.[68] During the 18th century between a third and a half of the population was said to be nonconformist[69] and although vicars were resident they failed to attract increased numbers despite a steady increase in population. In 1738 the vicar was giving 2 services each Sunday at Bloxham; he also reported that he catechized regularly during Lent and that at Easter and Christmas there were *c.* 60 communicants.[70] Although Sunday schools were started later in the century the number of services was not increased and there was a falling off in the number of communicants.[71] By 1778, on account of the vicar's failing health, a stipendiary curate had been appointed. The vicar remarked that although too many were absent on Sunday without excuse the situation was no worse than in other places.[72]

In 1802 there were *c.* 80 communicants at Bloxham. George Bell (1789–1852), who was resident, was an able and conscientious vicar;[73] he fought hard and successfully to rectify abuses of the town charities by the Bloxham feoffees,[74] and to improve the financial position of his parish clerk;[75] he also rebuilt the vicarage-house. In 1820, however, he was unwilling to hold more than 2 services on Sunday on the ground that no more had ever been held.[76] In later years he was infirm and although he had the help of a curate, and at times had congregations of 400 and 500 (including school children),[77] his successor considered that the parish was neglected and that the people were 'in a very low state of religious life'. James Hodgson (1852–86) was a High Churchman and was particularly distressed at his parishioners 'having no notion of a church as a place of worship'.[78] He began weekly communion services, daily matins and evensong, and 5 services on Sundays. He catechized either in church or the chapel of the grammar school, held a successful evening school for men, and opened a reading-room and library. His congregation of *c.* 300, however, was comparatively small, a fact which he attributed to long habits of neglecting the church, to dissenting feelings, and to his own inability to 'win the hearts of his parishioners',[79] who came readily to be confirmed but did not subsequently communicate. He was involved in quarrels over pews: Bishop Wilberforce's description of pews as 'the Devil's freehold in a church at which he can at any time stir up malice and hatred' was made with particular reference to Bloxham.[80] In 1853 J. W. Hewett became Hodgson's curate without stipend and in 1855 moved from the vicarage to the grammar school which he had opened.[81] Through the school he aimed to give a biblical education 'in the principles of the Catholic and apostolic church'; the attempt involved him in bankruptcy.[82] The vicar, along with the bishop and archdeacon, was a trustee of the deed of endowment of 1855 and so became involved in the chancery suit which followed.[83] Another outward sign of Hodgson's religious enthusiasm was the restoration of the parish church in 1864, with which he was actively concerned.[84] It was a part of his aim of impressing on people the value of the church.

The church of *ST. MARY*[85] consists of a nave,

59 MS. Rawl. D 1054, f. 32.
60 MS. Top. Oxon. c 55, f. 279.
61 Par. Rec.
62 Wood, *Fasti.* i. 288; Par. Rec., misc. pps. His will is P.C.C. 472 Ruthen.
63 *Calamy Rev.* 363; *V.C.H. Oxon.* viii, index; and see *Par. Colln.* i. 50 for Page's M.I.
64 See above.
65 MS. Rawl. D 1054, ff. 36, 36v.
66 MS. Oxf. Dioc. c 454, ff. 76, 78, 80–81.
67 In 1665 it had only 2 hearths: *Hearth Tax Oxon.* 141.
68 *Eton Coll. Reg. 1698–1752*, ed. R. A. Austen-Leigh.
69 See pp. 80–81.
70 *Secker's Visit.*
71 MS. Oxf. Dioc. c 327, pp. 283, 120.
72 Ibid. d 558.
73 Ibid. b 38, b 39.
74 Ibid. d 568, d 573, d 578.
75 Ibid. d 568, d 570; letter attached to visitation inquiry.
76 Ibid. 578.
77 Ibid. b 38.
78 MS. Top. Oxon. c 103, f. 95.
79 MS. Oxf. Dioc. c 332.
80 Ibid. d 178.
81 Ibid. d 701 and see p. 57.
82 Ibid. c 1736.
83 Ibid.
84 For correspondence with G. E. Street, see Par. Rec., misc. pps.
85 The church was dedicated in the 12th century to Our Lady; probably in the late 19th century the title of Our Lady of Bloxham was affected and is sometimes still used: *Godstow Eng. Reg.* i, p. 226; C. O. Moreton, *Bloxham Parish Church* (guide bk.), 1. In 1718 the church was dedicated to St. Giles and formerly a wake had been held the Sunday following the saint's day: *Par. Colln.* i. 49. By 1742 the dedication was St. Mary: Ecton, *Thesaurus.*

north and south aisles, south chapel, chancel with north vestry, north and south porches, and western tower.[86] It is, as Rawlinson described it in the early 18th century, 'a very large and handsome' parish church,[87] 110 ft. long and 70 ft. wide. It is one of a number of outstanding north Oxfordshire and Northamptonshire churches in the limestone belt: the spires of the three most notable are the subject of a local saying,

> Bloxham for length,
> Adderbury for strength,
> And King's Sutton for beauty.[88]

These churches form a distinctive group, built of the variety of limestone called 'Hornton'. The grandeur of Bloxham church may be attributed to the fact that the patronage belonged first to the Crown and from the time of Henry III to various rich feudatories. The existing church is predominantly of 14th-century date and apart from its tower and spire (198 ft.) is notable for the sculptured ornamentation on the exterior of the building.[89]

A rebuilding evidently took place in the mid-12th century and parts of this earlier church were used when there was a second rebuilding in the 13th century. There survive a doorway with carved tympanum reset in the north wall of the chancel and the voussoirs of the south doorway of the nave, which were re-used when the doorway was rebuilt in the early 14th century. The chancel arch also rests on 12th-century responds which appear too far apart to be in their original positions. The most unusual feature, however, is the use in the chancel of the 12th-century mouldings as the rear-arches for the tracery of the 13th-century windows. Cable, zig-zag, and beak-head motifs are used in these arches.[90]

The 13th-century church apparently consisted of a chancel, nave, north and south aisles, and possibly a western tower. The south aisle was probably added rather later than the north aisle. The chief 13th-century features now remaining are the chancel, including the windows in the north and south walls, the nave arcades with cylindrical piers on the north side, and clustered piers with early stiff-leaved capitals on the south side.

Soon after 1300 the north and south aisles were widened and the shallow north transept was constructed. The last is separated from the north aisle by a striking diamond-shaped pillar from which spring 2 arches. The clustered shaft of the pillar has an elaborately carved capital depicting the heads and shoulders of knights and ladies with linked arms, a feature found in other north Oxfordshire churches and possibly carved by the same mason.[91] The windows in the north wall of the north aisle and those in the south aisle still retain the tracery of this period. The north and south porches are contemporary with the widened aisles. The south porch is vaulted in 2 bays and is surmounted by a parvise, the upper part of which is of later date. The west tower and spire are also of early-14th-century date. The tower is richly ornamented and its west doorway has elaborate mouldings with a pattern of leaves, birds, and ball flower. Round the hood-mould of the door are the 12 apostles seated on thrones and above is portrayed the Last Judgment.[92]

The Milcombe chapel, the large east windows of both aisles, and the clerestory of the nave are Perpendicular in style and were added in the 15th century. It is considered that this chapel and the east windows were the work of the master mason, Richard Winchcombe, who was responsible for the rebuilding of Adderbury chancel (1418) and the Divinity School at Oxford (1430).[93] The chapel is separated from the south aisle by an arcade of 2 bays with 4-centred arches which evidently replaced a transept opening similar to that still existing on the north side of the church. The chapel is characterized by great lightness. Its east window has 7 lights and the windows on the south and west walls are of 4 or 5 lights. As in the Divinity School the recesses are carried down to form window seats and those at the east end, as at Adderbury, form a reredos. The east windows of both north and south aisles are in exactly the same style. The clerestory was also added in the 15th century, and the upper story of the south porch is the work of the builders of the Milcombe chapel. The exterior of the chapel has a number of boldly-carved gargoyles, a parapet without battlements, and square-topped pinnacles. The carving of the gargoyles and the treatment of the pinnacles are similar to Winchcombe's work at Adderbury.

There were few major alterations to the fabric between the 15th and the 19th centuries. Presumably something was done to the chancel in the early 16th century after it had been reported as 'ruinous'.[94] The roofs of the north and south aisles were reconstructed in 1686;[95] and at some unknown date the steeply-pitched chancel roof was replaced by a flat one. The line of the original roof is still visible at the west end. Probably in the 18th century the tracery of the east window was removed.[96] The expense of repair, as in the case of the Adderbury east window, was doubtless considered too great. The spire was several times repaired in this century, having been damaged by storms.[97] On the fourth occasion (1792) the architect S. P. Cockerell gave advice freely and a drawing of 1805 shows the date of this restoration on the spire.[98]

In 1864 a major restoration was begun with G. E. Street as architect. It was completed in 1866 at a cost of £6,000.[99] The aim was to restore all the fabric in the most 'solid manner' without making any fundamental alterations. The roofs of the nave

86 For earlier accounts of the church see *Trans. Bristol and Glouc. Arch. Soc.* xx. 352–4; lii. 41–4; C. O. Moreton, *op. cit.*

87 *Par. Colln.* i. 49.

88 Beesley, *Hist. Banbury*, 109.

89 For illustrations see Buckler drawings in MS. Top. Oxon. a 65, nos. 104, 105, 106; Skelton, *Oxon.* Bloxham Hund. i. 3.

90 For drawings see MS. Top. Oxon. a 65, no. 101; ibid. a 38, b 7.

91 C. F. Keyser, 'Sculptured cornices', *Antiqs. Jnl.* 1924, iv(1). 1–3.

92 For detailed drawings of 1805 and 1879–81 of architectural features of the church see MS. Top. Oxon. a 38, ff. 3–18.

93 For Winchcombe see J. Harvey, *Medieval English Architects*, 296; photo. in MS. Top. Oxon. c 484.

94 *Visit. Dioc. Linc. (1517–31)*, i. 127.

95 C. O. Moreton, *Bloxham Parish Church*, 12.

96 MS. Top. Oxon. a 65, no. 104: drawing of 1802 by J. Buckler, showing the east window without tracery.

97 Par. Rec., chwdns' accts. A vane was added in 1798.

98 Par. Rec., misc. pps.; MS. Top. Oxon. a 38, f. 3.

99 MS. Top. Oxon. c 103, ff. 94, 95, 116: details of this restoration.

and chancel were renewed and those of the north and south aisles were restored; the walls were stripped of plaster and the stonework repaired; the memorial slabs on the floor (63 in number) were removed and the whole of the floor was tiled; the the Milcombe chapel was also restored by G. E. Street; the figures in the niches were not added until 1894.[3]

In 1926 a new clock face was added on the west side of the tower; the church had had a clock at least since 1754.[4] Electric light was installed in 1935.[5] In 1956 major repairs were once again necessary; these included the repair of the spire, re-leading the nave and chancel, and re-roofing the south aisle and Milcombe chapel which had been attacked by the death-watch beetle.[6]

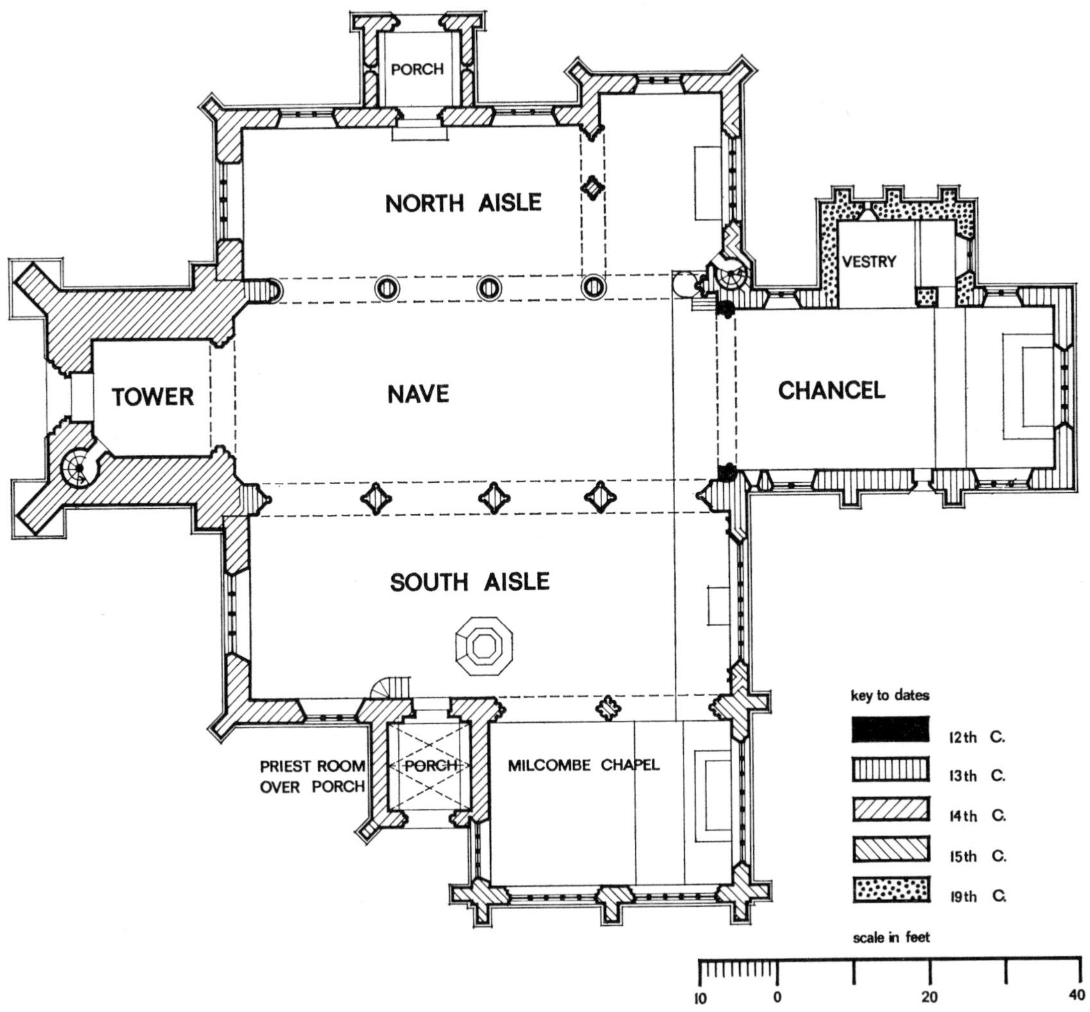

THE CHURCH OF ST. MARY, BLOXHAM

west gallery, probably an 18th-century addition, was removed and the tower was thrown open to the church by the removal of the lower floor; the pews, most of which had been introduced in the later 18th century were removed and the church was reseated. A vestry and organ-chamber were erected on the north side of the chancel and a new organ supplied by J. W. Walker was installed.

The church furniture also received attention: the 15th-century chancel screen was repainted, except for the panels, in what were believed to be the original colours, and it was restored to the chancel;[1] a new pulpit, litany stool, and sculptured reredos for the high altar were installed. The late-medieval font with its Jacobean cover was moved to its present position in the south aisle.[2] The ancient stone altar in

At one time the church walls were richly painted. There remain 3 late-medieval paintings. A giant St. Christopher and 2 other figures, one kneeling, beside him, is over the north doorway and the fragment of a doom is on the south side of the chancel arch. A 15th-century mural in the Milcombe chapel consists of a series of scenes which seem to tell the story of some youthful martyr.

A few fragments of the 14th-century glass, rearranged by Clayton and Bell in 1866, remain in the upper lights of a window in the north aisle.[7]

[1] The 4 doctors of the church, paired with the evangelist symbols, are painted on the lower panels: Howard, 'Screens and Rood Lofts, Oxon.', *Arch. Jnl.* lxvii, 176 and photo.

[2] For a Buckler drawing see MS. Top. Oxon. a 65, no. 102.

[3] MS. Oxf. Dioc. c 1735: faculty.

[4] Ibid. c 1736; drawing of 1805: MS. Top. Oxon. a 38, f. 3.

[5] MS. Oxf. Dioc. c 1736, faculty (1935).

[6] Ibid., faculty (1956).

[7] For drawings see MS. Top. Oxon. a 38, ff. 8, 10a.

The chancel east window (1869), a small window on the south side of the choir (1919), and the north aisle east window (1921) are by Morris and Co. The chancel east window was made up from designs by William Morris, Burne-Jones, and Philip West. The St. Christopher in the choir window is from a Burne-Jones design of 1868. The figure of St. Martin in the north aisle window is from a Burne-Jones design of 1878, and the other figures are probably from designs by J. H. Dearle.[8] The west window (1886) in the south wall of the chancel is by Kempe.

There are 3 late brasses: John Griffith of Penrhyn (d. 1632), Thomas Gabell of Bloxham (d. 1754), and Thomas Godwin, vicar (d. 1762).

There is a large marble monument in the Milcombe chapel to Sir John Thornycroft, Bt. (d. 1725); it is signed by Andrew Carpenter, London. This and other memorials to the family were originally at the east end and were moved to their present position during the restoration in 1866. The memorials include those of Elizabeth, Lady Thornycroft (d. 1704), wife of Sir John and daughter of Josiah Key of Milcombe, with the arms of Key and Thornycroft impaled; and John Thornycroft (d. 1687) and his wife Dorothy (d. 1717/18).

The following vicars are commemorated: Robert Pargiter (d. 1741); John Davis (d. 1789); Harry Davis, perpetual curate of Barford St. Michael (d. 1841); George Bell (d. 1852); James Hodgson (d. 1886). There are memorials to 19th-century members of the Holloway family.[9]

Rawlinson mentions *inter alia* an inscription to W. Dalby (d. 1695), member of a landed family at Milcombe; and Nicholas Page (d. 1696), vicar for 34 years.[10] These are no longer in the church.

The church now has no old plate: 2 silver chalices and a paten were melted down and recast when the church was restored in 1866.[11] The old plate included a communion cup and plate given *c.* 1685 by Ursula Cartwright of Aynho (Northants.).[12] The 19th-century set was given away when the vicar gave a new set in 1928.[13]

There is a ring of 8 bells, but all except the fifth, probably of *c.* 1570, and the tenor, dated 1648, have been recast in the 18th century or later.[14] A bell cast at the Reading foundry *c.* 1520 was in use until 1903.

The books given to the church and town in 1685 or 1686 by George Councer and John Cartwright of Aynho[15] consist of *The Acts and Monuments of the Church* and Piscator's *Commentaries on the Whole Bible* (3 vols. 1646). There is also in the church a *Book of Homilies* (1746), an 18th century *Hebrew Concordance* (2 vols. 1754) by John Taylor, and a *History of the Bible* (1752) by the Revd. T. Stackhouse. These books are now in the upper room above the south porch. In 1950 Miss E. M. Harper gave a Genevan (or Breeches) Bible (1583).

In the 16th century some of the income from the town estate was used for repairs to the church. By decrees of 1627 and 1635 a third share of the income of the estate was to be devoted to church repairs and to bridges. In 1824 it was found that this third was being spent as directed.[16]

The registers are complete from 1630.[17]

The chapel of Milcombe was in existence by *c.* 1200 when Robert, Abbot of Eynsham (1197–1205), gave Godstow Abbey a house in Milcombe for the chaplain,[18] and there are further references to it between 1215 and 1218.[19] In 1708 it was stated by the principal inhabitants of Bloxham that Milcombe was a 'distinct liberty'; that it and Bloxham were as 'two parishes in respect of all levies and taxes'; that the churchyard was not consecrated for burials; and that it was customary for the inhabitants to be buried at Bloxham and Wigginton.[20] A century later it was asked whether banns had been published there before 1753 and whether it was lawful to perform marriages there.[21] The Vicar of Bloxham reported that banns were and had been beyond living memory regularly published at Milcombe but that no solemnization took place except by favour of the minister on particular occasions. There had been only 4 marriages in the past 30 years. He also stated that Milcombe had no distinct register.[22] Local opinion was that banns had been published before 1753 and that the register had been lost.[23] On the last point at least it was correct. The Milcombe register has since been discovered: it began in 1562 when John Edyngson was made curate. The wording of the entry suggests that he was resident. There were then 2 churchwardens. The entry 'non marryed this year' suggests that marriages could be celebrated at Milcombe.[24] By the 19th century Milcombe had acquired its own burial ground and in 1854 marriages were said to have been performed there for many years.[25]

In the same year it was made a separate ecclesiastical parish. The living was to be a perpetual curacy, Eton presenting for 3 turns and the Rector of Wigginton for one.[26] As income the curate was to get £75 a year from the Vicar of Bloxham and part of the glebe of Wigginton, worth £25,[27] the Rector of Wigginton being no longer responsible for serving Milcombe one Sunday a month. By 1888 the living had been improved by £800 from Queen Anne's Bounty.[28] In 1917 the net value of Milcombe was *c.* £165.[29] In that year the Vicar of Bloxham was licensed to hold Milcombe in plurality and in 1921 the benefices were united.[30]

Before it became a separate parish Milcombe had been served by curates-in-charge or by the Vicars of Bloxham themselves. In the 16th century a former incumbent of the chantry of St. James in Chipping Norton was curate;[31] of his 16th-century successors

[8] This information was kindly given by Mr. A. C. Sewter.

[9] For a complete list of M.I. see list compiled by J. S. W. Gibson in MS. Top. Oxon. For list of M.I. covered up by tiles in the 19th cent. see Par. Rec. For the blazons of the arms on the monuments see Bodl. G. A. Oxon. 4° 685, p. 49 and G. A. Oxon. 16° 217, p. 70*b*; photos. in MS. Top. Oxon. c 484.

[10] *Par. Colln.* i. 49–50.

[11] Evans, *Ch. Plate.*

[12] MS. Top. Oxon. c 50, f. 100.

[13] C. O. Moreton, *Bloxham Parish Church*, 16.

[14] For full details see *Ch. Bells Oxon.*

[15] *Par. Colln.* i. 50.

[16] *12th Rep. Com. Char.* 201–6.

[17] Par. Rec.

[18] *Godstow Eng. Reg.* i, p. 352.

[19] *Rot. Welles*, i. 179.

[20] MS. Oxf. Dioc. c 454, ff. 80–81.

[21] Ibid. c 658, f. 177.

[22] Ibid.

[23] Ibid.

[24] Par. Rec. It is part of the Bloxham reg.

[25] MS. Oxf. Dioc. c 1894, order in council.

[26] Ibid. The Vicar of Bloxham had the first 3 presentations.

[27] Ibid.

[28] Ibid.

[29] Ibid. c 1735.

[30] Ibid.

[31] O.A.S. *Rep.* 1916, 49–50.

one, who died in 1571, served for 9 years and another for twenty.[32] For the 17th century no information has been found, but by 1738 the Vicar of Bloxham had no curate and supplied the chapel himself.[33] The division of duty at Milcombe chapel between the Rector of Wigginton and the Vicar of Bloxham[34] probably precedes the grant of Bloxham to Godstow. From the Wigginton register it appears that in the 17th and 18th centuries a quarter of the hamlet of Milcombe was reckoned as being in the parish of Wigginton. All baptisms, marriages, and burials of the inhabitants of this quarter were performed at Wigginton.[35] In the late 18th century the Rector of Wigginton continued to do duty every fourth Sunday at Milcombe.[36] Three communion services were held at Milcombe in 1738 and four by 1808.[37]

The first vicar after the creation of the new parish was Philip Hookins. He restored the church, and his successor, H. C. Blagden (1860–75), contributed to the building of the vicarage-house in 1862.[38] He reported an average attendance of 30 at morning service and 50 or about a third of the adult population in the afternoon. He considered that the main hindrance to his work came from the fostering of dissent in neighbouring parishes.[39]

The church of *ST. LAWRENCE*, Milcombe,[40] appears to have been built in the 13th century. It had a chancel, a nave with south doorway, and a north aisle. The existing nave arcade is of a plain 13th-century character, but the aisle was taken down in the 18th century and rebuilt in 'churchwarden style'.[41] The battlemented tower was added early in the 14th century. Windows were inserted in the body of the church in the 14th and 15th centuries, but these have since been removed or rebuilt. The nave was re-roofed in the 15th century,[42] and the chancel appears to have been re-roofed in the 18th century.

Rawlinson noted in 1718 that the church was indifferently kept.[43] Some repairs were done to the walls and battlements in 1742, to the wall and roof in 1789, and to the tower in 1837.[44] By 1859 the building was very dilapidated and it was restored in 1860 through the efforts of the incumbent Philip Hookins. The architect was G. E. Street. The faculty was for rebuilding the chancel and vestry, taking down the south wall of the nave and the arcade between the nave and north aisle, rebuilding the porch, providing a new roof, and moving the pulpit and lectern. All the windows in the church were restored and a new floor was put in. In addition the church was reseated and new benches were made after the pattern of the old. The old materials, including the lead, were sold.[45] Some of the lead was used to build the new school, and in 1869 this had 2 Perpendicular windows and a Decorated one from the old church.[46]

In 1906 an organ was installed and in 1945 a faculty was obtained to move it to the back of the church. In 1948 electric lighting was installed and in 1950 new heating.[47] In 1962 the church was again in need of repair.[48]

There is a much restored 15th-century chancel screen,[49] and tracery from the former medieval bench-ends is fixed to a panel at the east end of the north aisle. During the restoration a 15th-century mural painting, representing the Seven Deadly Sins, was uncovered.[50] The font dates from the 15th century.[51] There are 3 bells, of which 2 are dated 1607 and 1750.[52]

The earliest register dates from 1562 and extends into the 18th century, relating to Milcombe only. After the mid-17th century, however, entries for Milcombe are also regularly found in the Bloxham registers, and there are no further separate Milcombe registers until 1813.[53]

In the early Middle Ages besides Milcombe chapel there was another chapel on the king's Bloxham estate, called the church of St. John. It belonged to a small community of Benedictine monks and hermits and was situated at 'Felelia' in Bloxham Wood in Wychwood Forest.[54] The chapel and hermitage existed at least as early as the reign of Henry I, who granted it to Eynsham Abbey, with the assent of the Bishop of Lincoln. King Stephen confirmed the grant and gave the community an additional 7 a. of forest land. Waleran, Count of Meulan, also confirmed the grant when he became lord of Bloxham.[55] It seems that at this time all was not well with the house. The headship was sought by a monk of Tewkesbury, but eventually Geoffrey asked his friend Walter, Abbot of Eynsham, to undertake the care of the place. Geoffrey was supported in this by the Bishop of Lincoln, and the brothers of 'Felelia' were enjoined to be obedient to Eynsham Abbey which then seems to have absorbed the community.[56]

The chapel of St. John was still in existence in 1235, but in 1298 'Felelia' was described as 'le Forsakeneho'.[57] In 1315 it was uncertain to whom the site belonged. An inquiry was held as the bailiffs of the queen's manor of Bloxham claimed it as part of Bloxham, as in fact it had originally been. The abbot's claim, however, that it was part of his Charlbury manor was recognized as just and the royal bailiffs were ordered to stop interfering.[58]

ROMAN CATHOLICISM. In 1731 Dame Anne Lytcott and 4 women members of the Conquest and Brent families had small properties in Bloxham.[59] In the rest of the century the only Roman Catholics in this strongly Puritan area appear to have been some poor women, varying in numbers

[32] Bloxham Par. Rec., misc. pps.
[33] *Secker's Visit.*
[34] See above.
[35] Wigginton Par. Rec., reg., *sub anno* 1793; and see 17th-century reg. *passim*.
[36] Ibid. *sub anno* 1797.
[37] *Secker's Visit.*; MS. Oxf. Dioc. d 570.
[38] MS. Top. Oxon. c 104, ff. 43–49v.
[39] MS. Oxf. Dioc. c 332.
[40] Bacon, *Liber Regis*, 800.
[41] Beesley, *Hist. Banbury*, 137.
[42] Ibid.
[43] *Par. Colln.* ii. 209.
[44] MS. Oxf. Archd. Oxon c 84, ff. 52, 56v.; ibid. c 40, f. 484.
[45] MS. Top. Oxon. c 104, ff. 37, 41.
[46] The conversion of the school into a village hall has recently partly obscured the windows.
[47] MS. Oxf. Dioc. c 1736.
[48] Restoration appeal in church.
[49] For an account see Howard, 'Screens and Rood Lofts, Oxon.', *Arch. Jnl.* xlvii. 191.
[50] MS. Top. Oxon. c 104, ff. 37, 41.
[51] For sketch see MS. Top. Eccles. b 14.
[52] *Ch. Bells Oxon.*
[53] Bloxham Par. Rec.
[54] *Eynsham Cart.* i. 51–53.
[55] Ibid.
[56] Ibid. 53.
[57] Ibid. ii. 168, 93.
[58] Ibid. i. 365–6.
[59] O.R.O. reg. papist estates.

from one to four between 1738 and 1774.[60] The church of *ST. PETER* was built in 1938 and is served from Banbury.

PROTESTANT NONCONFORMITY. From the 17th century nonconformity flourished and was closely associated with the dissenting movement in Banbury and the neighbourhood. In 1669 it was reported that Quakers and Anabaptists each had meeting places in Bloxham, though in neither case were the numbers 'considerable'.[61] Nevertheless, seven years later 100 dissenters were recorded, 80 in Bloxham and 20 in Milcombe.[62] It is likely that some of these were Presbyterians attending the meeting-house at Milton[63] in Adderbury. Presbyterians probably first began to meet in Bloxham itself *c.* 1700. It appears that no chapel was built, but that the Town House was used.[64] The influential Councer and Huckle families were members of the sect[65] and the Presbyterians rapidly became the most important body of dissenters in Bloxham. In 1738 the vicar stated that four of the congregation were among the richest men in the village. The meeting had its own minister, who also looked after the Milton meeting-house. Presbyterians from other parishes came to the Bloxham meeting-house and Anabaptists also, so that the vicar was unable to be certain of their respective numbers, but he estimated that there were 30 Presbyterians and that their number had much lessened 'of late years'.[66] Nevertheless the vicar stated in 1768 that they formed a fifth of the parish and a very careful return made in 1808 recorded that they had formed as much as a third *c.* 1780.[67] As late as 1805 they were still the dominant sect but by 1817, when the vicar reckoned that there were 8 or 9 families of Presbyterian Unitarians,[68] they were losing ground to the Baptists.

Something is known of the ministers and the organization of the congregation.[69] Perhaps the first minister to reside at Bloxham was Andrew Durel (d. 1723), a Huguenot refugee, who had charge of both the Bloxham and Milton chapels.[70] He was not in principle a dissenter and is said to have often attended the parish church at Bloxham. The great popularity of the movement at this time may be gauged by the report that his congregation, gathered from the whole neighbourhood, numbered 500, of whom 20 were gentlemen, and the rest tradesmen, farmers, and labourers. It was reckoned that they had more than 20 votes for the county among them.[71] In the 1760s and 1770s the minister was Thomas Brabant,[72] formerly a classical tutor at a dissenting academy at Daventry (Northants.). He was never ordained as he had unorthodox views on baptism and was, in fact, known as an Anabaptist. He was minister for about 30 years and died at Bloxham in 1804. The vicar wrote in the burial register after the entry of Brabant's name 'formerly a dissenting minister here of respectable character and abilities but in doctrine *errans*'.[73] Another outstanding minister was Joseph Jevans (1799–1839), who had also been educated at a nonconformist academy and was, again like Brabant, a friend of leading nonconformists of the day. He was a man of outstanding piety and his great services to Bloxham, which included the opening of a Sunday school in his own house,[74] were recognized by the vicar when he 'made a point of conducting the (funeral) service himself instead of deputing his curate to perform the office as was his custom'.[75] The last of Bloxham's ministers was D. L. Evans. The congregation provided him initially with a stipend of £60. This must have entailed sacrifices, for Jevans, though originally paid £50, had been receiving only £20 in his later years. After two years' subscriptions, however, the congregation fell off, Evans left Bloxham, and the chapels at both Bloxham and Milton closed. During the previous century and a half the community had probably very much depended on one or two leading families like the Councers and Cakebreads. Jevans kept a register of baptisms which shows that he baptized the children of Lyne Councer, attorney, nearly a century after the family's connexion with Presbyterianism was first recorded.[76] George Cakebread, one of the family to be baptized by Jevans, and later a mason of some distinction,[77] signed a certificate of registration for the Particular Baptist meeting-houses at Bloxham and Milcombe.[78] Some of the Presbyterian community returned to the Church of England.[79]

The Bloxham Anabaptists were holding meetings once a month in the house of a member called Ingram in 1669, and the vicar complained of their not coming to church.[80] Another vicar reported in 1738 that there were 11 Anabaptists who had a licensed house but did not meet more than once a quarter; that Daniel Wilmot of Hook Norton was their visiting teacher; and that they were on friendly terms with the Presbyterians and attended their meetings.[81] By the beginning of the 19th century the Particular Baptists had become the most vigorous of the nonconformist bodies in the parish, and, in fact, in the neighbourhood. A meeting-house was registered in 1808 in the names of 6 local men of whom 3 belonged to the Gascoigne and Cakebread families.[82] The congregation of 'a few score' was apparently collected by the efforts of a labourer, who occasionally preached. There were said to be 10 families in the

[60] *Secker's Visit.*; MS. Oxf. Dioc. d 555, d 558, d 564.

[61] Lyon Turner, *Recs. of Nonconformity*, iii. 826.

[62] Compton Census.

[63] See p. 39.

[64] The meeting house was reported as licensed in 1738 (*Secker's Visit.*), but in 1805 the vicar reported that there had been a chapel for more than a century (MS. Oxf. Dioc. d 568); *Trans. Unitarian Hist. Soc.* ii(2). 14.

[65] George Councer and Robert Huckle both gentlemen of Bloxham, were trustees in 1708 of Milton Presbyterian chapel: see p. 39.

[66] *Secker's Visit.*

[67] MS. Oxf. Dioc. d 558, d 570; cf. a report of 1759, where half the parish was said to be Presbyterian: ibid. d 555.

[68] Ibid. d 568, d 576. Between 1771 and 1781 a family of Presbyterians at Milcombe was noted by the vicar (ibid. d 561, d 654, b 37, ff. 25, 113) but none are recorded in later visitations.

[69] The following statements, except where otherwise stated, are based on A. D. Tyssen, 'The Presbyterians of Bloxham and Milton', *Trans. Unitarian Hist. Soc.* ii(2). 9 sqq.

[70] Dr. Williams's Libr., Evans MS., list of ministers in 1715.

[71] Ibid.

[72] MS. Oxf. Dioc. d 558, d 561. For the complete list of ministers see Tyssen, *op. cit.* 14–25. Registers for 1789–1837 are at Somerset House.

[73] Par. Rec., reg.

[74] See p. 82.

[75] Tyssen, *op. cit.* 24.

[76] Ibid. 26 sqq.

[77] Gunnis, *Dict. of Sculptors*; see p. 71.

[78] See below; MS. Oxf. Dioc. c 644, 95.

[79] MS. Oxf. Dioc. d 576.

[80] Lyon Turner, *Recs. of Nonconformity*, iii. 826; MS. Oxf. Dioc. c 430, f. 6.

[81] *Secker's Visit.*

[82] MS. Oxf. Dioc. c 644, f. 95.

group at this time of whom some took communion in the parish church but more went to the Baptist chapel in Banbury.[83] In 1812 a chapel was built and registered.[84] In 1817 12 families with a preacher were reported; the vicar described them as 'Calvinistic Baptist Independents',[85] and there is no doubt that Baptists and Independents were closely allied in the neighbourhood. For instance George Cakebread, a Baptist, signed with the Independent minister of Banbury the registration certificate of the Adderbury Independent chapel,[86] but no other reference to Independents at Bloxham has been found. In 1821 a Baptist minister was ordained.[87] According to the 1851 Census the congregation numbered 100,[88] but this cannot be taken to mean a solely Baptist congregation, for many Church people went to dissenting meetings in the evening.[89] There was also a Baptist Sunday school.[90] A new and larger chapel was built in 1859.[91] In 1966 there were 11 members.[92]

Meanwhile the sect had also been making headway in Milcombe. In 1738 there were only 2 families of Anabaptists there. They had licensed a meeting-house and were visited monthly by the Hook Norton minister, Daniel Wilmot.[93] In 1774 only one family, qualified as 'pauper', was recorded, but in 1822 a meeting-house at Milcombe was registered by the Bloxham Baptists and their minister.[94] A chapel was built in 1824 and in 1851 a congregation of 51 was recorded in the Census return.[95] Some almost certainly came from outside the parish and when the chapel was rebuilt just before 1866 the vicar commented that this had been done through the efforts of a dissenting farmer from outside; that during the rebuilding many local dissenters had come to church; and that there were only about 8 *bona fide* dissenting families, some of whom normally attended church and school. Had there been no 'irritation' from without he considered that dissent might have died away.[96]

The influence of Bray Doyley of Adderbury and the strong Quaker community in Banbury and north Oxfordshire generally made itself felt in Bloxham in the 17th century. There were many Quakers in the parish who belonged to the Adderbury Meeting, and came under the jurisdiction of the Monthly Meeting of the Banbury Division, which in the early 18th century was fairly frequently held in Bloxham.[97] The village never had a permanent meeting-house, but meetings were held in the houses of Friends, and in the mid-17th century Milcombe seems to have been more zealous than Bloxham itself. In 1665 Quakers met in Edward Butcher's house in Milcombe; Butcher had been imprisoned in 1660 for refusing to take the oath of allegiance.[98] In 1669 the house of George Anson of Bloxham, apparently a weaver, was regularly used.[99] The vicar thought that the numbers attending were not great and in 1682 he described the local Quakers as 'so obstinate and ignorant' that it was 'vain to offer anything to their consideration'.[1] Quakers from Adderbury, Tadmarton, and Great Tew were arrested at meetings in Bloxham.[2] Those living in Bloxham suffered also for their attendance at meetings: between 1660 and 1665 George Tomkins and Edward Butcher, both of Milcombe, went to prison for several weeks 3 or 4 times for going to meetings at Banbury and in Milcombe, and 3 others were imprisoned for the same reason.[3] Refusal to pay ecclesiastical dues was a further source of trouble; one man was distrained on for refusing to pay towards church repairs. Edward Butcher, the first to suffer for withholding tithes, was imprisoned in 1659 and his goods were distrained on in 1665. Thomas Stranke, member of a leading Milcombe family, was also twice sent to gaol, once for 2 years, for the same offence. Many of those distrained on were poor, but Butcher, Tomkins, and Stranke from Milcombe, and Anson from Bloxham, who were the chief offenders, seem all to have been fairly well-to-do. After 1695 one of the most obstinate offenders was William Lamley of Bloxham, who was treasurer of Banbury Division in 1740 and represented the division at the Yearly Meeting in London in 1741 and 1748.[4] At least 6 other families were regularly fined in the earlier 18th century. These included Thomas Harris (d. 1757), whose family mostly attended Sibford Meeting and Joseph Harris of Sibford Ferris,[5] who evidently had a considerable amount of land in Bloxham since the tithe impropriators took from him in 1779 crops to the value of £20. Earlier in the century, in 1738, the vicar stated that the Quakers in his parish paid their dues on compulsion.[6]

As in Adderbury the Bloxham Quaker community increased greatly in the early 18th century. At least 18 family names from Bloxham and 7 from Milcombe appear in the Quaker registers in the 17th century; in the early 18th century there were 28 new names in Bloxham and 5 in Milcombe, with a higher proportion of new names to old than in Adderbury.[7] The society may have been declining by 1738, when the vicar reported that there were 8 Quaker families in Bloxham and 5 of low rank in Milcombe.[8] His figure for Bloxham, however, can hardly be correct. Thereafter the visitation returns give 6 families for Bloxham and 2 or 3 for Milcombe; they met in each others houses.[9] The parson in 1768 said that a house was licensed,[10] and in 1775 the house of William Harris, scrivener, was licensed.[11] Harris was probably the same man as William Harris, schoolmaster, who died in 1792, and also as

[83] Ibid. d 570.
[84] Dr. Williams's Libr., Wilson MS. F. 2, f. 135; *Baptist Mag.* xiv. 28.
[85] MS. Oxf. Dioc. d 576.
[86] See p. 41.
[87] *Baptist Mag.* xiv. 28.
[88] H.O. 129/163.
[89] *Wilb. Visit.*
[90] See p. 82.
[91] *Kelly's Dir. Oxon.* (1887).
[92] *Baptist Handbk.* (1966).
[93] *Secker's Visit.*
[94] MS. Oxf. Dioc. d 564; ibid. c 644, f. 264.
[95] H.O. 129/163.
[96] MS. Oxf. Dioc. c 332. Several houses for the meeting of unidentified sects were licensed in the 18th century: Richard Lovell's house at Milcombe (1708), Thomas Rundle's house (1737), John Allen's house (1742): O.R.O., *Cal. Q. Sess.* viii.
[97] Banbury M. M. Min. Bk. (1736–78).
[98] MS. Sufferings.
[99] Lyon Turner, *Recs. of Nonconformity*, iii. 826, 836. When Anson was fined in 1662 rolls of cloth worth £4 were confiscated: MS. Sufferings.
[1] MS. Oxf. Dioc. c 430, f. 6.
[2] Besse, *Sufferings*, i. 568, 570.
[3] Cases of sufferings cited below are to be found in MS. Sufferings or in Besse, *Sufferings*, i. 566, 569, 573.
[4] Banbury M. M. Min. Bk.
[5] Banbury Quaker reg.
[6] *Secker's Visit.*
[7] Banbury Quaker reg.
[8] *Secker's Visit.*
[9] MS. Oxf. Dioc. d 558, d 561, d 564.
[10] Ibid. d 558.
[11] O.R.O., *Cal. Q. Sess.* viii.

the William Harris of Bloxham who in 1770 was appointed to look after the abstracts of meeting-houses, burial grounds, and charities.[12]

By the 19th century the Bloxham Quakers had almost disappeared. Only two family names are to be found in the Quaker registers and the vicar recorded only 2 families in 1802 and 1805.[13] Thomas Gilkes, whose house at Milcombe was registered for meetings in 1835, may have been a Quaker.[14]

No Methodism was reported in Bloxham before the 1820s. In 1823, however, there were said to be 9 or 10 Methodists, meeting at a house registered in 1821.[15] In 1851 there was a congregation of between 120 and 150, but only 134 sittings and 'standing room'.[16] Church people used to go there or to the Baptist chapel in the evening. There was also a Wesleyan Sunday school.[17] The vicar would not give an estimate of numbers attending the chapel in 1854,[18] but in 1866 he said there were 210 dissenters (presumably mostly Wesleyans and Baptists) and in 1878 *c.* 100 in Bloxham and 17 in Milcombe.[19] A new Methodist chapel was built just before 1869[20] and in 1965 it seated 250. It was then served by ministers from Banbury and Brailes. There was a membership of 31.[21]

SCHOOLS. At some date between 1601 and 1627 William Hartley and his wife Mary granted the Bloxham feoffees 1 a. of arable land in trust for the use of a grammar school master, who might teach grammar at Bloxham. In default of such a master the grant was to be used for the poor living in the almshouse.[22] In 1627 it was found that the money accruing had been misapplied and it was ordered that School Acre should be handed over to new feoffees and be used for its proper purpose.[23] The school house, of which the door alone survives, was built next to the Court House in 1610. It is not known whether the building was still used as a grammar school when it was restored in 1674.[24] By 1738 it was occupied by a charity school supported by the subscription of local landowners, in which 20 boys were taught to read and write.[25] In 1771 the death of the principal contributor cut the value of subscriptions by half and the number of boys taught had been reduced to 10 by 1774.[26] The school seems to have come to an end soon after that date.

By 1808 there were 4 schools in Bloxham: a day school where 40 boys were taught reading, writing, arithmetic, and mensuration, and 3 schools for young children who were taught reading, needlework, and straw-plaiting. A Sunday school which had been started by the Presbyterians had ceased to exist by this date.[27] Ten years later the number of schools in the parish had doubled. Four day schools were attended by 83 children, 9 of whom came from neighbouring parishes. Three infant schools taught 29 children under the age of seven. Another school had 37 pupils, mostly boys, and a further 27 young adults attended in the evenings. In addition to these schools a long established girls' boarding school now took 6 local girls as day pupils. Two Sunday schools, which were receiving the endowment from School Acre in the form of £1 worth of coal and candles, were the sole means of education for 34 children. They were also attended by 30 of the children who went to the day schools. The vicar considered it a matter for congratulation that 14 per cent. of the children in his parish were receiving some sort of education. He strongly recommended the establishment of a National school in the parish and the provision of more evening schools so that the children might be free to earn during the daytime.[28]

Elementary education in the parish had been put on a sounder footing by 1831 when a free school was established, supported by a bequest from Job Faulkner. By his will dated 1807 this money, amounting to £30 a year, had been left, after the life interest of a wife and brother, to the vicar and churchwardens, who were to pay a schoolmaster to teach reading, writing, arithmetic, and mensuration to 28 boys between the ages of 5 and 14. The boys were to be the sons of poor persons not being farmers; they might belong either to the Established Church or to a dissenting body provided that they attended church or chapel regularly. Each boy leaving at the age of 14 after 2 years' regular attendance might receive 2*s.*, a Bible, and a certificate of good conduct. A prize of 1*s.* and a new prayer book was to be awarded at Christmas to the 2 best pupils and up to 6*s.* a year could be spent on books for each boy if the income allowed. Money collected at an annual charity sermon, for which an extra guinea had been allowed, was to be spent on coal for the schoolroom.[29] This school became the principal school in Bloxham and although the value of the Faulkner bequest had fallen by 1833 to £20 a year it was attended in that year not only by the 28 free pupils but also by 22 children paid for by their parents. In addition to the free school there were also at this time 2 day schools with 23 children, mostly boys, 3 infant schools with 46 children and the girls' day and boarding school. All these children were paid for by their parents. Two Sunday schools run by the Church of England taught 76 boys and 54 girls. Fifteen of these girls were given the opportunity to learn to write in a Wednesday class. The Baptists and Wesleyans also ran Sunday schools, the former with 45 and the latter with 7 pupils. In 1851 these had 25 and 27 pupils respectively.[30] All 4 Sunday schools were supported by subscriptions.[31]

In 1854–5 the vicar declared that new school buildings were urgently needed; that the girls' church day school was held in borrowed premises; that the boys' free school was in the very dilapidated school house owned by the feoffees, which was so

[12] Banbury Quaker reg.; Banbury M. M. Min. Bk.
[13] MS. Oxf. Dioc. c 327, f. 283.
[14] Ibid. c 646, f. 10.
[15] Ibid. d 580, c 644, f. 246.
[16] H.O. 129/163.
[17] Ibid.
[18] *Wilb. Visit.*
[19] MS. Oxf. Dioc. c 332, c 334.
[20] *Kelly's Dir. Oxon.* (1869).
[21] Ex inf. the Revd. A. J. Davies, Secretary of the Oxf. and Leic. District Synod.
[22] O.R.O., Bloxham feoffees' recs., decree of 1627. The statement (*12th Rep. Com. Char.* 207) that the land was granted in 1637 is an error.
[23] O.R.O., Bloxham feoffees' recs., decree of 1627.
[24] O.R.O., Bloxham feoffees' recs., townsmen's accts.
[25] *Secker's Visit.*
[26] MS. Oxf. Dioc. d 561, d 564.
[27] Ibid. d 707.
[28] *Educ. of Poor*, 719.
[29] Char. Com. file E 70180. For further information see Par. Rec., Job Faulkner, Sch. bk.
[30] H.O. 129/163.
[31] *Educ. Enq. Abstract*, 741. Faulkner's charity brought in £20 a year, less than had been intended by the donor. Char. Com., file E 70180.

overcrowded that infant classes were held in a loft accessible only by a dangerous ladder; and that there was no residence for the master or mistress. The Faulkner bequest, with the annual £5 from the feoffees for school sermons and voluntary subscriptions, was insufficient to finance the school and the vicar himself made up the deficiency of £14. He also contributed £11 to the girls' school and the Sunday schools.[32] The boys' free school and the girls' Church school were apparently regarded as an entity in 1857 when a copy of the school rules was attached to the report. The rules laid great stress on punctuality and cleanliness. Both boys and girls attended for 6 hours a day. Apart from the 28 free scholars, children of poor parents paid 2*d.* or 1*d.* a week according to age and the size of the family and those in better circumstances had to pay 4*d.* or 6*d.* The entry fee of 2*d.* was recharged if a child was away for more than 2 weeks without sufficient excuse. In addition to the usual basic lessons singing, religious instruction, and, to a slight extent, history, geography, and grammar were taught. Books had to be bought by the children and could be obtained at reduced prices or on hire purchase if necessary. They could be re-sold to the master if, when the children left school, they were clean and whole.[33]

With the help of a grant made by the Guardians of the Banbury Union in 1862 the free school was rebuilt on a new site and enlarged to take 100 pupils. It was opened in April 1863 as a mixed school in union with the National Society, supported by endowment, voluntary subscriptions, and a small Government grant.[34] An improvement grant of £142 was made in 1866.[35] Attendance in this year averaged 84, and most of the children also attended the Sunday school, which was the sole means of education for 16 children. The vicar regretted that he was unable to keep a hold on more of the children after they left day school. A night school was attended 3 times a week by 18 boys in the winter, but the library and reading room were not an attraction to the young, of whom only 15–20 were members in 1868. In this year there were also 2 dame schools with 12–15 pupils each. Most of the younger children, about 75 on average, attended the infant school, which had been established in 1866 with accommodation for 100, supported entirely by a lady of the parish.[36] This generous support continued until 1877 when the infant school came under the same management as the mixed school. It was held in part of the same block of buildings in a classroom built in 1875 with the aid of a Government grant.[37]

In 1890 the average attendance had reached 228, only 11 short of the maximum possible accommodation.[38] By 1902 the number of school places had been increased to 278, but average attendance had dropped to 209. The Education Department had spent a total of £274 on building grants to Bloxham schools up to this date and £1,033 had been subscribed for the same purpose.[39] In 1931 the mixed and infant departments were amalgamated and it was decided that no child under 5 would in future be admitted. Attendance in 1938 was 119. In 1965 Bloxham school still belonged to the Church of England with Controlled status and a roll of 133 children. New school buildings had been provided.[40]

All Saints School, later known as Bloxham School, a public school under the Woodard Foundation, is described elsewhere.[41]

No information about the education of children in Milcombe has been found before 1833, when it was reported that *c.* 20 boys and girls attended a day school and 40 attended 2 Sunday schools. All 3 schools were supported partly by subscription, partly by the poor rates.[42] In 1834 the Vicar of Bloxham noted that there were 2 day schools in Milcombe and that at least a seventh of the population in his parish had some schooling.[43] In 1859 some of the material from the dilapidated church was used to build a school on rented land, the ownership of which was disputed between the feoffees and the vicar.[44] The school was enlarged in 1883 and in 1889,[45] and by 1898 was receiving a Government grant.[46] It was used for evening classes in the winter, at least in 1878, and spasmodically as a reading-room.[47] Although there was accommodation for 110 children in 1903 there were only 34 pupils.[48] In 1920 the school closed and the children were sent to the school at South Newington.[49]

CHARITIES. A town estate, administered by feoffees and townsmen,[50] was made up of many charitable endowments of which only some were for the poor. The rents of much of the estate, given originally for a chantry,[51] were diverted in 1550 to the upkeep of the bridges and other uses. In 1603 the estate comprised 8 yardlands, several properties, including the Town House for keeping court in, and various sums of money; only those endowments specifically for the poor are listed below.[52]

Among the oldest was an annual payment to the poor of grain out of the rectory, commuted to a quarterly payment of 6*s.* 8*d.* which was still being paid by the lessees of Eton College in 1824.[53]

In 1603 it was stated that the almshouse in Bloxham South had belonged to the town 'beyond the memory of man'. In 1824 the almshouses consisted of 4 apartments on the north side of the churchyard. There were at that time 3 more ranges of buildings, used for housing paupers, who mostly paid no rent; two of these ranges seem to have been part of the town estate in 1603.[54] The almshouses were sold in the mid-19th century, the money was invested, and the interest carried to the poor's account.[55]

Before 1603 an ancestor of Christopher Pitt gave 3*s.* 4*d.* yearly out of Garner's land in Bloxham for

32 MS. Oxf. Dioc. b 70, f. 121; Char. Com., file E 70180; *Wilb. Visit.*
33 Ed 7/101/25.
34 *Ret. of Non-provided Schs.* (1906), 18; Ed 7/101/24.
35 *Schs. Aided by Parliamentary Grants* (1867–8), 694.
36 MS. Oxf. Dioc. c 332, c 335.
37 Ed 7/101/24.
38 *Ret. of Schs.* 212.
39 *List of Schs.* (1902), 198; *School Building Grants*, 105.
40 Ex inf. Oxfordshire County Council, Educ. Cttee.
41 See pp. 57, 75.
42 *Educ. Enq. Abstract*, 741.
43 MS. Oxf. Dioc. b 39.
44 Ibid. b 70.
45 *Kelly's Dir. Oxon.* (1902).
46 *Pub. Elem. Sch. Ret.* (1900), pt. 2, 672.
47 MS. Oxf. Dioc. c 344.
48 *Ret. of Non-provided Schs.* (1906), 347.
49 Ex inf. Oxfordshire County Council, Educ. Cttee.
50 For the administration of the estate see p. 64.
51 See p. 74.
52 *12th Rep. Com. Char.* 201–2. For other charities see pp. 64, 78, 82.
53 *12th Rep. Com. Char.* 201–2 and see p. 73.
54 Ibid. 201, 205.
55 O.R.O., Bloxham townsmen's accts.

the benefit of the poor. This sum was still paid out of Garner's land in 1824.

The following bequests also listed in 1603 have no further known history: William Dalby, Rector of Upper Heyford, by will gave £20 to his overseers, who appointed £16 to be used as a stock for the poor of Bloxham, and William Calcott of Williamscote gave £100 as a stock.

Between 1603 and 1627 Robert Samon surrendered a copyhold tenement subject to the payment of 3*s.* 4*d.* a year to the poor; this was probably the origin of the 3*s.* 4*d.* paid yearly out of a farm called Hawtin's Hook in 1824.

Between 1603 and 1627 Ann White gave by will 20*s.*, George Dalby of Milcombe 20*s.*, and Edmund Busby, of Shenington, and Philip Kendal each gave 40*s.* stock for the poor; by 1824 this money was all lost.[56]

The income from the sum of £40, left at an unknown date by John Gascoigne for apprenticing poor children, was thought by the Charity Commissioners in 1824 to have been used partly in building cottages, inhabited by paupers, and partly in repairing the church spire. Subsequently 40*s.* a year was set aside for the purpose of the bequest.[57]

The income of the town estate, which in 1692 was *c.* £92, rose steadily; in 1803 it was *c.* £235 and in 1877 *c.* £414, probably the highest figure, but by 1935 it had fallen to £211 10*s.*[58] At inclosure in 1794 and 1802 the open-field estate had been exchanged for *c.* 23 a. in Milcombe and *c.* 108 a. in Bloxham.[59] Between 1845 and 1871 the almshouses and 11 other cottages were sold and £325 stock bought. In 1930 the feoffees sold £335 stock to produce £184 for repairs and the extinction of manorial dues.[60] Between 1954 and 1959 more than 100 a., including the Milcombe land and 8 cottages, were sold.[61] The property then comprised the ancient Town House, *c.* 57 a. of land, and £6,379, of which over £1,100 represented reinvested accumulated income. The total annual income was £343 14*s.* 8*d.*[62]

In 1627 the Charity Commissioners, finding that the town estate had been administered badly and that able men rather than the poor had benefited from its income, decreed that henceforth the income should be divided into three and that a third should be spent on the poor. Until 1805, however, expenditure was recorded in one general account.[63] In 1811 the townsmen gave from the poor's third £129 15*s.*, to be distributed in doles by the overseers, as well as £50 worth of bread.[64] In 1818 £89 was carried to the poor's account, but this fell to as little as £33 in 1822;[65] such great fluctuations were due largely to property repairs which were allowed for before the total income of the estate was divided. At this time the poor's share was used to buy coal in summer to sell cheaply to the poor during winter.

The Charity Commissioners in 1824 criticized the manner of observance of the three-fold division of income: the use of houses and cottages to house paupers was seen as removing a burden from the town at large, and consequently it was considered unfair that the expense of repairs fell partly to the poor's account. The Commissioners thought that a third of the estimated value of the property should go to the poor.[66] The amount distributed to the poor remained in the region of £80 throughout most of the 19th century. From 1861 small sums were subscribed regularly to local hospitals. In 1887 £2 was given to a man to go to Droitwich, £6 2*s.* 6*d.* to help a man to emigrate to Canada, and £10 to a family for the same purpose. The last entry in 1892 was £1 5*s.* spent to supply clothing.[67] In 1955 the poor were given £44 10*s.* at Christmas and in 1959 96 poor people received £1 each.[68]

Two bread charities mentioned in 1603 were not merged in the town estate. William Huggins surrendered a cottage to feoffees in trust, and the rent of 6*s.* 8*d.* was being distributed in bread to poor widows in 1824. Thomas Hall of Bodicote gave 3*s.*, and in 1824 this sum, charged on lands in Bodicote, was being distributed to the poor of Bloxham North.[69]

In 1630 Roger Matthew, Vicar of Bloxham, gave £20 to the town as a loan charity for poor tradesmen and others who could give security; the money was soon lost owing to the insolvency of the borrowers.[70]

When in 1637 an acre of land was given to support a schoolmaster,[71] it was decreed that in default of a master the rent should go to the poor in the almshouse. After inclosure land allotted for School Acre was joined with a small fuel allotment, and the whole was leased for £3 3*s.*; although there was then no master, only the income from the fuel allotment was paid to the poor.[72]

Two legacies of £100 and £200 were bequeathed by the wills of John Potter (d. 1892), a Bloxham farmer, and of William Potter (d. 1894). The dividends were to be disposed annually among 10 poor men or 10 poor women living in Bloxham. The endowments in 1912 were represented by £101 5*s.* and £225 stock.[73]

Milcombe, like Bloxham, had an ancient town estate. The first known reference to it was in 1625, when it consisted of land and houses in Milcombe left by Thomas Stranke at an unknown date. As in Bloxham the charity was partly for the poor and partly for the upkeep of public roads and bridges and for other town uses; in 1688 the trustees were accused of refusing to apply the funds to the poor.[74] At inclosure in 1794 the town lands, which in 1786–8 brought in only £7 rent, were exchanged for 12 a. on Milcombe Heath and were subsequently let at £12, their full value. There were also 8 cottages let to poor people at a nominal rent of 6*d.* a week. In 1825 none of the income of the estate went directly to the poor, but in 1855 a third of the income of £33 went to the trustees of a fuel allotment.[75] The cottages were described in 1860 as very poor places, 'habitable and that is all', and by 1904 the whole

56 *12th Rep. Com. Char.* 202, 205.
57 Ibid. 205.
58 O.R.O., Bloxham townsmen's accts.
59 O.R.O., Milcombe and Bloxham incl. awards.
60 Char. Com., files E 15998, 70180; G file accts.
61 Ibid., file E 8279, G file corresp.
62 Ibid., file E 137261.
63 *12th Rep. Com. Char.* 203; O.R.O., Bloxham townsmen's accts. For expenditure up to 1805 see pp. 64–65.
64 O.R.O., Bloxham townsmen's accts. This had also been done in 1769 and 1800.
65 *12th Rep. Com. Char.* 206.
66 Ibid. 205–7.
67 O.R.O., Bloxham townsmen's accts.
68 Char. Com., G file accts.
69 *12th Rep. Com. Char.* 207–8.
70 Ibid. 208.
71 See p. 82.
72 *12th Rep. Com. Char.* 207.
73 Char. Com., file A 62279; G file accts.
74 C 5/78/72.
75 *12th Rep. Com. Char.* 208; Char. Com., file B 70163.

estate was almost derelict through neglect. Two of the cottages were converted in 1860–1 into a school-room[76] and the rest had been condemned before the whole estate, including the fuel allotment, which had been added to it, was sold in 1957 and 1958 for over £2,000. This money, by a scheme of the Charity Commissioners, was used for the building of the village hall.[77]

At inclosure in 1794 16 a. were allotted in lieu of common rights. This land was let for £19 in 1860, and coal tickets worth 11*s.* 5*d.* were distributed indiscriminately without regard to character or receipt of parish relief. The fuel allotment was amalgamated with the town lands in 1916 and was sold in 1958.[78]

It was recorded in 1603 that certain sums of money had been given as a stock for the relief of the poor of Milcombe. William Tay and Ellen Gurdon had each given 10*s.* and an unknown donor 20*s.*; John Hunt had left 10*s.* and this had been made up to 40*s.* by the inhabitants. The annual income was 7*s* 8*d.* Eton College were bound to pay out of the rectory of Bloxham a stick of wheat a year to Milcombe and this had been paid until within a few years of the inquiry. There is no further direct reference to any of these bequests.[79]

BROUGHTON

BROUGHTON parish (2,083 a.) lies some 2¼ miles south-west of Banbury and includes the townships of Broughton (975 a.) and North Newington (1,108 a.).[1] In 1592 Broughton was the larger township, containing 1,442 a.;[2] the present boundary between the townships dates from at least 1805.[3] The parish is bounded on the west, south, and north-east, by the Sor Brook and one of its feeders; on the north-west the boundary follows Padsdon Bottom and Padsdon Springs as far as Wroxton mill.[4] On the western boundary is an ancient ford over the Sor Brook, *Haeslford*, which occurs in a charter of 956.[5] There is an Iron Age fortification, known as Castle Bank, but otherwise there is no evidence of early settlement in the parish.[6] Roman coins and the remains of a Romano-British settlement have been found just beyond its boundaries, while the Roman road from Alcester may have skirted it on the south.[7]

In the valley of the Sor Brook the land is liable to flooding, but in the centre of the parish, at Claydon Hill (566 ft.) and Welshcroft Hill, and in the north-west and north-east, it rises to 500 ft. and over. The soil is red Marlstone overlain by Upper Lias clays, with Northampton Sands and Inferior Oolite Limestone on the hills.[8] Marl from the limestone quarries no doubt supplied the fuller's earth for Broughton's fulling-mills.[9] The Marlstone, apart from providing good corn-growing land, and plentiful building-stone,[10] lends colour to the landscape. Although the landscape retains an upland character, hedging of fields after inclosure in the 17th and 19th centuries, the creation of a park (58 a.) in the 18th century, and the making of coverts in the late 18th and 19th centuries[11] have diversified it. Ridge and furrow is visible on the high ground near Woad Mill Farm and elsewhere in the parish.

A secondary road from Banbury to Shipston runs through Broughton village, where it is crossed by a minor road from Bodicote to North Newington; it appears on a map of 1675 and was turnpiked in the 18th century.[12] The turnpike was altered in 1835 after the purchase of an acre of land, Lower Bretch, south of North Newington; part of the original route by Pike Farm is now a footpath.[13] Broughton toll-gate stood near the Bretch inclosure about a mile from the castle.[14] Another route which has lost its importance was the old Saltway from Droitwich to London which ran through North Newington and followed Crouch Lane, a name of British origin, at the foot of Crouch Hill.[15]

The parish roads probably carried much traffic in the Middle Ages: there were markets at Banbury and Chipping Camden (Glos.) and North Newington chapel seems to have had local importance as a pilgrim centre.[16] From the 17th century onwards growth of population and trade, and of Broughton's industries — fulling, dyeing, and later paper-making — added to the volume of traffic.[17] Especially at North Newington there were important wagoner's inns: in 1782 and 1783 the 'Roebuck' and the 'Three Lions' were licensed,[18] along with the 'Twisleton Arms' in Broughton village.[19] The 'Roebuck' and the 'Saye and Sele Arms' (successor to the 'Twisleton Arms') have obtained a new lease of life from modern motor traffic. North Newington contains another inn, 'The Bakers' Arms'.

Broughton village lies in the south-east corner of the parish.[20] Its name (O. E. *Broctun*) means 'the

[76] Char. Com., file B 70163.

[77] Ibid., file A 62279; G file accts.; *Oxf. Mail*, 3 May, 1954.

[78] Char. Com., Unrep. vol. 32, p. 456; file B 70163.

[79] MS. d.d. Par. Bloxham.

[1] O.S. *Area Bk.* (1882); *Census*, 1961.

[2] Bodl. MS. Rawl. D 892, f. 167.

[3] O.R.O., S. & F. colln. (uncat.), Broughton incl. schedule and map. Until 1861 the Census Reports state that Broughton contained 1270 a. and North Newington 680 a., although at inclosure in 1805 the acreages were 939 and 1090 respectively.

[4] O.S. Map 25″ Oxon. V. 10–12, 14–16, IX, 3 (1st edn.); O.S. Map 6″ SP 43 N.W., 44 S.W. (1955).

[5] *Saxon Oxon.* 70.

[6] *V.C.H. Oxon.* ii. 318–19.

[7] *V.C.H. Oxon.* i. 341 and map between pp. 266*a*–267.

[8] Agric. Research Council, *Soil Survey Report*, no. 9 (1956).

[9] For the importance of Broughton's mills see p. 96 and Par. Rec., newspaper cutting.

[10] Wood-Jones, *Dom. Archit. Banbury Region*, 2–3.

[11] See maps of castle and park *penes* Lord Saye and Sele: (i) map of 1803 with additions of 1839 and 1845, (ii) map of 1848 by Davis and Saunders; *P.O. Dir. Oxon.* (1864). When C. F. Wyatt wrote (*c.* 1880), the park had been reduced to 22 a.: Bodl., Bradford pps. (uncat.), MS. notes, hereafter cited as Wyatt's MS. notes.

[12] Ogilby, *Britannia* (1698), p. 7, pl. 23.

[13] Bodl., Bradford pps. (uncat.).

[14] Wyatt's MS. notes.

[15] Ibid. and Beesley, *Hist. Banbury*, 16, 332.

[16] See p. 101.

[17] See p. 96.

[18] O.R.O., Cal. Q. Sess. vi; Beesley, *Hist. Banbury*, 16, 332.

[19] O.R.O., Cal. Q. Sess. vi.

[20] O.S. Map 25″ Oxon. V. 15 (1st edn.).

inclosure or farm by the brook'.[21] The field name 'Chadwell',[22] which seems to be one of many invocations of St. Chad, Bishop of the Mercians (d. 672), perhaps provides additional support for the antiquity of the settlement.

The medieval castle and church lie close together on gently rising ground on the northern bank of the Sor Brook near its confluence with two small feeders. Nearby stood Broughton mill. In 1685 Broughton village comprised 19 houses standing in their own gardens and orchards. Most were grouped in Church Lane or spread out along both sides of the Banbury road between the mill and Danvers farm. Four of the houses, including 2 isolated fulling-mills on the Sor Brook, were right off the road.[23] In the 1660s the Danverses' house and one other had been taxed on 4 hearths and there were 3 other farm- or mill-houses with 3 hearths each.[24] The village expanded from the late 17th century to the 1820s, especially in the last decade of the 17th century and in the later 18th century.[25] In 1738 the rector said that there were 30 houses[26] and in 1805 that there were *c.* 37 families.[27] In 1827 Broughton contained 26 cottages, 5 farm-houses, a mill, and the rectory, and there were 2 isolated mill-houses.[28] Population was, however, then declining. It had reached its 19th-century peak in 1821, earlier in fact than in most Oxfordshire villages, and it fell fairly steadily to 132 in 1911, when it began to rise again.[29] In 1961 it was 158[30] but subsequently increased as commuters settled in the village.

Apart from the castle[31] the most imposing house in Broughton is the rectory-house. This house was originally built in 1694 by the rector John Knight on a new site.[32] It seems that the medieval rectory stood on rather lower ground, for remains of a 14th-century building were found there in the 19th century. In 1665 it was taxed on 7 hearths.[33] The medieval window now in the rectory out-buildings was placed there when the tithe barn was pulled down in the early 19th century.[34] Knight's house, of 2 builds, had five bays, two stories, and cellars, and still stands, though considerably enlarged in 1820 and 1842. The earlier work of 1820 involved the building of the bay-windowed drawing-room or west portion of the house with its wide-eaved roof after a design by S. P. Cockerell. New offices and kitchens and the upper coach house were designed by H. J. Underwood of Oxford in 1842.[35] The house retains its original 17th-century wainscoting, which Hannah Knight, the rector's relict undertook not to remove.[36] Most of the other houses in the village street date from the 19th century. They are built of local stone and in the Gothic style: Rectory Farm replaced the old farm-house in 1807–8; in 1841 twelve old cottages were pulled down and replaced by three new blocks, each block containing four tenements; in 1859 the almshouses were built by Elizabeth Bradford Wyatt; in 1864 the house opposite the 'Saye and Sele Arms' was built; in 1877 a Gothic lodge to the castle and in 1882 a brick Sunday school (now closed) were constructed,[37] and in 1892 the mill was converted into a dwelling-house.[38] This part of the village, which includes the 'Saye and Sele Arms', built in the 17th–18th centuries, remained substantially unaffected by modern developments, apart from the introduction of electricity in 1954. In 1816 many trees were planted in 'Townside'[39] which was notable for its trees in 1963.

A number of outlying farms in Broughton township were built after inclosure in the 17th century. They are Rectory Farm, Broughton Grange, Broughton Grounds Farm, and Pike Farm.

There has been considerable new building by Banbury R.D.C. and by private builders on the north side of Broughton. Since 1960, when there were only 48 dwellings,[40] the village has more than doubled in size.

North Newington hamlet is sited by a spring at a height of *c.* 400 ft.[41] Its position on the old Saltway and on the Banbury–Shutford road via Shutford bridge were factors in its growth. Non-agricultural work was available not only in Newington paper-mill but also in the weaving industry of Banbury and Shutford, with the result that by the early 18th century Newington's population was larger than Broughton's.[42] It reached a peak figure of 448 in 1841 and thereafter decreased to 265 by 1961.[43]

The village is irregular in shape; its houses lie chiefly on the Banbury–Shutford road (Main Street) and in Park Lane, which leads to Park Farm, probably the site of a medieval manor-house. A 14th-century doorway, now bricked up, visible in a cottage wall on Park Lane, most probably was part of the chapel of St. John:[44] it appears to be in its original position. Until the mid-19th century the remains of a medieval cross stood in Main Street.[45] In 1805 this part of the village was compact, since the west end of Main Street abutted on the green, where there had been very little encroachment.[46] After inclosure housing developed westwards along the Wroxton–Banbury road and the green disappeared. To the east of the village, south of Park Farm, a former lane and possibly buildings, which must have disappeared before 1805,[47] are shown by field markings.

In 1665 Newington contained William Dalby's manor-house, taxed on 8 hearths, 6 farms of 2 or 4 hearths, and 6 smaller houses. In 1662 17 houses

[21] *P.N. Oxon.* (E.P.N.S.), ii. 397; *V.C.H. Oxon.* ii. 328.

[22] See map of 1685 *penes* Lord Saye and Sele (photostat at O.R.O.: Misc. Saye I/1).

[23] Ibid.; cf. 12 tenements and 5 cottages listed in a 17th-century rental: MS. Rawl. D 892, f. 183.

[24] *Hearth Tax Oxon.* 141.

[25] The Broughton registers give the following figures: 1683–1693, 63 baptisms, 36 deaths; 1716–1726, 71 baptisms, 54 deaths; 1683–1755, 457 baptisms, 348 deaths; 1754–1812, 682 baptisms, 377 deaths; 1813–1870, 1,200 baptisms, 658 deaths.

[26] *Secker's Visit.*

[27] MS. Oxf. Dioc. d 568.

[28] Bodl., Bradford pps., valuation list.

[29] *V.C.H. Oxon.* ii. 217; *Census*, 1801–1961.

[30] *Census*, 1961.

[31] See pp. 89–92.

[32] Par. Rec., licence from Lord Saye and Sele to build on any part of the rectory ground; date 1694 on chimney stack.

[33] Wyatt's MS. notes; *Hearth Tax Oxon.* 141.

[34] Wyatt's MS. notes.

[35] Ibid.; MS. Oxf. Dioc. b 70, f. 145.

[36] Par. Rec., deed.

[37] Wyatt's MS. notes.

[38] Bodl., Bradford pps., photograph taken shortly before the mill's demolition. The present house has a date stone, 1700.

[39] Wyatt's MS. notes.

[40] Ex inf. Banbury R.D.C.; *Oxf. Mail*, 29 Mar. 1961.

[41] O.S. Map 25″ Oxon. V. 11 (1st edn.).

[42] *Secker's Visit.*; MS. Oxf. Dioc. d 568.

[43] *V.C.H. Oxon.* ii. 217; *Census*, 1911–61.

[44] See p. 101.

[45] Bodl., Bradford pps.

[46] O.R.O., S. & F. colln., Broughton incl. schedule and map.

[47] Ibid.

were taxed.[48] The present Park Farm, which lies outside the village, is perhaps identifiable with Dalby's manor-house. A moat is shown just to the north of it on a map of 1805.[49] In 1852 Park Farm was described as an ancient mansion called St. John's in the Wood. The house was later largely rebuilt, but retains a well-preserved 17th-century dovecot, built of ironstone rubble, circular in plan, with a moulded coved stone cornice.[50] Another 17th-century house, much altered, is the large house in Main Street, once an inn.[51] It is a 2-storied building of 5 bays, with cellars and attics. It has a central stone chimney-stack and a number of its original stone-mullioned windows. In 1883 it was used as a tenement house for labourers.[52]

In the early 19th century, when the population was expanding, the hamlet contained 65 houses, besides the 'Roebuck', a smithy, a malthouse, and 4 cottages and a shop belonging to the North Newington timber company. There were 8 farm-houses, of which 4 lay outside the hamlet; the paper-mill and house belonging to it were also outside.[53]

In 1963, although many of the stone houses survive, a few of them with thatch, there are new houses of red-brick in the main street, and slate roofs are predominant. Council houses have been built at the west end of the village, and there has been in-filling on Park Lane and School Lane.

Although the connexion of the parish with the families of Wykeham and Fiennes has brought it into touch with great national events,[54] the impact of these events on the parishioners is largely unknown. That families might be divided in their loyalties, however, is illustrated by the case of John French of Broughton who in 1644 supplied malt to the royalist army at Oxford while his son John was physician to Sir Thomas Fairfax's army.[55]

MANORS. Before the Conquest *BROUGHTON* was held by Turgot the *lageman* of Lincoln, who had estates in Yorkshire, Nottinghamshire, and Lincolnshire. Turgot's lands passed after the Conquest to Robert de Todeni and his son Berenger, and in 1086 Berenger held an estate assessed at 20 hides in Broughton which probably included North Newington.[56] The overlordship of Broughton evidently descended with the de Todeni lands to Berenger's niece Cecily of Belvoir, daughter of Adeliz de Todeni and Roger Bigod, who married William (I) d'Aubigny.[57] In the early 13th century Broughton and North Newington were held as three fees of the honor of Mortain of William (III) d'Aubigny of Belvoir (d. 1236).[58] The overlordship of the manors should have descended through Isabel, daughter of William (IV) d'Aubigny (d. 1242), to the de Ros family,[59] but their connexion with the lordship of Belvoir appears to have been lost in the later 13th century.

It seems that thereafter the mesne lords became overlords and that, in the early 14th century, the overlordship was transferred, not without difficulty, to Thomas, Earl of Lancaster; it was then deemed part of the duchy until the early 17th century. In 1224 the mesne lord of Broughton and North Newington was Richard of Waterville,[60] lord of Naburn (E. R. Yorks.) and North Dalton (E. R. Yorks.), manors which also had been held by the Saxon Turgot.[61] Richard undertook to provide additional service from his Yorkshire demesnes, that is to say the balance required to make up his three small fees in Broughton and North Newington to full knight's fees—*implementum quod deest ad tria feoda parva de Moretoing' ad facienda tria magna feoda*.[62] The mesne lordship of Broughton followed the descent of Naburn, which by 1242[63] was held by the Palmes family, until in 1318 William de Palmes quitclaimed the homage and service of the tenant of Broughton to Thomas, Earl of Lancaster.[64] The earl had already in 1315 claimed the wardship of the heir of Broughton and had taken possession of the manor. He held it until his execution in 1322, despite the claims of Robert of Wykeham, who actually held the manor for a week in 1315, before the earl seized it. Wykeham again took possession for a short while after the earl's death, until Broughton was taken into the king's hands. It was then found that the tenants of Broughton held of Robert in socage.[65] In 1331 Robert of Wykeham was again said to be overlord. Nevertheless, Earl Thomas's nephew Henry, Duke of Lancaster, was overlord of Broughton and North Newington at his death in 1361,[66] and thereafter the manors were consistently said to be held of the Duchy of Lancaster.[67]

In 1086 Broughton was held of Berenger de Todeni by Robert, Reynold, and Gilbert; it is not known whether any of these men were ancestors of the later demesne tenants, who took their name from the manor.[68] Ralph of Broughton was dead by 1224 when his heir, John, was in the custody of Richard of Waterville, who by 1230 had transferred his ward to the keeping of Michael Belet,[69] the founder of Wroxton Priory.[70] The heir, John of Broughton, was holding the manor in 1242–3,[71] and another John (d. 1315) was granted free warren at Broughton in 1301.[72] This John, a knight of Edward I, probably built the original castle; he served overseas and against the Scots, and may have died at Broughton,[73] for he is not known to have held other property, and an early 14th-century effigy in the church is almost certainly his. Coats of arms on

48 *Hearth Tax Oxon.* 141; E 179/164/504.

49 O.R.O., S. & F. colln., Broughton incl. schedule and map.

50 Gardner, *Dir. Oxon.* (1852); Dalby's house was mentioned in a late 16th-century survey: MS. Rawl. D 892, f. 169. For the dovecot see plate facing p. 182.

51 Wyatt's MS. notes. It was probably the 'Three Lions' mentioned above. By 1805 it was a farm-house: O.R.O., S. & F. colln., Broughton incl. schedule and map.

52 Bodl., Bradford pps. where there is also a 19th-century water-colour.

53 Ibid., valuation list.

54 See p. 92.

55 *Pps. of Capt. Hen. Stevens* (O.R.S. xlii), ed. Margaret Toynbee, 27; *D.N.B.*

56 *V.C.H. Oxon.* i. 417; *V.C.H. Yorks.* ii. 145–6.

57 For the descent see J. H. Round in Hist. MSS. Com. *Rutland*, IV, 106.

58 *Bracton's Note Bk.* ed. Maitland, ii, p. 589; *Bk. of Fees*, 448.

59 *Complete Peerage*, xi. 96.

60 *Rot. Welles*, ii. 17.

61 *V.C.H. Yorks.* ii. 145–6.

62 *Bracton's Note Bk.* ed. Maitland, ii, p. 589.

63 *Bk. of Fees*, 1101.

64 C 148/86/106; D.L. 42/2, p. 43.

65 *Cal. Inq. p.m.* vi, p. 207.

66 G. Metcalfe, *Broughton and N. Newington*, 4; *Cal. Inq. p.m.* xi, p. 109.

67 e.g. C 139/113/16; C 140/541/45; C 142/50/91; C 142/167/72; C 142/333/50.

68 *V.C.H. Oxon.* i. 417.

69 *Rot. Welles*, ii. 17, 32; Emden, *O.U. Reg.* for the career of Belet.

70 *V.C.H. Oxon.* ii. 101.

71 *Bk. of Fees*, 824.

72 *Cal. Chart. R.* 1300–26, 1; *Cal. Inq. p.m.* vi, pp. 207–8.

73 C. Moor, *Knights of Edw. I* (Harl. Soc. lxxx), 152.

this tomb show that he was allied with many important families, such as the Seagraves, lords of North Newington and many other manors, and with the Ardens of Drayton.[74] His son John came of age by 1327,[75] made a settlementof Broughton manor in 1333,[76] gave a rent in the manor to Wroxton Priory in 1340,[77] and was still alive in 1346.[78]

It is uncertain when the Broughtons became lords of North Newington. Late in the 12th century *NEWINGTON* was held by William Clement, lord also of Balscott in Wroxton and of Dunchurch (Warws.).[79] He left two daughters as his heirs, Christine and Alice. Christine and her husband, Avenel Butler, sent the child Alice to a convent and later persuaded her to become a nun, thus acquiring all the property.[80] When Alice came of age she repudiated her vows, married, and demanded half her father's inheritance. The lawsuit dragged on from 1201 to 1220, first against Avenel Butler and later against his son Jordan, who refused to restore the property on the plea that Alice was an excommunicated nun.[81] Eventually in 1220 Alice quitclaimed to Jordan Butler her inheritance in 2 fees and 4 hides of land in Newington, except for 20 a., in return for land in Wroxton.[82] Christine, daughter and heir of Jordan Butler, married John de Dunheved, who was returned in 1242 as one of the lords of the 3 fees in Broughton and Newington.[83] After 1244 there is no record of the family's connexion with these fees.[84] By the end of the century 2 fees in Newington had passed to John of Seagrave, who was granted free warren in his demesnes there in 1299.[85] Seagrave, one of Edward I's leading commanders, died in 1325. Although his grandson John was said to be lord of Newington in 1346,[86] the manor had probably already passed to the Broughtons. No further trace of the Seagrave's manor has been found and the property appears to have been divided earlier in the century. Perhaps a part was given in dower, for in 1316 John of Broughton was said to have been lord of both Broughton and Newington,[87] and the Seagrave arms on the earliest Broughton family tomb in Broughton Church imply that the families were allied. Newington was included in the settlement of the property of John of Broughton's son in 1333.[88] The two manors thereafter followed the same descent.

John of Broughton (d. *post* 1346) was succeeded by his son Sir Thomas by 1356.[89] Thomas was a knight of the shire for Oxfordshire in 1370 and 1372,[90] and died before 1377 without male heirs. It is likely that Margery, wife of Edmund Waldyff of Mollington in Cropredy,[91] and Joan, wife of John of Compton of Milcombe[92] in Bloxham, were Thomas's daughters and coheirs. By a series of deeds between 1377 and 1385 their husbands conveyed to a group of feoffees the manors of Broughton and North Newington except lands held in dower by Elizabeth, wife of Roger de la Chambre, relict of William of Adderbury and probably also of Sir Thomas of Broughton.[93] In 1392 the feoffees conveyed two-thirds of the manors and the reversion of the remaining third after Elizabeth de la Chambre's death to William of Wykeham, Bishop of Winchester, for life. After the bishop's death the property was to pass to Thomas, the son of William Perrot and Alice, the bishop's niece. He took the bishop's surname of Wykeham,[94] and had obtained possession of Broughton and North Newington by 1402,[95] two years before the bishop's death. On his own death in 1443, after being many times knight of the shire and sheriff, he was succeeded by his son William Wykeham, also a knight of shire and sheriff.[96] In 1448 William and his wife Joan settled the manors on themselves for life and then on Sir William Fiennes, husband of their daughter Margaret.[97] William Wykeham died in 1457;[98] Sir William Fiennes, who became Lord Saye and Sele in 1450,[99] was killed on the Yorkist side at Barnet in 1471, and Margaret held the manors until her death in 1477 when her heir, her grandson Richard Fiennes, *de jure* Lord Saye and Sele, was a minor.[1] During Richard's minority Broughton was placed in the custody of Sir Richard Harcourt, his maternal grandfather.[2] Richard died in 1501, leaving an infant son Edward as his heir,[3] and in 1502 a third part of Broughton and North Newington was assigned in dower to his relict Elizabeth[4] who survived until 1527. Edward Fiennes came of age *c.* 1521 and died in 1528 leaving his relict Margaret a life interest in Broughton and Newington, though her possession of the former was conditional on her not remarrying.[5] Margaret remarried before 1539;[6] Edward's son and heir Richard Fiennes came of age in 1541 and held Broughton until his death in 1573, while his mother retained a life interest.[7] In 1573 Margaret was still alive and holding North Newington.[8] Richard's son and successor, Richard, settled North Newington on his second wife Elizabeth, relict of William Paulet, in 1587, and in 1600 settled Broughton on his son William and William's wife Elizabeth, daughter of John Temple of Stowe (Bucks.).[9] In 1603 Richard obtained a patent confirming to him and the heirs of his body

[74] For the tomb see p. 100.

[75] *Cal. Inq. p.m.* vi, pp. 207–8; Metcalfe, *Broughton*, 4; cf. *Cat. Anct. D.* ii. B 2723.

[76] C.P. 25(1)/189/17/75, 76; for details see Metcalfe, *Broughton*, 6.

[77] *Cat. Anct. D.* ii. B 3544; cf. E 326/8839–40.

[78] *Feud. Aids*, iv. 178.

[79] See p. 178; *V.C.H. Warws.* vi. 80.

[80] *Cur. Reg. R.* v. 80; vii. 108.

[81] Ibid. ii. 81; iii. 41, 334; v. 79–80, 171, 183–6; vii. 108; ix. 241, 381–2. For a full account see *V.C.H. Warws.* vi. 80.

[82] *Fines Oxon.* 60–61.

[83] *Bk. of Fees*, 824; *V.C.H. Warws.* vi. 80.

[84] *Fines Oxon.* 60–61.

[85] *Cal. Chart. R.* 1257–1300, 481.

[86] *Feud. Aids*, iv. 178; *D.N.B.*

[87] *Feud. Aids*, iv. 166.

[88] Metcalfe, *Broughton*, 6.

[89] E 326/4433; *Cal. Inq. p.m.* xi. p. 109.

[90] *Cal. Close*, 1368–74, 476.

[91] Dugdale, *Warws.* 414.

[92] *Cal. Close*, 1368–74, 194.

[93] Ibid. 1374–7, 528; ibid. 1377–81, 493; ibid. 1381–5, 128; ibid. 1385–9, 78; C.P. 25(1)/191/23/22.

[94] C.P. 25(1)/191/24/24; for details see Metcalfe, *Broughton*, 7; *D.N.B.*

[95] *Cal. Chart. R.* 1341–1417, 419.

[96] C 139/113/16.

[97] C.P. 25(1)/293/71/336; *Oxon. Visit.* 296.

[98] C 139/166/29.

[99] For the descent of that peerage see *Complete Peerage*, xi. 482 sqq.

[1] C 140/541/45. Richard Fiennes's father Henry used the title of Lord Saye but was never summoned to parliament. The family's claim to hold the barony *de facto* was not admitted until 1603.

[2] *Cal. Pat.* 1476–85, 44.

[3] *Cal. Inq. p.m. Hen. VII*, ii, p. 272.

[4] Ibid. ii, p. 401.

[5] C 142/50/91.

[6] *Complete Peerage*, xi. 484.

[7] Ibid. 484n.

[8] C 142/167/72.

[9] C 142/333/50.

Effigies, probably of Sir Thomas Wykeham (d. 1443) and his wife Alice

Effigy, probably of Sir John of Broughton (d. 1315)

BROUGHTON CHURCH

Vaulted passageway, 14th-century

The Star Chamber, 16th-century chimney-piece

BROUGHTON CASTLE

the Barony of Saye and Sele.[10] At his death in 1612 or 1613 he was succeeded by his son William, who was created Viscount Saye and Sele in 1624.[11] He died at Broughton in 1662 and was succeeded by his son James who died in 1674 leaving two daughters as coheirs.[12] The barony then fell into abeyance while the viscounty and apparently the manor passed to James's nephew William Fiennes (d. 1696) and then to his son Nathaniel, who died unmarried in 1710.[13] In 1710 the viscounty passed to Lawrence Fiennes, Nathaniel's cousin,[14] but the manor thereafter seems to have followed the descent of the Barony of Saye and Sele, the abeyance of which terminated in 1715 by the death of one of the coheirs;[15] Cecil, daughter and heir of John Twisleton of Barley Hall (W. R. Yorks.) and his third wife Elizabeth, daughter and coheir of James, Viscount Saye and Sele (d. 1674), became Baroness Saye and Sele.[16] She married first George Twisleton of Woodhall (W. R. Yorks.) by whom she had a son Fiennes Twisleton, Lord Saye and Sele, who succeeded her on her death in 1723. He died in 1730 and was succeeded by his son John (d. 1763) and grandson Thomas Twisleton (d. 1788). The manors of Broughton and North Newington have continued to follow the descent of the barony.[17]

Lt.-Col. Ivo Murray Twisleton-Wykeham-Fiennes, Lord Saye and Sele, and brother of the previous baron, was lord of the manors in 1965.

CASTLE. Broughton Castle, probably begun by Sir John of Broughton (d. 1315),[18] is a notable example of a medieval fortified manor-house with 16th-century additions. It was built of stone from the local quarries.[19] It consisted of an exceptionally large hall (54½ ft. × 28¾ ft.),[20] flanked at one end by the lord's private apartments and at the other by the kitchen and other offices. The hall was much altered in the 16th century when its original timber roof was replaced by an upper floor, but surviving buttresses indicate that it was of four bays, lit by traceried windows, portions of which can still be seen built into both walls. The entrance appears to have been in the second bay from the west, where one jamb of the south doorway can be seen in the exterior wall. The lower doorways in the west wall, blocked in the 16th century, led to the buttery, pantry, and kitchen; those above them, also blocked, presumably gave access to a gallery, but the original arrangement cannot be fully reconstructed. At the other end windows with richly moulded jambs flanked the dais. The block to the east of the hall retains its medieval arrangements to a greater extent than any other part of the house. It is remarkable for a series of vaulted rooms and connecting passageways. The north passage led to a newel staircase mounting to the Great Chamber and further on, on the ground floor, to its undercroft, now used as the dining-room. Both the passage and the undercroft have vaulted roofs. From the south side of the hall another vaulted passage extends eastwards to the straight chapel stair and the south-east projection. The chapel is a rare example of an untouched 14th-century private chapel and can, perhaps, be exactly dated by the licence granted in 1331 to John de Broughton for divine service in his oratory at Broughton.[21] The chapel retains its original stone altar slab supported on stone brackets, and its only loss is the glass that once filled its lofty three-light east window. A blocked entrance in the south wall presumably led from the upper chamber to a gallery, and a squint still enables the altar to be seen from this upper chamber.

Bishop William of Wykeham bought the manor in 1377 and may have been responsible for some minor alterations to the castle. He may also have reconstructed the gatehouse, for the inner arch, the staircase turret, and the upper story all appear to date from the later 14th century. The gatehouse has no portcullis, but was provided with cross arrow-slits and two pairs of gates. The existing outer gates are dated 1617 and have wheels inset for raising a drawbridge. The building was repaired in 1655 by William Fiennes (d. 1662) whose initials W. F. appear on the battlements. In 1406 Sir Thomas Wykeham was given licence to crenellate his house,[22] and was probably responsible for building a battlemented wall, of which a portion remains to the south-west of the gatehouse. He may also have built the stable which adjoins the gatehouse to the east, as it is lighted by windows with Perpendicular tracery of the second quarter of the 15th century. His alterations to the house seem to have been comparatively slight: he appears to have filled in the two arches which span the space between the south end of the chapel and the south-east projection and inserted two Perpendicular windows in the upper chamber above the arches. Neither the Wykeham descendants nor Richard Fiennes, who succeeded in 1528, had the desire or the necessary means to make further large-scale alterations, and were evidently well satisfied with what Leland described as a 'fair manor place'.[23] It was not until the mid-16th century that Richard Fiennes, Lord Saye and Sele (d. 1573), transformed the ancient house into an Elizabethan mansion. Fiennes undertook his building operations while still a young man in 1554.

The alterations he made can be dated so exactly for two reasons: first there is the date 1554 on the chimney-shaft over the oriel window on the north front; secondly there is the evidence of the heraldry on the chimney-piece of the bedroom at the east end of the gallery which indicates that the room must have been built before 1556, the date of Richard Fienne's marriage. The heraldry in question consists of the crest of Danvers and the arms of Neville (i.e. the families of Richard's mother and his step-father), whereas one would expect that the arms of

[10] *Complete Peerage*, xi. 485 and App. I where this 'confirmation' is discussed in detail. The fact that the barony was from 1603 able to descend to heirs of the body led to the later separation of the viscounty and the barony: see below.

[11] *Complete Peerage*, xi. 485–6.

[12] Ibid. 488–9.

[13] C.P. 25(2)/709/Trin. 29 Chas. II; ibid. 956/Trin. 1 Anne; *Complete Peerage*, xi. 488–90.

[14] *Complete Peerage*, xi. 490.

[15] Ibid. 492.

[16] Ibid.

[17] Ibid. 492 sqq.

[18] See pp. 87–88.

[19] For early drawings of the castle see illustration facing p. 114; Bodl. Gough Maps 44, nos. 70, 73; Buckler views of 1822 in MS. Top. Oxon. a 65, nos. 123, 125. The following account except where otherwise stated has been based on an account by W. H. St. J. Hope in *Arch. Jnl.* lxvii, 382–6 and on an article by H. Avray Tipping in *Country Life*, Jan. 1930, pp. 50–57, 84–91, 126–134.

[20] Measurements from Wood-Jones, *Dom. Archit. Banbury Region*, 28.

[21] MS. Top. Oxon. c 394, p. 197.

[22] *Cal. Pat.* 1405–8, 161; for the Wykehams see p. 88.

[23] Leland, *Itin.* ed. Toulmin Smith, ii. 14.

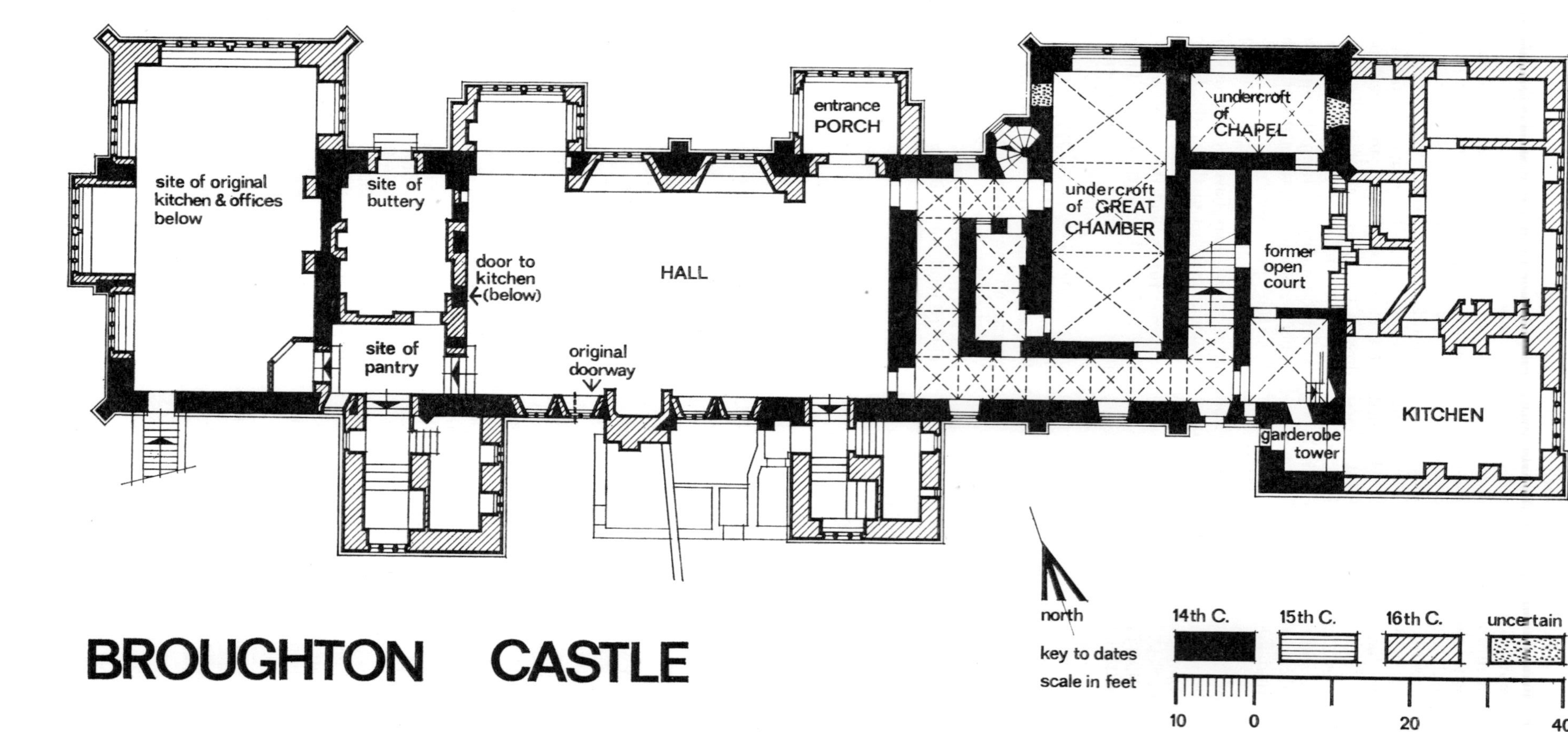
site of original
kitchen & offices
below
site of
buttery
site of
pantry
door to
kitchen
(below)
HALL
original
doorway
entrance
PORCH
undercroft
of GREAT
CHAMBER
undercroft
of
CHAPEL
former
open
court
garderobe
tower
KITCHEN
north
key to dates
scale in feet
14th C.
15th C.
16th C.
uncertain
10
0
20
40
BROUGHTON CASTLE

Fermor would have been portrayed had the chimney-piece been made after 1556. Furthermore, the architectural details of the oriel are in the short-lived Italianate style of the 1550s which was inspired by French examples. Similar details are found at Broughton round the opening at the top of the eastern staircase and in the projecting sills on the inner side of the window in the second-floor room at the east end of the gallery. These sills rest on consoles or brackets of classical character. Moreover in the room known as the Star Chamber there is a chimney-piece surmounted by a plaster relief. The subject is a scene of Dryads dancing round an oak, identified by the inscription '*QUERCUM ERISICHTONIAM DRYADES CINXERE CHOREIS*' as an illustration of Ovid, *Metamorphoses* VIII, 746. A relief representing the same scene formerly formed part of the decoration of the Galerie François I at Fontainebleau, and is known from an engraving by Boyvin. These features suggest that Richard Fiennes must have employed some of the craftsmen who executed similar work in England at Nonsuch (Surrey), Somerset House, Lacock Abbey (Wilts.) and Longleat (Wilts.). A further modernization of the house was carried on by Richard Fiennes (d. 1612 or 1613) after his father's death in 1573. The later work was in the usual Flemish Renaissance style of the late Elizabethan architecture.

The work carried out by the two men amounted to an almost complete remodelling of the principal rooms apart from the chapel. The medieval hall was given a flat ceiling and new windows; two floors were constructed above it and new staircases were made by adding two gabled projections on the south front. These staircases were themselves designed in accordance with the new square plan with wide treads and frequent landings. The south-west staircase rises to the Council Chamber in the top story, where William, Lord Saye and Sele, and his anti-royalist friends schemed against the government. The kitchen, buttery, and pantry were moved from the west end to buildings on the south side of the castle and the old screens passage of the medieval hall was done away with. Two symmetrical bay windows were added to the north front, the easternmost of which contains an entrance doorway in its west side. This arrangement of the entrance was unusual at this date though it later became common and is found at nearby Chastleton. Above the hall on the first floor there is a long gallery which evidently dates from this period, though its interior was remodelled in the 18th century. This appears to be the extent of the alterations carried out by the first Richard Fiennes by about 1570. In about 1598 his son Richard transformed the medieval west end, creating a range of two stories which balances the medieval east wing. This range contains little more than two great rooms, one on each floor. Each room is lit by mullioned and transomed windows of ample size. The ground-floor room (intended as a dining-room) is lined with contemporary wainscoting of unusually elaborate character. The plaster ceiling is correspondingly rich and ornate. The chimney-piece (14 ft. wide × 6 ft. high) has above it a seascape painting in oils by Jan Pieters representing Charles II's departure from Scheveningen on his return to England in 1660. There is also an elaborate interior porch with a cartouche of the Fiennes quarterings and the motto *Quod olim fuit meminisse minime juvat*. The motto is reputed to have been added by William Fiennes (d. 1662) after the restoration of Charles II when he was doubtless anxious to obliterate the memories of his Parliamentarian past. The White Room above has a plaster ceiling decorated with roundels of heraldic birds and beasts and shields of arms. At the south end is a lozenge with the date 1599 on it while at the north end another lozenge has the initials R.E.F. for Richard Fiennes and Elizabeth, his second wife. The room lacks original woodwork of any kind and was, perhaps, never completed. Until the end of the 17th century there was much painted glass in the windows, but it was removed to Belvedere House (Kent) in about 1830.[24] The two doorcases in the Elizabethan style date from the 19th century.

Since about 1600 very little has been done structurally to the house. It suffered in the Civil War when it was besieged,[25] and among the minor repairs done afterwards were those to the gateway already mentioned. Later at the time of James Fiennes's death in 1674, the house, park, and gardens were described by Celia Fiennes as 'much left to decay and ruin'.[26] For the hearth tax of 1665 it had been assessed on 26 hearths, 1 fewer than Shirburn Castle and 8 fewer than Wroxton.[27] During most of the 18th century the Twisletons resided,[28] and to them must be attributed the Georgian Gothic decoration of the Library and the Gallery. But in the early 19th century the house was leased[29] and Brewer noted in 1819 that the rooms were 'daily dilapidating from misuse'.[30] It was not until 1848 that the owners again took up residence at Broughton. In the 1850s Frederick Twisleton-Wykeham-Fiennes employed Sir Gilbert Scott to carry out a careful restoration of the castle,[31] but leased it again a few years before his death in 1887. It remained in the occupation of tenants[32] until 1912, since when it has been the residence of successive Lords Saye and Sele. Grants for the restoration of the house and gatehouse were made by the Historic Buildings Council in 1955 and 1962.[33] Among the contents of the house that are of special historical importance is the diary of Celia Fiennes. In the hall are some fine 19th-century examples of the furnishing fabrics of the Shutford plush industry.

At the end of the 16th century the castle was used by Richard Fiennes to house prisoners suspected of Roman Catholic and Spanish sympathies. His own family, in order to prevent any intercourse with prisoners, was removed by the Queen's orders to the rectory, but Fiennes petitioned that the prisoners might ride in the park with him for the sake of their health.[34] In 1604 and 1619 James I was a visitor;[35]

[24] MS. Rawl. B. 400b, ff. 143–147v.; Wyatt's MS. notes.
[25] O.A.H.S. *Proc.* N.S. v. 281.
[26] *The Journeys of Celia Fiennes*, ed. C. Morris, 25.
[27] *Hearth Tax Oxon.* 141.
[28] MS. Oxf. Dioc. d 568.
[29] The tenants were George Cobb (*c.* 1810–30), William Bushe (*c.* 1830–37) and H. C. Wilson (1842–8).
[30] Brewer, *Oxon.* 513.
[31] Bodl., Bradford pps.
[32] The tenants were George Granville Leveson-Gower (1885–6), H. F. Gladwin (1886–96) and Lord Algernon Gordon Lennox (1896–*c.* 1912): Wyatt's MS. notes.
[33] *Oxf. Mail*, 17 May 1962.
[34] *Acts of P.C.* 1589–90, 414–417; ibid. 1591, 16, 17, 62; ibid. 1592, 106–107; ibid. 1595–6, 517; *Cal. S.P. Dom.* 1591–4, 2, 11, 253.
[35] *Trans. Birmingham & Midland Institute* (1873), 88.

later the castle was made a centre of the opposition to the king and his son by William Fiennes (d. 1662), 'Old Subtlety' as he was nicknamed.[36] After his imprisonment in the Fleet for his attacks on the policy of James I he was confined at and within 4 miles of Broughton in 1622; in 1623 he was allowed a radius of 20 miles.[37] During Charles I's reign his active opposition to the king led Clarendon to describe him as 'the pilot that steered all those vessels which were freighted with sedition to destroy the government'.[38] Hampden, Pym, St. John, Nathaniel Fiennes, the Earls of Bedford, Essex, and Warwick, and Lord Holland were all visitors. It was at Broughton that William Fiennes (d. 1662) assembled a group of noblemen to arrange for their emigration to the New World. The founding of Saybrook (Connecticut) was the result.[39] When the Civil War broke out William Fiennes raised a regiment and garrisoned his house. According to tradition the regiment slept at Broughton on the eve of Edgehill. He and his sons fought there. He strongly disapproved of the execution of Charles I and lived in retirement at Broughton during the Interregnum. His second son Nathaniel Fiennes, M.P. for Banbury in 1640, became a colonel in the Parliamentary army and later played a prominent part in public affairs.[40] After the Restoration the Fiennes family continued to be active in the government of the country and James Fiennes (d. 1674) became a Privy Councillor and Lord Lieutenant of Oxfordshire.[41] In the late 19th century there were many royal and other distinguished visitors to Broughton, when Lord and Lady Algernon Lennox were the tenants. Among them was Lord Wolseley who was at Broughton in 1884 when ordered to take command of the Egyptian campaign.[42]

LOCAL GOVERNMENT. Broughton and North Newington were separately organized for poor law purposes from at least 1776.[43] At Broughton the cost of poor relief rose in the later 18th century. In 1776 £67 was spent; between 1783 and 1785 average expenditure was £96 and in 1802–3 £239 was spent, of which £176 was to provide out-relief for 20 adults and 46 children. This sum was raised by a rate of 3*s.* 4½*d.* in the pound.[44] In 1827 the rector and others successfully challenged the existing valuation; a new valuation brought in only £73 by a rate of 1*s.*, compared with £86 on the old system.[45] After the Poor Law Act of 1834 the cost of poor relief fell from £228 in 1834–5 to £178 in the following year.[46] Broughton became part of the Banbury Union; in 1851–2 expenditure was £79, raised by a rate of 11*d.* in the pound.[47]

Broughton's surveyors' accounts (1823–9) show that there were 2 surveyors. Levies for repair of the highways were 3*d.* or 6*d.* a year, which raised sums varying from £30 to £43 a year from about 14 contributors.[48]

At North Newington expenditure on poor relief almost trebled between 1776 and 1803. In 1776 £91 was spent. Between 1783 and 1785 there was an unaccountable fall in expenditure to an average £42; within 8 years, however, expenditure rose to £276. The rate was 5*s.* 6*d.*, one of the highest in Bloxham hundred. At that time £203 was spent on out-relief; 15 adults, of whom 10 were able-bodied, and 7 children received permanent relief, while 7 adults received occasional relief.[49] It may be that North Newington's many small freeholders suffered more than larger landowners from the Napoleonic wars and that the weaving industry was also affected. By 1834–5 expenditure on the poor was down to £119 and the following year to £38.[50] North Newington became part of the Banbury Union; in 1851–2 expenditure was £180, raised at a rate of 1*s.* 11¼*d.*[51]

ECONOMIC HISTORY. In 1086 the vill was assessed at 20 hides, which suggests that it was an ancient economic unit. It was under-cultivated, however, since only 10 ploughs were kept, although there was land for 16 ploughs. As 8 ploughs were in demesne, it seems that the lords held half the potential and three-quarters of the actual arable in their own hands. It is likely that the demesne farm of the pre-Conquest tenant Turgot was not divided when it came into possession of three Norman undertenants, for their holding was described as a single unit. There were 2 mills rendering 16*s.*, and 37 a. of meadow. In 1086 the estate was valued at £20 compared with its pre-Conquest valuation of £16. The recorded population of 4 *villani* and 10 bordars held 2 ploughs; there were 4 serfs.[52]

Broughton does not appear in the Hundred Rolls, nor are there any early extents. Tax assessments of the early 14th century show that the peasant community was poor compared with those in other parts of the county, for example in the Thames valley. All but 8 of the 48 assessed for the 1327 tax paid under 2*s.* and half paid less than 1*s.*[53] The relative prosperity of Broughton and North Newington is not illustrated by early records, but Broughton had the larger acreage and in the late 15th century was valued at £20, while North Newington manor was valued at £10.[54] In the 1540s Broughton was stated to be worth *c.* £35 a year and North Newington *c.* £25.[55]

Except in the Fiennes family there seems to have been no marked concentration of wealth in the parish in 1523 but there were several fairly substantial small farmers. There were 52 contributors to the first subsidy of that year, 47 to the second.

[36] *D.N.B.*; for his opposition to ship-money levies see *Cal. S.P. Dom.* 1636–9, 121, 122.

[37] *Acts of P.C.* 1623–5, 68, 81; *D.N.B.*; *Cal. S.P. Dom.* 1619–23, 487; ibid. 1623–5, 31, 168; 1636–9, 121, 122.

[38] Clarendon, *History of the Rebellion*, ed. W. D. Macray, iii. 26.

[39] *D.N.B.*

[40] Ibid.

[41] *Complete Peerage*, xi. 488.

[42] Wyatt's MS. notes.

[43] *Poor Abstract*, 398–9. The keeping of separate accounts by the churchwardens of Broughton and North Newington from at least 1719 suggests that the townships were then quite separate for all rating purposes: Par. Rec., chwdns' accts.

[44] *Poor Abstract*, 398–9.

[45] Par. Rec., vestry min. bk.

[46] *2nd Rep. of Poor Law Commrs. App. E*, H.C. 595–II, pp. 292–3 (1836), xxix (2).

[47] *Poor Law Unions*, 21.

[48] Par. Rec., surveyors' accts.

[49] *Poor Abstract*, 400–401.

[50] *2nd Rep. of Poor Law Commrs. App. E*, H.C. 595–II, pp. 292–3 (1836), xxix (2).

[51] *Poor Law Unions*, 21.

[52] *V.C.H. Oxon.* i. 417. The recorded population is small and suggests that not all the village was included in the survey.

[53] E 179/161/9. The 1306 assessment is incomplete and about a quarter of the sums in 1316 are illegible: E 179/161/10, 8.

[54] S.C. 6/1118/10; cf. *Cal. Inq. p.m. Hen. VII*, ii, p. 272.

[55] Bodl. MS. Rawl. D 892, f. 158.

About a third paid between 2*s.* and 4*s.* 6*d.*, that is were assessed on at least £4 worth of goods. Another third were assessed at 4*d.* and were either landless labourers or owned very few goods. Predominating over all were Sir Edward Fiennes and his mother, Elizabeth West, who paid between them the equivalent of the total contribution of the others and were the only persons assessed on lands.[56]

In 1444 the whole parish was included in a survey of the Wykeham estate. In general the survey shows that demesne farming in Broughton had declined, to the advantage of the small farmer. The demesne seems originally to have contained at least 21 yardlands (11½ in Broughton, 9½ in Newington) and a rabbit warren. In 1444 all except the warren and some meadow was leased to customary tenants; 22 tenants in Broughton and 12 in Newington held between ¼ and 1 yardland of demesne in addition to their customary tenements. The lord's farm equipment was also leased and 8 Broughton tenants held 6 carts and 8 ploughs formerly in demesne. Another unusual feature of the leases was that with one exception (where 10*s.* was paid for a yardland) tenants gave grain, not money, for demesne holdings, usually at the rate of 6 qr. for ½ yardland, as well as a cart-load and a sack of straw.[57]

There were only 5 free yardlands in Broughton and 6 in Newington, compared with 24½ customary yardlands in Broughton and 27 in Newington. They were held by 8 free and some 53 customary tenants, of whom as many as 37 lived in Broughton township itself. Tenants of free holdings held either by socage or knight service and rents varied from 1 lb. of pepper for a free yardland in Newington to 6*s.* 8*d.* for one in Broughton or 1*s.* 4*d.* for a croft held in socage. Two of the free tenants had substantial holdings of 3 and 5 yardlands respectively but the others held only 1 yardland or a toft or croft. The usual rent was *c.* 16*s.* for a yardland. Servile works were not mentioned and must have been commuted at an earlier date. Nevertheless, a contemporary court roll shows that the obligations of villein status were still insisted on, and two *nativi* who had left the manor were ordered to be at the next court. The distribution of customary land differed markedly in Broughton and Newington. In Broughton there had been little engrossment: only one tenant had as much as 2½ yardlands, the standard holding of customary land being ½ or 1 yardland, while 10 cottar-tenants held still less. In Newington, on the other hand, 8 tenants held between 2 and 4 yardlands each and 5 had 1 yardland only of customary land.[58]

The townships had separate fields. Some ordinances of 1441 include an order that no animals were to be allowed into ploughed land by night or day; at Broughton tenants had to keep the lord's pinfold in repair, and at Newington tenants were ordered to make a common pinfold. It was also laid down at Newington that none was to trespass in or make a road over the lord's warren or to break into a close of the lord or a tenant. All tenants of the manor had to scythe the lord's meadow. The grain rents show that maslin, dredge, and barley were the chief crops grown by the tenants, wheat being mentioned in only one instance.[59] Some land was laid down to leys, a common practice in north Oxfordshire.[60] There is little evidence for early consolidation of holdings: as late as the 16th century the glebe lay in scattered parcels of 1 a. or 2 a. and in lands and butts.[61] The yardland in Broughton contained *c.* 24 a.[62]

The pattern of farming established by the mid-15th century and practised throughout most of the 16th century was radically altered between 1589 and 1607 when Sir Richard Fiennes turned to large-scale farming, inclosed Broughton, and laid down much of the parish to pasture. About 500 a. of tenant land and some 12 tenements and 5 cottages were affected.[63] Sir Richard recorded in 1607 that he had taken over 3 yardlands of glebe in Broughton in exchange for 4 yardlands in Banbury and had resumed 9 yardlands of demesne in exchange for land in Bodicote. Other tenants had been persuaded to inclose: 50 a. of the parsonage, for example, once lying in common, were measured into 3 closes by 1607, and a few small tenants gave up their land altogether in return for common rights. At North Newington Sir Richard was only able to inclose 4 yardlands, which he had bought from a previous tenant.[64] After these changes Broughton manor, of which 1,295 a. were now in demesne, became the Fienneses' largest demesne farm in Oxfordshire. In North Newington they had only 217 a. in demesne.[65]

The object of inclosure was undoubtedly to convert land to pasture for sheep and cattle. In 1607 one tenant had none of his 60 a. of closes under the plough; and there were then only 4 or 5 plough-teams in the whole of Broughton township.[66] A survey of the demesne in 1592 records the changes in detail: 3 fields, about one-twelfth of the demesne, were arable, while the rest was meadow and pasture. The demesne estate was divided into some 20 closes. Some were exceptionally large, for example Stanwell pasture and meadow (171 a.), and Copthorn pasture (24 a.). There were only 146 a. of tenants' closes and houses in this township.[67] Over four-fifths (172 a.) of the demesne in Newington was pasture which was described in 1600 as on the 'east of the new hedge parting the great pasture' and worth £80 a year.[68] Newington, however, remained largely uninclosed. In 1592 the township, apart from the demesne, consisted of 22 a. of tenants' closes, 38 a. of meadow, and 449 a. of arable open field. In 1600 there were 23 yardlands in the common fields.[69] In 1607 it was recorded that the lord and tenants had 9 or 10 ploughs between them.[70] Despite the amount of open-field arable, however, many sheep were kept: one shepherd who died in 1637 had a flock worth £50.[71] Edward Broughton (d. 1613) was perhaps characteristic of Newington husbandmen with small mixed farms. At his death he had chattels worth £111 and carried, compared with many a south Oxfordshire farmer of the same class, a comparatively large amount of stock. He had a flock of 80 sheep, 8 horses, and a mare, and 7

[56] E 179/161/196, 198. Elizabeth Fiennes married William West as her second husband.
[57] B.M. Add. Roll 67029.
[58] Ibid.
[59] Ibid.
[60] MS. Oxf. Archd. Oxon. b 40, f. 76.
[61] Ibid.
[62] Deduced from the acreages given in 1589: Bodl. MS. Rawl. D 892, f. 183.
[63] MS. Oxf. Archd. Oxon. b 40, f. 76; Bodl. MS. Rawl. D 892, f. 183.
[64] Bodl. MS. Rawl. D 892, f. 183.
[65] Ibid. f. 166.
[66] Ibid. f. 183v.
[67] Ibid. f. 165.
[68] Ibid. ff. 63v., 167.
[69] Ibid.
[70] Ibid. f. 183v.
[71] MS. Wills Oxon. 18/2/13.

'beasts', accounting for over a third of the total value of his inventory.[72]

The effect of inclosure on the status of the villagers was marked. In return for the tenants' co-operation Sir Richard Fiennes substituted leasehold tenure for copyhold, at least at North Newington where he gave them 'all' leases.[73] He probably created a number of small freeholds also, for 7 people were said to hold land in chief in North Newington in the late 16th century.[74] Richard claimed that these changes were all to the benefit of the tenants and instanced increases in value by 1607 of three or four times the old value of 1589: e.g. one 60 a. holding had increased from £10 to £30 and the parsonage holding (50 a.) from £20 to £40.[75] Furthermore, he claimed that individual tenants 'now lived well' and 'brought up and bestowed their children well', and described Newington as a village where all had been tenants-at-will and 'lived poorly' but 'now live all welthily'.[76] The local farmer prospered still further in the later 17th century when Sir Richard's successors, unable to continue with large-scale demesne farming, because, no doubt, of their losses incurred during the Civil War, leased much of their estate.

Late-17th-century rent rolls show that the Fienneses by then drew mainly rents from Broughton, which was still, however, their most valuable possession in north Oxfordshire.[77] In 1688, for example, they received £1,452 from their property in the parish.[78] There were about 29 tenants on their rent rolls who had taken over much of the demesne land: a map of 1685 shows the various closes named after these tenants.[79] Rents for a house and close varied from 10*s.* to £1, but individual rents for closes were often high: £92 10*s.* for a 'bargain' in Newington and £58 for Chadwell Great Ground.[80] If Quaker opinion was typical of local feeling, William Fiennes, lord of Broughton at this time, was regarded as a grasping landlord. He is described in a Quaker pamphlet as 'one who would lay field to field and house to house, till there be no place for the poor'.[81]

An examination of inventories and wills made between the late 16th and early 18th century throws light on the status of the local husbandmen and yeomen. The value of the inventories ranged from £12 to £281, but the average yeoman's was well below £100: eight of the Newington farmers were worth between £33 and £68.[82] Richard Claridge (d. 1570), for instance, a husbandman of Newington, was probably the man assessed in 1546 on £10 worth of goods. His goods and chattels were worth £33 when he died; he was a carpenter as well, since he left 140 boards to one son and 200 to another.[83] Edward Tustian (d. 1622) of Newington is an example of a small husbandman, worth only some £14; he had corn in the barn and house (£1) and a crop on the ground (£1), a cow, three store pigs, and 6*s.* 8*d.* worth of hemp and yarn.[84] A similar small husbandman of Broughton was worth £15 in 1613 and his agricultural wealth was in 2 cows (£5) and 2 store pigs and poultry (7*s.* 8*d.*).[85] The miller of Broughton, on the other hand, was worth £85 in 1664, of which £35 was owed to him on bonds, while over a quarter of his wealth (*c.* £24) was in horses, cows, pigs, hay, and bees.[86] Samuel French (d. 1662), yeoman of Broughton, who was worth £281, was exceptional. He held a lease of Banbury Castle and Castle Orchard worth £150, which accounts for the high value of the property listed in his inventory. His actual wealth in grain and stock was £55 and included 2 yardlands of wheat and peas.[87]

Pasture farming continued to be the chief basis of wealth in the parish, and field names such as Dairy Ground, New Close Pasture, and Grazing Ground indicate the importance of cattle and sheep in the economy.[88] A tithe case of 1697 shows that of 977 a. half was pasture, a quarter meadow, and a third arable.[89] The Fienneses were receiving a considerable sum from cattle on their manors in north Oxfordshire,[90] while their tenants were keeping a large proportion of their land under pasture. William Dalby (d. 1684) was probably the largest tenant-farmer in the parish: he leased the Newington demesne closes[91] and in 1694 was worth £847, of which nearly half was in stock and a quarter in crops. His flock of 295 sheep was given an exceptionally high valuation of £212 and his herd of 150 cows and yearlings was worth £167.[92]

Even so arable land may have increased in importance in the course of the 17th century. In 1656 85 a. of the Bretch were tillage and by 1674 the deer park and warren were ploughed.[93] The Fienneses received considerable sums from crops: £320, for instance, in 1684 in four inclosures.[94] Between 1693 and 1695 tenant-farmers were said to have ploughed their closes for three years in succession and to have grazed others for one year and ploughed for two, or vice versa.[95] Inventories of local farmers indicate that the usual north Oxfordshire crops were grown, i.e. wheat, barley, and peas.[96] William Dalby also had oats in his rickyard, where he had £90 worth of grain, including wheat and barley, and another Newington farmer had rye listed in his inventory.[97] In the 18th century there was a tendency to convert to arable since there were then better profits for corn. To guard against the

72 MS. Wills. Oxon. 4/3/21.
73 Bodl. MS. Rawl. D 892, f. 183v.
74 MS. Dunkin 438/2, f. 153.
75 Bodl. MS. Rawl. D 892, f. 183v.
76 Ibid.
77 Ibid. D 915, rentals 1674–85; ibid. D 892, ff. 243–55, rentals 1687–89.
78 Ibid. D 892, f. 250.
79 Ibid. ff. 243 sqq.; map *penes* Lord Saye and Sele, Broughton Castle.
80 Bodl. MS. Rawl. D 892, f. 248.
81 *The Quakers' darkness avoiding the Scripture light* (Oxon. 1569). This is printed with Wm. Fiennes, *Folly and Madness made Manifest* (Bodl. copy in Wood 645(13)).
82 e.g. MS. Wills Oxon. 4/3/21; 18/5/11; 20/4/35; 22/1/42; 23/1/19; 23/4/10; 24/1/32; 30/1/58; 37/4/10; 58/3/67; 65/4/38; 83/2/17; 116/1/31; 148/3/10; 161/3/27; 184, f. 353; 185, f. 17; 187, f. 63.
83 Ibid. 185, f. 17.
84 Ibid. 65/4/38.
85 Ibid. 30/1/58.
86 Ibid. 37/4/10.
87 Ibid. 23/1/19.
88 e.g. Par. Rec., tithe case of 1697; map of 1685, *penes* Lord Saye and Sele, Broughton Castle.
89 Deeds *penes* Lord Saye and Sele.
90 e.g. Bodl. MS. Rawl. D 915, f. 97.
91 MS. Wills Oxon. 18/5/11. For his tenure of demesne closes in Newington see e.g. Bodl. MS. Rawl. D 892, f. 248.
92 MS. Wills. Oxon. 18/5/11.
93 Bodl. MS. Rawl. D 892, f. 168.
94 Ibid. D 915, f. 99.
95 E 134/9 Wm. III/Trin. 6 Oxf.
96 e.g. MS. Wills Oxon. 161/3/27; 23/1/19; 184, f. 353.
97 Ibid. 18/5/11; 161/3/27.

exhaustion of the soil and a diminution of stock leases often contained a clause similar to that found in a lease of a 220 a. farm in 1778, which specified that about a third of the farm was not to be ploughed and that £5 a year was to be paid for every acre of ancient meadow or pasture ploughed up without leave.[98] New crops such as flax, hops, sainfoin, clover, and woad were being grown.

In the 18th century tenant-farming predominated, the greater part of the parish still being owned by the Saye and Sele family.[99] In Broughton itself there were only three 40*s.* freeholds in 1754; in Newington, always a more independent village, there were 10.[1] Late-18th-century land taxes show that there were *c.* 14 other landowners in the parish besides Lord Saye and Sele, but only two or three were owner-occupiers.[2]

In 1778 farmers anxious to inclose North Newington Field met in Banbury. Disputes over tithe prevented agreement and in 1783 the attempt to inclose was abandoned[3] until the opening years of the 19th century. The inclosure award of 1805 dealt with 513 a. of common and waste.[4] Gregory, Lord Saye and Sele, as lord of the manor, received *c.* 2 a. for rights in the waste but had no other land in the open fields. The largest allotments were to Francis, Earl of Guilford (146 a.), to the rector (100 a.), and Mary Long (99 a.). Six allotments of 14 to 29 a. were made, and there were three of under 1 a.[5]

Throughout the 19th century the Saye and Sele family remained the chief landowners: in 1831 Gregory, Lord Saye and Sele, and Fiennes Trotman paid three-quarters of the land tax for the parish, the only other landowner of any size being the rector, who was assessed at £15 on house and land.[6] At this time there were *c.* 20 tenants holding land, 6 of them with rentals of over £100.[7] The small tenant farmer, however, disappeared in the course of the century. In 1851 3 farmers were recorded in Broughton and 6 in Newington. Of these, 3 had between 80 a. and 100 a., but there were 4 with 250 to 330 a., and almost a third of the total farmland (884 a.) was concentrated in the hands of one farmer, employing 41 labourers.[8] The labouring population at Broughton and Newington mostly lived in tied cottages, and benefited from the low rentals at which Lord Saye and Sele let them: 19 out of 21 cottages belonged to him in Broughton and were let at £2 10*s.* a year. It is noteworthy that at Newington the 17th-century tradition of independence persisted and over half of the 64 or so cottages there were owner-occupied.[9]

There is some evidence for rural distress. Between 1841 and 1851 the population dropped from 629 to 550, partly as a result of emigration;[10] later, however, agricultural depression and increasing population produced such bad overcrowding in the cottages that the rector urged that legislation should be introduced to prevent it.[11]

Both arable and pasture farming were practised in the 19th and 20th centuries, though there was perhaps a slight preference for corn growing in the early 19th century: in 1827 one farmer followed a 4-course rotation and his land in that year was divided between barley, fallow, wheat, and turnips;[12] woad was also still grown in the parish at this time.[13] Broughton Great Ground (190 a.) was mown for the last time in 1848.[14] There was a grazier living in the parish in 1851,[15] and the slump in corn prices in the 1870s undoubtedly encouraged the retention of permanent pasture. Before the First World War the highest rent was paid for land under grass;[16] about half the parish was then under permanent pasture and the other half was devoted to wheat and barley.[17] The farmland in the parish was particularly valuable and farms in North Newington, which were let for 24*s.*–35*s.* an acre, were among the most highly rented farms in Oxfordshire.[18] The area was described in the 1940s as the best land in the county.[19] In 1961 farming was still mixed. Leys farming was common and most farmers kept sheep and cattle. The chief crops were wheat and barley and there were very few root crops.[20]

By this date most of the inhabitants were employed in Banbury.[21] Both villages, however, have always had a non-agricultural aspect because of the mills.[22] Apart from the fullers, dyers, and paper- and bone-manufacturers and their employees, there are occasional references in the records to other craftsmen. In the 19th-century parish register the following occur: a stocking weaver, numerous carpenters, shoemakers, and maltsters, and two stone-masons.[23] A saddler's business recorded in 1920 was still in existence in North Newington in 1965.[24]

MILLS. Two mills were recorded in 1086 and by 1444 there were 3 on the Wykeham estate alone, one of which was a fulling-mill.[25] By the 17th century there were 2 fulling-mills in the parish and a paper-mill. At a later date there were mills making dyestuffs and bone manure.[26]

The best documented of the mills is Hazelford mill in Broughton township. Probably built on the site of one of the Domesday mills, it was held with 1 a. of land in 1444 by Thomas Hazelford as part of a knight's fee. The rent to the Wykehams was 13*s.* 4*d.*[27] In the late 16th and 17th centuries it was held by the Fiennes-Trotman family, lords of Shelswell manor, under their relatives the Fienneses of Broughton, and was leased to various tenants.[28] It was known then and as late as 1797 as Hazelford or Upper Fulling mill,[29] although by 1792 it had

98 MS. Top. Oxon. c 328, ff. 88–89.
99 O.R.O., land tax assess. 1785.
1 *Oxon. Poll* 1754.
2 O.R.O., land tax assess. 1785–1800.
3 MS. Top. Oxon. c 128, ff. 84, 86, 87.
4 O.R.O., incl. award. The act was dated two years earlier: Newington Incl. Act, 43 Geo. III, c 119 (priv. act).
5 O.R.O., incl. award.
6 O.R.O., land tax assess. 1831.
7 Ibid.
8 H.O. 107/1733.
9 Bodl., Bradford pps. (uncat.), valuation list (undated).
10 *Census*, 1841, 1851.
11 Bodl., Bradford pps. (uncat.), valuation list.
12 Ibid., 1827 survey.
13 Ibid., article on woad; and see p. 96.
14 Wyatt's MS. notes.
15 H.O. 107/1733.
16 Orr, *Oxon. Agric.* 65.
17 Ibid., statistical plates.
18 Ibid. 65.
19 *Land Utilisation Survey* (1943), pt. 56, 203.
20 Ex inf. Major J. F. Nicholson, Park Farm, Drayton.
21 Local information.
22 See p. 96.
23 Par. Rec., reg.
24 *Kelly's Dir. Oxon.* (1920).
25 *V.C.H. Oxon.* i. 417; B.M. Add. Roll 67029.
26 See below.
27 B.M. Add. Roll 67029; cp. Bodl. MS. Rawl. D 915, ff. 6 sqq. for the same rent being paid in the 17th century.
28 C 1/1123/56; C 142/115/33; C 142/127/39; O.R.O. Misc. Br. I/iii/1.
29 Map *penes* Lord Saye and Sele, Broughton Castle; Davis, *Oxon. Map* (1797).

already been converted to a paper-mill and had been leased to George King.[30] It was closed soon after 1851.[31]

A second Broughton fulling-mill was working on the Sor Brook in the late 17th century; it is shown on an estate map of 1685, and is mentioned in 1687 in the estate accounts of the Fiennes family.[32] The fulling-mills undoubtedly owed their existence to the flourishing state of the textile industry in the county, stimulated by an improvement in road transport and the proximity of Banbury, itself a flourishing centre of the industry. Plush-weaving at nearby Shutford was certainly in existence by 1747 and the connexion between Shutford and Broughton remained close until the mid-19th century.[33] By 1827 Lower Fulling Mill had a dye works attached to it and was dyeing cloth for Shutford.[34] The property consisted of shearing-houses, woad-houses, store-houses, and closes with racks for drying.[35] According to local tradition the woad was milled by horse power at Woad Mill Farm, which lies at some distance from the stream; the woad plant was certainly cultivated in the parish in the 19th century.[36] Lower Fulling Mill was evidently a prosperous concern. It was rated at over £54 in 1827 and in the 1860s the rental was about £155 compared with £60 paid for North Newington paper-mill and £135 for the corn-mill discussed below.[37] John Hutchings was the miller in 1852 and he was said to be able to produce very fine colours because of the excellent quality of the water; he dyed cloth for royal liveries, for the hangings of the new Palace of Westminster, and for policemen's uniforms.[38] The 1851 Census shows that, as was so often the case, dyeing was combined with farming. The dyer had a farm of 80 a., but he employed 12 labourers, more than enough for a farm of 300 a. In addition the Census recorded a dyer journeyman at Broughton.[39] The fulling and dyeing works seem to have come to an end in the early 20th century.[40]

A third mill in Broughton, close to the village, was used as a corn-mill. Its location suggests that it was an early manorial mill. In the mid-17th century its miller, Roger Jakeman (d. 1669), was a man of substance; he left chattels worth £85, of which £35 were in bonds.[41] Broughton mill was rebuilt in 1700 and was pulled down in 1892,[42] although the mill-house remains.

North Newington also had a water-mill named 'Collesmille' in 1444.[43] It was recorded as a paper-mill in 1684.[44] It is possible that the Fienneses had converted it into a paper mill long before the late 16th century and that Shakespeare had it in mind when he wrote *Henry the Sixth*. In that play Jack Cade taunts Lord Saye with building a paper-mill 'contrary to the king, his crown and dignity'; it is not known that the Fienneses had a paper-mill at any time on their Kentish property.[45]

Between 1687 and 1689 Nathaniel and Michael Hutton rented the Newington mill in succession.[46] The Huttons were connected with the family of that name who were paper-makers of Deddington. In fact Michael Hutton may have been identical with Michael Hutton of Deddington, paper-maker, who died in 1716.[47] William Elkins was described in 1753 as a paper-maker of North Newington in the Banbury marriage register; in 1760 John Jones occupied the paper-mill and its closes;[48] in 1801 the death of John Gauthern, paper-moulder of North Newington, was recorded,[49] and in 1816 William Emberlin occurs as a paper-manufacturer there. Since at least 1805 Thomas Cobb had been the owner.[50] When the mill was put up for auction in 1833 there were 4 engines for rags, a paper-making machine, and steam-drying apparatus.[51] The 1851 Census recorded 2 paper-makers, one employing 5 men, and another two.[52] Mrs. Rebecca Sellers, whose family had been tenants of Hazelford paper-mill,[53] was described as a paper-maker at North Newington mill between 1854 and 1869.[54] The present mill-building was constructed *c.* 1870. The mill-house was enlarged and reconstructed about that time by William Sellers.[55] The earlier mill is shown by some stones in one wall near the tail-race.[56] By 1887 Alfred Sellers, an artificial manure manufacturer, had converted the mill into a bone-factory,[57] which had ceased to work by 1920.[58] It has subsequently been used as a water-corn-mill.[59] The wheel, of pitch-back type, is still in operation and some apparatus, consisting of adjustable wooden slats formerly used for paper-drying, has been preserved in its original position in a long drying shed (80 ft. × 18 ft.).

CHURCH.[60] The written evidence for Broughton church begins in 1224, the date of the first known presentation,[61] but the font suggests that a church was in existence there *c.* 1100.[62] The rectory was never appropriated.

The advowson belonged to the lords of Broughton

[30] Bodl. MS. d.d. Oxon. c 7, 1792.
[31] Wyatt's MS. notes.
[32] e.g. Bodl. MS. Rawl. D 892, ff. 6, 8, 12, 24v.; map of 1685 at Broughton Castle.
[33] R. P. Beckinsale, 'Plush industry of Oxfordshire', *Oxoniensia*, xxviii. 65.
[34] Bodl., Bradford pps. (uncat.): 1827 poor rate assess.
[35] Ibid.
[36] O.S. Map 25" Oxon., V. 15 (1st edn.); article by E. A. Walford in *Banbury Advertiser*, 12 Dec. 1901.
[37] Bodl., Bradford pps. (uncat.): 1827 poor rate assess. and valuation list.
[38] Gardner, *Dir. Oxon.*; Wyatt's MS. notes.
[39] H.O. 107/1733.
[40] Local information
[41] MS. Wills Oxon. 37/4/10.
[42] Bodl., Bradford pps. (uncat.).
[43] B.M. Add. Roll 67029.
[44] For an account of the chronology of paper-mills see Rhys Jenkins, 'Early Papermaking in England, 1495–1788', *Library Assoc. Rec.* II (ii). 479 sqq.
[45] Shakespeare, *II Henry VI*, IV, vii.
[46] e.g. Bodl. MS. Rawl. D 915, ff. 68v., 73, 75; ibid. D 892, ff. 246, 248, 250v., 252v., 254.
[47] MS. Wills Oxon. 133/5/12; O.R.O., S. & F. colln. (uncat.).
[48] N. Riding of Yorks R.O. ZKF/39.
[49] cp. Bodl. MS. Oxon. Shutford, for a reference to him in 1795.
[50] H. Carter, *Wolvercote Mill*, 70; O.R.O., land tax assess. 1831.
[51] Bodl. G. A. Oxon. b 85a (27): *Sale cat.*
[52] H.O. 107/1733.
[53] MS. dd. Oxon. c 7 (1793).
[54] Billing, *Dir. Oxon.* (1854); *Kelly's Dir. Oxon.* (1869); Bodl. Bradford pps.; Harding, paper-maker of North Newington, occurs in the Broughton Register in 1856 and Mallins in 1854, 1859 and 1862.
[55] Ex inf. Mr. J. F. Carter; a date stone on the mill-house records W.S. 1876, and a name plate over an adjacent shed, William Sellers, paper-maker.
[56] Ex inf. Mr. J. F. Carter.
[57] *Kelly's Dir. Oxon.* (1887).
[58] Ibid. (1920).
[59] Ex inf. Mr. G. Clark, the Mill House.
[60] Some of the material for this section was kindly supplied by Frances Riddell Blount.
[61] *Rot. Welles*, ii. 17.
[62] See p. 99.

manor from at least 1230.[63] In 1317 during the minority of John of Broughton, there was a dispute over the advowson closely connected with that over the manor in 1315;[64] Thomas, Earl of Lancaster, won the right to present.[65] The advowson then followed the descent of the manor until after 1710 the manor passed to the Twisleton family, while the advowson was apparently retained by the Fiennes family; in 1732, for instance, Lawrence, Viscount Saye and Sele, presented.[66] The Twisletons later claimed the advowson and between 1766 and 1771 the living was vacant while the case was tried.[67] Judgement was given in their favour in 1771, but by 1806 they had sold the advowson to Charles Wyatt (d. 1821), a Banbury banker.[68] It continued to be held by the Wyatt family, two members of which were also rectors, and by their cousins the Bradfords,[69] until the Revd. B. W. Bradford (d. 1947) left it to his nephew, Lt.-Col. Charles J. Bradford of Adderbury. In 1950 the latter transferred it to Lord Saye and Sele, who was patron in 1963.[70]

The medieval rectory, consisting of the tithes of Broughton and North Newington, as well as some glebe, was a moderately valuable one, although perhaps not so 'abounding in revenues' as it was said to be in 1400.[71] It was valued at £10 (or £12) in 1254; and at £13 6*s.* 8*d.* in 1291, together with a pension of 10*s.* to the Abbess of Winchester[72] (probably of Nunnaminster), the origin of which has not been found. The pension was still being paid in 1428, but was not mentioned in 1535, when the value of the rectory was £18 16*s.*[73]

By the early 17th century the living was said to be worth £100[74] but its subsequent value was affected by a prescriptive modus of £40 agreed with the lord when he inclosed a large part of his demesne. By 1697, however, when much of that land was no longer in demesne, the rector, John Knight, sued 13 of William Fiennes's Broughton tenants for tithes in kind, claiming that the modus was invalid. The court found in his favour but confirmed several customary moduses for small tithes, among them 3*d.* for a milk cow, 1½*d.* for a dry cow pastured in tithable lands, and 1 lb. in 30 for tithe wool.[75] The rectory was valued in 1697 at £140 a year.[76] In the 1770s, when it was proposed to inclose Newington, the rector refused the farmers' offer of a seventh of the land and insisted on getting more than he had at Tadmarton (of which he was also rector), and on getting a fifth of the arable and a ninth of the greensward.[77] Inclosure was postponed and in 1783 the next rector leased the open-field tithes of Newington to farmers there for 12 years at £3 a yardland.[78]

When North Newington was inclosed in 1805 all the tithes in the parish were commuted for land, the rector receiving what he had asked for in Newington (100 a.), mostly for the tithes of open-field land, and 192 a. in Broughton for those of inclosed lands.[79] To this land was added the ancient glebe, first mentioned in 1341,[80] and which before inclosure in the 16th century had consisted of 3 yardlands with commons for 6 horses, 6 'beasts', and 60 sheep.[81] At the inclosure it was apparently exchanged for 28 a.[82]

In the 19th century the endowment of the rectory was therefore entirely in land: Tithe farm in Newington (*c.* 100 a.) and Rectory farm in Broughton (*c.* 232 a.).[83] By 1807 the rectory was worth £500 a year and it was thought that improvements would increase its value to £700.[84] Although its value fluctuated with that of land, it remained comparatively rich.[85] In 1943 and 1944 most of the land was sold.[86]

In 1356 a chantry was founded in Broughton church by Sir Thomas of Broughton for the souls of his family. It was to be served by a canon of Wroxton and was being so served in 1457.[87]

The medieval church had numerous lights for which bequests were left. In wills dated between 1527 and 1545, besides the light on the high altar the following lights are mentioned: the High Rood light, the Sepulchre light, the Five light, the Trinity light, St. George's light and the Twelve light. An obit supported by lands worth 8*d.* a year was also recorded.[88]

One of the medieval rectors, Ralph de Bereford (1317–62), came of a knightly family and was probably related to the Broughtons.[89] His successor, Roger Gledston (1369–?1399) a Newington man, was wealthy enough to give Wroxton Priory a house and yardland and to enlarge his own rectory-house.[90] With Master John of Wykeham (1399–1415)[91] the parish began to have rectors who were university graduates but who were, at the same time, pluralists and often non-resident. One was dispensed to hold Broughton in plurality with a Norfolk rectory in return for repairing the churches and rectory-houses of both parishes.[92] His successor, Thomas

63 Michael Belet presented in 1230 for his ward, John of Broughton: *Rot. Welles*, ii. 32 and see p. 87.

64 See p. 87.

65 Linc. Reg. ii. 169.

66 MS. Oxf. Dioc. c 266, f. 142v.; see also C.P. 25(2)/1186/Mich. 8 Geo. II, a fine on the manor but not on the advowson.

67 MS. Oxf. Dioc. d 558; the presentation of Robert Harrison was in 1766 and his institution in 1771: ibid. d 740; b 21, f. 86. See also C.P. 25(2)/1388/Trin. 6 Geo. III, East. 8 Geo. III. The legal record of the suit has not been traced.

68 MS. Oxf. Dioc. d 746, 1806/4. The patron in 1805 was Wm. Curtis: O.R.O., incl. award.

69 See M.I. in church to Eliz. Bradford, daughter of Chas. Wyatt; Wyatt family papers: notes by M. L. Dix Hamilton *penes* Banbury Hist. Soc.

70 MS. Oxf. Dioc. c 1748, letters.

71 *Cal. Papal Regs.* v. 282.

72 Lunt, *Val. Norw.* 309; *Tax. Eccl.* (Rec. Com.), 31.

73 *Feud. Aids.* vi. 377; *Valor Eccl.* (Rec. Com.), ii. 163.

74 MS. Dunkin 438/2, f. 153.

75 Par. Rec., 1697 depositions. The original tithe agreement could not be produced and the case was based on a lease of 1615.

76 E 134/9 Wm. III/Mich. no. 8.

77 MS. Top. Oxon. c 128, ff. 84–84v., 86.

78 Ibid. ff. 97–97v.

79 43 Geo. III, c 119 (priv. act); O.R.O., incl. award.

80 *Inq. Non.* (Rec. Com.), 138.

81 MS. Oxf. Archd. Oxon. b 40, f. 76; undated terrier of time of H. Leigh (1596–1605), but referring to some years earlier.

82 Ibid. f. 77; Bodl., Bradford pps. (uncat.), 1805 copy of incl. schedule. For an exchange of land in 1796 see MS. Oxf. Dioc. c 434, ff. 125 sqq.

83 Bodl., Bradford pps., valuation lists.

84 MS. Oxf. Dioc. d 549, p. 161.

85 *Rep. of Comm. on Eccl. Revenues*, H.C. 54 (1835), xxii.

86 Par. Rec.

87 E 326/4433; *V.C.H. Oxon.* ii. 101.

88 Bodl., Bradford pps., transcripts; *Chant. Cert.* 30.

89 e.g. E 326/4433, where Sir Robert de Bereford is a witness. The arms of Bereford are among those depicted on the tomb of John (d. *c.* 1350) or Thomas (d. *c.* 1375) of Broughton in Broughton Church.

90 *Cal. Pat.* 1367–70, 338.

91 Emden, *O.U. Reg.*

92 *Cal. Papal Regs.* vii. 203, 278; ibid. viii. 82, xi. 641.

Broke, not only paid him to resign but in return for his presentation paid the patron's debts.[93] He was excommunicated for simony but in 1446 received papal absolution on condition that he spent a year's income from the church on its fabric.[94] The rector in 1518 and 1520 lived on another cure in Derbyshire;[95] he was charged with failing to maintain a lamp, to pay the deacon who served Broughton and to keep a bull and a boar for the use of the parish.[96] His successor paid a curate and also leased the living.[97] The curate, Richard Crowley,[98] was involved in a tithe dispute with a parishioner who accused him of favouring the supremacy of Rome and commanding his congregation to offer alms on 'relics' Sunday.[99] These charges were denied.

Although several members of the Fiennes family were Puritans in the early 17th century and William Fiennes (d. 1662) was described by Clarendon as 'the oracle of those who were called Puritans in the worst sense'[1] it is not clear to what extent Puritanism affected Broughton parish generally. John Crayker, rector 1583–96, was a 'good preacher'.[2] His successor was deprived in 1605, perhaps for refusing to conform with standard Church practices and Crayker, then Rector of Tadmarton, was reinstated.[3] Ralph Taylor (1615–46), a 'faithful pastor' was shown much kindness by Nathaniel Fiennes, a strong Puritan.[4] John Taylor, his successor, was chaplain to Lord Saye and Sele, was made Fellow of Lincoln College, Oxford, in 1648 on a special order from the London Committee, and in 1654 was put on a commission to eject unfit ministers in Oxfordshire.[5] After the ejection of the next incumbent, Nathaniel Coney, in 1662[6] no evidence has been found of Puritan leanings among the rectors of Broughton. Richard White (1662–83) was a countryman and farmed his own glebe. He was not, however, without intellectual interests, for at his death he left £14 worth of books out of goods valued at £97.[7]

In the later 17th and 18th centuries the Fienneses sometimes presented their relatives to the living. Of those relatives one, Beaumont Percival, memorable for the account Celia Fiennes wrote of his Hawarden (Flints.) living, was only at Broughton for a few years,[8] but John Knight (1692–1704) who married a grand-daughter of William Fiennes (d. 1662), spent much of his life in Oxfordshire, being formerly Vicar of Banbury.[9] He rebuilt the rectory-house on coming to Broughton,[10] prosecuted both Protestant and Quaker farmers for non-payment of tithes, was also 'a good scholar, very loyal, and of a good name and esteem', and *strenuus schismaticorum et sacrilegorum impugnator*. He was a noted preacher,[11] which was of particular importance in Broughton, 'the genius of this neighbourhood, relishing nothing but sermons'.[12]

Eighteenth-century rectors served for long periods, were resident, and closely connected with the castle. John Eddowes (1732–66) held regular services: 2 on Sundays with 2 sermons in summer and 1 in winter, administered the sacrament 4 times a year to between 15 and 20 communicants, and catechized.[13] In his dotage he was helped by a curate.[14] Similar services were held during the rest of the century, but a later return adds that there were prayers on Wednesdays and Fridays in Lent and daily in Passion Week and that Lewis's *Exposition*[15] was used in catechizing the children.[16] At the beginning of the 19th century the rectors did not reside. The parish was cared for by a resident curate, with whom the parishioners were 'particularly well pleased', and it was said that 'no parish has greater pains taken with it or the duty done more conscientiously than at Broughton'.[17]

In the early 19th century because of the distance from the church, some Newington people, although not nonconformists, attended the Methodist chapel, and some of the aged and infirm as well as a few 'rich reprobates', attended no church.[18] The latter were probably Newington farmers, who had long been in disagreement with the rectors over tithes and who in their 'haggling manner' tried to beat one rector down from £3 to 5*s*. a yardland when he offered to lease the tithes to them.[19]

For nearly a hundred years the parish was connected with the Wyatts, father and son holding the living and also being patrons. The rise in standards of living and the size of clerical families had made the rectory too small and one of C. F. Wyatt's (rector 1819–70) first acts was to enlarge it.[20] Bishop Wilberforce, who held a conference in 1867 at Broughton, did not estimate Wyatt's spiritual influence very highly: he noted that he was 'a man more to cast up accounts, but anxious to have good curates'.[21] Nevertheless, he eventually increased the number of communions to one a month, had a large Sunday school, opened an evening school in 1853, and reported increasing congregations which by the 1860s reached 300.[22] In 1870 he resigned in favour of his son, C. F. Wyatt, who was a local antiquary, did much research into the history of the parish,[23] and was largely responsible for the restoration of the church. He was succeeded by his cousin

93 Beesley, *Hist. Banbury*, 173.
94 *Cal. Papal Regs.* ix. 561–2.
95 *Visit. Dioc. Linc. (1517–31)*, i. 127; MS. Top. Oxon. c 394, p. 206.
96 *Visit. Dioc. Linc. (1517–31)*, i. 127.
97 *Valor Eccl.* (Rec. Com.), ii. 163.
98 *Subsidy 1526*, 269.
99 *L. & P. Hen. VIII*, xxii(2), pp. 196–7, 225.
1 Clarendon, *Hist. of the Rebellion*, ed. W. D. Macray, i. 241.
2 *Seconde Parte of a Register*, ed. A. Peel, ii. 136; MS. Rawl. D 872, f. 182. Crayker was Rector of Tadmarton from 1590: see p. 157.
3 MS. Oxf. Dioc. c 264, f. 19v.
4 M.I. in churchyard; *Calamy Rev.* 479.
5 Beesley, *Hist. Banbury*, 465.
6 *Calamy Rev.* 131.
7 MS. Wills Oxon. 176; Beesley, *Hist. Banbury*, 487 where he is mistakenly identified with the Vicar of Banbury of the same name.
8 *Journeys of Celia Fiennes*, ed. C. Morris, 179.
9 M.I. in chancel. For pedigree see *Journeys of Celia Fiennes*, xlvi.
10 See p. 86.
11 For him see Wood, *Fasti*, ii. 348, where the names of his printed sermons are given.
12 Par. Rec., Broughton doc.
13 *Secker's Visit.*
14 MS. Oxf. Dioc. d 555; Par. Rec., reg.
15 Perhaps this was *The Sacrament: A plain and rational Institution* (1751), by Edward Lewis, Rector of Waterstock.
16 MS. Oxf. Dioc. d 558.
17 Ibid. c 660, ff. 191–2; Par. Rec., reg.
18 MS. Oxf. Dioc. d 576.
19 MS. Top. Oxon. c 128, f. 97.
20 MS. Oxf. Dioc. b 70; ibid. c 660, f. 191, c 661, f. 21.
21 Ibid. d 550, f. 23.
22 *Wilb. Visit.*; MS. Oxf. Dioc. c 332.
23 Wyatt's MS. notes.

B. Wyatt Bradford, who had already been curate since 1900.[24] The parish in 1963 had a resident rector: since 1946 the living has been held with Tadmarton.[25]

The church of *ST. MARY* consists of a chancel, nave, south aisle, and western tower surmounted by a broach spire.[26] It dates almost entirely from the 14th century and contains some excellent work of that period. The circular font with its cable-moulding[27] is the only evidence of a previous 12th-century church, but the arcade of 4 arches which separates the nave from the south aisle appears to date from the mid-13th century, and indicates the addition of a south aisle at that time. Some fragments of 13th-century roll-mouldings were discovered during the 19th-century restoration and are preserved in the vestry. The existing nave, south aisle, and tower were probably built during the lifetime of Sir John of Broughton (d. 1315), and may be compared with contemporary work in other north Oxfordshire churches, notably Bloxham. There is a straight joint in the masonry between the tower and the body of the church, but this is probably to be regarded as a structural expedient to avoid the dangers of unequal settlement, rather than as evidence of any difference of date. The chancel is slightly more advanced in architectural character, and was evidently rebuilt at a slightly later date than the nave, probably in *c.* 1320–30. It is separated from the nave by a contemporary stone screen.

Towards the end of the 14th century the walls of the south aisle were raised and clerestory windows were added. The original parapet and corbel table were re-used. When in the 15th century it was decided to add a nave clerestory, this heightening of the aisle walls made it necessary to raise the nave walls to an unusual height so that the nave clerestory might rise above the aisle roof. The main timbers of the existing low-pitched roof date from this rebuilding, though the roof has been frequently repaired, notably in 1684.[28] Another 15th-century addition to the church was the large 5-light window in the south wall of the south aisle.

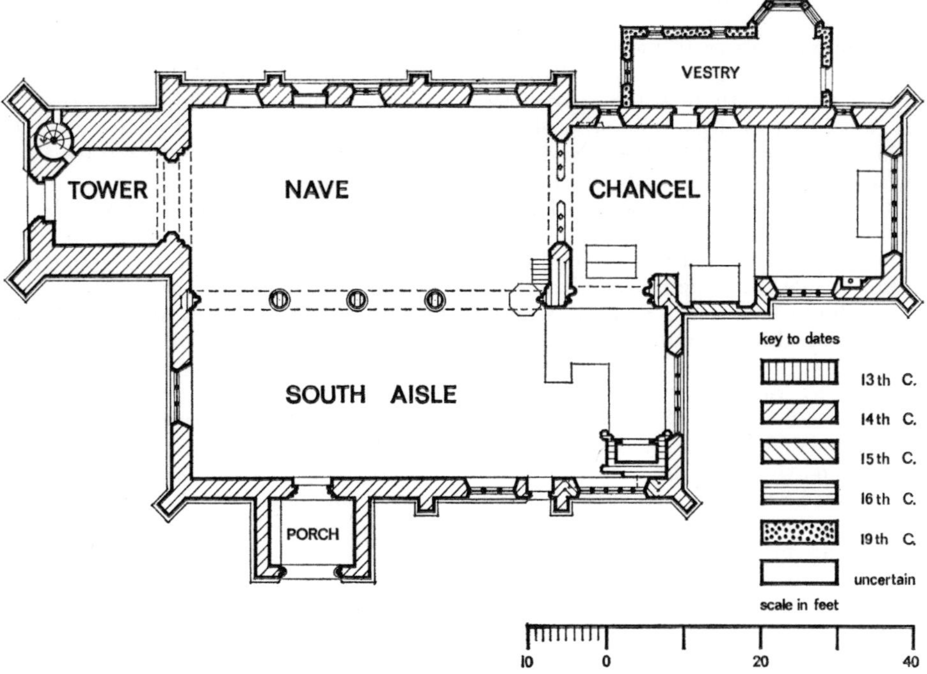

THE CHURCH OF ST. MARY, BROUGHTON

Apart from the repair of the nave roof in 1684 few details have survived before the 19th century of any alterations to the fabric. It may, however, be noted that the altar rails were erected in 1637, the re-opening of the blocked west window of the south aisle was ordered in 1756, the south aisle clerestory was restored in 1819, and the spire was partly rebuilt in 1823.[29] A small-scale general restoration took place in 1825.[30] In 1858 Gilbert Scott restored the sedilia and piscina, which had been walled-up until 1846 and whose tracery had been broken into a 'thousand atoms'.[31] Finally, between 1877 and 1880, a complete restoration was carried out by Sir Gilbert Scott and his son G. G. Scott.[32] An open timber roof in the Gothic style (builder, Davis of Banbury) replaced the flat (probably 18th-century) chancel roof of deal, the pitch being the same as that of the original medieval one;[33] the nave roof was rebuilt, some of the original 15th-century beams being retained; the south clerestory wall was

[24] For him see *Who's Who in Oxon.* (1936).

[25] See p. 157.

[26] For 19th-century illustrations of the most notable features of the church see Buckler drawing in MS. Top. Oxon. a 65, no. 122 (S.E. view 1822); Skelton, *Oxon.* Bloxham Hund. plates 6, 7; and for modern photographs see *Country Life*, 11 Jan. 1930, pp. 56–7, and N.B.R.

[27] For a drawing of the font see MS. Top. Oxon. a 65, no. 121 and *Arch. Jnl.* lxvii. 381 for an account.

[28] Wyatt's MS. notes. This date was found on one of the timbers during the restoration of 1877.

[29] Bodl. Bradford pps.; MS. Oxf. Archd. Oxon. d 13, f. 27; Par. Rec., chwdns' accts.

[30] Par. Rec., chwdns' accts.

[31] Wyatt's MS. notes.

[32] Bodl. Bradford pps.; *Parl. ret. for rebuilding churches and cathedrals* (1892), 116.

[33] Bodl., Bradford pps : a water-colour of 1805 shows the weather moulding of the medieval roof.

rebuilt from the window sills upwards; and the south aisle roof was entirely renewed and so constructed that it cleared the hood-mould and rear arch of the east window, which the original 14th-century roof had not done. The mutilated east window of the chancel was restored to its supposed original height and new tracery in the Decorated style was inserted.[34] The alterations also included the installation of a new pulpit in the Gothic style, replacing one made in 1741.[35]

Twentieth-century changes include the installation in 1908 of new heating apparatus and of electric light in 1939 and 1954.[36] In 1906 the floor of the chancel was raised by two steps to its original level and a reredos was erected. The tower and spire were repaired in 1960. In 1944 a tapestry reredos, the work of Marion, Lady Saye and Sele, was placed over the altar in the south aisle.[37]

In 1959 the 12th-century font was restored to its former position beside the westernmost pillar of the north nave arcade, its base and a draining hole in the ground having been found during recent restoration work.[38]

The church was richly furnished with wall paintings. At the restoration of 1878 many of these were uncovered, and others were discovered in 1938. The whole of the north wall of the chancel appears to have been painted with scenes from the life and death of the Virgin, attributed by E. W. Tristram to *c.* 1340. It seems probable that Sir Thomas of Broughton was the benefactor. His beneficence to the church was once commemorated in the glass of the east window of the south aisle as follows: *Multimodis ornamentis hanc ecclesiam adornavit.*[39] Besides the chancel murals there was a Doom over the chancel arch, a crucifixion on the pier beside the font, and a St. Christopher on the north wall of the nave.

The church was also once notable for its heraldic glass. Richard Lee noted 52 coats-of-arms in 1611 in the east window of the south aisle.[40] Among the coats was that of the Wykehams.[41] In 1963 only 3 circular panels of Elizabethan date survive in the cinquefoils of the tracery. Each has a quartered shield, including an achievement of Fiennes, wrongly reset.[42]

There are several examples of the work of Victorian glass-painters: a window of Munich glass was placed at the west end of the south aisle in 1862–6; the south window of the chancel was designed by G. G. Scott the younger and executed in 1870 by Burlison & Grylls (London); in 1871 the south-east window of the south aisle was made by Bowers & Westlake; in 1878 Clayton & Bell executed the glass in the east window of the chancel, and in 1880 another window in the south aisle was made by C. E. Kempe.[43]

The church has some notable monuments, of which 3 are medieval. They were considerably damaged, presumably during the Civil War, and were so zealously restored in 1846 that identification has been rendered difficult. The architect then employed was T. L. Donaldson, and 4 men were engaged on the 'reparations' during 4 months.[44]

The earliest monument is that of a cross-legged knight lying in an elaborately canopied recess in the south aisle. The knight's shield is charged with the arms of Broughton, and there are 13 shields surmounting the tomb. This is almost certainly the tomb of Sir John of Broughton (d. 1315). D. T. Powell, who wrote a careful description of the tomb in 1805, noted that it retained much of its original painting and gilding, and that most of the coats-of-arms could be deciphered.[45] The existing coats were painted in 1846 and are identical with Dugdale's drawings of *c.* 1636.[46]

A second effigy of a knight, probably representing the founder's son John of Broughton (d. *c.* 1350) or his grandson Thomas of Broughton (d. *c.* 1375), wears plate armour of the time of Edward II or Edward III, and carries an uncharged shield. In *c.* 1800 this effigy was placed on a table tomb of 15th-century date.[47] The tomb bears the arms of Fiennes but it has not been discovered for whom it was made. In a canopied recess in the chancel there are 2 fine alabaster effigies of a knight and his wife. In 1805 they were lying on the ground sadly 'hacked and broke'.[48] The canopy of the chantry has been destroyed, but stone panelling of mid-15th-century workmanship remains. This tomb is likely to be that of Sir Thomas Wykeham (d. 1443) and his wife. A fourth tomb, surmounted by muzzled bears supporting uncharged shields, may have been intended for Edward Fiennes (d. 1528). It was evidently unfinished and when the tomb was opened in the 19th century it was found to be empty.[49] William, Viscount Saye and Sele (d. 1662), and his wife Elizabeth (d. 1648) are commemorated by a marble table-tomb in the chancel. There are also numerous 17th-century and 18th-century inscriptions to other members of the Fiennes family, including Lawrence, Viscount Saye and Sele (d. 1742). There is a memorial to Charles Wyatt (d. 1821).

The following rectors are buried in the church: Robert Harrison (d. 1780), Rector of Broughton and Tadmarton; John Knight (d. 1715); Richard Crosse (d. 1732); and John Marcy (d. 1806).

There is a brass to Philippa Byshopsden (d. 1414), daughter and coheir of William Wilcotts and sister of the wife of Sir Thomas Wykeham.[50]

The church is not mentioned in the Edwardian inventory of 1552. In 1963 its most valuable possession was a large silver standing cup with cover, given in 1662, as the inscription testifies, by James, Viscount Saye and Sele (d. 1674). It is surmounted by the arms of Fiennes. There are 2 silver patens of 1686 and 1760, a silver chalice of 1783, and another presented in 1849.[51]

The tower has 5 bells, an additional clock bell,

[34] Bodl., Bradford pps.
[35] Ibid.; Par. Rec., chwdns' accts.
[36] MS. Oxf. Dioc. c 1748, faculties.
[37] Ibid.; *Oxf. Mail*, 19 Nov. 1960.
[38] Ex inf. Lord Saye and Sele.
[39] *Par. Colln.* i. 59.
[40] Ibid. 59–61; MS. Wood E 1, ff. 171–2.
[41] *Coll. Top. & Gen.* iii. 235.
[42] These are fully described in Lamborn, *Armorial Glass*, 114 sqq. (For an annotated copy with photos. see Bodl. 17031 e 17 and for tricks of the three shields see G. A. Oxon. 4° 688, p. 58*b*.) Photographs by P. S. Spokes are also in N.B.R.
[43] Bodl., Bradford pps.
[44] Ibid.
[45] Ibid. and drawings. For the blazons of the arms as seen today on the monuments see Bodl. G. A. Oxon. 4° 685, pp. 59–61; ibid. 4° 688, pp. 58–9; ibid. 16° 217, pp. 74–9. See plate facing p. 88.
[46] Bodl. MS. Dugdale II, f. 156.
[47] Bodl., Bradford pps., MS. notes by D. T. Powell and C. F. Wyatt.
[48] Ibid. See plate facing p. 88.
[49] Wyatt's MS. notes.
[50] Charles Boutell, *Monumental Brasses* (Lond. 1847), 48.
[51] Evans, *Ch. Plate.*

and a sanctus bell; all date from the 19th century.[52] A clock was installed in the tower before 1788.[53]

The registers are complete from 1683.[54]

A chapel dedicated to St. John the Baptist existed in 1331 when John of Broughton endowed it with 3 houses, 2 yardlands, and 16 a. in North Newington to found a daily chantry for himself and his wife Margaret.[55] It probably stood in what is now Park Lane in Newington.[56] It never became parochial despite an attempt to that end made with papal intervention in 1400.[57] At about the time that that attempt was made, and perhaps in compensation for the failure, the Pope granted indulgences to those who left goods to the chapel and released penance to those who visited it.[58] In consequence the chapel became something of a place of pilgrimage and in the early 16th century the curate of Broughton was accused of saying Mass for pilgrims on Midsummer Day there instead of in Broughton church.[59] In 1521 there was a brotherhood of St. John the Baptist attached to the chapel, with two keepers or wardens.[60] The chapel is not known to have survived the Reformation.

NONCONFORMITY. Roman Catholicism barely survived in this strongly Protestant parish. Apart from those recusants imprisoned in the castle between 1589 and 1593[61] the only other references are reports that 2 papists were living in the parish in 1768 and 1811.[62]

Until the 19th century Quakers were the only nonconformists in the parish. The opposition of William Fiennes, Viscount Saye and Sele (d. 1662), whose violent attitude to the Quakers is revealed in his two pamphlets, *Folly and Madnesse Made Manifest* (1659) and *The Quakers' Reply Manifested to be Railing* (1660), prevented the growth of a strong community in Broughton itself.[63] Fiennes went so far as to evict two Quakers from his Broughton cottages;[64] he also gave information which led to the imprisonment of one of them, William Potter, after a meeting in Broughton.[65] Potter moved to Tadmarton and played a leading part in establishing Quakerism there.[66] Only 5 Broughton families are recorded in 17th-century Quaker registers. In the 18th century numbers dwindled to 2 families and in the 19th century none is recorded.[67]

At North Newington, however, where there were many freeholders, Quakerism was stronger. Nathaniel Ball, a freeholder,[68] was particularly prominent. Until 1698 his house was used for meetings and it was there that Bray D'Oyley of Adderbury, one of the most influential Quakers in north Oxfordshire, was arrested in 1666.[69] Ball was imprisoned at least twice in the 1660s and again in 1678; he regularly suffered distraint for non-payment of tithes.[70] He was appointed by the Quarterly Meeting of the Banbury Division to carry out responsible tasks for the Oxfordshire Quakers.[71] The Quarterly Meeting was held at North Newington in 1683 and 1685 and occasionally the Monthly Meeting of Banbury Division was also held there.[72] In 1698, however, Ball was disgraced for scandalous drunkenness;[73] about the same time another North Newington Quaker achieved notoriety for interpreting literally St. Matthew's Gospel (xix. 12) and so castrating himself 'for the Kingdom of Heaven's sake'.[74] There were *c.* 12 families of Quakers in the hamlet in the 17th century.[75] In the 18th century, although the Fardons, Thompsons, and Graftons, all yeomen farmers, were constantly in trouble over tithes, Quaker affairs were less dramatic.[76] Fardon's house was licensed for meetings in 1731[77] but normally the Newington Quakers attended the Banbury meeting. In 1738 the rector reported that 9 families went there; thirty years later the reduction in numbers was attributed to the lack of a meeting-house.[78] In 1784 only 6 Quaker families lived in the whole parish.[79] The 19th-century registers give only 2 names for North Newington.[80] Most of the 15 Quakers reported by the rector in 1811 must have been at the North Newington boarding school,[81] for a private census of North Newington inhabitants in 1820 listed only five, forming one family.[82]

Methodism, too, had more success in North Newington than in Broughton; the rector attributed the growth of dissent to the hamlet's remoteness from the parish church.[83] A meeting-house in John Tysoe's house at Newington was registered in 1805 and the signatories' names suggest that they were Methodists.[84] In 1811 8 or 10 enrolled Methodists were meeting on a Newington farm, served occasionally by licensed travelling teachers.[85] In 1814 there were said to be 20 Methodists and in 1817 10 or 12 Methodist families.[86] In 1820, however, a private census listed 14 Methodists and 15 Calvinists.[87] No further reference to Methodists has been found.

Independents, probably the 'Calvinists' of the census, became predominant. In 1832 the minister

52 *Ch. Bells Oxon.*

53 Par. Rec., chwdns' accts. It was repaired in 1788.

54 Par. Rec., reg.

55 G. Metcalfe, *Broughton*, 4; C 143/212/22.

56 See p. 86.

57 *Cal. Papal Regs.* v. 282.

58 Bodl. MS. Rawl. A 269, f. 50, which refers to a bull of Pope Boniface (i.e. probably Boniface IX (1389–1404)).

59 *L. & P. Hen. VIII*, xii (2), p. 225.

60 Bodl., MS. Rawl. A 269, f. 50.

61 See p. 91.

62 MS. Oxf. Dioc. d 558; ibid. d 572.

63 Wm. Fiennes, *Folly and Madnesse made Manifest* (Oxf. 1659); ibid. *The Quakers' Reply Manifested to be Railing* (Oxf. 1660).

64 *The Quakers' Reply Manifested to be Railing*; MS. Sufferings.

65 MS. Sufferings.

66 See p. 158.

67 Banbury Quaker Regs.

68 For list of freeholders see Oxon. Q.M. Min. Bk. (1671–1746), *sub anno* 1679.

69 MS. Sufferings.

70 Ibid.; Besse, *Sufferings*, i. 567, 571.

71 Oxon. Q.M. Min. Bk. 1678, 1679, 1683, 1692.

72 Oxon. Q.M. Min. Bk. 1683, 1685; Banbury Prep. M. Min. Bk. (1696–1720).

73 Banbury Prep. M. Min. Bk. (1696–1720).

74 Plot, *Nat. Hist. Oxon.* 208.

75 Banbury Quaker Regs.

76 MS. Sufferings, *passim.*

77 O.R.O. Cal. Q.Sess. viii.

78 *Secker's Visit*; MS. Oxf. Dioc. d 558. In 1774 two Newington families were attending Shutford meeting-house: ibid. d 564.

79 MS. Oxf. Dioc. b 37.

80 Banbury Quaker Regs.

81 MS. Oxf. Dioc. d 570; the school was recorded in 1808: see p. 102.

82 Ibid. d 572; Bodl., Bradford pps. (uncat.): Gauthern's census. Visitation returns of 1817, 1820, and 1823 (MS. Oxf. Dioc. b 7) mention only two Quakers.

83 MS. Oxf. Dioc. d 576.

84 Ibid. c 644, no. 83.

85 Ibid. d 572.

86 Ibid. d 574, d 576.

87 Bodl., Bradford pps. (uncat.).

of the Independent Church at Banbury registered a private house as a meeting-house and in 1837 a chapel was built at North Newington.[88] At the 1851 census there were congregations of 80 and 93 (including children), presumably gathered from neighbouring villages as well.[89] The rector's estimate of 30 must have applied to the congregation drawn from his parish alone.[90] The chapel was rebuilt in 1876.[91] North Newington members, however, appear to have been decreasing, for in 1866 there were an estimated 20 dissenters, and in 1878 only 3 or 4 families of them in the parish.[92] By 1963 the chapel was disused.

SCHOOLS. In 1818 it was observed that the parish poor were without sufficient means of education. At that date there was a Sunday school at Broughton supported by private subscription. It was attended by *c.* 40 children in 1818 and 1833. A room for this school was built in 1836 at a cost of £150 and by 1866 the numbers attending had doubled.[93] There has never been a day school in Broughton village.[94]

At North Newington, apart from a private boarding school kept by a Quaker, recorded in 1808,[95] there seems to have been no school until 1814 when a Sunday school, supported by voluntary subscriptions, was started. In 1832 it was attended by 63 children and had a lending library attached.[96] There was also in 1832 a school for 12 boys and 6 girls who attended at their parents' expense.[97] In 1853 a school with a master's house attached was built at North Newington.[98] The site was purchased in 1861 by the trustees of the Saye and Sele charity, which thereafter supported a schoolmaster and paid for repairs to the school.[99] In 1866 80 children were attending. Evening classes were held in the winter months until in 1878 they were discontinued because of the school-master's ill-health.[1] At that date there were 5 voluntary instructors, but no pupil teachers; religious instruction was also given.[2] Between 1892 and 1901–2 attendance varied from 85 to 73.[3] The school was enlarged in 1911.[4] In 1944 it was recognized as a Junior Primary school, retaining its status as a Church school. In 1962 it had a roll of 66.[5] In 1963 it was still receiving £15 from the Saye and Sele charity.[6]

CHARITIES. At an unknown date an unknown donor gave 1 a. of land in Horley to the poor of Broughton parish.[7] In 1738 the land was being let for £1 7*s.* a year.[8] By 1823 it had become customary for the churchwardens to demand the rent of £2 2*s.* every two or three years and to distribute it equally between the poor of the two townships.[9] In 1871 the rent was £3.[10] In 1926 £12 was disbursed in 40 cash payments. In 1932 the rent was £1 and the balance in hand was £23.[11]

Christabella, Viscountess Saye and Sele, by will dated 1787, left in trust the residue of her estate, of which part was to benefit the poor of North Newington. The amount due to the trust was settled in Chancery in 1803, and the annual share of income for the township was £80. Half of this was spent in apprenticing two legitimate boys at £20 each, and £40 was given away at Christmas to the unrelieved poor. The trustees were somewhat negligent in their management so that large sums accumulated; the balance was distributed in 1824 and the proportion received by North Newington was £68 6*s.*[12] The charity was regulated by a Scheme in 1850, by which any interest not used for apprenticeships was to go to a school account; North Newington school was still receiving support from the charity in 1963.[13] A further change in 1897 allowed the £40 to be spent on apprenticing an unspecified number of deserving children or giving them outfits on entering service or trade.[14] In 1931 the trustees were enabled to pay instruction fees and travelling expenses of persons under the age of 21, or to help them in any way to earn their living.[15] In 1949 £24 was spent on outfits for three girls and £5 on tools.[16] The scheme of 1850 reduced the £40 originally given away to the poor to £25, but it was later increased to £30.[17]

In 1859 Elizabeth Bradford Wyatt conveyed in trust 4 cottages and *c.* ½ a. in Broughton village for the housing of poor and aged agricultural labourers, their relicts, or spinster daughters, who had resided in the parish for 21 years, were of good character, and were communicants of the Church of England.[18] An endowment of £500 for the maintenance of the cottages was probably given at the same date. In 1920 the stock was £716 and the income £16 a year. Because of difficulties in finding qualified occupants for the cottages the Charity Commissioners reduced the qualifications to 10-year residence and 'membership' of the Church of England. Between 1941 and 1950 £300 had accumulated and was invested, bringing the stock to *c.* £1,050.[19] From 1951 to 1959 the occupiers paid a yearly contribution totalling *c.* £40.[20]

[88] MS. Oxf. Dioc. c 645, nos. 52, 198.
[89] H.O. 129/163.
[90] *Wilb. Visit.*
[91] *Kelly's Dir. Oxon.* (1920).
[92] MS. Oxf. Dioc. c 332; ibid. c 334.
[93] *Educ. of Poor*, 720; *Educ. Enq. Abstract*, 742; MS. Oxf. Dioc. c 332, b 70.
[94] The school 'at Broughton' mentioned in the returns of mid-19th-century vicars is clearly that at North Newington: MS. Oxf. Dioc. c 332, c 335 and see below.
[95] MS. Oxf. Dioc. d 707.
[96] Ibid. d 574; *Educ. Enq. Abstract*, 742.
[97] *Educ. Enq. Abstract*, 742.
[98] Par. Rec., notebook of the rector, C. F. Wyatt, jnr.
[99] See below.
[1] MS. Oxf. Dioc. c 332; ibid. c 344.
[2] Ibid. c 334.
[3] *Schs. Special Grants*, H.C. 336, p. 57 (1892), lx; *Pub. Elem. Sch. Ret.* (1900), 674; *List of Schs.* (1902), 200.
[4] *Kelly's Dir. Oxon.* (1920).
[5] Ex inf. Oxfordshire County Council Educ. Cttee.
[6] Ex inf. the rector.
[7] *12th Rep. Com. Char.* 208.
[8] *Secker's Visit.*
[9] *12th Rep. Com. Char.* 208.
[10] *Gen. Digest. Char.* 12–13.
[11] Char. Com., G file, accts.
[12] *12th Rep. Com. Char.* 208 sqq.
[13] Char. Com., file E 79, 446; see above.
[14] Char. Com. B 14, 939.
[15] Ibid. E 72, 300.
[16] Ibid., G file, accts.
[17] Ibid. file E 79, 446.
[18] Ibid., Unrep. vol. 276, p. 359.
[19] Ibid.; Char. Com., file E 98, 495.
[20] Ibid., G file, accts.

DRAYTON

THIS small and narrow parish lies in the Oxfordshire wolds some 2½ miles north-west of Banbury.[1] In 1881 it covered 926 a. and in 1932, after a part had been annexed to Banbury, 871 a.[2] A tributary of the River Cherwell forms most of its long western boundary and divides it from Wroxton. Its southern boundary with Broughton is artificial. The parish lies within the 400 and 500 ft. contours, and is characterized by woodless undulating fields and valleys. There is no natural woodland, but its upland aspect was diversified after inclosure, some of it of 17th-century date, with timbered hedges. Trees have been planted, by the Norths, on the hill slopes between Park Farm and the boundary with Wroxton so that this part of the parish has the appearance of park land. There is a small covert in the south near Withycombe Farm. Withycombe, probably meaning willow valley,[3] gives a clue to the early character both of this part of the parish and of the western valley where Drayton village itself lies.

The road from Banbury divides ½ mile to the east of the village, one branch continuing northwards to Hanwell, the other going west to Wroxton and Alkerton. Banbury way, Bloxham path, and the highway called Drayton lane, are mentioned in a terrier of 1601.[4] A Drayton lane turnpike committee met in 1753 under the chairmanship of Francis, Earl of Guilford, and in March 1754 Drayton lane was being levelled for the turnpike road through Wroxton and Upton.[5] That economy was observed is suggested by one man's request to have charge of the turnpike gate if it was fixed at Drayton Town's End: as his house stood near the road, it could be used and would save the expense of building one.[6] Conditions before the turnpike was made are described in the Act of 1747: the road for several months of the year was dangerous for horsemen and almost impassable for carriages.

In the 19th century a mineral railway was built in the north of the parish in connexion with the ironstone works.[7]

The good water supply and the sheltered slopes of the valley probably attracted early settlers. Roman remains — the tessellated pavement of a villa and coins[8] — have been found near the church, lying on the 400 ft. contour on the hillside above the stream; hereabouts was the nucleus of the original village. The first element of the name Drayton derives from the Old English *drag* which is sometimes used of a portage,[9] and the village may have got its name because of the necessity of pulling corn from the mill and other goods up and down the steep valley sides.

The modern village is mostly scattered along the curving road to Wroxton on a rocky hill about 450 ft. up,[10] but there are still (1964) 3 cottages in the valley to the south-west of the church where the mill lay.[11] As the agricultural land was comparatively restricted the village was never large. In 1377 only 47 persons were assessed for poll tax;[12] the total male population of 18 years and over in 1642 probably numbered 51, a figure which agrees fairly well with the 104 adults recorded for the Compton Census of 1676;[13] according to 18th-century incumbents there were *c.* 20 families.[14] It was believed, however, that the village had once been larger. Rawlinson, writing in 1718, said that Drayton formerly called 'Little London', had suffered from fire and that burnt stones were frequently dug up. There were about 34 houses in his time.[15] In the 19th century there was a marked increase in population, numbers rising from 183 in 1801 to 224 in 1831.[16] In 1841 there were 42 houses and by 1868 these were mostly in a bad state.[17] Thereafter there was a decline until the expansion of industry at Banbury after the First World War attracted workers to the village. In 1931 the population numbered 210 compared with 172 in 1901,[18] and numbers have since continued to rise.

In the later 17th century there were 3 fair-sized houses in the village: the parsonage which was assessed on 5 hearths for the Hearth Tax of 1665 and 2 farm-houses assessed at 7 and 5 hearths; there were also 6 small farm-houses, assessed at 1 or 2 hearths each and an unknown number of cottages.[19] The largest farm-house, then occupied by John Cleaver, was probably the old manor-house of the Ardens and Grevilles, which has now totally disappeared. In the Middle Ages it must have been a considerable building: in 1329 Sir Robert Arden was licensed to crenellate it[20] and in the late 14th and 15th centuries it was the principal seat of the Greville family.[21] Sir Lewis Greville was outlawed in 1406 for receiving in his house an Alkerton man, who had committed murder, and for 'consorting in the crime'.[22] When Leland visited the village about 1540 a Greville was still living there, though in impoverished circumstances.[23] In the late 16th century the Greville's house was occupied by the wealthy yeoman Thomas Webb; after the murder of his brother Richard by Lewis Greville,[24] the manorial estate was split up and the village never again had a resident lord of the manor. In 1819 Brewer stated that the mansion, once of 'some importance', lay on the south-east side of the church and that the remains of the building were used as a poor-house.[25] By 1841 the house had entirely gone.[26]

1 O.S. Map 6″ Oxon. V (1st edn.); ibid. 2½″ SP 44 (1951).
2 O.S. *Area Bk.* (1882); *Census*, 1931.
3 *P. N. Oxon.* (E.P.N.S.), ii. 397.
4 MS. Oxf. Archd. Oxon. c 141, f. 473.
5 MS. North b 24, ff. 180–7; ibid. d 6, ff. 169, 171; the Act was 26 Geo. II, c 78 A.
6 MS. North d 2, f. 47.
7 See p. 171.
8 *V.C.H. Oxon.* i. 329, 336.
9 *P. N. Oxon.* (E.P.N.S.), ii. 397, when the editor comments that it is difficult to see in what sense 'portage' can be used in this particular name.
10 O.S. Map 25″ Oxon. V. 7 (1st edn.).
11 Mill Ham is mentioned in the incl. award (O.R.O.), and the site of the mill is shown on an early-19th-century map (Par. Rec.).
12 E 179/161/44.
13 *Protestation Ret.* 51 men signed; Compton Census.
14 MS. Oxf. Dioc. d 555, d 558, d 561, d 564.
15 *Par. Colln.* ii. 123; *Secker's Visit.*
16 *V.C.H. Oxon.* ii. 217.
17 *Census*, 1841; *Agric. Employment Women and Children*, 351.
18 *Census*, 1901, 1931.
19 *Hearth Tax Oxon.* 143.
20 *Cal. Pat.* 1327–30, 357.
21 Greville monuments in the church.
22 *Cal. Pat.* 1405–8, 394.
23 Leland, *Itin.* ed. Toulmin Smith, ii. 12–13.
24 See p. 106.
25 Brewer, *Oxon.* 517.
26 Beesley, *Hist. Banbury*, 174.

The 16th-century parsonage-house stood on the site of the present large 19th-century rectory house, the cellars of which are of 17th-century date.[27] This house was occupied by a number of rectors in the 16th and 17th centuries who were leaders of the Puritan movement in the English church; their memorials remain not only in stone in the church but in the their theological writings.[28] A bill of 1674 for repairs to the parsonage, the barn, and the stable, survives and it includes a sum for wainscoting the parlour.[29] In 1862 this house was pulled down and rebuilt to the designs of A. W. Blomfield.[30] A photograph of the earlier house shows a 2-storied house with attics, a thatched roof, and sash windows.[31]

The second large farm-house of 1665, then occupied by Elias Jackman, father of a Rector of Wigginton,[32] can perhaps be identified with the present Park Farm, which belonged to the Norths' estate and was bought in 1935 by Trinity College, Oxford.[33] This connexion with the North family perhaps explains the 18th-century castellated archway, standing on high ground in the fields of Park Farm, which was evidently a part of the design for landscaping the park at Wroxton on the opposite hillside. The detail of this 'folly' strongly suggests that Sanderson Miller was the architect, as he was of other ornamental buildings in Wroxton Park. Park Farm itself stands just above the church and is a house of 2 stories. It seems to have been built originally on the 2-unit plan, common in this area, with kitchen and parlour on either side of a through passage, but it has been added on to at both ends.[34] On a panel over the front door is the date 1683 and the initials C. J. G.

The Roebuck Inn probably dates from the same period. It is a 2-storied building of coursed rubble, which retains some stone-mullioned windows of 2 and 3 lights, with square moulded labels, and a doorway with a classical architrave and cornice.[35] The earliest record of licences being issued to Drayton victuallers, however, is between 1753 and 1772. In 1782 the innkeepers of both the 'Roebuck' and the 'Hare and Hounds' were licensed.[36] The second house is not recorded after 1806, perhaps because the traffic on the road was not sufficient to supply 2 inns at such a short distance from Banbury, but the 'Roebuck' flourished.

Although there was no resident squire in the 18th century, his place was taken in the second half of the century by the Metcalfe family, which presumably lived at Drayton Lodge,[37] a late 18th-century house in the north of the parish. It appears to be on the site of an older one and, though now a farm-house, there are indications that this was once a gentleman's residence; the grounds have fine trees planted in them and there are fishponds nearby. The Metcalfes supported the school and endowed a charity. The 'benevolent, munificent, and charitable' Elizabeth Metcalfe (d. 1791) is commemorated in the church.

Another outlying house is Drayton Fields Farm, built after the inclosure of the open fields in 1802. Withycombe farm-house dates from the 17th century; it is a 2-storied ashlar house with attic dormers and has a few brick cottages nearby, built in 1881.

There was some 18th- and 19th-century rebuilding and expansion, when the traditional materials, ironstone rubble and thatch, were mostly used, although the elementary school of 1868 is of brick. Today the village has few ancient cottages left. The modern houses have not followed the traditional pattern but are built of red brick, roughcast, Welsh slate, and various types of tile.

MANOR AND OTHER ESTATES.[38] The English thegn, Turchil of Arden, was one of the few Englishmen to retain land after the Conquest and in 1086 he was still holding 5 hides at *DRAYTON*.[39] But when William II created the Earldom of Warwick, probably in 1089, he gave Turchil's estates to Henry, the first earl.[40] Henceforth until the 1380s the Arden family held by knight service of the earls of Warwick. Although the Ardens were holding land in Warwickshire and elsewhere in the 12th century,[41] no reference to their tenancy of Drayton has been found before 1204, when a Thomas Arden is recorded as holding a ½ fee there.[42] There is considerable doubt about the identity of this Thomas. The 17th-century pedigrees disagree but according to Dugdale he was the son of William Arden of Radbourn, a younger son of Henry Arden, who was directly descended from Turchil; Henry's eldest son was Thomas (I) Arden whose son and heir was Thomas (II), who married Eustacia.[43] Thomas, son of William, again according to Dugdale, married Lucy and was lord of Drayton, which must have reverted to the senior branch in about 1224. Sir Thomas Arden, presumably Lucy's husband, presented to the church in 1223, but in 1224, when a plea was heard about land in Drayton, Thomas was said to be dead.[44] In 1229 Thomas (III) Arden, son and heir of Thomas (II), of the senior line, seems to have been in possession of Drayton. In the same year his mother Eustacia, the relict of Thomas (II), who no doubt already held part of the manor in dower, was also at law about Drayton land.[45] In 1243 Eustacia was returned as holding the whole vill in dower and in 1248 she was evidently holding the advowson also.[46] She was a sister of Savari de Mauléon, a Poitevin favourite of Henry III.[47] She clearly lived to a great age: in 1272 she may have been dead when Thomas alone was returned as lord.[48]

[27] A stone-mullioned cellar window remains; it is visible from the interior.

[28] See pp. 109–10.

[29] Par. Rec., reg.

[30] MS. Oxf. Dioc. c 1799, report, specifications and plans.

[31] Par. Rec., photo. *ante* 1862. See also drawing of 1865.

[32] *Hearth Tax Oxon.* 143.

[33] Ex inf. Bursar.

[34] For this regional type see Wood-Jones, *Dom. Archit. Banbury Region*, 125 and *passim*.

[35] cf. ibid. 270.

[36] O.R.O., victlrs' recogs.

[37] No other house of any size exists in the parish.

[38] Some material for this section was collected by Jane Sayers.

[39] *V.C.H. Oxon.* i. 422.

[40] *Complete Peerage*, xii(2), 358, and below.

[41] Dugdale, *Warws. passim.*

[42] *Pipe R*, 1204 (P.R.S. N.S. xviii), 111.

[43] Dugdale, *Warws.* 676; cf. *Visit. Warws. 1619* (Harl. Soc. xii), 179, 182.

[44] *Cur. Reg. R.* xi. 456.

[45] Ibid. xiii. 460.

[46] *Bk. of Fees*, 823; *Rot. Grosse.* 490.

[47] Dugdale, *Warws.* 676–7.

[48] *Cal. Inq. p.m.* i, pp. 233, 256. She was certainly dead by 1286 when Ryton upon Dunsmore (Warws.), having reverted to Sir Thomas Arden of Ratley, was granted to the hospitallers: *Cal. Pat.* 1281–92, 225.

There is no reference to her at Drayton after 1243, but it may be supposed that she was still in possession at the time of her death.

Eustacia's sucessor at Drayton as in her other manors was evidently her son Thomas, but in the 1280s he seems to have been in financial difficulties and was alienating his lands.[49] He had been one of the barons to rebel against Henry III, he was taken prisoner at Evesham,[50] and that, as Dugdale guessed, was probably 'the ruin of him'.[51] In 1281 he granted lands in Warwickshire to Sir Thomas Arden of Hanwell.[52] It was alleged in 1375 that he had also granted him Drayton *juxta Hanwell*[53] and there seems no reason to doubt this. The relationship of these two Thomases has not been fully established. Some 17th-century pedigrees make Sir Thomas of Hanwell the son of Eustacia, but this is demonstrably false. Dugdale makes him an Arden of Radbourn.[54] It may be that he was a younger son of William Arden (fl. 1267) but if so he certainly never held Radbourn.[55] He married Rose, the daughter of Ralph Vernon, and thereby obtained an estate in Hanwell;[56] he is known to have gone on an expedition to Wales in 1277;[57] and he was in debt in 1281.[58] It is difficult to distinguish him with certainty from his more important relative Sir Thomas of Ratley (Warws.),[59] but Dugdale stated that he had found 'little memorable about him'.[60] He died some time before 1306 when his relict Rose was assessed for tax on Drayton.[61] In the following year she obtained the grant of a chantry in Godstow nunnery for the soul of her late husband.[62] It is possible that he was the Thomas of Arden who was killed at Hamstall Ridware (Staffs.) in 1299,[63] but this was more probably Sir Thomas of Ratley.

Rose presumably held Drayton in dower for she was still in possession in January 1316,[64] apparently the year of her death, for Sir Robert Arden was returned as lord the same year and was assessed for tax levied in 1316 on Drayton.[65] Rose's lands mainly descended to her son Ralph,[66] but she had already granted Drayton in 1309–10 to Sir Robert Arden and his heirs, arranging to hold it of him during her life.[67] The relationship of this Sir Robert is by no means certain. He may possibly have been an elder brother of Sir Thomas of Hanwell.[68] He was in any case an important knight possessed of many manors in Northamptonshire, Oxfordshire, and Sussex; he was on the king's side in the baronial wars and in 1322 Banbury Castle was in his keeping.[69] In 1329 he was licensed to crenellate his Drayton house.[70] He died in 1331 and his relict Nicole subsequently married Sir Thomas Wale who is found holding the family's Sussex property in 1332 and 1349.[71] Nicole probably held Drayton in dower, for Sir Thomas presented to Drayton church in 1342, 1344, and 1349, and was returned as holding 1 fee in Drayton in 1346.[72] She seems to have been still alive in 1356 when Sir Giles Arden was pardoned for outlawry incurred because he had disseised her of her rents in Duns Tew.[73]

On Nicole's death Drayton reverted to this Giles, the son and heir of her first husband.[74] In 1366 his tenure was disputed by Elizabeth of Swinford, who claimed possession as the descendant of Sir Thomas Arden of Hanwell and Rose Vernon. She claimed to be the great-grand-daughter of Thomas, grandson of Sir Thomas Arden of Hanwell, but the defence asserted that this Thomas was a bastard and she evidently lost her case.[75] Sir Giles died in 1376 and, as his only son Sir Giles (II), predeceased him, his lands descended to his grandchildren, Margaret and Joan, both minors.[76] Their inheritance, according to Leland, had been greatly enlarged by their father's marriage with Philippa, 'a woman borne to faire landes'.[77] Sir Henry Arden, the children's cousin, was made guardian, and in 1380 he leased two-thirds of Drayton manor to the Rector of Drayton,[78] the other third being held as dower by Sir Giles's widow Margaret.[79] In 1384 or 1385 she and her second husband Walter Power leased her life interest in Drayton to Sir Richard Abberbury.[80] Meanwhile the remaining two-thirds had reverted to the Crown on the ground that Sir Giles had held in chief, and in 1381 this portion was committed to the custody of Sir Reynold de Malyns during the minority of the co-heirs.[81]

The eldest girl, Margaret, married Lewis

49 *Cal. Fine R.* 1272–1307, 51.
50 *Cal. Inq. Misc.* i, p. 280.
51 Dugdale, *Warws.* 677.
52 *Visit. Warws. 1619* (Harl. Soc. xii), 179; Bridges, *Northants.* i. 211; *V.C.H. Warws.* v. 62.
53 C.P. 40/191, m. 46.
54 *Visit. Warws. 1619* (Harl. Soc. xii), 178–80; Dugdale, *Warws.* 676.
55 Wm. Arden held Radbourn in 1267, and Wm. son of Wm. Arden in 1316: *V.C.H. Warws.* vi. 199.
56 Dugdale, *Warws.* 677.
57 *Cal. Pat.* 1271–81, 220.
58 *Cal. Close*, 1279–88, 131.
59 For further details of the Arden family at this date see C. Moor, *Knights of Edw. I* (Harl. Soc. lxxx), 18. Two generations of Arden of Ratley seem to be confused there, and Arden of Ratley is confused with Thomas Arden of Hanwell.
60 Dugdale, *Warws.* 677.
61 E 179/161/10.
62 Linc. Reg. ii, f. 155.
63 *Cal. Pat.* 1292–1301, 476. As Thomas of Hanwell also held Wappenham (Northants.), he may have been the Thomas who was Sheriff of Northants. and Constable of Northampton Castle in 1298: *Cal. Fine R.* 1272–1307, 103, 119.
64 *Cal. Inq. p.m.* v, p. 402.
65 *Feud. Aids*, iv. 166; E 179/161/8.
66 *V.C.H. Warws.* iv. 62.
67 C.P. 25(1)/189/14/64.
68 *Visit. Warws. 1619* (Harl. Soc. xii), 179, 182; cf. Dugdale, *Warws.* 676, where he is described as the younger brother. If he was one of the Ardens of Radbourn he cannot have been the eldest son, for William was holding Radbourn in 1316.
69 *V.C.H. Sussex*, vii. 203; Bridges, *Northants.* i. 211; C. Moor, *Knights of Edw. I* (Harl Soc. lxxx), 18.
70 *Cal. Pat.* 1327–30, 357. For grants of free warren at Drayton see ibid. 1300–26, 366; 1327–41, 25, 50, 91.
71 *V.C.H. Sussex*, vii. 203; *Cartwright's Topography of the Rape of Bamber*, ii(2), 237. For Nicole see also N.R.A. *Rep.* Earl of Bradford (Staffs.), B/160.
72 See list of presentations in MS. Top. Oxon. d 460; *Feud. Aids*, iv. 179. The statement that Drayton was once held by Richard Arden seems to be a clerical error for Robert Arden.
73 *Cal. Pat.* 1354–8, 415.
74 For pedigree see *Visit. Warws. 1619* (Harl. Soc. xii), 179.
75 C.P. 40/429, m. 396.
76 C 136/18/2; Leland, *Itin.* ed. Toulmin Smith, ii. 12.
77 Leland, *Itin.* ed. Toulmin Smith, ii. 12.
78 N.R.A. *Rep.* Earl of Bradford (Staffs.), D/146.
79 C 136/18/2. Margaret was the daughter of Sir John Molineux: *Visit. Warws. 1619* (Harl. Soc. xii), 179.
80 C.P. 25(1)/191/23/46.
81 *Cal. Fine R.* 1377–83, 279. For Malyns see *V.C.H. Oxon.* viii. 61. The custody was disputed by the Earl of Warwick in 1383 when he claimed guardianship against Sir Reginald de Malyns: *Cal. Close*, 1381–5, 274.

Greville, son and heir of William Greville of Chipping Campden (Glos.).[82] Lewis was evidently lord in 1398 when he presented to the church; he was recorded as such in 1417 and 1428.[83] Margaret's sister Joan married Sir Richard Archer,[84] and the Archers appear to have surrendered their claim to half the manor to the Grevilles,[85] for no evidence of two manors in Drayton during the 15th century has been found. Lewis Greville died in 1438[86] and was followed by his son William, and then by his grandson and great-grandson Ralph and John.[87] Both William and Ralph married heiresses.[88] Sir Edward Greville (d. 1528/9), John's son, and his wife Ann were at law over the manor in 1507, and Sir Edward's son John may have been in possession by 1523, when he presented to the church.[89] It was of this Greville, presumably, that Leland wrote. He said that he was a man of 400 marks a year, though the family possessed court rolls showing that the property was once worth 3,300 marks a year; the land had been enfeoffed to the use of a certain 'mean gentleman' of Drayton and he had sold much of it and diverted some to his own heirs.[90] Sir John died in 1548 and was followed by his son Sir Edward (d. 1559 or 1560), and his grandson Lewis (II) Greville[91] who, owing to his extravagant mode of life, was forced to sell in 1565 to Thomas Webb.[92]

Webb, a wealthy yeoman whose family may possibly have been tenants of the manor for over 100 years,[93] was still holding the whole manor in 1575 when the sheriff reported that he was a man of great wealth and had purchased Drayton manor.[94] He had died before 1588 when his relict Katherine and his brother Richard were claiming his lands in Drayton from Lewis Greville.[95] This dispute ended tragically. It seems that Greville invited Richard Webb to stay at his Sezincote house in Gloucestershire with the object of obtaining all his property by trickery. The man was persuaded, while drunk, to make a will in Greville's favour and was then murdered. The crime was discovered and in 1589 Greville, who refused to plead, was found guilty and pressed to death at Warwick.[96]

Meanwhile Drayton manor had been divided into four; in 1587 and Easter 1588 Richard Webb had sold or leased two separate quarters to John Fox and William Buckbye.[97] Fox died in 1593 and left the whole site of the manor-house and his share of the manor to his wife and son for their lives.[98] William Buckbye sold or leased his share to William Saunders of Welford (Northants.) in 1590.[99]

It is not clear how the dominant share of the manor and advowson came into the hands of Sir Anthony Cope of Hanwell, but he presented in 1598 and again in 1607,[1] and in 1602 he settled the manor on William his son and Elizabeth Chaworth on the occasion of their marriage.[2] There is no doubt that the manor was divided at this time, for in 1602 Sir Anthony Cope received fractions of one eighth and one fortieth from two different sources,[3] and *c.* 1630 the manor was still made up of four separate parts.[4] William Cope succeeded his father in 1614[5] and the manor descended directly with the Cope family of Hanwell until in 1676 Mary Gerard, relict of Anthony Cope (d. 1675),[6] was declared insane. Sir Anthony's younger brother Sir John succeeded,[7] and on his death in 1721[8] Drayton passed to the Bruern Copes and so to Arabella Diana, daughter of Charles, 2nd. Bt., of Bruern. She married first John Frederick Sackville, Duke of Dorset (d. 1799), then Charles, Earl Whitworth (d. 1825), and died herself a few months after her second husband.[9] Her daughter and heir Elizabeth married George John West (afterwards Sackville-West), Earl de la Warr (d. 1869). Elizabeth, created Baroness Buckhurst, died in 1870.[10] The Norths of Wroxton already owned more than a third of the parish and the manorial rights passed to them, but have since lapsed.[11]

In about 1629 William Fiennes, Lord Saye and Sele, bought 388 a. of the land of the manor, later Drayton farm and Withycombe, from Sir William Cope.[12] This property was settled in 1653 on Lord Saye and Sele's third son John Fiennes and his wife Susanna.[13] There is no record of its descent in the 17th century, but the property may have passed to their son Laurence Fiennes, who became Viscount Saye and Sele in 1710 and died in 1742, being succeeded by his cousin Richard, Viscount Saye and Sele (d. 1781).[14] By 1763, however, Drayton farm and Withycombe were in the possession of Francis North, Earl of Guilford (d. 1790).[15] The Norths thus came to hold more property than the lord of the manor, i.e. 326 a. of old inclosure in 1802.[16] The Drayton property followed the descent of the family's Wroxton manor, and was held by them until Trinity College, Oxford, purchased it in 1935 and 1942.[17]

LOCAL GOVERNMENT. In the Middle Ages local government was presumably conducted through the manorial courts. In 1329 Robert Arden was

[82] *Visit. Warws. 1619* (Harl. Soc. xii), 179.
[83] MS. Top Oxon. d 460; *Cal. Fine R.* 1413–22, 221; *Feud. Aids*, iv. 187.
[84] *Visit. Warws. 1619* (Harl. Soc. xii), 179.
[85] C 137/28/56.
[86] See M.I. in Drayton church. For pedigree see Dugdale, *Warws.* 530.
[87] Dugdale, *Warws.* 530.
[88] Leland, *Itin.* ed. Toulmin Smith, ii. 12.
[89] C.P. 40/980/m. 431; Linc. Reg. xxvii, 178v.
[90] Leland, *Itin.* ii. 12.
[91] Dugdale, *Warws.* 530.
[92] C.P. 25(2)/196/Mich. 8 Eliz. I.
[93] A Thos. Webb witnessed a release by Margaret, relict of Sir Giles Arden in 1378: N.R.A. *Rep.* Earl of Bradford (Staffs.), 0/35.
[94] Hist. MSS. Com. *Salisbury, II*, p. 95.
[95] *Acts of P.C.* 1588, 264–5; cf. C 3/230/34.
[96] *V.C.H. Warws.* v. 200; Dugdale, *Warws.* 534, 675; *Acts of P.C.* 1589–90, 324, 345–6.
[97] C.P. 25(2)/197 East. 30 Eliz. I; Mich. 31 & 32 Eliz. I.
[98] C 142/234/29.
[99] Hants R. O. 213 (419).

[1] MS. Dunkin 438/2, ff. 281, 285.
[2] C 142/392/99.
[3] Hants R. O. 214 (444); ibid. 215 (714).
[4] Ibid. 1004 (426).
[5] Sir Anthony's will is P.C.C. 22 Cope. For Sir William's settlement see C 142/570.
[6] C 142/734/65. For the Copes of Hanwell see pp. 115–6.
[7] He probably had a life estate: cf. p. 116.
[8] *Complete Peerage*, v. 636.
[9] Burke, *Extinct and Dormant Baronetcies*, 130–1; *Complete Peerage*, iv. 428–9; xii(2). 620.
[10] *Complete Peerage*, iv. 163–4.
[11] Ex inf. Bursar, Trinity Coll., Oxf.; and see p. 176.
[12] Fiennes is associated with Sir William Cope in transactions over land in that year: MS. North c 30, nos. 76, 77, 79.
[13] MS. North c 30, nos. 28, 29.
[14] *Complete Peerage*, xi. 491–2.
[15] MS. North b 15, f. 107; cf. ff. 234v.–235v.; *Complete Peerage*, vi. 213.
[16] O.R.O., incl. award.
[17] Ex inf. Bursar, Trinity Coll. Oxf.

granted view of frankpledge, *infangenetheof* and *outfangenetheof*, and waif.[18]

No records of the vestry have survived. In the year 1775 to 1776 £42 was spent on relief out of £44 raised. This sum fell to £37 out of £50 between 1783 and 1785, but by 1803 had nearly trebled. Out of £212 raised, at a rate of 2*s.* 6*d.*, £94 was spent on out-relief, another £94 on other objects, including the county rates and militia, and £23 on removals and other expenses. Twenty-six adults and children received permanent out-relief, and 4 adults were relieved occasionally. Seven of the 17 adults relieved were either over 60 or unable to work through illness.[19] Expenditure was still at a high level in 1834–5, for of £171 raised £129 10*s.* was spent on relief.[20] The parish became part of the Banbury Union, and in 1851 the cost of relief was still high: £129 raised by a rate of 2*s.* 5½*d.* on a rateable value of £1,059.[21]

ECONOMIC HISTORY. In 1066 the manor was worth £5, but its value rose after the Conquest to £8 in 1086.[22] In the latter year there was land for 5 ploughs, although in fact 6 were kept, 3 on Turchil of Arden's demesne farm and 3 in the hands of the peasants. There was a mill rendering 4*s.* The recorded population consisted of 12 *villani* and 4 bordars, and of 2 serfs on the demesne.[23]

No record of Drayton's economic condition has been found again before the early 14th century when between 15 and 20 tenants were listed on the tax rolls of 1306, 1316, and 1327. The village was clearly neither populous nor rich: nearly half the assessment of 1306 was paid by the lady of the manor; the highest assessments of 4*s.* and 3*s.* were again paid by the lord in 1316 and 1327, while all save 2 of the other contributors paid less than 2*s.* each.[24] Robert Arden's attempt to foster the prosperity of the village by obtaining the grant of a yearly fair there in 1329 had little apparent success.[25] For the tax of 1334 Drayton's assessment was the lowest in the hundred.[26] In 1523 there were 10 contributors paying small sums; only the lord of the manor was taxed on land and he paid the comparatively modest sum of £1.[27] The village remained small and poor in the 17th century; there were 12 contributors to the hearth tax in 1662 and 9 in 1665, of which 2 were discharged on account of poverty.[28]

Drayton remained partly an open-field parish until the early 19th century. The earliest description of the lay-out of the fields occurs in 17th-century terriers. In 1607 2 yardlands of glebe lay mostly consolidated in blocks of 12, 19, and 20 'lands' in Withycombe, the Close, and the water-furrows. The glebe also included a meadow called 'Parsons Ham' near the mill brook, and there were common rights for 10 cows and a bull in Withycombe between 14 September and 11 November, and for 80 sheep and 4 horses after Lammas (1 August).[29] Open-field agriculture is illustrated more clearly in a terrier of 1699 of a ¼ yardland, which lay in butts, balks, ridged acres and 'lands' in the field, and included leys, meadow ground, and 1 cow-common.[30] By this date the field was divided into quarters, implying a 4-course rotation, a practice followed in the 17th century in many north Oxfordshire parishes.[31] In the early Middle Ages there had been 2 fields, South and East Field,[32] and there is no evidence of an intervening stage of 3 fields. The open fields lay to the north-east of the parish near the Banbury road. Nickling Lane Quarter, for example, included a hedge 158 yards long between Drayton and Hanwell Fields.[33] By 1802, the date of the inclosure award, only 198 a. were uninclosed. Holdings still included rights in the cow-pasture and Town Green.[34] Early inclosure for sheep and cattle farming had probably been encouraged by the thriving Banbury cloth industry and made easier by the fewness and poverty of the inhabitants.

In Elizabeth I's reign most tenants of the manor were customary tenants. They usually took their tenements for life although a widow could continue to hold her tenement during her widowhood. A customary tenant was admitted in the court by the steward on payment of 1*d.* and the heriot due was his best beast or piece of property; one heriot, for example, was a black horse.[35] When Thomas Webb purchased the manor in 1565, he inclosed Withycombe Field which lay compactly in adjoining furlongs.[36] He was said to have converted in all 17 yardlands from tillage to pasture, 'the most part of Drayton manor', and to have reduced the number of ploughs from 14 to one. The value of the manor had increased from £40 to £340 a year, but the tenants accused Webb of unjust dealing.[37] They accused him of depriving the customary tenants of 5 houses, 16 yards of arable, and the appurtenant meadow, whereby they would be 'utterly undone', for it was their beasts' common and they could not live without it.[38] It was said that previously the lord of the manor had kept only 200 sheep in Withycombe, in the due season, but Webb retorted that the demesne lands lay together and that he could improve them, while he was willing to offer the tenants commons elsewhere. The tenants were only customary tenants, admitted for life in the manor court at the will of the lord, and Webb reminded them that they paid only 1*d.* for an entry fine although as lord he could exact £10 from them. The former lord of the manor, Lewis Greville, and two gentlemen of the neighbourhood, Richard Fiennes and George Danvers, had been chosen by the tenants to mediate, but no settlement had been reached.[39]

18 *Cal. Chart. R.* 1327–41, 118.
19 *Poor Abstract*, 398.
20 *2nd. Rep. Poor Law Comms.* 294.
21 *Poor Law Unions*, 21.
22 *V.C.H. Oxon.* i. 422.
23 Ibid.
24 E 179/161/8, 9, 10.
25 *Cal. Chart. R.* 1327–41, 118.
26 E 179/161/17.
27 E 179/161/196.
28 *Hearth Tax Oxon.* 143; E 179/164/504.
29 MS. Oxf. Dioc. b 40, f. 114.
30 MS. d.d. Risley A II/9/1.
31 In 1699 the quarters were Dunstall Mill, Hanwell, Banbury, and Barkham Quarters: ibid. In the late 18th century they were Town, Banbury Lane, Nickling, and Barkham Quarters: ibid. 9/18: undated survey, probably *c.* 1784.
32 *Cal. Close*, 1279–88, 429.
33 MS. Oxf. Dioc. b 40, f. 114; MS. d.d. Risley A II/9/1, 18; Davis, *Oxon. Map* (1797).
34 O.R.O., incl. award. The Inclosure Act of 1801 states that there were 270 a. of open field and commonable land, but this may have been before surveying: Incl. Act. 41 Geo. III, c 43 (priv. act).
35 Req. 2/87/76.
36 Ibid.; Req. 2/34/69.
37 Hants R.O. 43 M 48/212.
38 Req. 2/87/26; ibid. 2/34/69.
39 Ibid. 2/87/26.

The Court of Requests decided in favour of the plaintiffs, but probably Webb was induced to offer more favourable terms and the land was inclosed, for there is no later record of tenants' common rights in Withycombe. Moreover, in 1637 a number of the older inhabitants, some of over 80 years of age, when questioned on the 'decay of tillage' in Drayton, said that part of the parish had been inclosed before they were born, and that the Fiennes property in particular was ancient inclosure. It had once mostly been 'a park wood and warren ground', and was demesne land, belonging to the manor-house.[40] The Fiennes property adjoined their North Newington land in Broughton and lay mainly in the south around Withycombe, where they had bought some 388 a. in about 1629 from Sir William Cope of Hanwell.[41] In the 1630s this comprised Withycombe pasture and meadow (150 a.), High Field or Great Ground (100 a.) near Drayton village, again pasture, and 4 other closes (30 a., 20 a., 48 a., and 40 a.) lying on the east side of the brook between Drayton and North Newington.[42] Withycombe had formerly been open pasture ground but in 1635 it was described as inclosed. This land had all been pasture and meadow at one time, but in about 1627–9 Sir William Cope ploughed some of it, and in 1635 Elms close (48 a.) and Baynford's meadows (40 a.) were described as 'lately ploughed'.[43] When Lord Guilford bought Withycombe farm in 1764 he paid £2,150 for it.[44] At the time of the inclosure in 1802 there were about 666 a. of ancient inclosure and of the 17 people holding or occupying farm land in the parish only 3 seem to have had land in the open field. In particular Drayton farm (198 a.), Withycombe farm (125 a.), and 4 other holdings of between 40 and 140 a. were inclosed.[45]

The type of farming practised before inclosure can be deduced from the inventories of local farmers. In the late 17th century, for example, wheat, barley, oats, and peas were the chief crops mentioned; sheep, cattle, and in particular horses, a feature of these northern parishes, were kept. In 1668 the rector had corn in the field (worth £22) as well as hay, and a crop of oats (worth £52), and a rick of wheat in the barn; he also had horses and colts worth £20 and kept a bull.[46] A yeoman farmer, who died in the same year, had 2 wheat ricks (worth £23), barley, peas, and hay, and 97 sheep; and although he was only taxed on a single hearth in 1665 the total valuation of his goods came to the comparatively large sum of £270.[47] There is little doubt that the progressive farmers were those with inclosed land, where there was more scope for good husbandry. On Withycombe farm in 1764 both rye grass and clover were grown and in 1765 it was all grazing ground.[48] It is noteworthy that in 1809 Thomas Payne, who owned 140 a., and his brother James Payne, who occupied 43 a., both farms of 'old inclosures', were praised for their 'willingness to experiment'. Thomas Payne considered that the Drayton soil was 'too loose and hollow' for wheat, but that it could produce fine turnips, barley, peas, beans, and oats. According to Arthur Young, Payne carted off 20 loads of turnips an acre and still left 'a good sprinkling' for sheep. The brothers experimented with the cultivation of carrots, parsnips, lucerne, and rhubarb, and particularly with cabbages, which they advocated as 'superior to all other plants' for stock.[49]

By the inclosure award of 1802 Charles, Lord Whitworth, received 36 p. for manorial rights in the waste, and 121 a. for his 9½ yardlands in the open fields; two others received 13 a. and 3 a. respectively.[50] At this date all save some 188 a. was tenant-occupied land, mainly belonging to the Earl of Guilford, Charles, Lord Whitworth, and the rector.[51] In 1831 the picture was much the same: there were 3 proprietors of land valued at over £150, 3 of land valued at between £28 and £87, one of them an owner-occupier, and 2 proprietors of land valued at £3 and £4.[52] In 1851 there were 3 farms of 180 a., 225 a. and 266 a. respectively, and one small one of 20 a.[53] Throughout the late 19th and early 20th centuries there continued to be 3 or 4 farmers in the parish.[54] An agricultural expert writing in 1854 described Drayton as being on some of the best red land in the country with soil well adapted for growing barley and turnips; he particularly mentioned good pasture and grazing land on which some of the best Cotswold sheep were reared.[55] In 1961 the farming was described as mixed.[56]

In the 19th century the inhabitants were mostly farmers and labourers, of whom some were shepherds.[57] There were also 4 families of weavers recorded throughout the century, probably plush-weavers as in 1851, though one recorded in the 17th century was a silk-weaver.[58] There were also paper-makers, who were doubtless employed at North Newington paper-mill.[59]

After 1086 no reference occurs to a mill until 1589.[60] There were millers in the parish in 1851[61] but none is recorded later.

CHURCH. Drayton church is not mentioned until 1223,[62] the date of the first recorded presentation. This was made by Sir Thomas Arden, lord of the manor,[63] and thereafter the advowson seems to have descended with the manor,[64] passing in the 14th century from the Ardens to Sir Thomas Wale, second husband of Nicole Arden,[65] then to the Grevilles by marriage, and in the 16th century to the Webbs.[66] In the 1580s the advowson, like the

[40] MS. Rawl. D 872, ff. 189, 190.
[41] MS. North c 30, 64, 71, 76.
[42] Ibid. 53, 64, 71.
[43] Ibid. 64; MS. Rawl. D 892, f. 190.
[44] MS. North, c 64, f. 17.
[45] O.R.O., incl. award.
[46] MS. Wills Oxon. 13/5/13.
[47] Ibid. 18/3/31; *Hearth Tax Oxon.* 143.
[48] MS. North d 2, f. 103.
[49] Young, *Oxon. Agric.* 139–40, 173–5, 181, 201, 203. For rhubarb for medicine cf. p. 28.
[50] O.R.O., incl. award.
[51] Ibid.; cf. O.R.O., land tax assess. 1785–1802.
[52] O.R.O., land tax assess. 1831.
[53] H.O. 107/1733.
[54] *Kelly's Dir. Oxon.* (1854–1939).
[55] C. S. Read, 'Farming in Oxon', *Jnl. Royal Agric. Soc.* (1854), 198, 227.
[56] O.S. Land Utiliz. Survey Map, sheet 83 (1931–7); ex inf. Major J. F. Nicholson, Park Farm, Drayton.
[57] Par. Rec., reg.
[58] H.O. 107/1733; Par. Rec., reg.; MS. d.d. Risley A II/9/1.
[59] Par. Rec., reg.
[60] C.P. 25(2)/197/Mich. 31 & 32 Eliz. I; Mill Brook and Mill Ham were mentioned in 1601: MS. Oxf. Archd. Oxon. c 141, f. 473. For the site of the mill see p. 103.
[61] H.O. 107/1733.
[62] *Rot. Welles*, ii. 13.
[63] Ibid.
[64] For a list of incumbents and patrons see MS. Top. Oxon. d 460.
[65] See p. 105.
[66] MS. Top. Oxon. d 460; O.A.S. *Rep.* 1916, 45.

manor, was divided into quarters but by 1598 had been reunited in the hands of Sir Anthony Cope and thereafter continued to follow the descent of the manor.[67] In 1677, however, since Mary, Sir Anthony's relict, had been declared a lunatic, trustees presented, and again in 1683 and 1685, William Spencer, her guardian, acted on her behalf.[68] In 1688 John Dover of Barton-on-the-Heath (Warws.), who had presumably purchased a turn since Mary was still alive, presented his son.[69] In 1770 John Cleaver, possibly the previous incumbent, presented;[70] in 1813 Arabella Cope's husband, Lord Whitworth, did so,[71] and in 1858 the next turn was sold for £1,800 to Richard McDonald Caunter. Caunter intended to present his son, but in 1861 he accepted the rectory himself and was presented by the Earl and Countess de la Warr to whom the advowson had descended with the manor. It was afterwards held that Caunter had thereby lost his right to present his son in spite of having purchased a turn.[72] Charles, Earl de la Warr presented on Caunter's resignation in 1871, and the subsequent presentation was made in 1878 by the last incumbent's relict, Mrs. Hannah Roberts. Since 1905 the Oxford Trust has been the patron.[73]

The rectory was valued at £5 in 1254, at £7 6*s*. 8*d*. in 1291 and 1428, and at £13 6*s*. 6*d*. in 1526 and 1535.[74] At the end of the 18th century its annual value was £130, in 1831 the average net income was estimated at £316.[75]

This came from both tithes and glebe. At inclosure in 1802 *c*. 37 a. were allotted to the rector for tithes with an annual corn rent of £137, adjusted to £110 in 1920.[76] Judging from the land tax assessments the parson was better off after inclosure.[77]

The glebe was worth £4 in 1342 and in 1601 comprised 2 yardlands and commons for 10 cows and a bull, 80 sheep, and 4 horses.[78] A terrier of the rectory made in 1805 recorded about 40 a. of glebe, a house and out-buildings standing in nearly an acre of land, 2 cottages, and various appurtenances.[79] In 1918 the rector sold part of the glebe to the Oxford Ironstone Co., who sold it to Trinity College, Oxford.[80] In 1960 there were only 4½ a. of glebe left.[81]

A temporary vicarage was created by the Bishop of Lincoln in 1223 or 1224 to allow the rector to attend the schools at Oxford. The rector was to receive £2 a year and the vicar all the rest of the living. It was arranged that when the vicarage became vacant it was to be consolidated with the rectory provided that the rector had attended the schools and had studied properly.[82]

The church was not poor and as the parish was so small and Drayton not far from Oxford the living was sometimes used to subsidize scholars at Oxford; it frequently had graduates as rectors and often provided a comfortable living for the relations of patrons. For example William Wale, acolyte, was licensed to study in Oxford in 1335 and 1336,[83] and his patron, Sir Thomas Wale, was no doubt a kinsman.[84] The only known pluralist was Edmund Moore (rector 1523–47), who held a Warwickshire cure in 1535 and had a curate at Drayton to whom he paid £5 6*s*. 8*d*.[85] His predecessor, however, was also non-resident and had a curate, a canon of Wroxton, who resided in the abbey; his rectory was in lay ownership at the time of the bishop's visitation in 1518.[86] At the Reformation the parish had land for the maintenance of a light in the church.[87]

The rector subscribed to the Elizabethan settlement of 1559. Instituted in 1549 he had lived through all the religious changes of the period and had conformed.[88] However, with the presentation in 1598 of Robert Cleaver of St. Edmund Hall, Oxford, a favourer of the Presbyterian discipline,[89] the parish became strongly Puritan. Cleaver was a friend of the leaders of the movement in north Oxfordshire, Harris of Hanwell and Whateley of Banbury, and was noted as 'a solid text man'.[90] He collaborated with John Dod of Hanwell in his work entitled *An Exposition of the Ten Commandments* and delivered many notable sermons.[91] He was later suspended from his ministry by Bishop Bridges of Oxford, for failing to comply with the ceremonial laid down in the Prayer Book.[92] His friends Dod and Lancaster[93] were also suspended and this 'darkening' of 'three shining stars' was described by a contemporary as a 'fearful eclipse upon the church'.[94] When Archbishop Bancroft, finding no compliance in the silenced pastor, tried to collate to Drayton by lapse, Sir Anthony Cope intervened. When sitting in Parliament he took one or two of his fellow members with him and presented his choice to the archbishop, who after a long struggle admitted him.[95] In 1607, therefore, Drayton was 'furnished with a godly prudent man' Henry Scudder (1607–19). He was a Presbyterian of note: he and his

[67] See p. 106; O.A.S. *Rep*. 1916, 45; MS. Dunkin 438/2, ff. 284, 285v.

[68] MS. Oxf. Dioc. c 69, nos. 77–82.

[69] Ibid. d 106, f. 113.

[70] Ibid. d 561.

[71] Ibid. c 660, f. 144. The letter about this presentation says that the Duke of Dorset (Arabella Cope's first husband) had presented, but he died in 1799.

[72] Ibid. c 1798–9.

[73] Ibid. c 1799.

[74] Lunt, *Val. Norw*. 309; *Tax. Eccl*. (Rec. Com.), 32; *Feud. Aids*, vi. 378; *Subsidy 1526*, 269; *Valor Eccl*. (Rec. Com.), ii. 164.

[75] MS. Oxf. Archd. Oxon. b 24, no. 23; *Rep. of Com. on Eccl. Revenue* H.C. 54, p. 778 (1835), xxii. On the dorse of the presentation deeds of 1861 and 1871 the net yearly value of the rectory is stated as being between £300 and £400: MS. Oxf. Dioc. c 1798.

[76] O.R.O., incl. award and Drayton Corn and Tithe rents.

[77] cf. Diana McClatchey, *The Oxfordshire Clergy*, 109.

[78] *Inq. Non*. (Rec. Com.), 138; MS. Oxf. Archd. Oxon. c 141, p. 473; ibid. b 40.

[79] MS. Oxf. Dioc. c 448, no. 48.

[80] Ex inf. Bursar of Trinity Coll., Oxf.

[81] Ex inf. the rector.

[82] *Rot. Welles*, ii. 16.

[83] Emden, *O.U. Reg*.; MS. Top. Oxon. d 460.

[84] *Rot. Welles*, ii. 13. For other medieval rectors see MS. Top. Oxon. d 460.

[85] MS. Top. Oxon. d 460; MS. Oxf. Dioc. d 105, p. 124, *Subsidy 1526*, 269.

[86] *Visit. Dioc. Linc. 1517–31*, ii. 39.

[87] *Chant. Cert*. 36.

[88] O.A.S. *Rep*. 1916, 45.

[89] Ibid.; Foster, *Alumni*.

[90] W. Durham, *The Life and Death of . . . Robert Harris* (Lond. 1660), 15–20.

[91] See e.g. *Two sermons on the Third of Lamentations presented at Hanwell in the first Yeere of his Majesties reigne 1602. The one by I. D. the other by R. C.* (Lond. 1610).

[92] MS. Dunkin 438/2, f. 285v.

[93] For Lancaster see W. Durham, *The Life and Death of . . . Robert Harris* (Lond. 1660), 10–11.

[94] W. Durham, *The Life and Death of . . . Robert Harris* (Lond. 1660), 10–11; cf. S. Clarke, *A Collection of the Lives of Ten Emminent Divines* (Lond. 1662), 278.

[95] MS. Dunkin 438/2, f. 285v.; S. Clarke, op. cit. 279.

brother-in-law William Whateley, Vicar of Banbury, whose life he wrote, and Robert Harris of Hanwell were accustomed to meet together weekly to translate and analyse chapters of the Bible. Scudder's devotional work *The Christian's Daily Walk in Holy Securitie and Peace* was widely read in the 17th century.[96] Drayton had other incumbents of puritanical views: Thomas Lodge, presented in 1619, 'a burning and a shining light' for 32 years, witnessed the will of Robert Cleaver who died in the parish in 1640;[97] and Robert Clarke, who resigned in 1677, was 'a pious and painful minister'.[98] Richard Coghlane (1652–68) was one of the comparatively rare Irishmen to hold a benefice in the county; his theological views are not known but he was clearly a man of learning and wealth, for on his death in 1668 his goods were valued at £401, of which nearly £77 was for books.[99] Adam Morton (1677–83), '*fidei antiquissime patronus strenuus*', regarded the 'conventiclers' as 'seminaries of sedition and rebellion'.[1] His opinions are reflected in two books he left to his nephew along with his Bible — Cradock's *Harmony of the Evangelists* and *Apostolical Historie*.[2] With the institution of John Dover (1688–1725), who had started life as a barrister, there was a return to low church principles: an inscription to him in the chancel reads 'Lo, here your late unworthy rector lies, Who, though he's dead, loud as he can still cries, Repent'. Anthony Wood confirms that he was something of a sectary by saying that he was resorted to by many fanatical people.[3]

From the beginning of the 18th century the parish was served by curates. Dover or his successor employed a curate,[4] and Edmund Stone (rector 1742–69) lived at Chipping Norton, while his curate lived in Drayton parsonage and received £30 a year. At this time there were two services every Sunday and communion 4 times a year for which there were usually *c.* 40 communicants. Another pluralist followed Stone and lived at Bodicote and a third, William Lloyd (1813–61), was also Rector of Hanwell and twice obtained licence to be absent for a year from his cure in 1820 and 1832.[5] The unsatisfactory state of affairs at this period, despite the regular reports from churchwardens that all was well, is revealed in Lloyd's correspondence with the bishop over the charge of 3 guineas each Sunday made by his curate for serving the church during a vacancy of 22 weeks. Lloyd said that there were two or three clergymen in Drayton who would have done it for a guinea and that the curate's high charge was because he served the cure from Oxford, a distance of some 24 miles.[6] Of Lloyd himself, who had not been ordained when he was presented, the Archdeacon of Oxford wrote sternly that he was 'one of these galloping candidates who think nothing of their profession till their expected preferment is vacant'.[7] He did not appear to improve with age: he allowed the rectory-house to get in a very dilapidated state and so involved his successor in much trouble; as late as 1854 he was only administering communion four times a year and at great festivals.[8] With his successor, however, Drayton at last obtained a resident rector and monthly celebrations of communion.[9] The Tractarian movement passed Drayton by; so far as is known there has never been a cross on the Lord's Table and the north celebration has always been used. Since 1778 all the rectors have been Evangelicals and seven out of eight have served as missionaries overseas in the Arctic, Africa, India, and China.

The church of *ST. PETER*[10] consists of a chancel, nave, north and south aisles, and a western tower. It is mainly of 14th-century date, but the plain font is earlier.[11] The nave is separated from the aisles by arcades of 3 arches and is surmounted by a contemporary clerestory. One of the nave pillars has a capital carved with sculptured busts of knights with interlaced arms which are similar to those found at Bloxham and elsewhere in north Oxfordshire.[12] The south aisle has a piscina and sedilia.

No major alteration to the main structure was recorded before the early 19th century. A gallery, paid for by subscription, was erected in 1738,[13] the church was ordered to be whitewashed in 1755,[14] and in 1773 communion rails were set up at the rector's expense.[15] The tower, being in a ruinous condition and beyond repair, was pulled down and rebuilt in 1808 on a smaller scale.[16] Its low roof can be seen in Buckler's drawing of 1820.[17]

By the early 19th century the fabric generally was much in need of attention: in 1813 the chancel was reported out of repair and in 1818 the roof.[18] The latter was repaired in 1822 and in 1826 further unspecified repairs were in progress.[19] In 1877 a vestry decided to petition for a faculty for the restoration and enlargement of the building. It was planned to alter the tower and to add a spire, a south and a north porch, and an organ chamber and vestry on the south side of the church. The roof of the nave was renewed, the roofs of the aisles were releaded, and general repairs were carried out. The chancel floor was re-laid and new seats were provided both in the chancel and the church. The architect was Edwin Dolby of Abingdon.[20] The elevation of the new tower shows that it was to have a belfry and stone spire in the Early English style,[21] but this part of the plan was not carried out.

[96] S. Clarke, op. cit. 280; *D.N.B.*

[97] *Gent. Mag.* 1831, ci (2), 299; MS. Wills Oxon. 13/2/23.

[98] *Gent. Mag.* 1831, ci (2), 300.

[99] MS. Wills Oxon. 13/5/13; Foster, *Alumni.*

[1] MS. Oxf. Dioc. c 430, f. 17; MS. Wills Oxon. 91, f. 362v.; *Gent. Mag.* 1831, ci (2), 299.

[2] *Gent. Mag.* 1831, ci (2), 299.

[3] Wood, *Athenae*, iv. 597; for his many plays see *D.N.B.*

[4] Diana McClatchey, *The Oxfordshire Clergy*, 119; MS. Oxf. Archd. Oxon. b 24, no. 22.

[5] McClatchey, op. cit. 50; Le Neve, *Fasti*, 119.

[6] MS. Oxf. Dioc. c 328, nos. 52, 54; MS. Oxf. Archd. Oxon. c 38.

[7] MS. Oxf. Dioc. c 661, f. 8.

[8] Ibid. c 660, ff. 144–7; ibid. c 1799; *Wilb. Visit.*

[9] MS. Oxf. Dioc. c 332.

[10] In the early 18th century a wake was kept on the Sunday following St. Peter's day: *Par. Colln.* ii. 123.

[11] For a Buckler drawing see MS. Top. Oxon. a 66, no. 220.

[12] See *Antiq. Jnl.* 1924, iv(i), 1 sqq.

[13] Par. Rec., chwdns' accts. 1770–1904.

[14] MS. Oxf. Archd. Oxon. d 13, f. 11.

[15] Par. Rec., chwdns' accts.

[16] MS. Oxf. Dioc. c 658, ff. 67–67v.; MS. Oxf. Archd. Oxon. c 65, f. 207. The tower was reduced in size on account of the expense of a larger one.

[17] MS. Top. Oxon. a 66, nos. 221, 223.

[18] MS. Oxf. Archd. Oxon. c 65, ff. 214, 222.

[19] Ibid. ff. 228, 235.

[20] MS. Oxf. Dioc. c 1798.

[21] For the architect's plans see ibid.

Besides an unidentified medieval tomb (? 13th-century) in the north aisle,[22] there are two medieval memorials to the Grevilles. The tomb of Lewis Greville (d. 1438) was once in the chancel.[23] The alabaster slab which covered it is now on the belfry floor. It bears the incised figures of Lewis Greville (almost obliterated) and of his wife Margaret and their arms. The tomb of his son and heir William (d. 1440) is in the vestry.[24] There are also memorials to several rectors: Robert Cleaver (d. 1640); Thomas Lodge (d. 1651); Richard Coghlane (d. 1668); Adam Morton (d. 1683); John Dover (d. 1725).[25] Elizabeth Metcalfe (d. 1791), the donor of a charity, is also commemorated. Her ledger stone bears a coat of arms.

The earliest silver is a chalice inscribed 1808.[26]

The new tower of 1808 was built so that it might contain the present 3 bells: one is dated 1634 and the other two 1670.[27]

Two sums of £50 each for the upkeep of the churchyard were left by David Robert Smythe in 1920 and Emmanuel and Elizabeth Jones in 1924.[28] The amalgamated stock in 1958 was £126 and the annual income of £5 was less than the average labour cost for the previous five years.[29]

The registers date from 1577; there is a gap between 1686 and 1721.[30]

NONCONFORMITY. The absence of any dissent at Drayton at the time of the Compton Census in 1676, despite the strong nonconformist influence in north Oxfordshire, may perhaps be accounted for by the Puritan views of several of the 17th-century incumbents.[31] By 1682, when the cleavage between the Established Church and nonconformity had become distinct, one Quaker and one Anabaptist family were reported and four or five more, all, with one exception, yeomen, were said to attend a 'conventicle' at Banbury in the afternoon, although they went to their parish church in the morning.[32] By 1738, however, only one Presbyterian was left,[33] and no dissenters were recorded in later 18th-century visitation returns.

At the turn of the century Methodism took root, and in 1802 there was a meeting-house at Drayton attended by 30 Methodists, probably mainly from outside the parish.[34] Three years later the rector said there were many Methodists with a teacher and a licensed meeting-house.[35] In 1814 it was reported that they had visiting teachers occasionally, that there were only two 'professed' families of Methodists, but that many parishioners attended their meetings.[36] Houses were licensed in 1810 and 1817, when the community was said to number 8 to 10, and also in 1836 and in 1843.[37] In 1854 the incumbent estimated that a third of the parish were Methodists, though many of them attended the parish church, as they had no chapel of their own.[38] By 1866 the sect was said to have died out.[39]

SCHOOLS. No record of any school has been found before 1800; a day school was established then, supported first entirely by the rector and afterwards partly by a sum bequeathed by a parishioner, Elizabeth Metcalfe.[40] It had 12 or 15 pupils in 1808. There was no Sunday school, nor, in 1815, any wish to introduce the National Society's new plan of study.[41] By 1818 the day school itself had been discontinued, owing to the difficulty of finding a teacher and because the parents did not show sufficient interest.[42] Another day school was, however, begun in 1821 in which children were taught at the expense of their parents and by 1833 3 boys and 7 girls attended it, while another day school with 41 boys and 2 girls was supported by subscription and by payments from the parents.[43] There was also a free Sunday school where in 1833 15 children were taught and in 1854 thirty-two.[44] Only one of the day schools existed in 1855; the average attendance was 35, and the schoolroom, which consisted of 2 converted cottages, was given rent-free by Lord and Lady de la Warr.[45] Accommodation for the mistress was provided free by the rector, who in 1866 and 1868 claimed to be maintaining the school at his own expense with the help of a few half-yearly subscriptions.[46] This may not have been quite accurate since in the year ending December 1867 Drayton school received an annual Parliamentary grant of £15 6*s*.[47] The rector gave the number of children attending in these years as 16 boys and 15 girls daily, and 12 boys and 16 girls on Sundays. He was unable to retain any children in the Sunday school once they had entered 'service'. His many attempts to establish an evening school had not been successful.[48]

In 1871 accommodation in the school was given as 32.[49] The cottages which had formed the original school building were said to have been practically rebuilt by 1891,[50] but the following year the school was in poor condition. Accommodation was estimated at 43 in 1894 but the condition of the school was still not satisfactory and in 1899 a threat was made to withdraw the Government grant unless a separate room was found for the younger children. This was

[22] For a Buckler drawing see MS. Top. Oxon. a 66, no. 220.

[23] *Gent. Mag.* 1831, cl(2), 299.

[24] An inaccurate translation, reading John (d. 1441) for William (d. 1440), has been incised round the edge of the slab; this translation was followed in *Gent. Mag.* 1831, cl(2). 299.

[25] There are lists of inscriptions with full details in *Par. Colln.* ii. 127–8; *Gent. Mag.* 1831, cl(2), 298–300. For the blazons of the arms see Bodl. G. A. Oxon. 16° 217, p. 129; ibid. 4° 686, p. 127.

[26] Evans. *Ch. Plate.*

[27] *Ch. Bells Oxon.*

[28] Char. Com., Unrep. vol. 186, p. 447; 215, p. 309.

[29] Char. Com., file 99883; G file accts.

[30] Par. Rec.

[31] See pp. 109–10; Compton Census.

[32] MS. Oxf. Dioc. c 430, f. 17. An Anabaptist woman from Drayton was buried at Horley in 1699: Horley Par. Rec., reg.

[33] *Secker's Visit.*

[34] MS. Oxf. Dioc. d 566.

[35] Ibid. c 327.

[36] Ibid. d 574.

[37] Ibid. c 644, f. 109; d 576; c 645, f. 94; c 646, ff. 33, 264.

[38] *Wilb. Visit.*

[39] MS. Oxf. Dioc. c 332.

[40] MS. Oxf. Dioc. d 566, d 574 and see p. 112.

[41] MS. Oxf. Dioc. d 707; ibid. c 433.

[42] *Educ. of Poor*, 722.

[43] *Educ. Enq. Abstract*, 746.

[44] Ibid.; Billing, *Dir. Oxon.* (1854).

[45] Ed. 7/101/72; *Wilb. Visit.* 50; MS. Oxf. Dioc. b 70, f. 282.

[46] MS. Oxf. Dioc. c 332, 335.

[47] *Schs. aided by Parliamentary Grants.* (1867), 694.

[48] MS. Oxf. Dioc. c 332, 335.

[49] *Elem. Educ. Ret.* 326.

[50] Ed 7/101/72.

provided the following year giving places for 24 infants and raising the total school accommodation to 67.[51]

Lord North, who had become the owner of the school by 1891, died in 1932. After his death the existence of the school was threatened, as his successor wished to sell the site.[52] When he failed to find a buyer, the school managers kept the school open with local support, despite falling attendances and the Education Authority's wish to close the school. In 1941 Trinity College, Oxford, bought the site and let it to the managers. In 1948 the school finally closed and the children were transferred to North Newington Primary and Banbury Secondary Schools.[53]

CHARITIES. During the 18th century various sums of money, known as the Town stock, were vested in Sir Jonathan Cope, lord of the manor, for the benefit of the poor of the parish. The benefactions of unknown donors amounted to £60; £10 was left by the will of Dr. James Jenkinson (d. 1731), Rector of Drayton, and £10 by Mrs. Mary Metcalfe (d. 1760). The income of £4 was received regularly from the successors to the Cope property. By 1823 it had been amalgamated with the following charity.

By will dated 1774 Elizabeth Metcalfe (d. 1791) left in trust £527, the income to be given in clothes to poor children of the parish at Whitsun; and £700, the interest to be spent on clothes and coal in equal parts for the aged poor at Christmas. Her personal estate was insufficient to pay all the legacies and in 1799 the money available was re-apportioned in Chancery. Some of the income in 1814 was used to support a school. In 1823 the stock standing to the children's account was £328, and the dividend of £10 was spent on linen for poor children at Midsummer. The stock for the aged stood at £421 and to the interest of £13 was added the £4 from the town stock. From this each family received annually 7*s.* worth of coal or clothing at their choice;[54] £123, supposed to be the accumulation of unapplied income, was treated as capital.[55] By 1871 the total value of the stock was £872 and the dividend £26. Half the income was given to the parents of poor children for clothes, at Midsummer, and half was spent on coal for poor people over the age of 50.[56] During the early years of the 20th century some attempt was made by the trustees, with the approval of the Charity Commissioners, to distribute the charity in accordance with the needs of modern life. Ratepayers were not eligible, nor newcomers to the parish until they had resided there for 2 years.[57] In 1925 £8 was spent on children's clothes and £10 on the aged. From 1953 to 1956 the major part of the charity was given annually in coal, £20 worth to 50 households, while about 25 children received 3*s.* each.[58]

HANWELL

HANWELL is a small irregularly shaped parish lying 3½ miles north-west of Banbury. It covers 1,240 a.[1] and no boundary changes are known. Its short north-western boundary divides the parish from Warwickshire and the western and eastern boundaries follow the course of tributaries of the Cherwell.[2] The land lies mainly within the 400 ft. contour, but rises in the north-west to about 500 ft. Its landscape is of a typically upland character. There is no woodland and there was none in 1797, although there was at one time more heath and moor.[3]

The modern Warwick–Banbury road running from north to south through the western end of the parish follows the same line as an ancient highway.[4] This road was turnpiked in 1744, when Hanwell's toll-gates were set up, and dis-turnpiked in 1871.[5] A minor road crosses this route, running westwards to the ancient Moor Mill[6] and to Wroxton, and eastwards through Hanwell village to Bourton and the north Oxfordshire border. This was the Anglo-Saxon Hana's *weg* after which the village was originally named.[7] A minor road connected Hanwell with Horley; its eastern end is now a footpath.

The village was sited on Hana's *weg* beside a 'never failing' spring[8] and later the form *welle* was substituted for *weg*. Although there was a Roman villa near the main road and other Roman remains have been found in the parish[9] there is nothing to suggest that the village itself was settled before the Anglo-Saxon period.

The medieval village was of medium size for the area.[10] Eighteenth-century estimates vary between 40 and 60 houses or families; although the population rose from 264 to 301 in the earlier 19th century, there were only 68 houses in 1851.[11] Thereafter the number of inhabitants declined to 176 in 1901; in 1961 the figure was 218.[12]

The original centre of the village was almost certainly the spring near Park (formerly Spring) Farm, which supplied the village and the fishponds of Hanwell Castle. Here were the pound, the smithy, and the green. Hanwell Castle and the church stood apart, the church on high ground overlooking the village.[13] In later centuries the village expanded both to the south-west and east, its cottages lying mostly on one side of a winding street stretching from below the 'Red Lion' up the hill to the church. This linear expansion was made necessary by the large area

51 Oxfordshire County Council, Educ. Office, T/SL 20: *List of Schools* (1902), 199.
52 Par. Rec., sch. letter bk.
53 Ex inf. Oxfordshire County Council, Educ. Cttee.
54 *12th Rep. Com. Char.* 213; MS. Oxf. Dioc. d 574.
55 Char. Com., file E 9619.
56 *Gen. Digest. Char.* 24–25.
57 Par. Rec.; Char. Com., file E 9619.
58 Char. Com., G file accts.
1 O.S. *Area Bk.*
2 O.S. Map 25″ Oxon. V. 3, 4, 8 (1st edn.); ibid. 2½″ SP 44 (1951).
3 Davis, *Oxon. Map.*
4 Ogilby, *Britannia* (1751), 219.
5 Buckingham to Warmington Turnpike Act, 17 Geo. II, c. 43; ibid. 34–35 Vic., c. 115.
6 See p. 118.
7 *P.N. Oxon.* (E.P.N.S.), ii. 398.
8 Bodl. G.A. Oxon. b 91(2): *Sale cat.*
9 *V.C.H. Oxon.* i. 337–8; O.S. Map 25″ Oxon. V. 3 (1st edn.).
10 See p. 189.
11 *Secker's Visit.*; MS. Oxf. Dioc. d 556; *Census*, 1801–51.
12 *Census*, 1861–1961.
13 O.S. Map 25″ Oxon. V. 4 (1st edn.).

occupied by the castle on one side of the road and of the position of the open fields and commons which lay on all sides of the old village.[14] The village contracted in the late 19th century and in 1904 comprised about 45 thatched cottages with gardens and 28 a. of allotments, 4 farms, the inn, the Post Office, the school, the chapel, and rectory-house; largest house in Hanwell.[18] When it was leased in 1549, it was said to have dove-houses and outbuildings.[19]

It is doubtful whether there were any resident lords of the manor before the Copes[20] and the early manor-house was presumably leased or occupied by bailiffs. The present house, Hanwell Castle, dates

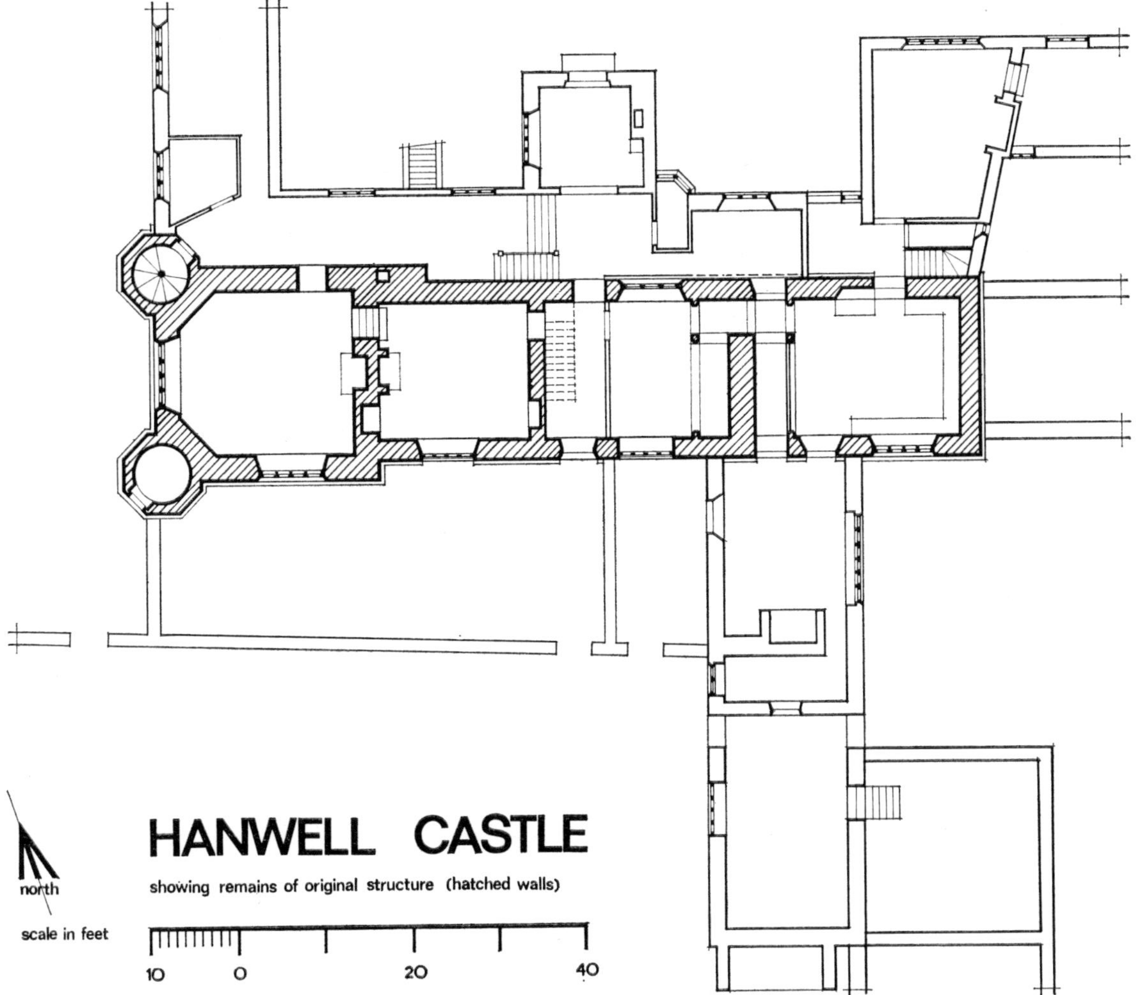

2 farms and Moor Mill lay outside the village.[51] Except for the addition of council houses there have been few 20th-century changes. Most of the houses are 2-story structures of coursed ironstone rubble. Some retain the once universal thatch, although there is some Welsh slate. Wooden casement windows and brick chimney-stacks are common. The 'Red Lion' is a 17th-century house, first mentioned by name in 1792.[16] Of the Victorian additions the school was built in the Gothic style of local stone; the Methodist chapel, a plain stone structure, was built at the end of the village, opposite to the inn; while the rectory-house, rebuilt *c.* 1843, lies some way off the main village street. The new house incorporated part of the old parsonage, which had evidently been large.[17] It was assessed on 6 hearths for the 1665 tax and after the manor-house was the

from the grant of the manor in 1498 to William Cope, Cofferer to Henry VII.[21] He already had a house at Hardwick, near Banbury, and his will makes it clear that he began building or rebuilding at Hanwell. His executors were to cause his house there 'to be finished and made according as it is begun and according to a platt thereof made'.[22] The property was left to Cope's second son Anthony and some time after 1518 William Cope's executors brought a chancery action against Anthony for refusing to finish the rebuilding of the house.[23] Later, however, he carried out his father's wishes. He bought a considerable amount of land in Oxfordshire in 1536,[24] became High Sheriff in 1548, and evidently used Hanwell as his country house until his death in 1551.[25]

Leland, who visited Oxfordshire between 1535

[14] Davis, *Oxon. Map*.
[15] Bodl. G.A. Oxon. b 91(2): *Sale cat.*
[16] O.R.O., victlrs' recogs.
[17] MS. Oxf. Dioc. c 1843. Plans and specifications are included.

[18] *Hearth Tax Oxon.* 143.
[19] Hants R.O., Cope pps. (uncat.).
[20] See p. 115. [21] Ibid. [22] P.C.C. 12 Fetiplace.
[23] C 1/399/39. [24] *D.N.B.*
[25] Ibid.; G.E.C. *Baronetage*, i. 36–7.

and 1545, described the house as 'pleasant and gallant'.[26] It was lived in by four generations of Copes until the death in 1714 of the relict of Sir Anthony Cope (d. 1675).[27] In the latter's lifetime her relations the Spencers also lived in the house.[28] It was probably converted into a farm house after the death of Sir Charles Cope of Bruern in 1781.[29] Only the south-west tower and the south side of the quadrangle were left, but some of the bricks from the demolished building were used to construct farm out-houses.[30] By 1902 the building, when let to G. F. Berkeley, was dilapidated. Berkeley's first wife, Caroline, was responsible for the restoration of the house and the gardens. She also added the modern east wing, which was built in the same style as the surviving Tudor wing.[31] In 1957 a private tutorial establishment was opened in the Castle.[32]

The grounds, covering 17½ a. in 1904, with fish-ponds and woods,[33] were more elaborate in the 17th century when the royalist Sir Anthony Cope (d. 1675) was living at Hanwell. Plot said that there were waterworks in a 'House of Diversion' built on an island in one of the fishponds to the north-east of the house. There was a ball tossed by a column of water and an artificial shower.[34] He also described the mill erected in the Park by the ingenious and 'great virtuoso' Sir Anthony. It was of 'wonderful contrivance' and not only ground the corn for the house, but also turned a very large engine for cutting the hardest stone, after the manner of lapidaries, and another engine for boring guns. It was similar to a mill at Tusmore.[35] There are traces of the foundations of unidentified buildings on the slope of the hill to the south of the house. The park had another mechanical curiosity in the 17th century which was still there in the mid-18th century, when Jonathan Cope of Bruern Abbey, M.P. for Banbury, seems occasionally to have lived there. This was a water-clock which showed the hour 'by the rise of a new gilded sun moving in a hemisphere of wood'.[36] The castle grounds were still considerable in 1962, but the original plan has been much altered. A lake has taken the place of a 'succession of ponds one below another'.[37]

Hanwell Castle was originally known as Hanwell House or Hall.[38] It was built of brick with stone dressings, and was one of the earliest examples of the use of brick in the area. Prints and drawings suggest a quadrangular plan with towers at each of the four corners, but in fact, as the plinth of the existing south range demonstrates, the house was built round three sides of a court, which was open to the east.[39] The main entrance was in the west front, which, according to Skelton, measured 109 ft. and formed a symmetrical composition with the gate-house in the centre.[40] It was approached by a road, now overgrown, which ran past the parsonage, down the hill, and through a gateway, of which the 17th-century piers remain. In the gatehouse itself was an oriel window with a medallion above it containing the portrait of a man. Bays projected from the ranges on either side of the gateway. The corner towers were similar to the remaining south-west tower: they were each of 3 stories, with 2 octagonal turrets rising above the roofs at the angles. The remaining south range is of 2 stories, and contains the kitchen, with 2 capacious fire-places placed back to back. The centre of the north front is marked by an oriel window, beneath which projects the modern porch. In the 18th century there was a 'gallery' connecting the house with the chancel of the adjoining church.[41]

The house was assessed on 27 hearths for the tax of 1665, one more than Broughton Castle.[42] When Rawlinson wrote in the early 18th century he thought the most remarkable things about the house were its 'fine gallery and many excellent paintings in the windows'.[43] This gallery was mentioned in an inventory of the house made in 1557 in which the following rooms were listed: hall, parlour, 2 great chambers, middle chamber, back chamber, gallery, gallery chamber, sepulchre, armoury, Thos. Hyll's chamber, My Lady's chamber, buttery, kitchen, dish-house, and store-house. The 'household stuff' was valued at £87 10*s*.[44] When Sir John Cope died in 1638 about 30 rooms were listed including the Queen's chamber and Mr. Dod's chamber.[45]

During Elizabeth I's reign Sir Anthony Cope (d. 1614) and his family kept great state at Hanwell. Ten of his children were baptized in the church from 1587 onwards.[46] Although his hopes of entertaining the queen there were never fulfilled he did entertain James I in 1605 and 1612.[47] Besides royal visitors Sir Anthony entertained Puritan divines.[48] Fuller tells how 'some riotous gentlemen, casually coming to the table of Sir Anthony Cope, were half-starved in the midst of a feast, because of refraining from swearing (meat and drink to them) in the presence of Mr. Dod'—i.e. John Dod, minister of Hanwell and friend of Sir Anthony.[49] His son Sir William (d. 1637) also twice entertained kings, James I in 1616 and Charles I in 1637.[50]

During the Civil War Sir William's grandson

[26] Leland, *Itin.* ed. Toulmin Smith, ii. 40.

[27] Beesley, *Hist. Banbury*, 508; Par. Rec., reg.

[28] e.g. William Spencer, and Chas. Spencer: Par. Rec., reg.

[29] Brewer, writing in 1818 (Brewer, *Oxon.* 519) says the house was pulled down *c.* 40 years past. Sir Charles died in 1781 and his property was divided.

[30] There is a photo by F. T. S. Houghton (n.d.) in N.B.R. and a drawing (1824) from the west by Buckler in MS. Top. Oxon. a 67, no. 298. There are plans in N.B.R.

[31] Tablet in the church; ex inf. the late G. F. Berkeley.

[32] Ex inf. the Headmaster, the Revd. C. Browne.

[33] G.A. Oxon. b 91(2): *Sale cat.*

[34] Plot, *Nat. Hist. Oxon.* 235–6.

[35] Ibid. 264–5.

[36] Ibid. 235; *The Beauties of England* (1764), 139.

[37] J. Murray, *Handbk. for Travellers in Oxon.* (1894). Remains of the fishponds are marked on O.S. Map 25″ Oxon. V. 4 (1st edn.).

[38] MS. Wills Oxon. 2/2/29; Ogilby, *Britannia* (1751), 219.

[39] Bodl. Gough Maps 44, no. 71 (N. view and S. view, n.d.); cf. ibid. no. 72, showing castle and church; MS. Gen. Top. f. 15, f. 69v. (1844); Skelton, *Oxon.* (Bloxham Hund.), pl. viii; Brewer (*Oxon.* 519) saw an 'ancient drawing' showing the four towers.

[40] Skelton, op. cit., plate viii. See plate facing p. 114.

[41] Brewer, *Oxon.*, 519. This was perhaps made for Mary, Lady Cope (d. 1714).

[42] *Hearth Tax Oxon.* 143.

[43] *Par. Colln.* ii. 162.

[44] Hants R.O., Cope pps. no. 123.

[45] C 8/120/72. Mr. Dod was presumably John Dod, Rector of Hanwell: see below.

[46] Par. Rec., reg.

[47] *D.N.B.*: Beesley, *Hist. Banbury*, 238–41.

[48] See p. 119.

[49] T. Fuller, *Ch. Hist. of Britain* (1845), vi. 306.

[50] *Cal. S.P. Dom.* 1580–1625, 556. For him and other Cope members of Parliament see W. R. Williams, *Parl. Hist. of the County of Oxford*, 49 sqq.; see also J. M. French, *Milton in Chancery*, 124–144 and *passim.*

Broughton Castle in 1729

Hanwell Castle before its partial demolition

1.

2.

3.

4.

1. Hanwell nave arcade, 14th-century. 2. Adderbury chancel, 15th-century. 3. Adderbury nave arcade, *c.* 1300. 4. Tadmarton font, 13th-century.

CHURCH CARVING

Anthony was a minor and nothing is known of the treatment of the house, but the church and parsonage evidently suffered damage from the Parliamentary troops quartered in the village.[51] During the first siege of Banbury in 1644 Colonel Fiennes, commanding the Parliamentary forces, made a stand south of Hanwell; on 27 June Sir William Waller was there and demanded reinforcements; two days later he moved nearer to Banbury and the Battle of Cropredy Bridge was fought.[52] In the next year the inhabitants of Hanwell petitioned the Warwickshire Committee of Accounts for the payment of charges when troops were quartered for 9 weeks.[53] Elizabeth Cope is said to have had Royalist sympathies, and her son when he came of age engaged at Hanwell in secret plans which led up to the restoration of Charles II.[54] After the Battle of Worcester Richard Allestree, who had acted as an intermediary between Charles II and the Royalists, was persuaded by Sir Anthony to live with him at Hanwell. He was there for several years and continued his activities as a go-between.[55]

MANOR AND LESSER ESTATE. Both before the Conquest and in 1086 *HANWELL* manor was held by the Saxon Lewin or Leofwine,[56] who also held lands in Cowley and Chinnor.[57] In the 12th century Hanwell, like Chinnor, was probably in the possession of the Vernons.[58] Hanwell was certainly held in 1218 by Warin, son of Richard de Vernon.[59] The manor was described in 1235–6 as 1 knight's fee and in 1242–3 as ½ fee held of Roger, Earl of Winchester.[60] Since this Winchester overlordship is not mentioned again it may well be an error arising from an association of Hanwell with Chinnor, which had been forfeited by Warin's kinsman Walter de Vernon and subsequently granted to Saer de Quincy, Earl of Winchester.[61] Warin survived his eldest son Warin (fl. 1234),[62] and died between 1247[63] and 1249 when his lands were divided between his widow Alda, his son Ralph,[64] and his grandson Warin son of Warin.[65] Hanwell fell to the share of Ralph,[66] who died in 1251.[67] The custody of his heir, a minor, was granted to Guy de Lusignan,[68] but Hanwell was entrusted to a Richard de Vernon who claimed rights as overlord.[69] Ralph's heir was his daughter Eustacia, but Hanwell later passed to his illegitimate son Sir Ralph, to whom Eustacia formally released her right *c.* 1311.[70] The Ralph de Vernon who was lord of Hanwell in 1316[71] was probably the son of Sir Ralph[72] and evidently held the manor in his father's lifetime.[73] The younger Ralph was dead by 1319 when his father granted Hanwell to his daughter-in-law Margaret for her life.[74] 'Old Sir Ralph' was still alive in 1329[75] but was probably dead by 1334 when his younger son Richard, Rector of Stockport (Ches.) and ultimate remainder man of his father's lands under a settlement of 1325,[76] granted the reversion of Hanwell after Margaret's death to his kinsman John de Vernon.[77] Margaret seems to have been dead by 1340 when Sir Ralph de Vernon, who was probably son of another Richard, illegitimate son of 'old Sir Ralph', and who succeeded to the barony of Shipbrook about this time,[78] granted Hanwell to John de Vernon.[79] John, who was perhaps a younger son of Ralph and Margaret de Vernon,[80] was lord of Hanwell in 1346[81] and was succeeded there by his son Edmund[82] by 1379.[83] Edmund died in 1380[84] and in the following year a group of feoffees, probably his executors, conveyed Hanwell to Sir Richard Abberbury.[85] Sir Richard, the founder of Donnington Hospital (Berks.), was dead by 1401[86] and was probably succeeded first by his brother Thomas and then by his nephew, Sir Richard the younger.[87] In 1415 the latter conveyed Hanwell to Thomas Chaucer and a group of feoffees.[88] In 1426 the manor was claimed against Thomas Chaucer by James de Vernon, great-grandson of Sir Thomas de Vernon of Lostock (Lancs.) a younger son of 'old Sir Ralph',[89] but Chaucer held Hanwell at his death in 1434.[90] Chaucer's relict Maud then held the manor, but on her death in 1436[91] it passed to her daughter Alice, wife of William de la Pole, Duke of Suffolk. Hanwell then followed the descent of the Dukedom of Suffolk[92] until Edmund, Duke of Suffolk (d. 1513), conveyed it to William Cope in 1498.[93]

William Cope died in 1513 and by his will Hanwell manor was to pass to his second son Anthony when he reached the age of 26.[94] Anthony

[51] See p. 120.
[52] *Cal. S.P. Dom.* 1644, 287, 288, 290, 291.
[53] Ibid. 1625–49, 689.
[54] *D.N.B.*
[55] Ibid.
[56] *V.C.H. Oxon.* i. 424.
[57] Ibid. 394.
[58] Ibid. viii. 57–8. For the difficult pedigree of the Vernons see particularly Ormerod, *Ches.* iii. 252; cf. *Ches. Visit. 1580* (Harl. Soc. xviii), 230–5.
[59] *Fines Oxon.* 56; cf. *Cur. Reg. R.* vi. 286.
[60] *Bk. of Fees*, 448, 823.
[61] *V.C.H. Oxon.* viii. 58; *Bk. of Fees*, 252, 613, where he is called William.
[62] *Ex. e Rot. Fin.* (Rec. Com.), i. 255.
[63] *Fines Oxon.* 147.
[64] His eldest legitimate son: *Cal. Pat.* 1381–5, 434.
[65] *Ex. e Rot. Fin.* (Rec. Com.), ii. 49; cf. Farrer, *Honors and Knights' Fees*, ii. 88.
[66] *Cat. Anct. D.* iii. B 4087.
[67] *Ex. e Rot. Fin.* (Rec. Com.), ii. 117.
[68] *Cal. Pat.* 1247–58, 121.
[69] *Close R.* 1247–51, 519. Richard's relationship to Ralph is uncertain.
[70] Ormerod, *Ches.* iii. 252; *Genealogist*, N.S. xii. 111.
[71] *Feud. Aids*, iv. 166.
[72] Constable of Beeston Castle in 1312: *Cal. Pat.* 1307–1313, 482.
[73] *Cat. Anct. D.* iii. B 4185.
[74] E 210/6450.
[75] *Cal. Pat.* 1327–30, 392. He is alleged to have lived to the age of 150 and may well have reached the age of 90: *Ches. Visit. 1580* (Harl. Soc. xviii), 230–3; cf. Ormerod, *Ches.* iii. 248 n. 6.
[76] Ormerod, *Ches.* iii. 247–8.
[77] E 212/56.
[78] Ormerod, *Ches.* iii. 248.
[79] E 212/67.
[80] Ormerod, *Ches.* iii. 246: i.e. brother of Rawlin, son of Ralph, son of 'old Sir Ralph'; a son of Margaret is a more likely successor than another John (of Lostock), for whom see *Ches. Visit. 1580* (Harl. Soc. xviii), 235.
[81] *Feud. Aids*, iv. 179; cf. *Cal. Fine R.* 1347–56, 37.
[82] *Cal. Inq. p.m.* x, p. 221.
[83] E 210/2377.
[84] *Cal. Close*, 1377–81, 288; *Cal. Inq. p.m.* (Rec. Com.), iii, p. 23.
[85] C.P. 25(1)/191/23/21.
[86] *Cal. Pat.* 1399–1401, 486.
[87] After Sir Richard's death the advowson at least was retained for a time in the hands of feoffees who presented 4 times between 1406 and 1409: see p. 118. For the Abberbury family see C. C. Brookes, *Hist. of Steeple and Middle Aston*, 51 sqq.; *V.C.H. Oxon.* vi. 304.
[88] C.P. 25(1)/191/26/9; cf. *V.C.H. Berks.* iv. 91.
[89] *Genealogist*, N.S. xvii. 112; Ormerod, *Ches.* iii. 252–3.
[90] *Feud, Aids*, iv. 187; C 139/70/35.
[91] *Cal. Close*, 1429–35, 325; C 139/83/53.
[92] *Cal. Inq. p.m.* (Rec. Com.), iv, p. 242; C.P. 40/942/218; *Complete Peerage*, xi. 443 sqq.
[93] C.P. 25(1)/191/31/34; Hants R.O., Cope pps. 187, 188 (quitclaims, 1498, 1500).
[94] C 142/28/31; J. C. Wedgwood, *Biographies of the members of the Commons house, 1439–1509*, 219.

had obtained Hanwell by 1518;[95] he was knighted in 1547 and died in 1551.[96] His eldest son and successor Edward Cope died in 1557 leaving as heir his eldest son William, a minor.[97] William appears to have died before reaching his majority, for Hanwell descended to Anthony, his younger brother, three times Sheriff of Oxfordshire and a prominent member of Parliament for both Banbury and Oxfordshire under Elizabeth I. He was knighted by her and created a baronet in 1611. He died in 1614 leaving debts amounting to over £20,000 and having settled Hanwell on his heir William and William's wife Elizabeth.[98] Sir William, several times M.P. for Banbury and Oxfordshire, died in 1637, and his son Sir John in 1638.[99] The latter's son, Sir Anthony, succeeded to the baronetcy at the age of six, and throughout the Civil War Hanwell manor was probably in the keeping of his mother Elizabeth (née Fane), daughter of Francis, Earl of Westmorland (d. 1629). Sir Anthony was several times M.P. either for Banbury or Oxfordshire between 1660 and his death in 1675.[1] All his children died in his lifetime; his relict, Mary Gerard (his cousin), became insane in 1676[2] and William Spencer her brother-in-law was appointed her committee under a commission of lunacy. By his will in 1675 Sir Anthony gave his brother and successor in the baronetcy, Sir John Cope, a life estate in Hanwell but laid down that Sir John should be succeeded only by a son, if any, by some other wife than his present one, Anne Booth. Mary, Lady Cope lived at Hanwell until her death in 1714, and since Sir John had not married a second wife Hanwell passed at his death in 1721, under a further provision of Sir Anthony's will, to Sir Jonathan Cope, of Bruern, grandson of Jonathan Cope of Ranton Abbey (Staffs.), a younger son of Sir William Cope (d. 1637).[3] Sir Jonathan died in 1765 and his grandson and successor Sir Charles in 1781. Sir Charles's only son, Sir Charles, also died in 1781, and his estates were divided between his sisters Catherine Ann and Arabella Diana.[4] Catherine, relict of the elder Sir Charles, married Charles Jenkinson, later created Earl of Liverpool, who held Hanwell in trust for his step-daughter Arabella[5] until her marriage in 1790 to John Frederick Sackville, Duke of Dorset.[6] After the duke's death in 1799 Arabella married Charles, Earl Whitworth, with whom she held Hanwell until her death in 1825.[7] Hanwell then passed to her younger daughter Elizabeth, wife of George John West, later Sackville-West, Earl de la Warr (d. 1869).[8] In 1946 Herbrand, Earl de la Warr, made over the estate to his son William, Lord Buckhurst, by a marriage settlement.[9]

In 1540 Sir Thomas Pope (d. 1559) was holding 5½ yardlands in Hanwell which may have been part of his Wroxton manor.[10] Sir Thomas sold this land to the Crown in 1540 and it was still retained by the Crown in 1553.[11] The further descent of this land is not known.

LOCAL GOVERNMENT. Almost nothing is known in detail of parish government at Hanwell until the end of the 18th century. An undated entry in the parish register indicates that the law relating to vagrants was strictly enforced: a widow, who was taken by the watch for begging, with her five children, was whipped according to law by the constable and sent with a pass to Herefordshire, where she was born.[12]

Parish rates in 1776 raised £104, of which £98 was spent on poor relief. By 1784–5 expenditure on the poor had risen to £170 out of £183.[13] Of the parish records only overseers' accounts for the periods 1792–9 and 1821–7 survive. Two overseers were chosen yearly, each accounting for 6 months. Weekly payments were given, ranging from *c.* 4*s.* 6*d.* to *c.* 9*s.* 6*d.*, to a number of persons. Between 1794 and 1796 the number on the list rose from 8 to 15 or more, at a cost of £40 to £70 a half year. The parish also used the roundsman system; between 6 and 11 men were paid weekly in the winter months of 1794–5, rising to 16 or more in 1797–8. In the summer this number fell considerably and then cost between £10 and £20 compared with £40 or more. Occasional expenses included payments of rent and repairs to the houses of the poor, payments for illness and for medical care, payment of an apprentice's premium, and an £8 fine to the justices for not finding a man for the Navy. The overseers regularly met the constable's disbursements. They also bore the loss made on the sale of cheap coal and bread to the poor. In 1794 the loss on coal, and in 1795 the loss on bread was *c.* £10. In all £230 was spent on poor relief in 1794–5, and £285 in 1796–7, the peak year in the first set of accounts.[14] Apart from some charity, and relief of the itinerant poor by the constable or by the churchwardens when he was absent,[15] this was the sum of poor out-relief. In 1796–7 £2 was spent on timber and boards at a workhouse but no expenditure on a workhouse is mentioned elsewhere.[16]

Expenditure had fallen by 1802–3; £102 was spent of £167 raised, all on out-relief, the remainder going on church rates, county rates, and highways. Five adults, with 19 children, received permanent relief, 50 occasional relief. Of the total number 5 were permanently unable to work.[17] By 1821 costs had risen enormously. There is no direct reference to roundsmen but a note on the last page of the account book states that, no payments for labour 'to roundsmen or otherwise' would in future be allowed in the overseers' accounts. The weekly list now had 16 to 20 people on it. Occasional payments

[95] C 1/399/39.
[96] C 142/94/43.
[97] C 142/112/139.
[98] C 142/392/99. For the Copes of Hanwell see G. E. C. *Baronetage*, i. 36–7. Anthony's will is P.C.C. 22 Cope. For his debts and other details see J. M. French, *Milton in Chancery*, 124 sqq.
[99] Par. Rec., note in reg. (1754); C 142/486/148.
[1] Beesley, *Hist. Banbury*, 471, 474.
[2] Ibid. 484; C 142/734/65.
[3] Par. Rec., reg.; Beesley, *Hist. Banbury*, 508; G.E.C. *Baronetage*, v. 19. For pedigrees of the Copes of Bruern see MS. Top. Oxon. c 49, f. 88; MS. Eng. Misc. d 18.
[4] G.E.C. *Baronetage*, v. 19; cf. C.P. 43/825/330; ibid. 842/441.
[5] G.E.C. *Baronetage*, v. 19; O.R.O., land tax assess.
[6] *Complete Peerage*, iv. 428–9; Gardner, *Dir. Oxon.* (1852).
[7] O.R.O., land tax assess.; ibid., gamekprs' deps.
[8] Ibid.; *Complete Peerage*, iv. 163 sqq.
[9] MS. Oxf. Dioc. c 1843; Burke, *Peerage* (1959).
[10] *L. & P. Hen. VIII*, xv, p. 169.
[11] Ibid.; L.R. 2/189, f. 180v.
[12] Par. Rec., reg.
[13] *Poor Abstract*, 398.
[14] Par. Rec., overseers' accts. 1792–99.
[15] Par. Rec., chwdns' accts. 1810–82.
[16] Par. Rec., overseers' accts., 1792–99; *Poor Abstract*, 398.
[17] *Poor Abstract*, 398.

increased and the supply of cheap coal and bread was continued. In 1821–22 total payments were £350; they fell in the next year to £263 but rose again and remained at *c.* £350 until the end of the accounts in 1827.[18]

The parish became part of the Banbury Union after the 1834 Act, and in 1834–5 of £243 10*s.* levied £175 was spent on out-relief. This fell to £130 out of £195 in the next year,[19] and again in 1851–2 to £129, raised by a rate of 1*s.* 7½*d.*[20]

ECONOMIC HISTORY. In 1086 there were 10 ploughs in use in Hanwell (although there was said to be land for only 8), of which 3 with 6 serfs were on the demesne, while 20 *villani* and 2 bordars worked 7 ploughs. The value of the manor had risen from £5 to £7 since 1066. Besides the arable 14 a. of meadow land were mentioned.[21]

In the 14th century Hanwell was a village of medium size and, with the exception of the lord, there was no villager of outstanding wealth. For the tax of 1316 only one tenant paid as much as 2*s.* 6*d.* and in 1327 all 24 tenants paid under 2*s.*[22] A great part of the tax was paid by the lord — in 1306 he and his daughters paid nearly a third of the village's total assessment.[23]

At this time the economy was based, as in other north Oxfordshire parishes, on a 2-field system. One field lay to the west of the village and the other to the east, and holdings were probably equally divided between the two.[24] Evidence for the size of holdings is lacking except for a survey of Sir Thomas Pope's land in Hanwell made in 1553 when it was in the king's hands; there were then 13 tenants holding some 5½ yardlands. All, save Sir Edward Cope, held by customary tenure at rents ranging from 5*s.* for ¼ yardland to 30*s.* for 1½ yardland.[25] By 1680 and possibly earlier the 2 fields had been replaced by 4 and a terrier of the rector's yardland records that it was divided between the fields into about 47 parcels.[26] An earlier terrier of 1601 shows that, as in other neighbouring parishes, each field contained leys. There was or had once been a dole meadow where land was assigned by lots.[27]

Some farmers probably profited by the price revolution of the 16th century. There were 8 contributors to the subsidy of 1523, though their assessments were small, one being assessed on £8 worth of goods and the rest on £4 to £6 worth.[28] In 1572 there were 5 farmers prosperous enough to be assessed besides Sir Anthony Cope, who was by far the richest man in the parish.[29] Although there may have been others of equal wealth who escaped taxation, it seems plain that by this time there had been some concentration of wealth in a few hands. Inventories of members of those yeoman families who were assessed in 1572 show considerable wealth, particularly when compared with those made in the poorer Chiltern country. James Hazelwood (d. 1689), for example, was worth £228 in goods.[30] Other families like the Bullers and Grants acquired wealth in the 17th century, or were newcomers to the parish. Edward Buller (d. 1666) had £109 worth of chattels, and two Grants had goods worth as much as £317 and £386 in the early 18th century.[31] The Bullers remained a leading Hanwell family into the 20th century: in 1904 they were renting three of the principal farms, but by the 1950s they had almost died out.[32] Other 17th-century families such as the Bortons and the Haineses were represented in the 20th century by cottagers.[33] The prosperity of Hanwell's farmers is also reflected in the number of substantial farm-houses. There were 7 with 3 or 4 hearths in 1665 and many of these were later enlarged.[34]

The crops normally grown were wheat, pease, barley, and oats, but there were at least 100 a. under woad at the end of the 16th century.[35] Although most farmers kept a few cattle, pigs, and sheep, arable farming was their mainstay. In the selection of inventories examined at least two-thirds of the value of each farmer's property was in his arable crops;[36] 17th-century terriers of the rector's glebe of 1 yardland show that the greater part of his land was arable,[37] a characteristic of the economy which persisted into the late 18th century when the only pasture or meadow in Hanwell were the fields around the mill and along the brook in the east of the parish.[38]

There is little evidence of early inclosure and Hanwell probably remained largely an open-field parish until the 18th century. In *c.* 1768 Sir Charles Cope, lord of the manor, who probably already owned most of the land,[39] bought out the common rights of copyholders, life- and lease-holders, and other proprietors than the rector, and inclosed the parish. New farm-houses outside the village were built; the trend towards farms of bigger acreage was encouraged, and capital investment accompanied experiments in farming practice.[40] In 1785 there were 9 farms of which 3 were probably over 150 a., and 6 smaller holdings of under 50 a.[41] By 1832 the number of landholders had declined to 10; there were still 3 large farms but some of the smallholders had disappeared.[42] From *c.* 1788 Thomas Wyatt had been the chief farmer in the parish.[43] Arthur Young considered him a progressive farmer and his farm an example of 'capital husbandry'; he noted his 'remarkably fine cows' of the long-horned

[18] Par. Rec., overseers' accts. 1821–27.
[19] *2nd Rep. of Poor Law Com.* 294.
[20] *Poor Law Unions*, 21.
[21] *V.C.H. Oxon.* i. 424.
[22] E 179/161/8, 9.
[23] E 179/161/10.
[24] Gray, *Eng. Field Systems*, 487.
[25] L. R. 2/189, f. 180v. See also p. 116.
[26] Par. Rec., reg. (1754). A terrier of 1676 mentions Lotzym Quarter: MS. Oxf. Archd. Oxon. c 141, f. 477; Gray, *Eng. Field Systems*, 493.
[27] MS. Oxf. Archd. Oxon. c 141, f. 484.
[28] E 179/161/196, 198.
[29] E 179/162/341.
[30] MS. Wills Oxon. 34/3/17.
[31] Ibid. 6/3/7; 28/2/8, 41.
[32] Bodl. G.A. Oxon. b 91(2): *Sale cat.*; local information.
[33] Bodl. G.A. Oxon. b 91(2): *Sale cat.*
[34] *Hearth Tax Oxon.* 143–4.
[35] B.M. MS. Lansdowne, xlix, 142.
[36] e.g. MS. Wills Oxon. 2/2/29; 6/3/7; 26/2/37; 28/2/37, 41; 34/4/3.
[37] MS. Oxf. Archd. Oxon. c 141, pp. 477, 484.
[38] Davis, *Oxon. Map.*
[39] In 1754 the only 40*s.* freeholder was the rector: *Oxon. Poll 1754.*
[40] Gray, *Eng. Field Systems*, 116; *C. J.* xxxix. 148: petition 5 Feb. 1783. This was confirmed in Hanwell Incl. Act. 23 Geo. III, c 43 (priv. act), which concerns only the glebe and the poor's allotment. There is no incl. award.
[41] O.R.O., land tax assess. 1785. The acreage is obtained by dividing the total assessment £87 11*s.* 5*d.* by the number of acres in the parish, which results in *c.* 14 a. for £1 of land tax. This calculation is very approximate.
[42] O.R.O., land tax assess. 1832.
[43] Ibid. 1788, 1832. His farm was assessed at £15 16*s.* 6*d.* in 1832 and rented for £39 12*s.*

breed, which though they gave less milk than his short-horns were less voracious and yielded milk of a rich quality. By tethering his horses on vetches, a custom of which Young disapproved, he was able to follow his vetches with swedes, which lasted for April and May feeding, and then he sowed the same land with roots again. Young also described the machine which Wyatt used for slicing swedes for sheep fodder; he commented also on this introduction of Swedish turnip, which was beginning to be preferred in Oxfordshire, on Wyatt's sowing of spring wheat, which he used twice in a course, and on his use of a scuffler in preparing the land for wheat.[44] Praise was also given to another Hanwell farmer, who benefited both the poor and himself by leasing land to them for potatoes and then planting the enriched land with wheat.[45]

Hanwell's farmers at this time were all tenants and the whole parish belonged to the lord of the manor as it continued to do into the 20th century. In 1904 there were 6 farms: Hanwell Fields or Bismore Hall, the only farm in the south of the parish, Spring farm and Hanwell Park farm, all between 240 and 300 a. in extent; and 3 of between 110 and 160 a.[46] Arable no longer predominated and there was 51 per cent. permanent pasture.[47] Some sixty years later mixed farming was still the rule, and the number of farms was approximately the same.[48]

Although Banbury was close at hand and the parish was not large, the village had its own craftsmen or tradesmen in the 18th century and was largely self-sufficient.[49] In 1811 52 out of 56 families were engaged in agriculture.[50] In the later 19th century the agricultural depression caused a decrease in the number of agricultural workers and rural craftsmen, and in the 20th century new farm techniques, improved transport and the industrial growth of Banbury, led villagers to find work in Banbury rather than on the farms.[51]

A rent of ½ mark from Hanwell's mill, which stood on a tributary of the Cherwell in the extreme west of the parish[52] and was known by the 16th century as Moor Mill, was granted by Sir Warin de Vernon (d. *ante* 1249) to the canons of Ashby (Northants.), for the souls of himself and his wife Alda.[53] Warin's son Ralph granted the mill, the ½ mark rent and a cottage there, with land and a meadow, and the multure and suit of Hanwell's tenants. He also promised to build no other mill.[54] In 1291 the mill was valued at £1 13*s.* but by the 16th century the priory let it for only 26*s.* 8*d.* a year.[55] Edward Bailly, husbandman of Drayton, took a 24-year lease of it in 1527; in 1535 he demised the remainder of the lease to John Wright of Hanwell, miller, who conveyed it in 1538 to Anthony Cope, of Hardwick, the lord of the manor.[56] Cope paid rent to the king, who had taken over the priory's possessions in 1536.[57] In 1545 the mill was granted to two members of the Lawley family.[58] In 1615 Sir William Cope mortgaged it to Manasses Cowper, of Arlescote (Warws.) for £300. Part of the agreement was that Cowper should have land on Mill Hill in the South-West Field on which to build a windmill.[59] Presumably Sir William paid off the mortgage within three years, as stipulated, for the proprietorship of the mill remained in the Cope family. The Misses Cope of Hanwell were the owners in 1784 when an attempt was made to improve the mill by increasing the flow of water. Apparently this proved impracticable and led to trouble with local farmers. Sixteen proprietors of Wroxton meadow alleged that the water in the brooks had been more than doubled and that this, with the removal of trees, mere-stones, and other landmarks, had caused an estimated £66 worth of damage to their meadow.[60] The mill was being worked by the Allen family in 1854; it was still in operation as a water-corn-mill in 1891 but by 1895 it had closed down.[61]

CHURCH. The earliest indication of a church at Hanwell is a reference to its rector in 1154.[62] The advowson probably belonged to the lord of the manor in the mid-12th century as it did in 1234 when the first recorded presentation was made.[63] Since then the descent of the advowson has followed that of the manor. Four presentations were made by feoffees between 1406 and 1409.[64] There was a royal presentation in 1558 on account of the minority of William Cope, and another in 1694 because of the lunacy of Mary, Lady Cope.[65] In 1946 Lord de la Warr transferred the patronage to his son, Lord Buckhurst, but the last two presentations have been nominations by the Bishop of Oxford at the request of the patron.[66]

The rectory, which was never appropriated, was endowed with all the tithes in the parish and with a small glebe. The living was valued at £6 13*s.* 4*d.* in 1254, at £7 6*s.* 8*d.* in 1291, and at £17 16*s.* in 1535, when Anthony Cope, lord of the manor, was leasing the tithes and glebe and paying the rent to the rector.[67] In the early 17th century the rectory was worth £100 and in the early 18th century £160.[68] In 1768, when the parish was being inclosed, Sir Charles Cope, who owned the whole parish except for the glebe, arranged with the rector to pay £146 a year in place of all tithes, and at the same time the rector was released from the obligation of keeping a bull and a boar. This agreement was ratified by the

[44] Young, *Oxon. Agric.* 80, 147, 180–1, 280, 312.
[45] Ibid. 185.
[46] Bodl. G.A. Oxon. b 91(2): *Sale cat.*
[47] Orr, *Oxon. Agric.* plate facing p. 161.
[48] Local information.
[49] For 18th-century craftsmen see MS. Wills Oxon. 80/3/28, 130/1/32; for 19th-century craftsmen see *Kelly's Dir. Oxon.* (1864–91) and H.O. 107/1734.
[50] *Census*, 1811.
[51] *V.C.H. Oxon.* ii. 217; local information.
[52] O.S. Map 25" Oxon. V. 3.
[53] Hants R.O., Cope pps. 185; *Cat. Anct. D.* iii. B 4094.
[54] *Cat. Anct. D.* iii. B 4087.
[55] *Tax Eccl.* (Rec. Com.), 44; *Valor Eccl.* (Rec. Com.), iv. 337; Hants R.O., Cope pps. 182, 183; for a 14th-century lease see *Cat. Anct. D.* iii. B 4088.
[56] Hants R.O., Cope pps. 182, 183.
[57] *L. & P. Hen. VIII*, x, p. 970.
[58] Ibid. xx, p. 222.
[59] Hants R.O , Cope pps. 186.
[60] MS. North b 16, f. 141.
[61] Billing, *Dir. Oxon.* (1854); *Kelly's Dir. Oxon.* (1891, 1895).
[62] *Eynsham Cart.* i. 39.
[63] *Rot. Welles*, ii. 45.
[64] The descent of the manor at this date is in some doubt. See p. 115. For a list of medieval presentations see MS. Top. Oxon. d 460.
[65] MS. Oxf. Dioc. d 105, f. 196; d 106, f. 149. A second presentation in 1712 was by her guardian: ibid. c 266, f. 188v.
[66] MS. Oxf. Dioc. c 1843.
[67] Lunt, *Val. Norw.* 309; *Tax. Eccl.* (Rec. Com.), 32; *Valor Eccl.* (Rec. Com.), ii. 165.
[68] Dunkin MS. 438/2, f. 153; *Par. Colln.* ii. 162.

Inclosure Act of 1783. It stipulated that the sum the rector received, which had been calculated as the equivalent of 71 qr. of wheat, could be reassessed every 21 years.[69] From that time the value of the rectory depended largely on the price of grain.[70] The open-field glebe of apparently 1 yardland or *c.* 20 a. was described in terriers of 1601 and 1680.[71] At inclosure the glebe with its right of common was exchanged for 27 a., which the rector still owned in 1946.[72]

Almost no record has been found of medieval church life at Hanwell and little is known of its medieval rectors. The rector in 1154 seems to have been a rural dean; reference was made to the Rector of Hanwell's deanery, presumably the later Deddington deanery.[73] In the 13th century Ralph de Vernon, a member of the family of the manorial lords and patrons, may have been rector[74] and Robert de Vernon certainly held the living in 1343.[75]

From the 13th century onwards a high proportion of rectors (about one third) were university graduates. Among them were two who were probably members of prominent local families — the Ardens of Drayton and the Danverses of Calthorpe. Gilbert de Arden (*ante* 1295–1317) was a pluralist and a prominent royal servant, and John Danvers (1390–1406) was a Fellow of New College, Oxford.[76] Both these men were likely to have been non-resident for at least part of the year. At the end of the 15th century, on the other hand, Master William Andrew (1491–1528) seems to have resided. The churchwardens made a number of complaints against him at the visitation of 1517–20, of which the chief were that he kept a woman in the parsonage and that he allowed sheep to pasture in the churchyard. A charge that he refused to open the churchyard gates to allow old people in perhaps means that the normal entrance was by way of a stile.[77] Non-residence seems to have been common in the 16th century at Hanwell: in 1541 the rector obtained a licence to be non-resident[78] and his successor's absence is perhaps implied by the fact that the parsonage was let in 1549.[79]

Non-residence may have stimulated the growth of Puritan sentiment which became important in Hanwell in the 17th century through the influence of the Cope family, patrons of the living. The Copes were deeply concerned with theological problems. Sir Anthony (d. 1551) was engaged in a theological dispute with the Vicar of Banbury in 1540, and among other works wrote a meditation on the Psalms.[80] His grandson, Sir Anthony (d. 1614), was a 'hot Puritan' who was imprisoned in 1587 for introducing into the House of Commons a Puritan version of the Prayer Book and a bill for abrogating the existing ecclesiastical law.[81] As early as 1584 the curate Jonas Wheler, who may also have been schoolmaster at Banbury,[82] was excommunicated for refusing to say services on Fridays and Saturdays. His church wardens were also excommunicated for not presenting him and for obstinately refusing to present him.[83] Wheler's crime was evidently a refusal to conform rather than any neglect of his flock, for he preached every Sunday and once during the week.[84] In 1584 Sir Anthony Cope, having been 'much wrought upon' by the preaching of John Dod, a young Cambridge Fellow, presented him to the Hanwell living.[85] There Dod spent 20 years and there his 12 children were born. His house became a centre of Puritanism for a far wider area than north Oxfordshire: on Sundays and Wednesdays he usually had 8 to 12 people dining with him and he spent much time 'among them in spiritual exhortation and conference'. He preached twice every Sunday as a rule, catechized on Sunday afternoon, held a lecture on Wednesdays, and also lectured at Banbury.[86] Other ministers were sometimes invited to preach at Hanwell, notably Robert Cleaver, Rector of Drayton, and his close friend, the Puritan divine Thomas Cartwright.[87] Dod and Cleaver together published a work on the Ten Commandments in 1603 which was based on sermons preached at Hanwell and probably also at Drayton. The volume, dedicated to Sir Anthony Cope, earned for Dod the title of the Decalogist.[88] He was said to have converted 'hundreds of souls' and was consequently envied by neighbouring ministers, who, although they did not preach themselves, did not care to see their congregations go elsewhere. He was 'questioned' from time to time in the bishop's court, and in 1593, after a special examination at the request of Archbishop Whitgift, he agreed to conform in all ways except for wearing the surplice and crossing children in baptism.[89] Complaints must have continued, however, for in 1606 or 1607 he was deprived. Nevertheless he went on living at or near Hanwell and received 'good affection' from Sir Anthony Cope.[90]

Dod's popular support created difficulties for his successor, Robert Harris, another learned divine and eminent preacher.[91] Harris found that his new congregation remained loyal to their ejected pastor, particularly as Harris differed in his preaching from Dod on several points. He was in time accepted, however, for he had the backing of Sir Anthony Cope and of Dod himself. He married the sister of William Whateley, the Puritan Vicar of Banbury, and again the parsonage became a resort for earnest Puritans, particularly for young Oxford Fellows, so that it seemed 'a little academy'.[92] Harris

[69] Hanwell Incl. Act, 23 Geo. III c. 43 (priv. act).

[70] e.g. *Oxf. Mail,* 2 Oct. 1950.

[71] MS. Oxf. Archd. Oxon. c 141, ff. 477–84. It had lot meadows for 1 yardland: ibid. f. 484.

[72] MS. Oxf. Dioc. c 448: 1806 terrier; c 1843: 1946 collation.

[73] *Eynsham Cart.* i. 39, 424–30.

[74] According to Ormerod (*Ches.* iii. 246, 252), but he gives no reference for the statement. There is a long gap in the list of known rectors at this point.

[75] MS. Top. Oxon. d 460.

[76] For them see Emden, *O.U. Reg.*

[77] *Visit. Dioc. Linc. 1517–31,* i. 126.

[78] *L. & P. Hen. VIII,* xvi, p. 501.

[79] Hants R.O., Cope pps. 184. The lease evidently did not run its full 99 years for in the late 16th century the rectors were again in possession. See also MS. Oxf. Archd. Oxon. c 141, f. 484.

[80] Reprinted in 1848 by W. H. Cope with a biographical preface.

[81] A. F. Pollard, *Political Hist. of England,* 458; *D.N.B.*

[82] *Archdeacon's Ct.* i. 86n.

[83] Ibid. i, 86; ii, pp. vii–viii.

[84] *The Seconde Parte of a Register,* ed. A. Peel, ii. 137.

[85] S. Clarke, *Lives of Twenty Two English Divines* (1660), 200; O.A.S. *Rep.* 1916, 57.

[86] For Dod, except where otherwise stated, see Clarke, op. cit. 199 sqq.; *D.N.B.*

[87] For Cartwright see W. Durham, *Life and Death of Robert Harris* (1660), 87–8; S. F. S. Pearson, *Thos. Cartwright,* 392.

[88] J. Dod and R. Cleaver, *A Plaine and Familiar Exposition of the Ten Commandements* (1607).

[89] *V.C.H. Oxon.* ii. 42; MS. Oxf. Dioc. d 4, f. 54.

[90] Durham, op. cit. 18–19.

[91] MS. Dunkin 438/2, f. 285v.

[92] Durham, op. cit. 16, 20 sqq.

maintained strong links with other north Oxfordshire Puritans, among them Cleaver of Drayton, and Lancaster, an outstanding Cambridge scholar,[93] while with Dod he daily read a chapter of the Bible in Hebrew.[94]

Harris was at Hanwell for about 40 years and his influence was felt much further afield, for he sometimes preached in London, Banbury, Deddington, and Oxford.[95] It was said that at Easter and Whit Monday 'troops of Christians from all quarters, many miles distant' flocked to Hanwell.[96] The sermon which he preached at Sir Anthony Cope's funeral in 1614 and published as a pamphlet[97] acquired a great reputation, especially among the Banbury Puritans. He is said to have had such success at Hanwell itself that there was no one who would refuse to be prepared for the Lord's Supper by him.[98] He was in no sense a Presbyterian or Independent, being tolerant on matters concerning church government.

In August 1642 he was driven from his house by royalist soldiers who had occupied the village.[99] He returned later, had royalist soldiers quartered on him, and held services which were attended by the royalists, but before the end of the year he had been ejected.[1] What then happened at Hanwell is uncertain. The parish register was carried off by soldiers in 1642 and was not found again until 1649;[2] Harris's goods were 'seized upon' and his living was said to have been given to another; in 1653 Harris, who had been appointed President of Trinity College, Oxford, called himself 'late pastor of Hanwell',[3] and in the same year, when a new register was begun for Hanwell in accordance with the Act of Parliament, a Walter Harris appears as 'minister and register'.[4]

With the new rector, George Ashwell (1658–94), Puritan influence ended. He was a royalist who had been preacher to Charles I during his stay in Oxford.[5] He was utterly opposed to all heresies and schisms and remained until his death in 1694 a strong supporter of the Established Church. In his will he professed his faith in it and his gratitude for having been able to serve it.[6] He was a scholar and in 1663 published his *Gestus Eucharisticus*, which he dedicated to Sir Anthony Cope, and much of his later writing was devoted to preserving church unity against the threat of the nonconformist movement in Banbury. He was also a devoted parish pastor: he preached 2 sermons on Sundays and catechized in Lent; he visited the sick; and baptized the young and old; when he came to the parish there were several who had not been baptized, but by 1682 there was none.[7] He lived a frugal life, despite his large house, 3 servants and goods valued at over £422, and set a vigorous example of piety and simplicity to his parishioners. In his will he desired his executrix to give 'small practical books' to those of his parishioners who would profit by them and others to his friends among the gentry, the Wenmans, the Dentons, and the Spencers.[8]

Ashwell's successor, William Wyatt, cannot have been resident for more than half the year, for he was Public Orator at the University and Principal of St. Mary Hall.[9] He had a curate, however, to serve Hanwell.[10] Another rector, John Loggan (1717–22), son of the engraver David Loggan, was formerly a Fellow of Magdalen College, Oxford.[11] Later in the century non-residence became common: one rector (1725–49) spent part of his time in Hanwell and part in his other parish, while his successor, who held office until 1802, was never resident,[12] but had resident curates. During the years when Hanwell was served by Thomas Gill, curate in 1797 and after, the parishioners were well cared for. He was a 'conscientious, discreet, diligent man' who was content with his small stipend, as he had an adequate income from two other churches.[13] Throughout the century 2 Sunday services were held, the sacrament was given 4 times a year, and the children were catechized in Lent.[14] The lively interest of the parishioners in their church is demonstrated by the great attention paid to maintaining its fabric.[15]

The patron Lord Whitworth presented in 1805 L. K. Pitt, who had been chaplain to the British Factory at St. Petersburg when Whitworth was Ambassador in Russia, but Pitt never came to Hanwell having received permission from the bishop to stay on at St. Petersburg.[16] His resident curate at Hanwell was stimulated by the increase of Methodism in the neighbourhood into making great efforts,[17] particularly in the field of education.[18] After Pitt's death in 1813 members of the Pearse family were rectors or curates for a century.[19] Vincent Pearse (1861–1912), who followed his father as rector, rebuilt the parsonage, repaired the church, increased the number of communion services from 4 to more than 12 a year, held a Sunday school and a night school in the winter for the boys, and ran a clothing club. Dissent nevertheless remained strong: Pearse reported that a half to two-thirds of the population attended church but that many of these also attended dissenting services.[20]

Since 1946 the living of Hanwell has been held in plurality with the vicarage of Horley and Hornton. Hanwell parsonage was sold and the rector lives in the larger village of Horley, a mile distant.[21]

The church of *ST. PETER* comprises chancel, nave, north and south aisles, south porch, and western tower.[22] It was almost entirely rebuilt early in the

[93] S. Clarke, *Collection of the Lives of Ten Eminent Divines* (1662), 278–81.
[94] Ibid. 282.
[95] e.g. sermons at London in 1626, 3 at Oxford in 1626, and 1 in the House of Commons in 1642.
[96] Durham, op. cit. 24–25; Clarke, op. cit. 283–6.
[97] *Samuel's Funerall* (1618).
[98] Clarke, op. cit. 286.
[99] Beesley, *Hist. Banbury*, 288, 301.
[1] Durham, op. cit. 30–33.
[2] Par. Rec., note in reg. (1754).
[3] Durham, op. cit. 33; *The Works of Robert Harris* (1654): title page to sermons.
[4] Par. Rec., reg.
[5] Wood, *Athenae*, iv. 396–7.
[6] MS. Wills Oxon. 2/2/29.
[7] MS. Oxf. Dioc. c 430, f. 21.
[8] *Hearth Tax Oxon.* 143; MS. Wills Oxon. 2/2/29. The books left included Digby's *Treatise* and Ward's *Book against Mr. Hobs.*
[9] Foster, *Alumni.*
[10] Par. Rec., reg.
[11] Foster, *Alumni*; *D.N.B.* under D. Loggan.
[12] *Secker's Visit.*; MS. Oxf. Dioc. d 556; d 559; c 327, p. 123; Par. Rec., reg.
[13] MS. Oxf. Dioc. c 653, f. 74; d 562.
[14] *Secker's Visit.*; MS. Oxf. Dioc. d 556; d 559; c 327, p. 123; Par. Rec., reg.
[15] e.g. Par. Rec., reg.
[16] MS. Oxf. Dioc. d 746; d 570; c 659, ff. 155, 194, 196; Foster, *Alumni.*
[17] MS. Oxf. Dioc. d 566.
[18] See p. 122.
[19] Foster, *Alumni*; MS. Oxf. Dioc. b 41; *Wilb. Visit.*
[20] MS. Oxf. Dioc. c 1843; c 332; c 344; Par. Rec., reg.
[21] Local information.
[22] There is an account of the building with photographs by C. E. Keyser in *Jnl. Brit. Arch. Assoc.* N.S. xxvii. 137–146; also see Beesley, *Hist. Banbury*, 118–19.

14th century, and has many of the characteristic features of the Decorated style as practised by the Oxfordshire masons. The only remaining features earlier than 1300 appear to be the font, which is ornamented with intersecting arcading of *c.* 1200, the north and south doorways (both 13th-century), the tracery of the east window of the south aisle (late-13th-century, perhaps reset), and the northern portion of the east wall of the same aisle. The disparity between the sizes of the north and south aisles may be due to the influence of the plan of the former church, and differences between the tracery of their windows suggest that the northern (and narrower) aisle may be slightly later in date. Both north and south nave arcades are, however, of identical design, and form part of a single build with the tower, which stands on arches within the west end of the nave. As the west wall of the tower is also of one build with the west walls of the two aisles, it is clear that the rebuilding of the church, although possibly spread over a period of years, formed part of a single architectural scheme.

The principal feature of the interior is the sculptured decoration of the nave arcades, whose capitals are ornamented with the busts of men and women with linked arms. On the north side the capitals have a battlemented cresting, and on the south they are surmounted by standing figures of minstrels playing musical instruments.[23] Similar carvings are found at Adderbury, Bloxham, and Drayton. At Hanwell the full scheme of decoration was never completed, for the capitals beneath the tower remain in a rough state ready for the carver. The external cornices of the north and south walls of the chancel are also elaborately decorated with grotesque sculpture, similar to that at Brailes (Warws.), Alkerton, Adderbury, and Bloxham.[24]

In the late 14th or early 15th century the clerestory was added and a new roof was constructed. The weather-mould of the earlier roof can be seen above the chancel-arch and on the east wall of the tower. Buckler's drawing of 1824 shows the new roof,[25] of which the main timbers still remain. Late in the 15th or early in the 16th century 3 flat-headed mullioned windows were inserted in the north wall of the north aisle. In the south-west angle of the south aisle there is a medieval fire-place: its chimney is decorated with crocketed pinnacles and is similar to one at Horley.

In 1686 altar rails were given by William Spencer and the rector George Ashwell wainscoted the chancel.[26] In the 18th century the fabric was maintained in good order: in 1775 the archdeacon found it necessary to order only minor repairs, including the repaving of the floor.[27] In 1763 when the leads of the nave were stripped off on the north side by a violent wind, the estimated cost of repair was £310 and it was 1767 before the money was raised. The work was then begun and completed in the same year.[28] The new paving of the church with Hornton stone was begun in 1773 and completed in 1774. The porch was also paved and the way from the parsonage gate to the north church door. The church was re-pewed at the same time, a new gallery was erected as well as the 'long seat' in the south aisle for farmers' men and servants. During the paving of the church the pulpit, reading desk, parsonage pews, and clerk's seat were removed to new positions for the 'greater convenience of the whole congregation'.[29] In 1774 the church clock, which has no face, was repaired and placed in a specially made recess.[30] The proportions of the chancel were impaired in 1776 when a vault was made beneath it for the Cope family. The floor was raised so high that the seats of the sedilia were level with the floor and 5 steps had to be built between the sanctuary and the nave. Two windows had already been blocked by large memorials to the Copes. In the 19th century the floor was restored to its former level,[31] but the church largely escaped 19th-century restoration: its external appearance still closely resembles Buckler's drawings of 1823 and 1824.[32]

New heating apparatus was installed in 1880,[33] and in 1949 and 1951 faculties were granted for installing electric lighting and heating in the chancel. A faculty for an organ was obtained in 1923.[34] The stone pulpit is dated 1940.

The church once had a series of wall paintings extending the whole breadth of the chancel. These were uncovered in 1841 when the whitewash was removed, but they could not be preserved.[35]

The heraldic glass described by Rawlinson[36] has been destroyed, but a few fragments of medieval glass survive in the west window.

The Creed and the Lord's Prayer are painted on the wall in the south aisle and the Commandments on boards in the north aisle.

In the south aisle there is the recumbent effigy of a woman, once part of a mid-14th-century tomb; above the altar in the north aisle there is a fragment of 14th-century sculpture which probably came from the side of this tomb: it consists of 5 figures of weepers in niches.[37] In the chancel is a large alabaster monument with figures of Sir Anthony Cope (d. 1614) and his wife. It is flanked by Corinthian columns supporting obelisks.[38] On the floor are two brasses of 1662 and 1671 to the infant children of Sir Anthony (d. 1675); on the south wall are memorials to Jonathan Cope (d. 1765) and his wife Mary (d. 1755), and to Sir Charles Cope and his son (both d. 1781).[39] A cartouche in the south aisle commemorates Dorothea (d. 1656/7), wife of Walter Harris, and there are memorials to a rector and a curate, George Ashwell (d. 1694), and Thomas Gill (d. 1777). A memorial slab, now in the south aisle, to another rector, Fitzherbert Potter (d. 1749), was

[23] Illustrated by Buckler in MS. Top. Oxon. a 67, no. 296. See plate facing p. 115.
[24] C. E. Keyser, *Antiq. Jnl.* iv. 1–10.
[25] MS. Top. Oxon. a 67, no. 298.
[26] MS. Rawl. B 400 b, f. 167.
[27] MS. Oxf. Archd. Oxon. d 13, f. 10.
[28] Par. Rec., reg.
[29] Ibid.
[30] Ibid.
[31] MS. Oxf. Archd. Oxon. c 73, ff. 71, 87–90.
[32] MS. Top. Oxon. a 67, nos. 297, 298; cf. a view of 1844 in MS. Gen. Top. f. 15, f. 69v.
[33] Par. Rec., chwdns' bk. 1809–82.
[34] MS. Oxf. Dioc. c 1843.
[35] Beesley, *Hist. Banbury*, 612.
[36] *Par. Colln.* ii. 164.
[37] The defacement of the medieval monuments perhaps occurred when troops were stationed in the village.
[38] For notes on the heraldry, see Bodl. G.A. Oxon. 4° 686, pp. 163–4; G.A. Oxon. 16° 217, p. 152, 156. For photos see N.B.R.
[39] For inscriptions see *Jnl. Brit. Arch. Assoc.* N.S. xxvii, 139–141.

part of a tomb accidentally destroyed in 1952.[40] In the north aisle 3 funeral helms of the Cope family are preserved.

The church possesses a fine Elizabethan chalice and paten cover, which is engraved 1574.[41] This may have been the gift of Charles Spencer, who lent a silver flagon, chalice, and paten for the use of the parishioners, intimating that he might later make it a gift.[42]

There is a ring of 5 bells, all cast in 1789 and 1790.[43]

The registers, which date from 1586, are complete except for a gap for the Civil War period.[44]

NONCONFORMITY. There was only one nonconformist in Hanwell in 1676,[45] probably an Anabaptist woman of whom the rector complained in 1682. Apparently some Hanwell parishioners also attended the Presbyterian conventicle in Calthorpe House, Banbury.[46] In 1714 William Glaze, 'a professed Presbyterian', late of Hanwell, was keeping a school at Neithrop,[47] and there were occasional references to a Hanwell Anabaptist throughout the 18th century.[48]

From 1802 the Horley Methodist chapel apparently attracted some Hanwell parishioners.[49] By 1814 there was at least one professed Methodist family,[50] in 1822 William Gunn's house in Hanwell was licensed for meetings which were clearly Methodist,[51] and in 1823 an itinerant preacher was visiting the village.[52] Although there were said to be no dissenters in 1834[53] there was an average attendance at William Gunn's house of 47 in 1851; in 1854 meetings were held there on Sunday evenings but there were no regular teachers.[54] By 1878 nearly half the inhabitants of Hanwell were thought to be dissenters and the 'Unionists' held meetings on the village green.[55] A Methodist chapel, built in the later 19th century, with seating for 80, was in use in 1965. It was served by ministers from Banbury and Brailes (Warws.), and its membership was five.[56]

SCHOOLS. About 1812 the curate established two Sunday schools,[57] one for 12 very young children, and another for about the same number of older boys. They were supported by the parish and were conducted to a very limited extent on the National Society's plan. Although the Sunday school teachers in 1815 were willing to adopt the new scheme proposed by the National Society, it was then considered that there were not enough children in the surrounding area to warrant it.[58] In 1823 the school received money from a charity.[59]

By 1834 a day school had been established, though there was still no infants' school. Twelve boys and 14 girls attended at their parents' expense and in the Sunday school, supported by contributions, there were 20 boys and 15 girls. Both schools received support from the lord of the manor, the rector, and some of the farmers.[60] In 1848 George, Earl de la Warr, gave a cottage to be used both as a school and a residence for the schoolmaster.[61] In 1854 the parish clerk was master and *c.* 30 children attended the day school and *c.* 50 the Sunday school.[62] In 1859 there were 33 children attending the day school and 38 the Sunday school. It was reported that it was not possible to retain the children in Sunday school after they had left the day school, and that a night school had been attempted without success.[63] Seven years later, however, the rector was able to report that a night school for labouring boys was fairly attended for so small a parish.[64]

A school was built in 1868 through the exertions of the rector, and the old cottage school was converted into a teacher's house.[65] The school, which was run in conjunction with the National Society and the Church of England, was intended for the children of labourers and other poor persons. The parents paid rates of 3*d.*, 2*d.*, and 1*d.* weekly according to their means, and in 1869 an annual grant covered all other expenses.[66] Attendance had risen from 30 in 1869 to 35 in 1871.[67] Although there was accommodation for 53, the situation seems to have been considered unsatisfactory, since in 1872 a School Board was formed compulsorily. This Board leased the school under restrictions approved by the National Society,[68] and in 1875 there were 49 pupils, of whom 45 paid 1*d.* and 4 paid 2*d.* weekly.[69] The maximum accommodation at the school was 65, and the average attendance about half that.[70] By 1890 the school received a Parliamentary grant, which, with payments from the rates and fees, made up the whole income.[71] The 1894 and 1900 returns, however, do not mention payments of school pence.[72] The school, which had had a roll of only 17 in 1952, was closed in 1961 and the infants transferred to Horley, the juniors to Hornton, and others to Banbury.[73]

CHARITIES. In 1728 James Jenkinson, Rector of Drayton and formerly Rector of Hanwell (1723–5), gave £10 for the use of the poor, and Mrs. Butterfield gave £3; both sums were vested in the lord of the manor and his successors. The income of 13*s.* was received and distributed regularly until 1780; payment then ceased until 1818 when arrears of

[40] For other memorials in the church before 1718 see Rawlinson's notes in *Par. Colln.* ii. 162–4. The Purbeck marble slab covering Potter's tomb may have formed the top of a much earlier altar tomb. A note in the parish register says that 'it belongs to the church and may be removed to its original position without risk'.

[41] For a full account of the church plate see Evans, *Ch. Plate.*

[42] Par. Rec., reg.

[43] *Ch. Bells Oxon.*

[44] See p. 120. The registers are kept at Horley. There are transcripts in the Bodleian Libr.

[45] Compton Census.

[46] MS. Oxf. Dioc. c 430, f. 21.

[47] *Oxon. Peculiars*, 274.

[48] *Secker's Visit.*; MS. Oxf. Dioc. d 556, 566.

[49] MS. Oxf. Dioc. d 566.

[50] Ibid. d 572, d 574.

[51] Ibid. c 644, f. 272. The certificate was signed by Joseph Wilson, a Methodist minister from Banbury.

[52] Ibid. d 580.

[53] Ibid. b 39.

[54] H.O. 129/163; Billing, *Dir. Oxon.*; *Wilb. Visit.*

[55] MS. Oxf. Dioc. c 344.

[56] Ex inf. the Revd. A. J. Davies, Sec. of the Oxf. and Leic. District Synod.

[57] MS. Oxf. Dioc. d 572.

[58] Ibid. c 433.

[59] See p. 123.

[60] Ibid. b 39.

[61] Ibid. b 70.

[62] Billing, *Dir. Oxon.* (1854).

[63] MS. Oxf. Dioc. d 180.

[64] Ibid. c 332.

[65] *P.O. Dir. Oxon.* (1869).

[66] Ed. 7/101/100.

[67] *Elem. Educ. Ret.* 655.

[68] MS. Oxf. Dioc. c 344; *Sch. Boards*, (*1900*), 318.

[69] *Ret. of Sch. Fees* (1875), 266.

[70] *Pub. Elem. Sch. Ret.* (1894), 500; *List of Sch.* (1906), 526.

[71] *Ret. of Sch.* (1890), 217.

[72] *Pub. Elem. Sch. Ret.* (1894), 500; ibid. (1900), 678.

[73] Ex inf. Oxfordshire County Council Educ. Cttee.

£16 5*s.* were collected. From this sum every adult received 2*s.* 6*d.* and every child 6*d.* Except in 1823, when the income was used to augment the school funds, the money was distributed annually to deserving poor for about a century.[74] In 1926 the charge was commuted for £26 and invested.[75] Between 1928 and 1932, when accounts ceased for 20 years, the interest was 14*s.* a year and 13 poor persons were each given 1*s.* yearly. In 1955 the income was 13*s.* and the balance in hand £7 8*s.* 10*d.*, of which £3 was spent on logs given to 6 aged or needy families.[76]

When Hanwell was inclosed *c.* 1768 34 a. and a cow pasture of 15 a. were allotted to the poor in return for their right to gather fuel on the commons. By the Inclosure Act of 1783 this land was put under the guardianship of the churchwardens and the overseers.[77] No further reference to it has been found.

HORLEY AND HORNTON

THE ancient parish of Horley covered 2,563 a. and was composed of Horley township (1,141 a.) and Hornton township (1,422 a.).[1] It lies in the extreme north-west of the county on the Warwickshire border, and is largely bounded by streams which eventually flow into the Sor Brook, a tributary of the Cherwell.[2] The woodless upland parts of the parish are well over 600 ft. and lie on Middle Lias rocks; they are divided by steep-sided gullies lying between the 450 and 500 ft. contours at Hornton village and along the boundary streams. At Bush Hill in the north of the parish there is rough land (*c.* 23 a.) at a height of 600 ft. and on the north-western boundary are extensive quarries of Hornton stone, some still working.[3]

The parish lies between the Banbury–Warwick and Banbury–Stratford roads, turnpiked in 1744 and 1753 respectively.[4] A secondary road connects Horley with both; a road from Hornton to Balscott crosses the main Stratford road and another meets it at Wroxton. The hard-bottomed ford on the Banbury road was not bridged until modern times, and the bridge over the Wroxton Brook dates from 1916.[5]

Horley lies near the eastern boundary of the parish crowning a hill 500 ft. high, some 3½ miles from Edgehill. The village lies between two streams, Wroxton Brook and Horley Brook; Horley means 'clearing in a tongue of land'.[6] The village has an irregular plan. One long street of cottages and farm-houses ascends the hill from Horley Mill to the church on the hill-top, still 'large and handsome' as it was when Rawlinson described it in 1718.[7] Here the houses are mainly concentrated on the west side of the hill in a rough parallelogram. On the west is the vicarage-house and on the south side of the hill-side are the manor-house of the sometime prebendal manor, and what is evidently the manor-house of the lay manor of Horley, now a farm-house.[8] The fishponds once existing to the west of the village presumably belonged to one or both of these manors.

At one time it was a more scattered village: in 1705 there was a substantial house called Yellow Well Hall on the edge of the village and there were still houses at Yellow Well on the north of it in the 19th century. There is a tradition that there were once houses in the Town Gore.[9] It seems always to have been a smaller village than Hornton and in the mid-17th century, when it is first possible to make a rough estimate of the village population, 47 men took the Protestation Oath compared with 73 at Hornton.[10] In 1801 it had a population of 269 and reached the peak figure of 425 in 1841. There were then 90 houses in the village. By 1901 the population had fallen to 247 and in 1961 it was 232.[11]

In general the houses and cottages are built in the local ironstone and in the regional style. They mostly date from the period 1580–1640 but many may have been altered in the 18th century, Later buildings include some early-19th-century cottages, with their gable end to the road, and the mid-19th-century vicarage-house, 'a small, neat, modern residence' built for the curate.[12] In the 20th century many old cottages have been reconditioned; and council houses in Lane Close were built after the Second World War.[13] Well-kept grass verges in the main street are a feature of the village.

There is now only one inn, the 'Red Lion', but in 1783 there was also the 'Crown'.[14] The latter house had probably long retailed beer, for it was occupied early in the century by a maltster, John Bray.[15] The churchwardens met in one or other of these inns in the 1780s.[16] Growing population led to the appearance of the 'Buck' in 1786 and the 'Bull' in 1806.[17]

The most imposing house is the Manor House, lying a little south of the church. Its medieval predecessor was occupied by the prebendaries[18] from time to time. They alone had a right to a seat in the chancel of the church, with which the house is directly connected by a right of way. The older part of the house, the present long east–west range, belongs to the 16th and 17th centuries. It is a 2-storied structure of coursed ironstone rubble with mullioned windows. It has been little altered since 1624 when John Austin bought the manor from Richard Light, who had resided there.[19] Some

74 *12th Rep. Com. Char.* 215; *Char. Don.* 976; *Secker's Visit.*
75 Char. Com. file E 68786.
76 Char. Com. G. file, accts.
77 Hanwell Incl. Act, 23 Geo. III, c. 43 (priv. act).
1 O.S. *Area Bk.* (1882).
2 The following maps have been used for this article: O.S. Map 25″ Oxon. II. 10, V. 3 (1st edn.); ibid. 6″ Oxon. II. SW (1st edn.); ibid. 2½″, SP 34 (1959), SP 44 (1951).
3 See p. 131.
4 Buckingham to Warmington Turnpike Act, 17 Geo. II, c. 43; Drayton Lane Turnpike Act, 26 Geo. II, c. 78.
5 Bodl. G.A. Oxon. 4° 593: MS. hist. of Horley by A. Stockton.
6 *P.N. Oxon.* (E.P.N.S.), ii. 399.
7 *Par. Colln.* ii. 180.
8 See below.
9 Hants R.O., Cope pps. no. 311; Bodl. G.A. Oxon. 4° 593.
10 *Protestation Ret.* 47; cf. p. 189.
11 *Census*, 1801–1961.
12 Gardner, *Dir. Oxon.* (1852).
13 Ex inf. Banbury R.D.C.
14 O.R.O., victlrs' recogs.
15 Par. Rec., memo. in reg.
16 Par. Rec., chwdns' accts.
17 O.R.O., victlrs' recogs.
18 See p.127.
19 Ibid.

interior panelling of about that date may well have belonged to the 17th-century house. In 1665 John Austin returned 5 hearths for the hearth tax and in 1718 Rawlinson reported that Nathaniel Austin was living there.[20] It was probably Nathaniel who remodelled the east end of the old house, which has an east wing of about 1700 as its front elevation. It consists of 5 bays, is of 2 stories with a hipped roof in which are 3 dormers, and has a central doorway surmounted by a broken pediment and approached by semi-circular steps; its large sash windows have moulded architraves with keystones and the interior is elegantly designed. The house was inhabited after 1741 by Edward Metcalfe.[21] By 1802 no person 'of note' resided in Horley;[22] but in 1852 the house was recorded once again as a gentleman's residence.[23] In 1892 it was bought by James Stockton, a Banbury solicitor.[24]

The manor-house of the lay manor, lying south of the prebendal manor, is now Bramshill Park Farm and may well have been used as a farm-house since the early 18th century, when the Copes bought it.[25] It was occupied in the 17th century by the Danvers family. Daniel Danvers died there in 1624[26] and his Puritan son Anthony seems to have lived there until the 1660s when he went to London.[27] In the last quarter of the century the new lord, Richard Thomson, occupied the house. His wife and 3 of his children were buried in the church between 1678 and 1690,[28] and it is likely that Thomson himself remained in the house until 1718 when he sold it to Sir John Cope of Bramshill. As only this Horley house and the arms of Thomson are shown on Michael Burgher's map of Oxfordshire,[29] it was evidently then the most important house in the village. The existing house appears to represent only the southern portion of a larger building, the northern part of which has been demolished. This may have been the result of a fire, as local tradition has it. Three 18th-century sketch-plans of a house at Horley, now among the Cope papers, may represent Bramshill Park Farm soon after the Copes obtained possession, though it is difficult to relate them to any part of the existing building.[30] One gives the measurements of the rooms and shows that the hall, then divided into two, was 9–10 ft. high and once measured 30 ft. × 20 ft. The dining-room was 17 ft. × 20 ft. There were three flights of stairs — the great stairs, the back stairs, and the little stairs. A list of the chief rooms made in 1735 enumerates the great parlour, the hall, the dining-room, 3 bedchambers, and 3 garrets.[31] The surviving portion of the mansion appears to date partly from the 16th and partly from the 17th century. The rectangular bay which projects from the east front has a lead rainwater-head with the initials 'T.R.D.', which no doubt are those of the owner Richard Thomson who bought the manor in 1668. The outbuildings in the farm yard date from c. 1600. They retain a doorway and two 3-light mullioned windows of that period.

Park House, once a Cope property, incorporates parts of a medieval structure. It was originally built on the 3-unit plan with the 2 ground-floor rooms both of about the same size, though on different levels, and separated by a through passage. To the right of this passage there is a doorway of 14th-century date and in the rear wall there is a small medieval window with an ogee head. The back entrance is through another medieval doorway. In the west gable of the house is a 2-light 14th-century window, now blocked. The chimney once backed into the left side of the through passage.[32]

Besides the farm-houses there are several 17th- and 18th-century cottages. One thatched cottage abutting on the Methodist chapel retains some of its 17th-century mullioned windows; some cottages have cellars. The schoolmaster's house and schoolroom were originally built c. 1630,[33] backing upon the churchyard. It is a substantially built stone house with mullioned windows and thatched roof. The master's house appears to have been enlarged in 1711, the date on the chimney stack. The schoolroom was extended in 1842 by the addition of a classroom with small Gothic windows; was again enlarged in 1899, and yet again in 1961, when glass and steel were the main building materials.[34]

Horley House, lying rather apart from the village, is a large early-19th-century mansion built of local stone in a plain late Georgian style. The main front has 5 sash windows and a stone pilastered porch. The house was perhaps built for John Hitchcock, one of the chief landed proprietors, who was living there in 1852.[35]

Hornton village lies mainly at the bottom of a steep sequestered valley at a height of 500 ft., but has spread up the hill which rises to 600 ft. The original settlement, as in the case of Horley, was on the land between two small tributaries of the Sor Brook, and the Old English name of the village signifies 'dwellers on a tongue of land'.[36]

It was among the larger villages of north Oxfordshire in the Middle Ages and by the 17th century the population may have been c. 300.[37] In 1662 there were 18 householders with sufficiently substantial houses to be taxed, and in 1665, besides the manor-house, there were 3 other farm-houses of about the same size, all assessed on 4 hearths; 8 others were assessed on 2 or 3 hearths.[38] By 1801 the population was 485; it rose rapidly to just over 590 in 1841 and 1851, and fell to 362 in 1901 and to 318 in 1961.[39]

The comparative isolation of the village has resulted in the preservation of many of the 16th-

[20] *Hearth Tax Oxon.* 148; *Par. Colln.* ii. 180.
[21] Par. Rec., reg.
[22] MS. Oxf. Dioc. d 566.
[23] Gardner, *Dir. Oxon.* (1852).
[24] Bodl. G.A. Oxon. 4° 593. See plate facing p. 137.
[25] See p. 127.
[26] Par. Rec., reg.
[27] Macnamara, *Danvers Family*, 413, 421, 431. Many Danvers children were baptized in the church down to 1661: Par. Rec., reg.
[28] Par. Rec., reg.
[29] Plot, *Nat. Hist. Oxon.* frontispiece.
[30] Hants R.O., 43M 48/764, 765, 766. There is no other house in Horley which fits the plans; it is possible, however, that they belong to the demolished Yellow Well Hall.
[31] Ibid. no. 735.
[32] For further details, see Wood-Jones, *Dom. Archit. Banbury Region*, 118; for photo. see MS. Top. Oxon. c 490.
[33] Par. Rec., reg.
[34] Date stones and ex inf. Mrs. Saunders, the schoolmistress.
[35] Gardner, *Dir. Oxon.* (1852).
[36] *P.N. Oxon.* (E.P.N.S.), ii. 399.
[37] *Protestation Ret.* 47, where, with few exceptions, the 73 people listed belonged to different families. See also p. 189.
[38] *Hearth Tax Oxon.* 176, 236.
[39] *Census*, 1801–1961.

and 17th-century farm-houses and even of cottages. The village has in recent years attracted commuters who have modernized and restored carefully. Local pride in the appearance of the village is evident not least in the exceptionally well-tended church and churchyard, a well-known feature of Hornton in the 19th century.[40] In 1959 'by a quiet communal effort' the villagers were awarded the Marlborough trophy for the best-kept small village in the county;[41] a century earlier Bishop Wilberforce had called Hornton the 'fringe of civilization'.[42] The older houses are built of the local ironstone rubble or, in the case of the better ones, of ironstone ashlar. The steep pitch of the roofs indicates that thatch was once used generally and it is still common.

Several notable examples of 17th-century yeoman houses survive. The manor-house, described as a cottage in 1852, and now a farm-house, bears the inscription '1607 C.E.'.[43] Though considerably altered at later periods its original construction can be traced. It is a 2-story house with attics, built on the common regional plan of a through passage with a large hall and kitchen on either side, and a third room, the parlour, adjoining the hall. A newel staircase in the north-east corner, which provides access from the ground floor to the roof, may be a part of the original house, and several original windows with flat-splayed stone mullions and moulded labels survive. The thatched roof has parapet gables and the dormer windows, flush with the second floor, project into it. The roof, of the tie-beam type with a single collar, shows an early example of a roof truss that was to be generally adopted in the 17th and 18th centuries for the more important houses in this region. The farm has an out-building with kitchen and oven, probably provided for farm labourers in the 18th century.[44] The Mount is a 2-story house dating from the end of the 17th century. It is of special architectural interest as it presents the 'final stage in evolution of the three-unit "upland" plan'. Built on the hill-side and facing down the valley, it comprises a parlour, with a cellar underneath, a small hall with a broad straight-flight stair against the rear wall, and front and rear entrance doorways. There is a kitchen containing a large fire-place and smaller second stair. The house is solidly built with walls 2½–3 ft. thick, and the architectural detail is of good quality, notably the moulded jambs and camber arch with lozenge-shaped stops to the label mould of the main doorway. The cellar has a well in it and a gutter to run off superfluous water. Eastgates Farm is similar in plan to the Mount, and like the Mount has its gable-end on the road and retains its original mullioned windows and doorway. It has masonry enrichment of the high quality found in small manor-houses in this area, and wrought iron casement fasteners, comparable with those at the Cope farm-house at Horley. Cromwell cottage is of the same 3-unit type, but is only 1½ story except over the kitchen bay where there are two. Wheeler's Farm, also on the hill-side, is of the 3-unit type and dates from the late 17th century. Other examples are the Glen, a smithy for much of its history, the adjoining Profitts House, and a house on the north side of the Hornton–Wroxton road, with a date-stone in the west gable inscribed '1661 T[homas] H[icks]'.

The village's two inns, the 'Bell' and the 'Red Lion', were probably licensed between 1753 and 1772, but they were not mentioned by name until 1782.[45] The name of a Hornton inn-holder, however, was recorded in 1709.[46] The 'Dun Cow' had opened by 1854 when it was a butcher's and beer-retailer's combined. Rock Tavern, lying isolated from the village near the quarries, was mentioned in 1854 and was clearly used mainly by quarry men.[47]

Outside the village Hornton Grounds House dates from the early 19th century and Hornton Hill House from 1864. The latter was built of Hornton stone in the Georgian style, and was notable in 1910 for its avenue of 'grand ornamental' beeches and other trees.[48]

MANORS AND OTHER ESTATES. Hornton was not mentioned in Domesday Book but clearly was included under Horley, where there were 2 large and 2 small estates in 1086. One 10-hide estate, held by Berenger de Todeni and of him by Ralph, had been held before the Conquest by Queen Edith and Turgot the law man (*lageman*).[49] Like another of Berenger's estates, Hutton Bardolf (N.R. Yorks.), this estate, the later lay manor of *HORLEY AND HORNTON*, was held in the 13th century by the Bardolf family.[50] It formed part of the honor of Brandon, which, according to Dugdale, comprised 10 fees attached to Brandon Castle in Wolston (Warws.).[51] The overlordship of Horley and Hornton may thus have followed the descent of Brandon which passed from Geoffrey de Clinton to his daughter Lesceline, who in the early 12th century married Norman de Verdun.[52] In the 1220s Nicholas de Verdun was recorded as overlord.[53] On the death of Theobald de Verdun in 1316 a fee in Horley and Hornton was among the lands which were to be divided between his four daughters and in 1344 it formed part of the inheritance of his daughter Margery and her husband Mark Hussee.[54] As in the case of other manors granted to the Hussees all trace of the overlordship then disappears.[55] In 1458, however, Horley and Hornton were said to be held of the Earl of Warwick;[56] this may perhaps be explained by the fact that the earls of Warwick held the overlordship of Brandon in the 13th century.[57]

In 1222 Hugh Bardolf and Robert the Chamberlain, both descendants of Osbert, Sheriff of Lincolnshire and Yorkshire (d. by 1116)[58] made a

40 *Banbury Guardian*, 9 Sept. 1893.

41 *Oxf. Mail*, 24 Oct. 1959.

42 MS. Oxf. Dioc. c 1865.

43 Gardner, *Dir. Oxon.* (1852). The initials have not been identified.

44 For a description of this and other houses see Wood-Jones, *Dom. Archit. Banbury Region*, index, *sub* Hornton.

45 O.R.O. QSD/VI; ibid., victlrs' recogs.

46 Hants R.O., Cope pps. no. 1041.

47 Billing, *Dir. Oxon.* (1854).

48 G.A. Oxon. b 91(13), 14: *Sale cat.*

49 *V.C.H. Oxon.* i. 417. Broughton, also held by Berenger, followed a completely different descent, but in 1501 Hornton was said to be held of William Fiennes as of his Broughton manor, and in 1516 Horley was similarly held: *Cal. Inq. p.m. Hen. VII*, ii, p. 271; C 142/31/18.

50 *V.C.H. Yorks. N.R.* ii. 153 and see below.

51 Dugdale, *Warws.* (1656), 29.

52 *V.C.H. Warws.* vi. 276.

53 W. de G. Birch, 'The Cistercian Abbey of Stanley', *Wilts. Arch. Mag.* xv. 286.

54 *Cal. Inq. p.m.* vi, p. 38; *Cal. Close*, 1343–6, 278, 346. For Margery's husbands see *Complete Peerage*, vii. 5–6.

55 e.g. *V.C.H. Warws.* v. 36, 67.

56 C 139/170/1.

57 *V.C.H. Warws.* vi. 276.

58 For Osbert see *Regesta Regum Anglo-Normannorum*, ii, p. 295, and the refs. given there.

division of lands, Hugh taking the ½ fee in Horley and Hornton.[59] Hugh made a grant in the 1220s to Stanley Abbey (Wilts.)[60] and sold the rest of the ½ fee to Robert Lexington, a royal judge.[61] He held it in 1230 but had granted it before 1236 to his brother John, who in 1239 was allowed free warren in his demesne lands in Horley and Hornton.[62] John Lexington died in 1257 holding 10 hides in Horley and Hornton and leaving as heir his brother Henry Lexington, Bishop of Lincoln.[63] On the bishop's death in 1258 Horley passed to his nephew William Sutton, a member of a Nottinghamshire family.[64] William was dead by 1276, and his widow Eve was married to Robert Paynel, who held the manor during her lifetime,[65] and claimed free warren in the parish.[66] William Sutton's son Robert was already dead, and the manor eventually descended to his grandson Sir Richard Sutton, whose son John married Margaret, the sister and later the coheir of Sir John de Somery.[67] In 1307 Richard agreed with Agnes de Somery, Margaret's widowed mother, that he would hold Horley and Hornton and other manors for life, and that he would not alienate them so that they could not descend to his son.[68] Richard Sutton held a fee in Horley and Hornton in 1316, and still held it in 1344 and 1346.[69] The family descended in the male line,[70] but no later reference has been found of any connexion with Horley.

A manor of Horley is next found in the possession of the Arden family of Drayton, but it is not clear that this was the Sutton holding. Robert Arden had held land there by at least 1327, when he was granted free warren in his demesne lands.[71] In 1329 he was allowed view of frankpledge there.[72] Sir Giles Arden held Horley manor with his wife at his death in 1376.[73] He left two young coheirs one of whom, Margaret, married Lewis Greville.[74] Their son William, on whom Horley was settled in 1398, was living there in 1406, but later lived at Drayton,[75] and the family connexion with Horley came to an end.

By 1428 John Langston, presumably John Langston of Caversfield, held the lands in Horley and Hornton which had once belonged to Richard Sutton.[76] They seem to have passed to the Dynhams, for on his death in 1458 Sir John Dynham and his wife Joan held the manors of Horley and Hornton. This is the first time they are described as 2 manors.[77] They passed to his son John Lord Dynham, who died childless in 1501,[78] and for the next 40 years the 2 manors followed a somewhat different descent. In the end, however, both were acquired by the Light family.[79] Hornton had been settled by Lord Dynham on his brother-in-law Sir John Sapcote of Elton (Hunts.), the husband of Elizabeth Dynham, and his heirs.[80] Sapcote died in 1501 and in 1541 his son Sir Richard Sapcote sold Hornton manor to Christopher Light.[81] Horley manor, on the other hand, which in 1501 was held for life by Sir Reynold Bray (d. 1503) by gift of Lord Dynham,[82] was divided into quarters among the families of Lord Dynham's four sisters.[83] One quarter, which must have been that which went to Joan Dynham and her husband Lord Zouche, was bought in 1540 from Joan and Prudence Coke by Christopher Light (d. 1546);[84] in 1544 Light bought another quarter from Sir Michael Dormer, who in 1542 had bought it from Sir William FitzWilliam and his wife Anne, said to be the daughter and heir of Sir Richard Sapcote, who died in 1542;[85] in 1553 the younger Christopher Light bought another quarter from Sir John Arundell, the grandson of Sir Thomas Arundell and Katherine Dynham;[86] while the fourth quarter, which had gone to the Carew family, passed like their quarter of Souldern to the Comptons,[87] and was bought in 1580 by Christopher Light.[88] Light died at Horley in 1584, leaving half the manor-house and his demesne in Horley to his wife Margaret for life, and the rest of the two manors to his son Richard, aged four.[89] Richard Light probably sold off the land of Hornton manor, for there are no later references to it.[90] By 1617 he had left Horley for Banbury, and in that year he and his mother, who was again widowed, sold Horley manor to Daniel Danvers and his son Anthony.[91] In 1661 Anthony transferred the estate to his son

[59] *Fines Oxon.* 232–3; but see *Yorks. Fines, 1218–31* (Yorks. Arch. Soc. Record Ser. lxii), 42, which says 1 fee, and lists the Lincs. lands but none in Yorks.

[60] See p. 128.

[61] *Cal. Inq. Misc.* i, p. 308. For him see *D.N.B.*

[62] *Fines Oxon.* 87–88; *Bk. of Fees*, 448, 823; *Reg. Antiquiss.* i. 180–1.

[63] *Cal. Inq. p.m.* i, pp. 102–3. For them both see *D.N.B.* Horley is not mentioned in the bishop's inquisition.

[64] *Feet of Fines, Essex* (Essex Arch. Soc.), i. 232–3; *Cal. Inq. p.m.* i, p. 109. For the Suttons see *V.C.H. Essex*, iv. 277.

[65] *Cal. Inq. Misc.* i, p. 308; *Cat. Anct. D.* iv. A 7099.

[66] *Rot. Hund.* (Rec. Com.), ii. 32.

[67] *Cal. Inq. p.m.* ii. p. 43; *Complete Peerage*, xii (1). 115 n.

[68] *Cal. Close*, 1302–7, 536. Horley is not mentioned in a division of his estates in 1307: P.R.O. *Lists & Indexes*, xvii, p. 101.

[69] *Feud. Aids*, iv. 166, 178; *Cal. Inq. p.m.* vi, p. 38; ibid. vii, p. 499: *Feud. Aids*, iv. 178.

[70] For them see H. S. Grazebrook, 'An Account of the Barons of Dudley', *Hist. Colln. Staffs.* (Wm. Salt Arch. Soc.), ix (2). 51 sqq.

[71] *Cal. Chart. R.* 1327–41, 25.

[72] Ibid. 117, 118.

[73] C 136/18/2.

[74] Linc. Reg. xxi, f. 88v.

[75] C.P. 25 (1)/191/24/71; *Cal. Pat.* 1405–8, 282; *Par. Colln.* ii. 127.

[76] *V.C.H. Oxon.* vi. 336; *Feud. Aids*, iv. 186.

[77] C 139/170/1.

[78] *Cal. Inq. p.m. Hen. VII*, ii, pp. 270–1. For family see *Complete Peerage*, iv. 377–82.

[79] For them see *Oxon. Visit.* 141–2.

[80] *Cal. Inq. p.m. Hen. VII*, ii, p. 271.

[81] *V.C.H. Hunts.* iii. 161; C.P. 25(2)/34/228/49; Bodl. MS. Ch. Oxon. 3678.

[82] *Cal. Inq. p.m.* ii, p. 271. For him see *D.N.B.*

[83] For details see *V.C.H. Oxon.* vi. 305.

[84] C.P. 25(2)/34/228/48; Bodl. MS. Ch. Oxon. 3670; Hants. R.O. 43 M 48/625.

[85] C.P. 40/1120, rot. 6; C.P. 25(2)/34/229/11. *L. & P. Hen. VIII*, xix (2), p. 469. For the Sapcotes see *Visit. Hunts.* (Camd. Soc. 1st ser. xliii), 12. Since the family descended in the male line it is not clear why Anne was Sir Richard's heir. For the FitzWilliams see Burke, *Peerage* (1959), under FitzWilliam.

[86] C.P. 25(2)/62/494/41; Hants R.O. 43 M 48/626, 629; *V.C.H. Oxon.* vi. 305. His father had held this at his death in 1545: C 142/86/11.

[87] Peter Compton held a quarter at his death in 1544: C 142/72/68. For a transaction of 1567 about it see C.P. 40/268, rot. 652; Hants R.O. 43 M 48/627, 628.

[88] C.P. 25(2)/260/Mich. 22 & 23 Eliz. I; C.P. 40/386, rot. 151; Hants R.O. 43 M 48/629, 630.

[89] C 142/247/46; Par. Rec., reg.

[90] e.g. O.R.O. Misc. Pe. 111/28. For a recovery of 1578 see C.P. 40/368, rot. 302.

[91] C.P. 25(2)/340/Mich. 15 Jas. I; Hants R.O. 43 M 48/631–4. For the Danvers pedigree see Macnamara, *Danvers Family*, 408.

and heir John Danvers, a London sugar refiner,[92] and in 1663 the Danvers family sold the manor to Sir Charles Wolseley, Bt.[93] Wolseley, who was connected with the neighbourhood through his marriage to a daughter of William, Lord Saye and Sele, sold the manor in 1668 to Richard Thomson of Edgcott (Northants.).[94] By 1680 Thomson was living at Horley, but in 1718 he sold the property to Sir John Cope of Bramshill (Hants), the son of Sir John Cope, Bt. (d. 1721), lord of the neighbouring manor of Hanwell.[95] While Hanwell went in 1721 to another branch of the Cope family, Horley descended with the title in the main branch.[96] By 1663, however, Horley manor consisted of only 6 yardlands,[97] and it is doubtful whether any manorial rights belonged to it. This manor is constantly referred to in 18th-century deeds,[98] and until at least 1813, but the inclosure award and other records refer only to the lords of the prebendal manor.[99] The Copes, however, continued to be landowners in the parish, their chief farm being Bramshill Park Farm.[1]

The second manor, known later as the *PREBENDAL MANOR OF HORLEY AND HORNTON*, probably descended from the 10-hide estate held in 1086 by Robert, Count of Mortain.[2] Robert's tenant Ralph may have been Ranulf Flambard (d. 1128), the royal minister,[3] who in the early 12th century held land in Horley of the king. In 1115 Henry I granted Horley with the church of King's Sutton (Northants.) to augment the prebend which Ranulf and his son Elias held in Lincoln Cathedral. By the terms of the grant the prebend was to be held by Elias for life with reversion to Ranulf for life and remainder to the cathedral.[4] By 1146 Horley was listed among Lincoln's prebendal endowments[5] and the manor, which also included land in Hornton, was held by the prebendaries of Sutton-cum-Buckingham.[6]

In the early 13th century the archdeacons of Buckingham were usually the prebendaries: in 1212–14, for example, the archdeacon is found defending his right to 4 yardlands in Hornton;[7] in 1239 he was granted free warren in his demesne lands in Horley and Hornton;[8] and in 1243 he was returned as holding half Horley vill in free alms of the Bishop of Lincoln's fee.[9] Later the archdeacons of Buckingham ceased to be prebendaries and in 1276 the Archdeacon of Northampton claimed, as prebendary, free warren in the parish.[10] In the 14th century several cardinals held the prebend.[11] In 1535 the prebend was leased by the prebendary, Richard Pate, to John Pate, who was in the service of Bishop Longland.[12] On Richard Pate's attainder his successor, Richard Cox, a royal chaplain and later Bishop of Ely, was appointed in 1542 by Henry VIII.[13] Cox's rapid advancement under Edward VI[14] owed something perhaps to the fact that in 1547 he surrendered the endowment of this 'noble prebend' to the Crown.[15] Soon afterwards it formed part of a large grant to the Duke of Somerset, on whose attainder in 1552 it reverted to the Crown.[16] The prebend itself was never formally dissolved, but being 'disseised of its estate' the bishop's attempts to fill it were unsuccessful.[17]

During the rest of the 16th century the estate was leased by the Crown, first to Sir John Mason, who was in possession in 1554,[18] and in 1569 to Henry Seymour for life, a grant which was renewed in 1595.[19] In 1609 the estate was granted by James I to Sir Robert Brett, a gentleman usher of the Privy Chamber,[20] who at once divided it and sold the part in Horley and Hornton to Richard Light, the lord of the other manor in the parish.[21] It was charged with a rent of £20 to the Crown which was paid until it was redeemed in 1769.[22] In 1624 Light sold the manor to John Austin who settled it on his son Robert.[23] On John's death in 1639[24] the property passed to his son Robert, and then to the latter's son John, who was probably the John Austin, the elder, who died in 1687.[25] He was succeeded by his son Nathaniel (d. 1728),[26] and by his grandson, John Austin of Drayton, who sold the property to Edward Metcalfe in 1741.[27] At the time of the Inclosure Act in 1765 Metcalfe was the only lord of the manor in the parish.[28] He only owned about 6½

[92] Hants R.O. 43 M 48/638; Macnamara, *Danvers Family*, 435.
[93] C.P. 25(2)/707/Trin. 15 Chas. II; Hants R.O. 43 M 48/639–43.
[94] G.E.C. *Baronetage*, ii. 62; C.P. 25(2)/708/Mich. 20 Chas. II; Hants R.O. 43 M 48/650–53.
[95] *Par. Colln.* ii. 181; Hants R.O. 43 M 48/672–6. For a settlement on Thomson's son Knightley in 1695 and other deeds see ibid. 657–76. For the family see G.E.C. *Baronetage*, i. 37.
[96] See p. 116; Burke, *Peerage* (1959).
[97] Hants R.O. 43 M 48/639, 644.
[98] e.g. ibid. 43 M 48/1077.
[99] Ibid.; C.P. 43/734, rot. 43 (Mich. 7 Geo. III); O.R.O., gamekprs' deps.
[1] Ex inf. Mr. W. P. Astell, Bramshill Park Farm.
[2] *V.C.H. Oxon.* i. 409.
[3] *D.N.B.*
[4] *Regesta Regum Anglo-Normannorum*, ii, p. 128.
[5] *Reg. Antiquiss.* i. 199, 207.
[6] By the early 13th century Buckingham church had been added to the prebend's endowment: *V.C.H. Bucks.* iii. 487.
[7] *Cur. Reg. R.* vi. 241; vii. 10, 48, 91, 113.
[8] *Reg. Antiquiss.* i. 180–1.
[9] *Bk. of Fees*, 832.
[10] *Rot. Hund.* (Rec. Com.), ii. 32.
[11] *Feud. Aids*, iv. 166; *Cal. Pat.* 1381–5, 417; *Cal. Papal Regs.* vi. 196. For a list of prebendaries see Browne Willis, *Survey of Cathedrals* (1742), ii. 245–8; Le Neve, *Fasti*, ed. T. D. Hardy, ii. 216–17.
[12] *Linc. Chapter Acts, 1526–36* (L.R.S. xii), 186–7.
[13] *L. & P. Hen. VIII*, xvii, p. 216.
[14] *D.N.B.*
[15] Willis, op. cit. 248. The actual surrender has not been found.
[16] *Cal. Pat.* 1547–8, 190.
[17] H. Bradshaw & C. Wordsworth, *Lincoln Cathedral Statutes*, ii (2). 656, 671. The tenant of the estate, and later the owner of the Sutton part of it, continued to make the payments to the cathedral formerly made by the prebendary: ibid.; Willis, op. cit. 245.
[18] Lipscomb, *Bucks.* ii. 575; Linc. Reg. xxviii, f. 106v.
[19] Lipscomb, *Bucks.* ii. 573; *V.C.H. Bucks.* iii. 483; *Cal. S.P. Dom.* 1595–7, 5.
[20] *Cal. S.P. Dom.* 1603–10, 526; K.B. 28/6, m. 4.
[21] K.B. 28/6, m. 4; Sir J. H. Seymour, *A Plain Statement of Facts* (2nd ed. Banbury, 1839), 47–48: copy in Bodl. G.A. Oxon. 8° 1308.
[22] Seymour, op. cit. 49.
[23] K.B. 28/6, m. 4 where the descent of the Austin family is given; C.P. 25(2)/340/Mich. 22 Jas. I.
[24] C 142/492/46.
[25] C.P. 25(2)/588/East. 9 Chas. II; *Par. Colln.* ii. 180.
[26] He apparently mortgaged the manor in 1689: C.P. 25(2)/863/Trin. 1 Wm. & Mary; C.P. 43/425, rot. 37 (Trin. 1 Wm. & Mary); O.R.O., S. & F. colln. (uncat.); MS. Oxf. Archd. Oxon. c 156, f. 40v.; ibid. b 60, f. 45.
[27] Seymour, op. cit. 48.
[28] Horley Incl. Act, 5 Geo. III, c. 25 (priv. act).

yardlands, all in Horley, but also had manorial rights in Hornton.[29] After his death the estate was held by his relict Elizabeth until her death in 1791 when it passed to John Metcalfe Wardle, a relative by marriage.[30] In 1828 either Wardle or his son of the same name sold it to Daniel Stuart, the owner of Wickham Park,[31] and on his death in 1846 he left it for life to his daughter Catherine.[32] She never married and after her death it was sold in 1892 to James Stockton, a Banbury solicitor.[33] At this time the estate consisted mainly of Horley Manor farm (306 a.), the manor-house, and the manorial rights of Horley and Hornton manors, which were worth about £5 a year.[34] The property passed to Stockton's son, Lt.-Col. Arthur Stockton.[35] By 1965 manorial rights had lapsed.

In 1086 1 hide in Horley and Hornton was held in chief by Robert of Stafford, and of him by Richard.[36] Another hide was held of the Count of Mortain by the 'monks of St. Peter', tentatively identified as the monks of Préaux Abbey.[37] Nothing further is known of these estates.

In 1222 or 1223 Hugh Bardolf, tenant of the lay manor, with the consent of his overlord Nicholas de Verdun, granted 3 carucates in Hornton in free alms to Stanley Abbey (Wilts.).[38] The Abbey still held the land in 1229[39] but no further record of it has been found.

LOCAL GOVERNMENT. In the Middle Ages the lay and prebendal manors held view of frankpledge for their tenants.[40] In the early 17th century, when the manors were jointly owned, the manorial rights of the lay manor appear to have lapsed. Some late records (1772–1894) of the prebendal manor, have survived;[41] the early court rolls were said to have been lost in the Civil War.[42] In the late 18th century there were usually one or two courts baron yearly for tenants in both Horley and Hornton but by 1839 the court was being held biennially.[43] Courts were held by the steward, with a bailiff, and the business was chiefly the admission of tenants and the payment of fines and heriots. The view of frankpledge was usually held in October or November. The homage, constable and tithingman were then sworn, and various village nuisances presented. In 1778, for example, the surveyors of the highways at Horley were presented because the footbridge across the ditch leading from Horley to Moor Mill in Hanwell was dangerously out of repair, and there were other presentments for not cleaning ditches.[44] The last court leet was held in 1920 at the manor-house.[45]

The townships of Horley and Hornton each had their own parish officers. The earliest record of their work in Hornton is the constable's book, 1798–1834.[46] The normal term of office was one year but one man served from 1797 to 1801. The constable's duties were the usual ones, although Hornton's constable spent very little on the travelling poor.[47] His most important item of expenditure was on the militia, particularly after the Acts of 1802–3. In 1803 their operation took up most of the expenses, and he also had to provide substitutes for 2 men chosen in the ballot at Banbury. These men were hired in Warwick and were paid £41 5*s.* in all. The rate for substitutes had doubled by 1808, and the whole expenses came to £106 17*s.* 4*d.*, of which £73 16*s.* was paid by William Gardner, probably one of the overseers. Throughout the period the constable's expenses rose steadily; in 1793–4 they were over £5 and by 1834 £30–£40 a year, without the militia expenses.

No overseers' accounts for Horley and only one set for Hornton have survived. In 1776 Horley spent £100 on relief and Hornton £59 10*s.*, and the mean average for 1783–5 was £170 and £150 respectively. In 1802–3 Horley and Hornton raised £380 and £343 respectively by poor rates, and they spent £340 and £310 respectively on out-relief alone. Hornton's population was almost twice as large as Horley's in 1801 and after; 37 Hornton people received permanent out-relief compared with 23 at Horley, and 101 children of all ages compared with 37. Occasional relief was given to 43 persons at Hornton and to only 7 at Horley. The poverty of Hornton is confirmed by the fact that a rate of 7*s.* 6*d.* there raised less money than a 6*s.* rate in Horley.[48] In 1834–5 Horley spent £176 on the poor out of £243 raised, Hornton £359 out of £438, the rest being spent on removals and county rates.[49] The overseers' accounts of 1831 to 1836[50] show how Hornton's affairs were managed. Expenditure on relief, which in 1831–2 was £699, dropped steadily to £422 by 1835.[51] The receipts came mainly from levies, but there was also a small income of about £7 a year from rents, probably of the parish houses which were insured by the overseer in 1833. Two overseers were appointed yearly and each accounted for six months. The accounts were approved yearly by a small group of four or five. Unlike Horley, Hornton had no assistance from charitable funds.[52]

The bulk of the money for the poor was spent on regular weekly payments: in April 1831, for example, there were 49 persons, receiving between 1*s.* and 7*s.* There were occasional payments for rent and house repairs, for medical attention, and household equipment. The overseers also paid the constable's and mole-catcher's bill, and supplied coal to the

[29] Seymour, *A Plain Statement*, 48. It is probable that the estate had been reduced by Richard Light who seems to have sold off part of the lay manor in the early 17th century: see p. 126.

[30] Seymour, op. cit. 48; O.R.O., land tax assess.

[31] Seymour, op. cit. 48.

[32] MS. Top. Oxon. d 42, f. 73.

[33] Bodl. G.A. Oxon. b 85a (35): *Sale cat.* (1892).

[34] Ibid.

[35] Bodl. G.A. Oxon 4° 593: MS. hist. of Horley.

[36] *V.C.H. Oxon.* i. 409, 412.

[37] Ibid.

[38] W. de G. Birch, 'The Cistercian Abbey of Stanley', *Wilts. Arch. Mag.* 1877, xv. 286; *Fines Oxon.* 68; *Cur. Reg. R.* x. 339.

[39] *Close R.* 1227–31, 252, 382.

[40] *Cal. Chart. R.* 1327–41, 117, 118; S. & F. Colln. (uncat.).

[41] There are court rolls and drafts for years between 1772–1801, 1838–81 in O.R.O., S. & F. colln. (uncat.), and there is a court book containing records of some Horley and Hornton courts and of some land transactions at other courts from 1843–94.

[42] Bodl. MS. Ch. Oxon. 3673.

[43] O.R.O., S. & F. colln. (uncat.).

[44] Ibid.

[45] Bodl. G.A. Oxon. 4° 593: MS. hist. of Horley.

[46] Horley Par. Rec.

[47] During the half year ending Nov. 1805 only 10*s.* out of £7 13*s.* 4*d.* was spent on the poor.

[48] *Poor Abstract*, 400.

[49] *2nd Rep. Poor Law Com.* 292.

[50] Horley Par. Rec.

[51] The discrepancy between the latter figure and that from the parliamentary paper suggests that different items were included.

[52] See p. 139.

poor at cheap rates. It was evidently bought in the summer and stored, for there are entries relating to the purchase of coal in June and to the rent of the coal shop. Nearly £4 was 'gained' by the sale of coal over the whole year. Roundsmen were mentioned occasionally, in the winter months. The largest number of men paid was 13 in a seven-day period from 14 February 1835, and the total soon fell again.

Both Horley and Hornton became part of the Banbury Union, and Hornton overseers started to pay to the Banbury Board of Guardians from July 1835. The needs of the two parts of the parish varied widely; in 1851–2 Horley, with a population of 392 and a rateable value of £1,848, spent £80 on poor relief, while Hornton, with 591 inhabitants, spent £356. Though Hornton was larger in extent than Horley its rateable value was only £1,779, and its rates were three times as high.[53]

ECONOMIC HISTORY. In 1086 there was land for 20 ploughs in the parish but only 16 ploughs were in use: there were 9 ploughs on the demesne of the 4 manors, while the tenants had 7 ploughs. All estates had some share in the meadow which was estimated at 46 a., and 1 furlong by 30 perches. Woodland (9 sq. furlongs) was only mentioned on one estate. There were 2 mills, one on Robert of Stafford's estate worth 5*s*., the other divided between the 2 10-hide estates and worth 1*s*. 4*d*. to each. The total value of the parish had increased from £12 in 1066 to £15 in 1086; 3 of the estates had risen in value, while the Mortain estate remained at £5. The recorded peasant population was 31, of whom 14 were serfs, 12 were *villani*, and 5 were bordars. No population was recorded on one of the 1 hide estates.[54]

In 1306 there were 39 tenants assessed for tax in Hornton and 19 in Horley. In 1316 and 1327 the 2 villages were assessed together, when 71 and 51 names were listed. The lord of a Horley manor paid 2 or 3 times as much as the highest peasant contributor in 1306 and 1316; most tenants were poor, for in 1306 three-quarters paid 2*s*. or less for the thirtieth and in 1316 and 1327 over half paid 2*s*. or less.[55] The parish's assessment was set at £10 1*s*. 11*d*. in 1334, the third highest in the hundred.[56]

For the 1523 subsidy the villages were assessed together and there were 18 names for the first assessment and 24 for the second. Christopher Light was assessed on £80 worth of goods, a few wealthier farmers at between £9 and £4, and as many as 9 at only 4*d*. for the first assessment, and 15 at between 4*d*. and 1*s*. 6*d*. for the second.[57] In 1577 the lord of the manor was again assessed highest, on £8 worth of land.[58] By the 17th century, however, the parish seems to have been dominated by a number of fairly wealthy farmers rather than by any one man. Of the 9 Horley and 13 Hornton men assessed for the hearth tax of 1665 only one had 5 hearths, 5 had 4 hearths, and 6 had 3 hearths; on the other hand 9 were discharged for poverty.[59] Richard Arne (d. 1665), 'gentleman' of Hornton, had chattels at his death worth £205; two 3-hearth householders, Thomas Hicks, 'yeoman' of Hornton, and Nathaniel Kinch, 'yeoman' of Horley, had chattels at their deaths worth £305 and £129 respectively.[60]

Most tenants held by copyhold and records of the terms of tenure of tenants of the prebendal manor have survived. In 1652 a widow was admitted tenant after her husband to 2 yardlands, and paid an entry fine of only 2*d*.;[61] entry fines were still low in the late 18th century.[62] Although some tenements were granted for 2 or 3 lives it was customary to make grants to the tenant and his heirs for ever according to the custom of the manor, eldest sons being admitted as rightful heirs. Heriots were paid in money and ranged from 8*s*. for a croft to £1 3*s*. 4*d*. for a house.[63] The manorial court's main concern was to keep a check on encroachments on the lord's waste. A late 18th-century rental shows that buildings on the waste included, for example, a house, a shop, and a stable, and payments for those were exacted in the courts.[64]

There are few records of the exploitation of the land in the Middle Ages. The lords had a warren in the parish by 1239, recorded also in 1272.[65] Both villages retained separate open fields until the mid-18th century. There was a 2-field system at Hornton,[66] which may have survived, as in neighbouring parishes, into the 16th or 17th century and have then been converted into a 4-field system. Certainly at Horley in 1766 there was a 4-course rotation of crops on the Cope estate.[67] The situation of the fields is not shown on any map but the arable probably lay on the hill slopes while the valley bottoms, being a heavy clay and badly drained, probably provided meadow and pasture.[68] Maps of 1797 and later show that the common and wastes lay near Horley village, to the south-west of Hornton village, and on Bush Hill, which was still marked on maps as rough pasture in 1882 and in the 1930s.[69] When Sir Anthony Cope purchased the manor in 1609, he bought 40 a. of heath as well as 150 a. of pasture, 50 a. of mead, and 240 of arable.[70] Although some of the farming was conservative there are indications that many farmers had introduced improvements within the framework of the open fields. Whereas a yardland and holding in 1645 lay in 39 parcels, partly arable and partly greensward, the glebe some 30 years later was consolidated into 3 parcels of 10 a. to 16 a. and 4 parcels of 12 to 32 ridges.[71] On both holdings the system of leys farming had been adopted. In 1631 a grant in Horley included 3 leys, and the terrier of ½ yardland made in 1672 lists 8 leys, some lying in the plain and some on the hill.[72] Variety was further introduced by the use of 'hitches', and vetches and clover were grown on 2 such hitches in Horley in 1712.[73]

53 *Poor Law Unions*, 21.
54 *V.C.H. Oxon*. i. 409, 412, 417.
55 E 179/161/8, 9, 10.
56 E 179/161/44.
57 E 179/161/196, 198.
58 E 179/162/341.
59 *Hearth Tax Oxon*. 136, 148.
60 MS. Wills Peculiars 32/1/44; 42/1/27; 44/5/18.
61 Bodl. MS. Ch. Oxon. 3673.
62 e.g. O.R.O., S. & F. colln. (uncat.).
63 Ibid.
64 Ibid.
65 *Cal. Chart. R*. 1226–57, 241; *Rot. Hund*. (Rec. Com.), ii. 32.
66 W. de G. Birch, 'The Cistercian Abbey of Stanley', *Wilts. Arch. Mag*. xv. 286; 52 a. in one field and 24 a. in another were granted to Stanley Abbey.
67 Hants R.O. 43 M 48/741.
68 Cf. O.S. Land Util. Survey Map 1″, sht. 83.
69 Ibid.; Davis, *Oxon. Map* (1797); O.S. Map 25″ Oxon. II. 10, 11, 14, 15; V. 2, 3 (1st edn.).
70 Hants R.O. 43 M 48/225.
71 Ibid. 43 M 48/682; Linc. Dioc. R.O. Ter., 20/11, 12.
72 O.R.O., S. & F. colln. (uncat.); Hants R.O. 43 M 48/695.
73 Hants R.O. 43 M 48/669 a.b.

The keeping of comparatively large animal stock made the provision of pasture and commons and the regulation of their use a matter of importance. By a 12-year agreement of 1712, which in general confirmed a previous 12-year arrangement,[74] it was decided by the lord and tenants of Horley that a common cow-pasture should be inclosed and set out, that a 'horse hitch' should be taken out of the fallow each year, and that Upper and Middle Moors should be divided by lot. Everyone sharing in the cow-pasture was to stint 8 sheep 'for the better making' of it; if sheep were put on it without permission, 1*d.* was to be deducted from their shepherd's wages. The horse-hitch was to be 'mounded' and prepared by everyone sharing in it, and was to be divided by lot in proportion to each man's number of yardlands. Each man was to sow 3 peck of vetches on his lot for every horse, mare, or gelding which he wished to keep there, and was to stint 1 sheep. The owners of tithes on this land agreed in the one case to take only $\frac{1}{15}$ of grain there and in the other case not to take any tithes from the new hitches, save rent for small tithes. It was specifically laid down that no one should put animals of Hornton men on this common, but Hornton men were evidently allowed to pay for the privilege of sowing in the new hitches. All common grass growing in the corn-field was to be sold and the money, together with the money from Hornton men, was to be used to trench the fallow, i.e. to drain the heavy soil.[75] Regulations were laid down at the same time for the grazing of cattle and sheep in other parts of the commons and open fields: animals were not to be put on the gores and moors until after harvest, nor on the stubble field before Michaelmas, nor on the hitch when sown, nor on any greensward after mowing, save for one or two horses for working purposes; and no horse was to be tied within 60 yards of any standing or cut corn, nor to be tethered on any balk or common ground in the field unless the grazing had been bought. Another order said that no one was to dig or take away the earth of the commons.[76]

The fields and commons were supervised by two fieldsmen chosen annually, and the grazing by two 'tellers', who in 1712 were to be the fieldsmen as well. Each commoner was obliged to inform the tellers of his stock turned out to graze, and the tellers could impound surplus animals; for payment they were given 8 sheep commons. Cattle were kept with the common herd under the herdsman, who received them night and morning and gave notice with his horn. Two bulls were to be kept each year to go with the herd; the providers of each bull were to have commons for 10 sheep and 3 lambs.[77]

Stints in the parish were diverse: in a dispute over the number of sheep-commons attached to the sale of 2 yardlands in Hornton the seller stated it to be 20 and the buyer 48, while the eventual agreement was for 40; and in 1611 the sale of 3 yardlands in Hornton included commons for 24 sheep, 5 beasts, and 4 horses to the yardland.[78] The Horley stint was changed by the 12-year agreement of 1712 to 24 sheep and 10 lambs in the cow-pasture and 12 sheep and 5 lambs in the field per yardland. At the end of the agreement the ancient stint of 40 sheep to a yardland was to be restored to the commoners and 67 sheep to a yardland to the parson.[79] There were a number of pasture and meadow closes[80] but when the open fields were finally inclosed in 1766 old inclosures amounted at most to 324 a.[81] It is not possible to locate these inclosures, but according to a grant of 1813 at least 68 a.lay in Horley township.[82]

The chief crops grown were wheat, oats, barley, and pulses; and cattle and horses were kept as well as sheep.[83] The sheep flocks, judging from inventories, were normally fairly small: few 17th-century farmers seem to have had flocks of more than 40 to 50. The following random selection of 17th-century inventories shows the mixed interests of the farmers. Thomas Allen (d. 1616) of Horley, whose goods were worth £82, had £18 worth of corn and grass, a flock of 45 sheep, 5 horses, 8 cows and calves, pigs, poultry, and 8 stocks of bees.[84] Another Hornton man had £45 worth of corn (oats, pease, and maslin), and horses (with harness) and cattle worth £27, out of a total valuation of £94.[85] A rather more prosperous man, Nathaniel Kinch (d. 1693) had a large flock of sheep (valued at £20), 7 horses, swine, and cows worth £24; his crops of wheat, pulse, barley, and hay were valued at £40, and he had cheeses worth £1 6*s.* 8*d.*[86] Another rich yeoman had more than two-thirds of the value of his goods in crops and stock: his barley, pease, winter corn, and oats were valued at £124; his horses, colts, cows, sheep, and pigs at £91.[87] A gentleman of the parish had £100 worth of wool stored in his house; at the time of his death his flock of 45 sheep was small, but this may not have been its normal size. He also kept a few horses and cows.[88]

The inclosure of 2,289 a. in Horley and Hornton Fields took place in 1766. The largest single allotments were made in Horley Field where Sir John Mordaunt Cope received 219 a., the vicar 181 a., and Edward Metcalfe 252 a. for his 6½ yardlands in Horley and impropriate tithes. No award was made for manorial rights over the waste, which Metcalfe evidently retained. There were 15 other allotments in Horley Field, of which only 5 were between 10 a. and 100 a. and the rest were under 10 a. In Hornton there were 34 allotments: Richard Calcott received 174 a. and 4 others between 111 a. and 122 a.; there were 14 allotments between 10 a. and 100 a. and 15 of under 10 a. Seventeen of the Hornton allotments included compensation for impropriate tithes.[89]

Inclosure did not immediately affect the pattern of landholding. In the late 18th century the land of the parish was still divided between a comparatively large number of proprietors: 27 in Horley and 36 in Hornton. There were 19 owner-occupiers

[74] Hants R.O. 43 M 48/669 a.b.

[75] This explanation was suggested by Mr. M. A. Havinden.

[76] Hants R.O. 43 M 48/669 a.b.

[77] Ibid.

[78] Ibid. 229; Bodl. MS. Ch. Oxon. 3681.

[79] Hants R.O. 43 M 48/669 a.b.

[80] Ibid. 700; O.R.O., S. & F. colln. (uncat.); Bodl. MS. Ch. Oxon. 3674; Linc. Dioc. R.O., Ter. 20/11.

[81] Gray, *Eng. Field Systems*, 537: calculation from a comparison with the 1902 acreage.

[82] O.R.O. Ta VIII/iii/1.

[83] e.g. MS. Wills Peculiars 32/1/31; 42/1/27; 44/5/18; Bodl. MS. Ch. Oxon. 3689.

[84] MS. Wills Peculiars 32/1/20.

[85] Ibid. 32/1/31.

[86] Ibid. 44/5/18

[87] Ibid. 41/1/27.

[88] Ibid. 32/1/44.

[89] Horley Incl. Act, 5 Geo. III, c 25 (priv. act); C P. 43/734 rot. 43 (Mich. 7 Geo. III). There is a copy of the award in O.R.O., S. & F. colln. (uncat.).

in the parish, of whom 4 had fair-sized farms in Hornton. Seven tenant-occupied farms in Hornton were assessed at between £2 and £7, and there were 4 in Horley assessed at between £6 and £21 but other holdings were all small.[90] In 1831 tenants farmed the 4 chief farms in Horley; there was one fair-sized owner-occupied farm. In all there were 24 assessed for tax in Horley and 28 in Hornton, where the 4 larger farms were owner-occupied, and there were 5 tenant farms with smaller rentals.[91]

In 1851 there were 21 farmers in all, of whom 2 had large farms of 345 a. and 330 a., one in Horley and the other in Hornton. There were 2 other farms of over 200 a., but the average size was much smaller: 9 farms in the parish were between 100 a. and 150 a., and 6 between 26 a. and 70 a.[92] By the end of the 19th century the number of farms in the parish had been reduced to 13, and by 1939 to 9 and 3 small-holdings.[93] In 1961 the average farm was small (*c.* 150 a.), although some like the Mount dairy farm in Hornton were under 90 a., and one, the Upton Estate, which lay in both Horley and Hornton, covered 1,000 a.[94]

Davis's map of 1797 shows a mainly arable parish[95] and 19th-century leases contained the proviso, often found elsewhere, for extra payment for the conversion of meadow and pasture into tillage, indicating that increased profits were to be expected from arable: in a lease of 1804, for example, an extra £20 a year was asked for every acre of meadow and pasture converted without licence; and a lease of 1840 asked for £50 for every acre converted.[96] An agricultural expert stated in 1854 that the red land at Horley was 'well adapted for growing barley and turnips',[97] and this was still recognized at the end of the century. In 1892, for example, the arable of Horley Manor estate (306 a.) was described as 'deep, staple turnip and barley land, growing heavy crops and very healthy for sheep'. This estate was then about a third under pasture.[98] A smaller farm in Horley (140 a.) was over half arable;[99] Hornton House estate (303 a.) was described in 1910 as 'rich old pasture and production arable' and again over half was arable.[1] A survey of the county's agriculture in 1914 estimated that 51 per cent. of the parish was permanent pasture, while 22 per cent. of the arable was under wheat, 23 per cent. under barley, and 13 per cent. under oats. There was a high percentage of root crops as compared with the rest of the county, i.e. 10 per cent. swedes and turnips. The proportion of sheep kept was high: 61 to every 100 a. of cultivated land, and there were 17 cattle to every 100 a.[2] The chief disadvantage of farming in this area was said to be the distance from Banbury, as the roads were too hilly for it to be profitable to carry large quantities of feeding stuffs and manures or to send produce away frequently.[3] Compared with the best Oxfordshire land the land of the parish was of average fertility. Many of the valley sides were so steep that they could not be ploughed easily, if at all, and the light land with the ironstone very near the surface was prolific of weeds. Mechanization, introduced during the Second World War, reached a very high level on the large farms with the result that the labour force dropped considerably, horses almost disappeared, and hedges were bulldozed so as to enlarge the fields to 20–40 acres. Farming remained mixed: about half the land was permanent pasture, although on the larger farms there was a complete change-over to arable with 1-year or 3-year leys, and the heavier soil of the bottoms was drained by irrigation. Barley, wheat, and roots were the main crops grown, though there were some oats and sugar beet. The rotation used on the largest farm (700 a.) was 2 years corn, 1 rape and turnips, 2 corn, and 3 leys, compared with 1 year each of corn, roots, corn, and leys before the war.[4]

The comparative isolation of Horley and Hornton resulted in village craftsmen and small traders persisting rather longer than elsewhere. In 1851 there were 4 tailors, a clockmaker, and 2 millers in each village, and at the end of the century fruiterers, grocers, shopkeepers, a blacksmith, and a watchmaker were still to be found.[5] Agriculture was the chief occupation up to the 19th century,[6] but quarrying and weaving had always been of some importance. The Hornton stone quarries supplied the principal building stone in the Banbury and Edgehill districts.[7] Quarrymen and masons are recorded in wills and registers from 1609, and in the 1851 census there were 19 stone-masons, 5 quarrymen and 10 labourers in Hornton, and 5 stonemasons in Horley.[8] In the 20th century the stone was quarried mainly for the ironstone by the Oxfordshire Ironstone Co. and very little was used for building.[9] Carr's Pit, the last of the Hornton quarries to be worked for Hornton stone proper, was closed in 1942. Besides its extensive use for building this stone has been much used for monumental work, especially blue Hornton, though a purple and brown Hornton was also used. The Stanleys have been masons for generations, and since the First World War their firm has been based on Edge Hill. Their market is world-wide, stone being sent to New Zealand and South America, as well as all over England. At one time the firm employed 50 per cent. Hornton men, but in 1963 only a few of its 40 employees came from the village. Gilbert Scott was an admirer of Hornton stone, and several modern sculptors, including Henry Moore, favour it.[10]

Plush-weaving was another minor industry carried on in Horley and Hornton down to the late 19th century: weavers are recorded in the parish from the 17th century. Two weavers were listed for the 1851 census, as well as two plush-weavers and a

[90] O.R.O., land tax assess. 1786.
[91] Ibid. 1831.
[92] H.O. 107/1733.
[93] *Kelly's Dir. Oxon.* (1903–39).
[94] Local information.
[95] Davis, *Oxon. Map* (1797).
[96] O.R.O., S. & F. colln. (uncat.).
[97] C. S. Read, 'Farming of Oxon.', *Jnl. Rly. Agric. Soc.* (1854), 198.
[98] Bodl. G.A. Oxon. b 85 a (35): *Sale cat.* (1892).
[99] Ibid. b 91 (12): *Sale cat.* (1896).
[1] Ibid. (13): *Sale cat.* (1910).
[2] Orr, *Oxon. Agric.*, statistical plates.
[3] Ibid. 65.
[4] Ex inf. the farm bailiff, Glebe Farm, Horley, and Mr. Passmore of Passmore and Nunneley Ltd.
[5] H.O. 107/1733.
[6] MS. Top. Oxon. d 42, f. 72.
[7] W. J. Arkell, *Oxford Stone*, 83.
[8] Hants R.O., 43 M 48/220; *Index to Banbury Peculiar Ct. Wills* (O.R.S. xl), 12, 14, 17, 25, 34, 49, 51; Par. Rec., reg.; H.O. 107/1733.
[9] Arkell, *Oxford Stone*, 83; ex inf. the Manager, Oxfordshire Ironstone Co.
[10] Ex inf. Mr. P. C. W. Stanley, Hornton; *Illustrated London News*, June, 1960.

shag-weaver.[11] In the 20th century most non-agricultural workers in the two villages are employed in Banbury.

The descent of the parish's 2 mills[12] in the Middle Ages is not recorded, but it is probable that one was the water-corn-mill at Horley, which later belonged to the prebendal manor and which descended with it in the 17th and 18th centuries.[13] In 1631 it was rated at £12 a year.[14] In 1804 it was leased for £90 a year.[15] There was a miller, usually described as both farmer and miller, at Horley until 1920, but he was no longer recorded by 1924.[16] The fate of the other Domesday mill is not known. There was a windmill marked near Hornton village in 1797 and 1882, but no miller was recorded there after 1869.[17]

CHURCH. Architectural evidence shows that both Horley and Hornton churches were in existence by the late 12th century. In 1115 Henry I granted land in Horley, and the church of King's Sutton (Northants.), which Ranulf Flambard held of him, to augment the prebend which Ranulf and his son Elias held in Lincoln.[18] There is little doubt that from this date the churches and tithes of Horley and Hornton were appropriated to the prebend, which was known as the prebend of Sutton-cum-Buckingham.[19] Until the mid-15th century Horley and Hornton, like Buckingham, were chapelries of King's Sutton.[20]

In 1231 Horley church belonged to the Archdeacon of Buckingham,[21] who held the prebend; from then until the mid-15th century it was served by a curate nominated by the Vicar of Sutton.[22] Hornton church was recorded in 1403 as a chapel of Sutton;[23] the nature of its relationship with Horley at that time is not known.

Between 1438 and 1448 a vicarage of Horley and Hornton was ordained.[24] The ecclesiastical revenue of the parish was divided between the prebendary and the vicar. The prebendary was patron and made the first presentation in 1452.[25] After the surrender of the prebend in 1547[26] presentations were made by lessees of the prebendal manor, who occasionally sold turns.[27] In 1609, when James I granted the manor to Sir Robert Brett, he retained the advowson; since then Horley and Hornton has been a Crown living.[28]

The prebendaries and their successors in the rectory had all the great tithes of Horley, except those of 6 yardlands which were paid to the vicar, as well as $6\frac{1}{2}$ yardlands of glebe: at inclosure the impropriator was allotted 252 a.[29] In 1839 Daniel Stuart, lord of the prebendal manor, declined to take sole responsibility for the upkeep of Horley chancel; although the vicar also held great tithes he claimed that he was exempt from repairing the church or the chancel.[30] Stuart repaired the chancel in 1840.[31] The great tithes of Hornton also presumably belonged to the medieval prebendaries. When the land of Hornton manor was split up, however,[32] the great tithes were apparently sold off in small quantities.[33] From this time they belonged usually, if not always, to the holders of the land,[34] and at inclosure in 1766 were extinguished.[35] Since the land-holders and tithe-owners were the same, the repair of Hornton chancel was paid for out of the church rates.[36]

In 1526 the vicarage was valued at £11 and in 1535 £16 13*s.* 4*d.*[37] After inclosure in 1766 the value of the living, which before then had been worth *c.* £120,[38] rose sharply and by 1789 the vicar was said to be receiving £500.[39] In the 1860s the net value of the living was *c.* £400, but agricultural depression later in the century caused a fall in the letting value of the glebe, from which most of the vicar's income came.[40]

In the 17th and 18th centuries the vicar was receiving the great and small tithes of 6 yardlands and a few acres in Horley except from the rectory's 3 yardlands there, and all Hornton's small tithes, which by 1765 had been commuted for 6*s.* a yardland.[41] The vicarial glebe comprised 3 yardlands in Hornton and a close of *c.* 5 a.; there was a vicarage-house in Horley and a cottage in Hornton. The vicar also received £6 13*s.* 4*d.* from King's Sutton rectory,[42] which was still paid in the 19th century.[43]

In the Middle Ages the Dean of Lincoln had the right to visit the prebend of Sutton-cum-Buckingham, and therefore Horley and Hornton, once every

[11] *Index to Banbury Peculiar Ct. Wills*, 34; Par. Rec., reg.; H.O. 107/1733.

[12] See p. 129.

[13] e.g. C.P. 25(2)/340/Mich. 22 Jas. I; C 142/429/46; C.P. 43/325, rot. 37; Bodl. MS. Ch. Oxon. 3675.

[14] MS. Oxf. Archd. Oxon. c 155, f. 18.

[15] O.R.O., S. & F. colln. (uncat.).

[16] H.O. 107/1733; Gardner, *Dir. Oxon.* (1852); Kelly's Dir. Oxon. (1869–1924).

[17] Davis, *Oxon. Map* (1797); O.S. Map 25″ Oxon. II. 14 (1st edn.); *Kelly's Dir. Oxon.* (1869–1924).

[18] *Regesta Regum Anglo-Normannorum*, ii, p. 128.

[19] For the prebendal manor see p. 127.

[20] Lipscomb, *Bucks.* ii. 575. Horley was first mentioned as a chapel of Sutton in 1277: *Rot. Graves.* 255.

[21] *Fines Oxon.* 89.

[22] Lipscomb, *Bucks.* ii. 575.

[23] *Cal. Pat.* 1401–5, 153.

[24] Lipscomb, *Bucks.* ii. 575.

[25] Linc. Reg. xix, ff. 60, 76.

[26] See p. 127.

[27] Sir John Mason was patron in 1554, William Collingston had a grant of the patronage in 1569, and Robert Johnson of Buckingham was patron in 1599: Linc. Reg. xxviii, ff. 106v., 70v.; xxx. 109.

[28] e.g. MS. Oxf. Dioc. c 1864, presentations.

[29] C.P. 43/734 rot. 43 (Mich. 7 Geo. III).

[30] For this dispute see Sir J. H. Seymour, *A Plain Statement of Facts in a Matter in which the Parishioners of Horley are Interested* (Banbury, 1839): copy in Bodl. G.A. Oxon. 8° 636(5). Stuart printed a pamphlet giving his side of the case, and Seymour answered with an enlarged edition of his *Plain Statement* (Lond. 1839): copy in Bodl. G.A. Oxon. 8° 1308(2). In 1839 the officials of Lincoln empowered the churchwardens to compel Stuart to put the chancel in repair.

[31] Bodl. G.A. Oxon. 4° 593: MS. hist. of Horley.

[32] See p. 126.

[33] e.g. C.P. 25(2)/339/Mich. 8 Jas. I: sale by Richard Light of tithes on 20 a.

[34] e.g. in 1712 a Hanwell yeoman held in fee simple the great tithes on $\frac{1}{2}$ yardland which he held by copy: MS. Wills Peculiars 28/2/8. For other deeds about Hornton tithes see Bodl. MS. Ch. Oxon. 3689–90; O.R.O. Misc. Gr. 2/x/5; C.P. 25(2)/1389/Trin. 15 Geo. III; ibid. 1390/Trin. 23 Geo. III.

[35] C.P. 43/734, rot. 43 (Mich. 7 Geo. III).

[36] Seymour, op. cit. 14.

[37] *Subsidy 1526*, 243; *Valor Eccl.* (Rec. Com.), iv. 240. Of the last sum £1 was paid by the prebendary: ibid. 238.

[38] Bacon, *Liber Regis*, 800; MS. Oxf. Dioc. c 654, f. 105.

[39] MS. Oxf. Dioc. c 654, f. 105.

[40] Ibid. c 1865, Bishop Wilberforce's statement.

[41] MS. Oxf. Archd. Bucks. c 241: 1706 terrier; Horley Incl. Act 5 Geo. III, c 25 (priv. act).

[42] MS. Oxf. Archd. Bucks. c 241; Linc. Dioc. R.O. Ter. 20/11, 20/12.

[43] Par. Rec., Horley reg. 1813 (fly leaf).

3 years. The Bishop of Lincoln instituted to the vicarage of Horley and Hornton and the chapter inducted.[44] After the Reformation and the formation of the Diocese of Oxford the parish formed part of the Peculiar of Banbury, Horley, and Hornton;[45] in the early 17th century the chapter's official held visitations sometimes at Horley and sometimes at Hornton and sometimes at Banbury, but later only at Banbury.[46] From the later 18th century the bishops of Oxford tried unsuccessfully to end the jurisdiction of the Dean and Chapter of Lincoln.[47] In 1838, however, it was the chapter that dealt with complaints about Horley chancel and until 1858 Horley wills were proved in the Peculiar court.[48] In 1853 the parish was formally transferred to Oxford Diocese.[49] Before that date, however, the Bishop of Oxford licensed curates and occasionally visited.[50]

The connexion of the medieval prebendaries of Sutton with Horley and Hornton was sometimes close; in the 14th century there was a prebendal house at Horley[51] and prebendaries were responsible for rebuilding the chancel. Two prebendaries, Henry Roworthe (1416–20) and Robert Gilbert (1420–36), have their portraits in the church windows.[52] Another, Richard Lavender, left 13*s*. 4*d*. to Horley church in 1508.[53] By contrast an Italian cardinal who held the prebend in 1383 was said to have spent little on the churches annexed to it.[54]

The earliest known clerk connected with the parish was Thomas, who held a yardland in Horley in 1231.[55] According to the ordination of King's Sutton vicarage in 1277 the Vicar of King's Sutton was to receive 2 marks a year from Horley chapel[56] and the likelihood is that he chose and paid the chaplains of both Horley and Hornton. By 1438 at least Hornton had its own churchyard and it appears that Horley people were buried there; the dean and chapter at that date considered the possibility of providing a more convenient burial place for Horley, since the inhabitants had a *via nimis tediosa* to Hornton chapel.[57] The Vicar of Sutton apparently found chaplains difficult to find and keep and it was at the request of the prebendary, Nicholas Dixon (1438–48), that the Bishop of Lincoln ordained Horley and Hornton vicarage.[58]

Thereafter the Vicar of Horley probably nominated and paid a curate for Hornton; in 1526 he was paying the curate £5.[59] Later the curate probably lived in the 'very small' house of some 2 bays[60] which in the early 19th century was still known as the Vicarage.[61] Occasional references to individual curates have been found between the 1590s and 1736;[62] separate registers were kept and Hornton's churchwardens made regular presentments to the Peculiar court.[63]

Only one pre-Reformation vicar, David Caunton (1489–1502), was a graduate.[64] Hugh ap Richard (or Pritchard), vicar from 1583 to 1599, was a pluralist but lived at Horley where he was said to preach sometimes;[65] his curate at Hornton, however, was described as 'no preacher'.[66] In 1606 the vicar was said to read and preach the word faithfully.[67] His successors, John (1612–52) and Thomas Clarson (1652–68), sadly neglected the fabric and furniture of both churches.[68] One of their problems may have been church rates; in 1631 the rate for Horley was 7*s*. a yardland and that for Hornton 5*s*. 8*d*., but Hornton people refused to pay rates for the upkeep of Horley church.[69] Stephen Goodwin (1669–1722), member of a prominent local family,[70] rebuilt the vicarage-house;[71] he was, however, probably the last resident vicar for over a century. During his incumbency there was trouble over pews erected in the south aisle 'to the disturbance and great prejudice' of Richard Thomson, who had sole right to sit there, and they were ordered to be removed.[72]

Goodwin's successor was also Vicar of Banbury and a succession of curates served Horley.[73] With the institution of John Dechair in 1758 the parish fell into a state of deep neglect and became a subject of scandal in the neighbourhood. Complaints about Dechair were made not only to the Bishops of Lincoln and Oxford, but to the Archbishop of Canterbury and the patron, the Lord Chancellor.[74] By 1790 the 'venerable parsonage' was in ruins, the churchwardens' presentments having been consistently ignored,[75] while the vicar wrung every penny he could from the living by selling the materials of the farm buildings as they fell down and cutting and selling the timber from the glebe.[76] In 1804 Dechair spent several months in the parish, but as he was at this time 77 and subject to many infirmities, he gave 'little satisfaction' to his parishioners.[77] Of his curates,[78] one was dismissed for drunkenness;[79] the curate in 1805–6, Joseph Jones, aroused opposition by nonconformist tendencies. The latter distributed nonconformist literature, including a

[44] The institutions are in the Lincoln registers; *Linc. Chapter Acts, 1526–36* (L.R.S. xii), 158. The Bishop did not visit: *Visit. Dioc. Linc. 1517–31*, i. 45n, 126.
[45] MS. Oxf. Archd. Oxon. b 60, f. 17; c 28, *passim*.
[46] MS. Oxf. Archd. Oxon. c 155, ff. 7, 9; c 156, f. 6v.; MS. Oxf. Dioc. c 649, f. 101.
[47] MS. Oxf. Dioc. c 657, ff. 36v., 37v.; see *V.C.H. Oxon.* vii. 201.
[48] Seymour, op. cit. 42; B. G. Bouwens, *Wills and their Whereabouts* (2nd ed. 1951), 57, 59.
[49] *V.C.H. Bucks.* i. 344.
[50] MS. Oxf. Dioc. c 327, p. 290; d 549, p. 168; d 566. They also visited in 1805, 1820, 1838 (ibid. d 568, d 578, b 41) and from 1854 onwards: *Wilb. Visit.*
[51] C 136/8/2; see p. 123.
[52] A. B. Emden, 'Oldest Portrait of a Principal', *St. Edmund Hall Mag.* 1931, iii, no. 7, 56–59; *Jnl. Brit. Arch. Assn.* N.S. xxvii, 150.
[53] Lipscomb, *Bucks.* ii. 573n.
[54] *Cal. Pat.* 1381–5, 417.
[55] *Fines Oxon.* 89–90.
[56] *Rot. Graves*, 255.
[57] H. Bradshaw & C. Wordsworth, *Statutes of Lincoln Cathedral*, ii(2), 476.
[58] Browne Willis, *Buckingham*, 76.
[59] *Subsidy 1526*, 243.
[60] MS. Oxf. Archd. Bucks. c 241.
[61] MS. Oxf. Dioc. d 568.
[62] A. Peel, *Seconde Parte of a Register*, ii. 137; MS. Oxf. Archd. Oxon. b 53, ff. 75, 82–5; ibid. b 60, ff. 54, 87.
[63] *Oxon. Peculiars*, 267–274.
[64] Emden, *O.U. Reg.*
[65] Peel, op. cit. ii. 137.
[66] Ibid
[67] MS. Oxf. Archd. Oxon. b 53, f. 8.
[68] *Oxon. Peculiars*, 263, 264.
[69] MS. Oxf. Archd. Oxon. c 155, ff. 12–14.
[70] For the family see *Misc. Gen. et Her.* 4th ser. ii. 32–39; for Stephen see ibid. 38.
[71] Par. Rec., reg.
[72] MS. Oxf. Dioc. c 157, ff. 488–9.
[73] There were 3 different curates in the 1730s: MS. Oxf. Archd. Oxon. c 4, ff. 44, 55; ibid. b 60, f. 49.
[74] MS. Oxf. Dioc. c 654, ff. 105, 124; c 659, f. 218.
[75] Ibid. c 654, f. 124.
[76] Ibid. f. 105.
[77] MS. Oxf. Dioc. c 657, f. 71.
[78] For a list see Par. Rec., marriage reg. 1755.
[79] MS. Oxf. Dioc. c 656, f. 117.

Presbyterian catechism, and indulged in 'violent and ranting' preaching. In 1806 a neighbouring rector wrote that he considered the churches of Horley and Hornton as 'meeting-houses', and the bishop insisted on a change of curates.[80] A later curate spent much of his time in Warwick, where he had 'some fortune', so that both sets of churchwardens complained to the Bishop of Oxford about the irregular hours of services and the 'indecent and scandalous' delay in burials. The bishop sent a sharp order to Dechair to engage and pay a reasonable stipend to a satisfactory curate.[81] As a final proof of Dechair's negligence lands which before inclosure had been used for the upkeep of the church were omitted from the inclosure award and were therefore 'melted down in the common mass' and divided among the landowners.[82]

On Dechair's death in 1810 the parishioners without success petitioned the Lord Chancellor to present their curate to the living.[83] Two non-resident pluralists followed, although the second, Sir John Hobart Seymour, Bt.,[84] was responsible for considerable repairs to the church fabric,[85] persuaded the lay rector to repair the chancel,[86] and provided allotments for churchgoing parishioners.[87]

The parish obtained a resident and devoted vicar in 1853 on the presentation of W. J. Pinwell, who had been curate since 1848.[88] He held 3 services on Sundays in the 2 churches in summer and 2 in winter,[89] but growth in population, Dissent in both places, and long neglect made the parish a difficult one. Accordingly it was decided to make Hornton into a separate parish, so that it could have a resident minister and two Sunday services. Plans for the separation drawn up in 1864 and 1870 came to nothing largely because of the difficulty of dividing up the endowments.[90]

When Charles Heaven came to the parish in 1879 he found it in a 'most deplorable condition', especially Hornton, which had a population of 600 'poor people'. There was no musical instrument there and no choir, no light or heating in the winter months, the roof let in the water, the churchyard was neglected, and there had been no Sunday school for many years. He at once tried to raise the very large sum of £5,450 to pay for the restoration of both churches and the rebuilding of the vicarage-house.[91] There were no large landed proprietors in the parish, however, and he soon found himself in serious financial difficulties. He had to pay a third of the profits of the living to his retired predecessor and himself farm the glebe at a time of falling prices.[92] By 1893 the condition of Hornton church had become a public scandal and was the subject of a series of articles and letters in Birmingham newspapers. Because of lack of heat services had to be held in the school in winter, a house had been built in the churchyard, and the registers were badly kept. In the vicar's defence attention was called to his financial difficulties, to the past neglect and 'gradual decay' of Hornton church, and to the difficulty of finding churchwardens. In the previous year it may be noted there had been a disputed election for parish warden in which a female candidate had obtained nearly half the votes. It was proposed both to secure the vicar's resignation and to separate Horley and Hornton,[93] but Heaven remained vicar until his resignation in 1914 and Horley and Hornton still form one ecclesiastical parish.[94]

In the 20th century local pride in both churches developed and both were restored in 1915 through the energy of the vicar, H. J. Buxton, who later became Bishop of Gibraltar. Much voluntary work has since been done in the church and churchyard, and church life is described as vigorous in both villages.[95] J. H. Clements-Ansell, who lived at Horley Manor, was a noted benefactor from 1910 to 1948.[96] Since 1946 the living has been held in plurality with Hanwell.[97]

The church of *ST. ETHELDREDA*,[98] Horley, consists of a chancel, a central tower, a spacious aisled nave, and a south porch, all built of Hornton stone.[99] The tower dates from the late 12th century; it has 2 belfry windows of that date to east and west. The arch upon which its western wall stands retains its Romanesque chamfered abaci, while the bases of the eastern arch are said to exist beneath the chancel paving, the responds and capitals having been remodelled in the 14th century.[1] Above the same arch there is visible the outline of what appears to be a large relieving-arch, though it is possible that it represents an attempt, afterwards abandoned, to enlarge the chancel-arch. The massive diagonal buttresses at the external corners of the tower were probably added in the 19th century, but the footings of the original buttresses at right-angles to the tower can still be seen at ground-level.

The existing chancel, though remodelled in the 14th century, appears to date substantially from *c.* 1200 and was probably built at approximately the same date as the tower. Internally it retains an aumbry with dog-tooth ornament and a heavy roll-moulding running beneath the windows in the north and south walls: externally the south doorway and the lower parts of the south wall are of the same date. Of the nave as it existed in the 12th century there is no trace except the outline of a steep-pitched roof on the west face of the tower. It may, however, be presumed that it was aisleless, as is still the case at Bucknell, a church of similar date and plan. During the earlier 13th century it was rebuilt with a higher roof and narrow lean-to aisles. The principal surviving portion of this 13th-century nave

[80] MS. Oxf. Dioc. c 657, ff. 93, 95, 102, 127.
[81] Ibid. c 658, ff. 116, 120.
[82] Ibid. c 658, f. 5.
[83] Ibid. c 659, f. 152.
[84] For him see Burke, *Peerage* (1890), under Culme-Seymour, the name he assumed in 1842.
[85] Par. Rec.
[86] See above.
[87] Bodl. G.A. Oxon. 4° 593, p. 42.
[88] Ibid. p. 40; Par. Rec., reg.
[89] *Wilb. Visit.*
[90] MS. Oxf. Dioc. c 1865, letter in *Banbury Guardian*; ibid., Heads of Inquiry.
[91] MS. Top. Oxon. d 42, ff. 72, 74–74v.
[92] MS. Oxf. Dioc. c 1865, correspondence of 1883; *Banbury Guardian*, 9 Sept. 1893.
[93] Par. Rec., chwdns' accts. and correspondence of 1893.
[94] *Census*, 1961.
[95] Ex inf. the vicar.
[96] M.I. in church.
[97] *Oxf. Dioc. Yr. Bks.*
[98] See K. E. Kirk, *Church dedications of the Oxford Diocese*, 51, 52.
[99] For a descriptive account see *Jnl. Brit. Arch. Assoc.* N.S. xxvii, 146–153 and figs. 44–60; Beesley, *Hist. Banbury*, 124; Skelton, *Antiqs. Oxon.* Bloxham Hund. n.p. There are drawings of 1820 by Buckler: MS. Top. Oxon. a 67, no. 337; and see plate facing p. 136.
[1] Par. Rec., reg. (notes by W. J. Pinwell).

is the west wall, in which the line of the original roof can still be traced externally. Two cusped niches and a doorway ornamented with attached shafts are features of the 13th-century west front.

Early in the 14th century the church was enlarged and remodelled. Both arcades were rebuilt with more lofty arches, and the south aisle at least was widened and re-windowed, though the original 13th-century south doorway was re-used in a new position. At the same time the chancel was largely rebuilt on its original foundations, though retaining much of the 13th-century masonry internally. Both in the chancel and in the south aisle the 14th-century masons conformed closely to the pattern of the 13th-century plinth still existing in the west wall of the nave. At the same time a clerestory was constructed in order to light the nave and a south porch was built. The buttressing of the tower probably took place at the same time as the general remodelling of the church. Like the relieving-arch already noted it may indicate some failure of the masonry in the east wall of the tower. A staircase turret formerly rose about 3 ft. above the parapet of the tower; it was removed early in the 19th century.[2]

In the early 15th century the north wall of the north aisle was rebuilt, both the fenestration and the external plinth being of that date. The original 13th-century north doorway was, however, retained and reset in the new masonry. The large square-headed west window of 3 lights with a transom dates from *c.* 1600, and no doubt replaces a medieval window that had fallen into decay.

As at Hanwell, there is a fire-place and chimney in the south-west corner of the south aisle. The tub-shaped font (restored in 1855)[3] may date from the late 12th or early 13th century.

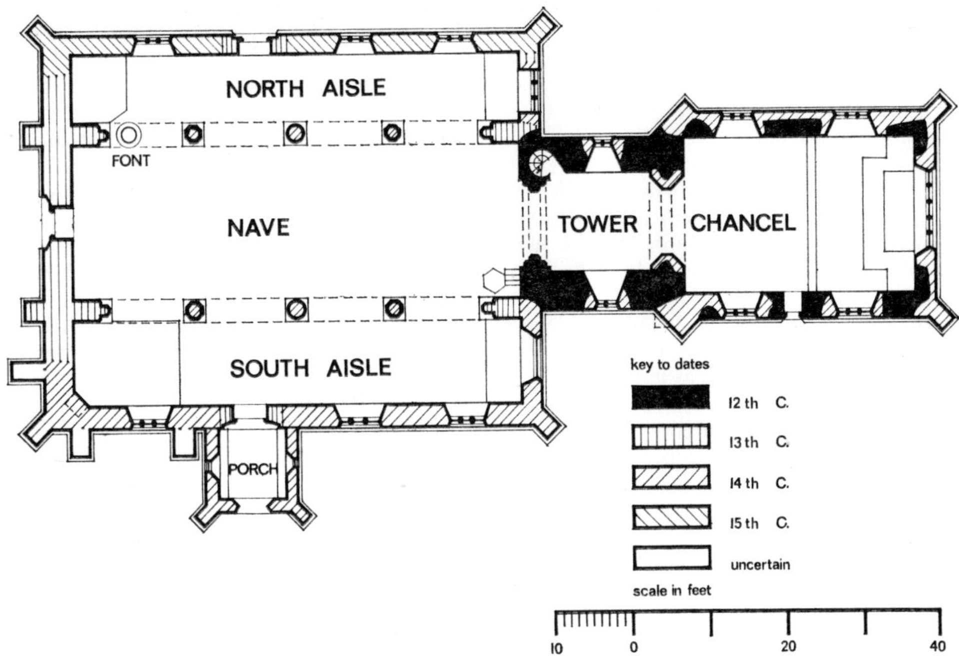

THE CHURCH OF ST. ETHELDREDA, HORLEY

The exposed position of the church no doubt helped to account for its early decay, though there seems to have been much neglect. The lay rector was constantly presented in the early 17th century for a dilapidated chancel. On one occasion some of the timber and one beam were said to have fallen down and in 1621 it was described as 'ruinous and much decayed' so that the rain came in.[4]

In 1632 the church itself was said to be 'ready to fall'.[5] In 1690 the roof of the 'north side' was ordered to be repaired with lead,[6] and in 1701, 1706, and 1714 repairs to the 'leads', generally, were again necessary.[7] Some time in the 18th century, perhaps about 1760,[8] the upper part of the east window of the chancel was rebuilt and new tracery was inserted in the westernmost of the 2 windows in the north wall of the chancel. In 1785 over £39 was paid for work on the tower and work in 1838–9 included new roofing and slating (not leading) the nave and the south aisle, repairing the north aisle, and reflooring and re-pewing the church. The work was paid for by subscription and was done as cheaply as possible, deal being used. The roof of the north aisle was not thoroughly repaired until 1855.[9] The pulpit and reading desk had been provided in 1836.

By 1879 a thorough restoration was required.[10] In a private letter the vicar wrote that the tower might fall any day.[11] In 1883 and 1884 the churchwardens examined the tower and found that it was necessary to do repairs at once to prevent the roof from falling in. Nothing was done, however, until 1915. The tower was then repaired and the fabric put in good order. The deal pews were replaced by chairs, and Persian carpets were given by the vicar.[12] Later, under the supervision of the architect, Mr. L. Dale, the rood, rood-loft, and rood-screen were erected;

[2] Par. Rec., statement by old parish clerk reported by W. J. Pinwell.
[3] Par. Rec., reg. (notes by W. J. Pinwell).
[4] *Oxon. Peculiars*, 262–4.
[5] Ibid.
[6] MS. Oxf. Archd. Oxon. c 28, f. 56.
[7] Ibid. b 53, ff. 28, 33, 41.
[8] Par. Rec.; W. J. Pinwell suggested this date.
[9] Par. Rec., chwdns' accts. 1785–1920.
[10] MS. Top. Oxon. d 42, p. 72.
[11] Ibid. p. 74.
[12] Ex inf. the vicar.

the pulpit was painted with scenes from the life of St. Etheldreda, and 2 new altars were installed in the north and south aisles.[13] The church is lit by clusters of candles.

Several coffin lids of the 12th or 13th century survive. A carved stone with cusped panelling at the east end of the south aisle appears to be part of a tomb of 15th-century date. There is also a brass indent of *c.* 1500 in the tower representing a civilian and lady with six daughters and several sons. Only parts of the brass itself remain.[14]

There is some ancient glass of the earlier 15th century: in a window in the north aisle is the kneeling figure of Henry Roworthe, rector until 1420 and Archdeacon of Canterbury. In the next window is the figure of Master Robert Gilbert, another rector, who became Bishop of London in 1436. There are fragments of the Beauchamp arms in the east window of the south aisle and in the westernmost window of the north aisle.[15]

The church is remarkable for its wall-paintings: the gigantic St. Christopher, dated *c.* 1450, is one of the largest and most perfect representations of the saint in this country.[16] Other scenes, the Annunciation, St. Michael weighing souls, St. George and the Dragon, and a representation of the Seven Deadly Sins, were uncovered by the vicar in 1853, but none could be preserved. A figure, probably of St. Etheldreda, remains on the western pier of the north arcade; on the north wall of the nave, near the tower, are some designs consisting of circles enclosing a character resembling the letter T. Some post-Reformation texts also remain on the south wall.

The painted Commandments in the chancel were put up in 1822, and the 18th-century organ and organ-case, said to have once belonged to Handel,[17] was acquired in the late 18th or early 19th century.

The church plate includes a pair of silver chalices of 1690, a silver paten of 1702 and a silver flagon of 1855. There were also a pair of pewter plates and a pair of tankard flagons, all of the 18th century.[18]

There is a ring of 4 bells by William and Henry Bagley dated 1706.[19]

The registers are complete from 1538.[20]

The church of *ST. JOHN THE BAPTIST*, Hornton, is built of the local ironstone and consists of chancel, clerestoried nave, aisles, western tower, and south porch.[21] It was originally built in the late 12th century, was enlarged in the 13th century, and again enlarged and considerably altered in the course of the next 2 centuries. Of the original church there remains the nave and the north aisle: the 3 arches of the nave arcade are in the transitional style between Romanesque and Early English and rest on cylindrical shafts which have capitals with square chamfered abaci. Another survival of the 12th-century church is the cylindrical font with an arcade of interesting arches and a base moulding of cables.[22]

In the 13th century the chancel seems to have been reconstructed, as the quoins at the east end are decorated with roll-mouldings of this period. The fourth arch of the north nave arcade indicates that the nave was lengthened westwards in the course of the 13th century.

Probably in the early 14th century the chancel was largely rebuilt and a chapel was added on the north side. Only one blocked-up arch remains of the 2 which formerly separated the chapel from the chancel. A south arcade of 2 bays was built, a clerestory was added, and a flat timber roof replaced the former steeply pitched one; nearly all windows and doorways in the body of the church and chancel were remodelled. A plain carpet was added to the exterior of the nave, aisles, and chancel. Later in the 14th or early in the 15th century the tower was built. In the 15th century the church was lightened by the insertion of a 4-light east window. An elaborately carved reredos, of which there are some remains at the east end, was probably also erected in the 15th century.

Minor repairs were carried out from time to time in the post-Reformation period but no structural alterations of importance have been made and the building remains an essentially medieval one. The roof was badly out of repair in 1629 and 1632 when the rain was coming in[23] but in 1670 and 1685 the church was stated to be in 'very good repair';[24] no further reports on the state of the fabric have been found before the 19th century.

When Beesley wrote in 1841, the church was in a very unsound and dangerous condition; the walls were 'fractured in an alarming manner and were much out of the perpendicular'.[25] In 1848 the curate was proposing to open up the blocked tower arch.[26] A west gallery, probably erected in the 18th century, existed at this time.[27] In 1881 the vicar reported that the roof was so much out of repair that moss, ferns, and plants flourished inside the church.[28] This neglect continued despite the efforts of the vicar. In 1893 the windows were broken and the kneelers were rotting from the damp. High pews in church and chancel, 'fantastically placed to face all points of the compass'[29] also aroused criticism. The building was not thoroughly repaired until 1919. Work, including the installation of heating and electric light, was completed in 1922.[30]

The church is notable for its wall-paintings. The whole of the south aisle was once brilliantly painted and traces of a 14th-century painting of the Virgin and Child remained at the east end in the 19th century. They were in too bad a state to preserve and have since been almost entirely covered with whitewash.[31] Over the chancel there is a Doom and

[13] Ex inf. the vicar.

[14] It was moved from the middle aisle in 1840: Par. Rec., reg. For a description see MS. Top. Oxon. d 186.

[15] Lamborn, *Armorial Glass* 133–4. For blazons of the hatchments in the chancel and for the epitaph on a monument to John Edwards, 1776, see Bodl. G.A. Oxon. 4° 686, pp. 180–1; G.A. Oxon. 16° 217, pp. xiv, 163.

[16] See *frontispiece.*

[17] Par. Rec., chwdns' accts. E. A. Walford, *Edge Hill*, 40. See plate facing p. 150.

[18] Evans, *Ch. Plate*, 88–89.

[19] *Ch. Bells Oxon.*

[20] Par. Rec., reg.

[21] For photographs of the church and a descriptive account see *Jnl. Brit. Arch. Assoc.* N.S. xxvii, 153–158, figs. 37b, 61–76. For drawings by Buckler in 1824 see MS. Top. Oxon. a 67, nos. 339, 340, and plate opposite.

[22] For a drawing see MS. Top. Oxon. a 67, no. 338.

[23] MS. Oxf. Archd. Oxon. c 155, ff. 3, 21.

[24] *Oxon. Peculiars*, 270–1.

[25] Beesley, *Hist. Banbury*, 126.

[26] Horley Par. Rec., Hornton reg. 1813–62 (note on fly leaf).

[27] Ibid.

[28] MS. Top. Oxon. d 42, f. 72.

[29] MS. Oxf. Dioc. c 1865.

[30] *Little Guide* (1924).

[31] Horley Par. Rec., Hornton reg. 1813–62, where these paintings are fully described by W. J. Pinwell.

Horley church from the south-east in 1820

Hornton church from the south-west in 1824

Hornton: Cromwell Cottage

Hornton: Manor Farm

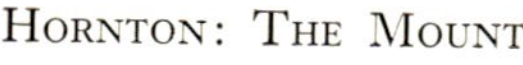

Hornton: The Mount

Horley Manor

over the pulpit the figure of St. George. There are also the remains of post-Reformation decoration on the north wall of the church and the south wall of the chancel, including the Creed written in English and other texts.

Only a fragment of painted glass remains — the coat of arms of one of the Verdun family in the east window of the south aisle.[32]

Late brasses in the chancel are to Richard Arne (d. 1665/6), and to John Goodwin (d. 1727), to Mary Zouch, his daughter (d. 1736), and to Mary, his wife (d. 1740). There is a brass effigy of a civilian and his son, Thomas Sharman, yeoman (d. 1586), in the south aisle.[33]

There is a silver Elizabethan chalice and paten of 1582.[34]

In 1706 the 3 bells and a sanctus bell were 'all broke' and they were ordered to be recast.[35] There are now 5 bells.[36]

The registers are complete from 1538.[37]

NONCONFORMITY. In 1656 Horley appeared in the lists of the Midland Association of General Baptists[38] and in 1693 Nathaniel Kinch of Horley was licensed to teach in any public meeting in the county.[39] He held a conventicle in the village attended by over 100 people, several of them described as gentlemen.[40] In the same year John Cox's house in Hornton was licensed for meetings.[41] In 1733 Horley was a member of the General Assembly of General Baptists; it was the only General Baptist community in Oxfordshire.[42] In 1768 the christening of 2 adult Anabaptists was recorded.[43]

In the 17th and 18th centuries there was a considerable group of Quakers living in Hornton and attending the Shutford meeting.[44] Prominent among them was William Rush who was imprisoned in 1688 and again later for failure to pay tithes; between 1697 and 1713 his goods were regularly distrained on for the same offence.[45] Of the 12 Hornton family names found in the Quaker register in the 18th century Jarrett was the most common.[46] In 1736 Stephen Jarrett was prosecuted for non-payment of tithes. The case involved a not uncommon subterfuge whereby Quakers allowed a man to pay their tithes and deducted the amount from his next bill; earlier Quaker tenants of the land farmed by Jarrett had done this, but Jarrett refused and was in trouble over tithes until 1747.[47] The family survived in Hornton until at least 1806, when the death of Joseph Jarrett, weaver, was recorded.[48] Hornton provided many of the most active members of Shutford meeting, William Stevens, Stephen and John Jarrett, and Joseph Tompson. These men had all died by 1787 and their deaths seem clearly related to the decline of Shutford meeting.[49]

Between the late 18th and mid-19th century other nonconformist groups appeared of which little is known. In 1794 2 houses had been registered at Horley. One of them, Elizabeth Adams' house, was to be used for the 'public worship of Almighty God according to the Orthodox Faith'.[50] The 1851 Ecclesiastical Census gives the date of the foundation of the Methodist chapel as 'before 1800'[51] and in 1802 the vicar spoke of a Methodist chapel as 'lately erected' and licensed, though without a licensed teacher.[52] In 1805 the vicar reported that the group was ministered to by licensed visiting teachers and that many Methodists absented themselves from church.[53] On the day of the census in 1851 the chapel had a morning congregation of 75 and an evening one of 90. In addition there was a Primitive Methodist meeting attracting a congregation of up to 60;[54] this meeting perhaps began as the group which in 1831 was meeting in the house of William Salmons.[55]

In Hornton a house was registered in 1790 and there were three further registrations in the 1830s.[56] It is not possible to be sure what sect used these meeting-houses although one was probably registered by Methodists.[57] The Primitive Methodists registered a building in 1836, a chapel was built in 1842, and by 1851 there was an average congregation of 120.[58] There was also an independent meeting in Hornton dating from 1834 which in 1851 had an average congregation of 45.[59] This may be identical with an 'independent' Methodists meeting held in a club room belonging to the 'Bell' in 1854.[60] No further reference to either meeting has been found.

By 1878 the vicar admitted that two-thirds of his parishioners were professed dissenters.[61] Methodism has survived in both villages. The death of older members has led to a decline in recent years, however, the total membership being 67 in 1965. Of that number 51 belonged to Hornton chapel.[62]

SCHOOLS. The parish had 2 schools with 17th-century endowments, one at Horley and one at Hornton. By his will, dated 1627, Michael Harding, a North Newington yeoman, left a house in Horley for a school-house, and *c.* 14 a. of land to maintain

[32] Lamborn, *Armorial Glass*, 134.
[33] *Jnl. Brit. Arch. Assoc.* N.S. xxvii. 155–7.
[34] Evans, *Ch. Plate.*
[35] MS. Oxf. Archd. Oxon. c 28, f. 112.
[36] *Ch. Bells Oxon.*
[37] There are transcripts with many gaps from 1668 in the Bodl. Libr.
[38] *Mins. of the General Assembly of General Baptists*, ed. W. T. Whitley, i. lxiv. In 1683 a chapel was mentioned in a Horley will: MS. Wills Oxon. 132/3/20.
[39] O.R.O., Cal. Q. Sess. viii. For Kinch see p. 129.
[40] Dr. Williams's Libr., Evans MS.
[41] O.R.O., Cal. Q. Sess. viii.
[42] *Mins. of Gen. Assembly of Gen. Baptists*, i. lxiv.
[43] Par. Rec., reg.
[44] Banbury Quaker Regs.
[45] Besse, *Sufferings*, i. 575; MS. Sufferings.
[46] Banbury Quaker Regs.
[47] *A Vindication of A Book intituled A Brief Account of . . . the Prosecutions of . . . Quakers so far as the Clergy of the Diocese of Oxford . . . are concerned in it.* (Lond. 1740): copy in Bodl. Vet. A 4 e. 1373, p. 399 sqq.; MS. Sufferings.
[48] Banbury Quaker Regs.
[49] Ibid.
[50] Ibid. c 644, no. 23; O.R.O., Cal. Q. Sess. viii.
[51] H.O. 129/163.
[52] MS. Oxf. Dioc. d 566. This chapel was presumably the building registered in 1802: MS. Oxf. Dioc. c 644, no. 61.
[53] Ibid. d 568.
[54] H.O. 129/163.
[55] MS. Oxf. Dioc. c 644, no. 195.
[56] O.R.O., Cal. Q. Sess. viii; MS. Oxf. Dioc. c 645, nos. 45, 202.
[57] The certificate was signed by John Goode of Adderbury, who was a known Methodist.
[58] MS. Oxf. Dioc. c 645, no. 38; H.O. 129/163.
[59] H.O. 129/163.
[60] Billing, *Dir. Oxon.* (1854).
[61] MS. Oxf. Dioc. c 344.
[62] Ex inf. the Revd. A. J. Davies, Secretary of the Oxf. and Leic. District Synod.

the schoolmaster on condition that John French of Broughton and his sons might have free education for 3 of their children for ever. A Commission of Charitable Uses in 1636 found that the house had 'fallen flat down', but that the rents of £13 6*s.* 8*d.* from the land were sufficient to repair the house, and then pay a schoolmaster.[63] The earliest known master was also described as curate.[64]

Another schoolmaster is commemorated by a grave stone, placed in the church by a pupil, which records his death in 1776 and says that he acquired much useful learning which he dispensed with great integrity.

In the early 19th century Horley school was in a very unsatisfactory state. Reading and writing were being taught to a maximum of 20 boys, but the trustees of the school had no knowledge of its lands or funds as a Banbury attorney held the deeds and refused to give any information.[65] When the master died in 1820, the trustees had to postpone appointing a successor until they could repair the building. The school re-opened 9 months later under new rules: girls were now also taken and taught knitting and sewing by the schoolmaster's wife; all children over 6 years in Horley were admitted free, and children from adjoining parishes, on the payment of a fee. The new schoolmaster was to teach according to the National system for a salary of £42 a year. The new arrangement was extremely unpopular in the village and in 1823 there were only 14 free pupils; the number of paying pupils, however, had risen to 32, some of whom came from neighbouring parishes. Petitions drawn up by the parishioners against the National system seem to have alleged that children learned faster before it was adopted. The Charity Commissioners found no substance in the charges and pointed out that 3 of the principal inhabitants were satisfied with the changed arrangements.[66] By 1833 the number of pupils had risen to 16 boys and 25 girls, and there was also a Sunday school, supported by local subscription and attended by *c.* 60 children.[67] This increase necessitated the building of a new schoolroom in 1842.[68] In 1860 the vicar gave the attendance figures at Horley National school as 46 daily and 13 on Sundays, making a total of 59. Presumably the 13 who attended on Sundays were in addition to the day pupils since he also stated that, at Horley at least, he was able in many instances to retain children at Sunday school after they had left day school. There were no adult or evening classes in this year and none in 1878.[69]

When the National school was inspected by the Charity Commissioners in 1867, it was found that the number of children attending was 42: that prizes were given to children who had attended for 2 or 5 years; that a weekly fee of 3*d.* was paid for the children of tradesmen, but nothing for those of labourers; and that there were 2 teachers, appointed by the trustees. The schoolmaster's house was very dilapidated, and the commissioners recommended selling part of the Harding land and rebuilding the house.[70] In 1871 2 National schools were returned for Horley with accommodation for 61 children.[71] Up to this date no Government grant had been received and in 1878 the schools were refused Government inspection unless extensive alterations were made in the buildings and additional apparatus provided, all of which would involve the parish in an outlay of at least £100.[72] The schools continued to exist for the next 20 years without financial aid from the Government; every child attending who was born in the village received his education free.[73] A new building to contain all the children was erected in 1899 and opened in May 1900.[74] There is no record of Government inspection or grant in this year but £28 was received in 1902.[75] Average attendance was 41 in 1900 and 50 in 1906.[76] The land of the original endowment was sold in 1918 when the school was handed over to the Board of Education, and the proceeds invested. The income of *c.* £50 is used to keep the school in repair. The old schoolhouse, probably the 17th-century building, has a thatched roof; a small stone school-room was added and later a large brick building.[77] In 1962 the school was called the Horley Endowed School; it had a roll of 19 and received a grant.[78]

The school endowment in Hornton dates from 1613 when John Fox left ½ yardland in Hornton for a schoolmaster to teach 3 children. In 1665 the Commissioners of Charitable Uses decreed that the rent of £3 had been misapplied, and should revert to its original purpose.[79] It does not appear to have done so, for there was no school in 1738.[80] When the open fields of Hornton were inclosed in 1766, however, a plot of land was set aside to maintain a schoolmaster to teach poor children in Hornton to read, write, and count. This plot was occupied by the Giles family, and towards the end of the 18th century Richard Giles claimed the land as his own. In 1800, after much trouble and expense, the vicar and parishioners gained possession of it. The plot was then let for £9 a year, and 34*s.* was set aside to pay for the education of 3 or 4 children, the remainder being reserved to pay legal expenses.[81] By 1815 Hornton free school was attended by 31 girls and 20 boys. There had evidently been some agitation to affiliate it to the National Society, but there was opposition and it was said that the old system provided employment for people in the village and gave satisfactory results.[82] By 1825 the legal expenses had been paid off, and the full rent of 12 guineas now went to pay the schoolmaster, and to supply books and coals for the school. As yet there was no school-house and no master's house.[83] Finally, in 1833, a National school was built.[84] In

[63] *8th Rep. Com. Char.* 486–90.
[64] MS. Oxf. Archd. Oxon. c 157, f. 490.
[65] *Educ. of Poor*, 725.
[66] *8th Rep. Com. Char.* 486–90.
[67] *Educ. Enq. Abstract*, 748. There were the same number at the Sunday school in 1854: *Wilb. Visit.*
[68] Char. Com., file E 70184.
[69] MS. Oxf. Dioc. d 180; ibid. c 334.
[70] Char. Com. file B 19473; *Schs. Enq.* 308–9.
[71] *Elem. Educ. Ret.* 326.
[72] *Schs. Ret.* 348; MS. Top. Oxon. d 42.
[73] *Kelly's Dir. Oxon.* 1891; *Ret. of Schs.* 214; *Pub. Elem. Sch. Ret.* 494.
[74] Ed 7/101/115.
[75] *Pub. Elem. Sch. Ret.* 1900 (2), 672; *List. of Schs.* (1902), 200.
[76] Ed 7/101/115; *List of Schs.* (1906), 22.
[77] Bodl. G.A. Oxon. 4° 593: MS. Hist. of Horley.
[78] Ex. inf. Oxfordshire County Council, Educ. Cttee.
[79] *12th Rep. Com. Char.* 215–16.
[80] *Secker's Visit.*
[81] *12th Rep. Com. Char.* 215–16.
[82] MS. Oxf. Dioc. c 433.
[83] *12th Rep. Com. Char.* 215–16.
[84] MS. Oxf. Dioc. c 344; ibid. b 70 gives the date as 1826.

this year 68 children at the school were supported by an annual subscription of £7 and by an endowment of £14. There was also an infants' school for 25 children, who attended at their parents' expense. A Sunday school had been founded by voluntary subscriptions in 1809 and in 1833 had 75 pupils.[85] The National school and the Sunday school were attended respectively by 35 and 40 children in 1854 and by 45 and 54 in 1860.[86] In 1853 £20 was raised by subscription to buy a cottage for the use of the schoolmaster.[87]

In 1867 the school was found to be 'as bad as it could be', an opinion which was apparently shared by the Diocesan Inspector. The schoolmaster was unqualified and was a tailor by trade, the instruction he gave was very limited and there was 'an entire absence of life and animation'; both the children and the school were dirty. The school's income came from rent paid by the schoolmaster, rent from allotment, subscriptions, and school pence. The school was open to Dissenters who were not obliged to learn the catechism.[88] In 1878 the School Board, compulsorily elected in 1875, was proposing to take over the school because there was insufficient accommodation for 30 of the children. The vicar complained that the Board had been forced on the parish and that they had been ordered to erect a Board school at a cost of £1,300. This order, in view of the poverty of the parish, was greatly resented. The vicar got the order suspended for 6 months and campaigned to raise a fund to enlarge the existing school at one-fifth of the cost.[89] He appears to have been successful and in 1882 a new school was opened. The old building had been thoroughly repaired and a new wing added to it. Whereas previously the school had not belonged to any religious denomination it now became a Church of England school and the new wing was to be used for a Sunday school, which had apparently been allowed to lapse some time ago. A night school in winter months was also to be started. The schoolmaster was certificated and a girl taught the infants. Children paid 2*d.* or 3*d.* according to the size of their families. The average attendance was 69.[90]

The school was destroyed by fire *c.* 1912 and the infants were accommodated temporarily in Hornton Reading Room, the older children in Hornton Primitive Methodist Sunday school.[91] In 1913 the Board of Education appointed Oxfordshire County Council as trustees of the school[92] and in 1914 a new elementary Council school was built.[93] It was decided in 1923 that the proceeds from the sale of the schoolmaster's house in 1881 should be used to promote the social and physical training of the poor in Hornton.[94] The school continued as a Council school and in 1962 had a roll of 42.[95]

CHARITIES. In 1671 Thomas Saul left a rent-charge of 6*s.*, which was given in bread to poor widows of Horley and Hornton every few years when sufficient money had accumulated. During part of the 19th century the landowner distributed this rent in pence to schoolchildren, but by 1903 the charity had reverted to its original purpose. In 1961 25*s.* was spent on logs of wood for pensioners. The rent-charge was redeemed in 1925.

A bequest was made by John Bray, maltster, in 1725 of an annuity of 10*s.* charged on his house and land to be given to 20 poor persons. The last distribution was in 1863. The tenant later refused to pay and by 1888 the Charity Commissioners considered recovery of the money impossible.[96]

SHENINGTON

SHENINGTON lies 6 miles north-west of Banbury on the border of the county. The parish covers an area of 1,628 a.[1] and its modern boundaries are the same as those of the ancient parish, which was a detached part of Tewkesbury hundred (Glos.) until 1844, when it was transferred to Oxfordshire.[2] The origin of the place-name is uncertain. Its earliest form was *Shenedon* and the first element may be *Sciena*, whose burial mound may have been Shenlow Hill. Alternatively the name may mean beautiful hill (*scenan dune*).[3] The Sor Brook divides Shenington from Alkerton, while a small tributary, Shenington Brook, defines almost the whole southern boundary. The western boundary follows the Edgehill escarpment. Shenington's land is a watershed of both the Severn and the Thames, for another of its streams flows into the Stour and eventually into the Severn. The parish lives mostly between the 500 and 625 ft. contour line, but Shenlow Hill, notable for its wide views of eight counties, rises to 740 ft.; Rough Hill rises to over 700 ft. in the south-west, while part of Edgehill is also within the parish. Shenington's soil of red loam lies on Middle Lias rock.[4] The flat rolling land in the north-west was used as an airfield during the Second World War and one of the earliest jet bombers was stationed there. The airfield has since been converted into a course for go-karting and a gliding club has its headquarters at Sugarswell Farm.[5]

There are fine examples of strip-lynchets in Shenington which were probably open-field selions.[6] There is no natural woodland and none has been planted. The parish is in the area of the Warwickshire Hunt, and in 1763 was advertised as open and fine sporting country.[7]

A turnpike from Banbury and Edgehill ran just

85 *Educ. Enq. Abstract*, 748; MS. Oxf. Dioc. c 433.
86 *Wilb. Visit.*; MS. Oxf. Dioc. d 180.
87 Char. Com., file E 70184. 88 Ibid. and file E 79457.
89 MS. Top. Oxon. d 42, p. 72; Kelly's Dir. Oxon. (1891).
90 Ed 7/101/116.
91 Char. Com. file 79457; Ed 7/101/116 A.
92 Ed7/101/116 A.
93 Char. Com., file 23256; Ed 7/101/116 A.
94 Char. Com., file 79457.
95 Ex inf. Oxfordshire County Council, Educ. Cttee.
96 *12th Rep. Com. Char.* 215; *Char. Don.* 976; Char. Com., files E 15594, 70184; G file accts. Horley; G file corresp. Horley and Hornton.

1 O.S. *Area Bk.* (1882). The following maps were used in this article: O.S. Map 25″ Oxon. V. 5 (1st edn.); 6″ Oxon. V. N.W. (1923 edn.); 2½″ SP 34 (1959).
2 Counties (Detached Parts), 7 & 8 Vic. c 61.
3 *P.N. Oxon.* (E.P.N.S.), ii. 402–3; *V.C.H. Oxon.* i. 367.
4 *V.C.H. Oxon.* i, map between pp. 4–5.
5 Local information.
6 J. E. G. Sutton, 'Ridge and furrow in Berks. and Oxon.', *Oxoniensia*, xxix/xxx. 106. See plate facing p. 151.
7 *Oxf. Jnl.* 17 Dec. 1763.

outside the parish and a branch-road went to Alkerton, Shenington, and Tysoe (Warws.). The village remains secluded and connected with its neighbours by minor roads only.

The village crowns the hill at a height of 576 ft. and faces Alkerton on the opposite slope of the Sor Brook valley. It lies close to the boundary. A map of 1732 shows that its dwellings were then grouped irregularly round a green and the parish church, which lay just off the green to the south-east. Rattlecom Lane, Stockin Way, and Stratford Way branched out from the village and passed through the surrounding open fields. The water-mill and the miller's house lay on Shenington Brook in the south-east corner of the parish.[8]

In 1551 there were said to be about 112 communicants, in 1603 80 communicants, and in 1676 110 adults in the parish.[9] In 1712 there were said to be about 280 inhabitants and 60 houses.[10] Only 42 houses had been listed in 1672[11] and it may be that the expansion of population noted in the 18th century[12] began at an earlier date. Numbers rose rapidly from 332 in 1811 to 463 in 1841, but declined thereafter to 205 in 1931.[13] The downward trend was reversed slightly by the expansion of industrial Banbury, and in 1961 there were 233 inhabitants.[14]

In 1672 2 houses were assessed on 6 hearths, 1 on 5 hearths, and 7 on 3 or 4 hearths. Thirty-two were assessed on 2 hearths or less.[15] The two 6-hearth houses belonged to the families of Owen and Pettifer and were possibly the two manor-houses.[16] Many of the houses and cottages, built of the local ironstone rubble or ashlar, survive and preserve such characteristic features as stone chimney stacks with moulded shafts, mullioned or transomed windows of stone or wood with square moulded labels, thatched roofs, and square stair-case projections. Of the 17th-century farm-houses Mill Farm, which stands on the south side of the churchyard, is notable. It is built of iron-stone ashlar, of 3 stories with cellars, and is still used as a farm-house. It retains many of its original stone mullioned windows of 2 and 3 lights with square labels. The Goodwin manor-house, which later passed to the Sadlers, can be identified with the largely 18th- and 19th-century house immediately east of the church.[17] The 'Bell', the only surviving inn, was rebuilt in 1700. It has a stone inscribed with this date and the initials 'E.S.E.'. In 1727 there were two inns and in 1755 three.[18] In the early 19th century the house on the south side of the green was the 'Red Lion'.[19]

Much damage was done, particularly to the cottages, by a fire in 1721.[20] Among the victims of the fire was the rectory-house, which was later rebuilt. It is a 2-story structure of ironstone ashlar with a stone slate roof in which are 3 small attic dormers. The adjoining stabling and coach-house with thatched roof and stone mullioned windows are survivals from the earlier house. Among the cottages Mizpah Cottage in Church Lane has a plaque inscribed 'This house was burnt May 13th 1721'. It was rebuilt and bears the initials 'L.J.A.' in an oval wreathed cartouche. A cottage lying south-west of the 'Bell' is distinguished by having a panel with the arms of the Masons' Company of London. Two houses on the green, 'Longwalls' and 'The Limes', appear to have been built or rebuilt in the 18th century as 'gentlemen's residences'; 'The Limes' may probably be identified with a large mansion house sold in 1763 with stabling for 10 horses, a summer-house, orchards, woods, and fish ponds.[21]

In the 19th and 20th centuries there has been some new building and modernization. The plain red brick Primitive Methodist chapel was erected in the early 19th century at the bottom of the hill outside the village; the school, built in 1871, was enlarged in 1905.[22] New houses were built in 1965 on the Shenington Building estate. At that time the village had two general stores, a butcher's shop, a post office, and a petrol station.

There are 4 outlying farms of which one, Sugarswell ('robber's spring'), stands on the site of an early hamlet inhabited from at least the late 12th century.[23]

The village acquired notoriety in 1810 when a prize fight was arranged by Morant Gale of Upton (Warws.) between Molyneaux, a Negro pugilist, and the English champion, Thomas Cribb. The ring was in Shenington Hollow, well away from the vigilant watch of the Gloucestershire J.P.s, and the match was fought on 3 December.[24]

MANORS. In pre-Conquest times Shenington was attached to the lordship of Tewkesbury (Glos.), which on the eve of the Conquest was held by Brictric, son of Algar, a prominent Anglo-Saxon thegn.[25] After the Conquest his lands, the later honor of Gloucester, were granted to Queen Maud (d. 1083), and in 1086 they were amongst her former possessions then held by the king.[26] *SHENINGTON*, assessed at 10 hides, was farmed for the king by Robert d'Oilly.[27] About 1087, however, William II gave Gloucester honor to Robert FitzHamon as a reward for his services and the overlordship of Shenington henceforth followed the descent of the honor.[28] Shenington, held as 1 fee, was among the lands confiscated on Prince John's rebellion in 1194 and was in the king's hands until 1197.[29] It presumably passed later with the honor to Geoffrey de Mandeville, and then to the Clares, Earls of Gloucester and Hertford. On Richard de

[8] Oriel Coll. Mun.

[9] 'Bishop Hooper's Visit.', *E.H.R.* xix, 107; B.M. Harl. MS. 594, f. 247; Compton Census.

[10] Atkyns, *Glos.* 338.

[11] E 179/24/14; cf. 46 families in 1650: C 94/1, f. 29.

[12] Between 1721 and 1800 births exceeded deaths by 118: Par. Reg.

[13] *Census*, 1811–1931.

[14] Ibid., 1961.

[15] E 179/24/14.

[16] Ibid.

[17] Oriel Coll. Mun., maps of 1732, 1787, 1813.

[18] Glos. R.O. Q/AV 2, rot. 2.

[19] Oriel Coll. Mun., map of 1813.

[20] Par. Rec., memo. in register.

[21] *Oxf. Jnl.* 17 Dec. 1763. For the summer-house and fishponds see Oriel Coll. Mun., maps of 1732, 1787.

[22] See pp. 149–50.

[23] *P.N. Warws.* (E.P.N.S.), 285.

[24] The tradition was recorded in 1900 by G. Miller in *Rambles Round the Edge Hills*, 184. For the contestants see T. C. Wignall, *The Story of Boxing*, 85 sqq.

[25] *Dom. Bk.* (Rec. Com.), i. 163*b*.

[26] *Complete Peerage*, v. 682.

[27] *Dom. Bk.* (Rec. Com.), i. 163*b*.

[28] *Complete Peerage*, v. 682 sqq. As late as 1500 land in Shenington was said to be held of the honor of Gloucester: *Cal. Inq. p.m. Hen. VII*, ii, p. 218.

[29] *Pipe R.* 1195 (P.R.S. N.S. vi), 56, 147; *Chanc. R.* 1196 (P.R.S. N.S. vii), 73; *Pipe R.* 1197 (P.R.S. N.S. viii), 37.

Clare's death in 1262 Shenington was given in dower to his relict Maud (d. by 1289).[30] When the honor of Gloucester was divided in 1314 between the three sisters of Gilbert de Clare, the overlordship of Shenington appears to have been divided between two of them, Margaret and Eleanor. In 1347 Hugh de Audley, Earl of Gloucester, who had married Margaret, held the overlordship of $\frac{3}{5}$ fee. Their heir was Margaret, the wife of Ralph, Earl of Stafford; Margaret's son Hugh, Earl of Stafford, died possessed of it in 1386.[31] The family held the overlordship of this part of the fee in the 15th century. In 1393 Anne, Countess of Stafford, was granted dower in it,[32] and her son Humphrey, Earl of Stafford and Duke of Buckingham, held it at his death in 1460.[33]

The other $\frac{2}{5}$ fee was held of Eleanor le Despenser, the wife of Hugh le Despenser, the younger.[34] The connexion with this family continued at least until 1420 when Lord Abergavenny, heir of Isabel le Despenser (d. 1439), was overlord of a half of $\frac{1}{5}$ part of a Shenington manor.[35]

The Sor family were under-tenants of the whole fee in the 12th century. Robert Sor (fl. 1132), a follower of Robert, Earl of Gloucester, probably held the manor as he did the church; he was succeeded by his son Odo and in 1166 Jordan Sor was a prominent tenant of Gloucester honor, holding in all 15 fees.[36] Jordan was succeeded by John Sor, whose land was taken into the king's hands for his share in John's rebellion in 1194, but was later restored; he is recorded as holding Shenington until about 1203.[37] His heir was probably a minor[38] and may perhaps be identified with the Robert le Sor, whose property in Warwickshire and Gloucestershire was restored in 1217 after the Barons' War.[39] A John Sor was recorded in 1233[40] but he was dead by 1241 when Wentliana his relict, was granted a third of Shenington manor in dower.[41] His son and heir, William Sor, was then a ward of Wentliana's second husband Nicholas, son of Roger, but by 1255 he had entered his estates, and was returned in 1263 as holding 14½ fees of the earl in Shenington and elsewhere.[42] By 1280 he had been succeeded by John Sor, who was appointed as assessor and tax collector in Gloucestershire in 1295.[43] By 1303, however, Shenington had been divided into fifths, probably between coheirs, and was held by Robert Wykeham (d. 1327) and his wife Elizabeth, daughter of John Sor (Lazore), Henry Huse (Heuse) and his wife Margery, William de Esthall and his wife Ela, William de Staur and his wife Imeyne,[44] and Symunda the daughter of John le Sor.[45] Simon Sor was a lord of the vill in 1316 and in 1346 John Sor held $\frac{1}{5}$ fee.[46] There is no later record of this family's connexion with Shenington and their $\frac{1}{5}$ fee appears to have passed to their under-tenants.

Sir John Walton (de Wauton), lord of Alkerton (d. 1277),[47] was evidently tenant of this land, for Isabel, his relict, and her second husband Henry le Foun were in 1278 granted a house and 4 yard-lands in Shenington together with other of Sir John's property, and in 1292 conveyed Isabel's dower in it to Sir John's daughter and heir Maud Walton and her first husband Sir John de Stradling.[48] Maud's second husband, Sir John L'Estrange, died in 1309 holding Shenington of the heirs of John Sor (d. by 1303) for 1*d.* a year.[49] The manor then followed the descent of the L'Estranges' manor in Alkerton until at least the mid-16th century.[50] In 1542 Shenington, like Alkerton, was sold to Robert Hopper of Henley.[51] Before 1601, however, Shenington had passed out of the Hopper family, for it was conveyed at that date by William Hawkins, his wife Katherine, and son Thomas, to Richard Goodwin.[52] Richard was a younger son of Thomas Goodwin of Alkerton; on his death in 1637 the manor passed to his son John, who settled it on his son Richard in 1686.[53] Richard's son, John, who had moved to Sutton Coldfield (Warws.), mortgaged Shenington in 1729.[54] This manor then passed to his daughter Ann Osborn, widow, and in 1775 was sold by her to William Sadler.[55] By 1780 it had passed from the Sadler family, like their Sugarswell manor,[56] to Oriel College, Oxford, for the college was said to be lord of all Shenington manor.[57]

A second *SHENINGTON MANOR* evidently developed from the one-fifth fee held in 1316 by Sir Thomas Hasting.[58] He was lord of Chebsey (Staffs.) and Leamington Hastings (Warws.), and the third husband of Maud Walton.[59] In 1347 he was recorded as holding one-fifth fee in his own right as well as the one-fifth fee which he held with his wife.[60] He was dead by 1348 and his own fifth descended to his son Sir John (d. by 1359) and grandson Sir John (d. 1362). On the latter's death his lands were inherited by his daughters Maud and Joan.[61] Maud married Ralph of Stafford of Grafton Manor (Worcs.), who was returned as tenant of

[30] *Cal. Inq. p.m.* i, pp. 137, 159.
[31] Ibid. ix, p. 62; C 136/76/77.
[32] *Cal. Close*, 1392–6, 47; cf. ibid. 1402–5, 219.
[33] C 139/180/59; *Cal. Inq. p.m.* iv, pp. 290, 295.
[34] *Feud. Aids*, ii. 255; *Complete Peerage*, iv. 269. The date of the annotation, giving Lady Despenser as holding $\frac{2}{5}$ fee, is not given, but it has been assumed here that Eleanor held it.
[35] *Complete Peerage*, iv. 267–82; C 138/30/5.
[36] *Montacute Cart.* (Som. Rec. Soc. viii), 288.
[37] *Red Bk. Exch.* (Rolls Ser.), 154; *Pipe R.* 1194 (P.R.S. N.S. v), 194; ibid. 1202 (P.R.S. N.S. xv), 282; ibid. 1203 (P.R.S. N.S. xvi), 41.
[38] In 1203 and 1205 a Peter de Stokes was responsible for the scutage of the fees: *Pipe R.* 1203 (P.R.S. N.S. xvi), 43; ibid. 1205 (P.R.S. N.S. xix), 92.
[39] *Rot. Litt. Claus.* (Rec. Com.), i. 313.
[40] *Close R.* 1231–4, 333.
[41] *Som. Pleas* (Som. Rec. Soc. xi), p. 127, where the name appears as Wenclina.
[42] *Close R.* 1254–6, 192; 1261–4, 284.
[43] *Som. Pleas* (Som. Rec. Soc. xliv), 245; *Cal. Pat.* 1291–1301, 171; in 1287 John le Sor claimed to have free warren: J.I.1/284, m. 13*d.*

[44] It is probable that Imeyne was the daughter of Imeyne, wife of John Sor, who figures in an undated charter with her eldest daughter Ela: B.M. Ch. Cott. xxix. 52.
[45] *Feud. Aids*, ii. 255; *Coll. Top. & Gen.* iii. 363. Elizabeth's marriage was arranged in 1290: ibid.
[46] *Feud. Aids*, ii. 272, 288.
[47] See p. 45.
[48] *Feet of Fines Warws.* i. (Dugdale Soc. xi), p. 203; ibid. ii. (Dugdale Soc. xv), p. 25.
[49] *Cal. Inq. p.m.* v. p. 111.
[50] See p. 46.
[51] C.P. 25(2)/52/377/9.
[52] C.P. 25(2)/147/1924/Trin. 43 Eliz. I.
[53] *Misc. Gen. et Her.* (4th ser.), ii. 150–1, 190; C 142/638/52; C 60/541, no. 24; Oriel Coll. Mun. DELL 6.
[54] Oriel Coll. Mun. DELL 6.
[55] Ibid. DELL 6; LR 6; S II. 1. 93.
[56] See below.
[57] Oriel Coll. Mun. S II. 1. 93: incl. act.
[58] *Feud. Aids*, ii. 272.
[59] *Complete Peerage*, vi. 341–2. For evidence that his wife was Maud Walton and not Maud Deiville (as ibid. 342), see p. 46 n.
[60] *Cal. Inq. p.m.* ix, p. 62.
[61] *Complete Peerage*, vi. 341–4.

one-fifth fee in 1393 and 1403.[62] He died in 1410 and his Shenington land evidently followed the descent of his manor of Leamington Hastings, passing to his son Humphrey (d. 1418), grandson Humphrey, and to Humphrey's son Sir Humphrey, whose lands were confiscated after his attainder in 1485.[63] The property was restored in 1514 to his son Sir Humphrey Stafford,[64] whose grandson, another Sir Humphrey, sold Shenington to Oriel College, Oxford, about 1565.[65]

Joan, the other daughter of Sir John Hasting (d. 1362), married first John de Salisbury, who was executed in 1388.[66] On Joan's death in 1420 she was said to hold a moiety of a fifth of Shenington manor.[67] The property is not recorded again, but it may have descended like Joan's share of Leamington Hastings and eventually have reverted to Sir Humphrey Stafford in 1514 and have been included in the manor granted to Oriel College.[68]

A third manor, *SUGARSWELL*, was first recorded in 1258 when it was held by William Sutton, nephew of Henry Lexington, Bishop of Lincoln.[69] The manor followed the descent of the lay manor of Horley and Hornton until at least 1316 when Sir Richard Sutton held $\frac{1}{5}$ fee in Shenington.[70] There is no further record of the Sutton connexion with Sugarswell. The under-tenants appear to have been John of Sugarswell (Shokereswell) and his wife Alice, who in 1299 acknowledged the right of John de Dunheved to land in Sugarswell and Tysoe (Warws.).[71] Dunheved's son John apparently sold the estate to John Pecche, who held houses in Sugarswell in 1318.[72] Sir John Pecche, probably a son, died in 1376, leaving a son John (III) who was a minor.[73] John (III) died in 1387 holding the $\frac{1}{5}$ fee.[74] This evidently passed like his Warwickshire manors to his daughter Margaret and her husband Sir William de Montfort (d. 1452) of Coleshill (Warws.),[75] and thence to their son Sir Baldwin de Montfort (d. by 1461), and grandson Sir Simon de Montfort. Simon supported Perkin Warbeck's insurrection and was hanged in 1495, his estates reverting to the Crown.[76] The king granted 'Shenington' manor (i.e. Sugarswell) to Gerald, Earl of Kildare, and Elizabeth St. John, his second wife, in 1496.[77] Sir Gerald died in 1513, his wife in 1516, and their eldest son Henry also in 1516. The manor was then held by Henry's brothers Sir Thomas (d. 1531) and Sir James FitzGerald.[78] Sir James was accused of complicity in the rebellion of his nephew in 1534 and was hanged in 1536.[79] The manor reverted to the Crown; in 1541 it was leased to Nicholas Dorell,[80] and later granted to John Cockes and John Bassett, who in 1550 were licensed to grant it to William Button.[81] Button's chief holdings were in Wiltshire and in 1555 he granted his Shenington manor, which included land in Sugarswell and Shenington, to Richard Wiggett (Wygatt, Wigate) of Shenington.[82] Wiggett, who was called yeoman or husbandman, died in 1570 holding the manor in chief.[83] In 1575 Thomas Clarke, grandson of Wiggett's sister and heir Agnes, was granted the freedom of the manor.[84] His right was disputed by John, son of William Wiggett, an uncle of Richard Wiggett. In 1578 John Wiggett was said to be heir to the manor[85] and in 1579 he granted it to Tristram Holcombe, who was licensed to alienate it in the same year.[86] The manor eventually came into the possession of Richard Braughton of Seaton (Rut.), who sold it in 1608 to a Thomas Gardner.[87] There was a lawsuit in 1609 over the conditions of the conveyance. By 1616 Calybut Downing held the manor with land in Shenington.[88] His son was the eminent divine Calybut Downing (d. 1644),[89] whose daughters Elizabeth and Ann sold their moiety of the manor in 1653 to John Goodwin.[90] Sugarswell then descended with the Goodwins' other Shenington manor and in 1732, for example, was described as 'the manor of Sugarswell within the manor of Shenington'.[91] In 1780 Edward Sadler was described as lord of such part of Shenington as lay within Sugarswell Closes.[92] Presumably his rights were purchased with Sugarswell by Oriel College at that date.[93] The descent of the other moiety has not been established.[94]

A fourth *SHENINGTON MANOR*, probably originating in the $\frac{1}{5}$ fee of Robert Wykeham and his wife Elizabeth or in that of William de Esthall and his wife Ela,[95] was recorded in the 15th century. In 1393 $\frac{1}{5}$ fee, held under the Countess of Stafford, was said to have been previously held by a Lambert de la More,[96] and in 1411 John More granted half the manor to Henry Vyall (Vyale, Vielle), presumably the man recorded as escheator in Somerset until *c.* 1421.[97] Vyall seems to have been succeeded by William Vyall (fl. 1434–53), whose son James was in possession of a Shenington manor in 1488.[98]

[62] *Cal. Close.* 1392–6, 47; 1402–5, 219. Although the estate was evidently divided it may be that only one branch of the family was responsible for the $\frac{1}{5}$ fee.

[63] *V.C.H. Warws.* vi. 151.

[64] Ibid.

[65] Oriel Coll. Mun. DLR 6; Fosbrooke, *Glos.* ii. 536. The original deed of conveyance does not seem to be at Oriel, but Sir Humphrey Stafford conveyed the manor to trustees in 1565.

[66] *Complete Peerage*, vi. 344; *Cal. Inq. Misc.* iv, p. 217. Joan's second husband was Rustin de Villeneuve and her third Roger of Swynnerton.

[67] C 138/37/6; *Cal. Close*, 1419–22, 36. Joan was said to hold of Lord Abergavenny, although Thomas Hasting's fees were previously said to be held of the Staffords. This may be an error in the inquisition or perhaps much of the land of the manor was held of this family.

[68] *V.C.H. Warws.* vi. 151.

[69] C.P. 25(1)/282/15/365. This Shenington manor may have included the later Sugarswell manor in Tysoe (Warws.): see *V.C.H. Warws.* v. 177.

[70] *Feud. Aids*, ii. 272; see p. 126.

[71] *Feet of Fines Warws.* ii. (Dugdale Soc. xv), p. 201.

[72] *Cal. Pat.* 1317–21, 100, 176; *V.C.H. Warws.* vi. 80.

[73] *Cal. Inq. p.m.* xiv. p. 277.

[74] C 206/14/1; *Cal. Close*, 1392–6, 47.

[75] Glouc. City Libr. Glos. colln. 27082.

[76] *V.C.H. Warws.* iv. 83; vi. 80; *Cal. Inq. p.m. Hen. VII*, iii. p. 489.

[77] *Cal. Pat.* 1494–1509, 84, 308; *L. & P. Hen. VIII*, i(1), p. 352.

[78] Fosbrooke, *Glos.* ii. 535; C 142/54/109; cf. *L. & P. Hen. VIII*, iv(3), p. 2737.

[79] *Complete Peerage*, vii. 236.

[80] *L. & P. Hen. VIII*, xvi. p. 424.

[81] *Cal.Pat.* 1549–51, 246.

[82] Ibid. 1554–5, 256.

[83] Ibid. 1558–60, 203.

[84] C 142/155/152; C 60/391, no. 22.

[85] C 142/181/101.

[86] C 66/1179, m. 34. Sugarswell manor in Tysoe has a different descent: *V.C.H. Warws.* v. 177.

[87] C 3/271/12.

[88] Ibid.; C.P. 43/137, m. 13.

[89] Foster, *Alumni*; *D.N.B.*

[90] Oriel Coll. Mun. DELL 6.

[91] Ibid. DLR 6: draft of estate sale.

[92] Ibid. S II. 1. 93.

[93] Ibid. DELL 6.

[94] Fosbrooke (*Glos.* ii. 536) noted in 1819 that Sugarswell manor had been divided.

[95] See below.

[96] *Cal. Close*, 1392–6, 47; cf. 1402–5, 219.

[97] C.P. 25(1)/79/85/51; *Cal. Pat.* 1399–1401, 476; 1416–22, 198, 370.

[98] *Cal. Pat.* 1429–36, 340; *V.C.H. Berks.* iv. 209; Oriel Coll. Mun. DLR 6: list of deeds.

A moiety of this Shenington manor was granted to Oriel College in 1503.[99] The descent of the other half is not known.

The Wykehams and Esthalls were recorded as holding $\frac{1}{5}$ fee in 1303 and as lords in 1316.[1] No later reference to the Esthall holding has been found, but Robert Wykeham's son Robert was holding in 1346 and John Wykeham (fl. 1360) was described as of Shenington.[2]

LOCAL GOVERNMENT. Records have survived of some views of frankpledge held between 1483 and 1540, and of the courts baron of Oriel College, Oxford, between 1693 and 1718.[3] It may be noted that college tenants not only owed suit to that court but paid 'frithsilver' to Tewkesbury court, presumably the hundred court.[4]

The records of the vestry perished in the fire of 1721[5] but the period 1777–1832 is fairly well documented.[6] Two overseers were appointed yearly, each accounting for 6 months. In Shenington, as elsewhere, expenditure on the poor began to increase rapidly in the late 18th century; in 1775–6 £87 was spent, and by 1802–3 the sum was £163, all of which went on out-relief; the rate was then 3*s.* 10½*d.* in the pound.[7] In 1810–11 over £364 was spent; this included the constable's charges and the county rate, and regular weekly relief accounted for £277. In 1817–18 the figure was nearly £650 of which £374 was spent on the weekly list; the cost of weekly relief rose to £536 in 1820–21, although total expenditure had fallen slightly. In the following year the dole may have been reduced; although the number receiving weekly relief changed little, the total expenditure was only £379 and it remained at a lower level of *c.* £300 until the 1834 Act reduced it still further.[8] Shenington became part of the Banbury Union; by 1851–2 only £118 was spent on the poor, and the rate in the pound was 1*s.* 1½*d.*[9]

In 1799 there were *c.* 16 people on weekly relief ranging from 1*s.* 4*d.* to 3*s.* 6*d.* By 1817–18 the number 'on the list' had reached 32, and 14*s.* a week was paid to a man and his wife. The roundsman system, in use by 1799, when there were about four roundsmen each week in the winter months, had by 1820 been largely replaced by labour on the roads with payment for so many days of unemployment. In the bad years there were sometimes 12 roundsmen even in summer, working 7 days a week. The overseers made the usual payments for clothes, fuel, apprenticing of orphans, and medical care, and built 7 parish houses which were let at sums varying from £1 6*s.* to as little as 8*s.* 9*d.* where an occupant was sick.[10]

The overseers paid the constable's account, and the constable also received the county rate and after 1824–5 'bridge money' amounting to £8 14*s.* The overseers also paid the mole-catcher, were responsible for the militia, and for settlement and removal. To cover expenses, except those for journeys and meetings, the overseers were allowed £6 10*s.* yearly from 1821.

ECONOMIC HISTORY. Shenington was a 10-hide estate but by 1086 3 hides, perhaps the demesne, were exempt from geld and royal service. On the demesne were 4 ploughs worked by 12 serfs and a mill worth 3*s.* a year. There may have been more than 4 ploughlands in demesne for the 17 tenants had as many as 8 ploughs and presumably ploughed some of the demesne. The tenants included 5 radknights, 8 *villani* and 4 bordars.[11] The drastic fall in the value of Shenington from £20 before the Conquest to £8 in 1086 may have been a result of Brictric's forfeiture.[12]

Details for only one small estate have survived for the 12th and 13th centuries. In 1195 Robert le Puhier's land was in royal hands and the farm for three-quarters of the year was £1 4*s.* 10*d.*; grain sold fetched £3 3*s.* and oxen £2 2*s.*[13]

Although Sugarswell was well-established as a separate hamlet by 1318,[14] it was not large enough to appear separately in 14th-century tax assessments. In 1327 of the 24 Shenington inhabitants assessed three-quarters paid less than 2*s.* Two men, neither of them manorial lords, paid over 4*s.*[15] The total assessment of £2 0*s.* 8*d.* suggests that Shenington was fairly prosperous.[16]

Nothing more is known of Shenington until the beginning of the 17th century, except that there was no dominant inclosing landlord in the parish. Only around Sugarswell Farm in the north of the parish did early inclosure of any importance take place; much had been inclosed by 1609 and probably earlier,[17] and in 1780 Edward Sadler of Sugarswell alone had 71 a. of old inclosure out of a total of 194 a. in Shenington, and there was evidently little inclosed land elsewhere in the parish.[18]

From the 16th century Oriel College began to accumulate land in Shenington but kept none in hand. By 1619 there were 20 tenants of the college manor, holding about 16½ yardlands, 4 cottages and other small parcels of land, and the mill. Six tenants held by lease and the rest by copy.[19] Leases show that the college used the manor as a source of grain by exacting it from their lessees. In 1569, for example, a house and yardland in Shenington was leased for 60 years at 16*s.* a year but in 1628, when it was again leased, the rent was 10*s.* 8*d.*, 1 peck of wheat, and 4 bushels 1 peck of malt.[20] Another lease

[99] Oriel Coll. Mun. DLR 6; *Cal. Pat.* 1494–1509, 314. It was said to be held of the king of the Earldom of Warwick. See Glos. R.O. D 184/M 14/2, 3 etc. for courts held by the earls.

[1] *Feud. Aids*, ii. 255, 272.

[2] Ibid. 288; *Coll. Top. & Gen.* iii. 360.

[3] Glos. R.O. D 184/M14/1–21; Oriel Coll. Mun. DLR 6. See also ibid. S II. 1. 2 for courts of 1751–6.

[4] Oriel Coll. Mun. DELL 2, no. 1.

[5] See p. 140.

[6] Par. Rec., surveyors' accts. 1777–1832, 1836; overseers' accts. 1799–1808, 1808–16, 1816–20, 1821–31. The following account is based on these records, except where otherwise stated.

[7] *Poor Abstract*, 182–3. The figure in the overseers' accts. is £2 less.

[8] *2nd Rep. Poor Law Com.* 128–9.

[9] *Poor Law Unions*, 21.

[10] At the end of the overseers' accts. for 1816–20 is a partial account for £112 for the building of these houses.

[11] *Dom. Bk.* (Rec. Com.), i. 163*b*. For radknights see *V.C.H. Salop.* i. 301.

[12] A. S. Ellis, 'Domesday tenants of Gloucester', *Trans. B.G.A.S.* iv. 96.

[13] *Pipe R.* 1195 (P.R.S. N.S. vi), 56.

[14] *Cal. Pat.* 1317–21, 100, 176.

[15] *Glos. Subsidy Roll 1327* (priv. print by Sir Thos. Philips, n.d.), 37–38.

[16] See p. 189.

[17] C 3/271/12.

[18] Oriel Coll. Mun. S II. 1. 14, p. 28; see p. 144.

[19] S.P. 14/vol. cx, p. 48.

[20] Oriel Coll. Mun. DELL 2, no. 1.

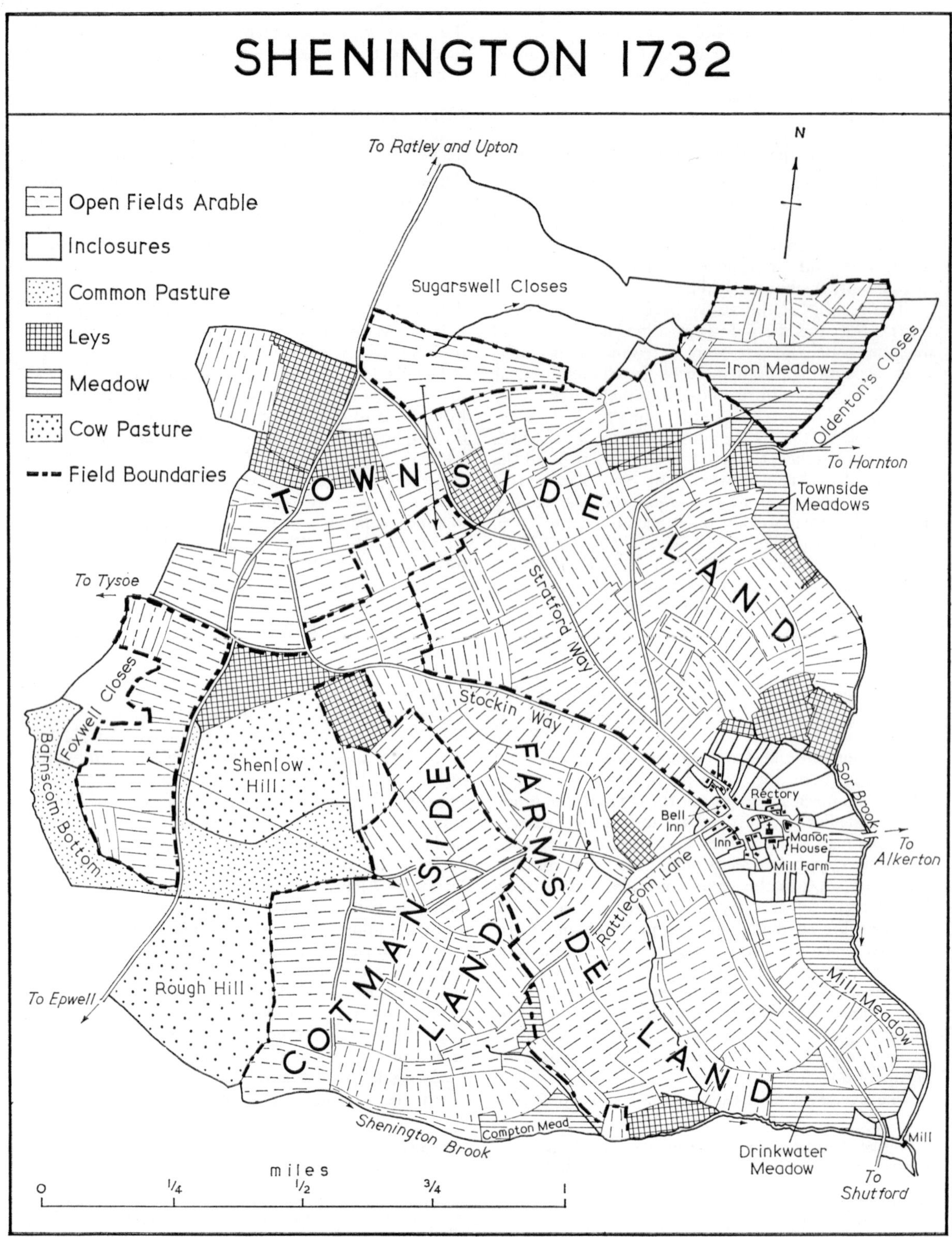

Based on a map by Robert Whittlesey at Oriel College, Oxford.

of $\frac{3}{4}$ yardland which had been for 7*s*. 6*d*. in 1569 was renewed in 1627 for 6*s*. 8*d*. and 2 bushels, $\frac{1}{2}$ peck of wheat, and 2½ bushels of malt.[21] Copyhold land was taken for three lives, each life to enjoy sole use, although the first taker had the right to surrender the copy if he so wished.[22] In 1699 it was said that the custom was to hold for one life in possession and two lives in reversion, and the executor to hold the customary premises for one year.[23] The land was handed over 'by the rod' in open court by the steward.[24] Court records survive for 1693 to 1718 and in these courts heriots were taken regularly.[25] The heriot was usually a horse or mare, i.e. the best animal, for a yardland or more, but other possessions might be taken, as in 1693 when the heriot from a cottager was a table worth 1*s*. 6*d*.[26] Rents were low: in 1619 a yardland was rented at 16*s*. and a cottage at 2*s*. to 3*s*. a year, and late-17th-century courts specified a 'customary rent', which evidently had changed little from the early 17th century.[27] On the other hand heavy fines were sometimes taken: £80 for the reversion of 3 yardlands in 1693, and £100 in another case; for 1½ yardland in 1699, however, it was only £15, while no fine was taken for a cottage.[28] Sub-letting of premises could be done with licence from the court: in 1713 the tenant of 4 yardlands paid 10*s*. for licence to sub-let for 50 years.[29]

Yeomen and husbandmen maintained a vigorous hold on the parish under this system, although the hearth tax returns of 1672 suggest that many had only a modest standard of living. Ten householders were assessed on 3 to 6 hearths, 8 on 2 hearths, and 24 on only 1 hearth each; 16 of these were discharged on account of poverty.[30] The land tax of 1724 indicates the distribution of wealth: John Goodwin, lord of Sugarswell, and the rector each paid about a sixth of the total land tax of £41, while 9 other contributors were assessed at between £1 and £4 and 9 between £1 and 4*d*.[31] Probably the largest farm in the parish was the Goodwins' Sugarswell farm, which had 5 yardlands (i.e. 150 a.) of arable, meadow, and pasture in 1687, as well as Sugarswell Closes.[32]

The size of holdings in the open field is given in a survey of 1732 when there were 26 tenants holding 26¼ yardlands of college customary or leasehold land, 21¾ yardlands of free land, and 76 a. of common, apart from Sugarswell. Six of the farms, consisting of 100 to 163 a. were comparatively large for that date; 9 were of 20 a. to 73 a. and 10 of under 20 a.[33] Much land was still copyhold and in 1737 Oriel College tenants included 3 leaseholders, 6 copyholders, and 6 cottagers, paying a total rent of £23 5*s*., of which the copyholders paid some £14 12*s*. for 20¼ yardlands in the open fields and 8 cottages. The land was valued at £10 a yardland. At inclosure in 1780 there had been a slight increase in the number of larger farms: there were 5 farms of 100 to 216 a., and the holdings of under 20 a. had decreased to five.[34] Oriel College had by this time increased the amount of its leasehold and there were 7 leasehold estates. A survey of the parish made for the inclosure commissioners shows that the college possessed 1,481 a., of which 739 a. were freehold and 527 a. copyhold and leasehold, and Edward Sadler had 48 a. in the open fields besides his 71 a. of old inclosure. The total annual value of this 1,601 a., presumably the whole parish, was *c*. £1,032.[35]

The open fields extended over most of the parish, particularly to the south and west. Field-names compounded with 'stocking', i.e. clearing, which are found near Shenlow Hill indicate the piecemeal clearing by which the hill land was added to the open field: by the 18th century the open field extended right up the hilly sides of the valley to the foot of Shenlow Hill. In 1732 Shenington Field was divided into three, Townside, Farmside, and Cotmanside, which may have represented the three original fields; each was in turn divided into four parts for cropping.[36] The system of cropping, however, was complicated and shows the extent to which flexibility could be introduced into open-field farming if the small farmer was willing. Three-quarters of both Townside and Farmside were ploughed and sowed each year with wheat, pease, and barley, and a quarter was fallow, or used, if so desired, as a pease 'hitch'. Cotmanside had one quarter sowed with wheat and another with barley; the rest was either fallow or 'hitch'. Thus, by this system one quarter of the land normally grew wheat, another barley, while pulses could be grown on a sixth to a half of the arable; the fallow could be omitted altogether if so desired.[37]

A certain amount of the parish was laid down in 'leys',[38] which were interspersed with the arable strips. This method of farming was characteristic of north Oxfordshire parishes. Shenington New House, for example, had some 17½ leys attached to its holding in the common fields in 1657,[39] and in 1732 the leys lying in furlongs were shown on the map.[40] Grazing ground was provided on Rough Hill, and at Barnscom and Shenlow: Rough Hill and Shenlow were cow-pasture each year and were broken about 12 May, while Barnscom was fallow for sheep every other year. The Hill ground near Iron Meadow was allotted in proportion to the number of yardlands every other year.[41] In 1732 the stint of common was 2 cows and 28 sheep a yardland, but in 1760 there were also said to be 2 horse commons to the yardland.[42] There was much meadow land available by Alkerton Brook: Iron Meadow, Drinkwater Meadow, Comptons Mead, Townside Meadow, and Mill Meadow were recorded in 1732.[43] Some of them were certainly lot meadows, for in

[21] Oriel Coll. Mun. DELL 2, no. 11.
[22] C 3/76/1.
[23] Oriel Coll. Mun. LR 6, Sept. 1699.
[24] Ibid., Oct. 1693.
[25] Ibid., 1693–1718.
[26] Ibid., Oct. 1693.
[27] C 3/76/1; Oriel Coll. Mun. LR 6.
[28] Oriel Coll. Mun. LR 6, Oct. 1693, Oct. 1697, Oct. 1699.
[29] Ibid., Feb. 1699, July 1713.
[30] E 179/247/14.
[31] Oriel Coll. Mun. S II. 1. 97.
[32] Ibid. DLR 6. There were 11 closes attached to this farm in 1731: ibid.
[33] Ibid. S II. 1. 19.
[34] Ibid. S II. 1. 14.
[35] Ibid.
[36] Ibid. S II. 1. 19.
[37] Ibid. For an explanation of the cropping see M. A. Havinden, 'Agricultural Progress in Open-Field Oxfordshire', *Agric. Hist. Rev.* ix (2), 79.
[38] Terriers give the impression that leys were not changed or ploughed up very often.
[39] Oriel Coll. Mun. S II. 1. 93.
[40] Ibid. R 8.
[41] Ibid. S II. 1. 19.
[42] Ibid.; S II. 1. 3.
[43] Ibid. R 8.

1692 one yardland included ½ a. of lot grass in 'Onlcaour' and 'Hartioum', in 1708 another holding had 1½ a. of lot meadow, part of it adjoining Sugarswell, and in 1732 Mill Meadow was shown divided into lots.[44] Other valuable rights were held over the furze and fern in the parish: a yardland holding in 1692 had a small plot of fern at Rough Hill and another of furze and thorns in Shenlow.[45] Coles Furze and Syms Furze are shown on the 1732 map.[46]

Holdings in the open field were not consolidated but lay in scattered parcels of single acres, butts, leys, and *hades* right up to the date of inclosure: in 1692, for instance, one yardland lay in 67 pieces, and in 1732 two yardlands were distributed in some 114 different pieces.[47] A farm of 209 a. in 1763, which had recently been two farms, had only 20 inclosed acres lying in two parcels.[48]

From the early 18th century, however, Oriel College had been preparing for inclosure, and specified in their leases that the lessee must assent if the college was at any time minded to inclose.[49] During the 18th century Oriel also acquired more leaseholds. In 1760, when a survey was made, there were 8 leaseholders, 6 copyholders, and 8 cottagers, and details were given of 'improved rents' which, for example, were as much as £53 for 4½ yardlands compared with the earlier rent of £3 4*s*. It was said that if the land were inclosed it could be let at 15*s*. an acre a year instead of £10 a yardland;[50] since in 1732 there were almost 30 a. to the average yardland in Shenington, this would be a significant increase.[51] In the award of 1780[52] 1,434 a. were inclosed, of which 1,034 a. were open field and 400 a. were waste and common.[53] The chief proprietors, Oriel College, William Harrison, and Edward Sadler, lord of Sugarswell, received 673 a., 187 a., and 146 a. respectively. Three others received 47 a., 36 a., and 28 a., whilst the remaining 8 received less than 15 a. each.

The changed appearance of the parish is shown by a map of 1781, made when the land had been grouped into consolidated farms.[54] It is difficult to judge the average size of holdings from one estate alone, but surveys of the Oriel copyhold and leasehold estates (699 a.) in the early 19th century suggest that the small tenant was gradually being eliminated, especially after the Napoleonic Wars. In 1813 there were still 7 holdings of under 1 a. and 9 holdings of 3 a. to 45 a., but in 1831 the 11 tenants of the estate each held over 20 a.[55] The rise in value forecast at the time of inclosure took place over the subsequent 30 years and in 1813 699 a. held by Oriel College were valued at £1,563, far more than the total value of the parish in 1780; this may have been artificially inflated by the war, for in 1831 the estate was valued at £1,040, still, however, a considerable increase.[56] The rise was partly due to more exacting leases and stricter farm management. By 1813 there were 15 leaseholders on the college estate[57] and leases of the early 19th century show that entry fines were increased: a yardland which paid only £9 in 1718 paid £90 for an entry fine in 1820.[58] In the mid-19th century the college began to introduce rack-rents: a holding which paid £11 rent in 1836, with a fine of £160, paid a rack-rent of £140 in 1854.[59] By 1881 there were only 11 a. of copyhold and the rest of the estate (839 a.) was let out at rack-rents.[60]

College policy to a certain extent dictated the type of farming in the parish. Leases, for example, still included the providing of grain and malt for the college: amounts of 216 and 180 gallons of wheat are recorded.[61] College leases from the 1820s demanded a sum of £50 a year for every acre of meadow and pasture ground converted into tillage; the premises were to be managed in a husbandlike manner, i.e. no meadow was to be mown more than once a year, and all dung, soil, and compost was to be used on the farm.[62] In 1854 an Oriel lease of Rough Hill farm (81 a.) claimed that most of the farm was of a high quality and easy cultivation, although it needed better drainage. The land was divided between wheat (26 a.), vetches and fallow (12 a.), clover (7 a.), fallow (11 a.), and 'old lay' (9 a.); in the following year 25 a. was under barley.[63]

By the mid-19th century there were about 12 farms in the parish or about half the number before inclosure.[64] Seven were of between 100 a. and 210 a., the remainder were between 30 and 80 a. and there was one smallholding of 7 a. The two largest farms employed 10 and 9 labourers.[65] In 1914 the parish contained much excellent cornland and the crops were wheat (20 per cent.), barley (21 per cent.), and oats (13 per cent.), with some roots: swedes and turnips (8 per cent.), mangolds (2 per cent.), and potatoes (1 per cent.). By this time 51 per cent. of the cultivated area of the parish was pasture.[66] In 1900 sheep flocks were common and dairy farming almost non-existent. Milk was used mainly for butter-making. A 7-course rotation was used.[67] During the Second World War the emphasis naturally shifted to arable and the first combined harvester to be used in Shenington was on Sugarswell farm in 1940. Some good farming land was taken for an airfield.[68] After the war there was a return to pasture farming. In 1962 Sugarswell farm (350 a.) was chiefly devoted to the production of beef cattle, seven-eighths of the produce being sent to Tipton (Staffs.) and only a small proportion to Banbury. Mill farm (160 a.), Lower farm (57 a.), and Rectory farm (200 a.) concentrated on grazing and dairy farming, while Oriel farm (180 a.) kept mainly pedigree Wessex Saddle Back pigs and had only 60 a. of arable; these farms mainly used Banbury for their market.[69]

Perhaps because of its distance from Banbury

[44] Oriel Coll. Mun. S II. 1. 94; DLR 6: terrier 1708.
[45] Ibid. S II. 1. 94.
[46] Ibid. R 8.
[47] Ibid. S II. 1. 94; R 8.
[48] *Oxf. Jnl.* Dec. 17 1763.
[49] e.g. Oriel Coll. Mun. DELL 2, no. 1.
[50] Ibid. S II. 1. 3.
[51] Ibid. S II. 1. 19.
[52] Shenington Incl. Act., 20 Geo. III, c 49 (priv. act); O.R.O., incl. award.
[53] Gray, *Eng. Field Systems*, 538.
[54] Oriel Coll. Mun.
[55] Ibid. S II. 1. 18.
[56] Ibid.
[57] Ibid.
[58] e.g. ibid. DELL 2, no. 1; cf. DELL 1, 3.
[59] Ibid. DELL 3.
[60] Bodl. G.A. Oxon. 8° 1357.
[61] e.g. Oriel Coll. Mun. DELL 2, no. 1; DELL 3.
[62] Ibid.
[63] Ibid. DLR 6.
[64] *Kelly's Dir. Oxon.* (1864).
[65] Bodl. G.A. Oxon. 8° 1357.
[66] Orr, *Oxon. Agric.* 171, and statistical plates.
[67] Ex inf. Mr. G. C. Middleton.
[68] Local information.
[69] Ibid.

Shenington supported a flourishing community of craftsmen and shopkeepers in the 19th century: in 1851 there were 4 carpenters, 2 blacksmiths, a wheelwright, a basket-maker, 2 shoemakers, a dressmaker, a milliner, 3 grocers, a maltster, a beerseller, and 2 butchers.[70] In 1869 among others a pig-dealer and a haulier and in 1895 a cattle-dealer were recorded.[71] Shenington also had a number of masons: in 1851 9 men were engaged as stone-masons, stone-cutters, or carvers; in 1864 2 masons and a stone-mason and in 1869 one stone-mason were recorded.[72] A blacksmith survived into the 1920s.[73] There was a surgeon in the village in 1895.[74]

Shenington mill descended with the manor from 1086.[75] Its ownership was divided similarly into fifths and by the 17th century four-fifths evidently belonged to Oriel College and one-fifth to the Goodwins' manor.[76] This must have been the reason for the later claim that one-fifth of Shenington mill was free land, by contrast with college customary land.[77] It was a water corn-mill. At the end of the 15th century the miller was regularly presented in the courts leet for taking excessive tolls.[78] Seventeenth-century courts record its tenure by the Grimes family, customary tenants; in the 19th century it was held by lease and in 1808 the tenant paid 15*s.* a year rent and an entry fine of £80.[79] In 1855 the mill worked with two pairs of stones and depended for its water on a few uncertain springs, sufficient for grinding wheat for a short period only each year. It was valued at £54 10*s.* a year and its fall in value was blamed at that time on competition from steam mills and farmers' hand mills.[80] Leases of the mill survive up to 1875 but it probably ceased to operate soon afterwards and was not marked on the Ordnance Survey map of 1882.[81]

CHURCH. Shenington was included in Worcester Diocese until it was transferred in 1541 to the newly created Gloucester Diocese. In 1837 it was restored to Worcester Diocese.[82] In 1900 Shenington was united with Alkerton and became part of Oxford Diocese.[83]

The church was in existence by the first quarter of the 12th century when Robert Sor gave the advowson to Tewkesbury Abbey.[84] Within a few years the grant was confirmed by Robert's son Odo and Simon, Bishop of Worcester.[85] The abbey did not always present;[86] at least one papal provision was made, for in 1310 Odo, son of John Colonna, was provided.[87] On Odo's death the Pope granted to his brother, Cardinal Peter Colonna, a faculty to present.[88]

On the eve of the Dissolution, in 1534, Tewkesbury granted away one turn of the advowson,[89] probably on condition that, if necessary, it would be used to provide one of the monks with a benefice. In 1544 the advowson, which had reverted to the Crown, was granted to Richard Andrews and George Lysle,[90] but by 1551 it had come into the possession of the Sheldon family of Beoley (Worcs.);[91] William Sheldon presented in 1560 and in 1567[92] and Thomas Sheldon in 1577.[93]

The Sheldon family were Roman Catholics from the time of Ralph Sheldon (1537–1613) and so disqualified from exercising their patronage, although they held the advowson until the mid-18th century.[94] The first turn was granted to Anne Dochin, who presented in 1615. In 1642 John Keyte and Thomas Child presented,[95] but the bishop at first refused to institute their nominee, having been warned against it by William, Lord Saye and Sele, who seems to have questioned their right to present.[96] Child, a member of the famous banking firm, made another presentation in 1658.[97] In 1677, Sheldon Beeby, presumably a Protestant relation of the Sheldons, presented.[98] In 1717 George Carter presented, and in 1720 Oxford University presented under the Act of 1606 regulating presentations by recusants.[99] By 1738 George Lee, Earl of Lichfield (d. 1742/3), had acquired an interest in the advowson.[1] The Lee family were recorded as patrons in 1743, 1750, and 1779.[2] Robert Child, however, presented in 1772[3] and his trustees were patrons in 1801.[4] The whole of his estate was left by will to his grand-daughter, Sarah Sophia, who married George, Earl of Jersey, and the advowson of Shenington thereafter followed the descent of Alkerton.[5]

Shenington was valued at £12 6*s.* 8*d.* in 1291[6] and £15 3*s.* 4*d.* in 1535.[7] In 1650 it was worth £80,[8]

[70] H.O. 107/1733.
[71] *Kelly's Dir. Oxon.* (1869, 1895).
[72] H.O. 107/1733; *Kelly's Dir. Oxon.* (1864, 1869).
[73] *Kelly's Dir. Oxon.* (1915 and later edns.).
[74] Ibid. (1895).
[75] *Dom. Bk.* (Rec. Com.), i, 163*b* and see pp. 140–1.
[76] E.g. *Cal. Pat.* 1554–5, 256; Oriel Coll. Mun. S II. 1. 85; C.P. 43/350, rot. 136.
[77] Oriel Coll. Mun. DLR 6.
[78] Glos. R.O. D 184/M14/1, 3, 4 etc.
[79] Oriel Coll. Mun. DLR 6, 1693; DELL 3, leases.
[80] Ibid. DLR 6, valuation 1855.
[81] Ibid. DELL 3, leases; O.S. Map 25″ Oxon. V. 5 (1st edn.). See also Oriel Coll. Mun., maps of 1732, 1781, 1813, and 1870.
[82] *Lond. Gaz.* Aug. 18, 1837 (p. 2174).
[83] MS. Oxf. Dioc. c 1997.
[84] Dugdale, *Mon.* ii. 71.
[85] Ibid.
[86] *Reg. Giffard* (Worcs. Hist. Soc.), ii. 167; for Tewkesbury's patronage see *Reg. Sede Vacante* (Worcs. Hist. Soc.), intro., pp. cviii, cxv; pt. iii, pp. xx, xxii.
[87] *Cal. Papal Regs.* ii. 69, 71.
[88] Ibid. 95.
[89] Hockaday Abs. cccxxxv.
[90] *L. & P. Hen. VIII*, xix (2), p. 76; Hockaday Abs. cccxxxv.
[91] 'Bishop Hooper's Visit.', *E.H.R.* xix. 107. William Sheldon was patron.
[92] Hockaday Abs. cccv. For the Sheldon family see E. A. B. Barnard, *The Sheldons, passim.*
[93] Hockaday Abs. cccxxxv.
[94] Ralph Sheldon was patron in 1603: B.M. Harl. MS. 594; f. 247. Atkyns, *Glos.* 338 has Mr. Sheldon as patron in 1768; cf. Par. Rec., chwdns' accts. *sub anno* 1752 when Mr. Sheldon was one of the chief contributors to the cost of the church gallery.
[95] P.R.O., Inst. Bks.; Hockaday Abs. cccxxxv.
[96] Hockaday Abs. cccxxxv.
[97] Ibid.
[98] P.R.O., Inst. Bks.
[99] Hockaday Abs. cccxxxv; Act to prevent and avoid dangers which may grow by Popish Recusants, 3 Jas. I c 5.
[1] Hockaday Abs. cccxxxv; F. G. Hilton-Price, *The Marygold by Temple Bar* (London 1902), 38, 63.
[2] Bacon, *Lib. Reg.* 322; G.D.R. 381 A, 397; Rudder, *Glos.* 648.
[3] P.R.O., Inst. Bks.; Bacon, *Lib. Reg.* 322; G.D.R. 381, which has both the Earl of Litchfield and Robert Child as patrons.
[4] G.D.R. 382.
[5] *Complete Peerage*, vii. 91–2; *V.C.H. Mdx.* ii, 109; F. G. Hilton-Price, *The Marygold by Temple Bar*, 85. See pp. 47, 49.
[6] *Tax. Eccl.* (Rec. Com.), 223.
[7] *Valor Eccl.* (Rec. Com.), ii. 503; MS. Ch. Oxon. 34.
[8] C 94/1, f. 29.

by 1738 £120,[9] and by 1779 *c.* £160.[10] In 1835 the benefice was valued at £332,[11] but in 1900 only £220.[12] In 1920 it was worth £325 with Alkerton annexed.[13] At inclosure in 1780 the rector was allotted *c.* 188 a. for tithes.[14] Details of the small tithes were given in 1721: tithe lambs and tithe eggs were taken in kind, but tithe of sheep, milk cows, colts, sucking pigs, and fruit was commuted.[15] Easter offerings were then charged at the rate of 2*d.* a head for adults, and by 1828 at 4*d.* a house.[16] In 1613 the glebe comprised 2 yardlands and 2 closes.[17] At inclosure the rector was awarded *c.* 43 a. for glebe.[18] In 1807, when the rectory estate was leased separately from the rectory-house, it comprised *c.* 212 a., a farmhouse, and other buildings.[19] Most of the glebe was sold in 1920 for £9,000; in 1963 *c.* 11 a. remained.[20]

An annual pension of 13*s.* 4*d.* paid to Tewkesbury Abbey[21] passed with the advowson in 1544 to Richard Andrews and George Lysle.[22]

On several occasions Tewkesbury Abbey presented incumbents who were in minor orders only,[23] and non-residence was common throughout the Middle Ages. A case of non-residence in 1286 resulted from the intrusion, when the rector was still alive, of Robert of Lechlade who already held St. Peter's, Bristol.[24] One rector, a papal chaplain, was not only non-resident in 1309 but was eventually deprived, and it does not seem likely that Odo Colonna, who held three prebends and one other benefice, was even resident in England.[25] At least two medieval rectors were granted long-term study leave.[26] It is not surprising to find that in 1317 the Dean of Worcester was charged with the discovery and punishment of those guilty of concealing the tithes, goods, and other profits of Shenington church.[27]

Several of the 16th-century rectors appear to have been non-resident also, for the parish was being served by curates; there was a curate in 1532,[28] who was still serving there in 1540 and 1544, and in 1545 a parishioner left 10*s.* for him to say a trental. In 1548 another curate was condemned as contumacious.[29] It is possible that Roger Hughes, presented in 1544, who was certainly non-resident, was also a pluralist since a man of this name was presented to Portishead (Som.) in 1543.[30]

The incumbent in 1560 was deprived for refusal to conform to the Elizabethan Settlement; in 1551 his replies to visitation articles had been only satisfactory (*mediocriter*).[31] At that time there were 112 communicants in the parish.[32] The next incumbent, although resident, was described in 1563 as 'a drunkard and a swearer', who said the services so indistinctly that the congregation could neither understand nor join in the responses; he was declared contumacious in 1566 and resigned the following year.[33] His successor, although perfect in scripture, was a pluralist and neglected the church building and goods.[34] The next incumbent, neither a graduate nor a preacher in 1584, had taken a degree by 1593;[35] his incumbency saw a fall in the number of communicants to eighty.[36] In 1615 he was succeeded by another non-resident incumbent.[37]

Nothing is known of the church life of Shenington in the 17th century, except that during the Interregnum it was served by a curate because the minister was aged.[38] For much of the 18th and 19th centuries Shenington was almost a family living. Edward Hughes held it from 1721 to 1735, another Edward Hughes from 1772 to 1801, then Robert Edward Hughes from 1801 to 1846 when his son of the same name was instituted.[39] In 1796 a relation was made assistant curate.[40] In the period 1738–72 Dormer Sheldon was rector. He held the living with another benefice and with a private chaplaincy.[41] There were frequent changes of curates, as many as three between 1739 and 1743.[42] R. E. Hughes also held Broughton after 1814. In 1835 he was instituted to Alkerton and until 1869 the livings were held jointly.[43] On the death of the second R. E. Hughes in 1869 the patron, Lord Jersey, attempted to unite the two livings. The disputes which followed and the later history of the livings after their union in 1900 are described under Alkerton.[44]

Two customs connected with Shenington church should, however, be mentioned here. One is the strewing of grass in the church for three weeks at Whitsun; the other is the Oddfellows or Amicable service which since 1841 has taken place every Trinity Monday.[45] The strewing of grass, brought from Shipton, is mentioned in 1720, and a visitor remarked on the custom in 1778.[46]

The church of *HOLY TRINITY* comprises a nave, chancel, south aisle, and western tower.[47] The earliest part of the church is the former chancel arch, enriched with chevron and cable mouldings, which dates from the 12th century; at the restoration of 1879 it was removed to its present position between the organ chamber and the chancel.[48] The south aisle was built in the 13th century. The dividing arches of the Early English arcade are supported on octagonal shafts with capitals

[9] Hockaday Abs. cccxxxv.
[10] Rudder, *Glos.* 648.
[11] Hockaday Abs. cccxxxv.
[12] MS. Oxf. Dioc. c 1997.
[13] *Kelly's Dir. Oxon.* (1920).
[14] O.R.O., Shenington incl. award.
[15] Shenington Par. Rec., chwdns' accts.
[16] Ibid.; G.D.R. 265A T5.
[17] G.D.R. 265A T1.
[18] O.R.O., Shenington incl. award.
[19] G.D.R. 265A T4
[20] Ex inf. the Rector of Shenington.
[21] *Valor Eccl.* (Rec. Com.), ii. 481; *Ch. Ch. Arch.* 167; Dugdale, *Mon.* ii. 85.
[22] *L. & P. Hen. VIII*, xix(2), p. 76; Hockaday Abs. cccxxxv.
[23] For a list of medieval incumbents see MS. Top. Oxon. d 460.
[24] *Reg. Giffard* (Worcs. Hist. Soc.), ii. 298, 326.
[25] *Reg. Reynolds* (Worcs. Hist. Soc.), 12, 150; *Cal. Papal Regs.* ii. 69, 71, 95.
[26] *Reg. Reynolds* (Worcs. Hist. Soc.), 87; *Cal. Papal Regs.* vi. 9.
[27] *Reg. Sede Vacante* (Worcs. Hist. Soc.), pt. iii. 186.
[28] Hockaday Abs. xxv.
[29] Ibid. xxxi.
[30] Foster, *Alumni.*
[31] Hockaday Abs. cccxxxv; 'Bishop Hooper's Visit.', *E.H.R.* xix. 107.
[32] 'Bishop Hooper's Visit.', *E.H.R.* xix. 107.
[33] Hockaday Abs. cccxxxv; ibid. xliii; B.G.A.S. Libr., MS. Furney B, p. 24.
[34] Hockaday Abs. xliv, xlvii, cccxxxv.
[35] Ibid. xlix, lii.
[36] B.M. Harl. MS. 594, f. 247.
[37] Ibid. Foster, *Alumni, sub* Richard Ingram.
[38] C 94/1, f. 29.
[39] Hockaday Abs. cccxxxv.
[40] G.D.R. 382.
[41] Ibid. 298; Hockaday Abs. cccxxxv.
[42] Hockaday Abs. cccxxxv.
[43] Ibid. and see p. 51.
[44] See p. 51.
[45] Par. Rec. and ex inf. the rector.
[46] Par. Rec., chwdns' accts.; Loveday MSS.
[47] There is a pre-restoration drawing of the church, dated 1844, in the vestry and one of 1833 by J. C. Buckler in MS. Top. Oxon. a 68, no. 456.
[48] Par. Rec.

decorated with stiff-leaf foliage. In the early 14th century windows were inserted in the chancel walls, a rood-screen was erected, and a canopied piscina, a locker, and one stone seat were installed. The south aisle was rebuilt in its present form, with Decorated windows and ashlar-faced walls. Also in the 14th century the nave was heightened and clerestory windows were inserted on the south side. A south porch was added in the 15th century. The west tower cannot be earlier than the late 15th century and the architectural details, in particular the belfry windows, might suggest an even later date. A bequest of 1504 'for the making of the steeple of Shenington' probably dates the work precisely.[49]

The medieval church contained a side altar dedicated to Our Lady.[50]

Box pews were installed in the late-17th or early-18th century.[51] In 1720–21 the roof of the tower was new-leaded, but it is clear that the fabric of the church was in general disrepair at that time. By will proved in 1734 Samuel Davenport, wharfinger of London, left £100 for repairing, rebuilding, or finishing the church.[52] In 1739 fairly extensive repairs to the nave and south aisle, including the rebuilding of a side wall, were carried out.[53] It seems from the large plumber's and carpenter's bills and the references to timber and lead that the work was chiefly connected with roofs.[54] In 1742 Oriel College was asked to give timber for the erection of a gallery for 'a company of singers'.[55] Before the end of the century the north walls of the nave and chancel and the east end of the chancel were rebuilt in 'a bald and tasteless style'.[56]

In 1840 a new church door was put in. In 1867 the west gallery was removed, 'four new windows' were inserted (apparently those now in the north wall of the nave), and the exterior of the church was stuccoed.[57] Restoration was carried out in 1879 by the architect J. L. Pearson, with G. Bartlett of Bloxham as builder.[58] A new chancel arch was built in the 'Early English' style and in the course of this work the upper doorway of the rood-loft staircase, which was in perfect condition in 1841,[59] was obliterated. A vestry was built in the Decorated style, its window partly a copy of the east window of the chancel. The east window itself was altered and placed higher in the wall. The west window of the south aisle and another window were entirely renewed and were copied exactly from the original windows. New bases were put to all the pillars. The whole church was re-roofed in oak. It was presumably in the course of this work that all '18th-century ugliness' was replaced by work in the Gothic style. The old box-pews were replaced by pitch pine open benches and the 14th-century rood-loft which formed the back of one of the box-pews in 1841[60] was presumably destroyed. Oak choir stalls, pulpit, and lectern were installed and a reredos erected. The chancel and the aisles of the nave were tiled. A new font, made before 1821, was removed from the chancel to the west end of the south aisle.[61] New heating apparatus was installed.

In 1948 the church acquired electric light.[62]

The earliest monumental inscriptions are to Mary Goodwin (d. 1666/7), and to Robert (d. 1699) and Elizabeth Pettifer (d. 1713), who did 'much good to their relations and the poor'. The tablet to the Pettifers was put up in 1716 by Samuel Davenport (d. 1734), whose own bequest to the parish was commemorated by the churchwardens in 1739. There is a tablet to Arthur Blythman, rector for 57 years (1869–1926), and a memorial window to R. E. Hughes (rector 1801–46).

In the external wall of the south aisle is a medieval sculpture representing a man and an ox. Stained glass windows, designed by Jones & Willis of Birmingham, were erected in 1909, 1920, and 1921.[63]

The church possesses a silver Elizabethan chalice and paten cover, both hall-marked 1576.[64]

The five bells were all cast in 1678 by Henry Bagley and were hung on a frame of 1615. They were rehung *c.* 1926.[65] A clock was placed in the tower before 1720.[66]

The registers of baptisms and burials are complete from 1721 and the register of marriages from 1753.[67]

NONCONFORMITY. A group of 6 Protestant nonconformists was recorded in 1676.[68] These may all have been Quakers, for the registers of the Banbury Division give 6 family names for Shenington in the late 17th century and 7 in the 18th century.[69] There was no meeting-house, and Shenington Friends seem to have attended the one at Shutford.[70]

In 1815 a Shenington blacksmith certified to the Bishop of Gloucester that his shop was used for a dissenting meeting and in 1818 and 1819 a Methodist minister of Banbury sent in certificates first for the blacksmith's shop and then for a chapel.[71] The chapel lay just on the Shenington side of the stream separating the villages of Shenington and Alkerton, and in 1851 was being shared by Independents and Primitive Methodists, the former having a congregation of 55, the latter of 80.[72] These figures probably included people from neighbouring villages. By 1869 the chapel was described as Primitive Methodist only.[73] In 1878 the rector found the dissenters still numerous and the Primitive Methodists 'very consequential and self-opinionated'.[74] The chapel was in use in 1962.[75]

SCHOOLS. 'School-house close' in Shenington was mentioned in 1732, but no further evidence of a

[49] Hockaday Abs. cccxxxv.
[50] Ibid.
[51] Ibid.
[52] Somerset House, P.C.C. Ockham 238.
[53] Par. Rec., chwdns' accts. 1720–89.
[54] Ibid. The total cost was *c.* £138.
[55] Oriel Coll. Mun. LR 6.
[56] Beesley, *Hist. Banbury*, 141.
[57] Par. Rec., chwdns' accts. 1720–89.
[58] Par. Rec. The following details of the work done at the restoration are taken from the faculty and a 19th-century MS. account of the church in the parish chest.
[59] Beesley, *Hist. Banbury*, 142.
[60] Ibid.
[61] MS. Top. Oxon. a 68, no. 455; MS. Top. Eccles. b 14.
[62] Par. Rec., faculty.
[63] MS. Oxf. Dioc. c 1997.
[64] Evans, *Ch. Plate.*
[65] Par. Rec., MS. acct. The faculty was obtained in 1926: MS. Oxf. Dioc. c 1997.
[66] Par. Rec., chwdns' accts.
[67] Par. Rec.
[68] Compton Census.
[69] Banbury Quaker Regs.
[70] Ibid.: evidence of burials. The last Shenington entry was in 1760.
[71] Hockaday Abs. cccxxxv.
[72] Gardner, *Dir. Oxon.* (1852); H.O. 129/163.
[73] MS. Oxf. Dioc. c 332.
[74] MS. Oxf. Dioc. c 344.
[75] Local information.

school before the 19th century has been found.[76] In 1819 a school was reported to which 'all the poor' sent their children. It was supported by voluntary subscriptions and was on the National plan. This school, which was also attended by children from Alkerton, was thought to be adequate for the needs of the population.[77] In 1833 it had 27 boys and 41 girl pupils, and was described as a day and Sunday school.[78] In 1871 a National Church of England school was built. Boys, girls, and infants were taught in one room and by one teacher who was appointed by the incumbent and churchwardens. A Sunday school was held and night school twice a week. Children's payments supplemented the parliamentary grant, subscriptions, and a small endowment. There was accommodation for 78, and an average attendance of 40[79] rising to 47 by 1896.[80] The number of children attending school had increased to 100 by 1903 and in 1905 the school was enlarged.[81] In 1962 Shenington school had aided status and there were 37 children on the roll.[82]

CHARITIES. One J. Davenport of London (d. 1734) gave £120, by will, for the poor. The bequest was partly lost through unsecured loans, but the rector, said in 1828 that his father, when rector, recovered some and invested £119 8*s.* In 1828 the rector received a dividend of £3 11*s.* 7*d.* which was distributed by him and the churchwardens. Samuel Davenport left £220, a bequest commemorated by a tablet put up in the church in 1739. No later information has been found.

One J. Ward, by will dated 1812, gave £40 to the minister and churchwardens, half for bread for the aged poor and half in cash to the same and to fatherless children in distress. In 1828 it was reported that the executor regularly paid interest to the churchwardens.[83]

TADMARTON

TADMARTON lies 5 miles south-west of Banbury.[1] The ancient parish covered 2,070 a. in 1801 and there have been no subsequent boundary changes.[2] Some of the landmarks of an estate granted to Abingdon Abbey in the 10th century can still be recognized as the boundary marks of the modern parish: *Haeslford* is the ford by the present Hazelford Mill: the northern boundary still runs near *Haeslburh*, an earthwork east of the Shutford road,[3] *Woh Burne* is the Sor Brook; and *Eald Ford* may possibly be at Lower Tadmarton Mill where Abingdon Abbey had a fulling-mill at the turn of the 13th century.[4] The medieval custom of perambulating parish boundaries was kept up into the post-Reformation period, but in 1759 the rector complained that this custom had been long neglected.[5]

The greater part of the parish to the north and south of Upper and Lower Tadmarton lies at about 500 ft., but the land drops to 400 ft. along the stream beds and rises to 600 ft. on Tadmarton Heath in the south-west, and to 641 ft. in the centre of the Iron-Age camp there. For the most part the landscape is one of undulating hills and heathland, but a couple of small copses were planted in the late 19th century,[6] and there are many elms and oaks in the post-inclosure hedges.

The parish lies on the Middle Lias or Lower Oolite strata. The land, composed of sand with a subsoil of limestone, is well-watered by streams, and there is even now much marsh. The upkeep of bridges has therefore been a constant burden.[7] In 1774, for example, £3 10*s.* was paid for the repair of the 'Town Bridge', and nearly £15 for Lower Tadmarton Bridge.[8] In 1866 the latter was pulled down and rebuilt with 3 arches.[9] The Town Bridge was recently rebuilt by the R.D.C. as the old bridge had been partially washed away.[10]

The chief road in the parish connects Swalcliffe with Bloxham and runs through Upper Tadmarton. Lower Tadmarton lies at the junction of this road with a road from Wigginton, which follows the line of a prehistoric track going from the Cotswolds through Tadmarton Camp to Northampton. Until well into the 19th century this route was used by Welsh drovers who could travel for over 100 miles without going through a toll-gate.[11] Eighteenth-century records testify to the parish's activities in the repair of roads; as many as 22 labourers were engaged in 1768 in mending the highways.[12] Bridle roads were also important: one led in 1775 from Tadmarton Field by the ford into Bloxham Field, another from Tadmarton village to Lower Fulling Mill in Broughton, another from Lower Tadmarton to Milcombe.[13]

The area was settled early: an Iron-Age camp lies *c.* 1½ mile south-west of the village and 2½ miles from Madmarston Camp, which lies just outside the parish boundary. Two barrows once lying on the heath north-west of Tadmarton Camp have been totally destroyed.[14] East of the centre of the camp was a medieval well, known as Holy Well; nearby, human remains, a spear-head, and Roman coins have been found. A spring rises on the hillside there and runs into Lower Tadmarton.[15] In the 20th century part of the heath has been made into a

[76] Oriel Coll. Mun. S II. 119.
[77] *Educ. of Poor*, 310.
[78] *Educ. Enq. Abstract*, 325; see p. 53.
[79] Ed. 7/101/177.
[80] *Schs. aided by Parl. grants* (1896), 191.
[81] *List of Sch.* (1906), 529; *Kelly's Dir. Oxon.* (1915).
[82] Ex inf. Oxon. Co. Educ. Cttee.
[83] *21st Rep. Com. Char.*
[1] The following maps were used for this article: O.S. Map 25″ Oxon. V. 14, 15, IX. 2, 3, 6, 7 (1st edn.); ibid. 6″ Oxon. IX. (1st edn.); ibid. 1/25,000 SP 33 (1959), SP 43 (1957).
[2] *Census*, 1801, 1961; O.S. *Area Bk.*
[3] O.S. Map 25″ Oxon. V. 14.
[4] *P.N. Oxon.* (E.P.N.S.), ii. 407; *Chron. Abingdon* (Rolls Ser.), i. 192–3, 198. For the mill see p. 154.
[5] MS. Oxf. Dioc. d 557.
[6] O.S. Map 25″ Oxon. IX. 6 (1st edn.).
[7] O.R.O., Cal. Q. Sess. viii.
[8] MS. Tadmarton Surveyors' accts. in Arkell's MS. Bk. *penes* Lord Saye and Sele, Broughton Castle.
[9] Ibid.
[10] Local information
[11] Beesley, *Hist. Banbury*, 12.
[12] MS. Surveyors' accts.
[13] O.R.O., S. & F. colln. (uncat.).
[14] *V.C.H. Oxon.* ii. 316–17, 347.
[15] Ibid. i. 344, 372; O.S. Map 25″ Oxon. IX. 6 (1st edn.).

Lower Tadmarton

Horley church: 18th-century organ

Tadmarton church: 12th-century nave arcade

Shenington: strip lynchets and ridge and furrow north of the village

Ironstone mining near Alkerton

golf course and Holywell Farm (dated 1783) has become the club house.

Upper Tadmarton village lies at a height of 400 ft., and its houses stretch for about ¼ mile along the main road. The church, the manor-house, the 'Lampet Arms', and the school form a nucleus in the north, while the pound and a group of farm-houses form another at the south and lower end. The hamlet of Lower Tadmarton is sited on a feeder of the Sor Brook about ¼ mile away; its farms and cottages are scattered except for a row of cottages and a farm near the mill.[16] The place name may derive from *tademere tun*, signifying the *tun* by the frog pool, but the early forms suggest that the second element was not *mere* but *gemaer*, signifying a boundary.[17] In either case it is likely that the ford was the original attraction for settlers, and Lower Tadmarton the earlier of the two settlements.

In the Middle Ages the two villages seem to have been among the smaller ones in the hundred.[18] In 1642 there were 77 subscribers to the Protestation Oath,[19] in 1738 there were said to be *c.* 30 families at Upper Tadmarton and 17 at Lower Tadmarton, and in 1750 the rector recorded 186 males and 153 females.[20] The number of houses in the parish rose sharply from 58 in 1768 to 80 or 90 in 1781.[21] The population increased from 387 in 1801 to 450 in 1851, the peak year.[22] In 1802 Upper Tadmarton had more than twice as many inhabitants as its hamlet.[23] By 1901 numbers were down to 301 but by 1961 had risen to 386.[24]

Both villages still retain much of their 16th- and 17th-century regional character, for many of the 26 houses listed for the Hearth Tax of 1665 survive.[25] Most are 2-storied structures of coursed ironstone rubble, sometimes with ashlar quoins; they have stone or later brick chimney stacks, casement windows, some with stone mullions and square labels, and thatched roofs. Some houses have large projecting bread-ovens or stair-cases. Several red-brick cottages with roofs of Welsh slate were put up in the 19th century and later. There has been much 20th-century building in yellowish brick in the main street and at the Banbury end.

The manor-house, now used as a farm-house, never had a resident lord, and was probably always leased.[26] In the 17th century the Pargiters may have been the lessees. If so it was a house with 3 hearths in 1665 when there were two Robert Pargiters in the village, each assessed for the Hearth Tax on 3 hearths.[27] The present house is mainly early-18th-century, when one wing was probably remodelled and the other new built, but in a traditional late-17th-century style. The stone and thatched barn belonging to this house is certainly the oldest structure in the village, and must have been built by Abingdon Abbey. With its arched brace tie-beams it is similar to the New College 14th-century barn at Swalcliffe, but its character and workmanship is more modest and is considered to be rather later in date.[28]

The Old Rectory was by far the largest house in Tadmarton in 1665, when it was assessed on 8 hearths. Ruinous in 1802–4, it was rebuilt in 1842 and was later described as a 'handsome modern structure'.[29] Nevertheless, it retains much of the earlier house at the back. Both parts are of coursed ironstone rubble; the older part was stone-slated while the new house was roofed with Welsh slates. A sundial on the stabling is dated 174 (?). The house was sold in 1946 and became a private house.[30] A large house in Lower Tadmarton, probably identifiable with that assessed on 5 hearths in 1665, dates partly from the 17th century and still has 2 original stone mullioned windows with a square label; the northern half of the house must have been rebuilt after its destruction by fire in 1826.[31] It has a late-17th-century dovecot. Old Malthouse Cottage, perhaps the oldest surviving dwelling, is a 16th- or 17th-century building, originally having a single-room plan of 1½ story, 2 rooms serving as a new hall and parlour. There was a cellar beneath the parlour. The house was modernized in 1954.[32] The 'Lampet Arms', which replaced the earlier 'Red Lion',[33] is a large red-brick Victorian structure named after Capt. W. L. Lampet, one of Tadmarton's principal landowners in the mid-19th century.[34] The Methodist chapel was built in 1861 and the stone school replaced an earlier schoolroom in 1876.[35]

Since the Second World War the R.D.C. has built a housing estate of 12 houses on the Swalcliffe road for the use of agricultural workers.

Outside the village Tadmarton House, just off the Bloxham road, was built in the 19th century. It was the home of Capt. W. L. Lampet in 1852 and the Lodge has the Lampet arms carved on it.[36]

MANOR. In the 10th century the land of the two Tadmartons formed a royal estate. In 956 King Edwy is reputed to have granted 10 hides of it to his thegn Beorhtnoth, 5 hides to another thegn Beorhtric, and another 5 hides to the *princeps* Beorhtnoth.[37] These 20 hides later came into the possession of Abingdon Abbey, who retained them until the Reformation. After the Conquest Abbot Aethelm was induced to grant the vill to Robert d'Oilly, Sheriff of Oxfordshire, but he subsequently regained possession in return for an annual rent of £10.[38] D'Oilly seems to have caused the abbey much trouble at this period, among other things taking possession of a meadow in Oxford which belonged to Tadmarton manor. He renounced his

[16] O.S. Map 25″ Oxon. IX. 2, 3.
[17] *P.N. Oxon.* (E.P.N.S.), ii. 406.
[18] See p. 189.
[19] *Protestation Ret.* 48–9. Actually 80 names are listed but 3 are identical with the 3 preceding ones. As one of that group bears the unusual Christian name of Organ, it seems likely that all 3 were re-copied in error.
[20] *Secker's Visit.*; Par. Rec., rector's census.
[21] MS. Oxf. Dioc. d 560, c 327.
[22] *Census*, 1801–51.
[23] MS. Oxf. Dioc. d 567.
[24] *Census*, 1901–61.
[25] *Hearth Tax Oxon.* 146–7.
[26] See p. 152.
[27] Robert Pargiter, sen., was 'collector' of the Protestation returns in 1642: *Protestation Ret.* 48; *Hearth Tax Oxon.* 146–7.
[28] Wood-Jones, *Dom. Archit. Banbury Region*, 22.
[29] *Hearth Tax Oxon.* 146; MS. Oxf. Archd. Oxon. c 108, ff. 198–200; Gardner, *Dir. Oxon.* (1852).
[30] Local information.
[31] *Hearth Tax Oxon.* 146–7; MS. Dunkin, 439/1, p. 328.
[32] Wood-Jones, op. cit. 64–67, 209–11.
[33] O.R.O., victlrs' recogs.
[34] Gardner, *Dir. Oxon.* (1852).
[35] See pp. 158–9.
[36] Gardner, *Dir. Oxon.* (1852).
[37] *Chron. Abingdon* (Rolls Ser.), i. 191–9.
[38] Ibid. ii. 7.

claim to the rent-charge on the manor, but did not restore the meadow.[39] His relatives continued to give trouble: in Henry I's reign Robert's brother and heir, Niel, was compelled, after a long dispute, to pay the customary rent (*gafol*) of 6*d.* for the meadow in Oxford.[40]

In 1086 the manor was still assessed at 20 hides, of which 5 were held of the abbey by an unnamed knight.[41] The latter's identity is uncertain, but in 1104 one Anskill and Robert his son exchanged the lands, church-houses, and meadows which they held of the abbey in Tadmarton for 1 hide of land in Chesterton (Warws.).[42] The deed states that the Tadmarton land was assessed for geld at 5 hides, and no doubt it was identical with the Domesday holding.

In Henry I's reign Simon le Despenser exchanged the lands which he held of the abbey in Berkshire for Tadmarton manor and 3½ hides at Garsington, to hold at a fee-farm rent of £15 a year.[43] There are no further references to the abbey directly exploiting land at Tadmarton and this grant probably covered the whole vill; its distance from the abbey's other Oxfordshire possessions probably explains its alienation at this early date. Simon le Despenser was a nephew of Reynold, Abbot of Abingdon.[44] In Stephen's reign Simon settled the manor on his daughter and her husband, Walter son of Hingham, to hold on the same terms as himself. Walter failed to pay the rent due to the abbey, so Abbot Ingulf seized the manor.[45] Owing to prevailing conditions his control does not appear to have been very effective. Both Walter and the Despensers gave trouble and, since its royal charters were said to 'profit it little or nothing', the abbey secured two bulls from Eugenius III in 1146 and 1152, confirming its possessions.[46] On the accession of Henry II a suit was begun before the king, between the abbey and Simon le Despenser's son, Thurstan, to whom the manor had reverted.[47] Although judgement was given in the abbey's favour, the Despenser family continued to hold land in Tadmarton until the end of the 13th century. In 1284 Adam le Despenser proved his title to 4 houses and 2 yardlands there, held in chief, claiming descent through his brother Thurstan, who had died without issue.[48] In the following year he conveyed the property to the abbey.[49] At the same time the family were disposing of their other manors in the county.[50]

The fate of the manor after 1154 is not clear. In 1243 the whole vill was stated to be held in free alms by the abbey, but no tenants are named[51] and there is no entry in the Hundred Rolls. In 1284 the abbot unsuccessfully claimed, in addition to the manor, one knight's fee in Tadmarton formerly held by John Bret of Mollington in Cropredy.[52] The abbot also claimed free warren in virtue of a grant by Henry III.[53] In 1291 the abbey had £24 14*s.* 6*d.* in lands and rents in the village.[54] No further evidence is available before the 16th century, when the abbey farmed out the manor.[55] In 1538 Abingdon Abbey surrendered Tadmarton with its other manors,[56] and in the following year the king granted it to Sir Thomas Pope and others.[57] By 1545 Pope had secured sole ownership.[58] He had already obtained much monastic property in north Oxfordshire. Tadmarton followed the descent of two of his estates, Ardley and Wigginton.[59] As in the case of Wigginton the proposed settlement on Trinity College, Oxford, did not take place and Tadmarton remained in the Pope family until sold after 1660 to Ambrose Holbech (d. 1662) of Mollington.[60] It then passed to Richard Brideoake who was lord of the manor in 1692.[61] The Brideoake family, who also held Wigginton, then held the manor until at least 1718 when Ralph Brideoake was returned as lord:[62] he was presumably the Ralph Brideoake who died in 1728 and was buried in the family vault.[63] Although another branch of the Brideoake family retained an interest in land in Tadmarton until the late 18th century,[64] the manor had passed by 1763 to Crescens Carter (fl. 1735–75), probably a kinsman of the George Carter (d. 1707) whose body was brought from London to be buried in the Brideoake vault and who was presumably related by marriage.[65] Crescens Carter was lord of the manor in 1775 but by 1785 it had passed to the Revd. Bartholomew Churchill of North Leigh who still held it in 1823.[66] In 1833 it was held by 3 men, perhaps trustees, i.e. John Dixon, Thomas Howard, and Jonathan Brundelt.[67] In 1839 it was bought by the trustees of John Charles MacDermot, of St. John's Wood, London, who was lord in 1852, but was not resident, the manor-house being used as a farm-house.[68] In 1892 the estate was put up for sale by order of the mortgagees, but only one farm was sold and the rest was either withdrawn or failed to reach the reserve.[69] MacDermot appeared as lord in 1895, when the manor-house was occupied by George Wade,[70] but thereafter manorial rights seem to have lapsed.

LOCAL GOVERNMENT. Records of the manorial courts have with a few exceptions disappeared.[71]

39 *Chron. Abingdon* (Rolls Ser.), ii. 12–15, 133; cf. Kennett, *Paroch. Antiq.* i. 97–98.
40 *Chron. Abingdon* (Rolls Ser.), ii. 133.
41 *V.C.H. Oxon.* i. 408. The abbey claimed that all the land had formerly belonged to its demesne: ibid.
42 *Chron. Abingdon* (Rolls Ser.), ii. 136–7.
43 Ibid. 166–8; cf. *V.C.H. Oxon.* v. 139. For the Despensers see J. H. Round, *King's Sergeants and Officers of State*, 190.
44 Round, *King's Sergeants*, 189.
45 *Chron. Abingdon* (Rolls Ser.), ii. 183.
46 Ibid. 190, 192, 197.
47 Ibid. 187.
48 Bodl. MS. Lyell 15, f. 166v.
49 *Fines Oxon.* 217–18.
50 *Manors and Advowsons of Great Rollright* (O.R.S. ix), 78.
51 *Bk. of Fees*, ii. 832.
52 Bodl. MS. Lyell 15, f. 167.
53 Ibid.
54 *Tax. Eccl.* (Rec. Com.), 43.
55 See p. 154.
56 C.P. 25(2)/52/372/36; *Valor Eccl.* (Rec. Com.), ii. 163; Dugdale *Mon.* i. 530.
57 *L. & P. Hen. VIII*, xiv, p. 588.
58 Ibid. xx, p. 216.
59 *V.C.H. Oxon.* vi. 10 and see p. 162.
60 See p. 162.
61 MS. Oxf. Dioc. c 456, f. 69.
62 *Par. Colln.* iii. 304 and see p. 162.
63 Par. Rec., misc. notes.
64 O.R.O., S. & F. colln. (uncat.).
65 O.R.O., gamekprs' deps.; Par. Rec., misc. notes.
66 Tadmarton Incl. Act, 15 Geo. III, c 77 (priv. act); O.R.O., gamekprs' deps.
67 O.R.O., gamekprs' deps.
68 Gardner, *Dir. Oxon.* (1852).
69 Bodl. G. A. Oxon. b 85*b* (56): *Sale cat.*
70 *Kelly's Dir. Oxon.* (1895).
71 For exceptions see p. 154.

Of the vestry records the earliest to survive are the churchwardens' accounts of 1725. In the early 19th century the vestry met 7 or 8 times a year, but later it lost its importance and met only once a year to deal with church business. In the earlier period 5*s.* was allowed for beer at each meeting.[72]

It is clear from the churchwardens' accounts that they and the overseers worked closely together. On one occasion in 1729 the same men held both offices,[73] and, as in most parishes, the churchwardens were to a certain extent responsible for occasional relief and the relief of vagrants. They also shared with the overseers the responsibility for maintaining the fire-engine which Tadmarton shared with Swalcliffe; from 1771 onwards there are records of payments to Swalcliffe for cleaning and oiling it, and an annual contribution of 10*s.* was made. The churchwardens were conscientious in fulfilling their obligations under the 1598 statute to reward destroyers of vermin.[74]

Between 1725 and 1735 there was a town estate, worth £15 10*s.* a year, in the hands of six different persons; it was carefully administered in the time of the rector, Robert Harrison (1745–80), after which there is no further mention of it nor of the use to which it was put.[75]

One constable was chosen each year but certain men, like Richard Hartley or William Austin, served the office again and again. From *c.* 1790, in addition to his regular duties, the constable took over from the churchwardens the job of rewarding the catchers of vermin. In other ways Tadmarton's constable encroached on what was often the responsibility of churchwardens and overseers; in 1747, for instance, he paid for the inquest on and the burial of a pauper, and in 1752 it was the constable who gave 1*s.* to a travelling woman, suspected of having smallpox. Although his expenses were originally met by a constable's levy the account was settled in 1793 by the overseer and this became the regular practice.[76]

There were 2 surveyors at Tadmarton and their expenses were met either by levy or by the system of 'selling the highways'. The average annual expenditure on the maintenance of the roads was £9, but very large amounts could be spent on occasion: the expenses of the surveyors for 1775–8 for instance totalled £65, spent chiefly on labour and digging stones. In 1814 it was decided that the surveyors' accounts should be examined at a vestry and signed by the majority of the inhabitants. From 1825, however, the accounts were verified on oath by one man and allowed by the others. The surveyors' duties included provision of a town bull: in 1766, for instance, they hired Crescens Carter's bull for the season.[77]

By 1801 there were 2 overseers a year, one accounting from April to October, the other from October to April. The office was filled on a rota system but substitutes were allowed: in 1828 Edward Hawtin was paid £3 for doing the overseers' office for John Colegrove. This is probably the origin of payments of £2 10*s.* for a term of office, which became customary after 1829. The overseers' accounts were approved in the Easter vestry by the churchwardens and 2 others. They made all the usual payments and were in addition responsible for the carriage of the poor's coal and for making up any deficit in that account. They rented cottages for the use of the poor, and in 1806 were paying £17 a year for the lease of 20 cottages. The overseers engrossed many more than their original duties with the passage of time. By 1803, for instance, almost all the most important financial burdens were borne by them: they paid the constable's account and the vestry, and had taken over from the constable the responsibility for the militiamen; in 1804 the overseer paid out £5 bounty money.[78]

The cost of poor relief had risen steadily throughout the 18th century from £21 in 1725 to £72 in 1776, and to about £159 in 1784.[79] In 1801 20 persons were being regularly relieved and in 6 months £345 was spent. The overseers' office was much more burdensome at some seasons than at others; the bill for bread in the winter was usually double what it was in the summer and autumn. The roundsman system was working by 1801, although only one or two men were involved each week. By 1805, however, 8 men were on the rounds. At some date between 1808 and 1828 it was thought expedient to keep the 'round' account separately. In 1828 the system cost the parish from £3 to £4 a month, except in December when the cost rose to £12 12*s.*, and in 1830 the 'round' account for the first half of the year came to £58. Medical charges for the poor cost a great deal and in 1802 one doctor's bill was nearly £8. Thereafter the overseers made bargains with doctors to treat the poor for a year at a fixed sum. Although in 1803 only 17 persons were being regularly relieved, by 1805 the number had more than doubled. Henceforth the number of those relieved rarely fell below 30 and there were usually 5 men on the rounds. By 1830 there were 40 on the overseers' books, including 9 widows and at least 6 orphans. In 1831 Tadmarton spent about £740 on poor relief including the sums which now began to be paid to the unemployed. Even before the passing of the Poor Law Amendment Act, however, expenditure had begun to decline and the total for 1833–4 was under £533. The old system of relief continued to operate until May 1835 when the last entry under the old system was made. The total expenditure on relief in 1836 was £342;[80] by 1851–2 this had been reduced to £235, raised by a rate of 1*s.* 11¼*d.*[81]

ECONOMIC HISTORY. Tenth-century references to plough-lands, headlands, and gores suggest that Tadmarton's open fields were by then established.[82] By 1086 there were 2 separate estates, one of 15 hides belonging to Abingdon Abbey, the other of 5 hides held by the abbey's tenant. The abbey demesne (6 hides) had 3 ploughs worked by 2 serfs; the other 9 hides were held by 15 *villani* and 7 bordars with 5 ploughs. The smaller estate had 2 ploughs and 1 serf in demesne, and the tenants,

[72] Par. Rec., overseers' accts. 1801–11.
[73] Ibid., chwdns' accts. 1725–1907.
[74] Ibid.
[75] Ibid.; MS. Oxf. Dioc. d 557.
[76] Ibid., constable's accts. 1742–1820; overseers' accts. 1801–11.
[77] Ibid., surveyors' accts. 1765–1836.
[78] Ibid., overseers' accts. 1801–11, 1828–36.
[79] Ibid., chwdns' accts.; *Poor Abstract*, 400–01.
[80] *2nd Rep. Poor Law Com.* 292–3.
[81] *Poor Law Unions*, 21.
[82] *Cart. Sax.*, ed. Birch, iii, pp. 148, 150, 152.

8 *villani* and 5 bordars, had 2 ploughs. Meadow (32 a.) and pasture (60 a.) were features of the abbey's estate; there was also a mill worth 4*s*. and a mill on the smaller estate worth 5*s*. The value of the abbey's manor had dropped from £16 before the Conquest to £12 in 1086, while the smaller estate, perhaps under direct exploitation, had increased in value from £2 to £6 over the same period. It was said that there was land in the vill for 16 ploughs and the fact that only 12 were working again indicates economic set-back, at least on the abbey's estate.[83] The total recorded peasant population of 38 was unusually large for a village in this hundred.[84]

The existence of a fulling-mill and a dispute between the abbey and 2 Milcombe tenants over pasture in Tadmarton may suggest that sheep were important by the mid-13th century.[85] In 1291 the abbey was still holding a large amount of land in demesne: its lands and rents there were worth £24 14*s*. 6*d*. a year, while stock and crops were valued at £4 6*s*. 8*d*. In 1306, the abbey's *curia* was assessed for taxation at £1 or at two-fifths of the total for the village.[86] The village itself was fairly prosperous: for the tax of 1316 19 tenants were assessed at between 2*s*. and 3*s*. and 26 at under 2*s*.; in 1327 10 were assessed at between 2*s*. and 4*s*. 6*d*. and 21 at under 2*s*.[87]

One of the Domesday mills was probably 'Edward's mill', recorded in 956.[88] The abbey's fulling-mill, leased with cow-commons worth 16*s*. a year in the 13th century,[89] may have survived beyond the Middle Ages for Fulling Mill Quarter was probably a late field name.[90] Two water-mills were recorded in 1627 and one in 1726 and 1790.[91] A water-corn-mill was marked on a map of 1882 but in 1903 only a saw-mill was in operation.[92]

In the late Middle Ages the abbey leased its demesne; Thomas Hale, assessed at 20*s*. for the 1523 subsidy was probably the abbey's farmer and in 1530 John Winter certainly was.[93] The yeomen and husbandmen seem to have prospered and for the 1523 subsidy nearly two-thirds of the 33 contributors were assessed at 2*s*. or over (i.e. £4 worth of goods), while only one was assessed at the landless labourer's rate of 4*d*.[94] In 1538 rent from the abbey's free and customary tenants came to over £40.[95]

The Pope family did not reside and it is possible that they did not even keep a large demesne farm; in the early 17th century several tenants held demesne.[96] Customary tenants held usually for one life and there is only one example of a grant for two lives. On the other hand a widow was allowed to take on a holding after her husband's death; and a son was regarded as heir to the property.[97] It was customary to exact only one heriot in the event of a widow succeeding. This, in the few recorded cases, was a horse; one worth £4 5*s*., for example, was taken for an estate of 3 yardlands of customary land and 1 yardland of demesne.[98] No entry fines were recorded and rents for customary holdings were low: in 1615 2 yardlands of customary land and 1 yardland of demesne were held at a rent of 15s. 1*d*. a year with customary services,[99] which in this and other cases included the obligation to plant trees.[1] Tenants who sub-let were fined: in 1605 the fine was set at £5.[2] Encroachment on the lord's waste was vigilantly noted.[3] On one occasion all the tenants of the manor were ordered to meet at the church in Whitsun week and to go together to survey encroachments.[4] Tenants were obliged to use the lord's mill, and in 1607 those using their own querns without good reason were threatened with confiscation of their copyholds.[5]

The court supervised the open fields and elected village officials, the hayward and the field-men.[6] In April 1607 two field-men for the 'over town' and two for the 'nether town', one of them a woman, were elected and each was to have for his pains 2 sheep-commons above the number allotted to other tenants according to the quantity of their lands.[7] These officials made sure that the regulations of the court were observed. Tenants were ordered not to mow, reap, or cut the grass balks or to heap stones on them. The homage was frequently ordered to place mere-stones on land in the fallow field or to settle disputes over the placing of boundary stones.[8] No doubt to prevent such disputes it was ordered in 1615 that everyone should leave in the fallow field ½ ft. for greensward between his lands and the balk and 1 ft. for each acre between each acre and land 'as every man's land lies in the field'.[9] Sheep commons were stinted and in 1606 the court ordered that none should keep more than 12 lambs for a yardland or 1 sheep for every 4 lambs.[10] The making of 'hitches' reduced the commons and in 1607 it was agreed that there should be 2 sheep commons less for every 'hide'; in 1614 tenants were ordered to abate 4 sheep for every yardland of the ancient stint, 2 sheep for the hide-land, and 1 sheep for every land and ley in the new hitch.[11] The letting of sheep commons was strictly supervised and anyone taking or letting them was to notify the tithingman.[12] There were many presentments for straying sheep and overburdening of commons.[13] More unusual cases included that of a tenant who allowed his flock to go without a bell and of tenants who allowed

[83] *V.C.H. Oxon.* i. 408.
[84] Ibid.
[85] Bodl. MS. Lyell 15, ff. 130, 131v., 137, 143.
[86] *Tax Eccl.* (Rec. Com.), 43; E 179/161/10.
[87] E 179/161/8, 9.
[88] *Cart. Sax.*, ed. Birch, iii, p. 150.
[89] Bodl. MS. Lyell 15, ff. 130, 131v.
[90] See p. 155.
[91] C.P. 43/179, rot. 60; C.P. 43/573, rot. 25; C.P. 43/827, rot. 290.
[92] O.S. Map 25″ Oxon. IX. 3 (1st edn.); *Kelly's Dir. Oxon.* (1903).
[93] E 179/161/198; *Visit. Dioc. Linc. 1517–31*, ii. 39.
[94] E 179/161/196, 198.
[95] Dugdale, *Mon.* i. 530.
[96] e.g. Bodl. MS. Ch. Oxon. c 49, no. 4470, Mar. ct. 1605.
[97] e.g. Bodl. MS. Ch. Oxon. c 49, no. 4470, Mar. ct. 1605; MS. Rolls Oxon. 106, Oct. ct. 1614.
[98] Bodl. MS. Ch. Oxon. c 49, no. 4470, Apr. ct. 1607.
[99] Ibid. no. 4471, Apr. ct. 1615.
[1] e.g. MS. Rolls Oxon. 106, Apr. ct. 1609. In this case they were oak, ash or elm.
[2] Bodl. MS. Ch. Oxon. c 49, no. 4470, Oct. ct. 1605.
[3] e.g. ibid. no. 4472, Oct. ct. 1617.
[4] Ibid. no. 4470, Apr. ct. 1607.
[5] Ibid.
[6] e.g. ibid. no. 4472; Bodl. MS. Rolls Oxon. 106, Apr. ct. 1614.
[7] Bodl. MS. Ch. Oxon. c 49, no. 4470, Apr. ct. 1607.
[8] Ibid. Mar. ct. 1605, Apr. ct. 1606; no. 4472, Apr. ct. 1617.
[9] Ibid. no. 4471, Mar. ct. 1615.
[10] Ibid. no. 4470, Apr. ct. 1606.
[11] Ibid. Apr. ct. 1607; Bodl. MS. Rolls Oxon. 106. Cf. the stint of 24 sheep to a yardland in the early 18th cent.: O.R.O., S. & F. colln. (uncat.).
[12] Bodl. MS. Ch. Oxon. c 49, no. 4471, Mar. ct. 1615.
[13] Ibid. nos. 4470, 4472, *passim*.

sheep to graze in the hitch.[14] The grazing of horses within the fields after Martinmas was prohibited in 1606, and in 1614 tenants were ordered to tie their horses in the field after Lammas, 1 horse at 1 rope's length, 2 horses at 2 ropes' length.[15] Cow commons were also stinted: in 1606 it was forbidden to put more than 2 beasts in the fields before August unless a field was 'whole grass', and in 1727 a yardland had 2 cow commons and an unstated number of horse commons.[16] The herdsman's work was almost full-time, and in 1616 it was forbidden to hire him to do any other work from the time the beasts went into pasture until Michaelmas.[17]

The regulations for the open fields imply that there were 2 fields only in the parish in the 17th century and that the hamlets did not have separate fields.[18] Like other north Oxfordshire parishes Tadmarton later changed to a 4-course rotation. A pease hitch was added by 1615 when it was decided that all tenants should tell the tithing- or field-men the number of lands and leys they possessed in the new hitch each year, 'either in writing or upon a scored stick'.[19] By 1676 the fields were divided into 4 quarters called Blackland, Fulling Mill, Lea Brook, and Ratmill Quarters.[20] The extent of consolidation of holdings is not known but as late as 1727 one yardland was divided into *c.* 50 lands, leys, and butts.[21] Pasture was available on leys scattered throughout the common fields, on the heath, on 'Lammascommon' and 'Outer Common'.[22] Meadow was assigned by lot: in 1676, for example, the glebe included 1 'hide' of lot ground in North Meadow.[23] Tenants also had the right to cut furze: in 1676 the glebe included 9 'lots' of furze on Tadmarton Heath and in 1727 a yardland holding had a '¼ of a ½ lot' there and a '¼ hide' in the commons in 'all lot thorns and bushes and fern'. The lot land was on the heath, Combe Hill, Wookbrash Hill, Bull Hill, and 'Sandpitts', while there were at least 6 'hides' of lot ground on Ushercombe.[24] These rights were mentioned in the negotiations before inclosure when 2 landlords had the right to cut 100 furze-bushes each year and 2 tenants had rights to cut furze once every 4 years.[25]

In the 17th century Tadmarton's farmers seem to have been reasonably prosperous. Although 5 of the 12 inventories examined had totals of £50 or less some farmers had goods valued at over £100.[26] In Upper Tadmarton 14 people were assessed for the hearth tax of 1665, 1 on 8 hearths, 8 on 3 or 4 hearths, and 5 (of whom 2 were discharged by poverty) on 2 hearths or less. In Lower Tadmarton 12 people were assessed, 1 on 5 hearths, 4 on 3 hearths, and 7 (of whom 3 were discharged) on 2 hearths or less.[27] One man, Robert Austin, who occupied the 5-hearth house, had goods valued at £2,280 at his death. Although large flocks of sheep were rare in Tadmarton Austin had £110 worth of wool.[28]

At the time of the inclosure award in 1776 the parish was almost entirely uninclosed; of the 37 small closes the largest was 4 acres. There were 15 proprietors including the rector and the church-wardens. The lord of the manor, Crescens Carter, held three-eighths of the land and together with John Wheatley had then recently bought up about another seventh. Eight other proprietors had holdings of between 3 and 6 yardlands and 2 of 1 yardland. Carter and Wheatley had at least 8 tenants.[29] There were in all *c.* 1,698 sheep-commons and 166 cow-commons held by some 14 proprietors.[30] In the award there were 14 allottees: the rector received 461½ a. for glebe and tithe, Carter 1½ a. for rights in the manorial waste, 405 a. for his lands in the open field, and, together with Wheatley, 237 a. for lands recently purchased. There were 4 allotments of just over 100 a., 6 of between 20 and 80 a., and 2 of less than 20 a.; of the last, one was for the poor, the other for a stone-pit.[31]

Inclosure evidently did not substantially affect the pattern of land ownership. In 1785 the land taxes show that there were 15 proprietors paying the land tax, a third of which was paid by one proprietor, Bartholomew Churchill, who had 9 tenants. There were only 5 owner-occupiers, none with land assessed at more than £6, and the greater part of the land was farmed by tenants. There were some 16 farmers in the parish, 2 with large farms assessed at £10 and £16 respectively, 12 with medium-sized farms assessed at £5 to £8, and 1 with land assessed at just over £2.[32] In 1831 13 proprietors were assessed for land tax, of whom only 4 were owner-occupiers. There were then 12 tenant-farmers.[33]

Agricultural labourers suffered unemployment in the 1830s and in 1831 a 'riotous assembly' attempted to destroy a threshing machine and a draining plough.[34] There was probably little alternative employment: in 1851 Tadmarton had only a lace-maker, a dyer, and 2 cabinet-makers, apart from a few village craftsmen dependent on agricultural prosperity. At that date there were 11 farms of over 100 a., 2 smallholdings of 12 a. and 32 a., and a farm of unknown acreage. Five were fairly large farms of *c.* 200 a. or more, three of them supporting 8 or more labourers each.[35]

The sandy soil was best suited to grazing land and by 1797 much of the parish seems to have been pasture or meadow.[36] In 1892 Lower Tadmarton Farm was described as a first rate sheep farm and two-thirds of another farm was pasture.[37] In 1903 3

14 Ibid. no. 4470, Mar. ct. 1605; no. 4472, Oct. ct. 1617.
15 Ibid. Apr. ct. 1606; Bodl. MS. Rolls 106, Oct. ct. 1614.
16 Bodl. MS. Ch. Oxon. c 49, no. 4470, Apr. 1606; O.R.O., S. & F. colln. (uncat.), 1727 terrier.
17 Bodl. MS. Ch. Oxon. c 49, no. 4471, Oct. ct. 1616.
18 Ibid. no. 4470, Apr. ct. 1607; no. 4471, Mar. ct. 1615.
19 Ibid. no. 4471, Mar. ct. 1615.
20 MS. Oxf. Archd. Oxon. b 41, ff. 127–30; cf. O.R.O., S. & F. colln. (uncat.), 1727 terrier; cf. Gray, *Eng. Field Systems*, 131–6.
21 O.R.O., S. & F. colln. (uncat.), 1727 terrier.
22 Bodl. MS. Ch. Oxon. c 49, no. 4471, Mar. ct. 1615; O.R.O., S. & F. colln. (uncat.), 1727 terrier.
23 MS. Oxf. Archd. Oxon. b 41, f. 130. 'Hide-lands' were smaller units than yardlands.
24 MS. Oxf. Archd. Oxon. b 41, ff. 127–30; O.R.O., S. & F. colln. (uncat.): 1727 terrier.
25 O.R.O., S. & F. colln. (uncat.).
26 MS. Wills Oxon. 1/6/6; 2/1/15; 2/2/14; 6/3/38; 11/5/22; 18/2/25; 51/1/37; 51/4/30; 72/4/26; 81/3/3; 113/2/4; 296/4/74.
27 *Hearth Tax Oxon.* 146–7.
28 MS. Wills Oxon. 2/1/15.
29 C.P. 43/775, m. 63: incl. award; O.R.O., S. & F. colln. (uncat.).
30 O.R.O., S. & F. colln. (uncat.).
31 C.P. 43/775, m. 63.
32 O.R.O., land tax assess. 1785.
33 Ibid. 1831.
34 *Oxf. Jnl.* 5 Mar. 1831.
35 H.O. 107/1733.
36 Davis, *Oxon. Map* (1797).
37 Bodl. G.A. Oxon. b 85*b* (56): *Sale cat.*

farmers were described as graziers or cattle-dealers.[38] Even so most of the farms remained mixed; in 1914 57 per cent. of the parish was estimated to be permanent pasture and it was calculated that there were 71 sheep and 19 cattle per 100 a., while barley, oats, and wheat were the chief crops.[39]

By 1939 there were 8 farms in the parish, 4 of them over 150 a.[40] After the First World War the creation of a golf course reduced the amount of grazing land on the heath.

CHURCH. The earliest evidence for the existence of a church in Tadmarton is early Norman work in the church building.[41] Tithes in Tadmarton were held by Abingdon Abbey in 1146.[42] The advowson was in the hands of the abbey until it was surrendered to the Crown in 1538.[43] Later in that year Charles, Duke of Suffolk, was given licence to alienate it to Sir Thomas Pope[44] in whose family it remained until sold after 1660 with the manor, the descent of which it followed until the early 18th century.[45] In 1715 the advowson was sold to Christopher Widmore; by 1730 it was in the hands of Mrs. Brideoake who conveyed it in that year to Ralph Brideoake, Fellow of New College, Oxford and his heirs. By will of 1761 Ralph settled the advowson on Jane Payne and her daughter, Elizabeth Farebrother. Jane and Elizabeth settled two-thirds of the advowson on Matthew Woodford, Jane Payne's nephew, and one-third on Elizabeth Farebrother.[46] In 1762 Elizabeth Farebrother and her husband conveyed their third share to Matthew Woodford.[47] By 1780 Matthew Woodford, presumably the son of Matthew and Mary Woodford, presented himself to the living.[48] In 1789 he sold the advowson to Henry Harrison.[49] By 1790 it was held by Thomas and Eleanor Harrison who sold it in 1805 to Worcester College, Oxford,[50] which still retained it in 1962.[51]

In 1546 the Bishop of Oxford collated, presumably by lapse, and in 1590 John Standish of Bold (Lancs.) presented.[52] On a number of occasions thereafter the Popes and their successors granted turns to others. In 1615, for example, Thomas Sacheverell of Leicester presented his son Ambrose[53] and in 1702 and 1720 Michael and Nicholas Woodhull made successive presentations.[54] In 1814 the Revd. Bartholomew Churchill, lord of Tadmarton manor, held the next turn. He is reported to have broken into the rectory-house in the absence of the curate in order to examine the property.[55]

In 1291 and 1341 the rectory was valued at £8 and in 1536 at £18.[56] The rector was assessed at £22 in the clerical subsidy of 1526,[57] a high rate compared with neighbouring parishes, and in 1615 the rectory was valued at £66 8*s.* 4*d.*[58] By 1883 the gross value was £436, the net value £392;[59] the income was derived from rents of the glebe (gross rental £375), surplice fees (£1), and the value of the house and gardens (£60). In 1931, when the glebe had been considerably diminished, the net income was £350.[60]

In the 12th century Abingdon Abbey took some at least of Tadmarton's tithes: its right to them was confirmed by the Pope in 1146, 1152, and 1200.[61] In the early 13th century the abbey appears to have accepted pensions of 40*s.* for the demesne tithes and 48*s.* 4*d.* for the rector's tithes.[62] The rector's pension was confirmed by Bishop Hugh of Welles and both pensions were confirmed in 1401.[63] They were still being paid to the abbey in 1536[64] but passed after the Dissolution to Sir Thomas Pope.[65] He was licensed in 1555 to put £3 18*s.* 4*d.* from the rectory to the endowment of Durham College, Oxford,[66] and this sum was still paid to Trinity College in 1962.[67] The rectory was also charged in the 17th century with a payment of 3*s.* 4*d.* to New College, Oxford, the origin of which is unknown. The tenant of Swalcliffe rectory was receiving it for the college in 1663–74.[68] At inclosure in 1776 the rector received 3 allotments for tithes, totalling 328½ a.[69] His subsequent request to the patron for a contribution of £200–£300 towards the cost of the new buildings at the rectorial farm was declined.[70]

A terrier of the glebe in 1676 gave no total acreage but a century later it was said to be 2 yardlands.[71] There was some doubt about the location of the glebe in 1759 when the rector suggested that the terrier be kept in the 'public chest' and that the bounds be inspected every 3 years, a long-neglected custom.[72] He repeated the suggestion in 1768, since the terrier was inadequate and out-of-date.[73] In 1776 the rector was allotted 54 a. for glebe which, with the tithe allotment, made up a compact estate of 462½ a. adjoining the rectory-house.[74] He was empowered to grant leases of up to 21 years, with the patron's consent.[75] Shortly before inclosure the glebe had been mortgaged to pay for new buildings

38 *Kelly's Dir. Oxon.* (1903).
39 Orr, *Oxon. Agric.*, statistical plates.
40 *Kelly's Dir. Oxon.* (1939).
41 The 'church-houses' mentioned in 1104 may have been connected with Abingdon Abbey rather than Tadmarton church: *Chron. Abingdon* (Rolls Ser.), ii. 136–7.
42 Bodl. MS. Lyell 15, ff. 15–16.
43 C.P. 25(2)/34/228/Hil. 29 Hen. VIII.
44 *L. & P. Hen. VIII*, xiii(2), p. 495.
45 See p. 152. Sir Thomas Pope was licensed to endow Durham College, Oxf. with the advowson in 1555, but this was not effected: *Cal. Pat.* 1554–5, 90–91.
46 Worc. Coll. Mun. Mr. J. Campbell kindly supplied notes on the college muniments.
47 Ibid.
48 MS. Top. Oxon. c 42(1), f. 53.
49 Worc. Coll. Mun.
50 Ibid.
51 Ex inf. the Bursar, Worc. Coll.
52 O.A.S. *Rep.* (1916), 53. Sir Thomas Pope is said to have assigned the advowson to his brother John, 'naturalis pater', of John Standish.
53 MS. Oxf. Dioc. c 264.
54 Bacon, *Liber Regis*, 799.
55 MS. Oxf. Dioc. c 662, ff. 2–3.
56 *Tax Eccl.* (Rec. Com.), 31; *Inq. Non.* (Rec. Com.), 128; *Valor Eccl.* (Rec. Com.) ii. 163.
57 *Subsidy 1526*, 269.
58 MS. Dunkin, 438/2, f. 153. There is no indication whether the value was gross or net.
59 MS. Oxf. Dioc. c 2042, surveyor's rep. 1883.
60 Worc. Coll. Mun.
61 Bodl. MS. Lyell 15, ff. 15–16.
62 *Chron. Abingdon* (Rolls Ser.), ii. 299, 328.
63 Bodl. MS. Lyell 15, f. 52; *Cal. Papal Reg.* v. 353 where the pension is stated to be 30*s.*; cf. *Feud. Aids*, vi. 377 where it is said to be £4.
64 *Valor Eccl.* (Rec. Com.), ii. 163; cf. *Subsidy 1526*, 269.
65 *L. & P. Hen. VIII*, xx(1), p. 216.
66 *Cal. Pat.* 1554–5, 90–91; *V.C.H. Oxon.* iii. 244.
67 For a payment in 1805 see MS. Top. Oxon. c 449.
68 *Woodward's Progress*, 89, 90, 92.
69 O.R.O., incl. award.
70 Worc. Coll. Mun.
71 MS. Oxf. Archd. Oxon. b 41; O.R.O., incl. award.
72 MS. Oxf. Dioc. d 557.
73 Ibid. d 560.
74 O.R.O., incl. award.
75 Tadmarton Incl. Act, 15 Geo. III, c 77 (priv. act).

and in 1788 the lands awarded for tithe (Holywell and Parsonage farms) were mortgaged for £300 to Matthew Woodford, patron and rector.[76] By 1920 more than 100 a. of glebe had been sold and in 1946 the last of the glebe was sold with the rectory-house[77].

In 1277 the Rector of Tadmarton was cited in the archbishop's court for not being ordained priest within a year of institution.[78] At least 6 of the medieval rectors were graduates[79] but it is clear that some of the more distinguished were non-resident. After vacating Tadmarton Master Geoffrey Crukadan became a proctor at the Roman curia;[80] Master John Blodwell was much at Rome while still Rector of Tadmarton (1413–*c.* 1419),[81] and John Incent, D.C.L., was at one time a royal chaplain and Wolsey's vicar general.[82] He paid a curate £5 6*s.* 8*d.*[83]

Thurstan Standish was instituted in 1546 and held the living through the Tudor religious changes until his death in 1590.[84] His successor, John Crayker (d. 1614), who held Broughton rectory until 1596,[85] was resident and farmed his glebe; at his death his goods were valued at the comparatively large sum of £240 which included £10 worth of books.[86] Ambrose Sacheverell (d. 1647) was probably resident in his early years. His family seem to have been lessees of the manor and many Sacheverell children were baptized in Tadmarton between 1617 and 1630.[87] His goods were sequestrated on the day of his death for assisting the king in the previous year.[88] Cresswell Whateley (1647–82)[89] and his successor Thomas Oldys (1682–1720)[90] also appear to have been resident.

The only 18th-century rector to make more than formal replies to the visitation articles was Robert Harrison (1745–80), described by Thomas Warton as his 'learned and ingenious friend'. During his ministry the church building was kept in repair,[91] there were only 3 regular absentees from services, and the number of communion services rose from 3 to 4 a year.[92] He attributed the decline in the number of communicants from 20–25 in 1759 to 16–20 in 1768 to the 'continued mistranslation of a certain celebrated text' in the Bible.[93] He originally catechized for as long as 6 months a year. In later years he took another cure at Broughton in 1771 and appointed a curate in Tadmarton. The period of catechizing was then reduced.[94] He reported that he said prayers on Holy Days if he could get a congregation and that he had been warned that his proposal to take an offertory would prevent most of his regular communicants from attending.[95] Harrison carefully safeguarded the rectory estate,[96] made sure that a perambulation of the parish boundaries was carried out triennially,[97] preserved what was left of the town stock,[98] and in 1750 made a census of his parish.[99] His immediate successors were non-resident and for 30 years Tadmarton seems to have been left largely to the care of poorly paid and transitory curates.[1] Despite increasing population the number of communicants in 1784 was only 10; it was said there were 24 in 1802 but only 12 in 1805.[2]

Church life revived with the institution in 1810 of John Keen, son of the previous incumbent.[3] Communicants numbered 60 in 1811 and *c.* 90 in 1817, and a Sunday school was started.[4] The revival proved temporary. There was trouble over church rates in 1814, the Sunday school was temporarily discontinued, and communicants declined to 30 in 1820 and rose only to between 40 and 50 in 1823.[5] A new rectory-house, however, was built in 1842 and Tadmarton once more obtained resident rectors.[6] Since 1946 the living has been held with Broughton.[7]

The small church of *ST. NICHOLAS* comprises a nave and chancel, both with north aisles, and a western tower.[8] The 12th-century church was on the same plan, except that there is no evidence of a tower. Of the original building there remains the north nave arcade, some blocked arches on the north side of the chancel, and the internal jambs of a low-side window on the south side. The church was enlarged in the 13th century: an Early English chancel arch was inserted within the Romanesque one, the chancel was largely rebuilt, and the nave aisle was rebuilt on a larger scale. The nave of 3 bays was lengthened to the westward by the addition of a narrow arch to the nave arcade; and the existing tower was built.

At a later date new windows were inserted in the walls: those in the chancel are the earliest, being in the Transitional style between late Decorated and Perpendicular; the rest are Perpendicular. The walls of the nave were raised and clerestory windows were inserted in the south wall; a new window seems to have been inserted at the west end of the north aisle but was blocked up subsequently; low-pitched roofs to the nave and aisle were built; the upper stage of the tower was added; and the original belfry windows were blocked.

No major structural changes appear to have been made before the restoration of 1893. Faculties for Richard Brideoake's vault and another one were

[76] MS. Oxf. Archd. Oxon. b 26.
[77] *Kelly's Dir. Oxon.* (1920); Worc. Coll. Mun.
[78] *Rot. Graves*, 232.
[79] MS. Top. Oxon. d 460: list of medieval rectors: Emden, *O.U. Reg.*
[80] Emden, *O.U. Reg.*
[81] Ibid.
[82] Ibid.
[83] *Subsidy 1526.*
[84] O.A.S. *Rep.* 1916, 53; Par. Rec., reg.
[85] See p. 98.
[86] MS. Wills Oxon. 11/5/23.
[87] Par. Rec., reg.
[88] *Cal. Cttee. for Compounding*, iii. 1732.
[89] A large number of his children were baptized at Tadmarton: Par. Rec., reg.
[90] He signed the affidavits for burial in wool up to 1685; Par. Rec., reg.
[91] MS. Oxf. Dioc. d 557. When so many churches were in bad repair he was ordered only to supply a communion cloth and copies of the commandments &c.
[92] Ibid. d 557, d 560.
[93] Ibid.
[94] Ibid. d 567, c 654, b 37.
[95] Ibid. d 557.
[96] See p. 156.
[97] MS. Oxf. Dioc. d 557.
[98] See p. 153.
[99] Par. Rec., reg., note on fly-leaf.
[1] MS. Oxf. Dioc. c 327, f. 287; c 654, ff. 156–8; Worc. Coll. Mun.
[2] MS. Oxf. Dioc. b 37, d 567, d 569.
[3] MS. Oxf. Dioc. c 659, f. 127.
[4] Ibid. d 573, d 577.
[5] MS. Oxf. Archd. Oxon. c 108, f. 218; MS. Oxf. Dioc. d 573, d 577.
[6] Worc. Coll. Mun.
[7] MS. Oxf. Dioc. c 2042.
[8] For an early-19th-century account of the building see Beesley, *Hist. Banbury*, 139.

obtained in 1692 and 1693;[9] a gallery was added at the west end and the tower arch blocked up,[10] probably in the late 18th century; the chancel was repaired *c.* 1780; some work was carried out on the porch, roof, and north side of the church in 1808;[11] and some new pews of painted deal with doors were added in 1825.[12] The porch was rebuilt in 1850 and the north aisle leaded in 1852.[13]

A report on the church in 1867 stated that it 'much needed the work of the diocesan architect',[14] but it was not until 1891 when the church had 'sadly fallen into decay' that plans were made for a general restoration. The architects were Milne and Hall of London, the builder J. S. Kimberley of Banbury.[15] It was proposed to restore the roofs of the nave and the north aisle, provide new floors and stair-case in the tower, remove the west gallery, open up the tower arch, make a new vestry in the tower, repair the mullions of the nave window which had subsided, remove all the interior plaster, and add a new door to the principal entrance. The pews, of which some high deal ones reached half-way up the chancel arch, were to be removed and replaced with chairs.[16] All this work was carried out in 1893.[17] When the plaster was stripped from the chancel the original Romanesque arches were exposed.

Electricity was installed in 1916.[18]

The 13th-century font with its vigorous row of grotesque heads remains.[19] An aumbry was placed in the east wall of the chancel in 1947.[20] There is a communion table of 1635; the pulpit, lectern, prayer desk, and pews date from the 19th century, but some carved bench ends of late medieval date were preserved as J. O. Scott considered them 'exceptionally good'.[21] The parish chest dates from the 17th century. The arms of George IV hang over the tower arch.

The following are among those commemorated: Mary Whateley (d. 1657), the wife of the rector;[22] and L. C. M. Gibbs (d. 1955) of Tadmarton Manor. A stained glass window was inserted by Mowbray of Oxford in 1916.[23]

There is a ring of 6 bells, of which 4 were originally cast in the early 17th century and one in 1761. Two of the 17th-century bells were recast in 1923 and 1939 and the treble was added in 1947. The sanctus bell was restored to its original position in 1893.[24]

The church has a silver paten and chalice of 1569.[25]

The registers are complete from 1548.[26]

NONCONFORMITY. In 1676 there were 20 Protestant nonconformists in Tadmarton.[27] These may all have been Quakers since no reference has been found to other sects before the late 18th century. One of the earliest Quakers in Tadmarton was William Potter who moved there after William, Lord Saye and Sele, had evicted him from a cottage in Broughton *c.* 1655.[28] Potter was subsequently imprisoned twice for attending meetings in Broughton and Banbury;[29] he and his family had their goods distrained on for tithes almost every year between 1673 and 1706.[30] In 1669 meetings were held every other Friday at his house in Lower Tadmarton: *c.* 80 people attended[31] and among the speakers were Potter himself and Benjamin Ward, an ex-quartermaster in Cromwell's army, who had been imprisoned several times in the 1660s, and in 1672 had sheep worth £20 distrained upon for his refusal to pay tithes.[32] Eight family names appear in the Quaker register[33] during the 17th century and the community was sufficiently important for divisional monthly meetings to be held there in 1699 and occasionally between 1700 and 1706.[34] Most Tadmarton Quakers, however, seem to have belonged to Shutford Meeting.[35] Seven family names are to be found in the register during the 18th century but after 1732 no Tadmarton Quaker suffered for conscience sake and the sect was clearly less vigorous; of the 6 Quakers recorded by the incumbent in 1738 2 attended church and in 1759 there were only two Quaker families and one that was partly Quaker.[36] By 1781 there was only one Quaker left and his family attended church.[37]

No dissenters were reported in the earliest 19th-century visitation returns but 2 houses were registered for worship in 1813, and another in 1814, when the parson reported the existence of a few dissenters, and a fourth in 1818.[38] In 1817 a dissenting teacher occasionally visited a licensed meeting which met weekly in a private house.[39] There is no certainty that these dissenters were Methodists but in 1820 there were *c.* 60 Wesleyans in Tadmarton.[40] In 1834 the rector claimed that the Wesleyans attended church as well as their own meetings.[41] In 1861 they built a chapel by subscription. It was a one-roomed structure of brick and corrugated iron in Upper Tadmarton.[42] The chapel had been closed for Methodist worship for some years before 1927, but had been used occasionally by Baptists as a preaching station, nominally under

[9] MS. Oxf. Dioc. c 456, f. 69; c 105, f. 59; cf. Par. Rec., reg.

[10] See below.

[11] MS. Oxf. Archd. Oxon. c 108, ff. 160, 207.

[12] Ibid., f. 235.

[13] Par. Rec., chwdns' accts.

[14] O.A.S. *Rep.* 1867, 10.

[15] MS. Oxf. Archd. Oxon. c 22, p. 15*a*. For drawings of the unrestored church see Buckler's drawing in MS. Top. Oxon. a 70, no. 544; ibid. a 39, f. 133 (*c.* 1879).

[16] MS. Oxf. Archd. Oxon. c 22, p. 15*a*. For the rector's correspondence about the restoration see MS. Top. Oxon. c 104, ff. 387, 389.

[17] There is a ground plan in the vestry.

[18] MS. Oxf. Dioc. c 2042.

[19] For a drawing of the font see MS. Top. Oxon. a 70, no. 543 and see plate facing p. 115.

[20] MS. Oxf. Dioc. c 2042.

[21] Par. Rec., Broughton pps.

[22] For details of inscriptions see MS. Top. Oxon. c 166, f. 221 and *Par. Colln.* iii. 304. For arms on the monuments and pewter plate see Bodl. G.A. Oxon. 4° 687, p. 304.

[23] MS. Oxf. Dioc. c 2042.

[24] *Ch. Bells Oxon.*; MS. Oxf. Dioc. c 2042. Mr. Bagley was paid £18 10*s.* in 1760 for repairing the bells: Par. Rec. chwdns' accts.

[25] Evans, *Ch. Plate.*

[26] Par. Rec.

[27] Compton Census.

[28] Wm. Fiennes, Lord Saye and Sele, *The Quakers' Reply Manifested to be Railing* (Oxf. 1660); see p. 101.

[29] Besse, *Sufferings*, i. 565.

[30] Ibid. i. 565, 576; MS. Sufferings.

[31] Lyon Turner, *Recs. Nonconformity*, iii. 826.

[32] Ibid.; Besse, *Sufferings*, i. 570, 573, 576.

[33] Banbury Quaker Regs.

[34] Banbury Prep. M. Min. Bk. (1696–1720).

[35] Banbury Quaker Reg., burials.

[36] *Secker's Visit.*; MS. Oxf. Dioc. d 557.

[37] MS. Oxf. Dioc. c 327, f. 127; cf. reports of 1768, 1771 and 1774; ibid. d 560, d 563, d 565.

[38] MS. Oxf. Dioc. c 644, nos. 133, 139, 142–3, 197; ibid. d 575.

[39] Ibid. d 577.

[40] Ibid. d 579.

[41] Ibid. b 39; cf. report of 1854; *Wilb. Visit.*

[42] Land was conveyed to trustees by a deed of 1861: Char. Com. file E 107, 329; ibid. G 48 (Corresp.), 2nd Bk

the chapel at Hook Norton. It was then sold to the Baptist Union Corporation and used by the Baptists until 1941. Thereafter it was used occasionally as an assembly room for the Friends' Evangelistic Band. In 1947 it was finally abandoned and in 1950 it was sold.[43]

SCHOOLS. In 1808 there were 3 schools in Tadmarton. One, which was described as 'endowed', had 70 pupils. The others each had 24 pupils and in them reading, writing, accounts, and grammar were taught; the salaries of the teachers, one of whom was a Baptist, were derived from 'Quarter Pence', quarterly payments by the children's parents. There was also a Sunday school, with 130 pupils, where reading and writing were taught in addition to Scripture.[44]

In 1811 only one school was recorded[45] and in 1815 there was one day school for young children (10 boys, 12 girls), kept by a woman in return for her support. A Sunday school, established in 1813, was supported by subscription; it was attended by 25 boys and 20 girls.[46] By 1818 both schools had closed and it was reported that the poor were in need of instruction.[47]

By 1833 3 day schools had been established, containing between 30 and 36 children paid for by their parents, but in 1834 the rector disparagingly described these as no more than dame schools in the parish; a Sunday school had been established in 1830 with 50 pupils and was supported by the rector and the landowners.[48] In 1834 a new Church of England school was built at Tadmarton at a cost of *c.* £700;[49] by 1854 it had *c.* 30 pupils while the Sunday school, supported by the rector, had 55.[50] The common complaint was that it was impossible to retain children in the Sunday school after they had left day school. A night school was held in the winter months.[51]

By 1871 the day school, which officially had room for 29 children, was badly overcrowded with 53 pupils.[52] In 1872 a School Board was selected to seek a means of improving the situation. In 1875 George Cookes of London granted land adjacent to the site of the recently-demolished Sunday school for the building of a new school, and in 1876 a new Church of England school was opened.[53] It had accommodation for 84 children and up to 1906 the average attendance was *c.* 44.[54] Fees of 4*d.*, 2*d.*, and 1*d.* were paid according to the parents' means. A Sunday school was held on the premises and a night school in the winter.[55] The school was united with the National Society by deed and received annual and fee grants as well as voluntary financial support and a bequest from MacDermot's charity.[56] In 1962 it was a Controlled school and had a roll of 36.[57]

CHARITIES. By will proved 1864 John Charles MacDermot left money to be used for public purposes at the discretion of trustees. The will was disputed and it was not until 1893 that the funds, then amounting to £3,000, became available. By a Scheme of 1897 a sum not exceeding £10 was allotted to both a Hospital and Provident Club, £30 to a coal fund, and between £20 and £25 to the school. The school spent the money monthly on outings and prizes. The residue of the charity's income was reserved for cases of special distress. A Charity Commission Scheme of 1905 allotted £1,000 of the capital to the Education Fund.

After 1946 the Hospital Club money was transferred to the coal fund; the amount allotted to the latter was increased to £45 in 1950. The Provident Club, which became a clothing club, came to an end in 1959 and its money was thereafter added to the coal fund.[58]

The coal fund was worth £50–£100 in 1963, of which £24 came from rent of 15 a. on Tadmarton Heath awarded at inclosure in 1776 for fuel.[59]

WIGGINTON

WIGGINTON lies half way between Banbury and Chipping Norton, on the River Swere. It covers 1,187 a. and is roughly triangular in shape with the river forming one side of the triangle.[1] The dominant features in the north are the sandy Wigginton Heath and Rye Hill where the land rises to 600 feet. Most of the parish lies between the 500 and 600 feet contour and in the Upper Lias area.[2]

The modern road from Hook Norton to Milcombe passes through the parish; it is connected with South Newington and Swalcliffe by minor roads. A cross track, which may be of great antiquity, joins the village to the Romano-British road through Tadmarton Camp,[3] and another ancient track runs from Stow to Banbury across Wigginton Heath—the 'great road' as it was called locally in the 18th century.[4] The line of at least one road has probably been changed: immediately after crossing the brook to the south of the village on the Swerford road what appears to be the pre-inclosure road can be seen ascending the hill to the left.[5] The Banbury–Chipping Norton railway, built in 1887 and closed

[43] Ibid.
[44] MS. Oxf. Dioc. d 707.
[45] Ibid. d 573.
[46] Ibid. c 433.
[47] *Educ. of Poor*, 731.
[48] *Educ. Enq. Abstract*, 756; MS. Oxf. Dioc. b 39.
[49] MS. Oxf. Dioc. b 70.
[50] *Wilb. Visit.*
[51] MS. Oxf. Dioc. d 180.
[52] *Elem. Educ. Ret.* 326.
[53] Par. Rec., trust deed; *Kelly's Dir. Oxon.* (1895); Ed 7/169/208.
[54] *Pub. Elem. Sch. Ret.* (1894), 498; ibid. (1900), 676; *List of Schools* (1906), 529.
[55] Ed 7/169/208.
[56] *Pub. Elem. Sch. Ret.* (1900), 676; see below.
[57] Ex inf. Oxfordshire County Council, Educ. Cttee.
[58] Char. Com. files. E 58, 984; G 48 (Corr.) 2nd Bk.; G48 (Accts.) 2nd Bk.; Unrep. vol. 99/128.
[59] Ex inf. the Trustees; *Char. Don.* 978.

[1] O.S. *Area Bk.* (1881). Mr. F. D. Price (Keble College and Wigginton) kindly read this history and made corrections and suggestions.
[2] The following maps have been used: O.S. Map 25″ Oxon. IX. 6, 10, 14 (1st edn.); O.S. Map 6″ Oxon. IX (1st edn.); O.S. Map 2½″ SP 33 (1959).
[3] I. V. Margerry, *Roman Roads*, ii. 18 and map facing p. 15; O.S. Map 1″, sheet 145 (1954).
[4] Par. Rec., overseers' accts. *passim.*
[5] Ex inf. Mr. F. D. Price, who points out that the ridge and furrow headlands, the hedge line at the point of divergence, and the position of gateways all support this interpretation.

in 1964,[6] crosses the parish north of the village.

The village took its present name from a Saxon lord, Wicga, who may have held extensive property in the neighbourhood, for there was a Wicga's tumulus in Hook Norton.[7] The rich red soil and the River Swere had already attracted Romano-British settlers. The site of a Roman villa of some size and wealth, and possibly a military post, lies north-east of the church. It was excavated in 1824 by the curate and Joseph Skelton, who described it in his *Antiquities*.[8] In 1965 further excavations were carried out. Air photographs show the outlines of small fields of the Iron-age or Roman period on Wigginton Heath near the cross roads.[9]

Wigginton has always had a small population; in the late 14th century it seems to have had no more inhabitants than Milcombe, a hamlet of Bloxham.[10] The Protestation Returns of 1641 were signed by 41 men of 18 and over, and the 112 adults of 14 and over listed by the Compton Census in 1676 may indicate an increase in population,[11] which took place in this period in other villages in the hundred. In 1738 and 1768 the incumbent reported that there were about 40 houses, inhabited by farmers and labourers.[12] The population increased rapidly in the early 19th century, rising from 192 in 1801 to 291 in 1821; there were then 66 families living in 55 houses. Since the peak year of 1861, when there were 338 inhabitants, there has been a decline to 211 in 1901, and to 159 in 1961.[13] Some of the inhabitants, at least in the 19th century, lived outside the village, in cottages at South Fields, Withycombe on the Heath, and at the mill-house.[14] Wigginton's isolated position and lack of any special industry has prevented it from developing: it has one person to every 5 acres. Bodicote with about the same amount of land was nearly ten times more thickly populated in 1965.

The village is sited at a height of 400 ft. on the hill above the Swere valley, just off the road from Swerford to Swalcliffe.[15] The original plan of the village has been obscured by later changes, but it seems once to have centred more upon the church.[16] Today scattered dwellings, houses, and orchards, lie mainly along the four sides of an irregular square, being mostly concentrated on the west side where the two public houses are. The church now stands rather isolated on the east side, but in the 19th century there were cottages on the north and west side and the village street from Mill Lane wound in a 'miserably circuitous' way between them, crossing what is now the north part of the churchyard, and behind the parish pound inclosure. Some of these dilapidated cottages were bought by J. R. Cobb in 1867, were ceded to the church to extend the churchyard in exchange for the parish pound, the inclosure of which may still be seen, and were demolished.[17] The well now by the road-side was once in a cottage garden. One of the cottages to the north of the church still stands and as late as *c.* 1920 was used as a blacksmith's shop. When the cottages were pulled down the village street was realigned along the line of the present garden wall of the rectory-house. Many of Wigginton's 2-storied cottages and farm-houses date from the 16th and 17th centuries, though they have been remodelled and enlarged at later periods. With the exception of a few 19th-century and modern brick buildings all are of the local ironstone, quarried round the village. Until recently thatch for roofing was general but Stonesfield slate was occasionally used. As late as 1907 there were 2 thatchers living in the village.[18]

Of the 13 houses taxed in 1665 10 were modest farm dwellings with 2 hearths apiece, and of the 3 larger houses one was the old rectory-house and one the manor-house.[19] The last can perhaps be identified with the present Manor Farm. John Blount was assessed on 5 hearths for it in 1665 and when George Blount died in 1700 his house was described as having a hall, parlour, and kitchen on the ground floor as well as an out-kitchen and buttery. There were chambers over the parlour and hall and two others, a 'best' and a 'middle' chamber. There was a closet and a 'garret'.[20] The present house is L-shaped and has been much enlarged. The rectory-house, also taxed on 5 hearths, was pulled down in 1844 and replaced by the present house, designed by the architect John Prichard of Oxford in the Tudor style.[21] The old house was nearer the church than the present one which was built on the site of a glebe farm-house, which it in part incorporates.

Another 17th-century house, 'Woodheys', inscribed 'W 1695' belonged to the Wyatts, a well-known local family of farmers and masons. It was still a farm-house in 1813. The present representative of the family inhabits a cottage that his family acquired in 1704.[22] The most striking of the 18th-century additions to the village was the 'Dolphin'.[23] It was built as a farm-house by James Eden, the principal farmer in the parish in the 1720s, and bears the inscription 'I:E. 1727'. Its façade of ironstone ashlar with keystoned windows is dignified by a shell hood over the doorway. The house is set off by the smaller houses in the street, all built in the regional style, and by the grass verges that edge it. On these verges stalls used to be erected in the late 19th century on St. Giles's Day, when the village held its wake. At the approach to the village from Tadmarton is the 'Swan' public house. It was first mentioned by name when licensed in 1782,[24] but it is an older house dating probably from the 17th century. It consists of one story and an attic and is T-shaped in plan. In the 19th century there were 3 inns in the village.[25]

[6] E. T. MacDermot, *Hist. of the G.W.R.* ii. 365; ex inf. British Railways, Western Region.

[7] *P.N. Oxon.* (E.P.N.S.), ii. 408.

[8] Skelton, *Oxon.* Bloxham Hund. 9–10, 12; *Gent. Mag.* 1842, xvii. 512; W. J. J. Knight, 'A Romano-British Site at Bloxham, Oxon.', *Oxoniensia*, iii. 41–56; O.A.S. *Rep.* 1929, 229–32.

[9] Ashmolean Mus. Allan 1,377.

[10] See p. 189.

[11] *Protestation Ret.* 49; Compton Census.

[12] *Secker's Visit.*; MS. Oxf. Dioc. d 560.

[13] *V.C.H. Oxon.* ii. 217; Par. Rec., reg. (copy of details of 1821 census); *Census*, 1911–61.

[14] H.O. 107/1733.

[15] O.S. Map 25" Oxon. IX. 10, 14 (1st edn.).

[16] This paragraph is based upon personal observation and Par. Rec., correspondence.

[17] Par. Rec., correspondence. A drawing at the rectory-house shows the cottages.

[18] *Kelly's Dir. Oxon.* (1907).

[19] *Hearth Tax Oxon.* 135.

[20] MS. Wills Oxon. 77/3/19.

[21] *Hearth Tax. Oxon* 135; MS. Oxf. Dioc. b 106, no. 8, which includes plans and specifications.

[22] Deeds *penes* Mr. W. F. Wyatt.

[23] For details and plans see Wood-Jones, *Dom. Archit. Banbury Region*, 186–9.

[24] O.R.O. QSD/VI.

[25] MS. Oxf. Dioc. d 179, c 332.

'Town houses' were built for the poor in 1777 and 1811.[26] The latter have been identified with a house (originally 3 tenements) at the extreme south-west corner of the village. The building called the 'Court' may originally have been the 'church house'[27] which was later used for the leet courts. The rear parts date from the 17th century, though the main structure was rebuilt in the 19th century as four tenements. The central gable has 'G. W. 1830' inscribed on it and over the two doorways below is the text 'Unless the Lord is with us we build in vain' in Latin. The architectural details are in a traditional Tudor style. The mason employed was Robert Cleaver,[28] a member of the family after whom Cleaver's Lane is named. Being in a dilapidated state, they were bought from the R.D.C. in 1963 and converted into one house.[29] Other 19th-century buildings in the village are the Baptist chapel (1835), the adjacent church school, built in 1832 and enlarged in 1859, and the Wesleyan Methodist chapel (1883).[30] Outside the village on the Swere is the 19th-century mill-house, and the adjoining mill, built by William Gilkes and inscribed 'W. G. 1823'. Both have been slated with Welsh slate, a comparatively rare material at Wigginton. The 19th-century 'Lodge' at Wigginton cross-roads once stood at the corner of a wood. Many of the fine trees in the wood have recently been cleared to make way for sand pits.

Apart from its rectors, one of whom signed a protest in 1649 against the execution of Charles I,[31] Wigginton has had no known inhabitants of any repute outside the village. Certain farming families, such as those of Hall, Stanbra, and Coles, and the Cleavers, who were masons, have long dominated village life. At one period in the 19th century a Stanbra had the 'White Swan' and another the mill.[32]

MANOR. In King Edward's time Levric held 10 hides in Wigginton and in 1086 this estate was held by Guy d'Oilly, a younger brother of Robert d'Oilly, Constable of Oxford Castle and lord of the neighbouring manor and barony of Hook Norton.[33] Guy d'Oilly's estate evidently came into the hands of the main branch of the d'Oilly family, the descendants of another brother Niel, who succeeded to Robert d'Oilly's barony of Hook Norton.[34] In later centuries Wigginton was attached to this lordship and held as part of 3 fees with Ardley, South Weston, and Wheatfield, all places held in 1086 by Robert d'Oilly.[35] The overlordship remained with the d'Oilly family for over a century, and then passed to Thomas, Earl of Warwick (d. 1242).[36] In 1242 Wigginton was held for a ½ fee of Thomas's sister and heir Margaret, Countess of Warwick.[37] Her husband John de Plescy (d. 1263), styled Earl of Warwick, succeeded in retaining after his wife's death some of the d'Oilly lands, among them Wigginton, which was retained by the Plescys until the late 14th century and followed the descent of Ardley and Bucknell.[38] Philip de la Vache successfully claimed overlordship of Wigginton, as held of his manor of Hook Norton, as late as 1391.[39] No further record of the overlordship has been found.

No mention occurs of the mesne tenancy of Wigginton in the 12th century, but since the manor was later held by the Fitzwyths it is probable that it followed the descent of Ardley and South Weston and was held by Roger son of Ralph, a nephew of Niel d'Oilly and an ancestor of the Fitzwyths.[40] He was followed at Ardley, and no doubt at Wigginton also, by his son Ralph (d. by 1201) and grandson Robert (d. by 1218).[41] In 1227 Ralph son of Robert was in possession of the advowson of Wigginton church and probably of the manor. His brother Guy who presented to the church in 1231, may have been already in possession of the manor, as he certainly was in 1242 when he was returned as holding a ½ fee.[42] Guy was dead by 1268 when his relict Iseult seems to have had dower in Wigginton.[43] Their son John was called 'of Wigginton' at the end of the century, and had been succeeded there by his son Robert Fitzwyth by 1306.[44] Both Robert and his son Guy died in 1316, and Elizabeth, Robert's relict, was said to be lady of the vill; when Wigginton was assessed for tax in that year she paid the highest assessment.[45] Guy's heir was his infant daughter Elizabeth, but the Fitzwyth estate at Wigginton, as at Ardley and South Weston, passed into the hands of a collateral branch, the Fitzwyths of Shotteswell (Warws.).[46] John Fitzwyth doubtless acquired the manor on Elizabeth's death and in 1342 his son Robert was probably in possession of the manor as he was of the advowson. Robert was returned as tenant of the ½ fee in 1346.[47] After the murder of Robert's nephew and successor Robert Fitzwyth in 1362 his relict Joan had dower in Wigginton manor, but released her rights in 1370 to Sir John de Beauchamp of Holt (Worcs.), later created Lord de Beauchamp, Baron of Kidderminster. Beauchamp had married Joan, daughter and heir of Robert Fitzwyth and his first wife, and thus he acquired her father's inheritance.[48] Wigginton followed the same descent as Ardley after Lord de Beauchamp's attainder in 1388, and on the death of his son John de Beauchamp in 1420 passed to John's daughter Margaret, relict of John Pauncefoot. Margaret may have leased the manor, as she did the advowson, for in 1428 Joan, relict of John Blount, was said to hold the Fitzwyth lands and the ½ fee.[49] By 1472, however, Wigginton manor was held by the three daughters of Margaret Beauchamp,

[26] Par. Rec., receipt and see p. 163.
[27] See p. 170.
[28] Ibid., vestry mins.
[29] Ex inf. Canon A. J. S. Hart.
[30] Kelly's Dir. Oxon. (1887) and see pp. 169–70.
[31] See p. 167.
[32] Par Rec.
[33] *V.C.H. Oxon.* i. 420, 386n. For Guy d'Oilly see ibid. vii. 126.
[34] Dugdale, *Baronage* (1675), i. 460; I. J. Sanders, *English Baronies*, 54.
[35] E.g. *Cal. Inq. p.m.* ix, p. 184; *V.C.H. Oxon.* vi. 8; vii. 254, 266.
[36] *V.C.H. Oxon.* vi. 348; I. J. Sanders, *English Baronies*, 54.
[37] *Bk. of Fees*, 823.
[38] *V.C.H. Oxon.* vi. 8, 73. For further information about the families holding Wigginton down to the 18th century see ibid. 8–10.
[39] C 145/241/91.
[40] *V.C.H. Oxon.* vi. 8.
[41] Ibid. 8–9.
[42] *Rot. Welles*, i. 65; ii. 22, 34; *Bk. of Fees*, 823.
[43] *Fines Oxon.* 196.
[44] Macnamara, *Danvers Family*, 61, 80; E 179/161/10.
[45] *Feud. Aids*, iv. 166; E 179/161/10.
[46] *V.C.H. Oxon.* vi. 9.
[47] Linc. Reg. iv, f. 289v.; *Feud. Aids*, iv. 179.
[48] *V.C.H. Oxon.* vi. 9.
[49] *Feud. Aids*, iv. 187.

Alice, Joan, and Elizabeth, and their husbands.[50] As at Ardley Elizabeth's third of Wigginton was divided on her death without issue between her two surviving sisters. In 1501 Joan and her husband John Croft were recorded as holding half the manor,[51] and Alice and her husband, John Guise, must have held the other half for it descended to their son John Guise. In 1518 he acquired the Croft portion and in 1539 sold the whole manor to the king, who seven years later granted it to Sir Thomas Pope of Wroxton.[52] The Blount family, however, appears to have been the lessee throughout this period and later.[53]

Sir Thomas Pope (d. 1559) had also acquired the neighbouring estates of Hook Norton and Tadmarton and, on the other side of the county, Ardley, whose descent Wigginton continued to follow.[54] In 1559 John Pope (d. 1584), his brother and heir, became the absentee lord of Wigginton and was succeeded by a nephew, Edmund Hochens (d. 1602).[55] The estates then reverted to John Pope's son William, created Earl of Downe in 1628, and on his death in 1631 passed, with the exception of Wroxton, to his grandson and heir Thomas Pope, Earl of Downe (d. 1660), then a minor.[56] As a royalist he had his north Oxfordshire estates sequestered in 1650 and let to various tenants.[57] After his death Wigginton's connexion with Ardley was broken, for his uncle and heir Thomas Pope, Earl of Downe (d. 1668), granted Wigginton and neighbouring estates to Ambrose Holbech (d. 1662) of Mollington, a noted lawyer.[58] Holbech's son Ambrose (d. 1701) was still in possession in 1670, but evidently sold the property to Richard Brideoake of Ledwell (in Wootton), son of Ralph Brideoake, Bishop of Chichester.[59] Brideoake held some of the Holbech estates by 1691 and was mentioned as lord of lands in Wigginton in 1694, by which time he presumably held the manor.[60] He obtained an Act of Parliament to sell part of his estate, including land in Wigginton, in 1710,[61] but apparently did not include the manor, for his son Richard (II), who had inherited the property by 1712, still held the manor at his death in 1715, and either a younger brother or a son, Ralph Brideoake, lord of Hook Norton and Swerford, was lord in 1718.[62] A Mr. Rowney, probably Thomas Rowney, M.P. (d. 1727), the Oxford attorney and a considerable landowner in the county, who already held the advowson, was named as joint lord.[63] Brideoake died in 1728.[64] The immediate descent of the manor has not been established,[65] but it must have been sold at some date before 1759 to the Argyll family for in that year Jane, Duchess of Argyll and Greenwich, was holding the leet court. It passed with her Adderbury property to Henry, Duke of Buccleuch, who held courts in the period 1770–93.[66] In 1795 William Walford had the manorial rights and was recorded as lord up to 1812.[67] By 1817 the manor had passed into the hands of Sophia Elizabeth Wykeham, Baroness Wenman of Thame Park, who was still lady in 1852. In 1854, however, it was held by R. S. Bolton Davis of Swerford Park,[68] the successor of the Brideoake family there. He was still lord in 1891; there is no later record of manorial rights, although Lady King who succeeded him at Swerford Park was returned as one of the chief landowners in Wigginton as late as 1920.[69]

LOCAL GOVERNMENT. The manorial court survived at least until 1825, although, after inclosure in 1796, its activities were limited. The constable, hayward, and thirdborough were chosen and sworn there, and breaches of manorial custom punished. The court regulated open-field farming and dealt with minor offences such as having an unauthorized garden or a dunghill in the street.[70]

From the 16th century the vestry was responsible for most local government; for Wigginton the surviving records are exceptionally complete.[71] Its officers, the constable, 2 churchwardens, 2 overseers of the poor, and 2 surveyors of the highways, were elected yearly.

The constable looked after the parish stocks and whipping-post,[72] the parish pound, the well, and the fences between Wigginton fields and neighbouring parishes. He paid the parish crow- and mole-catchers and hired a bull for the use of the town. He was responsible for the relief of the travelling poor; in 1694–5, for example, 336 persons received relief as they passed through Wigginton. The organization of the militia was also the constable's responsibility; usually militia men were chosen by lot but in 1780 the constable seized on 'an idle fellow for a soldier' and had to satisfy the justice in Banbury. The constable performed the usual duties of collecting national and local taxes, which he paid over at the Reindeer Inn in Banbury.

The surveyor of the highways relied largely on casual labour; in the 1790s labourers were paid 1*s*. a

50 *V.C.H. Oxon.* vi. 9. It is not certain which husband was the father of Margaret Beauchamp's daughters.

51 C.P. 25(1)/294/80/78, 102; C.P. 40/957, m. 21.

52 C.P. 25(2)/34/225/41; *L. & P. Hen. VIII*, xv, p. 411; ibid. xxi (2), p. 158.

53 See p. 163.

54 *V.C.H. Oxon.* vi. 10; 142/124/153.

55 C 142/271/178; C 3/355/15; *Cal. Pat.* 1554–5, 90–91. The permission to give Wigginton to Trinity College, Oxf., was not acted on.

56 *V.C.H. Oxon.* vi. 10. 57 Ibid.

58 C.P. 25(2)/707/Trin. 13 Chas. II.

59 C.P. 25(2)/708/Trin. 22 Chas. II; Foster, *Alumni*.

60 C.P. 25(2)/865/East. 6 Wm. & Mary; cf. M. Dickins, *Hook Norton*, 77.

61 Act for the sale of part of the estate of Richard Brideoake, 9 Anne, c 43 (priv. act).

62 For the Brideoakes see O.R.O., S. & F. colln. (uncat.); C.P. 25(2)/1049/Trin. 1 Geo. I; *Par. Colln.* iii. 292, 341; Tadmarton par. reg.

63 *Par. Colln.* iii. 341; *V.C.H. Oxon.* v. 217, 241.

64 Tadmarton par. reg.

65 Some property was purchased by the Marlboroughs (C.P. 25(2)/707/Trin. 26 Geo. II) and the Duke's son George is mentioned in connexion with it in 1869: O.R.O., gamekprs' dep. No deeds relating to this property have been found in the archives at Blenheim.

66 O.R.O., S. & F. colln. (uncat.); Par. Rec., steward's precepts to constable for summoning the court, 1770–85.

67 Wigginton Incl. Act, 35 Geo. III, c 21 (priv. act); O.R.O., gamekprs' dep.

68 O.R.O., gamekprs' dep.; Gardner, *Dir. Oxon.* (1852); Billing, *Dir. Oxon.* (1854). For the Baroness Wenman see *V.C.H. Oxon.* vii. 177.

69 *Kelly's Dir. Oxon.* (1864–1920).

70 O.R.O., S. & F. colln. (uncat.); Par. Rec., presentments, e.g. 26 Oct. 1770.

71 Par. Rec., constable's accts. 1690–1836; chwdns' accts. 1717–1837, 1842–92; accts. of surveyors of highways, 1772–95; overseers' accts. 1713–1826. Unless otherwise stated, all references are to these volumes. See also F. D. Price, 'A North Oxfordshire Parish and its Poor: Wigginton, 1730–1830', in *Cake and Cockhorse* (Banbury Hist. Soc.), ii (1). 1–6.

72 New ones were purchased in 1704 and 1736: Par. Rec., constable's accts.

day and annual expenditure was between £1 and £3. Most of this was spent on the Banbury–Stow road. Work done on the bridges was carried out by the Cleaver family of stonemasons.

In the first 60 years of the 18th century the cost of poor relief was comparatively small: in 1720 it was just over £3, and in 1770 it was £45. During this period few people received direct money payments; when they did so it was usually 1*s.* for a woman and 2*s.* for old men (presumably with their wives). The able-bodied poor were set to work on the roads, or bird-scaring, cow-keeping, stone-breaking, ditching, and picking up stones from the fallow. Women were employed making clothes for the aged poor. Occasional relief was given in kind, for instance in clothes, food, and coal. The overseers paid medical bills for the sick poor; in the 1820s they subscribed £2 12*s.* 6*d.* a year to the Radcliffe Infirmary, Oxford, to secure admission for Wigginton paupers.[73] If a patient died, they paid for the burial and tried to recoup themselves by selling the patient's effects. The overseers spent much time dealing with settlement problems[74] and with bastards and orphans; the care taken over the education of such children is shown by the terms on which 3 children were apprenticed in 1796 to a Hook Norton tailor, an agreement requiring a premium of £10.[75]

The impact of the Napoleonic wars led to a steep rise in the cost of poor relief. The year of inclosure the overseers spent £130 and in 1800 £237. After a fall to £150 in 1802–3 expenditure rose steadily.[76] In 1819 it reached £650, raised by a rate of 10*s.* in the £. It is clear that the overseers tried new methods in the face of growing expenditure. They began to build houses for the poor, the earliest in 1777 and 3 more in 1811. A workhouse was set up in 1785, and it was agreed to farm the poor to Thomas Wilkes, a wool-comber, who also seems to have been a publican in the village. He was paid £67 5*s.* a year, for which sum he agreed to clothe, feed, and care for the inmates. Food included 3 hot meals a week, as laid down by the workhouse rules. In return Wilkes had the labour of his charges free. In 1790 the overseers took a more constructive step. They tried to develop the sandpits on Wigginton Heath, in order to make money to ease the rates. Handbills advertising the sand were printed for distribution in Banbury market, and the Banbury town crier was paid 6*d.* for crying Wigginton sand there on market days.

Wigginton's population increased by a third between 1811 and 1821, and the returning officer attributed this to the 'frequent and early marriages of the labouring poor: to which the plan of relieving them by head money according to the number of their respective families no doubt operated as a very great inducement'.[77] After the wars the overseers had adopted the roundsman system. By 1822 the situation was so bad that they cut the rate of outdoor relief by as much as a third in some cases. Their accounts end in 1826. Their expenditure in 1834–5 was still high; it amounted to £319. The following year, after the parish became part of the Banbury Union, only £168 was spent.[78] In 1851–2 only £105 was spent on relief at 1*s.* 4½*d.* in the £ on rateable value.[79]

ECONOMIC HISTORY. On the eve of the Conquest Wigginton was assessed at 10 hides, a round figure suggesting that it was a well-established vill.[80] In 1086 there was land for 6 ploughs, although in fact there were said to be 3 ploughs on Guy d'Oilly's demesne farm and 5 in the hands of his tenants. The significance of this excess of ploughs, which was paralleled in the neighbouring parish of Hook Norton, is not clear, but it may have been related to the fact that Wigginton, like Hook Norton, lay in the path of marauding armies of the 10th and 11th centuries.[81] There is no indication that the village suffered at the Conquest, for the valuation of the estate both in 1066 and 1086 was £5. The other assets of the parish were a mill, rendering 8*s.*, and 16 a. of meadow. Of the 20 recorded peasants 9 were *villani*, 5 were bordars, and 6 were serfs attached to the demesne. The serfs presumably manned the 3 ploughs in accordance with the medieval custom of 2 men to a plough. Another tenant of the lord was a knight (*miles*), an unusual entry in the Oxfordshire Domesday.[82]

There seems to have been a considerable demesne estate belonging to the Fitzwyth manor, although nothing is known of its history. The lord was assessed at more than six times as much as the next highest contributor for the thirtieth of 1306, and at nearly 3 times as much in 1327.[83] There were no other tax-payers of substance. The highest number of contributors to these taxes was 24, and in 1316, when 21 contributed, the tenants' share of the tax was fairly evenly distributed, 9 paying between 2*s.* and 2*s.* 6*d.* and 11 between 1*s.* and 1*s.* 6*d.*[84] The contribution of the village was standardized at £2 15*s.* 8*d.* in 1334, only a moderate sum in comparison with other parishes of the same size in the hundred.[85] To the poll tax of 1377 73 adults were assessed.[86]

By Henry VIII's reign, in the absence of a resident lord, some farmers had risen to prominence and moderate prosperity. For the subsidy of 1523 there were 17 contributors of which most can be identified as yeomen and husbandmen. The almost landless labourer, paying the lowest sum of 4*d.*, who was a common feature of many parishes, had only a single representative at Wigginton.[87] By 1577 the 3 chief farmers were George Blount, Humphrey Hall, and Richard Croft.[88] They were members of families already well-established in the parish and prominent in the following century as well. The Blount family apparently farmed the land of the manor as early as 1428, when Joan, relict of John Blount, held it;[89] in 1523 George Blount paid the second highest contribution (8*s.*) in the parish; and another George Blount (d. 1604) was among the 7 contributors listed in 1577.[90] The property of the

73 Par. Rec., receipts from Radcliffe Infirmary.
74 Par. Rec., settlement orders.
75 Par. Rec., apprentice bonds.
76 *Poor Abstract*, 400–1.
77 Rec. Par.
78 *2nd Rep. Poor Law Com.* 294–5.
79 *Poor Law Unions*, 21.
80 *V.C.H. Oxon.* i. 373, 420.
81 Ibid. 393n. 413, 420.
82 Ibid. 420.
83 E 179/161/8, 9, 10.
84 E 179/161/8, 9.
85 E 179/161/17.
86 E 179/161/44.
87 E 179/161/196, 198.
88 E 179/162/341.
89 *Feud. Aids*, iv. 187. A Wigginton husbandman owed money to John Blount in 1441: *Cal. Pat.* 1436–41, 464.
90 E 179/161/196; E 179/162/341.

Blount family in the 17th century included at least 4 yardlands and by the middle of the century one of the family, John Blount, had risen into the ranks of the gentry.[91] He was probably the John Blount who paid tax on a comparatively large farm-house (5 hearths) in 1665; at his death his personalty was valued at £90.[92] The Hall family likewise flourished in the 16th century, and they continued to farm in the parish up to the mid-19th century.[93] For the subsidy of 1577 Humphrey Hall paid on £5 worth of goods,[94] and William Hall (d. 1683), who left 2 yardlands in his will, had moveable goods valued at £70.[95] Other members of the family, at their deaths, had goods valued at £45, £54, and £115, and Richard Hall (d. 1766) had goods worth £867, £620 of which was owing to him on debts and mortgages.[96] The Croft family also prospered: when John Croft died in 1666 he had £61 out on bond and debts and was worth in all £84; while Thomas Croft (d. 1667) had goods worth £320, of which a half was in farm equipment, stock, and grain.[97] Other Wigginton farmers were comparatively wealthy in the late 17th century: in 1677, for instance, Richard Calcott's goods were valued at £206, in 1695 Richard Humfreys's to £170, and in 1700 Thomas Giles's to £178.[98]

On the other hand hearth tax returns give the impression that the village as a whole was comparatively poor. Although 22 house-holders had been listed in 1662, only 9 farmers were assessed in 1665 and 3 were discharged on account of poverty. Only the Blount family and one other farmer had largish farm-houses.[99]

The structure of the village remained almost unchanged until the inclosure of the common fields in 1796. Nearly all the inhabitants at that date had a stake in the land and there were some 24 landholders, including the rector. There was, however, a very marked differentiation in the size of holdings: 2 were of 4 and 7 yardlands each, 12 between 1 yardland and 3½ yardlands, and 9 of a ¼ to ¾ yardland.[1] Assessments for land tax in the late 18th century show that there were *c.* 28 small proprietors in the parish. Of these only between 6 or 8 were owner-occupiers, but they included, in 1798 for instance, the largest farmer in the parish, John Hall, with land assessed at £9 10*s.*[2] His nearest rival was David Samman, assessed at £7 11*s.* The fact that Samman was a pauper by 1819–20 may illustrate the financial uncertainty of small-scale farming.[3]

The conservative character of agriculture until 1796 is indicated by the small amount of inclosed land (38 a.), most of it apparently lying close to the village, compared with 37½ yardlands in the open fields.[4] Within the framework of the open-field system, however, there had been developments since the medieval period. It is likely that an original 2-field system was preserved here as in other north Oxfordshire parishes until comparatively late.[5] There were certainly 4 fields or quarters by 1685, but they may not have existed in 1601, when a terrier described the position of arable lands, acres, or ridges by reference to furlongs and not fields.[6]

In 1685 the divisions were Milcombe Quarter (called Wheat Quarter in 1748), which evidently lay to the east of the church, South Quarter, sometimes called South Field, in the tongue of land in the south of the parish, Petye Bush Quarter (Pitchy Bush in 1748 and Pit a Bush in 1796) and Midnill Quarter.[7] The way in which the changes in field rotation could take place is indicated by the names 'the hitching', which is found attached to various lands in Pitchy Bush Quarter in 1748, and 'hitching leys', recorded in 1796: presumably this was land taken at one time from the fallow or leys for arable.[8]

The leys were a feature of Wigginton's agriculture as of that of neighbouring parishes. The rectory land in 1685, for example, included 'grass ground' in 'Sweet Leys', 'Morrall Leys', Rynell, Pit Furlong, the Heath, and 'shooting on to Tadmarton ditch and Castle ditch'.[9] In 1748 a description of leys belonging to a holding included leys at Marchwithys, under Hanghill and Withycombe leys, as well as leys 'in the Heath' (at Black Heath, Ling Heath, Lott Heath) and on Horsehill and Roundhill.[10] In 1797 there was heath or grassland around and to the north of the village itself and in the very north of the parish towards Tadmarton.[11]

Meadow lay near the streams and was divided into lots. In 1748 a holding included a ¼ lot in Tenury Meadow, and other lots in Oxhay, Sidemore, South Mead, and at Clownam Bridge.[12] At inclosure 4 tenants had rights to the first mowth of meadow in the Mill Ham, Flag Meadow, and Mill Acres.[13] Holdings in the open field carried common rights, which included the right to cut furze on the heath. The tenement described in 1748 included a lot of land on 'fuel moor', and at inclosure in 1796 the poor's right to cut furze and other fuel growing on the commonable lands was specifically mentioned.[14]

Farming throughout the 17th and 18th centuries was of a mixed character and there is no indication of any wholesale conversion to pasture, such as took place in some neighbouring parishes: Davis's map of 1797, for instance, showed a mainly arable parish.[15] Names such as Peas Furlong, Oat Furlong, Rye Hill, Hay Down, and Wheat Quarter indicate the cropping,[16] and farmers' inventories confirm

[91] He was John Blount, gent. of Wigginton who leased 2 yardlands in 1654: O.R.O., S. & F. colln. (uncat.).

[92] *Hearth Tax Oxon.* 135; MS. Wills Oxon. 77/3/19.

[93] e.g. O.R.O., land tax assess. 1785–1831; *Billing's Dir. Oxon.* (1854).

[94] E 179/162/341.

[95] MS. Wills Oxon. 132/3/20. For the Halls see also *Hearth Tax Oxon.* 135.

[96] MS. Wills Oxon. 35/1/17; 133/1/28; 133/2/39.

[97] Ibid. 18/1/64; 13/5/2.

[98] Ibid. 14/2/10; 34/4/33; 80/1/19.

[99] *Hearth Tax Oxon.* 135; E 164/504.

[1] O.R.O., incl. award.

[2] O.R.O., land taxes, 1785–1805. Most proprietors were assessed at under £1.

[3] Par. Rec., land tax assess., overseers' accts.

[4] O.R.O., incl. award. If the 1902 acreage is taken there must have been 63 a. of old inclosure: H. L. Gray, *Eng. Field Systems*, 538.

[5] Gray, *Eng. Field Systems*, 136.

[6] MS. Oxf. Archd. Oxon. c 141, ff. 497, 501.

[7] Ibid. f. 497; O.R.O., S. & F. colln. (uncat.); O.R.O., incl. award.

[8] O.R.O., S. & F. colln. (uncat.); O.R.O., incl. award.

[9] MS. Oxf. Archd. Oxon. c 141, f. 497.

[10] O.R.O., S. & F. colln. (uncat.).

[11] Davis, *Oxon. Map* (1797).

[12] O.R.O., S. & F. colln. (uncat.).

[13] O.R.O., incl. award.

[14] O.R.O., S. & F. colln. (uncat.); Wigginton Incl. Act 35 Geo. III, c 21 (priv. act); and see p. 170.

[15] Davis, *Oxon. Map* (1797).

[16] e.g. MS. Oxf. Archd. Oxon. c 141, f. 501.

that the usual crops were barley, oats, hay, and wheat. Most farmers kept sheep, horses, pigs, and cattle. The inventory of one wealthy yeoman (d. 1667) included £10 worth of wool in his house, 77 sheep, 30 ewes and lambs, a few horses and pigs, and 3 stocks of bees; among his stored crops was a rick of wheat and maslin, and he had 2½ yardlands of crops in the field.[17] Another man (d. 1676/7) had livestock (pigs, cows, and horses) worth £67, and winter corn in the field worth £49.[18] The inventory of William Hall (d. 1683) gives a picture of the type of husbandry practised by a small farmer with 2 yardlands: he had mares and colts (£9 10*s.*), cows and a bull (£8 5*s.*), sheep and lambs (£9 2*s.* 6*d.*), a crop of corn and hay worth £20 10*s.*, and wool and hemp worth £1 1*s.* His house also included a cheese chamber with cheese racks and boards.[19] Hemp was grown in the fields and spinning wheels are mentioned in the inventories of several farmers, as well as stored hemp and wool for spinning.[20]

The system of crop rotation followed at Wigginton included the fallow year or 'deads year'. A lease in 1654 of 2 yardlands of arable in the open fields enjoined good husbandry on the tenant, who was to leave all the fallows 'soiled' and ploughed 'ready for feed'; the lessor reserved all trees and right of entry to cut them. This lease was for 6 years at an improving rent of £19 for 4 years and then £20 a year.[21] Ordinances and presentments made in the courts leet of the late 18th century reveal some of the usual difficulties experienced in managing the open fields: in 1772 it was ordered that the cow pasture which was always hained (i.e. closed to cattle) on 21 April should in future be hained on 5 April, and that none should tie any horse, mare, or colt upon any bank between the cornlands in the fields. In 1781 3 tenants were presented for over-stocking the sheep-commons.[22]

In 1796 the inclosure award dealt with 1,124 a. of open field, waste, and common.[23] The lord of the manor received 2 a. for manorial rights. The largest allotments (194 a. and 188 a.) were made to the rector and to David Samman. Two allotments of 94 a. and 80 a. were made, but the remaining 29 allotments were much smaller: 17 of 10 a. to 60 a., 6 of 1 a. to 9 a., and 6 of under 1 a.[24]

Inclosure was not followed by any marked change in land-holding in Wigginton. Although there was great distress in the parish at this time, it was a consequence chiefly of the Napoleonic Wars and the difficult conditions after them.[25] In 1820 there were still 28 proprietors in the parish and in 1831 34 proprietors. The number of owner-occupiers had increased but the 2 largest holdings, with rentals of £263 and £145, were tenant-occupied.[26] Amalgamation of holdings, however, was undoubtedly taking place and by the mid-19th century small-scale farming was declining. In 1851 there were 12 farmers in the parish, 7 with farms between 97 a. and 250 a., and 5 with small-holdings of between 6 a. and 22 a.[27]

About 1842 the rector made available 35 allotments, known as the Dashlake allotments. In 1876 new rules were drawn up which made the holdings of an allotment dependent on attendance at church or chapel, and on good behaviour. Later these rules were found to be unworkable: from 1878 the rector let the ground for £30 a year to the tenant of Rectory farm, leaving him free to sub-let.[28] Farming remained mixed, although there was perhaps more permanent pasture after inclosure, and an 1827 lease specified an extra annual rent of £50 for every acre of meadow or pasture ploughed up, and another £50 for every acre sown or planted with flax seed, rape, hemp, woad, or teazels.[29] In 1914 57 per cent. of the parish was permanent pasture and there was a high proportion of cattle and sheep on the land compared with the south of the county. Wheat, oats, and barley were the main crops, with some mangolds, swedes, and turnips.[30] In 1919 over half (i.e. 100 a.) of Wigginton's glebe estate was pasture.[31] The ironstone is generally so close to the surface that in modern times large-scale arable farming has been considered unprofitable.

In the 1930s farming was still mixed with a substantial dairying side and there was a similar pattern of farming in 1961 when *c.* 65 per cent. of the parish was permanent pasture, running sheep and cattle. The crops were wheat, barley, and oats, and a small amount of roots. The average size of farms was small, ranging from 57 a. to 180 a., but all were fully mechanized.[32]

In the 1851 census the only non-agricultural workers recorded were 4 masons, a master carpenter, a waggoner, a timberer, a grinder, and a miller.[33] The mill or its millers are occasionally mentioned from 1086 onwards.[34] A miller continued to work the water-grist-mill until at least 1920, but other craftsmen and traders had disappeared rather earlier.[35] The village, nevertheless, had its own grocer, general store, butcher, baker, builder, blacksmith, thatcher, wheelwright, joiner, shoemaker, and tailor until after 1900.[36] Many women made gloves (for a Chipping Norton firm) and straw bonnets. The Wyatt family's building firm only came to an end after the Second World War. In 1962 many of the inhabitants worked in Banbury and Bloxham.[37]

CHURCH. The earliest documentary reference to the church is *c.* 1210.[38] About 1130, however, the canons of the church of St. George, Oxford, were in possession of part of the demesne tithes[39] and this may mean that some tithes were reserved for the incumbent of Wigginton.

The first recorded presentation was made by Ralph, son of Robert, an ancestor of the Fitzwyths,

[17] MS. Wills Oxon. 13/5/2.
[18] Ibid. 14/2/10.
[19] Ibid. 132/3/20.
[20] Ibid. 34/4/33; 80/1/19.
[21] O.R.O., S. & F. colln. (uncat.).
[22] Ibid.
[23] O.R.O., incl. award; Gray, *Eng. Field Systems*, 538.
[24] O.R.O., incl. award.
[25] See p. 163.
[26] O.R.O., land tax assess.
[27] H.O. 107/1733.
[28] Par. Rec., misc. pps.
[29] O.R.O., S. & F. colln. (uncat.).
[30] Orr, *Oxon. Agric.*, statistical plates.
[31] *Sale cat.*: Bodl. G.A. Oxon. c 317(14).
[32] Ex inf. Mr. Hawtin Checkley.
[33] H.O. 107/1733.
[34] *Close R.* 1227–31, 406; C.P. 43/495, rot. 147; ibid. 557, rot. 59; O.R.O., S. & F. colln. (uncat.); *Kelly's Dir. Oxon.* (1869–1920).
[35] *Kelly's Dir. Oxon.* (1869–1920).
[36] Ibid.
[37] Local information.
[38] *Rot. Welles*, i. 65.
[39] See below.

between 1209 and 1219, and he presented again in 1226.[40] The advowson followed the descent of the manor and so came into the hands of Sir John de Beauchamp in 1361.[41] In 1418 a presentation was made by John Eburton of Milcombe on the gift of Sir John and in 1419 by a group of men who were possibly Eburton's trustees.[42] Temporarily the manor and advowson descended separately: in 1459 Anne, relict of Thomas Sculle, presented; in 1483 and 1499 Sir William Berkeley, possibly her second husband, and in 1503 his relict Anne, presented.[43] By 1524 the advowson was sold to John Geyser who gave it to Richard Wye.[44] By 1546 the Crown had purchased it and reunited it with the manor, granting both to Sir Thomas Pope.[45] In 1555 Sir Thomas was licensed to settle the advowson on his new foundation, Trinity College, Oxford, but his intention was never carried out.[46] Turns of the advowson were sold or given away by the Popes on occasions: in 1572 Hugh and Elizabeth Powlett, for instance, presented.[47] In 1668, on the death of Thomas Pope, Earl of Downe, and the division of his estates, the Earl of Lindsey and other of Pope's heirs leased the advowson to Ambrose Holbech, who already held the manor, and others, and in 1676 they leased it to William Taylor.[48] In 1683 Sir Francis North presented[49] but by 1686 Thomas Rowney had acquired the advowson, for he gave it to Jesus College, Oxford, in that year.[50] The College has since regularly presented.[51]

In 1254 the value of the rectory was only £3 6*s.* 8*d.*[52] Its value had risen by 1428 to £8 13*s.* 4*d.*,[53] by 1526 to £13 6*s.* 8*d.*, out of which the rector was paying a curate £5 6*s.* 8*d.*, and by 1535 to £17 13*s.* 4*d.* gross or £17 2*s.* 8*d.* clear.[54] In the early 17th century it was said to be worth £100 a year.[55] In the early 18th century it was only worth *c.* £80, but by the end of the century its gross value was £290.[56] In 1834 the rectory was endowed with £3,000, apparently by Jesus College,[57] and in 1887 it was worth £400.[58]

Robert d'Oilly granted two parts of the demesne tithes to the canons of St. George's in Oxford Castle. Henry I confirmed this grant in *c.* 1130.[59] These tithes passed to Oseney Abbey in 1149.[60] Before 1270 these tithes were commuted for a fixed annual payment of 5*s.*[61] On two occasions, in 1272 and 1283, when the pension was withheld, Oseney Abbey brought successful actions in the ecclesiastical courts to recover it.[62] The pension was still being paid to Oseney at the Dissolution.[63] In 1542 it was granted to the Dean and Chapter of Christ Church, Oxford,[64] but appears to have been granted later to the lords of the manor, for in 1806 a fee-farm rent of 5*s.* was being paid by the rector to the Duke of Buccleuch,[65] who was then lord.

There is no record of the total value of Wigginton tithes, but when they were commuted in 1844 the rector was awarded 174 a. for them with an annual rent-charge of 18*s.* 8*d.* for the tithe on tenements.[66] The rector also had part of the tithes of Milcombe, a chapelry of Bloxham, and at the inclosure of Milcombe in 1794 received 32 a. for them.[67] Wigginton's claim to Milcombe tithes, the basis for which is not known, led to a long dispute with Godstow Abbey ending *c.* 1200, when it was agreed that the Rector of Wigginton was to get half the tithes from 2 hides belonging to Merton Priory and all the tithes from 2 more hides.[68] Later the rector's tithable land was reckoned as 14½ yardlands which lay intermixed in the open fields with land tithable to Bloxham.[69] In a tithe dispute in 1601 it was stated that 'much of it (i.e. Wigginton's land) cannot be known'.[70] John Dyde, Rector of Wigginton, alleged that the Vicar of Bloxham was withholding his tithes and that Eton College, Bloxham's lay rector, was trying to deprive him of his predial tithes.[71] In another dispute in 1674 it was said that before the Civil War the holders of some messuages in Milcombe had been buried at Wigginton church; and that an aisle was set apart in his church for his Milcombe parishioners.[72] The customs about the tithes of wool and lambs indicate the complications of the system: if a man had part of his land in Bloxham parish and part in Wigginton and his commons were not fully stocked with sheep, the curate of Milcombe had the whole tithe of what belonged to Bloxham and the parson of Wigginton lost his tithe. In the case of one farm, the tithe corn went to Wigginton, but not the hay tithe. Tithe of the mill at Milcombe also belonged to the rector.[73] At the time of inclosure at Milcombe in 1794 Eton College was paying Wigginton's rector £15 a year for Milcombe tithes.[74]

The usual disputes likewise occurred over the collection of tithes in Wigginton itself: in a case of 1574 all the witnesses were agreed that if a man kept no more than 6 black sheep no tithe wool was paid but only ½*d.* on every fleece.[75]

The glebe was valued at £3 in the 14th century.[76] Since so many rectors were non-resident, glebe and tithes must have been leased at an early date but the first certain reference to leasing occurs in 1574.[77] Two terriers of the glebe in 1601 and 1685 indicate

[40] *Rot. Welles*, i. 65, ii. 22; and see p. 161.
[41] See p. 161. For list of incumbents and patrons see MS. Top. Oxon. d 460.
[42] MS. Top. Oxon. d 460.
[43] Ibid.
[44] Linc. Reg. xxvii, f. 179v.; P.C.C. 26 Ayloffe (Will of Ric. Wye).
[45] *L. & P. Hen. VIII*, xxi (2), p. 332.
[46] *Cal. Pat.* 1554–5, 90–1.
[47] *Reg. Parker* (Canterbury & York Soc. xxxix), 1002.
[48] Jesus Coll. Mun.
[49] P.R.O. Institution Bks.
[50] Jesus Coll. Mun.
[51] P.R.O. Institution Bks.; MS. Oxf. Dioc. c 2071.
[52] Lunt, *Val. Norw.* 310.
[53] *Feud. Aids*, vi. 377.
[54] *Subsidy 1526*, 270; *Valor. Eccl.* (Rec. Com.), ii. 163.
[55] MS. Dunkin 438/2, f. 153.
[56] *Par. Colln.* iii. 341; MS. Oxf. Dioc. d 549.
[57] Jesus Coll. Mun.
[58] MS. Oxf. Dioc. d 549.
[59] Salter, *Oxf. Chart.* no. 50.
[60] *V.C.H. Oxon.* ii. 90, 160.
[61] Ibid. iv. 48.
[62] Ibid. 291–4.
[63] *Oseney Cart.* vi. 246.
[64] *L. & P. Hen. VIII*, xvii, p. 491.
[65] MS. Oxf. Dioc. c 449.
[66] Jesus Coll. Mun., terrier 1844.
[67] O.R.O., Milcombe incl. award.
[68] *Godstow Eng. Reg.* ii, p. 476–7.
[69] Par. Rec., reg. 1558 (fly leaf).
[70] MS. Oxf. Archd. Oxon. b 41, f. 155.
[71] MS. North c 5, ff. 48–9.
[72] E 134/26 Chas. II/Mich. no. 21, 26–7 Chas. II/Hil. no. 2.
[73] MS. Oxf. Archd. Oxon. b 41, f. 155.
[74] Milcombe Incl. Act, 33 Geo. III, c. 74 (priv. act).
[75] MS. Oxf. Dioc. c 21, f. 438.
[76] *Inq. Non.* (Rec. Com.), 138.
[77] MS. Oxf. Dioc. c 21, f. 438.

that the rector had arable and leys land amounting to *c.* 30 a. scattered throughout the open fields.[78] He also had 2 'lands' in the open fields of Milcombe.[79] When Jesus College revalued the rectory after tithe commutation in 1844, the property comprised the rectory-house, a small dwelling house in the village, 210 a. in Wigginton of which 30 a. had been allotted in lieu of glebe, and 32½ a. in Milcombe.[80] In 1887 the glebe, reduced to 225 a., was worth £326 a year; 218½ a. were sold in 1919, and by 1939 only 1 a. remained.[81]

The earliest known rector, instituted at some time between 1209 and 1219, was made subject to the rules of the Lateran Council by Hugh of Welles, Bishop of Lincoln, as he already had a benefice worth £2 10*s.*[82] He appears to have been followed by a younger brother of the lord of the manor, Gilbert son of Robert, a subdeacon.[83] In the 14th century another Fitzwyth, an acolyte, was incumbent.[84] In the later Middle Ages several incumbents were graduates. One of them, presented in 1507, had to pay an annual pension to his predecessor and was non-resident at the visitation of 1517–20. His successor was probably non-resident in 1526 and 1530 when he had a curate.[85] Wigginton had two educated incumbents during the Reformation period; the second, Hamlet Malbone (*c.* 1559–1572), had previously been master of the school maintained by the Trinity Guild in Chipping Norton and was 'a man well learned in grammar'.[86]

Wigginton's 17th-century rectors were usually resident. John Calcott (1594–1612)[87] evidently farmed his own glebe; agricultural implements, cows, horses, sheep, and crops on the glebe worth £32 were listed in the inventory drawn up on his death.[88] His successor, Gamaliel Holloway, also resided for some time,[89] and when he became rector of Kislingbury (Northants.) and resided there, his son Thomas acted as curate of Wigginton.[90] Thomas was reported as curate in 1635 and 1641 and later became rector.[91] The Holloways were a Royalist family. Gamaliel was present at the battle of Edgehill and actively supported the king on other occasions.[92] His son was ejected from Wigginton in 1646 and his wife was granted one-fifth of the issues of the rectory.[93] During the Interregnum Richard White was intruded as rector; the registers were not kept in this period.[94] After the Restoration Wigginton obtained in John Dyde (1662–83) another rector who had suffered for his loyalty to Charles I.[95] He was active in safe-guarding his church's temporal rights.[96] His will shows him to have been a man of some wealth and of studious inclinations.[97] His memorial inscription described him as *Pietatis, fortitudinis, charitatis, exemplar spectabile.*[98]

When Thomas Rowney granted the advowson to Jesus College in 1686, he stipulated that one of the five senior Fellows should be presented to the rectory whenever there was a vacancy, thereby preventing the danger of simony 'which too much is used by lay patrons' and at the same time enabling the college to elect as Fellows 'ingenious young men' who would otherwise be disappointed of promotion.[99] The college seems to have benefited at the expense of the parish in the 18th century. The meagre value of the benefice and possibly the remoteness of Wigginton led to non-residence and the employment of poorly-paid and often transitory curates. Between 1717 and 1738, for instance, there were at least four curates.[1] In 1738 the curate, who was paid £30 a year, was not licensed and lived four miles away, having 'no conveniency of boarding there'.[2] He also served Milcombe church once a month,[3] an obligation arising out of the payment of tithes by Milcombe villagers. The curate stated in 1738 that the rector, Francis Payn (1729–75), was then expected to reside[4] and he may have done so occasionally, but he was Dean of Jersey and lived there part of the year.[5] The parish does not seem to have been neglected, however, and the chancel was kept in good order.[6] Thirty years later the parish still had neither a rector or curate in residence. The curate held 4 communion services a year, performed Sunday duty at Wigginton, and took services at Milcombe 13 times a year. He catechized children in summer.[7] The absence of full visitation returns for the parish in the period 1768–1802 may be attributed partly to an aged rector and partly to indifferent ones. The poor state of repair in the church at this time and reports of small congregations confirm neglect.

From 1789 to 1872 the living was held by two graduates of Jesus College, one of whom lived in Guernsey,[8] the other, as Fellow and Tutor of his college, being only occasionally resident.[9] Their curates lived in the rectory-house and by 1814 were paid £70.[10] In 1834 the congregation was *c.* 150, roughly half the population, and there were 25 communicants.[11] The curate, John Thorp, catechized the children once a month in Sunday

[78] MS. Oxf. Archd. Oxon. b 41, ff. 155, 156.
[79] MS. Oxf. Dioc. c 449.
[80] Jesus Coll. Mun., terrier 1844.
[81] Kelly's Dir. Oxon. (1887); Par. Rec., misc. pps.
[82] *Rot. Welles*, i. 65.
[83] Ibid. ii. 22.
[84] Linc. Reg. ii, f. 148v.
[85] Ibid. xxvii, f. 179v.; *Visit. Dioc. Linc. (1517–31)*, i. 126, ii. 41.
[86] O.A.S. *Rep.* 1916, 52.
[87] The name was a very common one in Wigginton: MS. Wills Oxon. and Par. Rec., reg.
[88] MS. Wills Oxon. 296/1/59.
[89] There are regular entries in the register of his children's baptisms and in 1624 he was overseer of a parishioner's will: Par. Rec., reg.; P.C.C. 47 Byrde.
[90] *Walker Rev.* 280. His daughter Joan is described on her marriage in 1641 as of Kislingbury: Par. Rec., reg.
[91] *Walker Rev.* 297.
[92] Ibid. 280; MS. Oxf. Dioc. c 2071: MS. notes on the rectors of Wigginton.
[93] *Walker Rev.* 297.
[94] Par. Rec., reg.
[95] M.I. once in church; see *Par. Colln.* iii. 341.
[96] See p. 166.
[97] MS. Wills Oxon. 124/4/16.
[98] Jesus Coll. Mun.
[99] *Par. Colln.* iii. 341.
[1] MS. Oxf. Archd. Oxon. e 4, ff. 16, 23, 42; ibid. c 143, f. 50.
[2] MS. Oxf. Dioc. d 554.
[3] Ibid.
[4] *Secker's Visit.*
[5] On his visits to England he stayed sometimes, if not all the time, at Swerford Rectory with his son-in-law: Par. Rec., misc. pps.
[6] MS. Oxf. Archd. Oxon. b 27, ff. 354–7; Par. Rec., chwdns' accts. 1756.
[7] Par. Rec., reg.
[8] MS. Oxf. Dioc. b 38; ibid. d 575.
[9] Ibid.
[10] Ibid. d 575.
[11] MS. Oxf. Dioc. b 38.

school and gave a lecture, which was not part of his duty, on Sunday afternoons.[12] There were 8 communion services and 2 full additional services on Christmas Day and Good Friday.[13] A new parsonage was built in 1844.[14] The rector, John Williams, was an active parish priest. There were 2 services on a Sunday, evening service with a sermon once a week in Advent and Lent, and monthly communion; children were regularly catechized, and an evening school for adults was started with partial success.[15] Williams attempted to reform village morals by attaching moral conditions to the possession of the Dashlake allotments.[16] He felt that he was hampered in his work in Wigginton by a turbid spirit of excitement in his flock and by the facility with which publicans got licences: there were 3 inns in the village for a population of 320.[17]

The institution in 1876 of E. S. Ffoulkes, a former Roman Catholic,[18] was followed by a great increase in church services. Assisted by a permanent licensed curate he held 2 services on Sundays, matins daily, and communion twice a month.[19] He found that many of his parishioners had never been confirmed and, if confirmed, were non-communicants.[20] His religious and moral zeal brought him into conflict with his parishioners, particularly when he attempted to restore the original rules relating to the Dashlake allotments.[21]

In 1879 A. D. Mozley became rector. He was the nephew of Cardinal Newman and a Tractarian.[22] His successor H. J. Riddelsdell continued the High Church tradition. Canon A. J. S. Hart has been incumbent since 1922; since 1937 he has been perpetual curate of Barford St. Michael with Barford St. John.[23]

The church of *ST. GILES*, built of the local ironstone, comprises chancel, nave, aisles, western tower, and porch set at an angle at the west end of the north aisle.[24] The only surviving feature earlier than the 13th century is a Romanesque capital re-used as a corbel supporting the westernmost truss of the roof of the south aisle. The nave and aisles date from the 13th century, but the bases and capitals of the north arcade are earlier in character than those of the south. Both aisles are lit by lancet windows, arranged in grouped triplets. The original chancel arch has been replaced, but on the north side the newel stairs to the rood loft remain. A piscina indicates that there was formerly an altar at the east end of the south aisle.

Early in the 14th century the chancel was rebuilt, with the exception of the chancel arch, which survived until the 19th-century alterations. There are 'low-side' windows at the west end of both walls. Immediately to the west of the one on the south side there is a stone seat with an ogee-arched canopy, crocketed and decorated with ball-flower ornament. It is possible that this seat once surmounted the sedilia on the south side of the sanctuary, which shows signs of mutilation. Externally the chancel was decorated with a cornice with ball-flower ornament, which appears to have been re-sited later when a clerestory was added. Parker, writing in 1850, reported that there was a Decorated cornice 'stilted up above the Perpendicular clerestory'.[25] The cornice was restored to its original position during the restoration of 1870–1. The unbuttressed west tower dates from the late 14th or early 15th century. In the 15th century clerestories were added to both nave and chancel. In 1584 the churchwardens were cited because the church was 'in decay', but as they replied that it was under repair and would be finished in three weeks no extensive structural changes may have been involved.[26] Repairs were needed again in 1668, when the churchwardens were threatened with excommunication for not repairing the body of the church, and in 1671, when dissatisfaction with the progress of the work led to the substitution of new ones.

The churchwardens' accounts show that the fabric was in need of constant attention throughout the 18th century:[27] in 1734 and 1735 repairs, particularly to the porch, were carried out. The sundial on the tower was put up in 1745. In 1755 the churchwardens were ordered to have the south-east side of the church wall repaired and pointed, to have the south door mended and the porch paved, and to carry out many other minor repairs:[28] this work appears to have been carried out in 1757–65, but there were many other small payments to the plumber and the carpenter in 1770 and 1790. In the period 1787–97 in particular repairs were being carried out on the roof and south aisle. Between 1798 and 1807 about £100 was paid out for repairs. In 1808 a new gallery was erected and the church was re-paved. In 1809 there were plans for completing the re-seating of the church and in 1811 a new font was purchased. A new pulpit and a new desk staircase were included in the estimate for repairs.[29]

The church appears to have been unheated before 1856.[30] By 1870 the building was 'in rapid decay' and the south aisle in particular had become unsafe. It was said that the chancel could not safely be touched unless the south aisle and the chancel arch were also repaired. Plans for restoration were made by William White of London. George Anthony of Waddesdon (Bucks.) was employed as builder and the church was re-opened in 1871 after the most urgent part of the work, the repair of the south aisle and chancel, had been completed.[31] The chancel clerestory was removed and a high-pitched roof was added. The builder is alleged to have taken advantage of the rector's illness and to have done the work

[12] MS. Oxf. Dioc. b 38.
[13] Ibid.
[14] Par. Rec., misc. pps.; MS. Oxf. Dioc. b 106, no. 8.
[15] MS. Oxf. Dioc. d 179, c 332, c 338.
[16] See p. 165.
[17] MS. Oxf. Dioc. d 179, c 332.
[18] Ibid. d. 761.
[19] Ibid. c 344.
[20] Ibid.
[21] See p. 165.
[22] Par. Rec., misc. pps.
[23] *Oxf. Dioc. Yr. Bk.* (1965); *Crockford* (1964–5).
[24] For an account of the church in 1919 see *Jnl. Brit. Arch. Assoc.* xxv. 17 and figs. 40–42.
[25] Parker, *Eccles. Top.* no. 150. For pre-restoration views see MS. Top. Oxon. a 69, nos. 593, 594 (J. C. Buckler, 1823); MS. Top. Oxon. b 165, no. 223 (*c.* 1820); ibid. b 220, f. 87v.; drawing by A. J. W. (1863) at Wigginton Rectory.
[26] *Archdeacon's Ct.* i. 21.
[27] Par. Rec., chwdns' accts.; cf. MS. Oxf. Archd. Oxon. c 113, ff. 84, 85, 88; ibid. c 154, f. 85.
[28] MS. Oxf. Archd. Oxon. d 13, ff. 12v.–13.
[29] Ibid. c 154, f. 85.
[30] The first entry relating to the purchase of coke occurs at that date: Par. Rec., chwdns' accts.
[31] MS. Oxf. Archd. Oxon. c 104, ff. 471, 475, 477, 483

so badly that the south aisle had to be repaired again in 1873–4.[32] The second part of the work was carried out in 1886 by the architect J. L. Pearson.[33] During the restoration all interior plaster was removed so that any mural paintings there may have been were destroyed.[34]

A 19th-century pulpit (replaced in 1935),[35] communion rails, and a communion table were probably installed at the time of the restoration work, but the early-19th-century pews were retained and two of the ancient bench ends, re-used in 1809–11, have therefore been preserved. The previous communion table is preserved in the south aisle. New nave pews were installed in 1963 in memory of W. Osborne Smith, churchwarden 1952–62. An organ, designed by Norman & Beard of London, was obtained in 1913 and electric light was installed in 1934.[36]

There are two medieval monuments in the chancel, in arch recesses, which have been obscured by the raising of the chancel floor and the insertion of benches. The recumbent knight now on the north side was originally lying on a black marble gravestone on the south side and a stone coffin with a cross on it, described by Rawlinson as on the north side, has been destroyed. The effigy of a recumbent man with two small female figures, one on either side, now in the southern recess, was fixed to the outside of the south aisle in the early 18th century.[37] The ledger stone to John Blount (d. 1699/1700)[38] is now only just identifiable.

A few fragments of old glass remain in the chancel windows. The stained glass in the east window was designed by A. L. Moore of London in 1909.[39]

There is a silver chalice of *c.* 1670.[40]

Of the 3 bells one was formerly dated 1631, but the present ones were recast in the 18th and 19th centuries.[41] There is a clock of mid-17th-century date, arranged to strike the hours on the tenor bell. It has been disused since the 1920s.[42]

The registers are complete from 1558.[43] The other parish records are kept in a handsome parish chest, bought in 1796.[44] The earlier, 16th-century, chest is also preserved in the church.

NONCONFORMITY. The Compton Census of 1676 listed 16 Protestant nonconformists in the village. It is known that there was at least 1 woman Quaker,[45] but probably most of the nonconformists were Anabaptists, for in 1738 the rector reported 12 Anabaptists of 'no considerable rank', and said that their number had been constant over several years. They had no meeting house. The rector also reported 1 Quaker and the Quaker registers for the 18th century give the names of four.[46] Over 30 years later there were still Anabaptists in the parish though their numbers were 'lessening daily'.[47] In 1814 Robert Cleaver and his wife were reported as Baptists and in 1817 the rector said that there was only one dissenter 'who is sometimes an Anabaptist and (as I understand) at other times of another denomination'.[48]

The revival of dissent in this remote village was encouraged by the strong communities at Chipping Norton and Hook Norton.[49] By 1835 the Particular Baptists at Wigginton were sufficiently organized to have a chapel built with sittings for 100.[50] The 1851 Census recorded an average congregation of 50, many of its members doubtless coming from neighbouring villages; when the rector reported in 1854 that the chapel was 'not very numerously' attended he may have been referring to Wigginton members only.[51] The chapel (of exceptionally severe aspect) remains near the village hall, and is now used as a store-house.

In 1834 there were said to be 2 Wesleyan families, and a Wigginton house was registered for meetings by the Methodist minister of Chipping Norton.[52] A barn, belonging to one of the Stanbra family, was licensed in the same year.[53] The certificate, which was signed by a Hook Norton dissenter, gives no indication of the denomination, and some at least of the Stanbras were strong Anglicans.[54] Although the rector in 1878 stated that there were only 2 professed dissenters many more of his parishioners must have been willing to attend chapel, for in 1883 a Wesleyan chapel was built.[55] A Methodist family from outside the village, from the Heath, was and still is (1965) the backbone of the congregation. In 1955 the church's congregation was increasing; the building was redecorated and electric heating was installed.[56]

SCHOOLS. Until 1832 there was no regular day school in Wigginton. In 1738 there was a dame school in the parish, at which the rector and his curate paid to have 6 children taught reading. As soon as the children could read, they were replaced by others.[57] By 1808 this arrangement had come to an end and there was a Sunday school, where about 30 children were taught to read, write, and say the catechism. The parishioners contributed £6 yearly to its support.[58]

A small dame school, with 10 boys and 10 girls, existed in 1815, as well as the Sunday school which then had 33 pupils. According to the rector there was no great desire in the village for learning; the National Society's new plan for instruction could not be introduced since no one in the village was capable of understanding it; there was unconquerable

[32] Par. Rec., correspondence.
[33] Ibid.
[34] Traces of a painting of St. Christopher are reported to have existed in the north aisle.
[35] MS. Oxf. Dioc. c 2071.
[36] Ibid.
[37] *Par. Colln.* iii. 341.
[38] Ibid.
[39] MS. Oxf. Dioc. c 2071.
[40] Evans, *Ch. Plate.*
[41] *Ch. Bells Oxon.*
[42] For full details see *Oxon. Clockmakers*, 21, 73. The legend that it came from Bloxham almost certainly arises from confusion with Samuel Bloxham to whom payments for maintenance and repairs were made by the churchwardens in the early 18th century.
[43] Par. Rec.
[44] Ibid., chwdns' accts.
[45] Compton Census; Banbury Quaker Reg.
[46] *Secker's Visit.*; Banbury Quaker Reg.
[47] MS. Oxf. Dioc. d 560.
[48] Ibid. d 575.
[49] See below.
[50] H.O. 129/163.
[51] Ibid.; *Wilb. Visit.*
[52] MS. Oxf. Dioc. b 39; ibid. c 645, f. 16.
[53] Ibid. c 645, f. 15.
[54] E. R. Stanbra was churchwarden from 1833 at intervals until 1894.
[55] MS. Oxf. Dioc. c 344; *Kelly's Dir. Oxon.* (1915).
[56] *Oxf. Mail*, 4 Feb. 1955.
[57] *Secker's Visit.*
[58] MS. Oxf. Dioc. d 707.

indifference among the parents, who sent their boys to work as soon as possible, while their girls were sent lacemaking.[59] Even so, within 3 years another day school, under a master, had been set up and the Sunday school still flourished. Wigginton girls, however, were still employed in lace-making for the sake of the wage.[60]

A regular day school, allied to the National Society, was established by the curate, John Thorp, in 1832 and a proper building was provided; there were said to be 36 boys and 31 girls attending, compared with 35 and 34 in the Sunday school, but the room was so small that it is doubtful whether all could be accommodated at the same time. The school was supported partly by voluntary contributions and partly by payments of 4*d.* from farmers' children and 2*d.* and 1*d.* from labourers, the master receiving 12*s.* a week for himself and his wife.[61] There was also a small school kept by a woman, where 4 girls and 4 boys were taught at their parents' expense.[62]

Within a year the attendance at the National school had risen to 46 boys and 37 girls, ranging from 3 to 12 years old.[63] By 1854 50 children attended the school. The Sunday school numbers had dropped to 40 and the rector complained that it was impossible to keep children there after 11 or 12 years of age.[64] The day school had one uncertificated master, who was greatly underpaid, and there was little equipment. There was no charity support, and any financial deficit had to be borne by the rector, whom the trustees left in full control. In 1859 the school was enlarged, on ground given by the rector, to accommodate 72 children, although attendance remained on the same level.[65]

The rector's reports of 1866 and 1868 give attendance figures at the day school as 60 and at the Sunday school as 50. Of the Sunday school pupils 21 did not attend on weekdays. The rector considered the evening school to be very well attended.[66] The day school figures may have been optimistic since the average attendance in 1869 was reported to be only 40.[67]

In 1871 51 children attended the day school.[68] Children over 7 years paid 2*d.* a week, the others 1*d.*; the girls were taught needlework by the assistant mistress.[69] In 1878 the rector reported that there were no pupil teachers, but 5 voluntary teachers, 4 of them women; an evening school was held in the winter when pupils could be got to attend.[70]

Before 1894 accommodation was increased to 89. Attendance, however, barely reached half the capacity; in 1894 there were 30 day pupils,[71] rising to 39 by 1904.[72] The school was in receipt of a Parliamentary grant by 1890 and a fee grant by 1894 which, with voluntary contributions and an old grant, made up an income of £95 in 1897–8.[73]

In 1958 the school, which had a roll of 17 pupils, 16 of whom lived in Swerford, was closed and the children were transferred to Hook Norton Church of England school, until a new school for the children of Wigginton and South Newington could be erected.[74] Following the closure of the school the building was successfully claimed by the descendants of the former rector, John Williams, under the terms of the School Sites Act, the major part having been built on ground given by Williams in 1859. The claimants then (1965) presented the building to the parish as a village hall.[75]

CHARITIES. An almshouse, of which nothing further is known, may have existed in 1642, when an 'almswoman in the churchhouse' was mentioned.[76]

At the inclosure in 1796 *c.* 36 a. on Wigginton Heath were awarded for the provision of fuel for the poor.[77] At first part of the land was used to grow furze, but later it was let and the rent used to buy coal. Until 1804 the rent was £12, the price of 10 tons of coal, but by 1812 the parish was able to let the land for £30 a year. The poor were required to pay 1*d.* a cwt. to defray toll charges when the coal was brought from Banbury, although the farmers lent waggons and teams for the cartage free.[78] By a scheme of the Charity Commissioners in 1908 the income was not to be applied in aid of the rates. The distribution of coal in 1952 was 80 cwt. to 33 recipients. In 1962 the income was estimated at £25–£50 a year.[79]

[59] MS. Oxf. Dioc. c 433.
[60] *Educ. of Poor*, 732.
[61] *Educ. Enq. Abstract*, 757; MS. Oxf. Dioc. b 39; ibid. b 70. The school-room of 1832 was later used as a kitchen. For full account of Thorp's objectives in 1832 and the help he received in the form of financial subscriptions, collections at sermons, and gifts of materials and voluntary labour, see Par. Rec., reg. (memo.).
[62] *Educ. Enq. Abstract*, 757.
[63] MS. Oxf. Dioc. b 39.
[64] *Wilb. Visit.*
[65] MS. Oxf. Dioc. b 70; Ed 7/169/226.
[66] MS. Oxf. Dioc. c 332, c 335.
[67] Ed. 7/169/226.
[68] *Elem. Educ. Ret.* 326.
[69] Ed 7/169/226.
[70] MS. Oxf. Dioc. c 344.
[71] *Pub. Elem. Sch. Ret.* (1894), 498.
[72] *List of Schs.* (1906), 530.
[73] *Ret. of Schs.* (1890), 216; *Pub. Elem. Sch. Ret.* (1894), 498; ibid. (1900), 676.
[74] Ex inf. Oxfordshire County Council, Educ. Cttee.; *Oxf. Mail*, 5 Apr. 1958.
[75] Ex inf. Mr. F. D. Price.
[76] Par. Rec., reg.
[77] O.R.O., incl. award.
[78] Par. Rec., overseers' accts.
[79] Char. Com., Unrep. vol. 40, p. 222; Char. Com., files E 61285, G 53 accts.

WROXTON[1]

THE parish of Wroxton (2,543 a.)[2] lies 3 miles west-north-west of Banbury and includes the hamlet of Balscott.[3] It lies on a sandstone plateau covered by red loam, rising at Claydon Hill, its highest point, to 550 ft. Precipitous ravines, like Ragnell Bottom, cut by streams, form natural boundaries to the north, east, and south; the two villages themselves are situated at the head of other gullies that cut deep into the plateau from the south and east. To the west the parish boundary is marked off by no natural feature from the neighbouring parish of Alkerton.

The parish was once traversed by ancient trackways and by the Saltway, a route from the Worcestershire saltworks to London. It has not yet been possible to prove the existence of a Roman road, but there are slight traces of a Roman settlement.[4] The main road from Stratford-on-Avon to Banbury bisects the parish east and west, passing to the north of Wroxton village and leaving Balscott well to the south. This was always a busy thoroughfare: in 1391 the Prior of Wroxton complained of impoverishment due to the obligation to give hospitality to a stream of travellers on it, and it figures prominently as London Way on maps of Wroxton of 1684 and 1768.[5] Regular entries in Wroxton estate accounts from 1685 about Banbury market[6] suggest that there was considerable local traffic on this road. In the mid 18th century, when it was proposed to turnpike it, William Cartwright of Aynho argued that a good road between Banbury and Stratford 'would be a great convenience for bringing coals thence and carrying corn thence'.[7] The proposed alignment of the road caused disputes, however, and in 1753 30 inhabitants petitioned Francis, Earl of Guilford (d. 1790) asking that the turnpike should follow an existing driftway to avoid loss of good land.[8] The earl was himself concerned in case travellers might avoid the toll-gate by passing through Wroxton Park.[9] A Bill was brought in in 1753 and work began early in 1754.[10]

A stone guide-post, which stands on the Banbury road just outside the village, was set up in 1686 by Francis White, whose name is inscribed on it. The New Inn, also on the Banbury road, probably came into existence soon after the road was turnpiked. To the north of the highway is a mineral railway, a branch of the former G.W.R., built to facilitate the exploitation of ironstone in the parish. It was under construction in 1880.[11]

In the Middle Ages Wroxton was probably a larger settlement than Balscott.[12] In 1377 148 men and women contributed to the poll tax, but many died from plagues shortly afterwards.[13] A suit roll of 1569 lists 70 names, 12 of them of widows.[14] The parish register for 1563–71 shows a continued, if less marked, increase.[15] The Protestation Return of 1641 recorded an adult male population of 107, and in 1676 there were 219 communicants of 16 and over, both of which suggest a total population of *c.* 330.[16] After a period of stability the population began to rise about 1740;[17] the rate of growth was highest, however, in the second, third, and fourth decades of the 19th century. The total population was 613 in 1801, 652 in 1811, and 792 in 1821. By 1841 it had reached a peak of 819.[18] It fell steadily to 562 in 1901. In 1961 it was 598.[19]

Wroxton village lies on the slopes of a valley at a height of *c.* 500 ft. on the east side of the parish. The earliest spellings suggest an etymology *Wroces Stan* or the Buzzards' stone.[20] The extent of the village before the 18th century is unknown, but it can never have been large. In 1738 the vicar returned 50 houses.

In 1797 the village was described as 'tolerably large', and in 1841 there were 129 houses.[21] The main Banbury–Stratford road forms one side of the triangle in which the village lies. From it the village street descends southwards past the church, which stands high above the road, to the pond and school; it leaves Wroxton Abbey and its out-buildings isolated in their park in the south-east corner, and then ascends again to join the highway. Most of the cottages and houses date from the early 17th or 18th century and so the village has preserved to a remarkable extent its regional character. The cottages are mostly 2-storied, though some have cellars, and are built of coursed ironstone rubble, or occasionally of ashlar. They mostly have brick chimney stacks. Probably all were once thatched, for stone slates were little used in this area. There was still much thatch in 1965. A number (e.g. Ivy Cottage) retain ancient stone-mullioned windows or casements, while others have 18th-century casements. Two are dated: Wroxton Cottage is inscribed 'I.S. 1736' and another, some 30 yards to the west of the old school, has a sundial inscribed 'C:S.E. 1752, 30 May'.[22] Many were probably rebuilt after a serious fire in 1666. Collections after the fire were made in various parishes and over £50 was distributed among 18 'necessitated poor'.[23]

The 'White Horse' is first mentioned by name in 1782; the 'North Arms', although a 17th-century house in origin, does not appear to have been licensed until *c.* 1850.[24] It is of two builds and has been

[1] This article is based upon the investigations of Professor Lawrence Stone who wrote parts of it himself.

[2] O.S. *Area Bk.*

[3] The following maps have been used: O.S. Map 25″ Oxon. V. 2, 6, 7, 11 (1st edn.); O.S. Map 2½″ SP 44 (1957).

[4] *Oxoniensia*, xv. 108.

[5] *Cal. Papal Regs.* v. 436; map of Balscott (1684) by Hen. Dormer and map of Wroxton (1768) by Edw. and Thos. Smith in Trinity Coll. Bursary and printed in *Sixteen Old Maps of Oxon.* ed. J. L. G. Mowatt.

[6] MS. North c 50, *passim.*

[7] MS. North d 6, f. 149.

[8] MS. North d 6, f. 148v.

[9] L. Dickens and M. Stanton, *An Eighteenth-Century Correspondence*, 185.

[10] MS. North d 6, f. 148v.

[11] O.S. Map 25″ Oxon. V. 6 (1st edn.).

[12] See p. 189.

[13] E 179/161/44; see p. 179.

[14] Trinity Coll. President's Off., Wroxton and Balscott suit roll.

[15] Par. Rec., reg.

[16] *Protestation Ret.* 49, 50; Compton Census.

[17] Par. Rec., reg. There were 111 baptisms in 1750–59 and 96 burials, compared with 73 baptisms and 58 burials in 1700–40.

[18] *Census*, 1801–41.

[19] Ibid. 1851–1961.

[20] *P.N. Oxon.* (E.P.N.S.), ii. 409.

[21] *Secker's Visit*; MS. Oxf. Dioc. d 575; *Census*, 1841.

[22] For the dovecot at Sundial House see plate facing p. 182.

[23] Par. Rec., note at back of reg.

[24] O.R.O., victlrs' recogs.; Gardner, *Dir. Oxon.* (1852); MS. Top. Oxon. c 104, ff. 569–82.

refaced. There are many farm-houses in the village of 17th- or early-18th-century origin. A barn at Raydon Hill farm is dated 'W.L. 1677'. The 19th and 20th centuries have seen the addition of a few new buildings such as the nonconformist chapels, the vicarage-house, built in 1868 by the architect John Gibson, and the Roman Catholic chapel,[25] but they lie on the fringe of the old village. Since 1840, when its streets were taken in hand by Colonel North and pig-sties and rubbish dumps cleared away,[26] Wroxton has been almost a 'model' village.

The medieval village was no doubt dominated by the Augustinian priory founded there in the 13th century.[27] This brought it into contact with a wider world, and the parish benefited directly from the priory's charitable gifts: on Maundy Thursday bread and fish to the value of 40*s.* was dispensed to the poor, and at the obit of the founder 14 paupers received alms valued at £5 16*s.*[28] The village has also been made memorable by its connexion with Wroxton Abbey, which was built on the priory site in the early 17th century, and with the distinguished members of the Pope and North families who have resided there. Sir William Pope entertained James I, and William's grandson, the royalist Sir Thomas Pope, Earl of Downe (d. 1660), received Charles I and his queen after the two royal armies had joined forces at Edgehill.[29] Francis North, Lord Keeper, who had married a sister of the last Earl of Downe, was often at Wroxton. He spent much of his vacations at the Abbey with his two brothers and his sisters, a company he styled *societas exoptata.* In his last illness he retired to Wroxton, being partly drawn by the recent discovery of the medicinal qualities of the waters at Astrop near King's Sutton (Northants.). He took the great seal with him and carried on his work from Wroxton until his death in 1685.[30]

Among other distinguished members of the family who resided from time to time were the Keeper's brother Roger North, the historian of the family and an amateur scientist, who built a laboratory at Wroxton, and Frederick, Lord North and Earl of Guilford (d. 1792), 13 times M.P. for Banbury, and First Lord of the Treasury 1770–82.[31] Among the literary friends of the family who stayed at Wroxton were Francis Wise (d. 1767), Wroxton's incumbent,[32] and Horace Walpole.[33]

Many of the priory buildings presumably dated from the early 13th century, and in 1304 it was reported that they were out of repair. The prior and convent asked for the grant of three years' indulgence to those visitors who should assist them.[34] A clause in the first lease of the site to Sir William Raynesford, dated 1536, directed that most of the buildings should be destroyed.[35] There is a 13th-century arched recess and a 14th-century doorway in the cellars of the present house[36] and the greater part of the north wing appears to be part of the monastic buildings, the north wall of the existing hall being the original exterior south wall. In 1956 excavations in the grounds uncovered conduits and foundations of some of the monastic out-buildings and further excavations in 1964 revealed the monastic church lying immediately to the north east of the house.

The present house was built in the second decade of the 17th century by Sir William Pope, later Earl of Downe (d. 1631), at a reputed cost of £6,000.[37] The doors of the chapel bear the date 1618, by which time it may be presumed that the work was virtually complete. The house is of 3 stories, with stone-mullioned windows and numerous gables. The west front forms a symmetrical composition, with a central porch running up all 3 stories and flanked by projecting north and south wings. Though a south wing was clearly intended from the first, it was not in fact built until 1858–9. Eighteenth-century drawings show the house ending abruptly where the wing now joins the main structure.[38]

Of the original fittings the most remarkable are the carved wooden doors of the chapel already mentioned, the wooden gallery in the hall, elaborately carved with strapwork cartouches, caryatides, and other Jacobean motifs, and the glass, some by the brothers Van Linge, in the east window of the chapel. There is also a good deal of 16th- and 17th-century woodwork scattered about the house. Some of this was removed in the 18th century from the North family seat of Kirtling (Cambs.), and some was bought abroad by Colonel North in the early 19th century. At one time there was much 16th-century heraldic glass in the windows of the hall, some of which was original and some taken from other houses by the Norths. None of this now remains: some went long since to the Gothic Temple in the grounds of Stowe House (Bucks.), more was removed in 1901 to the Roman Catholic church at Kirtling, and the rest was sold to an American collector in the 1920s.[39] Of the moveables, such as pictures, furniture, and tapestries,[40] nothing now remains at Wroxton, as the entire contents of the house were sold by auction in 1933.[41]

Towards the end of his life Lord Keeper North (d. 1685) carried out some extensive works at Wroxton with the assistance of his brother Roger who was an architect of ability. Roger records that the Lord Keeper erected 'a large order of stabling very

[25] See pp. 184, 186–7.
[26] MS. Top. Oxon. c 104, f. 580.
[27] For an account of the priory see *V.C.H. Oxon.* ii. 101–2.
[28] *Valor Eccl.* (Rec. Com.), ii. 199.
[29] *Mercurius Civicus*, no. 8.
[30] *Lives of the Norths*, ed. A. Jessop, i. 347, 348, 414, iii. 221 and *passim*; for the Spa see Wood, *Athenae*, iv. 297.
[31] *D.N.B.; Lives of the Norths*, ii. 243.
[32] *D.N.B.*; MS. North d 4, d 5a, d 6 *passim* and see Bodl. MS. index to North pps.; *V.C.H. Oxon.* v. 117, 121.
[33] For his correspondence with and visits to the Norths see *Letters of Horace Walpole*, ed. W. S. Lewis and R. S. Brown, *passim.*
[34] Linc. Reg. iii, f. 90.
[35] J. Wilson, *Catalogus Cartarum*, 57. The list of buildings still standing in Aug. 1537 is given in T. Warton, *Life of Sir Thomas Pope* (1780), App. XXII. This transcript is both faulty and incomplete: for 'outside' read 'south side' for 'fourth aisle' read 'south aisle' and add: 'the prior's lodging on both sides and the great buttery' (Trinity Coll. President's Off., Wroxton and Balscott Misc., f. 2).
[36] A plan of these features is at the N.B.R.
[37] This is the figure alleged in the lawsuit of 1631: Trinity Coll., Treasury.
[38] Bodl. Gough Maps 26, ff. 68, 69 (view by Grimm, 1781). For west front and hall see plates facing p. 172.
[39] This glass is now at Roneale Manor, Elkins Park, Philadelphia, Pa., U.S.A.: cf. F. C. Eden, 'Heraldic Glass at Roneale Manor', *Connoisseur*, July 1930.
[40] Inventories of the contents of the house in 1631 and 1678 are to be found in MS. North c 47 (5) and g 12, ff. 399–406.
[41] Bodl. G.A. Oxon. c. 224* (3): Auction cat., contents of Wroxton Abbey.

The west front

The hall in the early 19th century

WROXTON ABBEY

The village street and pond

The old school

WROXTON

stately and convenient; and built from the ground a withdrawing room and back stairs and finished up the rooms of state, as they were called, and shaped the windows, which before had made the rooms like birdcages', all at a cost of over £2,000.[42] When Celia Fiennes visited the house about this time, she approved of the alterations 'all the new fashion way'.[43]

Further alterations were carried out in the 1740s by Francis, later Earl of Guilford (d. 1790).[44] In 1747 he invited Sanderson Miller to design a new Gothic east window for the chapel.[45] Apart from the erection of a new entrance gateway in 1771[46] no further changes took place for nearly a century. A Gothic library designed by Sir Robert Smirke was added on the east side of the house in the second quarter of the 19th century[47] and in 1858–9 Colonel North employed John Gibson (1817–92) to design the south wing in a Jacobean style matching the rest of the house.[48]

The gardens were laid out in 1733–48 by Francis, Earl of Guilford (d. 1790).[49] Alterations had been started even earlier, in 1728, when Francis, while his father was still alive, commissioned Tilleman Bobart, a member of the Oxford family of gardeners, to construct a rectangular pond, 240 ft. × 40 ft., and improve the terrace. In 1730 Bobart submitted a design for the kitchen garden, and was still at work at Wroxton two year later.[50] It is not known whether he was also responsible for the major alterations that then began. The main features of these were a dam, creating a large artificial lake; a cascade falling down 20 ft. and a serpentine river running through woods from the dam to the stream at the end of the park; a pillared Gothic rotunda on a mound, designed by Sanderson Miller in 1750 and equipped with 'curtains that, by turning screws, let down so as to afford shelter whichever way you please';[51] a Chinese summer-house, that was in being by 1749;[52] a Chinese bridge and a small Chinese shelter for a seat; an obelisk erected on a prominent position to commemorate the visit of Frederick, Prince of Wales, for the Banbury Races of 1739;[53] a hot house, and extensive planting of trees, shrubs, and flowers.[54] The result was greatly admired at the time, for example by Horace Walpole and Dr. Richard Pococke, but many of the features of the Georgian layout, including the shelter, rotunda, and summer-house, have since disappeared.[55] The house was modernized in 1964–5 and opened in 1965 as a college for American students of the Fairleigh Dickinson University, New Jersey.[56]

Balscott hamlet lies in the south-west of the parish at the head of a steep gully leading south. The earliest spellings are *Berescote* or *Belescote*, and the name probably derives from *Baelles cot* or the homestead of Baell.[57] The site, 500 ft. up, seems originally to have been triangular, the houses built round a green, with the church almost in the centre. Balscott was a hamlet of moderate size in the Middle Ages;[58] in 1738 the vicar returned 20 houses and in 1841 there were forty-eight.[59] In the 19th century a Wesleyan chapel was built in the apex of the triangle. The school of 1840, enlarged in 1867, was built of stone in the Gothic style.[60] It was not until the 20th century that the introduction of new building materials, yellow brick and concrete, began to make much effect upon the character of the village. The cottages are mainly 2-storied and of 17th- or 18th-century date. They are built of local ironstone, and, although thatch remains, Welsh slate is also common. The 'Butchers Arms', now much altered, dates from the 17th century.

Three farm-houses are of considerable architectural interest. Of these Grange Farm and the Priory Farm retain windows and doors of medieval date.[61] Wroxton Abbey had property in the hamlet and perhaps at least one of these houses and possibly both were originally built for the priory's tenants in the 14th century. In 1535 Richard Burden, a salaried official of the priory and general receiver of all its rents, farmed the priory's grange farm.[62] His family remained in Balscott and for the hearth tax of 1665 Robert Burden (d. 1677) was assessed on 5 hearths.[63] He lived in a house on the northern edge of the hamlet, bordering on the common. The priory also had a bailiff at Balscott, Richard Taylor. He was the receiver of rents for Balscott and Wroxton,[64] and he may have occupied Priory Farm. The occupant in 1665 may have been Edward Atkins who was assessed on 5 hearths for the tax.[65]

Priory Farm is set back from the road behind its farm-buildings. Its original medieval hall, though now subdivided, can be identified. It was unusually large (17 ft. × 19 ft.) and in the south wall there is a window of 4 lights, of which the heads have fine curvilinear tracery of the 14th or early 15th century. The walls are of medieval thickness and the roof is in part medieval although much altered in the 17th century. The house itself was much altered *c.* 1500 when the main entrance through a wide doorway with a 4-centred arch, contained within a square label, was constructed and a new service bay was

[42] Roger North, *Lives of the Norths* (1826), ii. 248; Norwich Publ. Libr. 7803/23, f. 2. In 1680 Ld. North was granted £50 worth of timber when his lease was renewed, because he 'intended great repairs and alterations': Trinity Coll. President's Off., letters between Ld. North and College and Reg. of Fines, 1658–1776, p. 8.

[43] *Journeys of Celia Fiennes*, ed. C. Morris, 26.

[44] MS. North c 59, ff. 23, 54, 177v. etc. Besides 'improvements' to the garden mentioned below the accounts include a payment of £397 for 'improvements' in 1742–3.

[45] L. Dickens and M. Stanton, *An Eighteenth-Century Correspondence*, 130, 183; MS. North c 63, f. 187. The Van Linge glass was rearranged; for descriptions see Bodl. G.A. Oxon. 4° 689, pp. 357–8, and H. T. Kirby, 'The Van Linge window at Wroxton', *Jnl. Brit. Soc. of Master Glass-Painters*, xiv(2). 117–22.

[46] MS. North c 64, ff. 196, 196v.

[47] Gardner, *Dir. Oxon.* (1852).

[48] Note at the back of Ld. North's copy of Warton's *Life of Sir Thomas Pope* (copied in Par. Rec., Compton's notebk.).

[49] MS. North c 58, c 59, *passim.*

[50] Ibid. b 28, f. 26; d 2, ff. 8, 9, 13, 14 (Cynthia Borough kindly supplied these references).

[51] Dickins and Stanton, op. cit., 167, 275; MS. North c 64, f. 151; *Travels through England of Dr. Richard Pococke*, ii. (Camd. Soc. N.S. xliv), 240.

[52] Dickens and Stanton, op. cit., 160, 167; cf. W. Halfpenny, *New Designs for Chinese Temples* (1750, 1751); drawings in Bodl. Gough Maps 26, f. 68.

[53] Hist. MSS. Com. *Dartmouth, III*, 113, 159–60.

[54] MS. North c 58, 59, 63, 64, *passim.*

[55] *Travels through England of Dr. Richard Pococke*, ii. 240; see plate facing p. 183.

[56] *The Times*, 28 Jun. 1965.

[57] *P.N. Oxon.* (E.P.N.S.), ii. 409.

[58] See p. 189.

[59] *Secker's Visit.*; H.O. 107/875.

[60] See pp. 187–8.

[61] For full architectural descriptions see Wood-Jones, *Dom. Arch. Banbury Region*, 42–59 and *passim.*

[62] *Valor Eccl.* (Rec. Com.), ii. 198–9.

[63] *Hearth Tax Oxon.* 147; MS. Rawl. B 400b, f. 191*b*.

[64] *Valor Eccl.* (Rec. Com.), ii. 199.

[65] *Hearth Tax Oxon.* 147.

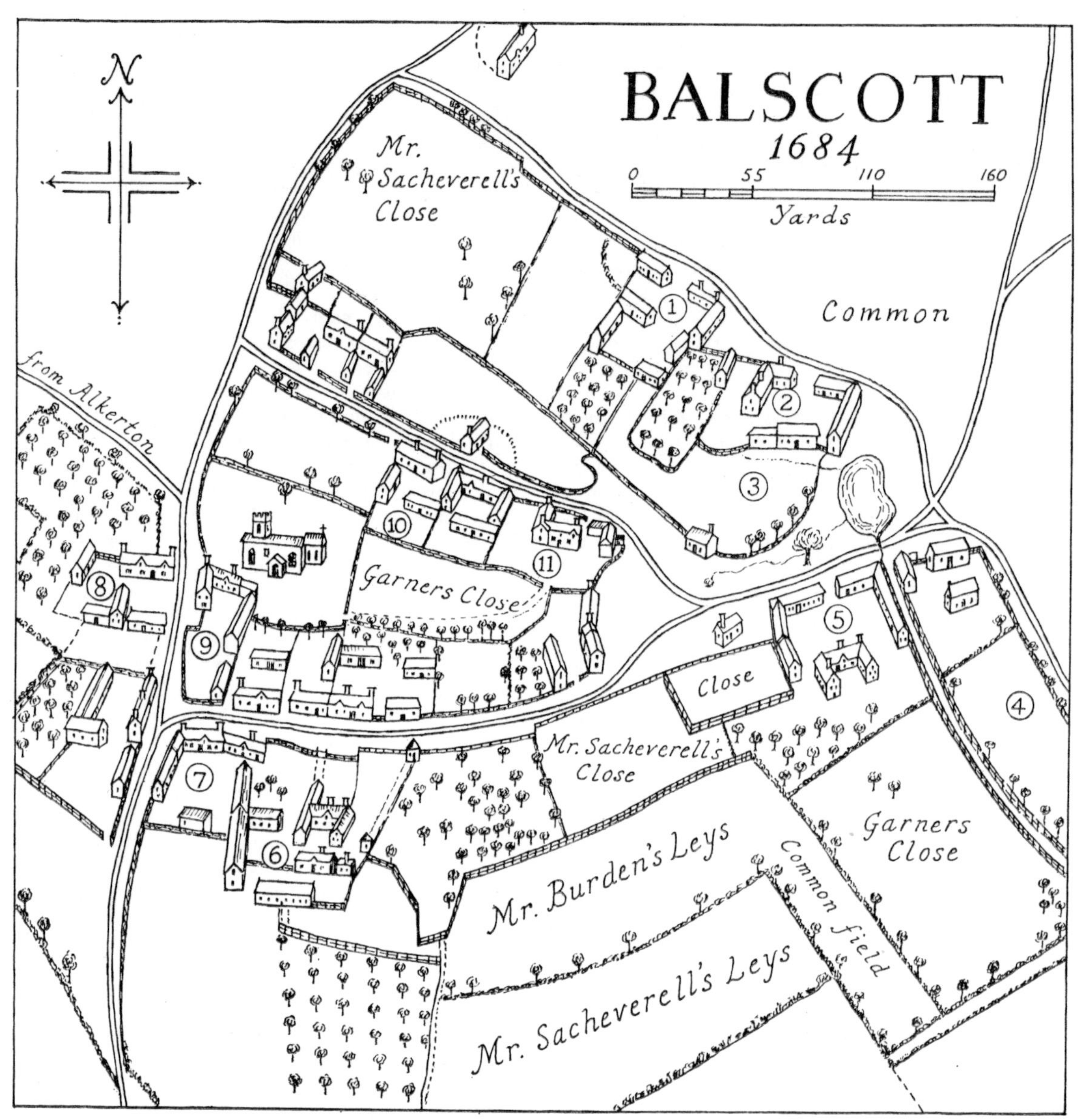

1. Mr. John Burden's house
2. Widow Adkin's house
3. Mr. John Burden's close
4. Mr. John Burden's grange close
5. Mr. Walter Garner's house
6. Mr. William Sacheverell's house
7. Mr. Banister's house
8. Mr. Henry Plum's house
9. Widow Plum's house
10. Mr. John Matthew's house
11. Mr. R. Gardner's house

From a map by Henry Dormer at Trinity College, Oxford.

added, separated by a through passage from the hall. There was a major rebuilding in the 17th century when the north wall of the hall was completely rebuilt and its roof structure altered. A stair-case was added and mullioned windows were inserted. In the mid 18th century there was a complete reorganization of the one-time service end of the building: the 17th-century parlour became the service room and the hall became the kitchen, a new canopied door was added to the south front, and sash windows were inserted.

The architectural history of Grange Farm is very similar. It can be identified with the house with two wings shown on a map of 1684, near to Grange Close from which it is separated by Grange Lane, and was then occupied by Walter Garner.[66] It lies close to Priory Farm and is entered by a fine and unusually large doorway with a 4-centred moulded arch of 15th-century date. A large window of 2 lights, once lighting the medieval hall, remains. It has a stone mullion and transom and Perpendicular tracery contained within a square head. There is a door at the rear with a 4-centred arch. A bread oven was built out into the road at a later date.

Manor Farm, once the manor-house, has an L-shaped plan and dates from the 17th century, though it was much altered in the 18th century. It was the chief house in the village in the 17th century and was occupied by the Sacheverell family. It was assessed on 7 hearths in 1665[67] and it figures on maps of 1677 and 1684.[68] The present house has an 18th-century front, while the rear wing is mainly 17th-century with mullioned windows of moulded stone and a 2-storied stair-case projection. The stable with a pigeon loft over it is also of 17th-century date. The house is approached through a 17th-century gateway and ascending stone steps.

Balscott House, another 17th-century house, consists of 2 stories and an attic. It was originally built on a 2-unit plan but was added to at later dates. A spiral stair-case is contained in a projecting square block at the back of the house. The hall chimney was placed against the screens passage and a large open fire-place still remains.

Outside the village there is another 17th-century house, Balscott Mill, a further illustration of the great revival in agricultural prosperity of this period. Home Farm, of late-18th-century date, is also of some architectural interest. It is built in the local style and with local materials.

Balscott and Wroxton have been chiefly distinguished by their connexion with Wroxton Abbey and its inhabitants. Thomas Pope's estate suffered damage during the Civil War,[69] but the parish played no prominent part in events.

MANORS AND OTHER ESTATES. In 1089 Wroxton, assessed at 17 hides, was held in chief by Guy de Reinbeudcurt, lord of Chipping Warden (Northants.). His son Ingram was holding of him,[70] but neither at Wroxton nor elsewhere is anything further heard of this son and by 1120–30 Wroxton had passed with the barony of Chipping Warden to Richard, another son. *WROXTON MANOR* followed the descent of the barony of Chipping Warden, known also as the honor of Rockingham.[71] Held as 1 fee of the lordship in the late 13th century and probably before, it made payment for castle-guard at Rockingham.[72] The overlordship passed from Richard to his daughter and heir, Margery, and to her husband Robert Foliot. In 1173–4 Foliot became a monk at Old Warden (Beds.) and was succeeded by his son Richard who came of age *c.* 1177 and died in 1203. Through his marriage with Richard's daughter and heir, Margaret, Wischard Ledet (d. 1221) then inherited the barony. His daughter Christine took it to her first and second husbands, Henry de Braybrooke (d. 1234) and Gerard de Furnival (d. 1241–2), and so probably to her third husband Thomas de Grelley (d. 1262), lord of Pyrton. Both in 1235 and 1242, however, for some unknown reason, Wroxton was said to be held by Wischard (II) Ledet, Christine's son by her first marriage, who died on crusade in 1241–2.[73] Christine died in 1271, seised of the barony, including Wroxton. Her heirs were Christine and Agnes, grand-daughters of Wischard (II) Ledet; Christine, to whose share of the barony Wroxton belonged, married Sir William Latimer.[74] The overlordship of Wroxton descended from Christine to her son Thomas Latimer (d. 1334). In 1335 his wife Laura was given dower of a third of the rent of Wroxton.[75] The connexion between Wroxton and the overlords probably became increasingly tenuous, but 6*s.* 8*d.* quit rent for Rockingham castle-guard was still being paid to the king in 1536.[76]

From at least the early 12th century the Belets were under-tenants at Wroxton.[77] Hervey Belet, the first recorded member of the family to hold Wroxton, was excused payment of danegeld for his Oxfordshire lands in 1136.[78] His son Michael, hereditary butler to Henry II and a prominent judge,[79] held Oxfordshire lands in 1155, and Wroxton was probably included in his 1166 return of 4 fees of the old enfeoffment held under Robert Foliot.[80] He was holding the Oxfordshire fee in 1199[81] but was probably dead by 1201.[82] In the office of royal butler and in his Oxfordshire lands at least he was succeeded by his son Master Michael Belet, civil lawyer and canonist.[83] Michael's rights in the property of his grandfather were confirmed by

[66] Trinity Coll. Bursary, Balscott map (1684).
[67] *Hearth Tax Oxon.* 147.
[68] Plot, *Nat. Hist. Oxon.*, frontispiece; Trinity Coll. Bursary, Balscott map.
[69] *Cal. Cttee. for Compounding*, 934–5.
[70] *V.C.H. Oxon.* i. 419. For the Reinbuedcurts see *Cartulary of Old Warden*, ed. C. H. Fowler (Beds. Hist. Rec. Soc. xiii.), 325.
[71] For the barony see Dugdale, *Baronage*, i. 679; Sanders, *Eng. Baronies*, 33–34; Bridges, *Northants.* i. 112.
[72] *Bk. of Fees*, 841; *Cal. Inq. p.m.* ii, p. 208.
[73] Ibid. For these families see *Cart. of Old Warden*, 323–8; *V.C.H. Oxon.* viii. 148 sqq.
[74] Sanders, *Eng. Baronies*, 33–34; *Cal. Inq. p.m.* ii, p. 208.
[75] *Cal. Inq. p.m.* vii, p. 424.
[76] *Valor Eccl.* (Rec. Com.), ii. 199.
[77] Blomfield, *Norfolk*, vii. 152.
[78] *Pipe R.* 1130 (H.M.S.O. facsimile), 6; *Cal. Chart. R.* 1226–57, 376.
[79] *D.N.B.*
[80] *Pipe R.* 1156–8 (Rec. Com.), 37; *Red Bk. Exch.* (Rolls Ser.), 331.
[81] *Red Bk. Exch.* (Rolls Ser.), 124.
[82] In this year his son bought a marriage for his sister: *Rot. de Ob. et Fin.* (Rec. Com.), 180.
[83] *D.N.B.*; Emden, *O.U. Reg.* Dugdale says that he succeeded an elder brother Hervey (*Baronage*, i. 614), but there is no evidence for this, and the references he gives refer to a Hervey Belet who was alive in 1214: *Rot. Litt. Pat.* (Rec. Com.), i. 120. The relict of Michael Belet's brother John claimed dower in Wroxton in 1205, but John is not recorded as holding Wroxton and may have died before his father: *Cur. Reg. R.* iii. 257; *Rot. Cur. Reg.* (Rec. Com.), ii. 57.

King John in 1205.[84] Like his father he too had a successful career as a royal servant, although he temporarily incurred the king's displeasure in 1211 and his property was confiscated for a few months.[85] The Belet family were pious benefactors of religious houses[86] and *c.* 1217 Michael founded a house of Augustinian canons at Wroxton and endowed it, among other properties, with his Wroxton manor-house and demesne.[87] His heirs, his sister Annora and her husband, Walter de Verdun, disputed the grant,[88] but apparently became reconciled to it later, for Annora herself endowed the priory with a mill and 6½ yardlands in Wroxton in 1263.[89] The priory was returned as under-tenant of Wroxton, holding of the honor of Rockingham in 1242 and 1271.[90] Wroxton Priory retained the fee throughout the Middle Ages and gradually extended its holding in the parish, acquiring the Clements' estate in 1242[91] and other small parcels of land.[92] In 1411 the priory was given a grant of free warren in all its Wroxton demesne lands, and by 1536, when it surrendered to the Crown, it held nearly all the land in the parish.[93]

In 1536 the Crown granted a 21-year lease of the site and demesne of the two manors of Wroxton and Balscott to William Raynesford of Wroxton.[94] In 1537 Thomas Pope, the Treasurer of the Court, obtained a reversion of Raynesford's lease in return for an exchange of land and some money, and a grant in fee of the two manors in exchange for Clapton manor (Northants.).[95] In November Pope bought out the remainder of Raynesford's lease for £200 and thus acquired full possession of the manors and demesnes.[96]

In 1551 he gave his brother and heir John a 99-year lease of the manors.[97] Shortly afterwards Thomas Pope conceived the idea of founding Trinity College, Oxford, and in 1554 he conveyed the manors for ever to the new foundation.[98] Pope's arrangements, however, were singularly unbusinesslike for so able and astute an administrator. He agreed with his brother John that his own steward should hold the manorial court, while John took the profits and signed the copies, a wholly illegal arrangement which caused much trouble for Trinity when it took over from Thomas Pope.[99] Worse still, the day after he transferred the property to Trinity he is alleged to have settled it in tail male on his brother John.[1]

The conveyance attesting the settlement has not survived, but the fact that John Pope's son William proceeded to spend £6,000 in the early years of the 17th century in erecting the existing mansion suggests that it was a reality. Some such arrangement for the manor house of Fyfield (Berks.) was certainly made at about the same time by Thomas Pope's old friend Thomas White in his foundation of St. John's College, Oxford,[2] and it is therefore probable that the Wroxton property was so entailed and that Trinity accepted the obligation to renew the lease to the heirs male. Created Earl of Downe in 1628, William Pope died 3 years later, by which time the remarkable situation had arisen of a great English land-owner whose main residence was held on lease. On the first earl's death his younger son Sir Thomas Pope seized Wroxton and Balscott, the evidences to the property, and the personal estate of the late earl, claiming it on the strength of a death-bed will. The heir to the title was the first earl's grandson, Thomas, aged 8, the child of his eldest son William who had died in 1624. It was alleged on the minor's behalf that Trinity College had made a 'confidence or agreement' with the first Sir Thomas Pope that the lease was to be renewed only to the heir male of the family, this document having been seized by Sir Thomas Pope. The President of Trinity College denied all knowledge of any such agreement and 9 years later took a surrender of the old lease from Sir Thomas Pope and issued a new one for 21 years.[3] Thus Thomas, Earl of Downe (d. 1660), never possessed Wroxton; on his death without issue in 1660 his uncle Sir Thomas (d. 1668) succeeded to the title. When the latter's son also died in 1668 there was a failure of the male line, and the property, including the Wroxton leases, was divided between 3 daughters. The second daughter Frances married the rising lawyer Francis North, later Lord Guilford, who in 1681 bought out the shares of the other two in the leases of manors and rectories for £5,100.[4] By this means the property, still held on 21-year leases from Trinity, passed into the hands of the Norths, Barons and later Earls of Guilford, where it remained until the failure of the male line in 1827. It then passed to Maria, Marchioness of Bute, the eldest daughter of George Augustus, Earl of Guilford (d. 1802), until her death in 1841, when it descended to the second daughter, Susan (d. 1884), who inherited the title of Baroness North. She married Colonel J. S. Doyle (d. 1894), who changed his name to North, and their son William, Lord North, continued to hold the estate on lease until his death in 1932. In that year the family found itself in financial difficulties, the lease was surrendered to Trinity, and the long connexion of the Popes and Norths with Wroxton manor ended.[5]

[84] *Cur. Reg. R.* iii. 157.

[85] *Pipe R.* 1211 (P.R.S. N.S. xxviii), 12; *Rot. Litt. Claus.* (Rec. Com.) i. 286.

[86] Blomfield, *Norfolk*, vii. 153.

[87] *Lib. Antiq.*, 90, 98; *V.C.H. Oxon.* ii. 101; *Cal. Inq. Misc.* i, pp. 160–1.

[88] *Cal. Papal Regs.* i. 85.

[89] *Fines Oxon.* 193; cf. 171.

[90] *Bk. of Fees*, 841; *Cal. Inq. p.m.* ii, p. 208.

[91] See p. 178.

[92] *Cal. Pat.* 1317–21, 23; 1321–4, 32; 1334–8, 318; 1350–4, 366; 1354–8, 464; 1391–6, 144; 1429–36, 464.

[93] *Cal. Chart. R.* 1341–1417, 443; *Valor Eccl.* (Rec. Com.), ii. 178–9.

[94] Trinity Coll. President's Off., J. Wilson, *Catalogus Cartarum*, 57. For Balscott manor see below.

[95] *L. & P. Hen. VIII*, xii (1), pp. 251, 341.

[96] Trinity Coll. Tower Mun., Wroxton bdle. C.

[97] Ibid. bdle. F.

[98] Trinity Coll. President's Off., *Catalogus Cartarum*, 58; C.P. 25(2)/76/650/24.

[99] Trinity Coll. President's Off., Wroxton and Balscott Misc.

[1] Alleged by Sir Walter Pye, attorney of the Court of Wards, in a suit brought on behalf of Thomas, Earl of Downe, a minor, in 1631: Trinity Coll. Tower Mun., Wroxton bdle.

[2] In his will of 1558 Sir Thomas White asked the College to continue to lease Fyfield to his heirs 'as long as the male line continues': W. H. Stevenson and H. E. Salter, *Early History of St. John's College* (O.H.S. N.S. i), 397.

[3] Trinity Coll. President's Off., Reg. A, f. 121.

[4] MS. North b 8, f. 127, an account of negotiations with the third daughter, Finetta Hyde. The marriage agreement of 1671 is to be found ibid. b 26, f. 153.

[5] *Complete Peerage*, *sub* Downe, Guilford and North; Trinity Coll. President's Off., Reg. Fines, i, ii.

The Wroxton and Balscott manors, when given to Trinity in 1554, formed a very substantial portion of the college endowment, being £80 out of a total of £191 8*s.* 4*d.*[6] The lease was surrendered in 1640 and from then onward was issued for 21 years at a time, at a rent of £24, 24 qr. of barley malt and 18 qr. of wheat, a fine being paid for each renewal. After 1680 the lease was regularly renewed every 4 years. The fine was set at £120 from 1684 to 1752, and rose to a peak of £1,162 in 1812.[7] The rent, with its substantial proportion fixed to the price of malt and wheat, also rose greatly in the late 18th century, reaching £248 in 1817. In 1860 a new agreement was entered into, providing for a rack rent to begin in 1881.[8] In that year a new lease was granted but in 1894 the agricultural depression obliged William, Lord North, to return to the college the 403 a. of agricultural land which he had rented at £725, leaving himself only the mansion and park at a rent of £510. In 1921 he took a 14-year lease of the mansion and park at a rent of £742, the unexpired portion being surrendered at his death in 1932.[9]

In 1086 *BALSCOTT*, assessed at 5 hides, was a part of the fief of Bishop Odo of Bayeux and was held by Wadard, one of his most influential and wealthy tenants.[10] Like other of Wadard's lands Balscott afterwards formed part of the barony of Arsic, of which Cogges was the head.[11] The later manor, not recorded until the 16th century, descended from the knight's fee for which Balscott was held under this barony, and as late as 1535 the Prior of Wroxton owed suit of castle-guard at Dover, part of the service for which the barony was held.[12] The overlordship was held by the Arsic family in the 12th and 13th centuries.[13] After the death in 1230 of Robert Arsic it formed part of the inheritance of Joan, one of his two daughters and coheirs, and was returned as held of her in 1242.[14] In fact Joan had granted her rights in Cogges to Walter de Grey, Archbishop of York, in 1241, and in 1244 she and her second husband granted the homage and services of tenants, identifiable as tenants in Balscott, to Walter son of Robert de Grey, the Archbishop's nephew, who obtained the barony and the knight's fees in Oxfordshire and elsewhere.[15] The overlordship is not recorded again until 1536.[16]

An under-tenant, William Leuke, perhaps the son of the Robert Leuke who held land in Balscott in 1200, was mentioned in 1204. He claimed to hold 1 carucate in Balscott by service of ½ fee of John le Pahier.[17] John le Pahier's connexion has not been traced further but from later evidence his land was clearly part of the Arsic fee. William Leuke granted it in 1206 to Walter of Sarsden (Cerceden) and his wife Gillian,[18] but the Leuke family had other land for in 1241 William Leuke's son William acknowledged the customs and services he owed for a ¼ fee in Balscott to Joan Arsic and acknowledged the payment of a due for castle-guard at Dover.[19] He was recorded as one of 4 co-parceners in the fee in 1242, and a Roger Leuke was one of the Arsic tenants in 1244.[20] The connexion of the family with the fee is not recorded further and in 1306 a William Leuke of Balscott, presumably the man who was accused of a killing in 1299, paid a very small tax.[21]

The Sarsdens, who were granted the ½ fee in 1206, had a longer connexion. The family seems to have already had land in Balscott, for a Richard of Sarsden was accused of unlawful disseisin there in 1204.[22] Walter of Sarsden, either the original grantee or his son, was a verderer of Wychwood in 1232, and a Robert of Sarsden was a co-parcener in the Arsic fee in 1242 and 1244;[23] John of Sarsden contributed to the tax levied in 1306, and was returned as one of the lords of the village in 1316.[24] By 1346 a John atte Halle held the ½ fee, said to have been formerly held by the heirs of Walter of Sarsden, but by 1428 it was again in the possession of the Sarsden family, as Thomas of Sarsden was lord.[25] There is no later record of his family's connexion with the ½ fee.

Another under-tenant of the fee was Master Simon of Walton, who held 1 yardland in Balscott in 1228 and 6 yardlands in Balscott and Tysoe (Warws.) in 1239–40, and was a co-parcener in 1242.[26] He was later Bishop of Norwich, and became lord in 1247 of an Alkerton manor also, with which his Balscott lands must have descended. His successors at Alkerton in 1277 held 4 yardlands and rent in Balscott.[27] No later reference to this family's holding at Balscott has been found.

The Prior of Wroxton was the fourth co-parcener in 1242 under Joan Arsic. He was joint lord in 1316, and it is likely that the abbey obtained the other holdings in the course of the Middle Ages.[28] In 1536 the abbey held Balscott grange, 5 yardlands, and the mill.[29] The manor, if manor it was, descended with Wroxton to the Popes. It seems likely that there was no medieval manor in the strict sense. By the time the records begin in the early 16th century there was certainly no manorial court.

In 1086 2 hides in Wroxton were evidently included in Miles Crispin's holding assessed under Alkerton.[30] The overlordship of this part of Wroxton followed the descent of the overlordship of Alkerton and was included in the 2 fees held under the honor of Wallingford.[31]

Richard Fitz Reinfrid, the mesne tenant of Alkerton, likewise held these 2 hides and before his death in 1115 or 1116 promised them to Abindgon

6 Trinity Coll. President's Off., Miscellanea i, f. 1.
7 Ibid., Reg. Fines, i, ii; Reg. B 1823; Calculation of Leases, 1820–88.
8 Ibid., Wroxton Copyholds and Leaseholds, 1865, p. 79
9 Trinity Coll. Bursary, Wroxton file; Burke, *Peerage* (1959), 1686–7.
10 *V.C.H. Oxon.* i. 379, 407.
11 Ibid. 379; Sanders, *Eng. Baronies*, 36–37.
12 *Bk. of Fees*, 823; *Valor Eccl.* (Rec. Com.), ii. 199.
13 For the descent see Sanders, *Eng. Baronies*, 36–37.
14 *Bk. of Fees*, 823.
15 *Cal. Chart. R.* 1226–57, 285; *Fines Oxon.* 238.
16 *Valor Eccl.* (Rec. Com.), ii. 199.
17 *Fines Oxon.* 9; *Pipe R.* 1204 (P.R.S. N.S. xviii), 112.
18 *Cur. Reg. R.* iv. 169, 252; *Fines Oxon.* 35.
19 *Fines Oxon.* 115.
20 *Bk. of Fees*, 823; *Fines Oxon.* 238.
21 *Cal. Pat.* 1292–1301, 477; E 179/161/10.
22 *Cur. Reg. R.* iii. 157.
23 *Close R.* 1231–4, 64; *Bk. of Fees*, 823; *Fines Oxon.* 238.
24 E 179/161/10; *Feud. Aids*, iv. 166.
25 *Feud. Aids*, iv. 179, 187.
26 *Cur. Reg. R.* xiii, 161; *Feet of Fines Warws.* (Dugdale Soc. xi), i, p. 117; *Bk. of Fees*, 823.
27 See pp. 45–46; *Feet of Fines Warws.* (Dugdale Soc. xi). i, p. 204.
28 *Bk. of Fees*, 823; *Feud. Aids*, iv. 166.
29 *Valor Eccl.* (Rec. Com.), ii. 198–9.
30 *V.C.H. Oxon.* i. 419; *Boarstall Cart.* 321.
31 *Boarstall Cart.* 321; and see p. 45.

Abbey, a gift which was confirmed by his son Hugh in the presence of the overlord Brian Fitz Count and his wife Maud.[32] Hugh presumably promised to do the foreign service for the holding, for although his immediate successors are not recorded as having any connexion with Wroxton, the manor was included in the 2 fees of Wallingford honor held in 1297 by Master Robert de Stokes, who had possession of this estate by 1293.[33]

Abingdon Abbey appears only to have drawn rent from its Wroxton holding and the under-tenant of Wroxton in 1115, William Clement, continued in possession.[34] He was probably followed by Ingram Clement (fl. 1154–61), lord of Dunchurch (Warws.), and by his grandson William (II) Clement, lord of Balscott and of Dunchurch.[35] Until at least 1244 this estate followed the descent of the Clements' estate in North Newington.[36] It may then have passed to Wroxton Priory which certainly before 1256 bought 3½ yardlands formerly held by Alice Clement.[37] About the same time Alice Clement, called of Wroxton, granted 15*s.* rent from 2 yardlands held of her in Wroxton to Abingdon Abbey.[38] The abbey's rights were acknowledged by Wroxton Priory who agreed to give 3*s.* a year to the abbey.[39] The estate thus acquired by Wroxton Priory was merged with its main manor, and the payment due to Abingdon Abbey was probably included in the annual pension paid to it by Wroxton Priory in 1536.[40]

Before 1219 Michael Belet granted the rectory estate to Wroxton Priory.[41] It then followed the descent of Wroxton manor[42] until in 1544 Thomas Pope made a 99-year lease to his mother, Margaret Bustard, and her heirs of all the tithes of Wroxton and Balscott except those of the manor and demesne.[43] He then professed himself dissatisfied with the Crown auditor's valuation of the rent for the rectory[44] and in 1545 sold the tithes back to the Crown, less the tithes of manor and demesne,[45] although he himself remained the reversionary lessee as inheritor of the Bustard lease. Eighteen months later Henry VIII granted the estate to the Dean and Chapter of Christ Church, Oxford, who thereupon became the lessors of Margaret Bustard.[46] Margaret died in 1557 and the lease passed to Thomas Pope's heir, John, who assigned it in 1560 and again in 1583.[47] In 1623 Christ Church challenged Sir William Pope to show his title, and took the case to Chancery. For 2 years he prevaricated, said he had lost the lease, launched a counter-suit against Christ Church accusing them of stealing it, and then finally produced it. The court upheld the lease in view of the long time it had passed unchallenged, but decreed that the property should return to Christ Church on its expiry. In 1631 the lease was surrendered and a new one granted to Sir Thomas Pope for 21 years; it was renewed to the lessee of the manors for 21 years in 1649, 1659, 1667, and thereafter every 7 years until the inclosure award of 1805.[48] After inclosure the property was leased to the North family as before.

Before the Dissolution the rectorial tithes of Wroxton were valued at £10.[49] From 1631 the rent of the estate consisted of £10 old rent taken two-thirds in cash and one-third in kind in the form of 4 qr. of best wheat and 8 qr. of malt at current Oxford market prices.[50] This relative fixity of rent was compensated for by a fine at will for renewal of the lease. Starting at £40 in 1667 it rose to £100 in 1729 and by 1799 had reached £383. In 1813 it reached a peak of £772, which was not surpassed until 1841; between 1848 and 1864 it was over £1,000. At the same time the rent fluctuated with the corn prices, reaching a maximum of £77 17*s.* in 1799.[51] In 1805 Christ Church and its lessee, Lord Guilford, were awarded 326½ a. for rectorial tithes.[52]

The grant of the church to Thomas Pope in 1537[53] included glebe, which probably belonged to the rectory. In 1623 William Pope was holding a house called the Parsonage, with a garden or orchard and a close.[54] In 1625 Chancery ordered that a search should be made for any glebe or parsonage-house which the Popes might have absorbed.[55] No further reference to rectorial glebe is known.

LOCAL GOVERNMENT. Manorial records are largely lacking, but it is known that the Prior of Wroxton had the assize of bread and ale for his manorial tenants, and also view of frankpledge. Trinity College succeeded to the prior's rights and was still holding the view with court baron in 1804. A copyholder was admitted in that year and a heriot taken.[56] Wallingford honor, later Ewelme honor, had the view for the 2 hides in Wroxton that belonged to its Alkerton fee, and suit was owed to the honor court down to 1720.[57]

Apart from some late 19th-century minutes, and the churchwardens' accounts of Balscott,[58] no vestry records have survived. The vicar recorded in 1751, however, that there were 2 overseers who acted jointly for the poor of Wroxton and Balscott, though the churchwardens of Wroxton and of Balscott kept separate accounts; each hamlet had a constable, though the vicar was unable to say whether they acted jointly or separately, and, as each hamlet repaired its respective highways,[59] each presumably had its own highways' surveyor.

In the early 18th century and probably earlier

32 *Chron. Abingdon* (Rolls Ser.), ii. 108–9.
33 *Cal. Inq. p.m.* iii, p. 481; *Boarstall Cart.* 301, 321.
34 e.g. *Chron. Abingdon* (Rec. Com.), ii. 109.
35 *V.C.H. Warws.* vi. 80.
36 See p. 88.
37 Bodl. MS. Lyell 15, f. 101v.: dated by the abbot, John (1241–56).
38 Ibid. f. 101.
39 Ibid. f. 102.
40 *Valor Eccl.* (Rec. Com.), ii. 198.
41 *Liber Antiq.* 98–99.
42 See above.
43 Trinity Coll. President's Off., Wroxton and Balscott Misc., no. 24.
44 Ibid.
45 *L. & P. Hen. VIII*, xx (1), p. 219.
46 Ibid. xxi (2), p. 334.
47 Ch. Ch. Treasury, Bk. of Evidences, 408.
48 Ibid. 407, 408 and index to Bk. of Leases, vol. 1. For the circumstances of the 1631 lease to Sir Thos. Pope see above.
49 *Valor Eccl.* (Rec. Com.), ii. 199.
50 MS. North c 37, f. 23.
51 Ch. Ch. Treasury, index to Bk. of Leases, *passim*.
52 O.R.O., incl. award.
53 *L. & P. Hen. VIII*, xii (2), p. 350.
54 Ch. Ch. Treasury, Bk. of Evidences, 408.
55 Ibid.
56 *Rot. Hund.* (Rec. Com.) ii. 32; MS. d.d. Morrell c 34.
57 *Rot. Hund.* (Rec. Com.) ii. 32; MS. d.d. Ewelme honor, d 1–3; O.R.O., Ewelme honor cts. (uncat.).
58 Par. Rec.
59 Ibid., correspondence.

the burden of poor-relief seems to have been alleviated by the intervention of the manorial lords: in Lord Guilford's estate accounts for 1709 there occurs an entry of £11 as an allowance for 22 weeks for the poor,[60] which suggests some kind of regular payment. In 1775–6 poor-relief cost the parish £232, but between 1783 and 1785 the average for some reason was only £140.[61] By 1803 there had been a sharp rise: £507 was raised at the rather high rate for a rural parish of 5*s.* 3*d.* of which £353 was spent on out-relief and £104 on in-relief.[62] A workhouse, consisting of 3 cottages, was first mentioned in 1768,[63] and in 1802–3 it had 14 permanent inhabitants. At that date 18 people were receiving permanent out-relief and 10 occasional relief.[64]

As a large proportion of the expenditure at Wroxton went on in-relief the 1834 Poor Law Act had little immediate effect. In 1834–5 £447 was spent and although there was a fall to £371 the following year this was proportionally a much smaller drop than in most other parishes in the county.[65] Expenditure was still at this level in 1851–2 when the parish was part of the Banbury Union and Wroxton's poor were being sent to the Union workhouse.[66]

ECONOMIC HISTORY. In 1086 there were 24 recorded tenants at Wroxton (2 serfs, 12 *villani*, and 10 bordars) and 9 at Balscott (3 *villani* and 6 bordars). There were 8 ploughs owned by the peasants and 3 on the demesne farm at Wroxton. At Balscott there was 1 plough on demesne while the tenants had 2 ploughs. There were 14 ploughlands and 60 a. of meadow at Wroxton and 5 ploughlands and 20 a. of meadow at Balscott. Wroxton was valued at £16 and Balscott at £6.[67]

Fourteenth-century tax lists suggest that Balscott was a slightly wealthier community than Wroxton. In 1316 9 out of 19 contributors were assessed at more than 2*s.* 6*d.* while at Wroxton only 1 out of 44 contributors was assessed at more than 2*s.* 6*d.* The richest man at Balscott was assessed at 6*s.*[68] In 1327 8 out of Balscott's 19 contributors were assessed at more than 2*s.* while at Wroxton only 13 out of 40 were assessed at more than 2*s.* One woman at Wroxton was assessed at 5*s.*[69] To what extent the villages were affected by the Black Death of 1349 is unknown; the population in 1377 was comparatively large[70] but in 1391 Wroxton Priory alleged that its lands were barren and almost uncultivated through the death, caused by epidemics, of cultivators.[71] No direct evidence has been found of the stock kept or the crops grown in the open fields in the Middle Ages, but it is likely that the priory kept large flocks of sheep in Wroxton as on its other estates. In 1217 its demesne contained a vineyard,[72] which presumably disappeared in the later Middle Ages like most other English vineyards.

Information about the economic history of Wroxton becomes fuller in the 16th and 17th centuries. For the second subsidy of 1523, to which there were 52 contributors, there were 24 assessed at the lowest amount of 4*d.* and even the 3 richest farmers were assessed only at 3*s.* 6*d.* and 4*s.* on goods worth £7 and £8.[73] The peasant farmer, however, profited from inflation, and his comparative prosperity is reflected in the rapid growth of population[74] and in wills and inventories. Terriers of 1571 and 1604 show little marked gradation of wealth in the village and no change except in the names of holders. The tendency of the open-field system to prevent capital accumulation thus receives further confirmation. In 1571, of 25 customary tenants 11 held under 3 yardlands, 7 just 3, and 7 over 3; in 1604 the pattern was 10, 5, and seven.[75] Holdings were divided into the usual multitude of small strips, marked out where necessary by merestones. In 1604 Thomas Burden, the largest copyholder, held 5½ yardlands in 117 separate pieces.[76] A substantial part of the manorial demesne, known as 'the abbey lands' and consisting of 30 yardlands, was scattered throughout the open fields and worked by tenants. By 1751 consolidation had taken place in each furlong, and the abbey lands consisted of a number of blocks, known as 'Abbey Piece', of 4 to 15 'halfs'.[77] As late as 1804 these blocks, still known as 'Abbey Piece', were separated from the rest of the open-field strips by wide green balks.[78]

Wroxton adhered to a 2-field system to a comparatively late date: in 1537 there is mention of Town Field and in 1571 of South Field or South Side of Wroxton Field,[79] but it is likely that, as in neighbouring parishes, the furlong was more important than the field. Experiments in crop rotation were being practised and leys farming had been introduced. At some time between 1604 and 1654 the 2-field system was altered into a 4-field system in which crops were grown 3 years out of 4, the quarters being known in the 17th century as Padgeon, Courseway, Rudon Hill, and Rowlow.[80] Owing to the unequal distribution of the strips this change could not be accomplished by a simple process of dividing the 2 fields into 4, and as a result some quarters consisted, at least by 1768, of detached blocks scattered over the parish.[81] It is not known whether any exchange of strips took place to assist this division but it does not seem unlikely.

Along with the open fields was the usual accompaniment of meadow lands, in small lots in the Great and Little Meadow. It is evident that originally

60 MS. North b 13, f. 315v.

61 *Poor Abstract*, 400–401. Totals are given to the nearest £.

62 Ibid.

63 Trinity College President's Off., Wroxton and Balscott, 1768; ibid. Wroxton Survey, 1804; ibid. Wroxton Valuation, 1840.

64 *Poor Abstract*, 400–401.

65 *2nd Rep. Poor Law Com.*, 292–3.

66 *Poor Law Unions*, 21.

67 *V.C.H. Oxon.* i. 407, 419.

68 E 179/161/8.

69 E 179/161/9.

70 See p. 189.

71 *Cal. Papal Regs.* v. 436.

72 *Rot. Welles*, iii. 95.

73 E 179/161/196.

74 See p. 171.

75 Trinity Coll. President's Off., Wroxton terriers (1571, 1604).

76 Ibid.

77 Ibid.

78 Ibid., Wroxton and Balscott Misc.: notes by President Chapman, 1804; cf. map of 1768 in *Sixteen Old Maps of Oxon.* ed. J. L. G. Mowat, pls. 15, 16.

79 Trinity Coll. President's Off., Wroxton and Balscott Misc., 24; ibid. Wroxton terrier 1571.

80 Ibid., Wroxton terriers (1571, 1604); Hants R.O. 43 M 43/917. By 1768 the names of the quarters had changed: see p. 180.

81 *Sixteen Old Maps of Oxon.*, ed. J. L. G. Mowat, pls. 15, 16.

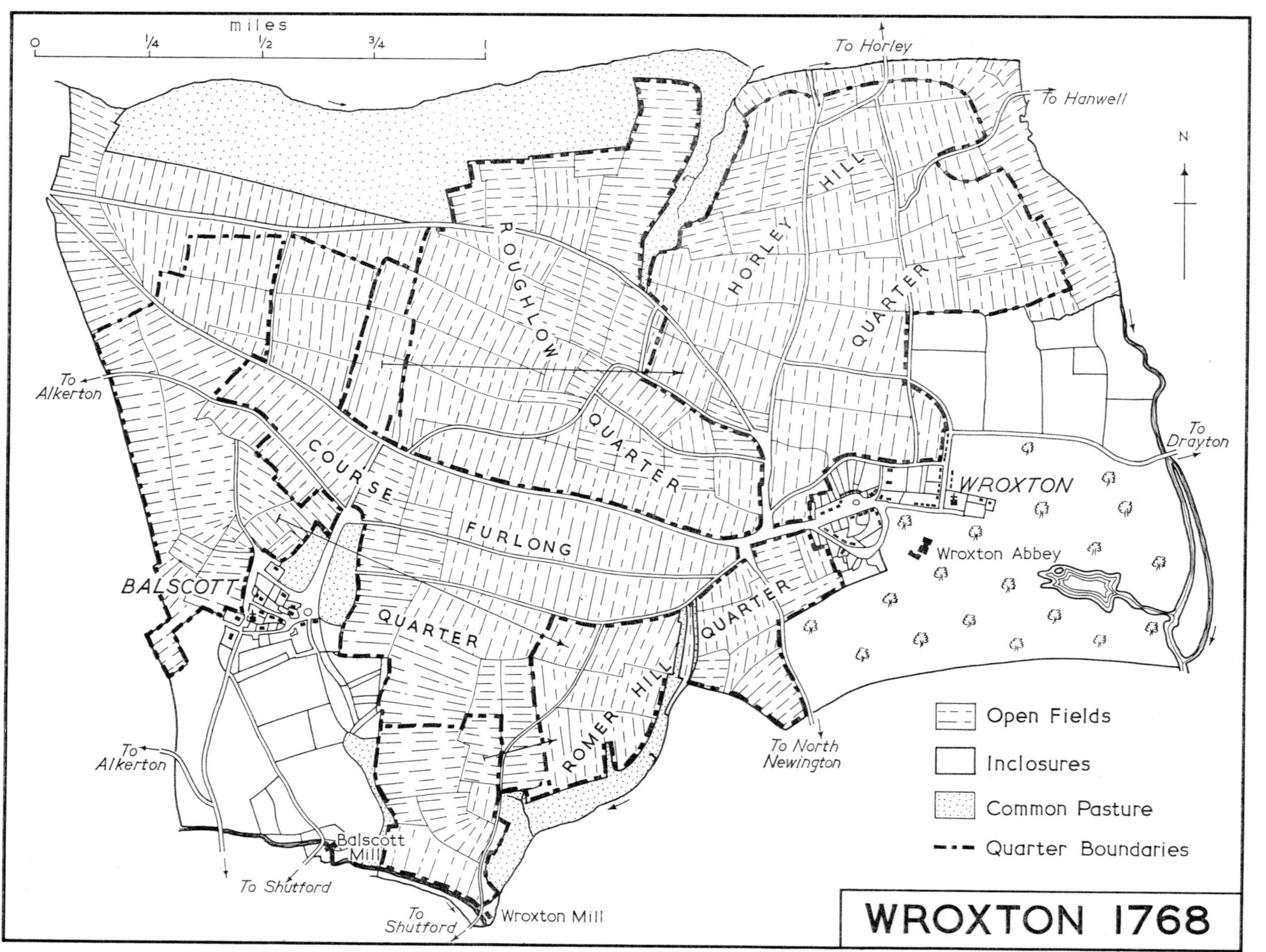

Based on a map by Edward and Thomas Smith at Trinity College, Oxford.

these parcels had been allotted annually, but by the 16th century the lots were firmly attached to each copyhold. In 1571 one tenant held a house, 80 strips of open-field land, 13 lots on the Great Meadow, and 7 lots on the Little Meadow, the whole comprising 2½ yardlands.[82] In addition there were common leys, and common or waste ground, amounting in 1768 to 120 and 216 a. respectively. Each holder of a yardland by the custom of the manor had the right of common for 3 horses or other beasts, and 20 sheep in winter and 30 in summer, while the poor had the right to cut furze on the common.[83] Thus the tenants of Wroxton alone had the right to keep about 1,300 sheep, and a series of orders issued by the manorial court in 1580 and the almost universal possession by the tenants of sheep-houses or sheep-cotes shown in the terrier of 1604 indicate that they were fully exercising this privilege in the late 16th and early 17th centuries. Indeed from the court orders it is evident that the pressure of sheep population in the village was threatening the smooth working of the open-field system, and limitations were placed on the number of lambs permitted on the fields between Lammas and Michaelmas, upon the right to employ shepherds, and upon the times of sheep shearing.[84] In addition to tenants' sheep there were 2,200 kept on the demesne in 1631 by William, Earl of Downe.[85] Probate inventories drawn up in the later 17th century show that tenant farmers usually kept sheep. Flocks were usually very small but some of the wealthier farmers had flocks of between 100 and 140.[86]

Copyholders in the 16th century held at fixed rents for 1, 2, or 3 lives, with the fine at the lord's will; they also paid heriot. By the early 17th century some heriots had been commuted for payments of 3*s.* 4*d.*, 6*s.* 8*d.*, or 13*s.* 4*d.*[87] A 1537 rent roll refers to day-works in addition to rent, but no details are given and there is no mention of them again.[88]

Comparatively little is known about the cottagers: a rental of Wroxton and Balscott of 1525 shows 10 cottagers and 25 tenants; an undated rent roll of the late 16th century or early 17th century 15 cottagers, 27 copyholders, and 4 leaseholders.[89] It was alleged in 1650 that the Popes had converted their copyholds into leaseholds during the Civil War, and had turned their tenants out so as to let their land and houses to others. The government was petitioned to restore the former position, but the outcome of the suit is not known.[90] By the early 18th century the term 'day labourer' was being used: a suit roll of 1718 lists 31 names, presumably tenants, and 21 day labourers.[91]

The largest and most continuously prominent tenant family in both Wroxton and Balscott was that of Lucas, records of which are continuous from the earliest court roll of 1514.[92] Other families, such as the Atkinses, were prosperous: Edward Atkins, 'yeoman' of Balscott, had 6 yardlands in 1633, of which 2 were leased out, and goods valued at over £168.[93] In 1686 another Edward Atkins, 'gentleman', and his wife had goods worth *c.* £394.[94] The latter's wealth, however, falls short of that of some of the Lucases. Edward Lucas, who was leasing out 2 yardlands in 1661, also farmed a good deal himself, for his crops were valued at £160 while the total valuation of his goods came to £518.[95] Joseph Lucas's goods amounted to over £370 and another Edward Lucas, who had evidently retired from active farming by 1681, had £258 in bonds.[96] Above them all, however, towered John Burden, 'yeoman', who was living in Balscott in 1684.[97] In 1687 he was farming 9½ yardlands and left goods valued at £645.[98]

A selection of some 30 inventories[99] suggests that the main wealth of the Wroxton farmer in this century came from his crops. Wheat, barley, pease, and hay were the chief crops grown, while oats and maslin were also mentioned. Sheep, cattle, and horses were kept in varying numbers in accordance with the wealth of each farmer; a herd of 20 cattle including calves was large. Some members of the Lucas family appear to have kept a common herd at Withycombe Grounds. John Lucas had a quarter of a 'stock of cattle' valued at £17 and Joseph Lucas apparently had another quarter.

William, Earl of Downe (d. 1631), appears to have devoted his land in the main to sheep and beasts. His inventory lists 2,200 sheep worth £1,300 and beasts and horses worth £400, while his crops (barley, maslin, pease, and oats) were worth only £66.[1]

From at least the end of the 17th century experiments began to be made in the cultivation of new crops. Cinquefoil was being grown by William Sacheverell on his inclosed ground in 1684.[2] In 1685 the purchase of a hop ground and mustard seeds were entered in the estate accounts;[3] in 1709 there is a reference to rape ground, in 1765 to turnips, in 1769 to Dutch clover and trefoil, and in 1757 and 1759 to rye grass.[4] Inclosures called Upper and Lower Rye Grass are also mentioned in the inclosure award of 1804.[5] Cape wheat was another crop which, as Arthur Young records in 1809, was grown with much success by a local farmer.[6]

Leases occasionally throw some light on farming practice. In 1765, for instance, the new tenant of a farm covenanted not to break up any old sward, or

[82] Trinity Coll. President's Off., Wroxton terriers (1571, 1604).
[83] Wroxton Incl. Act. 43 Geo. III, c 146 (priv. act).
[84] Trinity Coll. Tower Mun., Wroxton ct. roll A (1580).
[85] MS. North c 47 (5).
[86] e.g. MS. Wills Oxon. 8/5/5, 65/4/1, 29/2/7, 42/2/28.
[87] Trinity Coll. President's Off., Wroxton terriers (1571, 1604).
[88] Trinity Coll. Tower Mun., rent roll, 29 Hen. VIII.
[89] Ibid., Wroxton deeds; ibid. President's Off., Wroxton and Balscott Misc., 14.
[90] *Cal. Cttee. for Compounding*, 1643–60, 934–5.
[91] Trinity Coll. Tower Mun., Wroxton and Balscott, Coll. Min. Bk. vol. I.
[92] Ibid., ct. rolls 1514 sqq.
[93] MS. Wills Oxon. 113/1/23.
[94] Ibid. 76/2/11.
[95] Ibid. 41/4/7.
[96] Ibid. 42/2/28, 42/1/33.
[97] See p. 174.
[98] MS. Wills Oxon. 7/4/32; cf. MS. North c 50, f. 22v.
[99] MS. Wills Oxon. 42/1/1, 42/1/33, 42/2/18, 42/2/34, 42/3/13, 113/1/23, 14/4/4, 30/1/22, 15/1/36, 8/4/10, 8/5/5, 27/2/7, 78/3/25, 72/4/8, 131/5/31, 153/3/53, 76/2/11, 78/3/25, 1/2/54, 33/2/30, 8/5/5, 30/1/22, 29/2/7, 65/4/1, 41/4/7, 7/4/32, 76/2/11, 22/1/11, 41/3/21, 63/1/33, 58/4/24.
[1] MS. North c 47 (5).
[2] Trinity Coll. Bursary, map of Balscott (1684) by Hen. Dormer.
[3] MS. North c 50, ff. 7v., 8; cf. refs. to Ld. Guilford's hop ground in 1716; to the excise paid on 134 lbs. of hops in 1720; and to annual payments to the head gardener for tending the yard from 1756–80: MS. North c 52, ff. 54, 30v.; c 63, c 64 *passim*.
[4] Ibid. c 64, ff. 71, 151; ibid. d 2, f. 92.
[5] O.R.O., incl. award.
[6] Young, *Oxon. Agric.* 148.

to mow any of the meadow twice in a year under penalty of £5 a year; and to fallow a quarter part of the arable each year or sow it with turnips or grass seeds; and if he sowed with grass seed he agreed to take no more than one crop a year.[7]

The 18th century also saw a renewed interest in forestry. The Popes had done a great deal in this respect. When Sir Thomas Pope leased Wroxton Abbey to his brother John in 1551, the latter covenanted to plant within 20 years 2,000 oaks and 1,000 elm and ash trees, and to make the copyholders plant also.[8] Wroxton's woods, however, no doubt suffered like the rest of Oxfordshire from spoliation during the Civil War. A map of 1768 shows that all the woods in Wroxton parish had vanished, except those planted in the park. But the park itself had absorbed many of the old woods, whose names survived as Home Wood, Mill Wood, and the Great Wood. Extensive planting was undertaken by Lord Guilford in the first half of the century and by 1778 a fine growth of timber had developed. After long negotiations Lord Guilford finally bought the standing timber from the college for £3,553.[9] In 1805 a total of 633 trees, oak, ash, elm, and beech, were marked for sale.[10]

The final inclosure of the open fields did not come until 1804. There had long been some inclosed land, some at least dating from the Middle Ages. By the time of the Dissolution the priory had inclosed for pasture that part of the demesne that was concentrated to the east of the priory buildings comprising, according to a survey of *c.* 1535, 8 closes of 209 a., together with an orchard.[11] This inclosure may have been carried out by the early 14th century, judging from the amount of wool levied by the Crown from all the priory estates in 1339.[12] The estimate of 209 a. seems unduly low since the 1768 survey put the abbey inclosures at 342½ a., the 1778 terrier of house and park alone included 228 a., and an 1823 survey of the park and demesne included 359 a.[13]

Besides the abbey inclosures there were small inclosures round the two mills in 1571, and on the western extremity of Balscott field there were 11 yardlands, known by 1583 and probably at a much earlier date as 'inlands'.[14] In 1684 they measured 156 a. without the mill closes (5 a.) and comprised 19 closes. They were in the hands of Lord Guilford, William Sacheverell, and 2 others.[15] In 1710 there were 3 owners.[16] Later these inclosures passed almost entirely to the Copes: in 1728 Anthony Cope leased 130 a. of closes, Smith's close, and 6 yardlands in Balscott,[17] and in 1768 the Revd. Sir Richard Cope, Bt., was in possession and had recently 'taken in' from the open field another 27½ a.[18] By 1804, on the eve of inclosure, the old inclosures amounted to a total of 552½ a., of which *c.* 350 a. comprised the park and demesne, out of a total area in the parish of 2,495 a.[19]

As freeholders were never either numerous or prominent at Wroxton from the 14th to the 19th centuries, the bulk of the land was held by the lord of the manor, who was in possession of demesnes, abbey lands, mills, and extensive copyholds in the open fields. In 1768 a survey disclosed the following situation: Trinity College held 1,183½ a., comprising abbey inclosures (342 a.), abbey lands (293¼ a.), and other lands (547¼ a.); Brasenose College held 8 yardlands of open field or 75¼ a.; 10 freeholders (of whom 3 held between them 120 a. or 83 per cent.) held 145¼ a.; and common, leys, and waste totalled 336 a. In all there were said to be 1,741 a.[20] By the inclosure award of 1805[21] 2,251 a. were redistributed. The award allotted to Trinity College 1,603 a., to Christ Church 326½ a. for rectorial tithes, to 11 freeholders 194 a., to Brasenose College 101 a., to the poor 17 a., and to the churchwardens 10 a.

One of the effects of inclosure was to give great impetus to the break up of the old social pattern. In 1804, of the 65 copyholders of Trinity College other than Lord Guilford, 10 held 644 a. and the remaining 55 only 315 a.,[22] but by 1880 a life interest in 32 of Trinity's 74 copyholds was held by 2 men.[23] In 1894 most of the land was let at a rack rent, and only 36 unexpired copyholds for life remained.[24]

After inclosure the method of assessing the copyholders' fines, formerly paid at the will of the lord subject to heriot, was altered and they were calculated at 2 years' value. Heriots, which by the late 18th century seem to have been assessed at 2½ guineas a yardland, were not affected by inclosure.[25]

In 1851 there were only 2 large farms of 270 a. and 310 a. and 14 others of 50 a. to 120 a. The rest were small-holdings — 12 of 40 a. and under. The large farms employed 7 and 12 labourers each. One miller and farmer combined had 7 labourers.[26] In the 1860s the land was mainly under arable though the soil was better suited to grass and a 5-course rotation was used. Many sheep were kept and fed on turnips in the winter.[27] Labour conditions were somewhat better than elsewhere. Colonel North employed no boys under 12 years, no girls at all, and women only at special times. Though there was overcrowding in the cottages there was a good water supply and all married couples had an allotment of ¼ a. from Colonel North.[28]

The disastrous effects of the agricultural slump may be traced in the rents received by the Norths for the rectory estate. In 1864 gross rents had reached £633, falling off to £597 15*s.* eight years later. By 1883, however, Colonel North was only able to find

[7] MS. North d 2, f. 92.
[8] Trinity Coll. President's Off., J. Wilson, *Catalogus Cartarum*.
[9] MS. North accts. *passim*; map of 1768 in *Sixteen Old Maps of Oxon.*, ed. Mowatt, pls. 15, 16; Trinity Coll. President's Off., Wroxton and Balscott, 1768.
[10] MS. North accts.
[11] *Valor. Eccl.* (Rec. Com.), ii. 198; Trinity Coll. President's Off., Wroxton and Balscott Misc., 19, 27.
[12] *Cal. Pat.* 1328–40, 295.
[13] Trinity Coll. President's Off., Wroxton and Balscott, 1768; Trinity Coll. Tower Mun., Wroxton deeds; Trinity Coll. President's Off., Reg. B., f. 4.
[14] Trinity Coll. President's Off., Wroxton terrier 1571; Hants R.O. no. 837.
[15] Trinity Coll. Bursary, map of Balscott (1684).
[16] Ibid., map of Balscott (1710) by J. Perkins.
[17] Hants R.O. no. 873.
[18] Trinity Coll. President's Off., Wroxton and Balscott, 1768.
[19] Ibid., Wroxton and Balscott Misc., 25; ibid., Court Bk. of 1826, p. 24 and J. Wilson's notes.
[20] Ibid., Wroxton and Balscott 1768.
[21] O.R.O., incl. award.
[22] Trinity Coll. President's Off., Wroxton (1804).
[23] Ibid., Wroxton copyholds and leases.
[24] Ch. Ch. Treasury, Bk. of Evidences, Wroxton and Balscott: Trinity estates 1894.
[25] Trinity Coll. President's Off., Wroxton copyholds and leases.
[26] H.O. 107/1733.
[27] *Agric. Employment Women and Children*, 581. [28] Ibid.

1.

2.

3.

4.

1. Milcombe, Manor Farm 2. North Newington, Park Farm 3. Wroxton, Sundial House 4. Wroxton Park

DOVECOTS

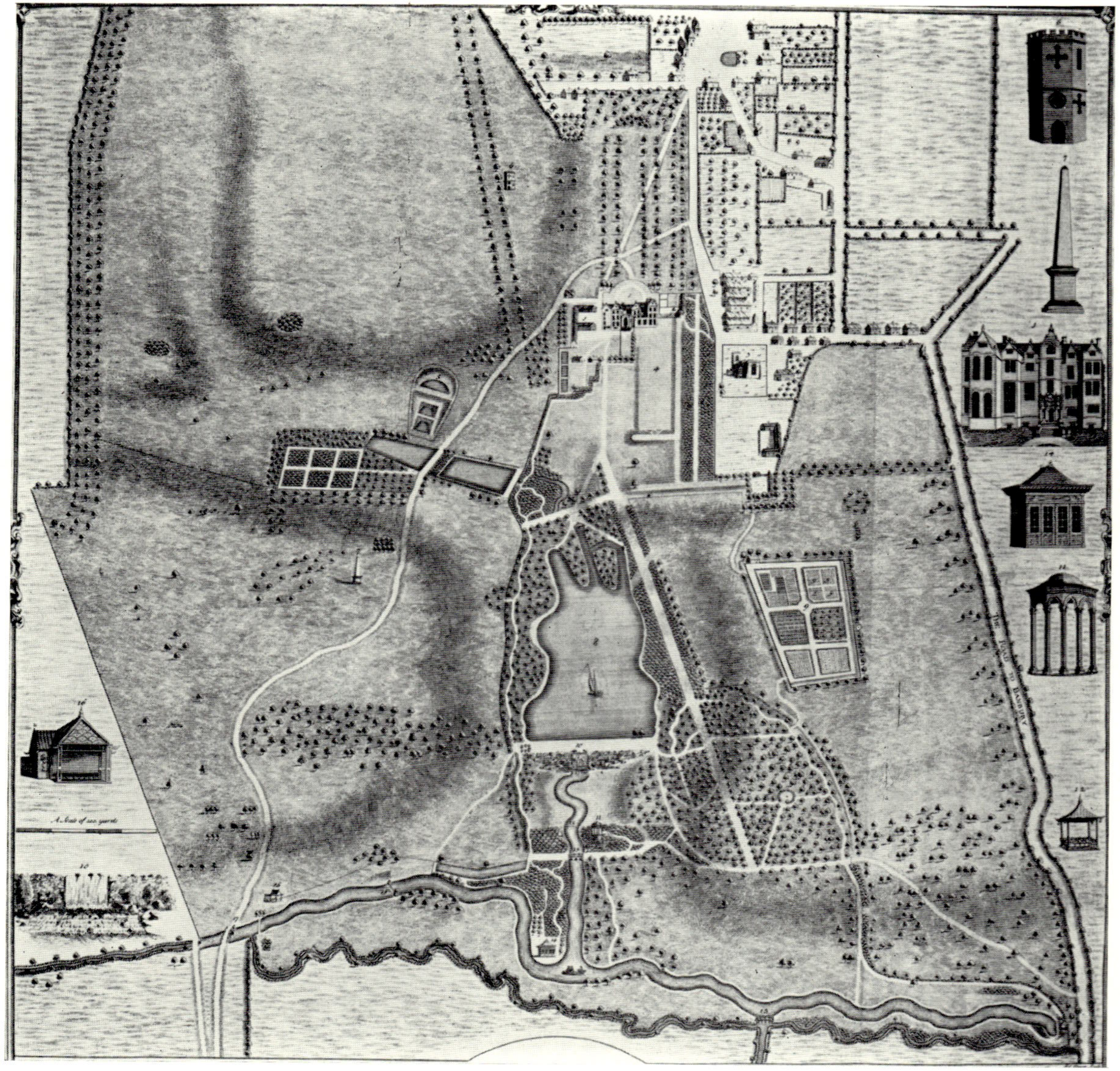

Wroxton Park in the 18th century, showing, in the margins, garden features and the west elevation of the house

The fingerpost of 1686

WROXTON

tenants for 105 a. the remaining 221 a. having been untenanted for 2 years and farmed by himself.[29] As late as 1943 it was considered that the land in this area was not being used to full advantage and that more should be devoted to grass and to arable sheep.[30] Since then there has been some improvement, though progress is retarded by the ironstone mining mentioned below. Some farms have increased their acreage, notably Laurels farm (425 a.) and Grange farm at Balscott (277 a.), and 4 have around 200 a. There are, however, still 5 holdings of between 15 a. and 100 a.[31]

Despite close proximity to Banbury with its weaving and other industries, Wroxton seems to have been chiefly an agricultural village before the 19th century. In 1571, however, 5 out of 25 tenants listed possessed kiln-houses, possibly used for smelting.[32] A Wroxton Quaker was apprenticed to a clothworker of South Newington in 1673, a member of the Lucas family was a silkweaver in 1698, and a weaver is mentioned in 1718–22.[33] Quarrying for building stone had been carried out on a small scale, as required locally, in the 18th century and probably before, but transport costs without easy water communication prevented its growth.[34] In the early 19th century the majority of the inhabitants of Wroxton, even if they did not farm land themselves, had occupations dependent on farming. The parish registers (1813–57) indicate that about half the population were labourers, and that there were the usual rural craftsmen such as blacksmiths and carpenters.[35]

In the 1851 census, besides such craftsmen, there were 2 masons, a lacemaker, a glover, a cork-seller, 2 plush-weavers, and a linen-weaver.[36] At the end of the 19th century came the large-scale exploitation of ironstone quarrying. Since 1917 the Oxfordshire Ironstone Co. Ltd. has been the lessee, and Christ Church and Trinity College have leased ground as the need for it arose. The company extracts ironstone at the rate of 30,000 tons an acre for conversion into steel; it works 45 yards at a time, preparing a third, digging a third, and restoring the level of a third. In 1963 it was employing 135–140 men, but at the height of the steel boom had employed 200. The product was sent to South Wales and to the Brinberg steel works at Wrexham (Denbighshire).[37]

MILLS. In 1086 a mill at Wroxton was valued at 8*s*.; it was probably this mill which Annora de Verdun granted to the priory in 1263.[38] Wroxton mill was probably reconstructed in 1475.[39]

A miller held land in Balscott in the early 13th century.[40] In 1504 'Ballam Mill' in Balscott was granted to the priory by Thomas Sidnell, Chaplain of Wroxton. The grant was disputed and in 1512 the priory began a lawsuit with Robert Wandell which ended with Wandell granting the mill to the priory in return for £20 in cash and a 30-year lease to himself at the old rent.[41] In 1535 Balscott mill, valued at 40*s*., was tenanted by John Sergeant, and Wroxton mill, valued at 26*s*. 8*d*., was let to Thomas Coventry.[42]

After the Dissolution the mills followed the descent of the manors and so passed to Trinity College, Oxford.[43] In 1536 John Pope, brother of Sir Thomas, leased the mills to John Burton for 24 years at a rent of £2 each yearly;[44] by 1686 one of the mills was let for £12.[45] In 1709 one was rebuilt,[46] and in 1768 the mills were valued at *c*. £12 and *c*. £16 and included 13 a. and 9 a. of land.[47] In the early 19th century the mills were said to have little value, having only 2 pairs of stones each and poor water supply. Trinity College carried out improvements at Balscott mill in 1824–8, and at both mills in 1852–4.[48]

In 1894 the agricultural depression and the advance of mechanized milling forced Lord North to surrender the lease to the college after it had been held in his family for at least 350 years. Because of failing water supply it was reported in 1914 that it was no longer a paying proposition to work the mills. Balscott mill has been a private house since the 1920s. In 1931 Wroxton mill was pulled down.[49]

CHURCH. The earliest documentary evidence for Wroxton church dates from 1217 when its rector was mentioned.[50] The dependent chapel at Balscott dates from the 12th century, however,[51] and it is likely that the mother church of Wroxton was still earlier.

When Michael Belet, Rector of Wroxton, founded the priory there *c*. 1217, he appears at first to have granted to it the advowson only.[52] In 1219 the Bishop of Lincoln confirmed that Wroxton Priory should appropriate the rectory, Michael Belet retaining his rights in it for life.[53] The chapel of Balscott was also included in Belet's grant.[54]

A vicarage had been ordained by 1219.[55] The vicar was to have a chaplain and clerk, the chaplain to serve at Wroxton and Balscott successively.[56] In 1395, however, the Prior and Canons of Wroxton

[29] Par. Rec., misc. notes.
[30] *Land Utilization Survey*, 203.
[31] Ex inf. the Bursar, Trinity Coll.
[32] Trinity Coll. President's Off., Wroxton terriers (1571, 1604).
[33] Ibid., Tower Mun., ct. rolls 1514 sqq.; Berks. R.O., Oxon. Q.M. Min. Bk. (1671–1746).
[34] The limiting factor of transport costs is well illustrated by the fact that when in 1681 Trinity wanted timber for some buildings it was found cheaper to buy wood at Oxford than to transport the logs down the Banbury–Oxford road: Trinity Coll. President's Off., Wroxton and Balscott Misc., 15.
[35] Par. Rec., notes made from regs. by Miss M. Stockton, Wroxton.
[36] H.O. 107/1733.
[37] Ex inf. the manager.
[38] *V.C.H. Oxon.* i. 419; *Fines Oxon.* 193.
[39] A stone bearing this date was incorporated in the present building on the destruction of the old mill in 1931: Trinity Coll. Bursary, Wroxton file.
[40] *Close R.* 1227–31, 404.
[41] Trinity Coll. Tower Mun., Wroxton box; Trinity Coll. President's Off., J. Wilson, *Catalogus Cartarum*, 56.
[42] *Valor Eccl.* (Rec. Com.), ii. 198.
[43] See pp. 176–7.
[44] Trinity Coll. Tower Mun., Wroxton box.
[45] MS. North c 50, f. 22v.
[46] Ibid. b 13, f. 315.
[47] Trinity Coll. President's Off., Wroxton and Balscott, 1768; Trinity Coll. Tower Mun., Wroxton box, terrier of Ld. Dartmouth's land.
[48] Trinity Coll. President's Off., Wroxton and Balscott Ct. Bk. of 1826, notes by J. Wilson.
[49] Trinity Coll. Bursary, Wroxton file.
[50] *Liber Antiq.* 90.
[51] See p. 186.
[52] *Liber. Antiq.* 90.
[53] Ibid. 98–99.
[54] Dugdale, *Mon.* vi. 485.
[55] *Liber Antiq.* 7; the date of the ordination is deduced from ibid. 99.
[56] *Rot. Welles*, i. 184, ii. 25.

petitioned that on the death of the vicar they might serve the church with one of their canons, or with a secular priest removeable at their pleasure.[57] The petition seems to have been granted for thereafter the living was treated as a perpetual curacy, the vicarage's endowments were lost,[58] and incumbents were paid a stipend by the impropriator[59] and were not instituted. In the 16th and early 17th centuries incumbents were called curates;[60] later incumbents called themselves indifferently curate and vicar;[61] the term 'minister' is also used.[62] In the early 19th century the Bishop of Oxford complained that the Norths had frequently done nothing more than nominate vicars orally; that vicars had no security of tenure and no real means of exacting their stipend; and that for some long time past incumbents had had no legal title since they had been unlicensed. The incumbent, however, supported the Norths, claiming, however mistakenly, that the living was a curacy since it carried with it not a foot of land.[63] In the course of the 19th century the vicarage once more received endowments[64] and any confusion over its status disappeared.

When the vicarage was ordained it was valued at £6 13*s*. 4*d*.[65] In 1395 it was worth £10 a year.[66] In 1526, however, the incumbent was paid only £5 6*s*. 8*d*.[67] In 1710 Lord Guilford was paying the vicar £30 a year, which had increased to £50 by the 1790s and to £60 in 1829.[68] In 1827 the living was endowed with £1,000 from Queen Anne's Bounty, and large private benefactions brought the total income of the vicar in 1862 to £133;[69] in 1879 Christ Church added a further £50 and the Ecclesiastical Commissioners granted an annual £50 out of the common fund.[70]

In 1226 the glebe comprised 2 yardlands to the east of the church, part of a hide held by Adam, clerk; the vicar was also granted a meadow, a house and other buildings, and all profits of the altar.[71] The vicar had only to supply sufficient altar lights and to pay the synodals; in 1395 the Prior and Canons of Wroxton agreed to continue paying the bishop's dues and other burdens of the church.[72] Although in 1625 Chancery ordered that a search should be made for any glebe or parsonage-house which the impropriators might have absorbed, it was reported in 1829 that the incumbent had neither land, tithes, nor fees, save for marriages; the churchyard, however, belonged to him.[73] Plans for a vicarage-house were set on foot in 1848 but the house was not completed until 1868; it was built on land given by Trinity College, Oxford.[74] In 1887 the glebe amounted to 1 a.[75]

The dependent chapelry of Balscott never acquired parochial status; it had no churchyard in the 16th century but had one by the beginning of the 18th century.[76] It is not certain that the stipulation made in 1226 that a curate should serve Balscott alternately with Wroxton was ever complied with. There was no separate curate at Balscott in 1526.[77] After the Dissolution the lessees of the rectory were to provide 2 chaplains for the parish, but in 1544 Thomas Pope was trying to get permission to demolish Balscott chapel and so obviate the need for more than one chaplain.[78] Between 1581 and 1594 the Rector of Alkerton served Balscott.[79] During most of the 18th century there was no curate, although in 1738 the incumbent of Wroxton was preaching there once a week, whereas his predecessor had held only one service there a month.[80] From 1754 a curate was intermittently employed; even so the number of times Holy Communion was celebrated there fell from 3 to 2 a year.[81] In 1834 the weekly Sunday service at Balscott was taken by the Curate of Horley.[82] In 1864 Christ Church made a grant of £80 a year for the stipend of Balscott's curate[83] but in 1900 the appointment finally lapsed.[84]

Three of Wroxton's late medieval incumbents, Thomas Balscott (fl. 1441), John Banbury (fl. 1526), and Robert Hanley (fl. 1540), were canons of Wroxton.[85] After the Reformation there is evidence that the Wroxton clergy were always on the move, shifting from one parish to another. In 1593, for instance, the curate was not returned in the Certificate of Oxford Clergy, and between 1565 and 1603 no incumbent stayed for more than two years.[86] From 1681, when the Guilfords became established at Wroxton, the church seems to have been treated by the family like a private chapel.[87] The connexion between the North family and the incumbent was especially close in the time of Francis Wise, philologist and antiquary, who was presented to the living by Francis, Lord Guilford, who had been his pupil at Oxford.[88] He held the living from 1723 until 1746, but for part of the period seems to have been non-resident. After 1726 he was Radcliffe Librarian and held the donative of Elsfield, also by gift of Lord Guilford, and was occupied with the collation of manuscripts in the Laud collection in the Bodleian Library for his edition of Plutarch's *Lives* (1729).[89] At various times, however, he certainly resided with the North family at Wroxton Abbey

[57] *Cal. Papal Regs.* iv. 523.
[58] See below.
[59] MS. North b 13, f. 312.
[60] O.A.S. *Rep.* 1916, 72–74; MS. Oxf. Dioc. e 9, f. 176v.
[61] e.g. MS. Oxf. Dioc. d 557; MS. Oxf. Archd. Oxon. e 4, ff. 31, 36; ibid. c 145, f. 44.
[62] MS. Oxf. Dioc. d 560, 563.
[63] Ibid. c 657.
[64] See below.
[65] *Rot. Welles*, ii. 25.
[66] *Cal. Papal Regs.* iv. 523.
[67] *Subsidy 1526*, 279.
[68] MS. North b 13, f. 312; MS. Oxf. Dioc. c 446.
[69] Hodgson, *Queen Anne's Bounty*, cccxxv; Ch. Ch. Treasury, Wroxton box.
[70] Ch. Ch. Treasury, Wroxton box; MS. Oxf. Dioc. c 2083.
[71] *Rot. Welles*, i. 184, ii. 25.
[72] Ibid.; *Cal. Papal Regs.* iv. 523.
[73] Ch. Ch. Treasury, Bk. of Evidences, 408; MS. Oxf. Dioc. c 446. Glebe mentioned in 1537 and the parsonage house mentioned in 1623 almost certainly belonged to the rectory estate: see p. 178.
[74] Par. Rec., Compton's notebk.; MS. Top. Oxon. c 104, ff. 581, 582, 669; Ch. Ch. Treasury, Wroxton box.
[75] *Return of Glebe*, H.C. 307, p. 123 (1887), lxiv.
[76] O.A.S. *Rep.* 1916, 72 and see below.
[77] *Subsidy 1526*, 279.
[78] Trinity Coll., President's Off., Wroxton and Balscott Misc. no. 24.
[79] O.A.S. *Rep.* 1916, 73; MS. Top. Oxon. d 386: MS. hist. of Wroxton by R. C. West.
[80] *Secker's Visit.*
[81] MS. Top. Oxon. d 386.
[82] Ibid. b 40.
[83] Par. Rec., Compton's notebk.
[84] MS. Top. Oxon. d 386.
[85] Emden, *O.U. Reg.*; *Subsidy 1526*, 279; O.A.S. *Rep.* 1930, 341.
[86] O.A.S. *Rep.* 1913, 165; ibid. 1916, 72–74.
[87] MS. Oxf. Dioc. c 657.
[88] Ibid. d 563; *D.N.B.*
[89] *D.N.B.*; *V.C.H. Oxon.* v. 121.

and his letters show that when there he acted as a steward of the estates, in the absence of the family.[90] It is evident that he was also an energetic incumbent. In 1738 he reported to the bishop that he took prayers twice every day at the Abbey; he preached every Sunday at Wroxton, and had increased the services at Balscott. He claimed, and the parish registers show, that he converted about 10 Anabaptists.[91]

At the beginning of the 19th century, too, the incumbent, besides serving Wroxton and Balscott, acted as chaplain to Lord Guilford, sleeping at his house 2 or 3 nights a week.[92] In 1834 the number of communicants had dropped from 30 to 20 and extra services were held only on Christmas Day and Good Friday.[93]

The influence of the Oxford Movement made itself felt in the second half of the century. By 1854 morning prayer was being celebrated every Wednesday and also on Saints' Days.[94] Psalms were first chanted in 1872 and in the same year candles were placed on the screen and altar for the harvest festival service. In 1885 the choir was seated in the chancel, and began to wear surplices; ten years later cassocks were added. In 1893 daily matins were begun and there were Holy Communion services on Sundays and the principal Saints' Days. A year later Holy Communion began to be celebrated chorally. These changes and increased parochial activity by the vicars resulted in a steep rise in the annual number of communicants in the 2 churches; between 1865 and 1872 numbers rose from 393 to 570. In 1941 the communicants numbered 1,048, but since then numbers have fallen off.[95]

The parish church of *ALL SAINTS*,[96] Wroxton, consists of nave, chancel, north and south aisles, south porch, and western tower. Structurally there is no sign of anything earlier than the 14th century, when the whole fabric appears to have been refashioned or altogether rebuilt.[97] In the 15th century the clerestory was added to the nave, and the nave aisles were given wooden roofs, substantial portions of which still survive. Traces of a medieval wall-painting remain above the chancel screen.

Some work must have been done on the tower in the early 17th century, to judge by a stone dated 1636 on the inside wall, but by 1748 it was in a perilous condition. With the assistance and encouragement of Lord Guilford, Sanderson Miller was employed to design a new tower. The work was carried out by his mason William Hitchcox of Ratley (Warws.) and the foundation stone was laid in April 1748. The tower was originally crowned with an 'octagon of stone', the squinches for which are still visible beneath the present roof. This octagon blew down almost as soon as it was erected, much to Horace Walpole's satisfaction.[98]

A gallery had been added at the west end of the church in 1738 by J. Banister;[99] in 1755 the chancel roof was repaired and the open medieval interior ceiled;[1] and between 1738 and 1823 the church was re-pewed.[2] In 1823 it was recorded that an annual income of £24 was used for painting the pews and that the church was in an excellent state of repair.[3] In 1845–6 the font was entirely recarved and the church was re-seated; an organ (by Halmshaw & Sons) was erected in the west gallery in 1879[4] and new heating apparatus and electric light were installed in 1932 and 1936.[5]

In 1885 Colonel North gave stained glass panels of the twelve apostles by Clayton & Bell in the chancel, and in 1884 and 1894 the windows by Burlison and Grylls at the east end of the north and south aisles. During the late 19th century Colonel North made extensive purchases of 16th- and 17th-century continental carved woodwork from different countries. These, some of which are very fine, are to be found let into the pulpit, on the back of the chancel screen, which mostly dates from the 15th century, on the front of the chancel pews, and as a frieze behind the altar at the east end of the chancel.

The church contains some notable monuments. In the chancel is a huge canopied tomb to Sir William Pope, Earl of Downe (d. 1631), and his wife Anne (d. 1625), with kneeling children. Among other monuments the most noteworthy are an elegant wall slab to Lord North, the Prime Minister, (d. 1792) carved by John Flaxman in 1800,[6] and another to the three wives of Francis, Lord Guilford (d. 1790), by Joseph Wilton (1783).[7] There are grave stones to Sir Thomas Pope, Earl of Downe (d. 1668), and to Francis, Lord Guilford (d. 1685), Lord Keeper. Among the local gentry and their wives who are commemorated are Thomas Sacheverell (d. 1675), son of the Rector of Tadmarton, Robert Burden of Balscott (d. 1677), and John Burden (d. 1687).

Among the brasses in the chancel is one to Margaret Bustard (d. 1557), wife first of William Pope of Deddington and then of John Bustard of Adderbury, and mother of Sir Thomas Pope, founder of Trinity College, Oxford.[8]

There are 5 bells, all cast by Henry Bagley in 1676.[9]

The plate includes a silver paten given by the Hon. Mrs. Ann North in 1722, and bought back by Lord North after its sale with other surplus communion plate by the vicar and parishioners in 1885.[10]

[90] *Secker's Visit.*; MS. North c 11, ff. 77, 132.
[91] See p. 186.
[92] MS. Oxf. Dioc. d 573.
[93] Ibid. b 40.
[94] Ibid. d 701.
[95] Par. Rec., Compton's notebk.
[96] A wake was kept on the Sunday after All Saints' Day in the early 18th century: *Par. Colln.* iii. 357.
[97] Linc. Reg. iii, f. 90.
[98] L. Dickens and M. Stanton, *An Eighteenth Century Correspondence*, 130, 167, 277. A copy of the contract is noted in Par. Rec., reg. and other financial details are recorded in MS. North, 59, f. 177v.; H. Walpole, *Memoirs*, ed. P. Toynbee, ii. 347.
[99] Par. Rec., receipt.
[1] MS. Oxf. Dioc. d 13, f. 11.
[2] In 1738 the vicar complained that the pews were decayed and inconvenient, that the parishioners were unwilling to purchase new ones: *Secker's Visit.*
[3] *12th Rep. Com. Char.* 219.
[4] Ch. Ch. Treasury, Wroxton box; Par. Rec., Compton's notebk.
[5] Par. Rec., faculty.
[6] For the date see Rupert Gunnis, *Dictionary of British Sculptors, 1660–1851*, 150.
[7] The original drawing for the monument is in the Metropolitan Museum, New York.
[8] For notices of other tombs and brasses, and for transcripts of inscriptions see *Gent. Mag.*, 1797, lxvii. 106–10; MS. Top. Oxon. c 167, ff. 65–6; Roger North, *Lives of the Norths* (1826), i. 169; the 7 brasses, all 16th and 17th century, are listed in MS. Top. Oxon. d 196, ff. 439–48. For blazon of the arms see Bodl. G.A. Oxon. 4° 687, pp. 360–1; ibid. 16° 217, p. 270*b*.
[9] *Ch. Bells Oxon.*
[10] Evans, *Ch. Plate.*

In 1805 *c.* 8 a. in lieu of open-field land were allotted to the churchwardens for church repairs; in 1823 the rent was as much as £24 a year. In the period 1941–*c.* 1955 the land was leased for mining and the royalties were spent mostly on reducing a debt of over £5,000 incurred in church restoration.[11] In 1902 Henry Fox vested Ragnell's Close (5 a.) in the vicar and churchwardens for the maintenance of the church clock and the upkeep of the churchyard. In the period 1941–*c.* 1955 the land was leased for mining, and in 1960, Trinity College were renting it for £189.[12]

The chapel of *ST. MARY MAGDALENE*, Balscott, consists of chancel, nave, south aisle, and a slender south tower. It appears to have been rebuilt in the early 14th century, but retains a tub-shaped font and part of a tympanum, both of which may be late-12th-century. The tower has an octagonal parapet, and the lowest stage serves as a porch. In the period 1800–23 the chapel was 'completely repaired' and given new pews and a gallery (since removed).[13] A small piece of land, administered by the Balscott churchwarden and leased in 1734 for £1 6*s.* and in 1801 for £8 8*s.*, had been sufficient to pay for all repairs in the 18th century; in the 19th century, however, the churchwarden was often in debt.[14] In 1849–50 the chancel roof was repaired at a cost of some £200 by Franklin.[15] There were extensive restorations in 1873;[16] in 1921 the chancel roof and in 1926–7 the nave and tower were restored. In the interior are two 14th-century piscinae and a pulpit made up of 16th- and 17th-century woodwork from the continent given by Colonel North.[17]

There are 2 bells, one probably 19th-century, the other re-cast in 1756 by Matthew Bagley.[18] The churchyard, mentioned in 1723, was probably extended in 1823.[19]

In 1805 the churchwarden of Balscott was allotted *c.* 2 a. for the church land held in the open field; the income was used as before for chapel repairs. In 1941 a mining lease was granted; some of the royalties were used for restoration of the chapel, but the greater part was invested.[20] A sum of £200, invested in 1923 and yielding £8 14*s.* 4*d.* a year in 1963, is said to derive from the Henry Gardner Trust for the upkeep of the churchyard.[21]

The Wroxton registers begin in 1548 but there are many gaps during the 16th century. There are transcripts for the period 1670–1865.[22]

ROMAN CATHOLICISM. No Roman Catholics were recorded at Wroxton before the late 19th century, except for a Flemish servant who was a recusant in 1706 and a woman who was said to be a papist in 1817.[23] Colonel North (1804–94) and his son, Lord North (1836–1932), were Roman Catholics and services were held in the chapel at the Abbey. In about 1883 a mission was established, the priest and chapel being located first in the 'North Arms' and later in an adjoining building.[24] In 1887 the chapel of *ST. THOMAS OF CANTERBURY* was built in the village by the Norths;[25] it is registered for marriages, and is served from Banbury.[26]

PROTESTANT NONCONFORMITY. The Compton Census of 1676 recorded 16 Protestant nonconformists in the parish, but this may well have been an underestimate, particularly for Balscott where there were both Quaker and Anabaptist communities. The Quaker registers for the Banbury neighbourhood give the names of 9 families in the parish in the 17th century, half of them living at Balscott.[27] Three of these persisted into the 18th century,[28] but the community was then a dying one. John Shelswell (d. 1717), who was distrained on for non-payment of tithes in 1717,[29] was one of the last of this Quaker family: the last Wroxton Quaker in the burial register was recorded in 1735,[30] and in 1738 the parson was probably correct in reporting that there were no Quakers in the parish.[31]

Anabaptists were not recorded until 1738 when they too were a dying community. The incumbent then said that there had been a licensed meeting house which had fallen out of use 15 years before; that he had baptized 'half a score of adults of that persuasion with their children'; and that there was only 1 left and this man's children often attended church.[32] One Anabaptist was reported at the beginning of the 19th century[33] and in 1834 the vicar said that there were Baptists in the parish but there is no record of any chapel.[34] Two or 3 Presbyterian families were mentioned in 1759,[35] but in 1778 there was only one.[36] In this year the first evidence of Methodism appears: 'a sort of Methodistical preacher, a drummer in the Northamptonshire Militia' came sometimes to Balscott and preached in a farm-house there,[37] but there was no meeting-house nearer than Banbury. There was a dissenting teacher with a licensed meeting in his house at Balscott in 1805[38] and 3 years later there were 10 'Calvinistic Methodists' in the hamlet, though they had no resident teacher.[39] The farm-house of a Mr. Williams was licensed[40] but in 1814 was disused as a meeting-house.[41] It is not possible to be certain whether Williams lived in

[11] *12th Rep. Com. Char.* 219; Char. Com., file E 123784, G file accts.; ex inf. the vicar.
[12] Char. Com., Unrep. vol. 160, p. 68; ibid., file E 123784; ex inf. the vicar.
[13] *12th Rep. Com. Char.* 219. There is a drawing of the church from the S.E. in 1824 by J. Buckler: MS. Top. Oxon. a 65 no. 54.
[14] Par. Rec., Balscott chwdns' accts.
[15] MS. Top. Oxon. d 386; Par. Rec., Balscott chwdns' accts.
[16] MS. Oxf. Dioc. c 750, 154–5; Par. Rec., faculty and plan showing layout before 1873.
[17] Ch. Ch. Treasury, Wroxton box; Par. Rec., Compton's notebk.
[18] *Ch. Bells Oxon.* There were 3 bells in 1718: Par. Colln. i. 16.
[19] MS. North c 53, f. 5; Par. Rec., Balscott chwdns' accts.
[20] *12th Rep. Com. Char.* 219; Char. Com., file E 123784; ex inf. the vicar.
[21] Char. Com., G file accts.; ex inf. the vicar.
[22] Par. Rec., reg.; MS. Oxf. Dioc. c 640; d 729, f. 150; c 143, f. 52.
[23] *Oxoniensia*, xiii. 82; MS. Oxf. Dioc. d 577. No papists were reported in the recusant return of 1767; MS. Oxf. Dioc. c 431.
[24] Stapleton, *Cath. Miss.* 58; *Cath. Dir.* (1964).
[25] *Kelly's Dir. Oxon.* (1887).
[26] *Cath. Dir.* (1964).
[27] Compton Census; Banbury Quaker Reg.
[28] Banbury Quaker Reg.
[29] MS. Sufferings.
[30] Banbury Quaker Reg.
[31] *Secker's Visit.*
[32] Ibid.
[33] MS. Oxf. Dioc. c 327, f. 288.
[34] Ibid. b 39.
[35] Ibid. d 557.
[36] Ibid. b 37.
[37] Ibid.
[38] Ibid. c 327, f. 288.
[39] Ibid. d 571.
[40] Ibid.
[41] Ibid. d 575.

Wroxton or Balscott or whether he is connected with the Williams who in 1822 offered facilities to the Independents.[42] In 1822 William Gardner's house in Wroxton was registered as a meeting-house by a Methodist minister of Banbury[43] and in 1834 the vicar said there was a Methodist place of worship in the parish, though he believed it not to be set apart for that purpose; the teacher was not resident.[44] William Gardner as steward returned in 1851 a Methodist congregation of 78 in the morning and 43 in the evening. Wroxton Methodist chapel was rebuilt in 1864.[45] There was also a Methodist chapel at Balscott, built in 1850, with a congregation of 57 in the morning and 95 in the evening.[46]

An Independent minister of Banbury, Thomas Searle, who had begun to preach in Wroxton in 1819, registered a small room as a meeting-house there the following year; immorality was said to be prevalent and 'gross darkness' to cover the people.[47] In 1822 Williams, a local farmer, offered part of his premises to be fitted up as a chapel which was registered in 1823.[48] It was said originally to hold 150, but to have been enlarged in 1824 to hold 200.[49] A church was formed in 1824 consisting originally of eight members but by the end of the year there were 28.[50] In 1825 the sect founded a flourishing Sunday school.[51] At the time of the 1851 Census there was a congregation of 60–70. The vicar, commenting on the Census figures for all the parish nonconformists, said that, as he could manage only one service in church, the Church people went to chapel as well and were counted in the dissenters' return. He also said that one of the churchwardens was a dissenter thrust into office against his will.[52] In 1878 there were reported to be 16 professed dissenters in the parish.[53] The Independent chapel disappeared between 1877 and 1883[54] but in 1965 the Methodist chapels at Wroxton and Balscott had memberships of 16 and 17 respectively. They were served by ministers from Banbury and Brailes.[55]

SCHOOLS. In 1709 there was a school at Wroxton, whose master was paid £20 a year by Lord Guilford.[56] For most of the 18th century there was no school at either Wroxton or Balscott.[57] By 1808 there were 2 unendowed schools, each supported by Francis, Earl of Guilford. There were about 20 children, of both sexes, in each school, the boys being taught reading and writing and the girls needlework.[58] To these another 'common school' had been added by 1815, but heavy taxation made the inhabitants disinclined to support a Sunday school; the National Society's new plan could not be put into effect, since the master and mistress were not capable of doing it.[59]

These difficulties, however, were overcome. In 1817 the Earl of Guilford leased 3 cottages, later 4, for the use of a school, and in 1818 it was reported that the two schools, with 44 children, supported partly by the earl and partly by voluntary subscription, were affiliated to the National Society.[60] A schoolmaster was appointed in 1821[61] and by 1833 the schools had been amalgamated, to form a National day and Sunday school. It was attended by 60 children between 6 and 12 years and had a master and mistress, who were paid £26 a year by Lady Georgiana North and £5 by Trinity College. There were also 2 small day schools, one kept by a churchwoman, the other by a dissenter, each with *c.* 12 pupils. Their instruction was paid for by their parents. Besides these there was a Sunday school, founded in 1825 by Independent dissenters, consisting of 22 boys and 20 girls, who were taught, free, by members of the sect.[62] In 1855 new buildings were erected for the National school, which was then managed by the vicar and a school committee. Graded fees were paid by the pupils.[63] The school had 67 pupils in 1860, and 20 attended an adult evening school, supported by the vicar, which was held in the winter months with moderate but steady success.[64] Attendance at the National school had risen by 1866 to 70 in the day and 85 in the Sunday school,[65] but though the schoolmaster was pensioned off in that year and a certificated schoolmistress appointed, to qualify the school for a government grant, this had still not been received by 1871.[66]

The school had been rebuilt in 1868, with accommodation for 112 children, though the average attendance up to 1906 was between 50 and 60.[67] The school building and site were handed over to trustees by a deed of 1871.[68] Annual and fee grants were received by 1894, and an aid grant by 1900, which provided most of the income, though some still came from voluntary contributions.[69] The school's status was that of a Controlled school in 1962 and it took about 50 pupils.[70]

Balscott school, with a teacher's residence attached, was built in 1840 largely through the efforts of E. J. Middleton, curate of the parish. A mistress was put in charge.[71] There were 68 pupils in 1860 and the school was supported by subscriptions. There was only one room for boys and girls and in 1862 the condition of the school was said to be 'very bad'.[72] By 1866 it was in receipt of a government

[42] See below.
[43] MS. Oxf. Dioc. c 644, no. 263.
[44] Ibid. b 39.
[45] *Kelly's Dir. Oxon.* (1903).
[46] H.O. 129/162.
[47] MS. Dunkin 439/1, f. 344v. (*Home Missionary Mag.* 1824); MS. Oxf. Dioc. c 644, no. 214.
[48] MS. Dunkin 439/1, f. 344v.; MS. Oxf. Dioc. c 645, no. 10.
[49] MS. Dunkin 439/1, f. 344v.
[50] Ibid.
[51] See below.
[52] *Wilb. Visit.*
[53] MS. Oxf. Dioc. c 344.
[54] *Kelly's Dir. Oxon.* (1877, 1883).
[55] Ex inf. the Revd. A. J. Davies, Sec. of the Oxf. and Leic. District Synod.
[56] MS. North b 13, f. 315v.
[57] The visitation returns for the 18th century regularly report 'no school'.
[58] MS. Oxf. Dioc. d 571.
[59] Ibid. c 433.
[60] Trinity Coll. President's Off., J. Wilson, *Catalogus Cartarum*, 113; Par. Rec., Compton's notebk.; MS. Oxf. Dioc. b 70; *Educ. of Poor*, 733.
[61] Par. Rec., misc. pps.
[62] *Educ. Enq. Abstract*, 758; MS. Oxf. Dioc. b 39 and see above.
[63] Ed. 7/169/234.
[64] MS. Oxf. Dioc. d 180.
[65] Ibid. c 332.
[66] Trinity Coll. President's Off., J. Wilson, *Catalogus Cartarum*, 113; Par. Rec., Compton's notebk.
[67] *Ret. of Sch.* (1890), 216; *Pub. Elem. Sch. Ret.* (1894). 498; ibid. (1900), 676; *List of Sch.* (1906), 530.
[68] *Ret. of Non-Provided Sch.* 26.
[69] *Pub. Elem. Sch. Ret.* (1894), 498; ibid. (1900), 676.
[70] Ex inf. O.C.C. Educ. Cttee.
[71] MS. Oxf. Dioc. b 70; Trinity Coll. President's Off., Wroxton and Balscott.
[72] Ed. 7/169/235.

grant, was affiliated to the National Society, and was managed by a committee instead of, as previously, by the vicar.[73] Then there were 48 boys and girls in the day school, and 30 in the Sunday school, since many children came from Shutford and elsewhere to the day school, and remained in their own parish for the Sunday school.[74]

The school premises were conveyed to trustees in 1866 and were rebuilt in 1867 when a playground was added.[75] There was accommodation for 45 in 1871, with an attendance of 6 boys and 29 girls.[76] A new school-house was built in 1888, with accommodation for 54 children.[77] Attendance, however, fell rapidly at the end of the century. In 1894 it was 41 and in 1904 nineteen. In 1931 the school was closed.[78]

CHARITIES. By the inclosure award of 1805 *c.* 17 a. were allotted to the poor in lieu of fuel rights vested in the inhabitants. The rent was to be applied to buying fuel, clothes, and necessities for parishioners, whether receiving relief or not.[79] In 1851 the land was let for £36 10*s.* which was spent entirely on fuel. Between 1884 and 1895 the rent was gradually reduced to £16 and coal was distributed by tickets worth 3*s.* 6*d.* each.[80] In 1941 a 36-year lease of the land was granted to the Oxfordshire Ironstone Co. Ltd., which relinquished the property *c.* 1955; the stock was then £3,050 and the interest £97 10*s.*[81] The land was subsequently held at a gradually increasing rent. In 1960 the money was spent on coal for the needy, on help for the sick and bereaved, and on educational expeditions to London.[82]

By the terms of Henry Fox's grant of 1902 for the upkeep of the church and churchyard any surplus was to be spent on relief of the poor.[83]

[73] MS. Oxf. Dioc. d 180.

[74] Ibid. c 332; *Ret. of Non-Provided Sch.* 29.

[75] Trinity Coll. President's Off., Wroxton and Balscott.

[76] *Elem. Educ. Ret.* 326.

[77] Trinity Coll. President's Off., Wroxton and Balscott; *Ret. of Schs.* (1890), 213.

[78] *Pub. Elem. Sch. Ret.* (1894), 498; ibid. (1900), 676; *List of Sch.* (1906), 530; ex inf. O.C.C. Educ. Cttee.

[79] Char. Com., Unrep. vol. 34, p. 186.

[80] Par. Rec., chwdns' accts.

[81] Char. Com. file E 123784; ibid. G file accts.

[82] Ibid. file E 76577.

[83] Ibid. Unrep. vol. 160, p. 68; see p. 186.

TAX ASSESSMENTS OF THE VILLAGES AND HAMLETS OF BLOXHAM HUNDRED, 1306–1523

	1306[a] a 30th		1316[b] a 16th		1327[c] a 20th		1344[d] a 15th	1377[e] poll tax	1523 lay subsidy			
									1st payment[f]		2nd payment[g]	
	£ s. d.	Contributors	£ s. d.	Contributors	£ s. d.	Contributors	£ s. d.	Contributors	£ s. d.	Contributors	£ s. d.	Contributors
Adderbury	5 6 6¼‡	35†	11 8 10	74	8 16 4	76	10 12 2	*	7 11 4	93	16 11 6	92
Barford St. John	*	*[h]	1 6 9	13	1 8 6	11	2 0 8	43	3 6 4	10	3 10 4	10
Bodicote	1 6 3¾	21	3 6 8‡	27†	2 6 6	22	2 13 0	89	4 17 0	17	5 5 6	22
Milton	*	*	2 1 8	16	1 14 7	17	2 18 3	*	1 7 6	16	1 8 8	14
Total	6 12 10	56†	18 13 11	130†	14 6 11	126	18 4 1	132†	17 2 2	136	26 16 0	138
Alkerton	*[i]	*	2 11 0	19	1 4 10	20	1 16 2	39	18 0	8	1 0 6	9
Bloxham	2 18 1[j]	45	5 0 0[k]	28	10 12 0	70	17 6 8	325	8 19 8	63	15 0 2	81
Milcombe	1 9 1¾	24	4 12 0	29	3 4 2	22	2 14 11	78	2 10 0	16	1 10 0	16
Total	4 7 2¾	69	9 12 0	57	13 16 2	92	20 1 7	403	11 9 8	79	16 10 2	97
Broughton North Newington	} (1 0 8¼)	} 14†	} 3 11 6	} 46	} 3 1 4	} 48	} 5 4 4	} 163	} 3 10 2	} 52	} 10 0 10	} 47
Total	(1 0 8¼)	14†	3 11 6	46	3 1 4	48	5 4 4	163	3 10 2	52	10 0 10	47
Drayton	18 9½	15	1 19 2	21	19 4	16	1 13 6	47	19 10	9	2 0 4	10
Hanwell	1 7 6¼	24	2 4 1	19	1 6 2	25	3 1 1	92	1 1 0	8	1 1 0	8
Hornton	(2 12 7¾)	39†	} 6 2 0	} 71	} 5 13 8	} 51	} 10 1 11	} 136	} 1 10 6	} 18	} 5 16 2	} 24
Horley	1 5 5	19										
Total	(3 18 0¾)	58†	6 2 0	71	5 13 8	51	10 1 11	136	1 10 6	18	5 16 2	24
Mollington[l]	*	*	2 9 4	23	1 0 0	13	2 8 2	*	19 6	9	1 4 0	7
Sibford Ferris[m]	*	*	2 4 6	23	2 4 6	26	} 8 19 8	} 37	1 8 2	12	1 3 4	11
Sibford Gower[m]	*	*	3 7 6	37	2 8 8	27			3 7 8	39	3 10 0	40
Tadmarton	2 11 2¼	32	4 0 1	45	3 8 8	31	3 18 4	84	4 15 7	33	4 16 8	20
Wigginton	19 2¼	16	2 8 1	21	1 19 1	24	2 15 8	73	2 7 4	17	2 7 4	17
Wroxton	2 10 5¼‡	43†	3 10 7	44	3 7 1	40	4 15 4	99	} 4 6 2	} 32	} 3 3 0	} 52
Balscott	(17 3¾)	17†	2 9 2	19	1 10 6	19	1 19 4	49				
Total	(3 7 9)	60†	5 19 9	63	4 17 7	59	6 14 8	148	4 6 2	32	3 3 0	52

* Missing from roll.
† Mutilated: number of names incomplete.
‡ Mutilated: rubric and some names missing.
() Mutilated: the total given is the sum of surviving payments.
[a] E 179/161/10.
[b] E 179/161/8.
[c] E 179/161/9.
[d] E 179/161/17.
[e] E 179/161/44.
[f] E 179/161/198.
[g] E 179/161/196.
[h] Barford St. John may be represented by the 8 unidentified names in the roll before Milcombe.
[i] May be the unidentified total of £1 2*s*. 7*d*. before Hanwell.
[j] Assessed for a 20th as ancient demesne.
[k] Bloxham *Almarice*.
[l] A hamlet of Cropredy (Banbury hundred).
[m] A hamlet of Swalcliffe (Banbury hundred).

INDEX

NOTE: A page-number in italic denotes an illustration; a page-number prefixed by a dagger † indicates a reference to a plate facing that page. The pages containing the substantive history of a parish are set in bold-face type. A page-number followed by *n* is a reference only to the footnotes on that page.

Among the abbreviations used in the index the following may require elucidation: adv., advowson; agric., agriculture; Alex., Alexander; And., Andrew; Ant., Anthony; Abp., Archbishop; Bart., Bartholomew; Bp., Bishop; bro., brother; cast., castle; Cath., Catherine; cent., century; chap., chapel(s) (of ease); char., charities; Chas., Charles; Chris., Christopher; ch., church(es); Coll., College; Ctss., Countess; ct., court(s) (manorial etc.); Dan., Daniel; dau., daughter; d., died; dom. arch., domestic architecture; Edm., Edmund; Edw., Edward; Eliz., Elizabeth; fam., family; fl., flourished; Fred., Frederick; Geof., Geoffrey; Geo., George; Gil., Gilbert; grds., grandson; Hen., Henry; Herb., Herbert; hosp., hospital(s); ho., house; Humph., Humphrey; hund., hundred; inc., inclosure; ind., industry; Jas., James; Jos., Joseph; jr., junior; Kath., Katharine; Laur., Laurence; Lawr., Lawrence; Ld., Lord; man., manor(s); Marg., Margaret; mkt., market(s); m., married; Mat., Matthew; Mic., Michael; Nat., Nathaniel; Nic., Nicholas; nonconf., nonconformity; O.E., Old English; par., parish; pk., park(s); Phil., Philip; pop., population; prehist., prehistoric; rly., railway; Reg., Reginald; rem., remains; Ric., Richard; riv., river; Rob., Robert; Rog., Roger; Rom., Roman; Sam., Samuel; sch., school(s); sr., senior; Sim., Simon; sis., sister; s., son; sta., station; Steph., Stephen; Thos., Thomas; Tim., Timothy; Vct., Viscount; Vctss., Viscountess; Wal., Walter; w., wife; Wm., William.

PRINTED IN GREAT BRITAIN BY
ROBERT MACLEHOSE AND CO. LTD
THE UNIVERSITY PRESS, GLASGOW